Torts II

Practicing Tort Law

Fourth Edition

Nelson P. Miller

Torts II–

Practicing Tort Law

Fourth Edition

Nelson P. Miller

Publisher:
Crown Management LLC – July 2018
1527 Pineridge Drive
Grand Haven, MI 49417
USA

ISBN-13: 978-1-7322387-6-3

All Rights Reserved
© 2018 Nelson P. Miller
c/o 111 Commerce Avenue S.W.
Grand Rapids, MI 49503
(616) 560-0632

Of man's first disobedience, and the fruit
　Of that forbidden tree, whose mortal taste
Brought death into the world, and all our woe,
　With loss of Eden, till one greater Man
Restore us, and regain the blissful seat,
　Sing, Heav'nly Muse, that on the secret top
Of Oreb, or of Sinai, didst inspire
　That shepherd who first taught the chosen seed
In the beginning how the heav'ns and earth
　Rose out of Chaos… .

　　　　　　　　John Milton, *Paradise Lost* (1668)

PREFACE

This Torts II course book continues, and is a companion to, a Torts I course book. These course books differ from the ordinary law school casebook. That difference is due in part to Thomas McIntyre Cooley. Justice Cooley had a polite and circumspect debate with Dean Christopher Columbus Langdell at Harvard Law School on the occasion of Harvard University's 250th anniversary, when Justice Cooley received Harvard's honorary degree. History credits (or shall we say *curses*?) Dean Langdell with inventing law school's case method and traditional casebook. Dean Langdell denigrated practical studies while championing science-like case studies. His Harvard comrade-in-arms Justice Oliver Wendell Holmes denigrated ethical studies. By contrast, Justice Cooley expressed concern that the law must not depart from the practical and ethical—hence Western Michigan University Cooley Law School's mission integrating knowledge, skills, and ethics to train law's sturdy practitioners.

Casebooks today do tend to include some introductory text and, often, author notes and questions. They also include statutes, law review articles, and other commentary. Going beyond those designs, this course book adds pedagogical (teaching), androgogical (learner-centered), and heutogogical (inclusive, learner-controlled) forms such as learner objectives, skills and ethics paths, tort-practice forms and vignettes, case studies, career advice, and explicit instruction on legal analysis. Especially when used with its companion workbook, these designs help you place tort law in its practice context while developing a professional identity as a member of a community of professional practice. Hence, its subtitle *Practicing Tort Law*.

The book's design is also to give you greater control over your learning. In its much-anticipated report *Educating Lawyers*, the Carnegie Foundation on Higher Education urged precisely these reforms—to integrate skills and ethics into a more explicit study of the knowledge or doctrinal dimension of law, to foster an apprenticeship of practice. Although professors at my law school already follow these practices (the Carnegie Foundation report vindicated the school's mission and programs), this book makes those practices clearer. It is another example of the student-centered innovation that lends Western Michigan University Cooley Law School its preeminence at practice preparation. I hope you appreciate this design. I welcome your comments, evaluation, and encouragement.

TABLE OF CONTENTS

Preface vii

Chapter

IX.	**Negligence—Defenses (continued)**	1
	C. Statutes of Limitations and Repose	1
	D. Immunities	6
X.	**Products Liability**	36
	A. Development	37
	B. Product Defect	47
	C. Types of Defect	58
	D. Proof and Procedure	74
	E. Defenses	82
	F. Product-Related Liability	103
XI.	**Strict Liability**	107
	A. Animals	108
	B. Abnormally Dangerous Activities	113
XII.	**Misrepresentation**	128
	A. Representation	129
	B. Knowledge of Falsity	139
	C. Reliance	150
	D. Loss	167
XIII.	**Defamation**	169
	A. The Common Law	170
	1. Defamatory Meaning	171
	2. Publication	178
	3. Of and Concerning	186
	4. Special Damages	192
	B. Constitution	197
	C. Privileges	221
	1. Absolute	221
	2. Qualified	226
	D. Remedies	232
XIV.	**Invasion of Privacy**	237
	A. Appropriation	238
	B. Intrusion	244
	C. Public Disclosure	247
	D. False Light	250
XV.	**Damages**	264
	A. Personal Injury	264
	B. Wrongful Death	283
	C. Property Damage	295
	D. Punitive Damages	297
XVI.	**Multiple Parties**	307

	A. Satisfaction and Release	307
	B. Joint-and-Several Liability	318
	C. Vicarious Liability	326
	D. Contribution and Indemnity	345
	E. Apportionment of Damages	354
XVII.	**NO-FAULT SYSTEMS**	358
	A. Motor Vehicle Accidents	360
	B. Workers' Disability Compensation	376
XVIII.	**MISUSE OF LEGAL PROCEDURE**	390
	A. Malicious Prosecution	390
	B. Abuse of Process	402
XIX.	**HARM TO COMMERCIAL INTERESTS**	412
	A. Injurious Falsehood	413
	1. Title	413
	2. Trade	416
	B. Tortious Interference	427
CONCLUSION		434
APPENDIX: TORT-PRACTICE PROCESS MODELS		436

Torts I—Practicing Tort Law

Chapter IX

Negligence—Defenses (Continued)

C. Statutes of Limitation and Repose

OBJECTIVE: Given dates and descriptions relating to various tort injuries, apply the law and principles relating to tort statutes of limitation and repose stated in this section of the text, to determine when the statutes would bar the tort claims.

Case Study: A business owner prepared financial statements for January 2002 in which he purposefully wildly exaggerated the business's profits. In December 2004, he showed the statements to a prospective buyer for his business, with the fraudulent intent of inducing the buyer to rely on them and purchase the business for substantially more than it was really worth. The buyer decided in February 2005 to make the purchase, based on the fraudulent financial statement. By July 2005, she had discovered that the statements were fraudulent. She spent the next six months trying to settle her claim. In January 2006, she sued the seller for fraud, for which the jurisdiction has a three-year statute of limitations. ***Discuss and evaluate whether the buyer filed her claim timely.***

Statutes of limitation bar tort actions within defined periods after causes of action arise. The common justification given for barring claims based on limitations periods is that too much time passing before suit compromises defendants' ability to gather and preserve evidence. Witnesses forget, move away, or die. Documents and other tangible evidence get lost or destroyed. Another concern involves defendants' interest in putting contingent liabilities to rest. How long must a professional who has retired or a manufacturer that has ceased operations remain insured against old claims? The quality of justice—its sensitivity and context, its ability to deter and compensate—also diminishes over time. Limitations periods address these concerns by extinguishing potential plaintiffs' rights to maintain claims unless filed within the applicable statute's reasonable time.

The plaintiff who files a tort lawsuit after the date on which the statute of limitations bars it will likely suffer its prompt dismissal on the defendant's motion. If the plaintiff filed the suit frivolously, without a credible argument to modify or extend law to authorize its filing as timely, then court may impose sanctions for the plaintiff and plaintiff's counsel to pay. Dismissals based on an expired limitations period are with prejudice, meaning that no opportunity exists for another suit between the same parties asserting the same claims. On the other hand, dismissal based on the limitations period does not decide the case's merits—a principle that may permit the plaintiff to file different claims against the same defendant or the same claim against a different defendant.

> **Skills**
> Limitations periods create significant practical issues for tort lawyers, especially plaintiff's counsel. Plaintiff's lawyers must know the limitations periods and then maintain a calendar system alerting them to the approaching end of any limitations period for any claim they have not yet filed, even for potential clients whose matter the lawyer has not yet firmly and finally accepted. The manner in which a law firm fields and records, and then reviews, evaluates, decides, and communicates the decision on, potential clients' requests for representation, determines a tort lawyer's competent and ethical service, and malpractice exposure. Consider again the example client-intake form, contingency-fee agreement, and decline letter provided in the companion Torts I text. Defense lawyers must also know limitations periods to ensure that they plead and pursue limitations defenses.

Claim Accrual. Evaluating a statute-of-limitations defense begins with determining when the cause of action accrued. Claim accrual starts the limitations period running. The law typically defines claim accrual to occur when all of the elements of the claim are present—for instance, in a simple motor-vehicle-accident claim, when the negligent driver's vehicle collides with another vehicle causing the plaintiff's injury. Accrual issues arise when continuing misconduct causes continuing injury—perhaps domestic or sexual abuse, or medical malpractice involving continuing mistreatment. A *continuing-tort* rule treat the conduct and injury occurring over time as a single tort with the last incident taken as the accrual date. *See* Feltmeier v. Feltmeier, 33 Ill. App.3d 1167 (2002) (years of spousal abuse treated as continuous act); Cusseaux v. Pickett, 279 N.J. Super. 335, 652 A.2d 789 (1994) (battered woman's condition treated as continuing-tort claim); Justice v. Natvig, 238 Va. 178, 381 S.E.2d 8 (1989) (cause accrues when medical treatment ends); *but see* Seaton v. Seaton, 971 F. Supp. 1188 (E.D. Tenn. 1997) (under Tennessee law, allowing a claim and recovery for only the final incident dates within the limitations period).

Discovery Rule. Claim accrual grows more complex in cases in which the defendant's misconduct occurs over time rather than in a single instant. Claim accrual is also more complex when the plaintiff's injury gradually coalesces over time rather than arising at a single moment, such as in toxic tort cases, or when the plaintiff cannot reasonably discover the injury until some time well after the defendant's misconduct. Courts treat the latter situation under a *discovery rule* holding that the claim accrues only when the plaintiff know or should have known of the injury and its connection to the defendant's conduct. In asbestos cases, where exposure to the allegedly defective product may gradually lead to the nonfatal lung disease asbestosis or, years later, to the fatal lung cancer mesothelioma, most courts allow plaintiffs to file claims based on accrual as late as the mesothelioma. Discovery-rule cases in other areas tend to find that the claim accrued with the symptoms of any related condition or disease, not the worst disease's full-blown manifestation. *See* Gnazzo v. G.D. Searle & Co., 973 F.2d 136 (2nd Cir. 1992) (limitations period triggered by earlier inflammatory disease from IUD, not by later discovery of infertility). Discovery-rule arguments, whether the courts recognize them or not, commonly arise in toxic-tort, defective-drug, medical-device-defect, child-sexual-abuse, and medical-malpractice cases. *Contrast* Doe v. Maskell, 679 A.2d 1087 (Md. Ct. App. 1996) (refusing to apply discovery rule to childhood sexual-abuse case where plaintiff claimed to have repressed the memories), *with* Doe v. Roe, 955 P.2d 951 (Ariz. 1998) (repression may support applying the discovery rule); *see also* Conn. Gen. Stat. §52-577d (West 1991) (childhood sexual abuse cases have no limitations period); Me. Rev. Stat. §752-C (West 2001) (childhood sexual abuse victims may sue up to 17 years after age of majority). Consider the following malpractice case involving claim accrual and the discovery rule.

Teeters v. Currey
Tennessee Supreme Court
518 S.W.2d 512 (Tenn. 1974)

HENRY, J. This malpractice action essentially involves a determination of whether the statute of limitation begins to run from the date of the injury or from the date of the discovery of the injury.

The admitted facts are that on June 5, 1970, plaintiff gave birth to a normal child. Defendant was the attending physician. Following delivery, because of edema, anemia and other medical complications, he recommended that plaintiff have a bilateral tubal ligation, the purpose of which was to avoid future pregnancies. Defendant performed this surgery on June 6, 1970, and her recovery was uneventful.

On December 6, 1972, she was hospitalized at Newell Clinic and was attended by Dr. Edgar Atkin. Dr. Atkin discovered that she was pregnant. He so advised her and referred her to other physicians for obstetrical care.

On March 9, 1973, plaintiff was delivered of a premature child and there were severe complications. Pursuant to medical advice, another bilateral tubal ligation was performed on March 11, 1973.

Plaintiff instituted suit on November 15, 1973, three years, five months and nine days after the operation, but approximately eleven months after discovering her pregnancy.

Plaintiff alleges that during the course of this latter surgery it was discovered that the earlier surgery performed by the defendant was negligently and inadequately done and was not performed in accordance with proper standards of care and good medical practice.

Specifically, she charges that defendant failed to properly or completely sever the left fallopian tube in a manner which would assure sterility and prevent future pregnancies. Further, she charges that he failed to identify the right fallopian tube in a manner which would assure sterility and prevent future pregnancies. Further, she charges that he failed to cut, sever or ligate this tube in any manner. …

It is readily apparent that the [Trial] Court, in effect, simply sustained a plea of the statute of limitations and that this is the decisive issue before this Court. …

Section 28-304, T.C.A. applies to malpractice suits and provides that the action be "commenced within one (1) year after cause of action accrued."

When does the cause of action accrue?

In Bodne v. Austin, 156 Tenn. 366, 2 S.W.2d 104 (1927) the Court said: ". . . we have been referred to no authority holding that mere ignorance and failure to discover the existence of the cause of action, or the consequential damages resulting from the breach of duty or wrongful act, can prevent the running of the statute of limitations."

But this was in 1927 almost half a century ago.

In Albert v. Sherman, 167 Tenn. 133, 67 S.W.2d 140 (1934), the Court followed Bodne.

This was forty years ago.

The time has come for us to re-examine the past holdings of our Appellate Courts in the light of contemporary standards of justice and of the holdings of the courts of last resort in other American jurisdictions. ...

... We find it difficult to embrace a rule of law requiring that a plaintiff file suit prior to knowledge of his injury or, phrasing it another way, requiring that he sue to vindicate a non-existent wrong, at a time when injury is unknown and unknowable. ...

... [T]he public policy of our state is opposed to requiring that suit be filed when circumstances totally beyond the control of the injured party make it impossible for him to bring suit.

We recognize that statutes of limitations are statutes of repose designed to promote stability in the affairs of men and to avoid the uncertainties and burdens inherent in defending stale claims.

In recognition of this, traditionally our courts have held that a right of action accrues immediately upon the infliction or occurrence of injury and that mere ignorance or failure of plaintiff to discover his cause of action or the subsequent resulting damage does not toll the statute. [C]

That this is a harsh and oppressive rule there can be little doubt. To counter the casualties it has produced the courts have fashioned the so-called "discovery doctrine," under which the statute does not begin to run until the negligent injury is, or should have been discovered.

This concept has been adopted by judicial interpretation in at least a majority of the American states. [C] Some of these jurisdictions limit the application of the doctrine to "foreign objects; the majority apply it to all medical malpractice cases."
...

Upon the basis of reason and justice, we hold that when an inherently unknowable injury, such as is here involved, has been suffered by one blamelessly ignorant of the act or omission and injury complained of, and the harmful effect thereof develops gradually over a period of time, the injury is "sustained" * * * when the harmful effect first manifests itself and becomes physically ascertainable. ...

[The opinion cites authority reflecting that 28 states have adopted the discovery rule.]

Add Tennessee to the list.

We adopt as the rule of this jurisdiction the principle that in those classes of cases where medical malpractice is asserted to have occurred through the negligent performance of surgical procedures, the cause of action accrues and the statute of limitations commences to run when the patient discovers, or in the exercise of reasonable care and diligence for his own health and welfare, should have discovered the resulting injury. All cases contra are overruled.

In the instant case the cause of action accrued when plaintiff discovered that she was pregnant, or in the exercise of reasonable care and diligence, she should have so discovered. ...

We here merely recede from prior cases in order to establish a rule which we are convinced will be productive of results more nearly consonant with the demands of justice and the dictates of ethics and morality.

Reversed and Remanded. Appellee will pay all costs incident to this appeal.

INQUIRY

Classifying Claims. The next step in evaluating a statute-of-limitations defense is to classify the type of claim, to determine the statutory period. State law defines state tort-claim limitations periods, according to the type of claim. Parties win and lose late-filed cases based on court rulings as to the true nature of the claim, when the plaintiff asserts one claim to satisfy a limitations period barring a more-obvious claim. *See* Kambury v. DaimlerChrysler Corp., 334 Or. 367, 50 P.3d 1163 (2002) (two-year products-liability claim, not three-year wrongful-death claim). The periods vary considerably from state to state and claim to claim. For example, one state's limitations periods allow 90 days for whistleblower claims, one year for libel or slander, two years for malpractice and assault and battery, three years for negligence and fraud, and five years for spousal battery. Mich. Comp. L. §§15.363(1), 600.5806. Statutes in the same state add 120-day administrative-agency notice periods for sidewalk-defect and highway-defect claims. Mich. Comp. L. §§67.7, 691.1404(1). (Notice-of-claim statutes are not statutes of limitations because they do not dictate the date by which the plaintiff must file a court case, and only require administrative notice—but they often have the same effect of barring a late-noticed case. *See* Keller v. Tavarone, 262 Neb. 2, 628 N.W.2d 222 (2001) (barring medical-malpractice case against county physician for failure to serve requisite agency notice).) Florida allows four years for negligence and battery claims but two years for malpractice claims. Fla. Stat. §95.11. Tennessee allows one year for all personal injury claims, defining the dates when the claims start to run. Tenn. Code §28-3-104. Administrative-filing deadlines for federal civil-rights actions add 180-day and 300-day limitations periods to this complex mix. *See* 42 U.S.C. §2000e-5(e). Once a claim accrues, these periods run until the time they allow expires. Once a lawyer determines a claim's accrual date and confirms the applicable limitations period, the next step is to consult a calendar to determine when the limitations period expires.

Tolling. Evaluating a statute-of-limitations defense does not end there. Instead, circumstances may toll the limitations period. *Tolling* means that the limitations period does not run while certain conditions exist. Statute, court rule, or common law dictate the conditions, based on various policies. The first example of tolling is when the plaintiff files a lawsuit. Once a plaintiff files the lawsuit, the suit may persist for months or years without concern that the limitations period will bar it. Issues can arise when the plaintiff attempts later to amend a complaint to add tort claims, and when the passage of time since the original filing would bar the added tort claims if filed in a separate action. Treatment of the added claims may depend on their similarity to the claims already pled and the fairness to defendant of responding to them. New claims that the court allows despite the putative bar of the statute of limitations are said to *relate back* to the original filing. Other issues arise when the plaintiff has misnamed or been unable to identify and name certain defendant parties in a pending action, until after the limitations period for claims against those other parties expires. Whether the court allows the plaintiff to add these parties despite the putative bar of the statute of limitations may depend on the same factors. Thus, counsel should identify and name all defendant parties, and name all plaintiffs (including consortium-loss claims, for example), in a suit filed before the limitations period expires.

Classes of Plaintiffs. Statute or common law may permit tolling under other circumstances. State statutes will often toll limitations periods for minority (infancy), *see* Mich. Comp. L. §600.5851(1) (tolling to one year beyond age 18), and insanity, *see* Mich. Comp. L. §600.5851(2) (defined as "mental derangement such as to prevent the sufferer from comprehending rights he or she is otherwise bound to know"). State statutes or common law may also toll limitations periods based on the defendant's fraudulent concealment of the claims. *See* Mich. Comp. L. §600.5855 (plaintiff may commence action within two years of when the plaintiff discovers or should have discovered the fraudulent concealment of a claim); Bernson v. Browning-Ferris Indus. Of California, Inc., 30 Cal. Rptr.2d 440, 873 P.2d 613, 7 Cal.4th 926 (1994) (anonymous publication of libel constitutes fraudulent concealment tolling limitations period). The federal Servicemembers Civil Relief Act, 50 App. U.S.C. §§501 et seq., provides tolling of any limitation period (state or federal) during active-duty military service. Tolling provisions may also exist for a term of imprisonment.

Statutes of Repose. One other accrual issue, not mentioned above, arises when the plaintiff's injury does not occur until some time (perhaps many years) after the defendant's misconduct—such as when a building collapses years after its design and construction, due to professional negligence by the architect or engineer, or defective construction. The law may treat the timeliness of these cases under a statute of repose. A statute of repose bars all claims that might arise, not a certain period after the dates that the claims accrue (like a statute of limitation), but rather, a certain period after the person or entity made the good or provided the service. *See* Or. Rev. Stat. §30.905 (1995) (product liability of manufacturer ends eight years after first sale). If, for example, an architect negligently designs a building, a statute of repose may bar actions against the architect a certain number of years after the design work—whether claims actually arise during that period or not. *See* Cal. Code Civ. Proc. §337.15 (10-year statute of repose for claims against architects and engineers); Mich. Comp. L. §600.5839 (barring architect- and engineer-malpractice claims the later of six years after building occupancy or one year after discovery of defect, but in no event longer than after 10 years). The policy behind statutes of repose has to do with the inability of persons and entities whose products and services have lasting effects, to evaluate and insure against latent risks, and preserve and gather evidence of actions performed long ago. Such actions probably also have significantly diminished deterrent effect, when the person or entity years ago ceased the particular practice at issue. Courts have both upheld statutes of repose, *see* Love v. Whirlpool Corp., 449 S.E.2d 602 (1994) (product-liability claim barred 10 years after first sale), and stricken them as unconstitutional, *see* De Young v. Providence Med. Ctr., 960 P.2d 919 (1998) (state constitution's privileges-and-immunities clause voids eight-year statute of repose for medical-malpractice actions).

D. Immunities

OBJECTIVE: Given various fact patterns involving tort injuries occurring within families, or committed by charities or federal, state, or local government, analyze the immunities involved so as to determine viable claims and responsible parties consistent with this section of the text.

Case Study: A driver worked for a transportation service operated by a charitable non-profit organization, taking patrons back and forth from an occupational rehabilitation agency to various work sites. On one of those trips, the driver negligently ran a red light, resulting in a collision in which a patron passenger was seriously injured. The driver's wife and minor child, who were not patrons but were along for the ride, were also seriously injured. *Identify the possible immunities relating to the potential claims of the three injured passengers.*

Immunities differ from other defenses in that they depend less on the occurrence's circumstance or misconduct's nature, but rather, on the special status of the putative defendant. Tort law has at times and in places recognized five immunities: intra-family, charitable, governmental, worker's compensation (employer), and motor-vehicle no-fault act. This text treats worker's disability compensation acts and motor-vehicle no-fault systems, both statute-based immunities, in a later chapter on no-fault systems. Statutes commonly modify each of the three traditional common-law immunities treated here, in some states eliminating them while in other states limiting them to certain claims or circumstances, although a few states retain intact the traditional common-law immunities. Even in states where the traditional immunities remain, their application can vary substantially based on differing case law. The following text treats immunities in broad brush. Practitioners must familiarize themselves with their state's peculiar immunity rules.

The two main intra-family immunities are inter-spousal immunity (immunity between spouses) and parent-child immunity (both ways, barring suits by children against parents and parents against children). The traditional justification for intra-family immunities begins with preserving family peace and tranquility, and hierarchical order (parent over child) within the family. A minor child's tort lawsuit brought against a custodial parent, for instance, or one spouse's tort lawsuit brought against the other spouse, could burden otherwise-trusting family relationships with strategic behaviors and strained feelings—especially considering the involvement of adversarial legal counsel on each side's behalf. The adverse parties may wish to cooperate, in itself raising a concern over collusion to defraud the insurer, but an insurance policy may instead require cooperation only with the insurer and defense counsel. A practical issue with intra-family lawsuits is that unless liability insurance covers the claim, the lawsuit's effect might be to merely move money from one household pocket to another, failing to alter the household's finances. What does a family gain by one member having a judgment against another? These instrumental and practical reasons to preserve intra-family immunities erode when one considers the less-than-ideal makeup of many families—especially those in which members have committed torts against one another. Tranquility may not exist within the family, or family order may improve with a tort action. The sacramental nature of family relationships—especially the marital relationship—and value society places on family ideals may separately warrant the immunities' serious consideration. Consider the following two cases.

Freehe v. Freehe
Washington Supreme Court
81 Wash.2d 183, 500 P.2d 771 (1972)

NEILL, J. Plaintiff, Clifford Freehe, seeks compensation for personal injuries allegedly sustained due to defendant's negligent maintenance of a tractor and failure to warn plaintiff of the tractor's unsafe condition. The claim for relief would be just the normal action in tort for personal injury but for the fact that the defendant is the wife of the plaintiff, thus bringing into issue the doctrine of interspousal tort immunity.

The farm on which the accident took place is the separate property of defendant, doing business under the name of Hazel Knoblauch. The tractor involved in this accident, together with all other assets and income of the farm, were and remain the separate property of defendant. The business of the farm is carried on separately from any community business of the parties. Plaintiff has no interest in the farming operation. Neither was he employed by defendant.

The trial court granted defendant's motion for summary judgment solely on the basis of interspousal tort immunity. Plaintiff appeals. …

The case which apparently established the doctrine of interspousal tort immunity in Washington is Schultz v. Christopher, 65 Wash. 496, 118 P. 629 (1911). In that case the court referred to the common law notion of "unity" of husband and wife… .

The "supposed unity" of husband and wife, which serves as the traditional basis of interspousal disability, is not a reference to the common nature or loving oneness achieved in a marriage of two free individuals. Rather, this traditional premise had reference to a situation, coming on from antiquity, in which a woman's marriage for most purposes rendered her a chattel of her husband. …

Things have changed. They had changed 88 years ago when the Rosencrantz court, noting the improved legal status of married women, held them as eligible as their husbands to serve on juries. Neither spouse is liable for the separate debts of the other. RCW 26.16.200. And either spouse may sue the other for invasion of separate property rights. RCW 26.16.180; Mattinson v. Mattinson, 128 Wash. 328, 222 P. 620 (1924). Recent legislation (Laws of 1972, 2d Ex.Sess., ch. 108) radically alters the relative right of the wife to manage and represent community property, rights and interests. Spouses are no longer individually liable for each other's torts unless they would be jointly liable if unmarried.

Modern realities do not comport with the traditional 'supposed unity' of husband and wife. In our view, this concept of legal identity is no longer a valid premise for a rule of this interspousal disability.

A second major reason given for the disability is the notion that to allow a married person to sue his or her spouse for tort damages would be to destroy the peace and tranquility of the home. On reflection, we are convinced that this is a conclusion without basis. If a state of peace and tranquility exists between the spouses, then the situation is such that either no action will be commenced or that the spouses—who are, after all, the best guardians of their own peace and tranquility—will allow the action to continue only so long as their personal harmony is not jeopardized. If peace and tranquility is nonexistent or tenuous to begin with, then the law's imposition of a technical disability seems more likely to be a bone of contention than a harmonizing factor.

We have previously discussed the family tranquility argument in an analogous context (parent-child disability: Borst v. Borst, 41 Wash.2d 642, 251 P.2d 149 (1952)) and in dicta in an interspousal disability case (Goode v. Martinis, Supra). On both occasions, the argument has been rejected. For the reasons stated here and in those cases, we now expressly reject the notion that the desirability of family peace and tranquility is a valid reason for precluding a cause of action in tort against the tortfeasor spouse. …

A third reason advanced in support of maintaining the common law rule of disability is the suggestion that the injured spouse has an adequate remedy through the criminal and divorce laws. It has been observed that neither of these alternatives actually compensates for the damage done, or provides any remedy for nonintentional (negligent) torts. ...

It has also been argued that to permit litigation between spouses over personal torts would flood the courts with a burdensome amount of trivial matrimonial disputes. As a matter of theory, this argument could be interposed against virtually all personal injury claims. Any validity to the argument would depend whether such a "flood" materializes in practice. In Goode v. Martinis, Supra, at page 234, 361 P.2d at page 944, we observed: "There is nothing in the experience of the dozen or more jurisdictions in this country which do permit spouses to sue one another for personal torts which would indicate that court calendars have become cluttered with trivial matrimonial disputes. We think it is fair to assume that few litigants would consider it worth-while to initiate such actions." ...

Respondent also suggests that another argument in favor of the disability rule is that to permit suits between spouses would encourage collusion and fraud where one or both of the spouses carries liability insurance. In Goode v. Martinis, Supra, at page 234, 361 P.2d at page 945, we rejected this "pessimistic premise," noting that "this line of argument presupposes that courts are so ineffectual and the jury system is so imperfect that fraudulent claims cannot be distinguished from the legitimate." In the analogous case of Borst v. Borst, Supra, 41 Wash.2d at page 653, 251 P.2d at page 155, we stated: "The courts may and should take cognizance of fraud and collusion when found to exist in a particular case. However, the fact that there may be greater opportunity for fraud or collusion in one class of cases than another does not warrant courts of law in closing the door to all cases of that class. Courts must depend upon the efficacy of the judicial processes to ferret out the meritorious from the fraudulent in particular cases. (Citation.) If those processes prove inadequate, the problem becomes one for the legislature. (Citation.) Courts will not immunize tort feasors from liability in a whole class of cases because of the possibility of fraud, but will depend upon the legislature to deal with the problem as a question of public policy."

We there cited, as an example of the ability of the legislature to cope with such a problem should it arise, the enactment of host-guest statutes (RCW 46.08.080, -.085, -.086) in automobile personal injury cases. We conclude that this possibility is not a valid premise for the common law disability rule.

Respondent also suggests that any change in the marital disability rule is a matter for the legislature, citing Schultz v. Christopher, Supra. This argument ignores the fact that the rule is not one made or sanctioned by the legislature, but rather is one that depends for its origins and continued viability upon the common law. In these circumstances, it is proper to echo the words quoted in Borst v. Borst, Supra, 41 Wash.2d at page 657, 251 P.2d at page 157: "Legislative action there could, of course, be, but we abdicate our own function, in a field peculiarly nonstatutory, when we refuse to reconsider an old and unsatisfactory court-made rule." [Cc]

Furthermore, we now observe that our prior cases which are cited as recognizing the common law rule, have contained statutory analysis focusing on the provisions of RCW 26.16.160 (equality). Another important statutory section is RCW 26.16.150. In Goode v. Martinis, Supra, we assumed, for purposes of argument, that section 150 is not a legislative abrogation of the doctrine of interspousal immunity. Section 150 expressly states that "Every married person shall hereafter have the same right and liberty . . . to sue and be sued, as if he or she were unmarried." Whatever may have been the view of this court as to the impact of RCW 26.16.150 on the common law doctrine here at issue, and it appears that we have not heretofore actually examined into the question, this court has never interpreted section 150. We are now of the view that the statute means what it says and that, to the extent that a spouse has an individual interest in compensation for personal injuries, the statute allows him or her to bring suit against the tort-feasor spouse. ...

We are cognizant of the long standing nature of the common law rule of interspousal tort immunity. But we find more impelling the fundamental precept that, absent express statutory provision, or compelling public policy, the law should not immunize tort-feasors or deny remedy to their victims. With this in mind, we have reviewed the stated reasons for the common law rule, and have found all of them to be insufficient. Therefore, the rule of interspousal disability in personal injury cases is hereby abandoned. To the extent that Schultz v. Christopher, Supra, can be read as inconsistent herewith, it is overruled.

Reversed and remanded.

> ***Knowledge***
> See the value in helping clients to recognize and define their objectives. Clients benefit greatly from this skill. Legal analysis involves more than identifying fighting pairs. You should also address whether maintaining a claim would meet the claimant's objectives. Clients may decline to sue their immediate family members. Just because claims exist does not mean that their prosecution is obvious or reasonable. The opposite may be true. No right-thinking client would sue an uninsured family member on whose income the client depends, where the judgment's enforcement would simply take money from one pocket in the household to put it in another, at substantial transaction costs (lawyer fees and litigation expenses). The same may be true for suing one's own partnership, business, or employer. Analysis thus requires determining whether maintaining the claim makes sense, even when the claimant could win the claim.
> Identifying a client's objective requires listening and questioning. Ask the client what the client hopes to achieve. Clients may have several objectives only some of which relate to law. A lawyer must sometimes clarify the law-related objective from among other objectives. A client who has suffered personal injury may want compensation, deterrence, punishment, or a combination of these results. The lawyer must compare these objectives to the available remedies, to determine which claims to pursue.

INQUIRY

Inter-Spousal Immunity. What is the most common type of inter-spousal tort claim? *See* Digby v. Digby, 120 R.I. 299, 388 A.2d 1 (1978) (motor vehicle accident). Do spouess assume the risk of certain negligent conduct—perhaps such as in food preparation or disease exposure? *See* Beaudette v. Frana, 366, 173 (N.W.2d 416 (1969) ("It would be an unusual case in which the trial court would not instruct the jury as to the injured spouse's peculiar assumption of risk....") (dicta). Among the eighteen remaining states not completely abrogating inter-spousal immunity, what modifications and exceptions would you expect to find? *See* McCulloh v. Drake, 24 P.3d 1162 (Wyo. 2001) (inter-spousal claim permitted for intentional infliction of emotional distress); Asplin v. Amica Mut. Ins. Co., 121 R.I. 51, 394 A.2d 1353 (1978) (inter-spousal claim permitted if either spouse has died); Childress v. Childress, 569 S.W.2d 816 (Tenn. 1978) (inter-spousal claim permitted after divorce); Lusby v. Lusby, 283 Md. 334, 390 A.2d 77 (1978) (inter-spousal claim permitted for intentional torts); Gaston v. Pittman, 224 So.2d 326 (Fla. 1969) (inter-spousal claim permitted after divorce, if the tort occurred before the marriage); Sanchez v. Olivarez, 94 N.J. Super. 61, 226 A.2d 752 (1967) (inter-spousal claim permitted after divorce, even if the tort occurred during the marriage). Consider now the next intra-family immunity—that between parent and child.

Renko v. McLean
Maryland Supreme Court
346 Md. 464, 697 A.2d 468 (1997)

KARWACKI, J. In Warren v. Warren, 336 Md. 618, 650 A.2d 252 (1994), and Frye v. Frye, 305 Md. 542, 505 A.2d 826 (1986), this Court declined to create an exception to the parent-child immunity doctrine in motor tort cases based upon the existence of compulsory automobile liability insurance coverage. We are asked in this case to reexamine those decisions. Having done so, we shall reaffirm the vitality of the parent child-immunity doctrine in this State and affirm the judgment of the Circuit Court for Anne Arundel County.

I.

The facts of this case are brief and undisputed. On December 8, 1992, Natasha Renko suffered serious injuries when her biological mother, Teresa Kaylor McLean, negligently drove the car both women were occupying into the rear of another vehicle. At the time, Natasha Renko was seventeen years old.

On January 18, 1994, and following her eighteenth birthday, Renko filed a Complaint and Election of Jury Trial in the Circuit Court for Anne Arundel County seeking damages in the amount of $100,000 for injuries she allegedly sustained in the December 8, 1992 automobile accident. The Complaint named Teresa McLean and her husband, Robert McLean,[] as defendants,[] here appellees. ...

II.

For nearly seventy years, the parent-child tort immunity doctrine has been, with few exceptions,[] a salient feature of Maryland law. See Schneider v. Schneider, 160 Md. 18, 152 A. 498 (1930).[] It remains so today.

Once an absolute bar to tort actions between parents and their minor children,[] the parent-child immunity doctrine grew out of an abiding belief that it served the compelling public interest in preserving, under normal circumstances, the internal harmony and integrity of the family unit and parental authority in the parent-child relationship. [Cc] In fact, the special relationship, with its reciprocal duties and obligations, that the minor child shares with his or her parents forms a major component of the foundation upon which the parent-child immunity doctrine is built—a relationship recognized both at common law[fn] and by the General Assembly.[fn] Other justifications offered for the rule include the prevention of fraud and collusion among family members to the detriment of third parties, and the threat that intrafamilial litigation will deplete family resources. [Cc] ...

In Frye, supra [305 Md. At 561, 505 A.2d at 836], we exhaustively surveyed the creation and refinement of the parent-child immunity doctrine both in this State and across our Country. Despite the growing chorus of criticism surrounding the doctrine,[] we determined that the parent-child relationship had changed little, if at all, in the ensuing years since our predecessors first recognized parent-child immunity. We thus concluded that "today's parent-child relationship, as recognized by this Court and the Legislature, furnishes no compelling reason to abrogate the rule." Id. at 561, 505 A.2d at 836; see also Warren, 336 Md. at 627-28, 650 A.2d at 256-57.

III.

Renko nonetheless mounts a three-pronged attack upon the parent-child immunity doctrine. She asserts that (1) adult children should be allowed to maintain actions against their parents for injuries occurring in their minority; (2) no contemporary justification exists to apply the doctrine to the facts of the case sub judice in light of compulsory motor vehicle liability insurance; and (3) any such application is violative of Articles 19 and 24 of the Maryland Declaration of Rights and of the Fourteenth Amendment to the United States Constitution. We shall address each of these contentions in turn.

a.

Renko correctly points out that we have permitted suits between parents and their minor children in limited circumstances. For instance, we have held that a minor child may maintain an action against a father's business partner for alleged negligence arising out of the operation of the partnership. [Cc] ...

Recognizing that reality sometimes belies the ideal of family life, our predecessors also deemed permissible a suit by a minor child against her father's estate for alleged injuries she sustained when, within the span of one week, the father both murdered the child's mother and committed suicide in the child's presence. Mahnke v. Moore, 197 Md. 61, 77 A.2d 923 (1951). The Court reasoned that

> "[i]n these circumstances, there can be no basis for the contention that the daughter's suit against her father's estate would be contrary to public policy, for the simple reason that there is no home at all in which discipline and tranquility are to be preserved.... [W]hen ... the parent is guilty of acts which show complete abandonment of the parental relation, the rule giving him immunity from suit by the child, on the ground that discipline should be maintained in the home, cannot logically be applied, for when he is guilty of such acts he forfeits his parental authority and privileges, including his immunity from suit... . Justice demands that a minor child shall have a right of action against a parent for injuries resulting from cruel and inhuman treatment or for malicious and wanton wrongs." Id. at 67-68, 77 A.2d at 926.

Renko contends that since this Court has already permitted children to maintain actions against their parents for acts occurring after the child reaches the age of majority, see Waltzinger v. Birsner, 212 Md. 107, 128 A.2d 617 (1957), we should take the logical step of allowing otherwise adult children to sue their parents for wrongful acts that occur during minority. We see no such logic. In fact, Renko's proffered solution to her particular dilemma would result in a de facto abrogation of the parent-child immunity doctrine in its entirety.

Maryland Code (1995 Repl.Vol., 1996 Supp.), §5-201[fn] of the Courts & Judicial Proceedings Article permits minors to bring tort actions for injuries sustained in minority at the hands of another within three years after reaching the age of majority. Thus, an injured minor child could simply wait until reaching the age of majority before initiating a suit that is otherwise barred in his or her infancy. In that circumstance, the parent-child immunity doctrine would serve not as a bar to actions between parent and child, but rather as an obstacle easily overcome with the passage of time. The looming specter of a lawsuit is as surely detrimental to family peace and harmony and parental authority as is the actual suit itself. Given this Court's long commitment to the parent-child immunity doctrine, we refuse to create an exception that would effectively negate the rule and open courthouse doors to every conceivable dispute between parent and child. See Warren, 336 Md. at 626, 650 A.2d at 256. Indeed, the rule was fashioned to prevent just that. Id.

b.

Renko alternatively contends that "with mandatory automobile insurance creating universal coverage for auto torts, there can be no rational objection to recovery by an emancipated child in" the case sub judice. ...

We recognized in Warren and Frye, supra, that an overwhelming majority of jurisdictions have abrogated the parent-child immunity doctrine in whole or in part. [cc] ... At the time we issued the Warren opinion, "[o]nly eight states, including Maryland, continue[d] to adhere to the doctrine of parent-child immunity without exception for motor torts." 336 Md. at 621 n. 1, 650 A.2d at 254 n. 1. Those same jurisdictions continue to stand their ground.[fn]

Other jurisdictions, however, have found persuasive arguments calling for the abolition of the parent-child immunity doctrine in motor tort cases. The seminal decision in this area is Sorensen v. Sorensen, 369 Mass. 350, 339 N.E.2d 907 (1975). There, the Supreme Judicial Court of Massachusetts observed: "In dealing with an automobile accident in which two passengers, one an unemancipated minor child of the defendant driver and the other a minor who had no familial relationship to the defendant driver, are injured, it would be incongruous to permit recovery against a parent and the parent's insurance company by the unrelated child but to deny recovery to the parent's child when culpability is admitted or established." Id. at 360, 339 N.E.2d at 913. Noting the basis of the parent-child immunity doctrine, the court commented that "[t]he primary disruption to harmonious filial relations is not the lawsuit brought for damages after the injury but the injury itself, resulting from the misconduct of a parent. Falco v. Pados, 444 Pa. 372, 380, 282 A.2d 351 [, 355] (1971). When the wrong has been committed, the harm to the basic fabric of the family has already been done and the source of rancor and discord already introduced into family relations. Tamashiro v. De Gama, 51 Haw. 74, 78, 450 P.2d 998[, 1001] (1969). Balts v. Balts, 273 Minn. 419, 429, 142 N.W.2d 66[, 73] (1966). It can hardly aid family reconciliation to deny the injured child access to the courts and, through them, to any liability insurance which the family might maintain." Id. at 360, 339 N.E.2d at 913.

Considering the same issue, the Supreme Court of Delaware concluded, that with the almost universal existence of motor vehicle liability insurance, "the domestic tranquility argument is, at best, hollow. Liability insurance impersonalizes the suit and negates the possible disruption of family harmony by easing the financial repercussions of the accident. In short 'when insurance is involved, the action between parent and child is not truly adversary; both parties seek recovery from the insurance carrier to create a fund for the child's medical care and support without depleting the family's other assets.'" Williams v. Williams, 369 A.2d 669, 672 (Del.1976)(citing Sorensen, 369 Mass. at 362-63, 339 N.E.2d at 914); see also Schneider v. Coe, 405 A.2d 682 (Del.1979)(affirming abrogation of parent-child immunity in auto tort cases where insurance coverage exists). ...

The fraud-collusion justification for the parent-child immunity doctrine too has suffered its critics, among them, the Mississippi Supreme Court—the birthplace of the parent-child immunity doctrine. See Hewlett v. George, 68 Miss. 703, 9 So. 885 (1891). In Glaskox, supra, the court majority observed that "'[t]he possibility of collusion exists to a certain extent in any case. Every day we depend on juries and trial judges to sift evidence in order to determine the facts and arrive at proper verdicts. Experience has shown that the courts are quite adequate for this task. In litigation between parent and child, judges and juries would naturally be mindful of the relationship and would be even more on the alert for improper conduct.'" 614 So.2d at 912 (quoting Nocktonick v. Nocktonick, 227 Kan. 758, 768-69, 611 P.2d 135, 142 (1980)). ...

Recognizing the continuing need to protect parental authority and family harmony, some jurisdictions have attempted to limit immunity to negligent conduct arising out of an "exercise of parental authority ... [or] an exercise of ordinary parental discretion with respect to the provision of food, clothing, housing, medical and dental services, and other care." Goller v. White, 20 Wis.2d 402, 413, 122 N.W.2d 193, 198 (1963); [cc].

California and New York have adopted their own unique brands of parent-child immunity. California courts apply a "reasonable parent" standard to determine the viability of tort actions between parent and child. [C] New York, on the other hand, seems to permit all such actions, except those arising out of a parent's failure to properly supervise the child. Under New York law, parents owe no legal duty to their children to supervise them properly. [C]

Despite the majority trend, even those most critical of the rule must acknowledge that its abrogation is not a panacea. At least with respect to motor tort cases, the argument for abrogation suffers from several infirmities.

In a normal case, liability insurance becomes relevant only after an insured's liability is fixed in an appropriate legal proceeding. Yet as between parent and child, it becomes the raison d'être of the suit. Thus, unlike a true adversarial proceeding, an insurer is forced into the unenviable position of attempting to defend a suit that its insured has every incentive to lose.[fn] ...

Further, many families carry medical insurance that would necessarily compensate the injured child, and therefore, his or her family, for injury-related expenses. Allowing children then to proceed to court and recover for pain and suffering and other noneconomic damages, which often far exceed medical costs, might potentially saddle a family with a judgment that they can ill-afford to pay because, as previously indicated, it exceeds available insurance.

Finally, Justice Lee of the Supreme Court of Mississippi cogently observed that many of the arguments against parent-child immunity "impl[y] that a child injured by the negligence of a parent is adrift in our current system with no rights of all.... [T]ort law cannot erase physical injuries or soothe human suffering. It can only insure that injured parties are compensated. [P]arents already have the legal responsibility of providing care for their children.... A policy of immunity in no way detracts from the seriousness of the issue of parental neglect or other forms of abuse. The proper remedy for these injuries, however, is eternal vigilance on the part of individuals and government agencies and vigorous enforcement of criminal statutes." Glaskox, supra, 614 So.2d at 916 (Lee J., dissenting).

In light of the foregoing observations and on balance, we remain convinced that the parent-child immunity rule "is still in the best interests of both children and parents to retain ... [and that] [a]brogating immunity would result only in further discord within the family and would interfere with the exercise of parental discretion in raising and disciplining children." Warren, 336 Md. at 626, 650 A.2d at 255. ...

... In light of the fact that parents are charged with the "support, care, nurture, and welfare" of their children, see n.8, supra, Maryland law has long recognized, save for extraordinary circumstances, that the parent-child immunity doctrine is a reasonable and well-founded limitation upon a child's access to our courts, serving to protect one of the most fundamental and sacred units in our society.

JUDGMENT AFFIRMED, WITH COSTS.

INQUIRY

Parent-Child Immunity. Where courts have completely abrogated parent-child immunity, to what standard of care do children and their children's tort lawyers hold parents? *See* Broadbent v. Broadbent, 184 Ariz. 74, 907 P.2d 43 (1995) (reasonably prudent parent standard); Anderson v. Stream, 295 N.W.2d 595 (Minn. 1980) (same); Gibson v. Gibson, 3 Cal.3d 914, 479 P.2d 648, 92 Cal. Rptr. 288 (1971) (same); *but see* Hartman v. Hartman, 821 S.W.2d 852 (Mo. 1991) (not an idealized standard). Should a child have a claim against a parent for negligent supervision? *See* Poole v. Poole, 1 P.3d 936 (Mont. 2000) (eleven-year-old child's allegation that parent failed to reasonably supervise child by letting child go to a friend's house without confirming adult supervision); Shoemake v. Fogel, Ltd., 826 S.W.2d 933 (Tex. 1992) (choice of home, food, and schooling not subject to review without culpability greater than ordinary negligence). Does imposing tort-law reasonable-parent standards run the risk of injecting cultural bias or missing cultural differences in raising and disciplining children? *See* Crotta v. Home Depot, Inc., 249 Conn. 634, 732 A.2d 767 (1999) (negligent supervision claims would ignore differences of culture). Should a child have a claim for emotional harm from a parent's failure to perform general parental duties? *See* Burnette v. Wahl, 284 Or. 705, 588 P.2d 1105 (1978).

Figure

Defense lawyer Sheila Birnbaum is a partner and the chair of the Complex Mass Tort and Insurance Group at the New York office of Skadden, Arps, Slate, Meagher & Flom LLP. She has been national or lead defense counsel for many Fortune 500 companies in complex and mass-tort litigation involving breast implants, medical devices, biogenetic corn, pharmaceuticals, salmonella-contaminated milk, DDT exposure, alcohol sales, asbestos and other building products, heavy machinery, cordless telephones, chemicals, and drinking-water contamination. She has argued or been lead counsel for defendant corporations on Supreme Court cases including State Farm's reversal of a $145 million punitive-damages award and in the *Buckley v. Metro North* case involving medical monitoring. She speaks and writes extensively, is the co-author of The

Practitioner's Guide to Litigating Insurance Coverage Actions, and has won many awards including the Louis D. Brandeis Award from the American Jewish Congress.

Policy. Recognizing that only approximately ten states have completely abrogated parent-child immunity, compared to the thirty-two states that have completely abrogated inter-spousal immunity, why do you think more states recognize some form of parent-child immunity, than inter-spousal immunity? How do the relationships and the likely effects of liability differ? *See* Small v. Morrison, 185 N.C. 577, 585-86, 118 S.E. 12, 16 (1923) (basis for parent-child immunity "was unmistakably and indelibly carved upon the tablets of Mount Sinai"). In those states that have not completely abrogated parent-child immunity, what permutations would you expect to find in its modification and exceptions? *See* Newman v. Cole, 872 So.2d 138 (Ala. 2003) (recognizing intentional tort claim for wrongful-death of child from parent's discipline); Herzfeld v. Herzfeld, 781 So.2d 1070 (Fla. 2001) (sexual assault and abuse); Eagan v. Calhoun, 347 Md. 72, 698 A.2d 1097 (1997) (child permitted to sue father for wrongful death of mother by manslaughter); Broadwell v. Holmes, 871 SW.2d 471 (Tenn. 1994) (parent-child motor vehicle accident suits allowed); Glaskox v. Glaskox, 614 So.2d 906 (Miss. 1992) (same); MFA Mut. Ins. Co. v. Howard Constr. Co., 608 S.W.2d 535 (mo. App. 1980) (parent-child suits allowed after termination of relationship by death of either party); Williams v. Williams, 369 A.2d 669 (Del. 1976) (child's suit allowed where parent has liability insurance coverage for the claims alleged); Fitzgerald v. Valdez, 77 N.M. 769, 427 P.2d 655 (1967) (child's suit allowed after emancipation); Gillett v. Gillett, 168 Cal.App.2d 102, 335 P.2d 736 (1959) (child may sue step-parent); *but see* Squeglia v. Squeglia, 234 Conn. 259, 661 A.2d 1007 (1995) (presence of liability insurance immaterial to existence of immunity).

Charitable Immunity. Charitable immunity traditionally extended to non-profit hospitals, religious organizations, service organizations, and the like, justified in that tort liability should not burden those organizations' good works. Indeed, a trust-fund theory exists that whatever assets charities hold are only in trust on their donors' behalf for public purposes—not subject to execution by a charity's tort creditors. Charities have traditionally served an important role in American society, providing needed goods and services, innovating, and diversifying goods and services in ways that contribute substantially to the economy and society. Yet a substantial majority of states abolished charitable immunity after the District of Columbia did so in Georgetown College v. Hughes, 130 F.2d 810 (D.C. Cir. 1942). One reason may be the sheer quantity of commerce charities conduct today in the United States—sometimes said to be the third leg of the economy after the private sector and government. The Internal Revenue Code's Section 501(c)(3) recognizes tens of thousands of tax-exempt charitable organizations operating, among other public services, schools, clinics, hospitals, ambulances, and nursing homes, not merely soup kitchens. Where law continues to recognize some form of charitable immunity, it often does so under legislative schemes like the following one in Texas, codified at Vernon's Tex. Stat. & Code Ann. §84.001 et seq.:

§84.002. Findings and Purposes

The Legislature of the State of Texas finds that:
(1) robust, active, bona fide, and well-supported charitable organizations are needed within Texas to perform essential and needed services;
(2) the willingness of volunteers to offer their services to these organizations is deterred by the perception of personal liability arising out of the services rendered to these organizations;
(3) because of these concerns over personal liability, volunteers are withdrawing from services in all capacities;
(4) these same organizations have a further problem in obtaining and affording liability insurance for the organization and its employees and volunteers;
(5) these problems combine to diminish the services being provided to Texas and local communities because of higher costs and fewer programs;
(6) the citizens of this state have an overriding interest in the continued and increased delivery of these services that must be balanced with other policy considerations; and
(7) because of the above conditions and policy considerations, it is the purpose of this Act to reduce the liability exposure and insurance costs of these organizations and their employees and volunteers in order to encourage volunteer services and maximize the resources devoted to delivering these services.

§84.003. Definitions
In this chapter:
(1) "Charitable organization" means:
(A) any organization exempt from federal income tax under Section 501(a) of the Internal Revenue Code of 1986 by being listed as an exempt organization in Section 501(c)(3) or 501(c)(4) of the code... .

§ 84.004. Volunteer Liability
(a) Except as provided by Subsection (d) and Section 84.007, a volunteer of a charitable organization is immune from civil liability for any act or omission resulting in death, damage, or injury if the volunteer was acting in the course and scope of the volunteer's duties or functions, including as an officer, director, or trustee within the organization.
...
(d) A volunteer of a charitable organization is liable to a person for death, damage, or injury to the person or his property proximately caused by any act or omission arising from the operation or use of any motor-driven equipment, including an airplane, to the extent insurance coverage is required by Chapter 601, Transportation Code, and to the extent of any existing insurance coverage applicable to the act or omission. ...

§84.005. Employee Liability
Except as provided in Section 84.007 of this Act, in any civil action brought against an employee of a nonhospital charitable organization for damages based on an act or omission by the person in the course and scope of the person's employment, the liability of the employee is limited to money damages in a maximum amount of $500,000 for each person and $1,000,000 for each single occurrence of bodily injury or death and $100,000 for each single occurrence for injury to or destruction of property.

§84.006. Organization Liability
Except as provided in Section 84.007 of this Act, in any civil action brought against a nonhospital charitable organization for damages based on an act or omission by the organization or its employees or volunteers, the liability of the organization is limited to money damages in a maximum amount of $500,000 for each person and $1,000,000 for each single occurrence of bodily injury or death and $100,000 for each single occurrence for injury to or destruction of property.

INQUIRY

Exceptions. In that minority of states where charitable immunity exists in some fashion, what form would you expect to find? Some states permit suits against charitable hospitals but not other charitable entities. Why? Would the fact that charitable hospitals hold as much as half of all hospital assets in the United States be a sufficient reason? Why? Other states prohibit suits by patrons against the charitable organization that served—and injured—them. *See* N.J.S.A. 2A:53A-7 (2004). Why? Other states tie charitable immunity to the organization obtaining liability insurance in a certain amount—permitting suits up to that amount only. *See* Md. Cts. & Jud. Proc. §5-632 (2003) ($100,000 liability insurance required to invoke immunity). How treat a charitable organization's intentional tort? *See* Mrozka v. Archdiocese of St. Paul & Minneapolis, 482 N.W.2d 806 (Minn. App. 1992) (punitive damages allowed for knowing misconduct). Should the law protect a charitable organization's volunteers while they perform the charitable service? *See* N.H. Rev. Stat. Ann. §508:17 (2004) (volunteer immunity with conditions); Moore v. Warren, 250 Va. 421, 463 S.E.2d 459 (1995) (volunteer protected by organization's immunity).

Governmental Immunity. Understand governmental immunity (traditionally called sovereign immunity) through a similar historical lens. Take as a starting point that a person could not sue the government without its permission, under the very laws that government had made. Governmental immunity also had a separation-of-powers aspect—that the judicial branch of government should not interfere with the administrative and legislative branches by imposing tort judgments against them. Legislatures can and do provide for compensation by legislative means, just as administrative bodies have some capacity to adjust rights and afford remedies administratively. Tort immunity did not usually extend to local government, only federal and state government. Yet today, government so heavily involves itself in the modern economy, engaging in activities so like those of private citizens and businesses (operating motor vehicles on the highway, for instance), that blanket governmental immunity seems unwise. Government insures itself, through inter-governmental liability pools and private insurance. Considering this history and policy, Congress enacted the Federal Tort Claims Act in 1946, waiving in part the federal government's common-law immunity. States followed by enacting their own partial governmental-immunity waivers. Statutory waivers of state immunity include features like providing for jurisdiction only in special courts of claims, not providing for jury trials, requiring strict notice of claims within periods much shorter than the general statute of limitations (a malpractice hazard for the uninformed tort practitioner), and capping damages. States waiving some immunity tend to retain immunity for judicial and legislative units.

Waivers. Waivers of governmental immunity (that is, where tort liability applies) are now common for the negligent operation of government motor vehicles, medical malpractice in government hospitals, and negligent construction and maintenance of defective sidewalks, highways, and buildings. *See, e.g.*, Mich. Comp. L. 691.1401 et seq. Other statutory waivers attempt functional distinctions—probably with significantly less clarity in the ensuing case law. For instance, states may preserve immunity for discretionary governmental decisions but not ministerial government actions. For example, the decision whether and how to salt roads against icing depends on discretion, implicating budget and labor policies, and judgments about the weather and salt reserves. *See* Lane v. State of Vermont, 174 Vt. 219, 811 A.2d 190 (2002) (road-salting decisions are discretionary and immune). Once an official exercises discretion to salt a road, operation of the salt truck—surely a ministerial act—would not be immune. Yet the discretionary-ministerial distinction can be notoriously difficult to make in any one case. *See* Aguehounde v. District of Columbia, 666 A.2d 443 (D.C. App. 1995) (decision on timing of traffic signals, made without judgment, is an immune discretionary function). Other statutes preserve immunity for governmental but not proprietary functions—another theoretically meaningful distinction that can be hard to make in practice. Consider the following case illustrating the complete waiver of governmental immunity.

Ayala v. Philadelphia Bd. Of Public Educ.
Pennsylvania Supreme Court
453 Pa. 584, 305 A.2d 877 (1973)

ROBERTS, J. Appellants, William Ayala and William Ayala, Jr., instituted this action to recover damages for injuries suffered by William, Jr., when his arm was caught in a shredding machine in the upholstery class of the Carrol School in Philadelphia. As a result of these injuries, the 15 year old student's arm was amputated.

Appellants alleged that appellee school district, through its employees, was negligent in failing to supervise the upholstery class, in supplying the machine for the without a proper safety device, in maintaining the machine in a dangerous and defective condition, and in failing to warn the children of the dangerous condition. Appellee, the Philadelphia Board of Public Education, interposed preliminary objections asserting the defense of governmental immunity. These objections were sustained and the Superior Court affirmed in a per curiam order. ... We granted allocatur.

We now hold that the doctrine of governmental immunity[]—long since devoid of any valid justification—is abolished in this Commonwealth.[] In so doing, we join the ever-increasing number of jurisdictions which have judicially abandoned this antiquated doctrine. ...

It is generally agreed that the historical roots of the governmental immunity doctrine are found in the English case of Russell v. Men of Devon, 2 T.R. 667, 100 Eng.Rep. 359 (1788). ... There, the court, in extending immunity to an unincorporated county, expressed the fear that if suits against such political subdivisions were permitted, there would be "an infinity of actions." Russell v. Men of Devon, supra at 672, 100 Eng.Rep. at 362. That court was also influenced by the absence of a fund "out of which satisfaction is to be made." Id. Finally, Justice Ashurst, expressing the eighteenth century societal evaluation of the individual and local governmental interests, observed that "it is better that an individual should sustain an injury than that the public should suffer an inconvenience." Id. ...

Whatever may have been the actual basis for Russell v. Men of Devon, the doctrine it advanced was soon applied in the United States. ...

Although the English courts abandoned the doctrine and permitted suits against municipalities and school districts,[] this Commonwealth continued to deny recovery. …

Thus, until the present action, we have retained the archaic and artificial distinction between tortious conduct arising out of the exercise of a proprietary function and tortious conduct arising out of exercise of a governmental function. …

Today we conclude that no reasons whatsoever exist for continuing to adhere to the doctrine of governmental immunity. Whatever may have been the basis for the inception of the doctrine, it is clear that no public policy considerations presently justify its retention.

Governmental immunity can no longer be justified on "an amorphous mass of cumbrous language about sovereignty… ." … As one court has stated:

"…it is almost incredible that in this modern age of comparative sociological enlightenment, and in a republic, the medieval absolutism supposed to be implicit in the maxim, 'the King can do no wrong,' should exempt the various branches of the government from liability for their torts, and that the entire burden of damage resulting from the wrongful acts of the government should be imposed upon the single individual who suffers the injury, rather than distributed among the entire community constituting the government, where it could be borne without hardship upon any individual, and where it justly belongs. Barker v. City of Santa Fe, 47 N.M. 85, 136 P.2d 480, 482. …" Molitor v. Kaneland Community Unit District No. 302, supra, 18 Ill.2d at 21-22, 163 N.E.2d at 94. …

We must also reject the fear of excessive litigation as a justification for the immunity doctrine. Empirically, there is little support for the concern that the courts will be flooded with litigation if the doctrine is abandoned. …

Equally unpersuasive is the argument advanced in Russell v. Men of Devon, and Ford v. School District that immunity is required because governmental units lack funds from which claims could be paid. It is argued that funds would be diverted to the payment of claims and the performance of proper governmental functions would be obstructed. Initially, we note our disagreement with the assumption that the payment of claims is not a proper governmental function.

Additionally, the empirical data does not support the fear that governmental functions would be curtailed as a result of liability for tortious conduct. …

Thus, we must agree with Chief Justice Traynor of the California Supreme Court that "the rule of governmental immunity for tort is an anachronism, without rational basis, and has existed only by the force of inertia." Muskopf v. Corning Hospital District, supra 55 Cal.2d at 216, 11 Cal. Rptr. at 92, 359 P.2d at 460. Moreover, the distinction between governmental and proprietary functions "is probably one of the most unsatisfactory known to the law, for it has caused confusion not only among the various jurisdictions but almost always within each jurisdiction." Davis, Administrative Law Treatise §25.07 at 460 (1958). …

Imposition of tort liability will, thus, be more responsive to current concepts of justice. Claims will be treated as a cost of administration and losses will be spread among all those benefited by governmental action. …

Moreover, "where governmental immunity has had the effect of encouraging laxness and a disregard of potential harm, exposure of the government to liability for its torts will have the effect of increasing governmental care and concern for the welfare of those who might be injured by its actions." Note, The Discretionary

Exception and Municipal Tort Liability: A Reappraisal, 52 Minn.L.Rev. 1047, 1057 (1968). ...

Having concluded that local governmental units—municipal corporations and quasi-corporations—are no longer immune from tort liability, the order sustaining appellee's preliminary objections is reversed and the record remanded for proceedings consistent with this opinion.

INQUIRY

Local Government. Other states in addition to Pennsylvania (above) have completely abrogated governmental immunity for local government. *See* Merrill v. Manchester, 114 N.H. 722, 332 A.2d 378 (1974); Kitto v. Minot Park Dist., 224 N.W.2d 795 (N.D. 1974). More states abrogate immunity for local government than for state government. *See* Mayor and City Council of Baltimore v. Austin, 40 Md. App. 557, 392 A.2d 1140 (1978); Henry v. Oklahoma Turnpike Auth. 478 P.2d 898 (Okl. 1970). Almost every state limits its own immunity in some manner. Why treat local government differently from state government? Municipalities are not sovereign like state government. State law authorizes local government, often as incorporated entities, taking on the character and even performing some of the activities of private corporations. Local government is more likely liable for its torts, and not immune, when engaged in proprietary rather than governmental functions. *See* Smith v. State, 93 Idaho 795, 473 P.2d 937 (1970). Can you tell the difference? *See* Casey v. Wake County, 45 N.C. App. 522, 263 S.E.2d 360 (1980) (immunity for providing for implantation a defective IUD contraceptive device, as governmental rather than proprietary function); Steelman v. New Bern, 279 N.C. 589, 184 S.E.2d 239 (1971) (immunity for defective street lighting, as governmental rather than proprietary function); *but see* Merrill, *supra*, and Kitto, *supra* (immunity abrogated even as to governmental function).

Skills

Mediation (sometimes called facilitation or facilitative mediation) is a common method of alternative dispute resolution for torts cases. The plaintiff's lawyer and defense counsel select a mediator they each trust and respect, and believe will interact well with their clients. The mediator receives some written information, and perhaps an elaborate brief with exhibits, from each side before the mediation. The mediation usually takes place at the law office of the mediator or some other neutral site with at least two private offices available, and lasts all day or a half day. The plaintiff and plaintiff's lawyer, the defendant (or corporate representative if the defendant is an entity) and defense counsel, the insurance claim representative, and the mediator begin the mediation in a joint session where the mediator lays the grounds rules and the lawyers may make brief opening statements. The mediator then separates the parties into private caucuses—separate offices where the mediator can discuss the case with only one side at a time.

Discretionary Functions. Some states waiving immunity in part continue to apply the distinction that government remains immune for discretionary rather than ministerial functions. How does one distinguish between a negligent decision and a discretionary function? *See* Harry Stoller and Co. v. City of Lowell, 412 Mass. 139,

587 N.E.2d 780 (1992) (firefighters' negligent decision not to use recently tested sprinkling system to put out fire, although discretionary, was not a policy decision and so did not have discretionary-function immunity). Is a state's enforcement of its restaurant-health code a discretionary or ministerial function, when a restaurant patron has died from bacterial infection related to eating shellfish, because of the state's failure to inspect and enforce its health code? *See* Gregor v. Argenot Great Central Ins. Co., 851 So.2d 959 (La. 2003) (holding state and restaurant jointly liable for patron's death because state enforcement was not discretionary but ministerial and mandatory). Is the decision to leave a two-year-old child alone a discretionary function? *See* Brantley v. Dept. of Human Resources, 271 Ga. 679, 523 S.W.2d 571 (1999) (no).

Categorical Approach. The text above states that some of the statutory schemes instead waive immunity for categories like the negligent construction or maintenance of a building. *See, e.g.,* Mich. Comp. L. §691.1406. Are these categories any easier to define than the discretionary-ministerial function distinction? *See* De Sanchez v. State, 467 Mich. 231, 651 N.W.2d 59 (2002) (bathroom-ceiling pipe on which suicide-watch inmate hung himself, not a building defect); *but cf.* Bonanno v. Central Contra Costa Transit Auth., 30 Cal.3d 139, 132 Cal. Reptr.2d 341, 65 P.3d 807 (2003) (bus stop's location could be a dangerous condition of public property). What would you think are some other common modifications and exceptions regarding the abrogation of governmental immunity? *See* Bollinger v. Schneider, 64 Ill. App.3d 758, 381 N.E.2d 849, 21 Ill. Dec. 522 (1978) (purchase of liability insurance is implied waiver of governmental immunity).

Liability Standards. Where government waives immunity and is liable for its torts, what standard of care does law impose? The issue often arises around the question of police protection. Although police agencies have a public duty to prevent violent crime, when are they liable to an individual for failing to do so? DeLong v. Erie County, 89 A.D.2d 376, 455 N.Y.S.2d 887 (1982), affirmed a verdict against a county and in favor of the estate of a woman who had telephoned the county's 911 system reporting that a burglar was trying to break into her house. The 911 dispatcher had said "okay" in answer to the caller's plea to "come right away" but sent police to the wrong address, with the coroner's evidence sufficient to infer that the caller might have survived the invader's fatal attack had the dispatcher not made the careless mistake. The court determined that the dispatcher's brief assurance "okay" was sufficient to take the case from the general public-duty rule and to find that the county had accepted a duty to a specific person as to whom existed a known, serious crime risk. *See also* Brandon v. County of Richardson, 624 N.W.2d 604 (Neb. 2000) (recognizing a special-relationship duty to protect a person who reports a crime against foreseeable retaliation by the reported suspect). *DeLong* represents a particularized-reliance exception to the public-duty rule. Consider the following extraordinary case, involving the public-duty rule, and distinguished in *DeLong*. The bizarre history of the following case is the subject of a contemporary film *Crazy Love*.

Riss v. New York
New York Court of Appeals
22 N.Y.2d 579, 240 N.E.2d 860, 293 N.Y.S.2d 897 (1968)

[KEATING, J. (dissenting), stated these facts: "Linda Riss, an attractive young woman, was for more than six months terrorized by a rejected suitor well known to the courts of this State, one Burton Pugach. This miscreant, masquerading as a respectable attorney, repeatedly threatened to have Linda killed or maimed if she did not yield to him: 'If I can't have you, no one else will have you, and when I get through with you, no one else will want you.' In fear for her life, she went to those charged by law with the duty of preserving and safeguarding the lives of the citizens and residents of this State. Linda's repeated and almost pathetic pleas for aid were received with little more than indifference. Whatever help she was given was not commensurate with the identifiable danger. On June 14, 1959 Linda became engaged to another man. At a party held to celebrate the event, she received a phone call warning her that it was her 'last chance'. Completely distraught, she called the police, begging for help, but was refused. The next day Pugach carried out his dire threats in the very manner he had foretold by having a hired thug throw lye in Linda's face. Linda was blinded in one eye, lost a good portion of her vision in the other, and her face was permanently scarred. After the assault the authorities concluded that there was some basis for Linda's fears, and for the next three and one-half years, she was given around-the-clock protection."]

BREITEL, J. This appeal presents, in a very sympathetic framework, the issue of the liability of a municipality for failure to provide special protection to a member of the public who was repeatedly threatened with personal harm and eventually suffered dire personal injuries for lack of such protection. The facts are amply described in the dissenting opinion and no useful purpose would be served by repetition. The issue arises upon the affirmance by a divided Appellate Division of a dismissal of the complaint, after both sides had rested but before submission to the jury.

It is necessary immediately to distinguish those liabilities attendant upon governmental activities which have displaced or supplemented traditionally private enterprises, such as are involved in the operation of rapid transit systems, hospitals, and places of public assembly. Once sovereign immunity was abolished by statute the extension of liability on ordinary principles of tort law logically followed. To be equally distinguished are certain activities of government which provide services and facilities for the use of the public, such as highways, public buildings and the like, in the performance of which the municipality or the State may be liable under ordinary principles of tort law. The ground for liability is the provision of the services or facilities for the direct use by members of the public.

In contrast, this case involves the provision of a governmental service to protect the public generally from external hazards and particularly to control the activities of criminal wrongdoers. [Cc] The amount of protection that may be provided is limited by the resources of the community and by a considered legislative-executive decision as to how those resources may be deployed. For the courts to proclaim a new and general duty of protection in the law of tort, even to those who may be the particular seekers of protection based on specific hazards, could and would inevitably determine how the limited police resources of the community should be allocated and without predictable limits. This is quite different from the predictable allocation of resources and liabilities when public hospitals, rapid transit systems, or even highways are provided.

Before such extension of responsibilities should be dictated by the indirect imposition of tort liabilities, there should be a legislative determination that that should be the scope of public responsibility [cc].

It is notable that the removal of sovereign immunity for tort liability was accomplished after legislative enactment and not by any judicial arrogation of power [c]. It is equally notable that for many years, since as far back as 1909 in this State, there was by statute municipal liability for losses sustained as a result of riot [c] Yet even this class of liability has for some years been suspended by legislative action [c], a factor of considerable significance.

When one considers the greatly increased amount of crime committed throughout the cities, but especially in certain portions of them, with a repetitive and predictable pattern, it is easy to see the consequences of fixing municipal liability upon a showing of probable need for and request for protection. To be sure these are grave problems at the present time, exciting high priority activity on the part of the national, State and local governments, to which the answers are neither simple, known, or presently within reasonable controls. To foist a presumed cure for these problems by judicial innovation of a new kind of liability in tort would be foolhardy indeed and an assumption of judicial wisdom and power not possessed by the courts.

Nor is the analysis progressed by the analogy to compensation for losses sustained. It is instructive that the Crime Victims Compensation and 'Good Samaritan' statutes, compensating limited classes of victims of crime, were enacted only after the most careful study of conditions and the impact of such a scheme upon governmental operations and the public fisc [cc]. And then the limitations were particular and narrow.

For all of these reasons, there is no warrant in judicial tradition or in the proper allocation of the powers of government for the courts, in the absence of legislation, to carve out an area of tort liability for police protection to members of the public. Quite distinguishable, of course, is the situation where the police authorities undertake responsibilities to particular members of the public and expose them, without adequate protection, to the risks which then materialize into actual losses [c].

Accordingly, the order of the Appellate Division affirming the judgment of dismissal should be affirmed.

KEATING, J. (dissenting). Certainly, the record in this case, sound legal analysis, relevant policy considerations and even precedent cannot account for or sustain the result which the majority have here reached. For the result is premised upon a legal rule which long ago should have been abandoned, having lost any justification it might once have had. Despite almost universal condemnation by legal scholars, the rule survives, finding its continuing strength, not in its power to persuade, but in its ability to arouse unwarranted judicial fears of the consequences of overturning it. ...

The foremost justification repeatedly urged for the existing rule is the claim that the State and the municipalities will be exposed to limitless liability. ...

The fear of financial disaster is a myth. The same argument was made a generation ago in opposition to proposals that the State waive its defense of "sovereign immunity." The prophecy proved false then, and it would now. The supposed astronomical financial burden does not and would not exist. ...

The statement in the majority opinion that there are no predictable limits to the potential liability for failure to provide adequate police protection as compared to other areas of municipal liability is, of course, untenable. When immunity in other areas of governmental activity was removed, the same lack of predictable limits existed. Yet, disaster did not ensue.

Another variation of the 'crushing burden' argument is the contention that, every time a crime is committed, the city will be sued and the claim will be made that it resulted from inadequate police protection. Here, again, is an attempt to arouse the "anxiety of the courts about new theories of liability which may have a far-reaching effect." [C] And here too the underlying assumption of the argument is fallacious because it assumes that a strict liability standard is to be imposed and that the courts would prove completely unable to apply general principles of tort liability in a reasonable fashion in the context of actions arising from the negligent acts of police and fire personnel. ... No one is contending that the police must be at the scene of every potential crime or must provide a personal bodyguard to every person who walks into a police station and claims to have been threatened. They need only act as a reasonable man would under the circumstances. At first there would be a duty to inquire. If the inquiry indicates nothing to substantiate the alleged threat, the matter may be put aside and other matters attended to. If, however, the claims prove to have some basis, appropriate steps would be necessary.

The instant case provides an excellent illustration of the limits which the courts can draw. No one would claim that, under the facts here, the police were negligent when they did not give Linda protection after her first calls or visits to the police station in February of 1959. The preliminary investigation was sufficient. If Linda had been attacked at this point, clearly there would be no liability here. When, however, as time went on and it was established that Linda was a reputable person, that other verifiable attempts to injure her or intimidate her had taken place, that other witnesses were available to support her claim that her life was being threatened, something more was required—either by way of further investigation or protection-than the statement that was made by one detective to Linda that she would have to be hurt before the police could do anything for her. ...

Although in modern times the compensatory nature of tort law has generally been the one most emphasized, one of its most important functions has been and is its normative aspect. It sets forth standards of conduct which ought to be followed. The penalty for failing to do so is to pay pecuniary damages. At one time the government was completely immunized from this salutary control. This is much less so now, and the imposition of liability has had healthy side effects. In many areas, it has resulted in the adoption of better and more considered procedures just as workmen's compensation resulted in improved industrial safety practices. To visit liability upon the city here will no doubt have similar constructive effects. ...

INQUIRY

Public Officials. Treat the immunity of individual public officials as an issue separate from the immunity of the governmental agencies for which they work. Assuming a common-law, constitutional-, or statutory-tort claim against a public official (the latter two meaning civil-rights claims), statutory or common-law public-official immunity may nonetheless exist. Statutory immunity would be in the state's governmental immunity act, like the employee immunity described below in the Federal Tort Claims Act, 28 U.S.C. §2679(b), for federal public officials. Many states bar at least some claims against public officials, so that ordinarily, the only recourse is against the government agency rather than the employee. *See* Mich. Comp. L.

§691.1407(2) (public officer or employee immunity for acts reasonably believed to be within the scope of employment and government function, and not grossly negligent). Common-law public-official immunity may also exist, based on a policy to preserve a sphere of action within which public officials can exercise judgment unfettered by fear of tort liability. *See* Restatement (Second) of Torts §895D. The general contours of common-law public-official immunity include absolute immunity for legislators, judges, prosecutors (in some states), and (for federal officials and in some states) also executive officers—meaning that these public officials gain protection even with evidence of their bad faith. *See* Nixon v. Fitzgerald, 457 U.S. 731 (1982) (president); Imbler v. Pachtman, 424 U.S. 409 (1976) (prosecutor); Pierson v. Ray, 386 U.S. 547 (1967) (judge); Barr v. Matteo, 360 U.S. 564 (1959) (federal executive officers); Tenney v. Brandhove, 341 U.S. 367 (1951) (legislator). Other states offer only qualified immunity to executive officers—meaning that they lose protection in the case of bad faith. Common-law public-official immunity may also be available for discretionary, but not ministerial, acts. *See* Restatement (Second) of Torts §895D. Constitutional challenge to public-official immunity, where the government agency is also immune and the victim has no remedy, has failed. *See* Carr v. United States, 422 F.2d 1007 (4th Cir. 1970).

Federal Government. Consider now federal government immunity. The United States government employs approximately five million federal employees. The Federal Tort Claims Act governs tort claims for injury or loss caused by their conduct within the scope of their federal employment. The Act waives governmental immunity—but is only a limited waiver. The Act's waiver provision, 28 U.S.C. §2674, states in relevant part that "The United States shall be liable, respecting the provisions of this title relating to tort claims, in the same manner and to the same extent as a private individual under like circumstances...." The Act's jurisdictional provision, 28 U.S.C. §1346(b), states in relevant part that the federal district courts "shall have exclusive jurisdiction of civil actions on claims against the United States, for money damages, ... for injury or loss of property, or personal injury or death caused by the negligent or wrongful act or omission of any employee of the Government while acting within the scope of his office or employment, under circumstances where the United States, if a private person, would be liable to the claimant in accordance with the law of the place where the act or omission occurred." The Act bars punitive damages and interest, *id.*, and limits attorney's fees to 25% (20% if settled administratively before suit), 28 U.S.C. §2678. The Act has other important procedural provisions. A tort claimant must present the claim to the federal agency and receive its denial (or wait six months, whichever occurs first) before filing suit. 28 U.S.C. §2675(a). Suit must be in federal district court, 28 U.S.C. §1402, and against the United States. No jury trial right exists. The judge tries all suits under the Act. 28 U.S.C. §2402.

Practice
Tort law, like other law fields, has had its globalizing trend. People, corporations, products, and media—and the torts they cause—increasingly cross national and continental boundaries. American tort lawyers may represent claimants or defendants in mass-tort cases against U.S. multinational corporations, on the other side of the globe, as was the case with the Bhopal, India disaster involving Union Carbide. Tort lawyers

practicing solely in the United States may also need to know something of international tort law. To know that Ghana's customary law recognizes causes of action for verbal insults that would fall short of actionable defamation in the United States, or that the French civil-law code imposes a duty to rescue that American law would not impose, can illustrate the boundaries of American tort law. Seeing how Germany and Italy treat non-economic damages, how the European Convention on Human Rights promotes privacy, or how malpractice law in Japan grants greater deference to physicians to decide what to tell or not tell patients, can help us preserve the strength and character of coordinate American provisions.

Federal law also authorizes what are essentially foreign tort actions, in United States courts. A remarkable federal act, known as the Alien Tort Statute or Alien Tort Claims Act, authorizes aliens to sue in United States courts for torts committed "in violation of the law of nations." 28 U.S.C. §1350. This act is not a product of any recent trend in the internationalization of United States law. Enacted in 1789, lawyers largely ignored it until a Paraguayan physician successfully brought suit in United States district court against a Paraguayan official for his son's alleged political torture and murder in Paraguay. Filartiga v. Pena-Irala, 630 F.2d 876 (2d Cir. 1980). The United States Supreme Court subsequently limited Alien Tort Statute claims to those based on international norms like the 18th-century paradigms of safe conduct, infringement of ambassador rights, and piracy. Sosa v. Alvarez-Machain, 542 U.S. 692 (2004). Some federal courts continue after *Sosa* to recognize causes of action for political assassination, torture, and genocide. The Torture Victim Protection Act of 1991, 28 U.S.C. §1350 note, separately authorized a civil cause of action in United States district courts, for both aliens and U.S. citizens, for official torture and political killings abroad.

Other federal acts authorize United States citizens to bring actions in United States courts against aliens or foreign governments. The Anti-Terrorism Act of 1991 provides United States nationals with a civil cause of action in United States district courts for injuries from acts of international terrorism. *See* Boim v. Quranic Literacy Inst. and Holy Land Fdn. for Relief and Dev., 291 F.3d 1000 (7th Cir. 2002) (recognizing claim over death of U.S. citizen allegedly killed by Hamas while visiting Israel); Gilmore v. Palestinian Interim Self-Government Auth., 422 F. Supp.2d 96 (D. D.C. 2006) (recognizing claim over death of U.S. citizen allegedly killed by PLO while visiting Jerusalem). The Foreign Sovereign Immunities Act, 28 U.S.C. §1605, permits U.S. citizens to bring causes of action in federal court against foreign governments, for injuries from torts or state-sponsored terrorism occurring abroad. International treaties can also affect what many would think are solely domestic torts. The Warsaw Convention, a treaty the Senate first ratified in 1934, is an example. In its present form, the Convention limits to a damages cap of $75,000, certain tort recoveries for individuals injured in international air transportation. The Convention applies to domestic legs of flights that passengers originated abroad. That interpretation means that passengers who begin a trip overseas but suffer injury in an air crash on a flight by a domestic airline, beginning and ending within the United States, may face a $75,000 cap on tort recovery. The Convention lifts the cap when the air carrier has engaged in "willful misconduct."

Exceptions. Although the Federal Tort Claims Act waives federal-government immunity, significant federal immunities do remain after passage of the Act. The Act expressly provides that federal government employees acting within the scope of their federal employment are immune from tort liability. 28 U.S.C. §2679(b)(1). The immunity of individual employees exists even if the federal government is also immune under one of the Act's many exceptions to the waiver of immunity. United States v. Smith, 499 U.S. 160 (1991). A second large exception to the Act's general waiver of immunity involves conduct of federal employees that involves "the exercise or performance or the failure to exercise or perform a discretionary function or duty …

whether or not the discretion involved be abused." 28 U.S.C. §2679(a). As state case law for similar state waivers and the federal cases below show, this *discretionary-function* exception itself requires substantial interpretation. The Act does not waive immunity for intentional torts, 28 U.S.C. §2679(h), meaning that the federal government remains immune from liability for its employees intentional torts. (Given that employers ordinarily have no vicarious liability for their employees' intentional torts, this exception has less significance than it may seem.) However, the Act states expressly that its tort immunity for federal employees does not extend to civil actions authorized by other statute for their violation of constitutional rights. 28 U.S.C. §2679(b)(2). Beyond these important limitations on the Act's waiver of immunity, the Act sets forth a long list of other exceptions to the waiver of immunity, including for acts done while exercising due care "in the execution of a statute or regulation," 28 U.S.C. §2679(a), and for postal delivery service, customs duties, admiralty, quarantines, fiscal operations, and combat activities. As to this last exception regarding combat, the Supreme Court has interpreted the Act to preserve immunity for injury and loss incident to active-duty military service. Feres v. United States, 340 U.S. 135 (1950). The *Feres* doctrine may seem like a callous limitation against those most deserving of recourse. Its justification lies in part in the federal benefits provided those who serve in the military and their dependents, and in preserving military discipline.

Loge v. United States
United States Court of Appeals, Eighth Circuit
662 F.2d 1268 (8th Cir. 1981)

HANSON, J. Lora Loge contracted paralytic polio after her infant son was inoculated with a trivalent, live, oral poliovirus vaccine trade named Orimune. She and her husband sued the United States and unknown employees of the Department of Health, Education, and Welfare[fns omitted] (HEW) under the Federal Tort Claims Act[] (FTCA) and the Constitution alleging liability based on negligent and willful acts and omissions committed in the regulating, testing, and licensing of Orimune. ... The district court[], 494 F.Supp. 883, dismissed the complaint "for failure to state a cause of action" (R. 83), and the Loges appeal. We affirm in part and reverse in part. ...

In June 1963, the Secretary of HEW licensed Lederle Laboratories to manufacture Orimune—a trivalent, live, oral poliovirus vaccine. ... See 42 U.S.C. s 262(a); 21 C.F.R. s 630.10(a). Orimune is composed of all three Sabin strains of live poliovirus corresponding to the three different types of polio (known as Types 1, 2, and 3), thus the designation "trivalent." A characteristic of live Sabin polio vaccines such as Orimune is that not only is the vaccine's recipient immunized from polio, but unimmunized persons who come into close contact with the recipient also are immunized through a shed virus which spreads from the recipient to the "contact." Because Sabin strains contain the live polio virus, there is a risk that either a recipient or a contact could develop polio. Accordingly, the Secretary has promulgated regulations pertaining to the safety and potency of these strains which serve to protect susceptible persons from contracting the disease.[fn omitted] Drug manufacturers must prove their product's conformity to these regulations before the Secretary will issue a license to manufacture. 42 U.S.C. s 262(d).

A risk-free alternative to inoculation with the live Sabin vaccine is the Salk vaccine in which the virus is killed so that the recipient cannot contract polio nor can the recipient shed a live virus to unimmunized contacts. But the Secretary has promoted the use of risk-bearing live vaccines because they are able to effect total immunization of the public through transmission of the shed virus with less than total inoculation.

Mrs. Loge was exposed to the shed virus in 1976 after a doctor inoculated her infant son Todd with Orimune. Within one month after her son's inoculation, Mrs. Loge was stricken with a vaccine-associated case of poliomyelitis, Type 2. As a result, she is now a paraplegic. ....

Before a cause of action against the United States can be stated, the hurdle of sovereign immunity must be overcome. This is the purpose of the FTCA.

The Federal Tort Claims Act is not a federal remedial scheme at all, but a waiver of sovereign immunity that permits an injured claimant to recover damages against the United States where a private person "would be liable to the claimant in accordance with the law of the place where the act or omission occurred." 28 U.S.C. s 1346(b); see also 28 U.S.C. s 2674.

... The district court construed the Loges' amended complaint to state several causes of action which failed to overcome this initial hurdle because they attacked acts or omissions by the Secretary of HEW that were "discretionary." The FTCA does not waive sovereign immunity for "(a)ny claim ... based upon the exercise or performance or the failure to exercise or perform a discretionary function or duty on the part of a federal agency or an employee of the Government, whether or not the discretion involved be abused." 28 U.S.C. s 2680(a). Insofar as the Loges' amended complaint alleged that the government was negligent in promulgating or failing to promulgate regulations that would ensure the safety of live, oral poliovirus vaccines and properly protect susceptible persons such as Mrs. Loge, the district court correctly found that such actions by the government were discretionary functions and therefore immune from suit under FTCA. ...

B. The district court did find that two causes of action under the FTCA were not barred by the discretionary function exception: the negligent failure of the government to require the mandatory tests of 21 C.F.R. s 630.10(b)[fn omitted] when Lederle was licensed to manufacture Orimune in 1963 and the negligent failure to follow mandatory tests when Lederle's Lot 451-162 was approved. The Secretary has no discretion to disregard the mandatory regulatory commands pertaining to criteria a vaccine must meet before licensing its manufacture or releasing a particular lot of vaccine for distribution to the public. See Griffin v. United States, 500 F.2d 1059, 1063-69 (3d Cir. 1974). ....

Nevertheless the district court concluded that the Loges had still failed to state a claim under FTCA because no circumstances were alleged "where the United States, if a private person, would be liable to the claimant in accordance with the law of the place where the act or omission occurred." 28 U.S.C. s 1346(b). ... Without deciding which venue's law applied, the district court concluded that neither the law of the District of Columbia—the place of the negligent acts and omissions—nor the law of Arkansas—the place of the harmful impact—imposes a duty of due care on a person for activity similar to the government's in this case. We find, however, that under the applicable choice of law principles, Arkansas law applies and further that a cause of action has been stated under the law of Arkansas. ....

... It can be said that the government increased the risk of harm to the Loges by licensing an allegedly untested product, Orimune, and by releasing to the public an allegedly untested or negligently tested lot of that vaccine: if either the product itself or a particular lot of that product failed to conform to standards established by the regulations, then proper testing or proof of testing would have revealed the nonconformity and the vaccine would never have been disseminated to Todd Loge. Likewise, it can be said that the government undertook a duty owed by the drug manufacturer to the Loges when it required that proof of the drug's safety be demonstrated to the government before releasing it to the public. Finally, the Loges alleged they relied on the government's use of due care in approving for release the particular vaccine lot that was eventually administered to Todd Loge. Therefore, the district court erred in concluding that the Loges had failed to state a claim under the law of Arkansas. ....

Accordingly, we affirm the district court's order of dismissal in all respects except for the dismissal of the Loges' two claims under the FTCA alleging the government's violation of its own regulations. As to these claims, we reverse and remand for further proceedings consistent with this opinion.

Deuser v. Vecera
United States Court of Appeals, Eighth Circuit
139 F.3d 1190 (8th Cir. 1998)

BOWMAN, J. ... The District Court dismissed appellants' claims under Federal Rule of Civil Procedure 12(b)(1) for lack of subject matter jurisdiction, holding that the government was protected from suit by the discretionary function exception of the FTCA. ...

... On July 3-6, 1986, the event known as the Veiled Prophet (or VP) Fair was held on the grounds of the Jefferson National Expansion Memorial in St. Louis, Missouri (the site of the Gateway Arch). Because the Expansion Memorial is a national park (a special use permit was issued to the city of St. Louis for the Fair), the Secretary of the Interior is responsible for maintaining the park and its facilities and for providing services to visitors, functions generally carried out by the National Park Service. [C] The park is within the jurisdiction of the National Park Rangers. On the evening of July 4, 1986, many thousands of people were in attendance at the Fair, including Larry Deuser. Rangers David Vecera and Edward Bridges observed Deuser grabbing women on the buttocks, to the obvious outrage of the victims and others. The rangers warned Deuser, and continued to keep an eye on him. When he urinated in public, the rangers arrested him. As the rangers made their way to their tent with Deuser, he was argumentative with them and continued making rude comments to female visitors.

After conferring with chief ranger Dennis Burnett, the rangers elected to turn Deuser over to St. Louis police. But the police department was overwhelmed with the additional workload created by the Fair, and officers were unable or unwilling to process Deuser's arrest. At this point, the rangers, together with St. Louis police officer Lawrence King, decided to release Deuser, but away from the park so that he would not return to the Fair that evening.

There is some dispute between the parties about where Deuser was released, and also some question of the timing of the events that occurred that night. It is sufficient for our purposes to know the undisputed facts: Deuser was freed in a parking lot somewhere in St. Louis, alone and with no money and no transportation. At some time after that, he wandered onto an interstate highway and was struck and killed by a motorist. Deuser's blood alcohol level was 0.214 at the time of his death, well above the legal limit for intoxication. ...

By enacting the FTCA, Congress opted to waive the sovereign immunity to civil suit enjoyed by the United States, and to give consent to be sued "for money damages ... for injury or loss of property, or personal injury or death caused by the negligent or wrongful act or omission of any employee" of the United States acting within the scope of his employment. 28 U.S.C.A. § 1346(b)(1) (Supp.1997). ... But, as is true in other cases where Congress on behalf of the United States has waived sovereign immunity, amenability to suit is not without exception.

The exception relevant here is commonly known as the discretionary function exception. It is statutory and shields the government from civil liability for claims "based upon the exercise or performance ... [of] a discretionary function or duty on the part of a federal agency or an employee of the Government, whether or not the discretion involved be abused." 28 U.S.C. §2680(a) (1994). ...

To determine whether the discretionary function exception applies here to protect the rangers and the United States from suit, we engage in a two-step inquiry.

A.

First, we must consider whether the actions taken by the rangers as regards Deuser were discretionary, that is, "a matter of choice." *Berkovitz[v. United States]*, 486 U.S. [531] at 536, 108 S.Ct. at 1958[(1988)]. "[C]onduct cannot be discretionary unless it involves an element of judgment or choice." *Id.* It is axiomatic that a government employee has no such discretion "when a federal statute, regulation, or policy specifically prescribes a course of action for an employee to follow." *Id.* If the rangers had a policy they were to follow in releasing Deuser, as the appellants contend, "then there is no discretion in the conduct for the discretionary function exception to protect." *Id.*

There are two written policies that the parties contend are of relevance here. The first is the Jefferson National Expansion Memorial Standard Operating Procedure for arrests (SOP), dated December 22, 1987.[fn] The opening declaration of the SOP suggests there is little room for discretionary decisionmaking on the part of the rangers in an arrest situation: "When an arrest is made by National Park Rangers within the jurisdiction of Jefferson National Expansion Memorial, the following procedures *will always be followed:* ..." Standard Operating Procedure-Arrests at 1 (emphasis added). The arrestee is to be searched, and if possible fingerprinted and photographed, before transport. The prisoner, handcuffed behind his back, is to be transported by two rangers. During business hours, the arrestee "will continue to be taken directly to the U.S. Marshall's [sic] Office." *Id.* at 2. At other times (or so we, and apparently the parties, infer from the SOP, although it is not clearly stated), "[t]he arresting Ranger plus a Shift Supervisor will transport the prisoner to the Fourth District Holdover Facility at 1200 Clark Avenue (Clark and Tucker) using the division vehilce [sic]," *id.* at 1, unless the facility is full, in which case prisoners are to be taken to one of the alternative locations noted in the SOP. ... This, appellants contend, is the procedure the rangers were compelled to follow with Deuser after they arrested him.

The rangers argue (and the District Court concluded) that the SOP arrest policy was abrogated temporarily by the VP Fair 1986 Operations Handbook. The Handbook emphasizes the "primary role" of the rangers during the Fair: "resource protection followed by the things we do best, visitor services and visitor care." [C &fn] The opening paragraph of the Handbook's General Enforcement Guidelines makes it clear that the guidelines are in fact quite general and are for use by the rangers "in enforcement contacts[,] but in no way should [they] be construed as a substitute for sound judgment and discretionary action on the part of the Ranger." The guidelines then cover the areas of concern for enforcement by rangers during the Fair: traffic control; liquor law violations; city ordinances in effect for the duration of the Fair concerning alcoholic beverages, glass containers, and pets; access to the Arch; and a variety of crimes against persons from simple assault to murder. The Enforcement section of the Handbook then wraps up with a paragraph that makes it clear the rangers have wide latitude in making enforcement decisions.... .

The rangers' argument—that the Handbook superseded the SOP for arrests on the grounds of the Expansion Memorial during the Fair—misapprehends the Handbook guidelines. The Handbook was intended to provide guidance to the rangers on the extent to which certain laws should be enforced during the Fair. Read as a whole, the Handbook suggests that enforcement in many circumstances might be relaxed during the event, so that arrests would be kept to a minimum. The rangers' "sound judgement and discretionary action" was to be exercised in the context of making decisions on *whether to make an arrest at all;* the Handbook never touches on the procedure to be followed in the event an arrest is made (except to note that holding facilities and rangers will be busy during the Fair). The Handbook did not override the standard operating procedures.[fn] Based on the record before us, it appears the SOP for processing arrestees remained unchanged during the Fair. Still, that conclusion does not mean that the rangers were required to complete an arrest, that is, to charge and incarcerate a suspect, once he was in custody. ...

... Law enforcement decisions of the kind involved in making or terminating an arrest must be within the discretion and judgment of enforcing officers. *See, e.g., Redmond v. United States,* 518 F.2d 811, 816-17 (7th Cir.1975) ("It cannot be denied that the Government has a duty to maintain law and order, but how best to fulfill this duty is wholly within the discretion of its officers ..."). It would be impossible to put into a manual every possible scenario a ranger might encounter, and then to decide in advance for the ranger whether an arrest should be made and, once made, under what circumstances an arrest could be terminated. Just as the rangers had discretion to decide (within constitutional limits, of course) when and whether to make an arrest, so they had-and here exercised-discretion to terminate an arrest without charging the suspect. Under the terms of the Handbook, that discretion became even broader during the Fair.

We hold that terminating Deuser's arrest, that is, releasing him without charging him with a crime, was a discretionary function reserved to the judgment of the rangers.

B.

We move now to the second part of our inquiry. Notwithstanding the judgment involved in terminating Deuser's arrest, we must ask "whether that judgment is of the kind that the discretionary function exception was designed to shield." *Berkovitz,* 486 U.S. at 536, 108 S.Ct. at 1959. To be protected, the rangers' conduct must be "grounded in the social, economic, or political goals" of the Handbook's discretionary enforcement guidelines. *United States v. Gaubert*, 499 U.S. 315, 323 ... (1991).

We think the conduct of the rangers here is the classic example of a "permissible exercise of policy judgment." *Berkovitz*, 486 U.S. at 539... . Social, economic, and political goals—all three—were the basis for the actions taken by the rangers.

An important function of the rangers during the Fair, according to the Handbook, was to serve and protect visitors to the park. Clearly, the decision to remove Deuser from the park served the social goals of protecting innumerable other fairgoers and ensuring that their enjoyment of the festivities was not diminished by the obnoxious and offensive behavior of a fellow attendee. Further, the decision to release Deuser, rather than to charge him for the offenses he committed, may have prevented a night of revelry that obviously was out of control from becoming a criminal conviction. And the rangers who otherwise would have spent considerable time booking Deuser were free to return to the Fair, possibly to prevent more serious or more dangerous crimes from being committed, or to apprehend the perpetrators of graver offenses, thereby continuing to further the goal of visitor protection.

The economic goals of the guidelines are clear, and are spelled out in some detail in the Handbook. Law enforcement manpower was expected to be stretched thin, both during the Fair and on the first business day following the Fair, when arrestees would have to be transported for court appearances. ... There were simply not enough officers to arrest and to charge all persons who might commit a crime at the park during the four-day Fair. The rangers' colleagues, St. Louis police department officers, were expected to be equally taxed with their own enforcement duties. Moreover, it was anticipated that the nearest holdover facility would be overcrowded with arrestees, meaning more miles and more manpower to transport suspects to alternative holdover facilities and to see to their arraignments. Releasing Deuser without charging him preserved already scarce law enforcement resources.

The political goals to be served by the guidelines concern law enforcement "territories." The Fair was not a National Park Service event. The Handbook acknowledges that "[t]he St. Louis Police Department is the lead agency for law enforcement." [C] As the chief ranger stated in the Handbook, the federal park rangers' "primary role is defined as resource protection followed by the things we do best, visitor services and visitor care." *Id.* When the police opted not to process Deuser's arrest, the rangers appropriately decided not to override the decision of "the lead agency for law enforcement." The Fair's success depended in part on all enforcement agencies involved working together toward a common goal, and the rangers acted properly to preserve that cooperation by releasing Deuser in this situation. Further, the Fair was designed to be an enjoyable event for the city, and it would have been unfortunate if overzealous federal law enforcement had dampened the festivities. ...

... We hold that the conduct of the officers here was grounded in the social, economic, and political policies of the Handbook. ...

... Thus the rangers' conduct falls within the discretionary function exception of the FTCA, and there is no federal subject matter jurisdiction for appellants' FTCA wrongful death claims.

The judgment of the District Court is affirmed.

INQUIRY

Discretion. In Berkovitz v. United States, 486 U.S. 531 (1988), the Supreme Court held that FDA employees had not exercised discretion, when deciding not to test all batches of a polio vaccine before public release, because the FDA had already required testing for all batches. *Deuser v. Vecera, supra*, applied the Supreme Court's test in *Berkovitz*. Did the court decide correctly, even though the federal agency in *Deuser* had required the same treatment for all arrests? Can you distinguish *Deuser* from *Berkovitz*? Is an FDA decision to approve a medical device a discretionary function? In re Orthopedic Bone Screw Product Liability Litigation, 264 F.3d 344 (3rd Cir. 2001) (yes). Would an OSHA decision not to inspect the machine that injured the plaintiff be discretionary? Irving v. United States, 162 F.3d 154 (1st Cir. 1998) (yes). Would an FAA decision to only spot-check airplanes for safety compliance be discretionary? *See* United States v. S.A. Empresa (Varig Airlines), 467 U.S. 797 (1984) (yes). When a federal employee times traffic signals without exercising any judgment, is the employee exercising discretion? *See* Aguehounde v. District of Columbia, 666 A.2d 443 (D.C. App. 1995) (yes—suit barred). The Supreme Court approved in United States v. Gaubert, 449 U.S. 315 (1991), that discretionary-function immunity extend to some instances where, although the employee *could* exercise discretion in considering policies, the employee did not do so. In short, and as the above cases suggest, the trend has been to construe the exception more broadly, allow fewer tort suits, and allow greater federal-employee carelessness without attendant liability for injury. Still, the discretionary-function exception does have its limits. *See* Hughes v. United States, 116 F. Supp.2d 1145 (N.D. Cal. 2000) (allowing suit for failure to warn of condition of road on military base); Andraloniz v. United States, 952 F.2d 652 (1991) (allowing suit for failure to warn of risk of rabies vaccine); Collazo v. United States, 850 F.2d 1 (1st Cir. 1988) (allowing medical-malpractice suit).

Active-Duty Service. As to the *Feres* doctrine barring suits for injury incident to military service, is a military experiment testing the effects of LSD on servicemen without their knowledge of the risks, incident to their service? United States v. Stanley, 483 U.S. 669 (1987) (yes—suit barred). When a military trainer holds a recruit underwater until the recruit dies, is it incident to service? Kitowski v. United States, 931 F.2d 1526 (11th Cir. 1991) (yes—suit barred). When a serviceman serving a 29-year sentence at Fort Leavenworth prison for kidnap-rape-murder suffers injury by a ceiling collapse, is the injury incident to service? Schnitzer v. Harvey, 389 F.3d 200 (D.C. Cir. 2004) (yes—suit barred). If military personnel sue a manufacturer who makes a military product to military specifications, may the manufacturer have the government's contribution or indemnity? *See* Stencel Aero Engg. Corp. v. United States, 431 U.S. 666 (1977), *rehg. Denied*, 434 U.S. 882 (1977) (no).

Choice of Law. What law is a federal district court applying when it adjudicates the merits of the liability portion of an FTCA claim? *See* Moos v. United States, 225 F.2d 705 (8th Cir. 1955) (applying Minnesota law to determine that plaintiff alleged a battery rather than negligence claim, and that the FTCA according barred the claim). Would the United States be strictly liable for its employees' torts under the Federal Tort Claims Act? *See* Laird v. Nelms, 406 U.S. 797 (1972) (no, with respect to allegations concerning sonic boom).

> **Practice**
> The practice vignettes throughout this text suggest some of the intercultural challenges tort lawyers face in dealing with diverse populations—from insurance company corporate officers and managers, to business risk and plant managers, product and process engineers, medical and accounting professionals, middle-class homeowners, jurors of all walks, and the homeless and destitute injured. Tort lawyers, as much or more than other lawyers, must exercise intercultural skills to effectively communicate with and serve diverse individuals. Consider a framework in which a lawyer's intercultural skills are in five areas: (1) communication, as the ability to speak with and listen to a client; (2) cognition, as the ability to adjust objective-setting, planning, implementing, and assessing to the client's preferences; (3) reference, as the ability to perceive and appreciate the client's worldview; (4) resource, as the ability to evaluate a client's material advantage and disadvantage in pursuing a legal objective; and (5) relationship, as the ability to adapt to the client's preferred manner of relating.

Chapter X

Products Liability

OBJECTIVE: Given fact patterns involving products causing injury, articulate the negligence, warranty, and products liability theories that are most likely to apply, as reflected in this section of the text.

Case Study: A climber purchased rock-climbing equipment over the Internet from an outfitter. The outfitter advertised one of the items that the climber purchased as appropriate for all-season use, when it was inappropriate for use in sub-freezing temperatures. The climber, who did not see the outfitter's advertisement, was not aware that the design of climbing devices might differ depending on use in freezing temperatures. The climber used the device climbing in the winter season during freezing temperatures. The device failed as a result, requiring that the climber undergo an embarrassing, hazardous, and expensive rescue in which she suffered exposure and scrapes. ***Choose and evaluate the most appropriate products-liability theory for the climber's claim against the outfitter.***

From the time of the earliest-known codes, tort law has provided for liability for loss caused by defective products. Nearly four millennia ago, Babylonians plied the Tigris and Euphrates Rivers under Hammurabi's Code providing liability for boat builders, owners, lessors, and navigators. Section 235 of the Code required builders to make their boats firm and strong, and pitch them thoroughly, that they not show any defect. Owners, lessors, and navigators had their own duties to exercise care maintaining and using the products. Those who failed in their duties had to repair or replace damaged boats and pay for loss of cargo. The ancient codes included liability provisions for personal injury or loss due to constructed walls, wells, and buildings, and domesticated animals. Products liability is frank recognition that careless actions are not the only causes of harm but that placing a defective good in commerce can also do so. In today's mass-production economy, with products so widely available for so many different uses, products liability occupies a prominent place in tort law. Processed foods, drugs, medical devices, construction equipment, vehicles, aircraft—products today have great capability both to improve and to harm life, depending on the care, caution, wisdom, judgment, foresight, and intentions of their designers, suppliers, assemblers, distributors, sellers, re-sellers, repairers, and users.

Products-liability law necessarily addresses these complex interests and responsibilities through a complex of liability theories. The products-liability framework in the United States today includes a negligence theory that each person or entity must exercise reasonable care with respect to design, manufacture, distribution, and sale of products. Negligence theories focus on the conduct of the person or entity more so than the qualities of the product (although conduct and quality closely relate). Breach of warranty is a second theory having to do with the transaction and communications between product supplier and user. Warranty is a contract-type theory, but courts extended it well beyond contract relationships, implying warranties as to a product's merchantability and particular fitness. A third class of theories, identified as strict products liability, focuses on the qualities of the product itself. Despite its name, strict products liability is not absolute liability. The several categorical and functional approaches to strict products liability each include some consideration of an objective standard and can involve fault-like analyses. The Restatement (Second) approach asks whether the product was in a defective condition unreasonably dangerous to users, with *defect* determined either by a consumer-expectation test or risk-utility test. The Restatement (Third) approach asks whether the product involved an alleged design, manufacture, or warning defect, and then follows different functional approaches for each type of defect. Consider how these theories developed.

A. Development

History shows the interplay of the negligence, warranty, and strict-products-liability theories. That history can help you appreciate how these theories operate in products-liability practice. This section outlines the history while addressing, negligence, express and implied warranties, misrepresentation, and some special categories like food products. The next section addresses strict products liability.

Negligence. During the industrial revolution that brought mass production of products, England's Exchequer of Pleas Court decided Winterbottom v. Wright, 10 M. & W. 109, 152 Eng. Rep. 402 (Exch. of Pleas 1842). *Winterbottom* held that the defendant repairer of mail coaches was not liable for the serious injury of a coach driver, where the defendant had failed to make any repair. The court meant the case to confirm the duty rule distinguishing nonfeasance from misfeasance—that tort liability to third persons extends only to injury from negligent performance of a contract, not the failure to perform the contract at all. Yet for the remainder of that century and into the next, the case also meant that the maker of an unsafe product had no liability beyond contract liability to the party in privity with the maker. *See* Losee v. Clute, 51 N.Y. 494 (1873) (neighboring property owner has no claim for damage due to explosion of negligently manufactured boiler). The privity rule applied except for the rare case where the product was inherently dangerous such as with guns, poisons, and other articles intended to injure. *See* Thomas v. Winchester, 6 N.Y. 397 (1852) (liability for mislabeled jar of poison).

Judge Cardozo set the misconception straight in MacPherson v. Buick Motor Co., 217 N.Y. 382, 111 N.E. 1050 (Ct. App. 1916), holding that "irrespective of contract, the manufacturer of this thing of danger is under a duty to make it carefully." If "the manufacturer of the finished product, who puts it on the market to be used without inspection by his customers[,]... is negligent, where danger is to be foreseen, a liability will follow." In so holding, Judge Cardozo "put the source of the obligation where it ought to be. We have put its source in the law[,]" because fundamentally, "foresight of the consequences involves the creation of a duty." *MacPherson*, which all American states eventually followed, cut the ties of privity, establishing negligence as a viable theory for product injury, even though doing so by intimating that it was relying on the inherently dangerous product formulation. Courts gradually abandoned that restriction. Today, where the facts support a negligence claim, practitioners continue to plead negligence even in cases where warranty or strict-products-liability claims also apply. *See* Connelly v. Hyundai Motor Co., 351 F.3d 535 (1st Cir. 2003) (affirming jury verdict for plaintiff on negligence claim and against plaintiff on strict-product-liability claim for airbag hazard); Buckingham v. R.J. Reynolds Tobacco Co., 142 N.H. 822, 713 A.2d 381 (1998) (affirming dismissal of strict-product-liability claim but permitting negligence claim to proceed as to second-hand smoke from defendant's tobacco products). Juries more-easily condemn careless wrongdoing, which is a more-compelling liability theory than the warranty and strict-products-liability theories having to do with product fitness, utility, and risk. Do not overlook negligence claims for products liability.

Warranty. A parallel history took place in warranty law. Parties make, distribute, and sell products in commercial relationship—through contracts of manufacture, distribution, and sale, accompanied by marketing, advertising, and negotiation. Misrepresentations may occur in commercial transactions—false advertising, false claims regarding a product's fitness, and other forms of intentionally deceitful, reckless or careless, or innocent misstatements influencing the purchase and use of an injuring product. See Williams v. Philip Morris Inc., 193 Or. App. 527, 92 P.3d 126 (2004) (upholding punitive-damage award for tobacco-company misrepresentations about smoking safety). The English common law early recognized both tort- and contract-based warranty actions based on product misrepresentations, between parties in privity to the product contract. Stuart v. Wilkins, 1 Doug. 18, 99 Eng. Rep. 15 (1778) (assumpsit—contract); Medina v. Stoughton, 1 Ld. Raym. 593, 91 Eng. Rep. 1297 (1700) (trespass on the case—tort). Why, though, when a product is placed into the stream of commerce for sale and use by foreseeable third parties, should the law restrict warranty claims to parties in privity with one another?

The first widely recognized inroad against the privity requirement for warranty actions was in the bad-food case Mazetti v. Armour & Co., 75 Wash. 622, 135 P. 633 (1913), fittingly, after nationwide concern over contaminated food supplies. Mazetti first implied a warranty that the food was fit and then extended the implied warranty beyond privity to end consumers. Cases today continue to make traditional distinctions between foreign versus natural substances in food. Thus, a chicken bone in a chicken enchilada does not create an unfit food product, *see* Mexicali Rose v. Superior Court, 1 Cal.4th 617, 4 Cal. Rptr.2d 145, 822 P.2d 1292 (1992), while metal or glass in an enchilada would mean an unfit product. Other cases follow a consumer-expectation test, imposing liability for an unfit product even where the unfit substance was natural to the foodstuff, if the reasonable consumer would not have expected it. *See* Jackson v. Nestle-Beich, Inc., 147 Ill.2d 408, 589 N.E.2d 547, 168 Ill. Dec. 147 (1992) (pecan shell in pecan candy). Other jurisdictions gradually followed *Mazetti* in imposing warranty liability beyond privity, in other bad-food cases. *See* Pillars v. R.J. Reynolds Tobacco Co., 117 Miss. 490, 78 So. 365 (1918) (ptomaine poisoned tobacco plug); Parks v. C.C. Yost Pie Co., 144 P. 202 (Kan. 1914) (ptomaine-poisoned pie).

One of those cases finally properly conceived that the implied warranty should run with the food product. *See* Coca-Cola Bottling Works v. Lyons, 145 Miss. 876, 111 So. 305 (1927); *see also* Ryan v. Progressive Grocery Stores, 175 N.E. 105 (N.Y. 1931) (implied-warranty recovery for pin in loaf of bread) (Cardozo, J.). Then, in a personal-injury case following *Mazetti* but involving not food but an advertisement for "shatter-proof" automobile windshield glass, Baxter v. Ford Motor Co., 168 Wash. 456, 12 P.2d 409 (1932), the court extended the manufacturer's express warranties beyond privity to end users. Significantly, *Baxter*, like the *MacPherson* case extending negligence-based product-liability claims beyond privity, involved that inherently dangerous article—a motor vehicle—although the *Baxter* court made no pretense of restricting its holding to vehicles.

Another motor-vehicle personal-injury case, Henningsen v. Bloomfield Motors, Inc., 32 N.J. 358, 161 A.2d 69 (1960), confirmed what was becoming increasingly obvious, that implied-warranty claims should also extend beyond bad-food products to other consumer products. *Henningsen* involved the defendant manufacturer's sale of an automobile through a distributor to a retailer, who sold it to Mr. Henningsen as a gift for his wife. Mrs. Henningsen suffered severe injury when the vehicle's steering failed. Unfortunately, the automobile industry at the time was using a standard sale contract that limited warranty liability to replacement of defective parts, effectively disclaiming warranty liability for personal injury. The court nonetheless held the manufacturer liable on an implied warranty of fitness for the vehicle's intended purpose, even though the manufacturer and retailer had each disclaimed warranties beyond an obligation to replace defective parts within strict time limits. *Henningsen* thus overcame the notorious "citadel of privity" as to warranty, much as *MacPherson* had done so for negligence claims several decades earlier. Implied-warranty claims remain viable today in many jurisdictions, even after adoption of strict products liability. *See* Denny v. Ford Motor Co., 662 N.E.2d 730 (N.Y. 1995) (implied-warranty theory applied to vehicle roll-over case under consumer-expectation test).

The Restatement (Second) of Torts §402B (1965) confirms the general availability of express-warranty liability, although somewhat curiously, it does so using only misrepresentation and not warranty language. Section 402B provides, "One engaged in the business of selling chattels who, by advertising, labels, or otherwise, makes to the public a misrepresentation of a material fact concerning the character or quality of a chattel sold by him is subject to liability for physical harm to a consumer of the chattel caused by justifiable reliance upon the misrepresentation, even though (a) it is not made fraudulently or negligently, and (b) the consumer has not bought the chattel from or entered into any contractual relation with the seller." *See also* Restatement (Third) of Torts: Products Liability §9 (1998) (misrepresentation liability for product injury).

The Uniform Commercial Code's §§2-314 and 2-315 provide for implied warranties of merchantability (that the product is fit for its intended purpose) and fitness for a particular purpose (if the seller specifies the product) between parties to the sale contract, while §2-318 extends those warranties to some third parties, in three alternatives. The federal Magnuson-Moss Warranty Act, 15 U.S.C. §§2301-12, also regulates the content and disclaimer of warranties. The Uniform Commercial Code's implied warranties are the basis for that form of products liability. The two UCC-warranty provisions state as follows:

UCC § 2-314. Implied Warranty: Merchantability; Usage of Trade.
(1) Unless excluded or modified (Section 2-316), a warranty that the goods shall be merchantable is implied in a contract for their sale if the seller is a merchant with respect to goods of that kind. Under this section the serving for value of food or drink to be consumed either on the premises or elsewhere is a sale.
(2) Goods to be merchantable must be at least such as: (a) pass without objection in the trade under the contract description; (b) in the case of fungible goods, are of fair average quality within the description; (c) are fit for the ordinary purposes for which such goods of that description are used; (d) run, within the variations permitted by the agreement, of even kind, quality and quantity within each unit and among all units

involved; (e) are adequately contained, packaged, and labeled as the agreement may require; and (f) conform to the promise or affirmations of fact made on the container or label if any.

(3) Unless excluded or modified (Section 2-316) other implied warranties may arise from course of dealing or usage of trade.

UCC § 2-315. Implied Warranty: Fitness for Particular Purpose.
Where the seller at the time of contracting has reason to know any particular purpose for which the goods are required and that the buyer is relying on the seller's skill or judgment to select or furnish suitable goods, there is unless excluded or modified under the next section an implied warranty that the goods shall be fit for such purpose.

INQUIRY

Reliance. What if the misrepresented character of a product injures a consumer (the first part of Section 402B express-warranty liability), but the injured consumer was not aware of and relying on the misrepresentation (the second part of Section 402B liability)? Most states follow the Restatement, holding reliance necessary, but a few states do not require reliance in all cases. *See* Pelman v. McDonald's Corp., 396 F.3d 508 (2d Cir. 2005) (no reliance necessary regarding food-value representations). Can you articulate why not? When one person or several people rely on a manufacturer's misrepresentation, can their reliance influence others who have not heard the misrepresentation, to purchase and use a product?

Puffing. What is the difference between advertising a product's cache or puffing its quality in a manner the consumer would expect, versus misrepresenting its essential character? *Compare* Smith v. Anheuser-Busch, Inc., 599 A.2d 320 (R.I. 1991) (advertisements inducing beer purchases not actionable misrepresentation with respect to plaintiff's drunk driving), *with* Klages v. General Ordnance Equip. Co., 240 Pa. Super. 356, 367 A.2d 304 (1976) (advertisement that mace gun will stop groups an actionable misrepresentation). In other words, how specific must a misrepresentation be under Section 402B in order to qualify as a "material" statement concerning the product's "character" or "quality"? *See* Collins v. Uniroyal, Inc., 64 N.J. 260, 315 A.2d 16 (1974) ("if it only saves your life once, it's a bargain" held to be an actionable misrepresentation).

Third-Party Beneficiaries—Alternatives. The concept of a third-party beneficiary is one typically associated with contract rather than tort law. As indicated above, the Uniform Commercial Code's §2-318 offers three alternatives for states to adopt, as to whether and to what extent express or implied warranties should extend to third parties, as a beneficiary of a contract or sale relationship between other parties. The three alternatives of Section 2-318 are below. What are the differences between the three alternatives? Which favors the injured person the most? Which alternative do you prefer?

UCC § 2-318. Third-Party Beneficiaries of Warranties—Express or Implied—and Obligations.
(1) In this section:
(a) "Immediate buyer" means a buyer that enters into a contract with the seller.
(b) "Remote purchaser" means a person that buys or leases goods from an immediate buyer or other person in the normal chain of distribution.

Alternative A to Subsection (2)
(2) A seller's warranty whether express or implied extends to any natural person who is in the family or household of his buyer or who is a guest in his home if it is reasonable to expect that such person may use, consume or be affected by the goods and who is injured in person by breach of the warranty. A seller's warranty to an immediate buyer, whether express or implied, a seller's remedial promise to an immediate buyer, or a seller's obligation to a remote purchaser under Section 2-313A or 2-313B extends to any individual who is in the family or household of the immediate buyer or the remote purchaser or who is a guest in the home of either if it is reasonable to expect that the person may use, consume, or be affected by the goods and who is injured in person by breach of the warranty, remedial promise, or obligation. A seller may not exclude or limit the operation of this section.

Alternative B to subsection (2)
(2) A seller's warranty whether express or implied extends to any natural person who may reasonably be expected to use, consume or be affected by the goods and who is injured in person by breach of the warranty. A seller's warranty to an immediate buyer, whether express or implied, a seller's remedial promise to an immediate buyer, or a seller's obligation to a remote purchaser under Section 2-313A or 2-313B extends to any individual who may reasonably be expected to use, consume, or be affected by the goods and who is injured in person by breach of the warranty, remedial promise, or obligation. A seller may not exclude or limit the operation of this section.

Alternative C to subsection (2)
(2) A seller's warranty whether express or implied extends to any person who may reasonably be expected to use, consume or be affected by the goods and who is injured by breach of the warranty. A seller's warranty to an immediate buyer, whether express or implied, a seller's remedial promise to an immediate buyer, or a seller's obligation to a remote purchaser under Section 2-313A or 2-313B extends to any person that may reasonably be expected to use, consume, or be affected by the goods and that is injured by breach of the warranty, remedial promise, or obligation. A seller may not exclude or limit the operation of this section with respect to injury to the person of an individual to whom the warranty, remedial promise, or obligation extends.

Warranty Disclaimers. How should the law treat a manufacturer's warranty disclaimers? Generally, courts and legislatures continue to give strong support for warranty theories, which remain important alternatives to negligence and strict-products-liability theories. Note that each of the above three alternatives ends with a limitation on warranty disclaimers. The UCC treats the enforceability of a warranty disclaimer as dependent on whether the disclaimer is "unconscionable" and defines the disclaiming of personal-injury damages as "prima facie unconscionable." *See* UCC §§2-302, 2-316, 2-719(3). Some states also prohibit disclaimers of consumer-product warranties, either within their commercial-code provisions or separately in consumer-product safety acts. What about disclaiming property damage and other economic loss? Defective products can cause substantial property damage or other economic loss, just as they can cause serious personal injury. Under UCC 2-318, warranty disclaimers as to property damage and other economic loss are not necessarily unconscionable. They may instead be quite effective in limiting the manufacturer's liability for property and economic losses from a defective product. Why not simply use a negligence or strict-products-liability theory in place of a warranty theory? In some cases, courts have employed the principle that the plaintiff may only sue on the products-liability theory that represents the gravamen or essence of the claim.

> **Ethics**
> Lawyer-ethics rules can seem daunting to the new torts practitioner. Fee agreements, trust accounts, ex-parte communications, soliciting—what are the rules and where are the issues and boundaries? A new lawyer joining a firm will have the added prospect of proving to the firm's other lawyers that the new lawyer knows and follows the ethics rules. On rare occasions, though, the new lawyer may observe something—or may even have a partner tell the lawyer to do something—that the new lawyer believes is unethical. Rule 5.2(a) of the ABA Model Rules of Professional Conduct provides that a lawyer must follow the rules even if directed by another person not to do so. When a subordinate lawyer observes a suspected violation, or the supervising lawyer directs the subordinate to engage in a violation, the subordinate lawyer should immediately seek the counsel of a supervisory lawyer. Rule 5.2(b) provides that a subordinate lawyer does not violate the ethics rules if the subordinate lawyer followed "a supervisory lawyer's reasonable resolution of an arguable question of professional duty." The subordinate lawyer may have misunderstood the rules or misunderstood what the subordinate lawyer observed or heard to do. Consultation with a supervisory lawyer may correct the misunderstanding. If, after any consultation, the subordinate lawyer knows what the rules require, then the subordinate lawyer must do what the rules require and not follow contrary instruction. Law is a self-regulating profession. Rule 8.3 of the ABA Model Rules of Professional Conduct requires that a lawyer must report another lawyer's violation of the rules when the violation raises a substantial question as to the other lawyer's honesty, trustworthiness, or fitness.

Economic-Loss Doctrine. Strict liability allows consumers to recover both economic and non-economic loss from personal injury. Yet what if no personal injury or property damage occurs, and the economic loss arises instead because of the defective product's destruction? The courts have generally restricted the owner of a defective product that damages only itself, to contract and warranty recoveries (in essence, the economic-loss doctrine). *See* East River S.S. Corp. v. Transamerica Delaval, Inc., 476 U.S. 858 (1986); Two Rivers Co., v. Curtiss Breeding Service, 624 F.2d 1242 (5th Cir. 1980); State Farm Mut. Auto. Ins. Co. v. Ford Motor Co., 225 Wis.2d 305, 592 N.W.2d 201 (1999) (vehicle manufacturer not liable in tort for defective ignition destroying vehicle); Alloway v. General Marine Indus., 149 N.J. 620, 695 A.2d 264 (1997); Moorman Mfg. Co. v. National Tank Co., 91 Ill.2d 69, 61 Ill. Dec. 746, 435 N.W.2d 443 (1982); *but see* Saratoga Fishing Co. v. J.M. Martinac & Co., 520 U.S. 875 (1997) (boat owner may recover in tort for boat equipment destroyed in fire started by defective boat engine); American Fire & Cas. Co. v. Ford Motor Co., 588 N.W.2d 437 (Iowa 1999) (tort claim permitted in truck-fire claim despite applicability of economic-loss doctrine, where personal). See how the court in the following case uses these principles and warranty disclaimers to limit the manufacturer's liability for economic loss due to a defective product. See if you can determine what claims might be more appropriate for warranty theories than negligence theories.

Spring Motors Distribs., Inc. v. Ford Motor Co.
New Jersey Supreme Court
98 N.J. 555, 489 A.2d 660 (1985)

POLLOCK, J. The fundamental issue on this appeal concerns the rights of a commercial buyer to recover for economic loss caused by the purchase of defective goods. More specifically, the question is whether the buyer should be restricted to its cause of action under the Uniform Commercial Code (hereinafter U.C.C. or the Code) or should be allowed to pursue a cause of action predicated on principles of negligence and strict liability. The difference is important because the buyer in the present case instituted its action beyond the four-year period provided by the U.C.C., N.J.S.A. 12A:2-725, but within the six-year period applicable to tort actions, N.J.S.A. 2A:14-1.

The defendants are a motor vehicle manufacturer, its dealer, and a supplier of transmissions. The gravamen of the complaint is that defects in the transmissions, which were installed in commercial trucks, caused the buyer to sustain a loss in the benefit of its bargain and consequential damages. Specifically, the buyer sought recovery for repair, towing, and replacement parts, as well as for lost profits and a decrease in the value of the trucks.

The trial court perceived the matter as sounding in contract and found that the plaintiff had not instituted its action within the four-year period provided by the U.C.C. N.J.S.A. 12A:2-725. In an unreported decision, the court granted summary judgment for defendants. The Appellate Division reversed on the ground that the action was more appropriately characterized as one in strict liability in tort, not contract, and that the six-year period of limitations applicable for tort actions had not expired. ...

We hold that a commercial buyer seeking damages for economic loss resulting from the purchase of defective goods may recover from an immediate seller and a remote supplier in a distributive chain for breach of warranty under the U.C.C., but not in strict liability or negligence. ... Accordingly, the four-year period of limitations provided by the Code, N.J.S.A. 12A:2-725, not the six-year general statute of limitations, N.J.S.A. 2A:14-1, determines the time within which an action must be commenced against the immediate seller and remote supplier. ...

... Plaintiff, Spring Motors Distributors, Inc. (Spring Motors), which is in the business of selling and leasing trucks, operates a fleet of 300 vehicles. Spring Motors agreed to purchase from defendant Turnpike Ford Truck Sales, Inc. (Turnpike) 14 model LN8000 trucks made by defendant Ford Motor Company (Ford) at a purchase price of $265,029.80. ...

In the agreement, Spring Motors specified that the trucks should be equipped with model 390V transmissions made by Clark Equipment Company (Clark), a supplier to Ford. Spring Motors specified Clark transmissions because of "excellent service and parts availability on past models" and because of Clark's advertisements and brochures.

At the time of the sale to Spring Motors, Ford issued a form warranty with each truck to "repair or replace any of the following parts that are found to be defective in factory material or workmanship under normal use in the United States or Canada on the following basis: * * * any part during the first 12 months or 12,000 miles of operations, whichever is earlier * * * transmission case and all internal transmission parts (including auxiliary transmission) * * * after 12,000 miles and during the first 12 months or 50,000 miles of operation, whichever is earlier, for a charge of 50% of the dealer's regular warranty charge to Ford for parts and labor. * * * For series 850 and higher trucks, any part of the * * * transmission * * * for the first 12 months or 100,000 miles of operation, whichever is earlier * * *."

The warranty also stated: "To the extent allowed by law, this WARRANTY IS IN PLACE OF all other warranties, express or implied, including ANY IMPLIED WARRANTY OF MERCHANTABILITY OR FITNESS." Furthermore, the Ford warranty expressly stated: "Under this warranty, repair or replacement of parts is the only remedy, and loss of use of the vehicle, loss of time, inconvenience, commercial loss or consequential damages are not covered."

The warranty that Clark extended to Ford provided: "WARRANTY. Clark Equipment Company ('Clark') warrants to Buyer that each new Clark axle, transmission, torque converter and drive train product, and components thereof, shall be free from defects and material and workmanship under normal use and maintenance" for 12 months or 12,000 miles for on-highway vehicles used on highways or 2,000 miles for off-highway equipment. At Clark's option, the warranty could be limited to repairs or replacements. The warranty also stated: "THIS WARRANTY IS IN LIEU OF ALL OTHER WARRANTIES (EXCEPT OF TITLE), EXPRESSED OR IMPLIED, AND THERE IS NO IMPLIED WARRANTY OF MERCHANTABILITY OR OF FITNESS FOR A PARTICULAR PURPOSE. IN NO EVENT SHALL CLARK BE LIABLE FOR INCIDENTAL, CONSEQUENTIAL OR SPECIAL DAMAGES."

… Spring Motors, which serviced the trucks during the period of the lease, began experiencing problems with the performance of the Clark transmissions as early as February 1977. The problems persisted, and Spring Motors communicated directly with Clark, writing in October 1977 that it had "had nothing but trouble" with the transmissions. Later correspondence, dated January 26, 1978, confirmed that Clark analyzed the transmissions and found that "the failure in these gear boxes was a result of improper angle degree in the way certain gears were cut," resulting "in additional strain on the actual gear and the mating gear and related shafts." Still later, Spring Motors pointed out that the transmission failures had cost it "several thousand dollars in out of pocket expenses plus many additional thousands of dollars in lost revenues, customer ill will, replacement equipment, etc."

Clark provided Spring Motors with replacement parts, but the transmission failures continued. On July 11, 1978, Spring Motors wrote to Clark that in the absence of a satisfactory response by August 1, it would remove and replace the Clark transmissions and "take whatever action is necessary to hold you financially responsible." Thereafter, on November 1, 1979, Spring Motors and Economic terminated the truck lease and, as part of a settlement, Economic purchased the trucks for $247,580.97. Four years and one month after the delivery of the trucks, on December 23, 1980, Spring Motors instituted this action.

In the complaint, which contained three counts, Spring Motors sought judgment against all defendants for consequential damages: the expenses of towing, repairs, and replacement of parts; lost profits; and decrease in market value of the trucks. The first count asserted that the defendants breached certain express and implied warranties; … and the third count sought recovery in strict liability and negligence. …

If the legal relationships among the parties are governed by the U.C.C., then plaintiff's action, which was instituted more than four years after the delivery of the trucks, is time-barred. Hence, one question is whether the Code provides the exclusive remedies available to Spring Motors. …

The Code provides for express warranties regarding the quality of goods, N.J.S.A. 12A:2-313, as well as implied warranties of merchantability, N.J.S.A. 12A:2-314, and of fitness for a particular purpose, N.J.S.A. 12A:2-315. ...

... A seller may exclude or modify its liability on warranties... . Furthermore, a buyer and seller may agree to limit the buyer's remedy to the repair and replacement of parts. N.J.S.A. 12A:2-719(1)(a). Similarly, the parties may agree to limit or exclude consequential damages, "unless the limitation or exclusion is unconscionable." N.J.S.A. 12A:2-719(3). Although a limitation of consequential damages for personal injuries in the case of consumer goods is prima facie unconscionable, a limitation of damages for a commercial loss is not. ...

... Because it presents a claim for economic loss, which is not normally recoverable in a tort action, rather than a claim for physical harm, this case probes the boundary between strict liability and the U.C.C. ... The delineation of that boundary requires a brief summary of the history and nature of strict liability.

One year before the adoption of the U.C.C. in New Jersey, this Court delivered its landmark opinion in Henningsen v. Bloomfield Motors, Inc., 32 N.J. 358, 161 A.2d 69 (1960). Henningsen involved a defective automobile that crashed and caused property damage to the car and personal injuries to the driver, who was the owner's wife. The Court affirmed a judgment in favor of the plaintiffs on the theory of breach of implied warranty of fitness. Justice Francis wrote in now familiar language: "[U]nder modern marketing conditions, when a manufacturer puts a new automobile in the stream of trade and promotes its purchase by the public, an implied warranty that it is reasonably suitable for use as such accompanies it into the hands of the ultimate purchaser." 32 N.J. at 384, 161 A.2d 69. By extending a warranty of safety to consumers of all products, not just those intended for human consumption, Henningsen removed the notion of privity of contract from all cases involving the sale of defective goods that cause physical injury. ...

Underlying the Henningsen decision was the Court's recognition that consumers were in an unequal bargaining position with respect to automobile manufacturers and dealers, who required them to sign standard contracts. [C] One of the main purposes of strict liability, as declared in Henningsen, is the allocation of the risk and distribution of the loss to the better risk-bearer. [Cc] Generally, the manufacturer, who is better able to eliminate defects from its product and who can spread the cost of the risk among all of its customers, is the better risk-bearer. [C] By contrast, the individual consumer is poorly situated to bear the entire risk of loss from injuries caused by a defective product. Through allocation of the risk of loss to the manufacturer, strict liability achieves its objective of protecting the consumer who, because of unequal bargaining power, cannot protect him or herself. ...

From the perspective of the injured party, strict liability generally provides a more congenial environment than contract principles, which may prevent recovery because of a lack of privity with the manufacturer. In addition to privity, the Code retains two other requirements that may pose considerable obstacles to a buyer. The first requirement is that of notice to a seller of a breach of warranty, [c]; the second arises from the seller's ability to limit or disclaim liability to an innocent purchaser. [C] A buyer who does not deal directly with a manufacturer cannot negotiate over the terms of a disclaimer and might find it impossible to give the manufacturer notice of the breach of warranty following an injury. [C] Strict liability, on the other hand, circumvents the technical requirements of the U.C.C. with respect to privity, notice, and limitation of damages. Avoiding those requirements is particularly important for persons outside the distributive chain who sustain physical damage caused by a defective product.

By comparison, the U.C.C. emphasizes the simplification of the law governing commercial transactions and the expansion of commercial practices through agreement. [C] Underlying the U.C.C. policy is the principle that parties should be free to make contracts of their choice, including contracts disclaiming liability for breach of warranty. Once they reach such an agreement, society has an interest in seeing that the agreement is fulfilled. Consequently, the U.C.C. is the more appropriate vehicle for resolving commercial disputes arising out of business transactions between persons in a distributive chain. ...

The considerations that give rise to strict liability do not obtain between commercial parties with comparable bargaining power. [C] Furthermore, perfect parity is not necessary to a determination that parties have substantially equal bargaining positions. [C] Suffice it to state that Spring Motors had sufficient bargaining power to persuade Ford to install Clark transmissions in the trucks that were the subject of the contract.

Insofar as risk allocation and distribution are concerned, Spring Motors is at least as well situated as the defendants to assess the impact of economic loss. Indeed, a commercial buyer, such as Spring Motors, may be better situated than the manufacturer to factor into its price the risk of economic loss caused by the purchase of a defective product. [C]

Presumably the price paid by Spring Motors for the trucks reflected the fact that Ford was liable for repair or replacement of parts only. By seeking to impose the risk of loss on Ford, Spring Motors seeks, in effect, to obtain a better bargain than it made. In such a context, the imposition of the risk of loss on the manufacturer might lead to price increases for all of its customers, including individual consumers. [C] As between commercial parties, then, the allocation of risks in accordance with their agreement better serves the public interest than an allocation achieved as a matter of policy without reference to that agreement.

Delineation of the boundary between strict liability and the U.C.C. requires appreciation not only of the policy considerations underlying both sets of principles, but also of the role of the Legislature as a coordinate branch of government. By enacting the U.C.C., the Legislature adopted a carefully-conceived system of rights and remedies to govern commercial transactions. Allowing Spring Motors to recover from Ford under tort principles would dislocate major provisions of the Code. For example, application of tort principles would obviate the statutory requirement that a buyer give notice of a breach of warranty, [c], and would deprive the seller of the ability to exclude or limit its liability, [c]. In sum, the U.C.C. represents a comprehensive statutory scheme that satisfies the needs of the world of commerce, and courts should pause before extending judicial doctrines that might dislocate the legislative structure. ...

For the preceding reasons, we hold that a commercial buyer seeking damages for economic loss only should proceed under the U.C.C. against parties in the chain of distribution. ...

What we have said about Spring Motors' strict liability claim applies substantially to its negligence claim. ...

The demarcation of duties arising in tort and those arising in contract is often indistinct, but one difference appears in the interest protected under each set of principles. [C] The purpose of a tort duty of care is to protect society's interest in freedom from harm, i.e., the duty arises from policy considerations formed without reference to any agreement between the parties. A contractual duty, by comparison, arises from society's interest in the performance of promises. Generally speaking, tort principles, such as negligence, are better suited for resolving claims involving unanticipated physical injury, particularly those arising out of an accident. Contract principles, on the other hand, are generally more appropriate for determining claims for consequential damage that the parties have, or could have, addressed in their agreement.

Although the nature of the damage may be a useful point of distinction, it also signals more subtle differences in the roles that tort and contract play in our legal system. The differences include judicial evaluation of the status, relationship, and expectations of the parties; the ability of the parties to protect themselves against the risk of loss either by contractual provision or by insurance, and the manner in which the loss occurred. [C] This evaluation reflects, among other things, policy choices about the relative roles of contracts and tort law as sources of legal obligations. As among commercial parties in a direct chain of distribution, contract law, expressed here through the U.C.C., provides the more appropriate system for adjudicating disputes arising from frustrated economic expectations. ...

It follows from our determination that Spring Motors should be restricted to its U.C.C. remedies as against Ford and Turnpike Ford that the appropriate statute of limitations is the four-year time bar contained in N.J.S.A. 12A:2-725. More than four years elapsed between the date of the delivery of the trucks and the institution of this action against Ford and Turnpike Ford. Consequently, Spring Motors' suit against them is time-barred. ...

Accordingly, we reverse the judgment of the Appellate Division and reinstate the dismissal of the complaint as to all defendants.

B. Product Defect

OBJECTIVE: Given the design, manufacture, distribution, and sale of products with defects causing injury, apply and analyze the products liability claims against the involved parties using the law, principles, definitions, and factors reflected in these pages of the text.

Case Study: A man owned a table saw from which he repeatedly removed and replaced the saw-blade guard to perform cutting operations, as shown in the table-saw manual. The man wearied of removing and replacing the guard and so decided to leave the guard off for all cutting operations. Unfortunately, a piece of material kicked back during a cutting operation, causing the man's finger to hit the saw blade, with resulting serious amputation injury. ***Choose and apply the most appropriate of the two product-defect tests under the Restatement (Second) of Torts §402A.***

Strict Products Liability. Turn, then, from negligence and warranty theories to the third form of liability for harm caused by products—what we know as strict products liability. Strict products liability has an equally interesting history. Again, having a sense of that history can help you understand the current products liability framework. In the midst of the above extension of warranty theories beyond food products, came the case of Escola v. Coca Cola Bottling Co., 150 P.2d 436 (Cal. 1944), involving an exploding soda-pop bottle. The majority opinion in *Escola* treated it as a negligence claim proven under the doctrine of res ipsa loquitur. It could have treated it under warranty theory, especially given that the case involved a food container (even if not a food product). What made the case most significant, though, was not the majority opinion affirming a plaintiff's verdict on the grounds of res ipsa loquitur but the concurring opinion of Justice Traynor laying the groundwork for an explicit theory of strict products liability. As you read Justice Traynor's opinion, identify and evaluate each rationale he offers for strict products liability.

Escola v. Coca Cola Bottling Co.
California Supreme Court
150 P.2d 436 (Cal. 1944)

GIBSON, C.J. Plaintiff, a waitress in a restaurant, was injured when a bottle of Coca Cola broke in her hand. She alleged that defendant company, which had bottled and delivered the alleged defective bottle to her employer, was negligent in selling "bottles containing said beverage which on account of excessive pressure of gas or by reason of some defect in the bottle was dangerous * * * and likely to explode." This appeal is from a judgment upon a jury verdict in favor of plaintiff.

Defendant's driver delivered several cases of Coca Cola to the restaurant, placing them on the floor, one on top of the other, under and behind the counter, where they remained at least thirty-six hours. Immediately before the accident, plaintiff picked up the top case and set it upon a near-by ice cream cabinet in front of and about three feet from the refrigerator. She then proceeded to take the bottles from the case with her right hand, one at a time, and put them into the refrigerator. Plaintiff testified that after she had placed three bottles in the refrigerator and had moved the fourth bottle about 18 inches from the case "it exploded in my hand." The bottle broke into two jagged pieces and inflicted a deep five-inch cut, severing blood vessels, nerves and muscles of the thumb and palm of the hand. ...

One of defendant's drivers, called as a witness by plaintiff, testified that he had seen other bottles of Coca Cola in the past explode and had found broken bottles in the warehouse when he took the cases out, but that he did not know what made them blow up.

Plaintiff then rested her case, having announced to the court that being unable to show any specific acts of negligence she relied completely on the doctrine of res ipsa loquitur.

Defendant contends that the doctrine of res ipsa loquitur does not apply in this case, and that the evidence is insufficient to support the judgment. ...

Upon an examination of the record, the evidence appears sufficient to support a reasonable inference that the bottle here involved was not damaged by any extraneous force after delivery to the restaurant by defendant. It follows, therefore, that the bottle was in some manner defective at the time defendant relinquished control, because sound and properly prepared bottles of carbonated liquids do not ordinarily explode when carefully handled. ...

Although it is not clear in this case whether the explosion was caused by an excessive charge or a defect in the glass there is a sufficient showing that neither cause would ordinarily have been present if due care had been used. Further, defendant had exclusive control over both the charging and inspection of the bottles. Accordingly, all the requirements necessary to entitle plaintiff to rely on the doctrine of res ipsa loquitur to supply an inference of negligence are present. ...

The judgment is affirmed.

SHENK, CURTIS, CARTER, and SCHAUER, JJ., concurred.

TRAYNOR, J. I concur in the judgment, but I believe the manufacturer's negligence should no longer be singled out as the basis of a plaintiff's right to recover in cases like the present one. In my opinion it should now be recognized that a manufacturer incurs an absolute liability when an article that he has placed on the market, knowing that it is to be used without inspection, proves to have a defect that causes injury to human beings. MacPherson v. Buick Motor Co., 217 N.Y. 382, 111 N.E. 1050, L.R.A.1916F, 696, Ann.Cas.1916C, 440 established the principle, recognized by this court, that irrespective of privity of contract, the manufacturer is responsible for an injury caused by such an article to any person who comes in lawful contact with it. [Cc] In these cases the source of the manufacturer's liability was his negligence in the manufacturing process or in the inspection of component parts supplied by others. Even if there is no negligence, however, public policy demands that responsibility be fixed wherever it will most effectively reduce the hazards to life and health inherent in defective products that reach the market. It is evident that the manufacturer can anticipate some hazards and guard against the recurrence of others, as the public cannot. Those who suffer injury from defective products are unprepared to meet its consequences. The cost of an injury and the loss of time or health may be an overwhelming misfortune to the person injured, and a needless one, for the risk of injury can be insured by the manufacturer and distributed among the public as a cost of doing business. It is to the public interest to discourage the marketing of products having defects that are a menace to the public. If such products nevertheless find their way into the market it is to the public interest to place the responsibility for whatever injury they may cause upon the manufacturer, who, even if he is not negligent in the manufacture of the product, is responsible for its reaching the market. However intermittently such injuries may occur and however haphazardly they may strike, the risk of their occurrence is a constant risk and a general one. Against such a risk there should be general and constant protection and the manufacturer is best situated to afford such protection.

The injury from a defective product does not become a matter of indifference because the defect arises from causes other than the negligence of the manufacturer, such as negligence of a submanufacturer of a component part whose defects could not be revealed by inspection ([cc]) or unknown causes that even by the device of res ipsa loquitur cannot be classified as negligence of the manufacturer. The inference of negligence may be dispelled by an affirmative showing of proper care. ... An injured person, however, is not ordinarily in a position to refute such evidence or identify the cause of the defect, for he can hardly be familiar with the manufacturing process as the manufacturer himself is. In leaving it to the jury to decide whether the inference has been dispelled, regardless of the evidence against it, the negligence rule approaches the rule of strict liability. It is needlessly circuitous to make negligence the basis of recovery and impose what is in reality liability without negligence. If public policy demands that a manufacturer of goods be responsible for their quality regardless of negligence there is no reason not to fix that responsibility openly. ...

... It is to the public interest to prevent injury to the public from any defective goods by the imposition of civil liability generally.

The retailer, even though not equipped to test a product, is under an absolute liability to his customer, for the implied warranties of fitness for proposed use and merchantable quality include a warranty of safety of the product. [Cc] This warranty is not necessarily a contractual one ([cc]), for public policy requires that the buyer be insured at the seller's expense against injury. [Cc] The courts recognize, however, that the retailer cannot bear the burden of this warranty, and allow him to recoup any losses by means of the warranty of safety attending the wholesaler's or manufacturer's sale to him. [Cc] Such a procedure, however, is needlessly circuitous and engenders wasteful litigation. Much would be gained if the injured person could base his action directly on the manufacturer's warranty.

The liability of the manufacturer to an immediate buyer injured by a defective product follows without proof of negligence from the implied warranty of safety attending the sale. Ordinarily, however, the immediate buyer is a dealer who does not intend to use the product himself, and if the warranty of safety is to serve the purpose of protecting health and safety it must give rights to others than the dealer. In the words of Judge Cardozo in the MacPherson case [217 n.y. 382, 111 N.E. 1053, L.R.A.1916F, 696, Ann.Cas.1916C, 440]: "The dealer was indeed the one person of whom it might be said with some approach to certainty that by him the car would not be used. Yet the defendant would have us say that he was the one person whom it was under a legal duty to protect. The law does not lead us to so inconsequent a conclusion." While the defendant's negligence in the MacPherson case made it unnecessary for the court to base liability on warranty, Judge Cardozo's reasoning recognized the injured person as the real party in interest and effectively disposed of the theory that the liability of the manufacturer incurred by his warranty should apply only to the immediate purchaser. It thus paves the way for a standard of liability that would make the manufacturer guarantee the safety of his product even when there is no negligence. ...

As handicrafts have been replaced by mass production with its great markets and transportation facilities, the close relationship between the producer and consumer of a product has been altered. Manufacturing processes, frequently valuable secrets, are ordinarily either inaccessible to or beyond the ken of the general public. The consumer no longer has means or skill enough to investigate for himself the soundness of a product, even when it is not contained in a sealed package, and his erstwhile vigilance has been lulled by the steady efforts of manufacturers to build up confidence by advertising and marketing devices such as trade-marks. [Cc] Consumers no longer approach products warily but accept them on faith, relying on the reputation of the manufacturer or the trade mark. [Cc] Manufacturers have sought to justify that faith by increasingly high standards of inspection and a readiness to make good on defective products by way of replacements and refunds. [C] The manufacturer's obligation to the consumer must keep pace with the changing relationship between them; it cannot be escaped because the marketing of a product has become so complicated as to require one or more intermediaries. Certainly there is greater reason to impose liability on the manufacturer than on the retailer who is but a conduit of a product that he is not himself able to test. [Cc]

The manufacturer's liability should, of course, be defined in terms of the safety of the product in normal and proper use, and should not extend to injuries that cannot be traced to the product as it reached the market.

INQUIRY

Rationales. Rank the following rationales in the *Escola* concurrence from the most to the least persuasive: (a) duty binds manufacturers to safeguard the consumer; (b) manufacturers have the greater capability of ensuring consumer safety than do consumers, and so liability should attach to manufacturers to encourage them to exercise that capability; (c) manufacturers have the greater resources than do consumers, and so liability should attach to manufacturers to spread the loss; (d) enterprises that market harm-causing products have a responsibility to compensate for those losses; (e) manufacturers of harm-causing products should restore those whom the products harm; (f) manufacturers have far greater litigation resources and advantages in products-liability litigation, and legal theories should restore a balance to the parties; and (g) law would have greater certainty and clarity if manufacturers were liable for harm their products cause, without requiring uncertain proof of fault. Can you articulate and distinguish the philosophical bases for the above rationales—deontological, economic, humanistic, probabilistic, pragmatic, and moral? Can you discern other rationales? In what other ways did Justice Traynor support his concurrence, in addition to policy?

Section 402A. Some years after *Escola*, Justice Traynor took the opportunity in Greenman v. Yuba Power Prods., Inc., 59 Cal.2d 57, 377 P.2D 897, 27 Cal. Rptr. 697 (1963) (below), to make his *Escola* concurrence the law in California. Within two years of *Greenman*, the American Law Institute drafted and circulated the Restatement (Second) of Torts §402A, adopting *Greenman*'s strict product liability. Section 402A, titled, "Special Liability of Seller of Product for Physical Harm to User or Consumer," provides:

> (1) One who sells any product in a defective condition unreasonably dangerous to the user or consumer or to his property is subject to liability for physical harm thereby caused to the ultimate user or consumer, or to his property, if
> (a) the seller is engaged in the business of selling such a product, and
> (b) it is expected to and does reach the user or consumer without substantial change in the condition in which it is sold.
> (2) The rule stated in Subsection (1) applies although
> (a) the seller has exercised all possible care in the preparation and sale of his product, and
> (b) the user or consumer has not bought the product from or entered into any contractual relation with the seller.

Expansion. An overwhelming majority of states soon adopted forms of strict products liability like that in *Greenman* and the Restatement's §402A. They did not limit this new form of strict products liability to food products, inherently dangerous products, or in other ways that lawyers might have expected from the above history.

States adopting *Greenman*-§402A strict products liability applied it to any product without categorical limitation. Privity was also no limitation. Law gradually became clear that strict products liability claims would be available not only to end users of the injury-causing product but also to bystander non-users whom the product defect injured. *See* Stegemoller v. ACandS, Inc., 767 N.E.2d 974 (Ind. 2002) (asbestos inhaled from clothers of a worker exposed to it); Jones v. Nordictrack, Inc., 274 Ga. 115, 550 S.W.2d 101 (2001) (fall against exercise machine); Hernandez v. Tokai Corp., 2 S.W.2d 251 (Tex. 1999) (defective lighter in hands of one child injures another). Elmore v. American Motors Corp., 451 P.2d 84 (Cal. 1969), was a leading case, holding that the manufacturer of a motor vehicle having a defective drive shaft could be liable not only to the motor vehicle's driver but to the driver of the oncoming vehicle into which the motor vehicle crashed because of the defect. The *Elmore* opinion stated that a prohibition on third-party recovery would be "only the distorted shadow of a vanishing privity which is itself a reflection of the habit of viewing the problem as a commercial one between traders, rather than as part of the accident problem." Authority even exists for strict products liability on behalf of bystanders suffering only emotional distress from a family member's injury by a defective product—just as similar bystander liability exists for negligence claims. *See* Shepard v. Superior Ct., 142 Cal. Rptr. 612 (Ct. App. 1977). As you read the progenitor case *Greenman*, consider whether other products-liability theories remain appropriate after adoption of strict products liability like that in *Greenman*.

Greenman v. Yuba Power Prods., Inc.
California Supreme Court
59 Cal.2d 57, 377 P.2d 897, 27 Cal. Rptr. 697 (1963)

TRAYNOR, J. Plaintiff brought this action for damages against the retailer and the manufacturer of a Shopsmith, a combination power tool that could be used as a saw, drill, and wood lathe. He saw a Shopsmith demonstrated by the retailer and studied a brochure prepared by the manufacturer. He decided he wanted a Shopsmith for his home workshop, and his wife bought and gave him one for Christmas in 1955. In 1957 he bought the necessary attachments to use the Shopsmith as a lathe for turning a large piece of wood he wished to make into a chalice. After he had worked on the piece of wood several times without difficulty, it suddenly flew out of the machine and struck him on the forehead, inflicting serious injuries. About ten and a half months later, he gave the retailer and the manufacturer written notice of claimed breaches of warranties and filed a complaint against them alleging such breaches and negligence.

After a trial before a jury, the court ruled that there was no evidence that the retailer was negligent or had breached any express warranty and that the manufacturer was not liable for the breach of any implied warranty. Accordingly, it submitted to the jury only the cause of action alleging breach of implied warranties against the retailer and the causes of action alleging negligence and breach of express warranties against the manufacturer. The jury returned a verdict for the retailer against plaintiff and for plaintiff against the manufacturer in the amount of $65,000. The trial court denied the manufacturer's motion for a new trial and entered judgment on the verdict. ...

Plaintiff introduced substantial evidence that his injuries were caused by defective design and construction of the Shopsmith. His expert witnesses testified that inadequate set screws were used to hold parts of the machine together so that normal vibration caused the tailstock of the lathe to move away from the piece of wood being turned permitting it to fly out of the lathe. They also testified that there were other more positive ways of fastening the parts of the machine together, the use of which would have prevented the accident. The jury could therefore reasonably have concluded that the manufacturer negligently constructed the Shopsmith.[fn] The jury could also reasonably have concluded that statements in the manufacturer's brochure were untrue, that they constituted express warranties, and that plaintiff's injuries were caused by their breach.

The manufacturer contends, however, that plaintiff did not give it notice of breach of warranty within a reasonable time and that therefore his cause of action for breach of warranty is barred by section 1769 of the Civil Code. Since it cannot be determined whether the verdict against it was based on the negligence or warranty cause of action or both, the manufacturer concludes that the error in presenting the warranty cause of action to the jury was prejudicial. ...

Although in these cases strict liability has usually been based on the theory of an express or implied warranty running from the manufacturer to the plaintiff, the abandonment of the requirement of a contract between them, the recognition that the liability is not assumed by agreement but imposed by law ([cc]), and the refusal to permit the manufacturer to define the scope of its own responsibility for defective products ([cc]) make clear that the liability is not one governed by the law of contract warranties but by the law of strict liability in tort. Accordingly, rules defining and governing warranties that were developed to meet the needs of commercial transactions cannot properly be invoked to govern the manufacturer's liability to those injured by their defective products unless those rules also serve the purposes for which such liability is imposed.

We need not recanvass the reasons for imposing strict liability on the manufacturer. They have been fully articulated in the cases cited above. (See also [cc]; Escola v. Coca Cola Bottling Co., 24 Cal.2d 453, 461, 150 P.2d 436, concurring opinion.) The purpose of such liability is to insure that the costs of injuries resulting from defective products are borne by the manufacturers that put such products on the market rather than by the injured persons who are powerless to protect themselves. Sales warranties serve this purpose fitfully at best. [C] In the present case, for example, plaintiff was able to plead and prove an express warranty only because he read and relied on the representations of the Shopsmith's ruggedness contained in the manufacturer's brochure. Implicit in the machine's presence on the market, however, was a representation that it would safely do the jobs for which it was built. Under these circumstances, it should not be controlling whether plaintiff selected the machine because of the statements in the brochure, or because of the machine's own appearance of excellence that belied the defect lurking beneath the surface, or because he merely assumed that it would safely do the jobs it was built to do. It should not be controlling whether the details of the sales from manufacturer to retailer and from retailer to plaintiff's wife were such that one or more of the implied warranties of the sales act arose. [C] ... To establish the manufacturer's liability it was sufficient that plaintiff proved that he was injured while using the Shopsmith in a way it was intended to be used as a result of a defect in design and manufacture of which plaintiff was not aware that made the Shopsmith unsafe for its intended use. ...

The judgment is affirmed.

INQUIRY

Standards. Are the Restatement (Second) of Torts §402A and the *Greenman* standard the same? Section 402A assigns liability based on a product's "defective condition unreasonably dangerous to the user or consumer...." This standard requires not only the "defect" that *Greenman* required but also that the defect was "unreasonably dangerous." To what extent does the "unreasonably dangerous" language of §402A add an element not required by *Greenman*? Does "defect" in itself imply an unreasonable danger? *Greenman* came first, then §402A. The California Supreme Court had the chance in Cronin v. J.B.E. Olson Corp., 501 P.2d 1153 (Cal. 1972), to decide whether to adopt §402A including its "unreasonably dangerous" language—but rejected it. *Cronin* involved a bread-truck driver's serious injury when an allegedly flawed metal hasp holding the bread racks broke in a collision, and the collision-freed racks forced the driver through the windshield. The *Cronin* opinion held that §402A's "unreasonably dangerous" language "burden[s] the injured plaintiff with proof of an element which rings of negligence," is inconsistent with the "clear and simple test" of *Greenman*'s strict liability for harm caused by product "defects," and places on the plaintiff "a significantly increased burden and represents a step backward in the area pioneered by this court." Do you prefer *Greenman-Cronin* or §402A?

Variety. Now that you have had an introduction to strict products liability, does law need three different causes of action to address products liability—negligence, warranty, and strict products liability? The Restatement (Third) of Torts: Products Liability §2, Comment n (1998), suggests that implied warranty is no longer necessary as a products-liability theory after adoption of strict products liability. Some cases disagree. *See* Castro v. QVC Network, Inc., 139 F.3d 114 (2d Cir. 1998) (separate warranty and strict liability instructions necessary in claim involving alleged defect in roasting pan); Denny v. Ford Motor Co., 87 N.Y.2d 248, 662 N.E.2d 730, 736 (1995) (it would be up to the legislature to abolish implied warranties that are provided for in the UCC); Lee v. Crookston Coca-Cola Bottling Co., 290 Minn. 321, 188 N.W.2d 426 (1971) (remanded for strict liability instruction after negligence and implied-warranty claims fail in exploding-bottle case). Other cases recognize the overlap between negligence, implied warranty, and strict products liability, and do not require jury instructions on the three different theories in all cases where they might apply. *See* Prentis v. Yale Mfg. Co., 421 Mich. 670, 365 N.W.2d 176 (1984) (claim for defective design of forklift properly instructed as negligence claim only) ("we adopt, forthrightly, a pure negligence, risk-utility test in products liability actions against manufacturers of products, where liability is predicated upon defective design"). Can you articulate scenarios in which each of the three theories might apply in the absence of the others, and separately, where all three might apply?

Experience. Beyond the question of which products liability theories to retain, what do you think of products liability generally? Although products liability has been one of the grounds for legislative reform of tort laws, empirical study has found less cause for alarm than popular portrayal may suggest. *See* Deborah J. Merritt & Kathryn A. Barry, *Is the Tort System in Crisis? New Empirical Evidence*, 60 Ohio St. L.J. 315 (1999). Would you expect products liability to retard or to promote product development? Would American products be better if their manufacturers did not face strict products liability? Are the costs of producing those products greater than the cost of producing competing products in countries not imposing strict liability? Would the strict products liability law of the state into which an importer sells a product that injures a consumer apply to the product's foreign manufacturer and domestic distributor? The European Union's EC Product Liability Directive adopts a form of strict products liability similar to the Restatement (Second) of Torts §402A.

Unavoidably Unsafe Products. How treat products—guns, knives, fireworks, tobacco, alcohol—dangerous in themselves rather than because of any anomalous characteristic? How does one judge whether the unavoidable danger is a defect and unreasonable danger? When the California Supreme Court declined in *Cronin* to add Restatement (Second) of Torts §402A's "unreasonably dangerous" element to its *defect* standard, it declined in part because of Comment i to §402A establishing the consumer-expectation test. Comment i addresses the problem of products that are in themselves dangerous at least to some consumers or for some uses. The examples it gives include whiskey (to alcoholics), butter (for artherosclerosis), sugar (to diabetics), and tobacco (to everyone, but with risks many accept). *See also* Buckingham v. R.J. Reynolds Tobacco Co., 142 N.H. 822, 713 A.2d 381 (1998) (second-hand tobacco smoke sufferers have no strict-products-liability claims) (citing Comment i); Joseph E. Seagram & Sons, Inc. v. McGuire, 814 S.W.2d 385 (Tex. 1991) (alcoholics have no warning-defect claim against alcoholic beverage manufacturers). Comment i states, "The article sold must be dangerous to an extent beyond that which would be contemplated by the ordinary consumer who purchases it, with the ordinary knowledge common to the community as to its characteristics."

Consumer-Expectation Test. The marketing of a recreation-quality flotation device as a "life preserver" is one example where the consumer-expectation test applies. The ordinary consumer might expect the flotation device to keep a user's air passages (mouth and nose) above water in the event of the device's use in an emergency. That function would be "life preserving" in the sense that an ordinary consumer might expect. On the other hand, recreation-quality flotation devices may merely be fashionable swimming aids. They may be "defective" if their buoyancy is not sufficient to keep a user's airways above water in a limb-disabling injury, if the seller markets them as "life preservers." *See also* West v. Johnson & Johnson Prods., Inc., 220 Cal. Rptr. 437 (Ct. App. 1985) (consumer-expectation instruction on products-liability claim against tampon manufacturer for allegedly associated toxic-shock syndrome). After all, what would the consumer expect of a product so named? Yet the consumer-expectation test does not always favor the plaintiff. What, for instance, would one expect of a handgun—that when the user pulls the trigger, it serves as a potentially lethal weapon? *See* Halliday v. Sturm, Ruger, & Co., 792 A.2d 1145 (Md. 2002) (dismissing claim brought on behalf of estate of three-year-old child who killed himself while playing with a handgun, because a consumer would expect that the gun be prove lethal if loaded and fired in the manner the father's gross negligence had permitted and the child had imitated and accomplished).

Outweighed Dangers. What, though, of controlled substances that, although dangerous in themselves, have therapeutic benefits outweighing their dangers? Many courts have followed Comment *k* to Restatement (Second) of Torts §402A, refusing to apply strict products liability to prescription drugs. *See* Brown v. Superior Ct., 44 Cal.3d 1049, 751 P.2d 470, 245 Cal. Rptr. 412 (1988). Other courts refuse to follow *Brown's* blanket-immunity rule and instead consider case-by-case whether drug makers have strict products liability for drug-design defects. *See* Freeman v. Hoffman-La Roche, Inc., 618 N.W.2d 827 (Neb. 2000). Most European Union members allow design-defect claims for prescription drugs but permit an ameliorating "development risk" defense that allows the manufacturer to show that during the design of the drug, the risk was unknown and not reasonably discoverable. The Restatement (Third) of Torts: Products Liability §6(c) (1998) assigns prescription-drug-defect liability only to drugs that have risks so great that reasonable care providers would not prescribe them. Should law afford this kind of heightened protection to drugs or medical devices that have production (manufacturing) defects rather than defects in design? *See* Transue v. Aesthetech Corp., 341 F.3d 911 (9th Cir. 2003) (no—give strict-products-liability instruction). Congress accepted the courts' invitation for legislation in this field, by enacting the National Childhood Vaccine Injury Act, 42 U.S.C. §§300aa-1 et seq., establishing a special federal court and compensation scheme for certain vaccination injuries.

Risk-Utility Test. As noted above, the consumer-expectation test is only one of two tests that the courts employ to determine whether a product is defective. The other widely recognized seven-factor *risk-utility test* articulated by Professor Wade in *On the Nature of Strict Liability for Products*, 44 Miss. L.J. 825 (1973), adopted by the New Jersey Supreme Court in Cepeda v. Cumberland Eng. Co., 76 N.J. 152, 386 A.2d 816 (N.J. 1978), is as follows:

(1) The usefulness and desirability of the product—its utility to the user and to the public as a whole.

(2) The safety aspects of the product—the likelihood that it will cause injury, and the probable seriousness of the injury.

(3) The availability of a substitute product which would meet the same need and not be as unsafe.

(4) The manufacturer's ability to eliminate the unsafe character of the product without impairing its usefulness or making it too expensive to maintain its utility.

(5) The user's ability to avoid danger by the exercise of care in the use of the product.

(6) The user's anticipated awareness of the dangers inherent in the product and their avoidability, because of general public knowledge of the obvious condition of the product, or of the existence of suitable warnings or instructions.

(7) The feasibility, on the part of the manufacturer, of spreading the loss by setting the price of the product or carrying liability insurance.

Knowledge

A simple way to analyze factors is to use a "factor-favors-because" formulation. For example: "The utility FACTOR heavily FAVORS the defendant, BECAUSE the product was absolutely necessary to the production of an important industrial component." "The location FACTOR somewhat FAVORS the plaintiff, BECAUSE mining typically does not occur so close to concentrated residences." "The pricing FACTOR very probably FAVORS the defendant, BECAUSE the cost of the only possible alternative design would have been astronomical." The formulation begins by identifying the factor. It then states in an evaluative manner whether that factor favors a party. It then reasons the assertion of favor. A similar "factor-favors-when-because" formulation ensures with the "when" trigger that you state the facts on which your analysis depends, as in, "The feasibility FACTOR strongly FAVORS the defendant, WHEN tests showed that plaintiff's proposed alternative design didn't work, BECAUSE proposing an infeasible alternative is

> nonsense, and without a feasible alternative design, one can hardly blame the defendant."

Choosing Tests. Which test for strict products liability does one use—consumer expectations or risk-utility? *See* Camacho v. Honda Motor Co., 741 P.2d 1240 (Colo. 1987) (product meeting consumer expectations can yet be unreasonably dangerous under risk-utility test). The answer often seems apparent from the allegedly defective product's nature. The more clearly that the product is a consumer product, and its failure relates to consumer expectations, the more likely that the consumer-expectation test applies. On the other hand, consumer expectations don't generally exist for industrial products or product risks involving highly technical judgments. In those cases, prefer the risk-utility test. *See* Knitz v. Minster Machine Co., 69 Ohio St.2d 460, 432 N.E.2d 814 (1982) (60-ton hydraulic press's defect measured by risk-utility test because "the consumer would not know what to expect"). The California Supreme Court faced that question in Soule v. General Motors Corp., 8 Cal.4th 548, 34 Cal. Rptr.2d 607, 882 P2d 298 (Cal. 1994), a vehicle-crashworthiness case where the evidence involved the force resistance of complex mechanical designs. The *Soule* court held that the parties were not to use the consumer-expectation test but must use the risk-utility test instead. *See also* Pruitt v. General Motors Corp., 86 Cal. Rptr.2d 4 (Ct. App. 1999) (rejecting consumer-expectation test for airbag-defect case); *but see* Bresnahan v. Chrysler Corp., 38 Cal. Rptr.2d 46 (Cal. App. 1995) (accepting consumer-expectation theory for airbag-defect case).

Scope of Consumer Expectations. Debate remains regarding the scope of the consumer-expectation test. Significant support exists to apply it to complex products. *See* Mele v. Howmedica, Inc., 348 Ill. App.3d 1, 283 Ill. Dec. 738, 808 N.E.2d 1026 (2004) (consumer need have no specific expectation about medical device's performance, to support application of consumer-expectation test to strict liability claim); McCabe v. American Honda Motor Co., 100 Cal. App.4th 1111, 123 Cal. Rptr.2d 303 (2002) (consumer-expectation test applied in airbag hazard case); Green v. Smith & Nephew AHP, Inc., 629 N.W.2d 727 (Wis. 2001) (the consumer-expectation test is favored for all products including sophisticated products); Potter v. Chicago Pneumatic Tool Co., 694 A.2d 1319 (Conn. 1997) (consumer-expectation test preferred over risk-utility test and applied to sophisticated product); Bresnahan v. Chrysler Corp., 38 Cal. Rptr.2d 446 (Ct. App. 1995) (consumer-expectation test used in airbag-design-defect case). What is clear from the procedural standpoint is that the jury decides a product's defectiveness where reasonable minds can differ. *See* Branty v. Hoffmann-La Roche, Inc., 262 Ga. App. 401, 585 S.E.2d 723 (2003).

Skills

For each of the following cases, consider which products-liability theory (negligence, express warranty, implied warranty, or strict products liability) would best fit the proofs, or which combination of theories would do so. Consider also how to prove the theories:

A Manufacturer's production process inadvertently produces ridge on gun-trigger safety, making safety malfunction.

B Retailer tells consumer that product is right for consumer's use, resulting in catastrophic loss.

C Supplier provides wrong material that, when incorporated into product, produces weaknesses that result in catastrophic failure.

> **D** Manufacturer specifies and incorporates fasteners that fail catastrophically after repeated use of product.
> **E** Product literature describes use of product exactly as it was used, resulting in catastrophic failure.
> **F** Manufacturer fails to include warning that if consumer uses product in a certain foreseeable manner, product will fail catastrophically.

C. Types of Defects

OBJECTIVE: Given fact patterns of products causing various injuries, analyze whether the incidents would give rise to manufacturing, design, or warning-defect claims, under the law reflected in these pages of the text.

Case Study: A couple was riding a Crosshare snowmobile along state trails when they came to a tree that had fallen across the path. It was clear that other snowmobilers had encountered the tree and managed to cross it in some fashion with their snowmobiles. So the rider dismounted from the snowmobile with its front skiis part way up over the tree trunk, and asked the operator to operate the snowmobile while the rider pushed and lifted the rear of the snowmobile to get it over the tree trunk. As the operator gunned the engine, the snowmobile track gears rotated sharply, catching and amputating the tips of the rider's fingers as he attempted to lift the rear of the snowmobile. ***Discuss and evaluate the rider's potential manufacturing, design, and warning-defect claims against Crosshare with respect to his injury.***

To this point, judges and tort scholars had led products liability's expansion—although their efforts certainly required the involvement of torts practitioners. Yet practitioners working with §402A's new product-defect standard soon found necessary developing a framework better suited to the different kinds of problems consumers encounter with products that result in loss or injury. *See* Barker v. Lull Eng. Co., 573 P.2d 443 (Cal. 1978) (distinguishing manufacturing- from design-defect claims). The conceptual difficulties presented in applying §402A's unified product-defect theory, together with criticism of its expansive nature, and enactment of legislation limiting its reach, led the American Law Institute to undertake a five-year study culminating in the Restatement (Third) of Torts: Products Liability (1998). After an introductory Section 1 stating simply that "[o]ne engaged in the business of selling or otherwise distributing products who sells or distributes a defective product is subject to liability for harm to persons or property caused by the defect," the Restatement (Third) of Torts: Products Liability then recognized three forms of product defect as follows:

§2. Categories of Product Defect
A product is defective when, at the time of sale or distribution, it contains a manufacturing defect, is defective in design, or is defective because of inadequate instructions or warnings. A product:
(a) contains a manufacturing defect when the product departs from its intended design even though all possible care was exercised in the preparation and marketing of the product;
(b) is defective in design when the foreseeable risks of harm posed by the product could have been reduced or avoided by the adoption of a reasonable alternative design by the seller or other distributor, or a predecessor in the commercial chain of distribution, and the omission of the alternative design renders the product not reasonably safe;

(c) is defective because of inadequate instructions or warnings when the foreseeable risks of harm posed by the product could have been reduced or avoided by the provision of reasonable instructions or warnings by the seller or other distributor, or a predecessor in the commercial chain of distribution, and the omission of the instructions or warnings renders the product not reasonably safe.

The Third Restatement's manufacturing-, design-, and warning-defect (failure-to-warn) framework reflects products-liability practice. Claims for manufacturing defects (unintended departures from design) require proofs of the product's condition at the time of the accident. The key in such cases is to preserve and inspect the injury-causing defective product, contrast it with the manufacturer's product exemplar, and reconstruct the accident to demonstrate the causal relationship between the injury-causing failure and the manufacturing defect, shown by contrast with the product exemplar. Claims for defects in design require quite different proofs regarding the safety, cost, feasibility, and utility of alternative design choices. The condition of the product itself at the time of the accident is much less significant in design-defect cases because the manufacturer made the product as designed. Instead, resolution depends on engineering judgments about the cost, efficacy, and feasibility of relative designs, including especially failure analyses of those various designs. Shortcomings in the warnings and instructions accompanying a product require yet a different treatment. Failure-to-warn cases raise questions of the manufacturer's knowledge of consumer behavior including product misuse, the form of product packaging and availability of other means of distributing product warnings and instructions, principles of good communication, and consumer sophistication regarding product risks. The text below addresses each of these three forms of defect, after considering questions the Third Restatement's framework raises.

INQUIRY

Refining Liability Standards. That the Third Restatement divides products liability cases into manufacturing, design, and warning claims is clear enough. But from the above quotations, can you tell which approach the Third Restatement took toward the defect standard—the simple *Greenman-Cronin* "defect" approach or the Restatement (Second) of Torts §402A's two-part "defective condition unreasonably dangerous" test? For manufacturing defects, the Third Restatement accepts a simple defect, defined as departing from design. However, for design defects, the Third Restatement requires proof of both a reasonable alternative design and that the chosen design rendered the product "not reasonably safe." The Third Restatement's addition of these requirements may well have been in recognition of the legislative response to the rapid expansion of strict products liability. Can you see why, from a conceptual standpoint, more is required for proof of design defects than for manufacturing defects? Likewise, for warning defects, the Third Restatement requires proof of reasonable alternative warnings and that their omission rendered the product "not reasonably safe." Does the Third Restatement's "not reasonably safe" mean the same as the Second Restatement's "unreasonably dangerous"?

Ethics

> Tort lawyers (as much or more than lawyers in other fields) use the help of nonlawyer assistants—secretaries, legal assistants, and couriers, to be sure, but occasionally also in-office physician and nurse experts, private investigators, and others with special skills. Rule 5.3 of the ABA Model Rules of Professional Conduct requires that a lawyer who supervises a nonlawyer assistant must "make reasonable efforts to ensure" that the nonlawyer assistant's "conduct is compatible with the professional obligations of the lawyer" and holds the lawyer responsible for the nonlawyer's violation of those rules, if the lawyer orders, ratifies, or fails to remediate the conduct. Put simply, a lawyer must be sure that nonlawyer assistants acting for the lawyer follow the lawyer-ethics rules, even though they are not lawyers, because they extend the lawyer's conduct.

Multiple Theories. Depending on the circumstances, a strict-products-liability claim may involve one, two, or all three forms of defect—manufacturing, design, and warning. The cases in which the plaintiff alleges only one defect form are relatively fewer. Do you sense why? For clarity's purpose, the cases below, as edited, illustrate only one form of defect at a time. As you read the following text and cases illustrating (in turn) manufacturing, design, and warning defects, try to generalize and articulate the circumstances in which each form of defect would arise and the different kind of proofs necessary for each defect form.

Manufacturing Defects. We begin with a manufacturing-defect case. Consider as an example the manufacture and sale of a chain saw for consumer rather than commercial use. The cutting chain of a chain saw ordinarily comes to a quick complete stop when the user releases finger-pressure on the chain saw's trigger. This quick-stop function is an important safety feature to keep the user's free hands from coming into contact with the cutting chain. The mechanical means by which the chain stops rotating about the blade and gear depends on a centrifugal clutch and the engine's revolution. As the user releases finger-pressure on the trigger, the engine RPMs slow and the centrifugal clutch turns more slowly until it no longer engages the gear that drives the cutting chain. If a chain saw's tendency for the chain to run-on after the user releases the trigger injures a user, then experts could inspect the chain saw's trigger and clutch, comparing them to an exemplar, to determine if the hazardous run-on was the result of manufacturing defects. If the trigger or clutch performance departs in a significant manner from the exemplar, perhaps because of differences in material composition or forming-process defects, and the differences are what produced the run-on, then the injured user may have a manufacturing-defect case. We will return to our chain-saw example later. Now consider a similar manufacturing-defect case.

Gower v. Savage Arms, Inc.
United States District Court
166 F. Supp.2d 240 (E.D. Pa. 2001)

McLAUGHLIN, J. The plaintiffs, John and Debra Gower, seek to hold Savage Arms, Inc. and Savage Sports Corporation liable for compensatory and punitive damages under a theory of "successor liability" for injuries John Gower sustained when his hunting rifle discharged inadvertently, shooting him in the foot.[fn] Gower alleges that the rifle was defective as … manufactured with a metal ridge that impaired the functioning of the safety mechanism (the "manufacturing defect"). … The plaintiffs assert causes of action in strict liability as well as negligence for the above defects. In addition, the plaintiffs assert causes of action for material misrepresentation, negligent misrepresentation, breach of warranty and loss of consortium.

The Court grants the defendants' motion with respect to punitive damages, the "unloading defect," insufficient warnings, misrepresentation, breach of warranty, and all negligence claims. ... The Court further denies the defendants' motion for summary judgment with respect to the strict liability claims concerning ... the manufacturing defect ... .

The plaintiffs claim damages for injuries sustained in a hunting accident in 1997. On December 15, 1997, John Gower was hunting with his two brothers, Clark and Craig, and with his brother-in-law, Robert Swan, at Long Pond, Pennsylvania. They spent much of the day hunting for deer in the woods. At approximately 4:30 p.m., after a day of hunting, the plaintiff left the woods and headed toward the truck in which they had driven to Long Pond. As he emerged from the woods, he turned around for one more visual sweep of the woods and field. Gower was preparing to unload his gun when the gun discharged, shooting him in the foot. [C][fn] Gower was wearing thick gloves, and his fingers were inside the trigger guard when the gun discharged. At the time of the discharge the plaintiff had not taken the gun off the "safe" position. The rifle was designed so as not to fire when in the "safe" position. ...

... As confirmed by expert inspections after the incident and conceded by both parties at oral argument, the rifle was not working properly at the time of the accident. [C] The safety mechanism could only be placed in the "safe" position with more than the usually required force. ...

The Pennsylvania Supreme Court has adopted Section 402A of the Restatement (Second) of Torts... . In order to succeed in a claim brought under 402A, the plaintiffs must show (1) that the product was defective, (2) that the defect existed at the time the product left the manufacturer's hands, and (3) that the defect caused the plaintiff's injury. [C] ...

The plaintiffs allege that there was a manufacturing defect in the rifle in the form of a metal ridge that affected the functioning of the safety mechanism: "The subject safety button has a shallow ridge on the bottom of its rear radius that contacts the rising radius of the slot. This contact limits (to about .133-inch) the free, unobstructed movement of the button to the rear when applying the safety. This defective condition was present at the time of manufacture." (Pl.Ex.H.) For purposes of summary judgment, the question of whether the ridge rendered the gun defective is not difficult to answer. In *Dambacher v. Mallis,* 336 Pa.Super. 22, 485 A.2d 408 (1984), the court stated: "In a manufacturing defect case, the question whether the product is defective is relatively simple. Since the allegation is that something went awry in the manufacturing process, so that, for example, the product lacked a component it should have had, the finder of fact need only compare the product that caused the injury with other products that were manufactured according to specifications." *Id.* at 426. [An expert witness] Mason undertook such a comparison and found that the subject rifle had the above-mentioned metal ridge, whereas an exemplar rifle of the same model did not.

The defendants, however, challenge Mason's claim that the defect was present at the time of manufacture as being entirely without a factual foundation. ...

The Court is not able to determine whether the statement lacks a factual foundation without allowing Mason to respond at a hearing, however. ...

For the above reason, the Court denies the defendant's summary judgment motion with respect to the "manufacturing defect" claim without prejudice to the defendant to renew the motion after the Court's decision on the *Daubert* motion. …

Skills

Cross-examination skills can be critical to the success of a products-liability claim, as with other tort claims. Plaintiffs' lawyers seeking deposition discovery of product information from manufacturer representatives will ask probing but open-ended questions. Cross-examination at trial is a very different art, employing close-ended questions that demand specific answers that the questioning lawyer already knows. Contrast the deposition discovery and trial cross-examinations below, by a plaintiff's lawyer of a defendant manufacturer's representative, for parallel questions.

DISCOVERY DEPOSITION:
Q. What consideration do you give to the product's safety, during design?
Q. What failure analyses did you perform during product design?
Q. What are your procedures for tracking consumer reports of product injury?
Q. Who is responsible for product safety, and what is their safety training?
Q. What product safety testing did you do before shipping this product?

TRIAL CROSS-EXAMINATION:
Q. Your company has no record whatsoever of having given any consideration to product safety during this product's design, isn't that true?
Q. You have no recollection at all of having performed any failure analyses for this product at any time, do you?
Q. Although you recall having had consumer reports of various problems with this product, in response to our requests you did not produce so much as a single record of any of those reports, did you?
Q. Your company does not designate anyone in particular, does it, as responsible for product safety?
Q. Among these few records your company produced of safety testing on this product, none of those records show any testing of the particular part of this product that failed, do they?

INQUIRY

Departures from Design. Manufacturing-defect cases are generally the easiest of the three forms of product-defect cases to prove. Can you articulate why? Significantly, under a strict-products-liability (rather than negligence) theory, the plaintiff does not have to show *why* the manufacturing defect arose. *See* Rix v. General Motors Corp., 222 Mont. 318, 723 P.2d 195 (1986) (broken flare in brake tube results in loss of vehicle brakes during operation). What must the plaintiff show for a prima-facie manufacturing-defect case? The above case suggests how relatively easy is comparing the manufacturing defect in the subject product to an exemplar without the defect. What if the defendant manufacturer offers evidence that the manufacturer used extraordinary care to prevent manufacturing defects but that a very small number of defects are bound to occur? The Restatement (Third) of Torts §2(a) provision reproduced above holds that manufacturing-defect liability arises "even though all possible care was exercised in the preparation and marketing of the product." Would the manufacturer's evidence of extraordinary care even be admissible?

Preservation of Evidence. On the other hand, what difficulties might a plaintiff face in preserving and recovering evidence of a manufacturing defect? The injury-causing incident often enough simultaneously destroys the product. Users also often dispose of or alter damaged products before lawyers can preserve and experts inspect them. Moreover, proof that a defect existed at the time of the incident is not alone sufficient to establish a manufacturing-defect claim. The plaintiff must also trace the defect back to the time of manufacture. Manufacturers commonly defend manufacturing-defect cases on the basis that the defect arose after the product left the manufacturer, either in distribution or use, or by deliberate alteration of the product, or even by wear and tear. *See* McNally v. Chrysler Motors Corp., 55 Misc.2d 128, 284 N.Y.S.2d 761 (Sup. Ct. 1967) (hydraulic-brake leak in 1963 not proof of manufacturing defect in 1961). One common response of the plaintiff is to allege a defect in the manufacturer's design that unreasonably contributed to the product's deterioration or alteration, including that the manufacturer should have anticipated and designed against risk-causing wear and tear. *See* Tucker v. Unit Crane & Shovel Corp., 256 Or. 318, 473 P.2d 862 (1970) (deterioration from prolonged use over nine years is a factor in determining whether a collapsed boom crane was defective when manufactured).

Design Defects. Consider, then, a design-defect case. Returning to our chain-saw example, another risk to chain saws in addition to chain run-on is the phenomenon of chain-saw kickback. Kickback involves the chain saw's blade snapping swiftly and forcefully back toward the user's face without warning. Kickbacks can instantly sever an artery in the user's neck, causing bleeding to death, or cause other serious injuries. Kickback occurs when the tip of the chain saw's blade buries in a log rather than remaining free on the opposite side of the log from where the user stands holding the handle and trigger of the chain saw. If the cutting chain at the buried tip of the chain saw grabs into the log and stops suddenly, rather than continuing to cut through the log, the centrifugal force of the suddenly stopped chain transfers to the blade causing it to snap back toward the user's face. A simple, inexpensive way to eliminate this form of kickback is to place a tip-guard in the blade near the far end of the blade away from the user, to keep the blade's tip from entering the log. Yet tip guards can also reduce a chain saw's utility by (among other things) decreasing the log diameters that the saw can cut. Whether the absence of a tip guard is a chain-saw design defect may depend on a range of considerations. We will return to our chain saw. Consider first a better-known design issue of a different kind of product.

Purvis v. American Motors Corp.
Louisiana Court of Appeals
538 So.2d 1015 (La. App. 1988)

CRAIN, J. This is an appeal of a damage award in an action resulting from an automobile accident. ...

Gerald and Shereen S. Purvis, Joe and Brenda K. Slade, Thomas and Debbie Brunet and a few other friends attended an outdoor music festival at Tangipahoa Beach and returned to the Brunet's house for a barbeque. Thomas Brunet and others went to the grocery for supplies. Shortly after they left, Debbie Brunet, Shereen Purvis, Brenda Slade, Terri Brewer Sprayberry and Howard Thomas decided to go to the store as well. They all got into a 1972 Jeep CJ-5 (Jeep) owned by the Brunets, with Debbie driving. In order to avoid striking a pothole, or after striking a pothole, Debbie Brunet steered the Jeep to her left into the path of an oncoming vehicle. She then steered it to the right and drove the Jeep into the ditch. She regained control of the Jeep and proceeded down the ditchline for some distance. When she turned left and attempted to return to the paved road the Jeep flipped on its side. Brenda Slade and Shereen Purvis were injured in the accident. The plaintiffs filed this action against American Motors-Jeep (AMC), Tangipahoa Parish Police Jury, Thomas and Debbie Brunet, and their liability insurer, Sentry Insurance Company (Sentry). A jury trial was held as to the action against AMC, the Brunets and Sentry. The trial judge heard the action against the parish.

A verdict was returned in favor of the plaintiffs finding fault on the parties in the following percent: Debbie Brunet, 70%, Thomas Brunet 0%, Tangipahoa Parish, 15%, American Motors-Jeep, 15%.

The jury further set damages as follows: Shereen Purvis, $95,000, Gerald Purvis $1,250, Brenda Slade $111,000, Joe Slade, $1,250. ...

a) *Acceptance of John Noettl as an Expert*

AMC argues that the evidence against it is insufficient because the trial court erred in admitting Mr. Noettl as an expert in the field of the dynamics of Jeep CJ-5 rollovers. ...

We find no abuse of discretion by the trial court in admitting Noettl as an expert witness or in allowing him to testify in his field of expertise. Noettl has investigated over five hundred cases involving instances of Jeep rollover. He has a bachelor and master's degree in engineering and had conducted extensive testing involving Jeep CJ-5 rollover characteristics as well as other diagnostic testing of automobiles.

b) *Sufficiency of the Evidence To Show a Design Defect*

AMC first argues that modifications to the vehicle altered it so much that it was no longer a "Jeep CJ-5". Consequently, it is argued, the original design of the Jeep CJ-5 is not pertinent to a resolution of this case.

The engine, transmission, and steering wheel had been changed on the vehicle. Coil springs had been added to the suspension to provide extra "stiffness" and the tires were larger than those originally provided with the Jeep. Despite the evidence of changes, the jury found AMC at fault, thus rejecting the contention that the modifications altered the vehicle to an extent that AMC was relieved of responsibility for its design. Findings of fact by the jury will not be disturbed on review absent manifest error. [C]

Noettl testified that the modifications to the suspension did not drastically affect the jeep's handling, and if anything, the modifications increased its resistance to rollover. He found that the engine, transmission and steering wheel had no effect on the accident. In addition, AMC stated, in a 1982 owner's supplement that was intended to be provided to all CJ-5 owners, that the vehicle could be used in off road racing by modifying the engine and suspension and changing the tires. AMC argues that the vehicle "tripped" over dirt "scooted up" by the right rear tire as it slid along the ditchline at the point of attempting reentry on the highway. This theory was provided by experts, but AMC failed to produce any physical evidence to support it, even though there were witnesses other than the parties involved present at the accident scene and photographs were taken. We find no manifest error in the determination of the jury that the modification to the jeep did not relieve AMC of responsibility for its design.

AMC next argues that it was error to admit into evidence a film of Jeep rollovers produced by Dynamic Science, Inc. ...

The tests were conducted at Dynamic Science's research center under the direction of Noettl. The tests were to determine the rollover characteristics of a 1980 Jeep CJ-5 under sharp turning maneuvers with optimum road conditions. Mr. Noettl testified that the test attempted to remove human error, braking, steering, tripping mechanisms and road conditions in testing the rollover characteristics of the CJ-5 produced only by lateral forces. Although the film might have been more objective and less dramatic had the testing "dummies" been removed, the test showed the tendencies of the vehicles to rollover in low speed situations which an automobile with a lower center of gravity would not have. Mr. Noettl testified that the 1972 CJ-5 and the 1980 CJ-5 test vehicle were virtually identical in handling characteristics. The tests were of situations which the average driver might encounter. After reviewing the film and the background information relating to the testing, we find no error on the part of the trial court in admitting the film into evidence.

In *Halphen v. Johns-Manville Sales Corp.,* 484 So.2d 110, 115 (La.1986) the Louisiana Supreme Court stated: "A product may be unreasonably dangerous because of its design for any one of three reasons: (1) A reasonable person would conclude that the danger-in-fact, whether foreseeable or not, outweighs the utility of the product.... (2) Although balancing under the risk-utility test leads to the conclusion that the product is not unreasonably dangerous per se, alternative products were available to serve the same needs or desires with less risk of harm; or (3) Although the utility of the product outweighs its danger-in-fact, there was a feasible way to design the product with less harmful consequences."

There was evidence from which the jury could have concluded that before the accident some of AMC's executive design personnel considered the CJ-5 to be unsafe because of its propensity to rollover due to its high center of gravity. They suggested lowering the ground clearance and widening the track width to lower its center of gravity and increase its stability.

After reviewing the record, we find the jury was not clearly wrong in its consideration of evidence to support finding AMC liable in part for the accident. Consequently, we find no manifest error on the part of the trier of fact. ... The judgment of the trial court is affirmed. All costs of this appeal are assessed against the appellants.

AFFIRMED.

INQUIRY

"Crashworthiness." The above case is one of many addressing the now well-known roll-over phenomenon. Design-defect cases do not stop at claims over defective designs that unreasonably increase accident injuries. They also include "crashworthiness" cases—claims that the maker should have designed the product (typically but not always a motor vehicle) to prevent injury in the event of a crash produced by other causes such as driver negligence or error. *See* Alami v. Volkswagen of America, Inc., 766 N.E.2d 574 (N.Y. 2002) (intoxication of vehicle driver does not bar, but may be considered comparative negligence in, driver's motor-vehicle crashworthiness case); D'Amario v. Ford Motor Co., 806 So.2d 424 (Fla. 2001) (intoxication of driver is immaterial to claim of alleged vehicle defect causing vehicle to burst into flame on crash); Hillrichs v. Avco Corp., 478 N.W.2d 70 (Iowa 1991) (farm combine); Tafoya v. Sears Roebuck & Co., 884 F.2d 1330 (10th Cir. 1989) (riding lawnmower); Leichtamer v. American Motors Co., 67 Ohio St.2d 456, 424 N.E.2d 568 (1981) (punitive damages warranted for defective design of uncrashworthy rollbar that displaced in accident); Smith v. Ariens Co., 375 Mass. 620, 377 N.E.2d 954 (1978) (snowmobile). Although initially controversial, crashworthiness cases today find overwhelming support for the proposition that manufacturers owe a duty to design reasonably crashworthy vehicles. *See* Blankenship v. General Motors Corp., 185 W. Va. 350, 406 S.E.2d 781 (1991); Restatement (Third) of Torts: Products Liability §16, Comment a (1998) (increased harm from product). Should evidence of the plaintiff's negligence in causing the crash be admissible in crashworthiness cases?

Alternative Feasible Design. Design-defect cases are the most difficult to address from both a conceptual and evidentiary standpoint. Can you articulate why? *See* Caterpillar Tractor Co. v. Beck, 593 P.2d 871 (Alaska 1979) ("there is no readily ascertainable external measure of defectiveness" for design-defect cases). One of the challenges that plaintiff's face in design-defect cases is to prove an alternative feasible design. Most jurisdictions impose that requirement (consistent with Restatement (Third) of Torts: Products Liability §2(b)) either by statute or by case law, as reflected in the above case. *See* Ohio Rev. Code §2307.75 (2005); Beech v. Outboard Marine Corp., 584 So.2d 447 (Ala. 1991); *but see* Vautour v. Body Masters Sports Indus., Inc., 784 A.2d 1178 (N.H. 2001) (proof of reasonable alternative not required in design-defect cases). The plaintiff is not required to build a prototype of the alternative design. *See* General Motors Corp. v. Sanchez, 997 S.W.2d 584 (Tex. 1999) (plaintiff need only show that reasonable alternative could be developed); *but see* Dhillon v. Crown Controls Corp., 269 F.3d 865 (7th Cir. 2001) (rejecting expert's testimony on basis in part that expert's proposed alternative had not actually been designed, built, or tested). Do *Daubert* requirements for expert testimony require that the expert's proposed design have been "tested"? *See* Colon v. Bic USA, Inc., 199 F. Supp.2d 53 (S.D. N.Y. 2001) (yes). Note, also, that the feasible-alternative-design requirement in design-defect cases may require an exception for products that have little or no utility or the manufacturer designed to injure without lawful purpose. *See* N.J. Stat. Ann. §2A:58C-3(b) (no requirement to prove alternative design for egregiously unsafe products having no utility); McCarthy v. Olin Corp., 119 F.3d 148 (2d Cir. 1997) (no requirement to prove alternative design for "Black Talon" bullets intended to increase wounding power, but affirming dismissal of claim against manufacturer).

Firearms and Defects. Gun cases raise their own troublesome issues in products-liability litigation. Generally, the cases hold that guns that work according to their lethal design are not defective simply because they fall into the wrong hands. *See* Perkins v. F.I.E. Corp., 762 F.2d 1250 (5th Cir. 1985); Halliday v. Sturm, Ruger & Co., 368 Md. 186, 792 A.2d 1145 (Md. 2002) (no strict liability for manufacturer when three-year-old child killed self with found gun); Hamilton v. Beretta U.S.A. Corp., 96 N.Y.2d 222, 750 N.E.2d 1055, 727 N.Y.S.2d 7 (2001) (gun manufacturer has no duty to keep products from reaching underground); Merrill v. Navegar, Inc., 26 Cal.4th 465, 110 Cal. Rptr.2d 370, 28 P.3d 116 (2001) (statute barring products-liability claims against gun manufacturers also bars negligence claim). On the other hand, the rare case will hold that liability may arise if a gun functions according to its design but in a way that departs from consumer expectations, creating unreasonable harzards. *See*

Smith v. Bryco Arms, 131 N.M. 87, 33 P.3d 638 (App. 2001) (manufacturer subject to strict liability claim for gun firing with clip removed if bullet was chambered). And some recent authority exists, following an older case holding a slingshot manufacturer potentially liable for marketing the device to children, Moning v. Alfono, 400 Mich. 425, 254 N.W.2d 759 (1977), for negligent-marketing claims for firearm sales reaching those who cannot legally purchase guns. *See* Ileto v. Glock Inc., 349 F.3d 1191 (9th Cir. 2003); Hamilton v. Accu-Tek, 62 F. Supp.2d 802 (E.D. N.Y. 1999); City of Cincinnati v. Beretta U.S.A. Corp., 95 Ohio St.3d 416, 768 N.E.2d 1136 (2002).

Date of Manufacture. Design-defect cases raise another nettling issue related to the feasibility of alternative designs. That issue is whether the manufacturer knew of an alternative design *at the time it manufactured the product*. If not, and if instead the alternative design was only apparent and feasible at the time of trial because of advances in knowledge and technology, then allowing a plaintiff to argue that the manufacture should have known and incorporated it years earlier when the product was designed and manufactured hardly seems fair. *See* Restatement (Third) of Torts: Products Liability §2, Comment d (1998) (evaluate industry knowledge at time of manufacture rather than time of trial). The question is whether the alternative design was within the "state of the art"—the defense's argument being that it was not within the state of the art and that the alternative design that the plaintiff has offered at trial is therefore irrelevant. "State of the art" sounds a bit like industry custom—that which an industry practices. Yet the plaintiff may occasionally use "state of the art" in a third manner, to argue that a product is defective because it is not "state of the art." This usage confounds the strict-products-liability *defect* standard, which does not require manufacturers to adopt the best design, or a current design, or certainly not a cutting-edge or "state of the art" design. Its proper usage is only in what was feasible and known at the time. A lawyer's best course may be to avoid the phrase.

Figure

Torts practitioner Mark Lanier is passionate about his commitment to the injured individuals whom he serves in complex, high-stakes tort-litigation. He recently won a plaintiff's verdict in the first pharmaceutical-liability trials over the prescription pain-killer VIOXX, which no longer sells after its connection to increased stroke and heart attack risk. A decade ago he won one of the largest asbestos-case verdicts in the nation's history for a group of twenty-one victims. He has also successfully represented small- and medium-size businesses in antitrust and fraud cases against industry giants. Mr. Lanier's success on behalf of tort victims have resulted in feature articles about his trial skills, in the *Wall Street Journal, New York Times, National Law Journal*, and other general and professional national publications, and frequent appearances on ABC's *Good Morning America*. He is also the founder of the Christian Trial Lawyers Association, a network of principled trial lawyers engaged in civic improvement, and leads a 300-member Sunday School class on Bible literacy.

Unusual Susceptibilities. How treat products that have risks only to those who have an unusual susceptibility? How should the law judge those products—by the expectations of the susceptible or non-susceptible consumer? The law could treat them under design-defect theories, that the maker should have weighed the risks and utility in a fashion different from that which led to the product. Yet at some point, and indeed in a large number of cases, design-defect theories begin to overlap with warnings and instructions issues. For instance, in Simeon v. Doe, 618 So.2d 848 (La. 1993), the appellate court held the defendant bar owner not strictly liable on a product defect theory for serving oysters that had a bacteria common to the region and not harmful to most people, but left the issue of a failure-to-warn claim to the jury. Most courts treat the question of the unusual susceptibility of a particular consumer to some product risk, as a warning-defect issue. For instance, in Livingston v. Marie Callender's, Inc., 85 Cal. Rptr.2d 528 (Ct. App. 1999), the appellate court held a jury question whether the defendant restaurant was liable for a customer's allergic reaction to monosodium glutamate in the restaurant's soup, about which the restaurant had failed to warn. The question thus becomes whether the risk was sufficiently substantial to a sufficient number of unusually susceptible, potential users or consumers, that a reasonable manufacturer would have warned those who had the unusual susceptibility. *See* Restatement (Third) of Torts: Products Liability §2, Comment *k* (1998) (duty to warn the susceptibility depends on the plaintiff showing a substantial number are susceptible).

Warning as to Defective Design. What if a product has what most would judge to be a design defect but the manufacturer has a clear warning with respect to it? The Restatement (Third) of Torts: Products Liability §2, Comment *l* (1998) states that a warning is not a substitute for a safe design. *See* Rogers v. Ingersoll-Rand Co., 144 F.3d 841 (D.C. Cir. 1998) (same) (District of Columbia law); Glover v. Bic Corp., 6 F.3d 1318 (9th Cir. 1993) (same) (Oregon law); Uniroyal Goodrich Tire Co. v. Martinez, 977 S.W.2d 328 (Tex. 1998) (same). One can see, again, how readily the three forms of defect overlap. One can also see how treating the three forms separately from a conceptual standpoint enables use of appropriate standards for each form of defect. Manufacturing-defect standards are most like strict liability. Design-defect cases begin to include aspects of fault both in consideration of consumer expectations and under risk-utility tests. And warning-defect cases are most clearly fault-based. *See* Vassallo v. Baxter Healthcare Corp., 428 Mass. 1, 696 N.E.2d 909 (1998) (plaintiff in warning-defect case must show reasonable foreseeability of risk and reasonableness of alternative warning).

Failure-to-Warn. Consider, then, a failure-to-warn claim relating to our chain-saw scenario. As described above, kickback is one of the risks of chain-saw use, at least when the chain saw lacks a tip guard. Users must prevent the tip of the chain-saw blade from entering the log where the chain at the tip might grab into rather than cut through the log. Users may feel that a tip guard reduces a chain saw's utility somewhat. Manufacturers might choose to design and manufacture chain saws without tip guards. Consumers might even demand them. The reasonableness of a manufacturer's forgoing a tip guard might depend on the warnings and instructions the manufacturer provides with the chain saw. Kickback is certainly a well-known phenomenon to the commercial chain-saw user but may be utterly unknown to the novice consumer. A manufacturer who sells to a consumer a chain saw without a tip guard and without a warning about kickback (including how kickback happens, what injury it produces, and how to avoid it) may well be strictly liable for the consumer's kickback injury, on a failure-to-warn theory. Now consider a less-plausible warnings case.

Mathews v. University Loft Co.
New Jersey Superior Court
387 N.J. Super. 349, 903 A.2d 1120 (2006)

STERN, J. Defendant, University Loft Company, appeals from a July 23, 2004 "order of judgment" based on a jury verdict awarding plaintiff $179,001, including prejudgment interest and costs... .

Plaintiff filed this products liability design, manufacturing, and warning defect case after falling from his loft bed and sustaining injuries. Summary judgment was granted dismissing plaintiff's case except for the claim "based upon lack of warning."

On this appeal defendant argues that summary judgment should have been granted on the failure-to-warn claim and that the case should have been dismissed at the end of plaintiff's case... [and] that the trial judge also "committed an error of law in allowing plaintiff's 'warnings expert' to testify concerning the retail standards for warnings and guardrails on loft beds[.]" ...

We agree with defendant that the failure-to-warn claim should have been dismissed, and we reverse the judgment for plaintiff. ...

I.

According to the proofs at trial, in the fall of 1999 plaintiff, then twenty-one years old, was a senior at Stockton State College. He lived with a roommate in a new campus apartment, where he slept in a new "loft bed" which was six feet off the floor.[fn: Defendant defines "loft bed" as "essentially a bunk bed, but instead of there being a top bed and bottom bed, there is a top bed and an empty space below, where the student can put a desk, dresser, etc."] Plaintiff began sleeping on the loft bed in the first week of September 1999. He had never slept on a loft or bunk bed before.

At about noon on October 11, 1999, plaintiff was asleep on the bed when his pager went off. The pager was on the "desk, or dresser area, below the bed." Plaintiff did not hear the pager at first, but his roommate, who also had been sleeping, woke up and yelled to plaintiff to "turn ... off" the pager. Plaintiff testified that "when he yelled over to me to wake up, or, you know, get up, I was startled, and I—the next thing I knew, I was—I fell off the bed, I was on the floor."

Plaintiff landed on his head and left shoulder, and felt "excruciating pain" in his shoulder, which looked "deformed" and had dislocated. After a few minutes he was able to "roll" the shoulder "back into the socket." He went to the school healthcare center from which he was sent to the hospital, where x-rays were taken and he was given pain medication and "a sling to wear for a few weeks."

Plaintiff resumed sleeping in the loft bed, but subsequently positioned himself "all the way against the wall," as far as possible from the open edge of the bed, because he "didn't want to fall off the bed again." There were no warning labels on the bed, and it had never "cross[ed his] mind" or "occurred to" plaintiff that he could fall or that the bed was dangerous in any way. He testified that had he seen a warning, he would have been "aware of the hazard that was present" and slept closer to the wall, as he had done after the accident. ...

George Widas, a consulting engineer, testified for plaintiff as an expert in "safety engineering, including safety in products, safety in falls from heights, and human factors." At plaintiff's counsel's request, Widas had examined the discovery in this case, as well as defendant's documentation concerning the loft bed in question and the applicable industry standard, which considered any bed higher than three feet off the ground to create a "fall hazard." According to Widas, this bed was six feet high, and thus constituted a "significant risk." In 1989 there had been over 8,000 reported falls from bunk beds by persons over fifteen years old.

Widas testified that when such a risk exists, the proper response is for the manufacturer to provide a "barrier to prevent a sleeping occupant from rolling or sliding out of the bed." If no barrier is provided or it is removable, industry standards require that the manufacturer affix a warning "that says make sure that you protect yourself from this fall hazard[.]" According to Widas, an adequate warning must include "a keyword, an alerting word, such as danger to get people's attention" and must "tell the people what the danger is and how to avoid it." The warning must be in certain colors to attract "attention," must "make the user aware of the means to mitigate the hazard," and must "be displayed on the end board of the bed at a prominent height, eye height, in a location that's readily visible to the user." Widas observed that although there was a manufacturer's sticker on plaintiff's bed, it was not a warning... . The label had "no alerting word, ... no description of a hazard ... and ... no description of any means to avoid the hazard."

Widas drew what he considered to be a proper warning, which was shown to the jury. In Widas's opinion, affixing a warning label conforming to the standards he described, with "black letters on an orange background and wording in the warning to identify the hazard and instruct ... how to avoid [it]," would have been "feasible" and would have made the bed "safe." The lack of such a warning rendered the bed unsafe, as there was a "hazard of significant risk that wasn't mitigated, either by device or warning."

Moreover, the danger was not "obvious," in Widas's opinion, because the risk occurred when the user was asleep... .

II.

... We agree with defendant that the judge should have granted summary judgment. ...

... [The Product Liability Act,] *N.J.S.A.* 2A:58C-4 defines what constitutes an "adequate product warning." It provides in relevant part: "An adequate product warning or instruction is one that a reasonably prudent person in the same or similar circumstances would have provided with respect to the danger and that communicates adequate information on the dangers and safe use of the product, taking into account the characteristics of, and the ordinary knowledge common to, the persons by whom the product is intended to be used...." [C]

Hence, if under those standards, no warning is adequate, none should be required; and under the facts of this case we are satisfied that summary judgment should have been granted to defendant. [C][fn] ...

... The PLA "has been interpreted as evincing a legislative policy to limit the expansion of products-liability law ... so as to balance [ ] the interests of the public and the individual with a view towards economic reality." *Zaza v. Marquess and Nell, Inc.,* 144 *N.J.* 34, 47-48, 675 *A.*2d 620 (1996) (internal citations and quotation marks omitted).

... We do not think that a "reasonably prudent person" would see a need to warn users of beds sold for use by college students about the obvious and generally known risks inherent to products that were not defectively designed as a matter of law. [C]

Based on the development of law by enactment of the PLA... , we hold that the obviousness of the danger is an absolute defense to plaintiff's failure to warn action in this case. [Cc] As noted in the *Restatement (Third) of Torts: Products Liability* § 2 comment j, warnings would lose their efficacy and meaning if they were placed on every instrument known to be dangerous, such as a knife, scissor, glass, bat, ball, bicycle, or other product that poses a generally-known risk of injury if misused, dropped, or fallen from. Moreover, as plaintiff's own expert stated, "when you're asleep you're not in control of your behavior; you roll over in your sleep." The risks are so obvious here that we fail to see what a college student would or could have done differently while asleep to protect himself from falling, or what a warning could have advised in addition to the obvious.

III.

We reverse the judgment for plaintiff and remand for entry of a judgment dismissing the complaint.

INQUIRY

Adequacy. What is an adequate warning? As the above case suggests, there is a (perhaps suspect) body of thought and some literature having to do with what constitutes an adequate warning. *Cf.* Restatement (Third) of Torts: Products Liability §2, Comment ("No easy guideline exists for ... assessing the adequacy of product warnings and instructions."). Failure-to-warn claims often present jury issues. *See* Schwoerer v. Union Oil Co., 17 Cal. Rptr.2d 227 (Ct. App. 1993) (jury issue whether solvent manufacturer provided adequate warnings). A conventional stance within that body of thought is that an adequate warning has three components: (1) a description of the hazard; (2) a statement of what injury the hazard may produce; and (3) an instruction on how to avoid the hazard. The alert factor is another question—what word the warning should use to call the user's attention to the hazard, where the word should appear, and how prominent it should be (size, color, and reflectivity, for example). *See* Pavlik v. Lane Ltd., 135 F.3d 876 (3d Cir. 1998) (jury issue whether warning that simply stated, "Do not breathe spray," was adequate). The word "danger," experts sometimes assert, is for risks of serious injury or death, "warning" for moderate injury or property damage, and "caution" for risks that the product might destroy or damage itself. *Cf.* Carruth v. Pittway Corp., 643 So.2d 1340 (Ala. 1994) (pamphlet describing installation hazard but failing to use "warning," "caution," or "danger" presents jury issue as to adequacy of warning). So, for instance, a warning that states, "Danger: rotating blade may cause serious amputation injury and death—keep hands from under housing," may, if properly placed and visible, sufficiently warn for a lawnmower blade, whereas "caution—rotating blade" may not. Do you think that warning is a field or science enough to find qualified expert testimony? Warnings experts are common in products-liability litigation, but they do not always garner the respect of the trial and appellate courts.

Foreseeability. As in the case of design-defect claims, most states require the plaintiff in a failure-to-warn case to prove that the defect about which the maker should have warned was known or knowable (within the "state of the art") at the time of the product's manufacturing and marketing. Carlin v. Superior Ct., 920 P.2d 1347 (Cal. 1996) ("failure to provide adequate warnings of known or reasonably scientifically knowable risks"); Anderson v. Owens-Corning Fiberglas Corp., 810 P.2d 549 (Cal. 1991) (same). A few states disagree and do not require proof of reasonable foreseeability. *See* In re Hawaii Federal Asbestos Cases, 960 F.2d 806 (9th Cir. 1992)

(Hawaii law); Sternhagen v. Dow Co., 282 Mont. 168, 935 P.2d 1139 (1997) (pesticide makers subject to strict liability despite inability to predict product hazards); Ayers v. Johnson & Johnson Baby Prods. Co., 117 Wash.2d 747, 818 P.2d 1337 (1991). Can you articulate policies why? How would a plaintiff prove foreseeability—or a defendant disprove it? Must a manufacturer foresee that a user might alter the product, perhaps by removing a guard, and warn against the hazards created by the modification? *See* Liriano v. Hobart Corp., 170 F.3d 264 (2d Cir. 1999) (affirming plaintiff's verdict in claim for manufacturer's failure to warn of hazards created by removing meat-grinder guard).

Product Safety Notices and Recalls. What if the industry discovers a risk only after a product's marketing? Should the manufacturer have a continuing duty to warn after the product's sale? Many courts follow the Restatement (Third) of Torts: Products Liability §10 (1998), weighing factors including the difficulty of locating current users, and requiring post-sale safety notices—the absence of which may contribute to failure-to-warn liability. *See* Schenebeck v. Sterling Drug, Inc., 423 F.2d 919 (8th Cir. 1970) (duty to warn physicians of newly discovered side effects of marketed drug); Comstock v. General Motors Corp., 358 Mich. 163, 99 N.W.2d 627 (1959); *but see* Gregory v. Cincinnati, Inc., 450 Mich. 1, 538 N.W.2d 325 (1995) (error to admit post-manufacture evidence in support of continuing duty to warn). Manufacturers may also have a post-sale duty to continue product research if evidence of product defects arises. Barson v. E.R. Squibb & Sons, Inc., 682 P.2d 832 (Utah 1984). Some authority also exists for liability based on a post-sale duty to repair. *See* Gracyalny v. Westinghouse Elec. Corp., 723 F.2d 1311 (7th Cir. 1983). Tort law, typically concerned with preserving the greatest degree of liberty, does not generally impose a duty to recall like that federal agencies may impose under consumer-safety laws and regulations. *See* Restatement (Third) of Torts: Products Liability §11 (1998).

Causation in Failure-to-Warn Cases. How does a plaintiff establish (the causation question) that a warning would have made a difference? The user's direct testimony would ordinarily go a long way toward establishing what the user would have done had there been a warning. But most states also presume that a product's user would have read and heeded a warning had the manufacturer given one. *See* Tenbarge v. Ames Taping Tool Systems Inc., 190 F.3d 862 (8th Cir. 1999); Reyes v. Wyeth Labs., 498 F.2d 1264 (5th Cir. 1974); House v. Armour of America, Inc., 929 P.2d 340 (Utah 1996) (plaintiff widower entitled to presumption that decedent would have read and heeded warning that body armor could be pierced by rifle fire); Coffman v. Keene Corp., 133 N.J. 581, 628 A.2d 710 (1993); Arnold v. Ingersoll-Rand Co., 834 S.W.2d 192 (Mo. 1992); Restatement (Second) of Torts §402A, Comment *j* (1965); *but see* Motus v. Pfizer Inc., 196 F. Supp.2d 984 (C.D. Cal. 2001) (no presumption under California law that Zoloft user who committed suicide would have heeded a warning if one had been given). Do you think that users read product warnings? Do sound reasons exist for a read-and-heed presumption even if users do not, on the whole, read warnings? *See* Coffman, *supra* (public policy warrants presumption despite showing warnings' general inefficacy). The presumption does not stop the defendant from proving that this individual plaintiff would not have heeded a warning. *See* Nelson v. Ford Motor Co., 150 F.3d 905 (8th Cir. 1998) (no recovery under failure-to-warn theory where plaintiff admitted that he did not read allegedly defective car-jack instructions); Jacobs v. Technical Chem. Co., 480 S.W.2d 602 (Tex.

1972) (manufacturer may rebut presumption). If the maker provided a warning, and the plaintiff is claiming a design defect related to the warned risk, then should law presume that the plaintiff read the warning—in other words, an equivalent read-and-heed presumption for the defendant? *Cf.* Nelson v. Ford Motor Co., 150 F.3d 905 (8th Cir. 1998) (plaintiff admitted he did not read provided warning); *see also* East Penn Mfg. Co., v. Pineda, 578 A.2d 1113 (D.C. Ct. App. 1990) (plaintiff admitted not reading given warning but permitted an inference that a better warning would have been read and communicated to him by others). Is there a problem with too many warnings? *See* Restatement (Third) of Torts §2, Comment *j* (1998) (too many needless warnings may reduce value of necessary warnings).

Sophisticated Users and Learned Intermediaries. What if the person injured by a product that would, for the layperson, have required a warning, is an expert in the field and already knows of the risk? The warning issue also involves a standard-of-care or causation question, the sophistication of the user. See Lawley v. Chevron Chem. Co., 720 So.2d 922 (Ala. 1998) (no warning of spark from static electricity from plastic pipe necessary for sophisticated gas company users); *see also* Christopher v. Cutter Labs., 53 F.3d 1184 (11th Cir. 1995) (no warning required for physician who already knows risks). What, too, if the end user does not know of the product's risk and would benefit by a warning but the warning is something that a learned intermediary would ordinarily have provided? The warning issue also includes evaluating whether responsible learned intermediaries exist, on whom the product manufacturer would have relied. Physicians prescribing drugs are learned intermediaries, particularly when their standard of care requires that they communicate drug risks. *See* Scharerrer v. Stewart's Plaza Pharmacy, Inc., 79 P.3d 922 (Utah 2003) (extending learned-intermediary rule to protect pharmacy from failure-to-warn liability, where physician had that duty); Restatement (Third) of Torts: Products Liability §6(d)(1) (1998) (physician will ordinarily communicate material drug warnings).

Over-the-Counter Drugs. What if the drug is over-the-counter, or even if prescribed, nonetheless advertised and marketed directly to consumers? Should the manufacturer of a drug that marketed to the end user have the protection of the physician learned-intermediary rule? *See* Perez v. Wyeth Labs. Inc., 161 N.J. 1, 734 A.2d 1245 (1999) (learned-intermediary doctrine will not apply for drugs and devices marketed directly to consumers); MacDonald v. Ortho Pharmaceutical Corp., 394 Mass. 131, 475 N.E.2d 65 (1985) (same for oral contraceptives); *but see* In re Norplant Contraceptive Prods. Liab. Litig., 165 F.3d 374 (5th Cir. 1999) (learned-intermediary rule bars consumers' failure-to-warn claim against manufacturer of drugs aggressively marketed to consumers). Can the government be a learned intermediary? *See* Macias v. State, 10 Cal.4th 844, 897 P.2d 530, 42 Cal. Rptr.2d 592 (1995) (yes) (state duty to warn of effects of malathion spraying protected spray manufacturer).

Employer Intermediaries. Employers are also potential learned intermediaries. *See* Adams v. Union Carbide Corp., 737 F.2d 1453 (6th Cir. 1984), cert. denied, 465 U.S. 1062 (1984) (under Ohio law, manufacturer satisfied duty by warning employer purchaser of product). The manufacturer would be especially likely to reasonably rely on the employer giving the warning, if the manufacturer sells the product to the employer in bulk. *See* Hoffman v. Houghton Chem. Corp., 434 Mass. 624, 751 N.E.2d 848 (2001); *see also* Restatement (Third) of Torts: Products Liability §2, Comment *i* (1998) (question is one of reasonableness of manufacturer's reliance on employer).

The possibility remains, however, that the manufacturer who provides a warning only to the employer and not, on the product container or otherwise, to the employee will nonetheless be subject to failure-to-warn liability. *See* Schwoerer v. Union Oil Co., 17 Cal. Rptr.2d 227 (Ct. App. 1993) (jury issue whether solvent manufacturer's providing material-safety data sheet to plaintiff's employer was adequate warning to plaintiff).

D. Proof and Procedure

OBJECTIVE: Given fact patterns of products causing injury, identify likely proof and procedural issues, under the law reflected in this section.

Case Study: A company manufactured a gearshift assembly to its own design and sold it to a distributor. The distributor supplied it to a racing team. The team incorporated it into a racecar it ran for three races at the end of the racing season and then sold to a family for the following race season. The company made the gearshift assembly out of tolerance in such a manner that it caused the vehicle to lurch forward in a pit area during the family's first race with it, pinning a pit-crew worker against another vehicle and seriously injuring him. ***Assuming that the accident was due to a manufacturing defect in the gearshift assembly, describe the relative products liability of the company, distributor, reseller, and final owner to the injured worker.***

Manufacturer. Keep in mind that products liability generally, and the theories the products-liability plaintiff pursues in particular, can raise significant proof and procedure issues—significant to the practitioner, as to the underlying theories. Proof problems include, as a first step, identifying the manufacturer. Makers do not adequately mark every product. Indeed, manufacturers deliberately mismark some products as if others manufactured them. Obviously, manufacturers are liable only for their own defective products and not for counterfeit goods. Just as obviously, the law would hold liable the counterfeiter for goods the counterfeiter manufactures under the name of another. The practical problem in such cases is locating and collecting from the counterfeiter. Counterfeit goods are much less of a problem as the product's cost and complexity grows. But even as to vehicles and other complex products where buyers readily identify the manufacturer, the manufacturer may not be insured, may be bankrupt, may have merged with another company, or may be a foreign manufacturer beyond the convenient reach of justice. Especially in the case of imported products with injury-causing defects, the plaintiff may face difficulties identifying, locating, or collecting from the foreign manufacturer. Foreign service of process through the Geneva Convention can be complex enough, but when a lawyer accomplishes service and obtains a judgment, foreign enforcement of the judgment may be even more difficult, expensive, and ultimately ineffective.

Retailers and Distributors. What is the plaintiff's recourse when the lawyer cannot identify and locate an injury-causing product's manufacturer, or the manufacturer no longer exists or is beyond the ordinary reach of execution? Product retailers and distributors are frequently additional defendants in products liability cases, especially when the manufacturer is beyond the plaintiff's effective reach for service or collection. Distributors and retailers (all those within the distribution chain below the point at which the defect arose) bear the same liability as the defective product's manufacturer. *See* Vandermark v. Ford Motor Co., 391 P.2d 168 (Cal. 1964) (extending defect-based liability to retailer); Restatement (Third) of Torts: Products

Liability §20 (1998). Is the rule fair? From a fault standpoint, distributors and retailers do not bear the same responsibility, especially when the maker packages and sells the goods in a way that consumers cannot discover the defect until after sale—as in the case of most products. Negligence theories fail against distributors and retailers unless the nature of the distribution and sale permits inspection and warrants imposing a duty—or distributors and retailers know the manufacturer's untrustworthiness and product's defects. Yet retailers and distributors are certainly a part of the enterprise that benefits from the product sale. And to address any inequity in holding a retailer or distributor liable for a manufacturer's product defect, retailers and distributors shift product-liability risk through indemnity clauses (on which, more is below). In the age of tort reform, about sixteen states have limited retailer and distributor liability to instances where the manufacturer is beyond reach. *See* Wash. Rev. Code §7.72.040 (2004).

Product Resellers. Should the same liability exist for re-sellers of used products? Courts split on the issue, some holding used-product sellers strictly liable for defects in the original manufacture, and others not. The Restatement (Third) of Torts: Products Liability §8 (1998) takes a middle ground, defining the strict liability of used-product sellers based on consumer expectations. A used-product seller would share the manufacturer's liability for a defective product if the seller was in the business of remanufacturing and reselling those products in such a way that the consumer would expect the seller to know the product's safety. Strict liability would also extend to a reseller who had a business relationship with the original manufacturer through which the reseller could obtain indemnity. By contrast, small-time used-car-lot sellers would have no such enterprise relationship or opportunity for indemnity—and so no strict liability. Indeed, UCC §2-316(a) permits a seller to exclude warranty liability for the sale of used goods, by using the phrases "as is" and "with all faults." One-time garage-sale sellers would not have strict products liability because they are not in the business of selling—although they may have negligence and even warranty liability depending on their knowledge and any misrepresentations. *See* Restatement (Third) of Torts: Products Liability §1, Comment *c* (1998). Consider the following representative case.

Peterson v. Idaho First Natl. Bank
Idaho Supreme Court
117 Idaho 724, 791 P.2d 1303 (1990)

BAKES, C.J. This is a products liability action. The appellant (Peterson) brought suit against respondent Idaho First National Bank (IFNB), claiming that the used mobile home he had purchased from IFNB was in a defective condition and unreasonably dangerous and, as such, caused Peterson and his wife to suffer illness (the illness stemmed from an alleged emission of a high formaldehyde concentration from the mobile home). The district court entered summary judgment in favor of IFNB on the grounds that a commercial seller of used products is not subject to strict liability in tort.

In March of 1984, the plaintiff, Kenneth M. Peterson, and his wife purchased on credit from IFNB a used mobile home which IFNB had financed and then repossessed. Prior to selling the repossessed mobile home to Peterson, the bank repaired the exterior skirting, cleaned the interior, and checked and winterized the water pipes. There is no evidence that it performed any repair, reconditioning or modification which would affect the level of formaldehyde emissions in the home. There also is no evidence to show that the bank was aware that the home had an unacceptable level of formaldehyde emissions or that the bank performed any inspection or tests that would show the presence of formaldehyde emissions. ...

On August 11, 1987, the plaintiff filed the instant action, alleging various physical ailments which were caused by the "uninhabitable condition of the mobile home purchased from defendant." ...

The single issue in this appeal is whether under either the statutes or the common law in Idaho a commercial seller of used products is subject to strict liability for the products it sells. ...

Not having addressed this issue in Idaho, we turn to the rulings of our sister states for guidance. There is currently a split of authority on the question. ...

Despite the conflicting results obtained by the various jurisdictions, most states generally concur that, in the absence of a statute resolving the issue, the resolution of this question hinges upon a common law analysis of the policies that underpin the doctrine of strict liability and whether those policies are promoted by applying the doctrine to sellers of used products. In *Tillman v. Vance Equipment Co.*, 596 P.2d 1299 (Or.1979), the Oregon Supreme Court identified three justifications for adoption of strict liability. They are: (1) compensation or ability to spread the risk (enterprise liability); (2) satisfaction of the reasonable expectations of the purchaser or user (implied representational aspect); and (3) overall risk reduction (the impetus to manufacture a better product). With respect to the concept of spreading the risk, the *Tillman* court stated: "While dealers in used goods are, as a class, capable like other businesses of providing for the compensation of injured parties and the allocation of the cost of injuries caused by the products they sell, we are not convinced that the other two considerations ... weigh sufficiently in this class of cases to justify imposing strict liability on sellers of used goods generally." 596 P.2d at 1303. ...

With respect to the implied representational aspect of strict liability, we think it apparent that, unlike the market for new products, the prevailing custom in the used product industry is that the seller does not offer, and the buyer does not expect, either express or implied representations of quality. As the Oregon court in *Tillman* explained: "Those markets, generally speaking, operate on the apparent understanding that the seller, even though he is in the business of selling such goods, makes no particular representation about their quality simply by offering them for sale. If a buyer wants some assurance of quality, he typically either bargains for it in the specific transaction or seeks out a dealer who routinely offers it...." 596 P.2d at 1303. ...

... A purchaser of used products from a person other than the manufacturer expects that the seller of the used product will not have personal knowledge of the product's design or manufacture, and will not have the same ability as the manufacturer to guard against those kinds of defects. Additionally, the purchaser of a used product will recognize that the commercial seller of such used products may have no information regarding how the product was used or whether it has been abused in its prior use. The average consumer is doubtless aware that products erode through use and the inevitable passage of time, and that the quality, durability, and safety of the product undergo a corresponding decline. But foremost, the purchaser of a used product will not expect that the commercial seller of the used products will be informed either as to the safety of the design or of defects in the manufacturing process.

Finally, regarding the risk reduction policy behind strict liability, the position of the seller of used products is not, like the manufacturer, distributor, and retailer, part of the original distribution chain of the product. As the *Tillman* court stated, "The dealer in used goods generally has no direct relationship with either manufacturer or distributors. Thus, there is no ready channel of communication by which the dealer and the manufacturer can exchange information about possible dangerous defects in particular product lines or about actual and potential liability claims." 596 P.2d at 1304. Theoretically, of course, a used dealer could obtain indemnity from the manufacturer, where the manufacturer is known and the defect in question can be traced to the manufacturer. But as the *Tillman* court stated with respect to this possibility, "[A]s a practical factor [the] risk prevention is considerably diluted where used goods are involved due to such problems as statutes of limitation and the increasing difficulty as time passes of locating a still existing and solvent manufacturer." 596 P.2d at 1304.

We therefore conclude that the policy considerations underlying the doctrine of strict liability do not justify imposing that doctrine as a common law rule on commercial sellers of used goods. ...

The judgment of the district court is therefore affirmed. Costs to respondent.

INQUIRY

Indemnity. The *Peterson* case, above, mentions a significant practical factor in this question of whether courts should hold other entities in the chain of distribution and sale strictly liable for a defect that originated with the manufacturer. Fault is only part of the products-liability equation. Retailers and distributors certainly stand within the overall enterprise benefiting from the manufacture and sale of the product. More significantly from a practical standpoint, retailers and distributors also have the opportunity to adjust their relative responsibilities and liabilities using their distribution and sale contracts. Common-law or contractual indemnity will most often pass liability back up the product chain to the entity responsible for the defect—a concern not for the plaintiff but for the defendants, as they sort out their common liability to the plaintiff. The traditional rule of distributor and retailer strict products liability for defective products has a supporting rationale. Do you recognize, as *Peterson* suggests, why that rationale is absent when it comes to most used-product sellers?

Suppliers and Lessors. Should the law hold a product's lessor to a strict-products-liability standard? *See* Baker v. Promack Prods. West, Inc., 692 S.W.2d 844 (Tenn. 1985) (yes); Restatement (Third) of Torts: Products Liability §20, Comment *c* (1998) (yes). What of the liability of component-parts suppliers—those parts manufacturers whose defective products are incorporated by the assembler-manufacturer into a finished product, and who are therefore above the assembler-manufacturer in the chain of the product's manufacture and distribution? Clearly, they, too, would have strict products liability for injuries caused by defects in their own products—as would the assembler-manufacturer, distributor, and retailer. What of the component parts supplier's strict products liability when the assembler-manufacturer incorporates a non-defective component into the product in a way that creates a defect? Then, the supplier's liability would depend on the supplier's knowledge of and warnings regarding the manufacturer's actions. *See* In re TMJ Implants Prods. Liab.

Litig., 97 F.3d 1050 (8th Cir. 1996) (Teflon suppliers not strictly liable for defective Teflon-coated jaw implants); Artiglio v. General Elec. Co., 71 Cal. Rptr.2d 817 (Cal. App. 1998) (silicone manufacturer not strictly liable for defective silicone-filled breast implants); Restatement (Third) of Torts: Products Liability §5(b) (supplier strictly liable if it participates in the defective integration of its component into the product). These dynamics of the liability and non-liability of others above and below the points of original manufacture and sale show again the value of retaining negligence, warranty, and strict products liability theories, to apply together or separately depending on the circumstances.

> **Figure**
> Corporate counsel Stacey Mobley, named by *Black Enterprise Magazine* as one of America's top African-American lawyers, is the senior vice president, chief administrative officer, and general counsel for the global science company DuPont. In those roles, Mr. Mobley oversees the giant company's legal and governmental affairs, including its management of and response to products-liability issues and litigation. His work has included development and implementation of the DuPont Legal Model, restructuring the company's relationship with outside counsel in order that all legal counsel representing and defending the company act as a virtual law firm consistent with the company's values, mission, and core business. Mr. Mobley is also on Howard University's board of directors and the board of a financial services holding company the Wilmington Trust Company, and is sufficiently active in charitable, philanthropic, and justice activities to have won leadership awards and be on several lists of the nation's leading lawyers.

Successors. What liability does a corporate successor have for injury from a defective product made by the corporate predecessor? Substantial case law exists on whether and when products liability will follow from the original manufacturer to an entity that merges with it, owns or acquires a controlling portion of its stock and is a corporate parent, or purchases the assets of the original manufacturer on the original manufacturer's dissolution. When a successor acquires the defective-product manufacturer's assets, strict liability will ordinarily extend to the successor only when the successor agrees to assume liabilities, the entire transaction is a fraudulent one to avoid those liabilities, or (the common fighting issue) the successor continues the original manufacturer's business. *See* Mettinger v. Glove Slicing Mach. Co., 153 N.J. 371, 709 A.2d 779 (1998) (acquisition of all assets and continuing the product line is sufficient for successor's liability). Although occasionally, successor liability becomes critical to the plaintiff's monetary recovery in products liability, for the plaintiff the recovery depends on finding at least one financially responsible entity among the retailer, distributor, and original manufacturer's insurer, leaving those entities to sort out the relative liability through subrogation and indemnification.

Franchisors and Endorsers. A company that franchises product outlets and then supplies a defective product or retains control over product quality can expect to be subject to strict products liability. If, on the other hand, the franchisee chooses the supplier and exercises sole control over product quality, then little basis exists for holding the trademark franchisor liable. What about product endorsers—not celebrity endorsers (do consumers rely on celebrity endorsements for product safety?) but consumer-protection entities that purport to test and approve products? *See* Hanberry

v. Hearst Corp., 276 Cal. App.2d 680, 81 Cal. Rptr. 519 (1969) (no strict liability, but other claims may apply).

Circumstantial Evidence. Other significant proof and procedural issues exist beyond these questions of identifying the appropriate, financially responsible defendants. Proof of the defect itself may entail circumstantial evidence that the incident would not have occurred but for the existence of that particular product feature. *See* Restatement (Third) of Torts: Products Liability §3 (1998). Although the approach of using the loss or injury to prove the defect sounds like res ipsa loquitur, this form of proof is not, strictly speaking, within the res-ipsa-loquitur doctrine when strict products liability (not negligence) is the underlying theory. *See* Myrlak v. Port Auth. of New York and New Jersey, 157 N.J. 84, 723 A.2d 45 (1999) (distinguishing res ipsa loquitur for products liability). Defectiveness, under the risk-utility test, exists in large part from the product's injury-causing risk. Must the plaintiff prove the specific defect that caused the injury, or is it enough that the plaintiff proves by circumstantial evidence that the injury was due to *some* defect? The Restatement (Third) of Torts: Products Liability §3, Comment *c* (1998), suggests that proof of a general (rather than specific) defect is sufficient. *See* Speller v. Sears, Roebuck & Co., 790 N.E.2d 252 (N.Y. 2003) (allowing circumstantial evidence to establish wiring defect in refrigerator that caused fire); *but see* Myrlak, *supra* (circumstantial evidence not sufficient to establish defect in collapsing chair). Consider the following illustrative case.

Welge v. Planters Lifesavers Co.
17 F.3d 209 (7th Cir. 1994)

POSNER, C.J.

Richard Welge, forty-something but young in spirit, loves to sprinkle peanuts on his ice cream sundaes. On January 18, 1991, Karen Godfrey, with whom Welge boards, bought a 24-ounce vacuum-sealed plastic-capped jar of Planters peanuts for him at a K-Mart store in Chicago. To obtain a $2 rebate that the maker of Alka-Seltzer was offering to anyone who bought a "party" item, such as peanuts, Godfrey needed proof of her purchase of the jar of peanuts; so, using an Exacto knife (basically a razor blade with a handle), she removed the part of the label that contained the bar code. She then placed the jar on top of the refrigerator, where Welge could get at it without rooting about in her cupboards. About a week later, Welge removed the plastic seal from the jar, uncapped it, took some peanuts, replaced the cap, and returned the jar to the top of the refrigerator, all without incident. A week after that, on February 3, the accident occurred. Welge took down the jar, removed the plastic cap, spilled some peanuts into his left hand to put on his sundae, and replaced the cap with his right hand—but as he pushed the cap down on the open jar the jar shattered. His hand, continuing in its downward motion, was severely cut, and is now, he claims, permanently impaired.

Welge brought this products liability suit in federal district court under the diversity jurisdiction; Illinois law governs the substantive issues. Welge named three defendants (plus the corporate parent of one-why we don't know). They are K-Mart, which sold the jar of peanuts to Karen Godfrey; Planters, which manufactured the product-that is to say, filled the glass jar with peanuts and sealed and capped it; and Brockway, which manufactured the glass jar itself and sold it to Planters. After pretrial discovery was complete the defendants moved for summary judgment. The district judge granted the motion on the ground that the plaintiff had failed to exclude possible causes of the accident other than a defect introduced during the manufacturing process.

No doubt there are men strong enough to shatter a thick glass jar with one blow. But Welge's testimony stands uncontradicted that he used no more than the normal force that one exerts in snapping a plastic lid onto a jar. So the jar must have been defective. No expert testimony and no fancy doctrine are required for such a conclusion. A nondefective jar does not shatter when normal force is used to clamp its plastic lid on. The question is when the defect was introduced. It could have been at any time from the manufacture of the glass jar by Brockway (for no one suggests that the defect might have been caused by something in the raw materials out of which the jar was made) to moments before the accident. But testimony by Welge and Karen Godfrey, if believed-and at this stage in the proceedings we are required to believe it-excludes all reasonable possibility that the defect was introduced into the jar after Godfrey plucked it from a shelf in the K-Mart store. From the shelf she put it in her shopping cart. The checker at the check-out counter scanned the bar code without banging the jar. She then placed the jar in a plastic bag. Godfrey carried the bag to her car and put it on the floor. She drove directly home, without incident. After the bar-code portion of the label was removed, the jar sat on top of the refrigerator except for the two times Welge removed it to take peanuts out of it. Throughout this process it was not, so far as anyone knows, jostled, dropped, bumped, or otherwise subjected to stress beyond what is to be expected in the ordinary use of the product. ... So the defect must have been introduced earlier, when the jar was in the hands of the defendants. ...

Of course, unlikely as it may seem that the defect was introduced into the jar after Karen Godfrey bought it if the plaintiffs' testimony is believed, other evidence might make their testimony unworthy of belief—might even show, contrary to all the probabilities, that the knife or some mysterious night visitor caused the defect after all. The fragments of glass into which the jar shattered were preserved and were examined by experts for both sides. The experts agreed that the jar must have contained a defect but they could not find the fracture that had precipitated the shattering of the jar and they could not figure out when the defect that caused the fracture that caused the collapse of the jar had come into being. The defendants' experts could neither rule out, nor rule in, the possibility that the defect had been introduced at some stage of the manufacturing process. The plaintiff's expert noticed what he thought was a preexisting crack in one of the fragments, and he speculated that a similar crack might have caused the fracture that shattered the jar. This, the district judge ruled, was not enough.

But if the probability that the defect which caused the accident arose after Karen Godfrey bought the jar of Planters peanuts is very small—and on the present state of the record we are required to assume that it is—then the probability that the defect was introduced *by one of the defendants* is very high. ...

... The strict-liability element in modern products liability law comes precisely from the fact that a seller subject to that law is liable for defects in his product even if those defects were introduced, without the slightest fault of his own for failing to discover them, at some anterior stage of production. [Cc] So the fact that K-Mart sold a defective jar of peanuts to Karen Godfrey would be conclusive of K-Mart's liability, and since it is a large and solvent firm there would be no need for the plaintiff to look further for a tortfeasor. ...

REVERSED AND REMANDED.

INQUIRY

Other Incidents. Another form of circumstantial evidence that may be admissible in products-liability actions is evidence of other incidents. *See* Uniroyal Goodrich Tire Co. v. Martinez, 977 S.W.2d 328 (Tex. 1998) (no error to allow evidence of other lawsuits involving same product). Should the absence of incidents, or lower incident rates, for the subject product be admissible? *See* Spino v. John S. Tiley Ladder Co., 548 Pa. 286, 696 A.2d 1169 (1997) (no error to allow evidence that there had been no reported similar incidents); Bittner v. American Honda Motor Co., 194 Wis.2d 122, 533 N.W.2d 476 (1995) (no error to allow evidence of lower accident rates for defendant manufacturer's ATV product).

Procedure. Strict products liability raises other procedural issues. For instance, should a tort or contract statute of limitations apply to strict products liability for harm caused by the manufacture, distribution, and sale of a defective product? *See* Greeno v. Clark Equip. Co., 237 F. Supp. 427 (N.D. Ind. 1965) (tort, not contract, limitations period applies). Under what circumstances should a court admit evidence of a change in the product's design and correction or elimination of the defect? Most courts, including the federal courts under Federal Rule of Evidence 407, will not admit such evidence, even though the theoretical basis for strict products liability might suggest otherwise, for which reason a few courts permit the evidence for strict products liability but not negligence. *See* Forma Scientific, Inc., v. BioSera, Inc., 960 P.2d 108 (Colo. 1998) (admissible in design-defect case); Ault v. International Harvester Co., 13 Cal.3d 113, 528 P.2d 1148, 117 Cal. Rptr. 812 (1974). Is there another basis on which to seek the admission of evidence of post-accident change in design, even in a negligence case? Evidence of a post-accident improvement in a product's design should be admissible if the defendant manufacturer denies the feasibility of the improvement. *See* Duchess v. Lanston Corp., 564 Pa. 529, 769 A.2d 1131 (2001) (admit remedial design if defendant asserts that it is not feasible).

Violation of Statute. How should products-liability law treat violation of a safety statute? Most courts, following the Restatement (Third) of Torts: Products Liability §4(a) (1998), treat a product as defective if the product violates a safety statute, and the product's injury-causing risk was what the statute's prohibition addressed. In that respect, products-liability law treats statutory violations much like traditional negligence law, where statutory violations are negligence per se, or give rise to a presumption or inference of negligence, if the tortious conduct was what the legislature intended the statute to address, and the plaintiff was within the class the legislature meant to protect. How does products liability treat a product's *compliance* with a safety statute? Again, like traditional negligence law, products liability accepts a product's compliance with a safety statute as admissible evidence of non-defectiveness (of the manufacturer's due care with respect to the product) but does not make compliance an absolute defense. The basis for this treatment is in the idea that safety statutes may establish minimum standards for product safety but do not guarantee that a complying product is reasonably safe. A court may still find that a product that meets safety statutes is unreasonably dangerous and defective. *See* Restatement (Third) of Torts: Products Liability §4(b) (1998); *cf.* Ramirez v. Plough, Inc., 6 Cal.4th 539, 863 P.2d 167, 25 Cal. Rptr.2d 97 (1993) (aspirin manufacturer complied with FDA safety standards by warning of syndrome risks in English and had no duty to provide Spanish-language warnings); *but see* Tenn. Code Ann. §29-28-104 (manufacturer's compliance with safety statutes and regulations raises a rebuttable presumption that the product is not unreasonably dangerous); Mich. Comp. L. §600.2946 (drug manufacturer not strictly liable if in compliance with FDA regulations), *cited in* Taylor v. Smithkline Beecham Corp., 468 Mich. 1, 658 N.W.2d 127 (2003). A section below treats federal preemption of state products-liability law.

E. Defenses

OBJECTIVE: Given fact patterns involving the use of a product causing injury, apply and analyze available defenses consistent with the law and principles reflected in this section of the text.

Case Study: The buyer had the leg protectors—chrome bars that extend around the foot pedals and beyond the operator's legs—removed from her motorcycle because she did not like the looks of them. The dealership where she bought the motorcycle new removed them. The motorcycle looked much better without them and was easier to store in the buyer's small garage next to her motor vehicle. One day the motorcycle tipped over as the buyer brought it to a sudden stop at an intersection. The weight of the motorcycle badly injured her leg. ***Identify, discuss, and evaluate the seller's defenses to the buyer's products-liability action.***

The emergence and rapid expansion of strict products liability, occurring largely through judicial decision, fascinated scholars. It also fueled an industry, legislative, and judicial backlash known as *tort reform*. The work of the Federal Interagency Task Force on product liability, established in 1976 in response to concern over expansive products liability, led to the Uniform Product Liability Act as a model and framework for reform. Some states adopted portions of the Uniform Product Liability Act or other provisions based on it. Yet the Uniform Act did not achieve the Task Force's recommendation for standardized products-liability laws. Congress did not enact broad federal products-liability legislation—only a few narrow provisions addressed, for instance, at aged aviation products and biomaterials. Broader state tort-reform statutes enacted in over forty states by the late 1980s, and aimed at personal-injury actions in general, affected products liability more broadly than any federal provision. The Uniform Product Liability Act's functional approach made its way into the Restatement (Third) of Torts: Products Liability (1998) and influenced states to alter their products-liability approaches. States have continued to legislate both broadly as to personal-injury actions and more narrowly as to products liability.

Consider the following defenses within that fluid body of statutory reforms of tort law generally and products-liability law in particular. Many of the traditional negligence defenses apply to products liability, including in particular comparative or contributory negligence, statutes of limitations, and statutes of repose. This section treats those defenses only briefly here because of their thorough treatment in the prior chapter on negligence defenses. The products-liability context, though, is unique. This section treats other defenses in depth. While studying defenses, keep in mind the rapid expansion of strict products liability, followed by marked retraction in many jurisdictions. Begin with the rudimentary treatment of the most obvious and common defense—comparative negligence.

Whitehead v. Toyota Motor Sales, U.S.A., Inc.
Tennessee Supreme Court
897 S.W.2d 684 (Tenn. 1995)

DROWOTA, J. ... [The Tennessee Supreme Court considered the case on certification of two issues from the United States District Court for the Eastern District of Tennessee. The first issue was whether the comparative negligence defense applied to a strict products liability action. The second issue was whether the defense applied even in an enhanced-injury claim in which the product defect did not cause the underlying accident.]

This is a products liability action that arises from an accident that occurred on January 22, 1992. On that day Mark D. Whitehead, plaintiff, was injured when a 1988 Toyota pickup truck that he was driving crossed the center line of the road and collided head-on with a vehicle that was traveling in the opposite direction from Mr. Whitehead's pickup truck.

The plaintiffs sued the defendants, the manufacturer and seller of the truck, based on the plaintiffs' contention that Mark D. Whitehead's injuries were enhanced beyond those he would have received had the truck he was driving been more crashworthy. The plaintiffs specifically contend that the seatbelt system of the Toyota pickup truck was defective. [C] The defendants answered the complaint, maintaining that there were no defects in the truck. The defendants also asserted, inter alia, the affirmative defense of comparative fault. ...

FIRST CERTIFIED QUESTION

On May 4, 1992, this Court decided McIntyre v. Balentine, 833 S.W.2d 52 (Tenn.1992), in which we adopted a system of modified comparative fault. We described the system as follows: "We therefore hold that so long as a plaintiff's negligence remains less than a defendant's negligence the plaintiff may recover; in such a case, plaintiff's damages are to be reduced in proportion to the percentage of the total negligence attributable to the plaintiff." 833 S.W.2d at 57. ...

Application of Comparative Fault to Strict Liability in Other States

Courts in a majority of states that have considered the issue of whether comparative fault should apply in products liability actions based on strict liability in tort have decided that comparative fault should apply in such cases. ...

Another leading case dealing with the application of comparative fault to strict liability is Daly v. General Motors Corp., 20 Cal.3d 725, 144 Cal.Rptr. 380, 575 P.2d 1162 (1978). In that case the Supreme Court of California stated as follows: "Those counseling against the recognition of comparative fault principles in strict products liability cases vigorously stress, perhaps equally, not only the conceptual, but also the semantic difficulties incident to such a course. The task of merging the two concepts is said to be impossible, that 'apples and oranges' cannot be compared, that 'oil and water' do not mix, and that strict liability, which is not founded on negligence or fault, is inhospitable to comparative principles. The syllogism runs, contributory negligence was only a defense to negligence, comparative negligence only affects contributory negligence, therefore comparative negligence cannot be a defense to strict liability....

While fully recognizing the theoretical and semantic distinctions between the twin principles of strict products liability and traditional negligence, we think they can be blended or accommodated."

"...We imposed strict liability against the manufacturer and in favor of the user or consumer in order to relieve injured consumers 'from problems of proof inherent in pursuing negligence ... and warranty ... remedies ...' As we have noted, we sought to place the burden of loss on manufacturers rather than 'injured persons who are powerless to protect themselves.'"

"The foregoing goals, we think, will not be frustrated by the adoption of comparative principles. Plaintiffs will continue to be relieved of proving that the manufacturer or distributor was negligent in the production, design, or dissemination of the article in question. Defendant's liability for injuries caused by a defective product remains strict. The principle of protecting the defenseless is likewise preserved, for plaintiffs recovery will be reduced only to the extent that his own lack of reasonable care contributed to his injury. The cost of compensating the victim of a defective product, albeit proportionately reduced, remains on defendant manufacturer, and will, through him, be 'spread among society.' However, we do not permit plaintiff's own conduct relative to the product to escape unexamined, and as to that share of plaintiff's damages which flows from his own fault we discern no reason of policy why it should ... be born by others. Such a result would directly contravene the principle ... that loss should be assessed equitably in proportion to fault." 144 Cal.Rptr. 380, at 385-387, 575 P.2d 1162, at 1167-1169. ...

An overwhelming majority of states have adopted the view that comparative fault should apply to products liability actions based on strict liability. ...

On the other hand, a minority of jurisdictions decline to apply comparative fault to strict liability actions. The minority view is expressed by the Supreme Court of South Dakota in Smith v. Smith, 278 N.W.2d 155 (S.D.1979), in which that court stated: "Strict liability is an abandonment of the fault concept in product liability cases. No longer are damages to be borne by one who is culpable; rather they are borne by one who markets the defective product. The question of whether the manufacturer or seller is negligent is meaningless under such a concept; liability is imposed irrespective of his negligence or freedom from it. Even though the manufacturer or seller is able to prove beyond all doubt that the defect was not the result of his negligence, it would avail him nothing. We believe it is inconsistent to hold that the user's negligence is material when the seller's is not." 278 N.W.2d at 160. ...

Most of the states which have a modified form of comparative fault, such as the one adopted by this Court in McIntyre, have concluded that the same type of modified comparative fault that applies generally should apply to strict liability actions. ...

CONCLUSION

In light of the foregoing discussion, our answer to the first question certified to us is that comparative fault principles do apply in products liability actions based on strict liability in tort. ...

The conduct that leads to strict products liability involves fault, as the word "fault" is commonly understood. [C] In keeping with the principle of linking liability with fault, a plaintiff's ability to recover in a strict products liability case should not be unaffected by the extent to which his injuries result from his own fault.

Two principal reasons for the adoption of the doctrine of strict products liability in Tennessee and elsewhere were (1) to encourage greater care in the manufacture of products that are distributed to the public, and (2) to relieve injured consumers from the burden of proving negligence on a manufacturer's part. Our decision today does not weaken these principles. …

[The opinion then concluded on the second certified question that the defense of comparative negligence applied equally to an enhanced-injury case in which the product did not cause the underlying accident.]

INQUIRY

Comparative Negligence. The *Whitehead* opinion typifies the majority of states recognizing comparative fault in strict-products-liability cases. *See* Murray v. Fairbanks Morse, 610 F.2d 149 (3d. Cir. 1979); Restatement (Third) Torts: Products Liability §17. The weak-fault basis for strict products liability provides a conceptual basis for comparing the plaintiff's fault to the defendant's actions in creating an unreasonably unsafe product. On the other hand, *Whitehead* extends comparative fault to enhanced-injury cases where the product defect did not cause the accident but worsened the injury. Would it be more logical to restrict plaintiff to recovering the enhanced injury, than to dividing the total fault by relative percentages? Are not enhanced-injury cases exactly that—cases in which the damage flowing from the product's uncrashworthiness are the worsening of plaintiff's injuries? As *Whitehead* makes clear, not all cases permit a comparative-negligence defense in strict-products-liability cases. Some of those cases, following Restatement (Second) of Torts §402A, Comment *n*, refuse the defense where the defendant argues that the plaintiff should have discovered the product's defect but permit the defense where the plaintiff's fault did not relate to the product's defect. *See* General Motors Corp. v. Sanchez, 997 S.W.2d 584 (Tex. 1999); Hernandez v. Barbo Machinery Co., 141 Or. App. 34, 917 P.2d 30 (1996) (defendant not permitted comparative-negligence defense relating to plaintiff's claim that saw blade rotating inside cabinet, with hidden on-off switch, presented concealed defect); *but see* Restatement (Third) of Torts: Products Liability §17, Comment *d* (1998) (no categorical limit to comparative-fault defense). Does this limited comparative-negligence defense offer the best of both worlds—strict products liability but with plaintiff's fault considered in appropriate cases?

> **Practice**
>
> "You know," the defense counsel was saying to the torts practitioner, "I think there's a real problem with bias against corporations generally and manufacturers in particular." "I imagine so," the torts practitioner replied with a half-smile. "I really mean it," the defense counsel continued, sensing that the torts practitioner needed convincing, and adding, "One of the first clients I ever served was just starting a business. He did nothing but work very hard and honestly all of his adult life. Over the years, his business grew to the point that it is now one of the leading charitable givers in the community, employing hundreds of individuals in decent jobs with full benefits. But from a legal standpoint, and maybe especially as to liability issues, it seems that all he gets is grief, when he's really never done anything intentionally wrong and has always tried to do things right. It's fine that you represent the injured and 'oppressed,' but we must be sure not to be biased against those who do more than just represent them—those who employ and, really, feed and clothe them and their families." The torts practitioner knew what the defense counsel meant. It was a good reminder.

Assumption of Risk. The *Whitehead* opinion also mentions that courts will recognize the assumption-of-risk defense in strict-products-liability cases. When the plaintiff voluntary encounters a known product risk, some courts follow the Restatement (Second) of Torts, holding that conduct to be a complete bar to the plaintiff's strict-products-liability claim. *See* Ferraro v. Ford Motor Co., 423 Pa. 324, 223 A.2d 746 (1966). An alternative followed in other states is not to recognize an assumption-of-risk defense but to allow the jury to consider the same conduct as a basis to apportion a greater degree of comparative fault to the plaintiff. *See* Bonds v. Snapper Power Equip. Co., 935 F.2d 985 (8th Cir. 1991) (comparative-negligence instruction for plaintiff's reaching under operating lawnmower); Restatement (Third) of Torts: Products Liability §17, Comment *d* (1998).

Statutes of Limitations. An above chapter on negligence defenses treats statutes of limitation in depth. Products liability raises some special statute-of-limitations issues. Because products liability trifurcates into negligence, warranty, and strict-products-liability theories, as many as three different limitations periods may apply to a products-liability case. Some states apply UCC 2-725(1)'s four-year limitations period to breach-of-warranty claims, including claims for personal injury. Other states hold that breach-of-warranty claims for personal injury are essentially tort actions governed by the limitations period for other, similar tort claims. *See* Victorson v. Bock Laundry Machine Co., 37 N.Y.2d 395, 373 N.Y.S.2d 39, 335 N.E.2d 275 (1975). Those states that follow the UCC limitation period likely also follow the UCC's claim-accrual rule in UCC 2-725(2), holding that warranty claims accrue on product delivery. Thus, the law may bar warranty claims before or shortly after the injury occurs, if the injury occurs some time well after the product's sale and delivery. *See* Waldrop v. Peabody Galion Corp., 423 So.2d 145 (Ala. 1982) (warranty claim, sole form of products-liability relief in state, barred under limitations period that began to run on garbage-truck product's delivery). Some states also have special products-liability limitations periods that may be as short as two years—shorter than a typical three- or four-year limitations period for negligence claims.

Statutes of Repose. As addressed in greater detail in the chapter on negligence defenses, statutes of repose bar actions a defined period after the defendant's tortious conduct—not (like statutes of limitation) after the tort claim accrues. Statutes of limitation are ubiquitous—one always finds an applicable limitations period. By contrast, statutes of repose for products exist in many states but do not exist in many other states. Product statutes of repose tend to be for relatively longer periods—ten to twelve years, commonly. Yet product life can be significantly longer. Statutes of repose are absolute bars to a tort lawsuit. Their presence in the field of products liability has to do with the inability of product manufacturers to insure against remote risks. They also have to do with the unfairness of calling upon a product manufacturer to defend product choices made remote in time and under an earlier state of the product art—assuming that company witnesses have survived, are available, and have the recollection to testify. Some claimants have made successful state-constitution challenges (on due-process, equal-protection, and jury-trial grounds) to statutes of repose that deny a products-liability plaintiff the right to sue even before the claim accrues. *See* Heath v. Sears, Roebuck & Co., 123 N.H. 512, 464 A.2d 288 (1983).

Open-and-Obvious Defense. One of the ways in which opposing interests balanced the rapid expansion of strict products liability was through the revival and expansion of the *open-and-obvious* defense. At the farthest extent of the expansion of products liability, indications existed that the consumer's awareness of an obvious product risk would have no bearing on liability. *See* Luque v. McLean, 501 P.2d 1163 (Cal. 1972) (plaintiff permitted to proceed against manufacturer for failure to guard against known access to lawnmower blades). Courts conceived the open-and-obvious defense as a bar to liability for harm caused by a product whose design included a safety risk that was readily apparent from casual inspection and would have been obvious to the ordinary consumer. *See* Killeen v. Harmon Grain Prods., Inc., 413 N.E.2d 767 (Mass. Ct. App. 1980) (danger that toothpick held in mouth might pierce lip was not hidden or unreasonable). No liability would exist if the consumer knew or should have known of the open and obvious risk and yet voluntarily encountered and accepted it in using the product—much like the assumption-of-risk and contributory-negligence defenses. A shallow pool is an example. Obvious risks exists for diving into a pool too shallow and not meant for diving—so obvious that some courts have held that no warning is necessary if the risk is open and obvious. *See* Glittenberg v. Doughboy Recreatonal Indus., 441 Mich. 379, 491 N.W.2d 208 (1992); *see also* Josue v. Isuzu Motors America, Inc., 87 Hawaii 413, 958 P.2d 535 (1998) (vehicle manufacturer had no duty to warn of obvious risk of serious injury from being thrown from pickup-truck bed in vehicle crash); Maneely v. General Motors Corp., 108 F.3d 1176 (9th Cir. 1997) (same).

Ameliorating Doctrines. A conceptual problem that the open-and-obvious defense immediately presents is that it appears to return tort liability to the all-or-nothing formula of the widely disfavored contributory-negligence defense. Thus, courts have wrestled with ways in which to soften or sensitize the open-and-obvious defense where the product risk, though open and obvious, yet remains unreasonably dangerous. *See* Perkins v. Wilkinson Sword, Inc., 83 Ohio St.3d 507, 700 N.E.2d 1247 (1998) (obviousness of lighter's capacity to start a fire is a factor but not determinative in evaluation of defect claim); Tabieros v. Clark Equip. Co., 85 Hawaii 336, 944 P.2d 1279 (1997) (harm from open and obvious hazard actionable only under risk-utility but not consumer-expectation test); Restatement (Third) of Torts: Products Liability §2, Comment *j* (1998) (jury decides obviousness of risk if reasonable minds could differ). Another important conceptual feature to recognize about the open-and-obvious defense is that it is not truly an affirmative defense but more like an element of the plaintiff's case—that the plaintiff has the burden of proving the product risk's non-obviousness. The case law addresses *open and obvious* both ways—as a question raised by the plaintiff's proofs regarding defect and as a response by the defendant manufacturer. Defense lawyers certainly plead open and obvious as an affirmative defense and argue it in that fashion. Yet in ruling on obviousness, the courts are not necessarily shifting the proof burden on that issue to the defendant in the manner typical of an affirmative defense like comparative negligence. As you read how the court in the following case resolved these tensions, consider the evidence that counsel for both sides presented on the obviousness issue.

McWilliams v. Yamaha Motor Corp.
United States Court of Appeals, Third Circuit
987 F.2d 200 (3rd Cir. 1993)

ROTH, C.J. Appellants, Larry P. McWilliams, Jr., and Larry P. McWilliams, Sr., brought a diversity action against Yamaha Motor Corporation, U.S.A. (Yamaha) and

D.T. Van Sice, Inc., claiming that the 1982 Yamaha Virago 920 motorcycle, which Larry P. McWilliams, Jr., (McWilliams) had bought from Yamaha distributor, D.T. Van Sice, Inc., was improperly designed and unreasonably dangerous. Appellants alleged in their Complaint that Yamaha could have mitigated lower limb damages by an effective and feasible design, known as crash bars. Appellants claim that, because there was not a heavy duty crash bar on the Yamaha Virago 920, that model was of a defective design. Appellants further allege that appellees were negligent due to their failure to give warnings regarding the unsafe conditions arising from the lack of a crash bar. Appellants assert that appellees are strictly liable. Appellee Yamaha moved for summary judgment on the ground that no basis for strict liability existed under New Jersey law because the risk of leg injury while operating a motorcycle is an open and obvious risk to the ordinary consumer or is a known danger. On November 20, 1991, the district court entered summary judgement in Yamaha's favor, dismissing the complaint in its entirety. ...

The accident underlying this litigation occurred on May 31, 1987, when McWilliams was operating his motorcycle eastbound on Route 625 in New Jersey. Albert Feise was parked in his automobile on the eastbound side of Route 625. Feise attempted to make a U-turn and in the process struck McWilliams and his motorcycle.[fn] The front bumper of Feise's car hit McWilliams's lower right leg. McWilliams's leg was pinned between the projection of the car bumper and the motorcycle. The leg was almost completely severed in the accident and was subsequently amputated below the knee. ...

McWilliams had been a dirt bike/minibike/motorcycle enthusiast since the age of 13 or 14. He purchased the Yamaha Virago 920 from D.T. Van Sice, Inc., in 1986. Although the Virago was a 1982 model, it was brand new when McWilliams bought it. The Virago did not have protective leg guards or crash bars. At that time, however, tubular metal crash bars to protect the rider's legs were available on some motorcycle models.

McWilliams had purchased his first motorcycle in about 1980. This was a Yamaha 750 Special which did have crash bars. ... McWilliams also acknowledged that he "knew motorcycles were dangerous, but he put it out of his mind and didn't think of it." [C] He knew from the day he bought his first motorcycle that his legs would be exposed when he was riding it. *Id.*

Appellants' claims in this case were supported by the opinions of proposed expert witnesses. Their design expert, Harry C. Peterson, asserted in his report that the Yamaha Virago 920 motorcycle was defectively designed in that, before it was placed on the market, impact-absorbing structures should have been installed to prevent serious, permanent injury to the legs of the motorcycle operator in the case of a collision. [C] Appellants' reconstruction expert, George P. Widas, asserted that Yamaha's failure to provide the warnings it should have "on the subject motorcycle relative to the unsafe conditions produced by ... the lack of collision protection for the lower limbs of the riders of the motorcycle" was a reasonably certain factor in the cause of McWilliams's injuries. [C]

In granting defendants' motion for summary judgment, the district court held that the New Jersey Products Liability Law (NJPLL), N.J.S.A. 2A:58C-1-7, was applicable. Section 3(a)(2) of the NJPLL provides a defense for harms caused by products if the harm "would be recognized by the ordinary person who uses or consumes the product with the ordinary knowledge common to the class of persons for whom the product is intended...."[fn] ... Following this reasoning, the district court granted summary judgment in favor of Yamaha and Van Sice. In doing so, it predicted that the New Jersey Supreme Court would rule "that a motorcycle, a vehicle specifically designed as an open-air, easily maneuverable, light-weight vehicle, contains an open and obvious risk of lower-leg injury." [C] ...

In their appeal, appellants initially challenge the district court's determination that a motorcycle is a product to which the inherent and obvious danger defense of Section 3(a)(2) applies. Next, even if Section 3(a)(2) were to be applied, appellants challenge the failure of the district court to go on to consider whether the installation of crash bars would eliminate the danger of lower leg injury without impairing the usefulness of the motorcycle; under the language of Section 3(a)(2) such a conclusion would except this case from the open and obvious danger defense.

In urging that Section 3(a)(2) should not apply at all, appellants contend that, unlike a match which must burn or a knife which must cut, a motorcycle is not intended to crash; that is not a basic function of its use. Appellants describe a motorcycle's basic function as providing a means of transportation, "to be a motor vehicle, to operate as a motor vehicle." [C]

However, a motorcycle is not the only type of vehicle available for motor transportation. An armored car or a dump truck also offers a means of motor transportation with minimal risk to the lower limbs of its operator. Nevertheless, a motorcycle devotee probably would not choose an armored car as an equivalent means of transportation. Motorcycle riders are interested in a vehicle which is open, light, maneuverable, speedy, and economical. The ensuing risk to the legs of operators of such an open and unprotected vehicle is well known. [Cc] Even Larry McWilliams acknowledged that he knew from the day he bought his first motorcycle that there was a risk to his legs—and to his arms and his body as well. [C]

McWilliams's expert witnesses also expressed their opinions that the risk of lower leg injury in motorcycle accidents was well known. ...

... [W]e concur with the district court's prediction that the New Jersey Supreme Court would rule that the open and obvious risk defense is applicable in a motorcycle case. A motorcycle is intended to be a light, open, maneuverable, relatively unencumbered motor vehicle; the risks of driving such a vehicle are well known to those persons who choose to operate one.

Nevertheless, although we conclude that the district court correctly anticipated the likelihood that the New Jersey Supreme Court would find the open and obvious danger defense applicable to the purchase of a motorcycle, we cannot agree with the next conclusion of the district court: that it need not consider whether the risk of leg injury could be eliminated by crash bars without impairing the usefulness of the product. After setting out the open and obvious danger exclusion from liability, Section 3(a)(2) of the NJPLL goes on to provide that this defense "is not intended to apply to dangers posed by products such as machinery or equipment that can feasibly be eliminated without impairing the usefulness of the product...."

The district court determined that this exception to the open and obvious danger exclusion was not applicable here because McWilliams bought his motorcycle for recreational purposes. [C] In ruling out the applicability of the "equipment and machinery" exception, the district court stated that it was clear from the language and legislative history of the NJPLL that the "New Jersey legislature did not intend the exception for machinery and equipment to apply to products purchased for recreational purposes. Indeed, one commentator stated that this exception is intended to preserve a line of cases requiring safety devices in industrial machinery." [C]

However, there is a second exception to the Section 3(a)(2) liability exclusions, which exception is specifically directed at industrial machinery ("this paragraph shall not apply to industrial machinery or other equipment used in the workplace"). In view of this specific provision for industrial machines, we believe that the district court misinterpreted the commentaries about the NJPLL. We cannot agree with the district court's prediction that the New Jersey Supreme Court would not apply the general machinery and equipment exception to a type of motor vehicle which manifested a danger that feasibly could be eliminated without impairing the usefulness of the product—even if such a motor vehicle might be used for recreational purposes.[fn] … If recreational equipment and machinery were to be given special treatment under the NJPLL, it would seem likely that such an intention would be clearly expressed in the provisions of the statute. It is not. …

… [W]e find that there is clearly a material issue of fact as to whether the addition of crash bars would have eliminated the risk of lower leg injury posed by the operation of a motorcycle without impairing the usefulness of that machine. Because such an issue remained to be resolved by the finder of fact, the district court erred in granting appellees' motion for summary judgment. [C]

We will, therefore, remand this case to the district court so that the finder of fact can determine whether the danger of injury to the operator of a Yamaha Virago 920 motorcycle could feasibly be eliminated by the installation of crash bars or similar protective devices without impairing the usefulness of the motorcycle.[fn] …

Skills

Discovery skills are critical to a practitioner's success with products-liability claims. In teams of three, choose which side you represent—the plaintiff employee or defendant manufacturer. Next, each team member choose the interrogatories, document requests, or deposition of the other side's principal witness (the plaintiff employee or the defendant manufacturer's design engineer). Then, each team member draft a list of the discovery topics for their form of discovery. Compare lists, and be prepared to report discovery topics to the class. **Facts:** The plaintiff is a 30-year-old married father of two children. He is a production engineer at an auto-parts plant. A plastic-injection molding machine at the auto-parts plant crushed his ring finger, resulting in the finger's amputation. He was inspecting the machine from the back of the machine opposite its operator station, when the machine operator cycled the machine at his request. He had his left hand on a metal support as the machine cycled. When the machine mold opened, the outside of the mold caught and crushed his finger against the metal support. The defendant is the manufacturer of the molding machine. The claims are for negligence, breach of implied warranty, and strict products liability.

Exclusive-Remedy Provisions. Another defense commonly encountered in the products-liability arena has to do with worker's compensation acts. As explained in greater depth in another chapter below, worker's compensation acts grant employees certain benefits without respect to fault, in exchange barring employee negligence suits against employers. The interpretation of these exclusive-remedy provisions of worker's compensation acts can prove significant when an employee wishes to maintain a claim regarding a product the defects of which the employer and its representatives had substantial knowledge. Consider the following case suggesting how the exclusive-remedy provision may—or may not—act as a bar to recovery for a dangerous product.

Millison v. E.I du Pont de Nemours & Co.
New Jersey Supreme Court
101 N.J. 161, 501 A.2d 505 (1985)

CLIFFORD, J. The New Jersey Workers' Compensation Act ... contains an exclusive-remedy provision in N.J.S.A. 34:15-8. The issue in these consolidated cases is whether that provision precludes employees who have suffered occupational diseases from maintaining a separate tort action against their employer and against company physicians. The employees charge the employer and physicians with intentionally exposing the employees to asbestos in the workplace, deliberately concealing from employees the risks of exposure to asbestos, and fraudulently concealing specific medical information obtained during employee physical examinations that reveal diseases already contracted by workmen. We hold that although the employees are limited to workers' compensation benefits for any initial occupational-disease disabilities related to the hazards of their employment experience, the Compensation Act does not bar plaintiffs' cause of action for aggravation of those illnesses resulting from defendants' fraudulent concealment of already-discovered disabilities.

I

Plaintiffs are former E.I. du Pont de Nemours (du Pont) employees and their spouses (reference to plaintiffs henceforth is to the employees). Defendants are du Pont and its company physicians who had worked at the du Pont plants at which plaintiffs-employees were stationed. Also named as defendants are certain manufacturers and suppliers of asbestos. Plaintiffs' claims against those defendants are unaffected by the disposition of this appeal; therefore, all subsequent references to defendants will include only du Pont and its company physicians. ...

Plaintiffs' brief before this Court summarizes their claims as follows: "The gravamen of the plaintiffs' claims [is] that du Pont and its doctors intentionally injured the plaintiffs by deliberately exposing them to asbestos and aggravated these injuries by conspiring to [conceal] and fraudulently concealing from the plaintiffs knowledge of diseases known by these defendants to have been caused by asbestos exposure and already contracted by the plaintiffs. Plaintiffs have suffered grievous and irreversible injuries both as a result of their initial exposure to asbestos and the failure of du Pont and its doctors to reveal diseases already contracted by the plaintiffs and known to the defendants."

Defendants filed a motion for summary judgment.... Defendants' argument in support of their motions was that plaintiffs' exclusive remedy was recovery under the Compensation Act. ... [T]he trial court granted summary judgment to du Pont but refused to dismiss the claims against the company doctors. ...

In an unreported opinion, the Appellate Division reversed the trial court's denial of the physicians' motion for summary judgment and affirmed the trial court's judgment in favor of du Pont. We ... now affirm in part and reverse in part.

II

... Plaintiffs-employees are all past or present workers at defendant du Pont's Chamber Works or Repauno plants. Both plants are involved in the manufacture of chemicals; each contains an extensive amount of piping through its facilities. As asbestos was often used for insulation purposes, the pipes in these plants were at one time surrounded by asbestos. It is therefore reasonably inferable that certain employees at the Chamber Works and Repauno plants were exposed to the asbestos insulation and inhaled asbestos fibers.

Defendants-physicians are Dr. W.E. Neeld, the medical director for the Chamber Works plant, and Drs. G.F. Reichwein and A. Smulkstys, former du Pont physicians at the Repauno plant. As medical director of Chamber Works, Dr. Neeld was required to supervise a medical staff of thirty-eight people responsible for meeting the health-care needs of the approximately 4,800 Chamber Works employees. The duties of Drs. Reichwein and Smulkstys, as plant physicians, included examining and treating plant employees, providing physical examinations, and being available for sick call and consultations.

The thrust of plaintiffs' allegations is that there was something akin to a conspiratorial agreement between du Pont and its medical staff that resulted in harm to plaintiffs. They assert generally that defendants, with knowledge of the adverse health consequences of asbestos use and exposure, and as part of a concerted plan for profit, deliberately exposed the plaintiffs to a dangerous work environment. ...

The first count of the complaint avers that defendants knew or should have known of the dangers associated with asbestos exposure, that they therefore had a duty to inform plaintiffs and to protect them from those dangers, but that they nonetheless acted intentionally to conceal from plaintiffs all information regarding the health hazards of asbestos. In count two of their complaint, plaintiffs allege that du Pont and the company physicians fraudulently concealed from plaintiffs the fact that company medical examinations had revealed that certain plaintiffs-employees had contracted asbestos-related diseases. They assert that each year the du Pont doctors would give employees complete physical examinations, including chest x-rays, pulmonary function tests, electrocardiograms, urine analyses, and blood tests.[fn] Plaintiffs contend that the results of these physical exams indicated that plaintiffs-employees had contracted serious pulmonary and respiratory abnormalities associated with exposure to asbestos. They further maintain that rather than provide medical treatment for these ailing employees, defendants fraudulently concealed plaintiffs' asbestos-related diseases and sent them back into the workplace, where their initial infirmities were aggravated by additional exposure to asbestos. Plaintiffs claim that the time from defendants' first knowledge of the employee's condition to the time when the employee was told of the danger was as long as eight years.

III

It is undisputed that plaintiffs' injuries, if proven, are compensable under the Compensation Act. The controversy presented, however, calls for a determination of whether the legislature intended that the Compensation Act should serve as a worker's sole and exclusive remedy under circumstances such as those alleged. The pertinent statute, N.J.S.A. 34:15-8, declares that when, by express or implied agreement, the parties have accepted the provisions of the Compensation Act and the employee qualifies for benefits under the conditions of the Act, the employee shall ordinarily be barred from the pursuit of other remedies.[fn] As the statute expressly indicates, however, an exception to the exclusivity provision is available when plaintiffs can prove an "intentional wrong." ...

... However, as noted by the Appellate Division in granting defendants' motions to dismiss, in order to satisfy the Compensation Act's definition of "intentional wrong," claimants have heretofore been required to show a deliberate intention to injure. [Cc]

... The approach of construing and applying the exception in the most limited fashion consistent with the purpose of the law is followed by the vast majority of jurisdictions that have considered whether allegedly egregious employer conduct warrants the recognition of a separate cause of action outside the compensation system. [Cc] ... [W]hat is equally clear is that although different jurisdictions may craft different formulations, whatever formulation is used represents a conscious effort to impose severe restrictions on the exception, bringing it as close to "subjective desire to injure" as the nuances of language will permit, while at the same time recognizing the problems of proof inherent in any attempt to demonstrate subjective intent. ...

V

Mindful of the origins of the Compensation Act and its subsequent development, we turn to the precise legal issue posed by this appeal: what categories of employer conduct will be sufficiently flagrant so as to constitute an "intentional wrong," thereby entitling a plaintiff to avoid the "exclusivity" bar of N.J.S.A. 34:15-8? Plaintiffs contend that du Pont and the doctors, in exposing the employees to asbestos and concealing medical information, acted knowingly and deliberately, not accidentally or negligently, so that defendants' conduct must be considered an "intentional wrong" within the meaning of the statute. Defendants, relying on the bulk of the authority on this topic, conversely assert that only conduct amounting to actual intent to injure employees will be sufficient to qualify as an "intentional wrong" in the context of a workers' compensation statute, and that the plaintiffs' complaints fall short of alleging "deliberate infliction of harm comparable to an intentional left jab to the chin." 2A A. Larson, supra, § 68.13 at 13-27.

Although we are certain that the legislature could not have intended that the system of workers' compensation would insulate actors from liability outside the boundaries of the Act for all willful and flagrant misconduct short of deliberate assault and battery, we are equally sure that the statutory scheme contemplates that as many work-related disability claims as possible be processed exclusively within the Act. Moreover, if "intentional wrong" is interpreted too broadly, this single exception would swallow up the entire "exclusivity" provision of the Act, since virtually all employee accidents, injuries, and sicknesses are a result of the employer or a co-employee intentionally acting to do whatever it is that may or may not lead to eventual injury or disease. Thus in setting an appropriate standard by which to measure an "intentional wrong," we are careful to keep an eye fixed on the obvious: the system of workers' compensation confronts head-on the unpleasant, even harsh, reality—but a reality nevertheless—that industry knowingly exposes workers to the risks of injury and disease.

The essential question therefore becomes what level of risk-exposure is so egregious as to constitute an "intentional wrong." ...

In adopting a "substantial certainty" standard, we acknowledge that every undertaking, particularly certain business judgments, involve some risk, but that willful employer misconduct was not meant to go undeterred. The distinctions between negligence, recklessness, and intent are obviously matters of degree, albeit subtle ones, as the thoughtful dissent so powerfully points out. In light of the legislative inclusion of occupational diseases within the coverage of the Compensation Act, however, the dividing line between negligent or reckless conduct on the one hand and intentional wrong on the other must be drawn with caution, so that the statutory framework of the Act is not circumvented simply because a known risk later blossoms into reality. We must demand a virtual certainty. ...

There is another significant component to the level of risk exposure that will satisfy the "intentional wrong" exception. Courts must examine not only the conduct of the employer, but also the context in which that conduct takes place: may the resulting injury or disease, and the circumstances in which it is inflicted on the worker, fairly be viewed as a fact of life of industrial employment, or is it rather plainly beyond anything the legislature could have contemplated as entitling the employee to recover only under the Compensation Act?

Examining the allegations in these cases in light of the foregoing principles, we conclude that count one of plaintiffs' complaints seeking damages beyond those available through workers' compensation for their initial work-related occupational diseases must fall. Although defendants' conduct in knowingly exposing plaintiffs to asbestos clearly amounts to deliberately taking risks with employees' health, as we have observed heretofore the mere knowledge and appreciation of a risk—even the strong probability of a risk—will come up short of the "substantial certainty" needed to find an intentional wrong resulting in avoidance of the exclusive-remedy bar of the compensation statute. In the face of the legislature's awareness of occupational diseases as a fact of industrial employment, we are constrained to conclude that plaintiffs-employees' initial resulting occupational diseases must be considered the type of hazard of employment that the legislature anticipated would be compensable under the terms of the Compensation Act and not actionable in an additional civil suit.

...

Plaintiffs have, however, pleaded a valid cause of action for aggravation of their initial occupational diseases under the second count of their complaints. Count two alleges that in order to prevent employees from leaving the workforce, defendants fraudulently concealed from plaintiffs the fact that they were suffering from asbestos-related diseases, thereby delaying their treatment and aggravating their existing illnesses. As noted earlier, du Pont's medical staff provides company employees with physical examinations as part of its package of medical services. Plaintiffs contend that although plaintiffs' physical examinations revealed changes in chest x-rays indicating asbestos-related injuries, du Pont's doctors did not inform plaintiffs of their sicknesses, but instead told them that their health was fine and sent them back to work under the same hazardous conditions that had caused the initial injuries.

These allegations go well beyond failing to warn of potentially-dangerous conditions or intentionally exposing workers to the risks of disease. There is a difference between, on the one hand, tolerating in the workplace conditions that will result in a certain number of injuries or illnesses, and, on the other, actively misleading the employees who have already fallen victim to those risks of the workplace. An employer's fraudulent concealment of diseases already developed is not one of the risks an employee should have to assume. Such intentionally-deceitful action goes beyond the bargain struck by the Compensation Act. But for defendants' corporate strategy of concealing diseases discovered in company physical examinations, plaintiffs would have minimized the dangers to their health. Instead, plaintiffs were deceived—or so they charge—by corporate doctors who held themselves out as acting in plaintiffs' best interests. The legislature, in passing the Compensation Act, could not have intended to insulate such conduct from tort liability. We therefore conclude that plaintiffs' allegations that defendants fraudulently concealed knowledge of already-contracted diseases are sufficient to state a cause of action for aggravation of plaintiffs' illnesses, as distinct from any claim for the existence of the initial disease, which is cognizable only under the Compensation Act. ...

VIII

... Affirmed in part, reversed in part. The cause is remanded to the Law Division for further proceedings consistent with this opinion.

INQUIRY

Product Misuse. Another defense commonly encountered in products-liability cases has to do with the product's misuse. As with the open-and-obvious defense, product misuse may either be an element of the plaintiff's case—that the plaintiff must show that the defendant manufacturer knew or should have known that consumers would use the product in the manner of the plaintiff's misuse—or an affirmative defense for the defendant to prove. Product misuse can also stand alone or fall within the defense of comparative negligence. The Restatement (Third) of Torts: Products Liability §17(b) adopts comparative fault rules and, in its Comment *c,* urges that courts not consider product misuse a separate doctrine. *See* Ford Motor Co. v. Matthews, 291 So.2d 169 (Miss. 1974) (rejecting that owner's misuse of tractor by standing beside it while turning the ignition key barred strict products liability claim). Only unanticipated misuses of a product would bar the plaintiff's claim, and they would do so, conceptually, because the plaintiff had failed to demonstrate a foreseeable risk to the product's anticipated use or misuse. *Contrast* Amatulli v. Delhi Construction Corp., 77 N.Y.2d 525, 571 N.E.2d 645, 569 N.Y.S.2d 337 (1991) (installing above-ground pool in a manner that makes it appear to be an in-ground pool is not an anticipated misuse); *with* Pavlik v. Lane Ltd., 135 F.3d 876 (3d Cir. 1998) (jury issue whether decedent's inhaling of butane lighter fluid was an unforeseeable misuse); Phillips v. Ogle Aluminum Furniture, Inc., 106 Cal. App.2d 650, 235 P.2d 857 (1951) (standing on a chair is a foreseeable misuse on which to base a negligent-construction claim).

Unforeseeability. Cases treat product misuse as a question of foreseeability. If an occurrence that relates to an arguable product defect is not something that a prudent manufacturer would necessarily foresee, then strict products liability should not exist. *Contrast* Griggs v. BIC Corp., 981 F.2d 1429 (3d Cir. 1992) (children's use of cigarette lighter not reasonably foreseeable); Erkson v. Sears, Roebuck & Co., 841 S.W.2d 207 (Mo. App. 1992) (child's riding as passenger on lawnmower, falling off, and having lawnmower run over child's leg, is not a foreseeable occurrence), *with* Larue v. National Union Elec. Corp., 571 F.2d 51 (1st Cir. 1978) (foreseeable that child's extremity might be injured slipping into vacuum-cleaner casement and coming into contact with fan). Some courts have held that if the general mechanism of injury is foreseeable, then the specific injury mechanism need not be. Meyering v. General Motors Corp., 232 Cal. App.3d 1163, 275 Cal. Rptr. 346 (1990) (object crashing through sunroof foreseeable even if concrete thrown from freeway overpass was not). The conceptual difference, if any, between product misuse and an unforeseeable occurrence is small, but misuse has more to do with the unintended purpose for which the consumer used the product, while unforeseeable occurrences have more to do with unexpected conditions under which the consumer used the product for its intended purpose.

Federal Preemption. Tort law is preeminently the domain of state, not federal, law. That fact is due in part to the regulatory orientation of Congress. Under the Constitution's Supremacy Clause, when Congress legislates within its constitutional authority, its enactments prevail over state laws. Thus, Congress could create private tort remedies within its Commerce Clause powers. The Federal Employers Liability Act, creating federal tort claims for injured interstate-railroad workers, is an example. Yet generally, Congress has not done so. It tends instead to exercise its authority over product manufacture, design, marketing, and warnings by authorizing federal-agency regulation—administrative, rather than private, enforcement of the national interest in safe products. The federal government heavily regulates products in certain fields including, for example, medical devices, tobacco products, fuels, and motor vehicles, but the legislation authorizing that regulation does not create private tort remedies. The way in which federal regulation comes into play in tort lawsuits is instead through the federal-preemption defense. Questions can readily arise whether state tort law should require greater care from manufacturers in those fields where federal regulations establish product standards. Certainly, state tort law cannot countermand duly authorized federal regulations. Federal regulations are supreme. But when the regulations are sufficiently comprehensive as to occupy the field of product safety regulation, that comprehensiveness may indicate Congress's intent that state tort law have *no* role shaping product manufacture, design, and warnings.

A series of Supreme Court cases have refined these preemption principles—regulatory supremacy, congressional intent, and comprehensive occupation of the field—beginning with a smoking-warning case, Cipollone v. Liggett Group, Inc., 505 U.S. 504 (1992). Congress required specific and progressively stronger smoking smoking warnings in 1965, 1970, and 1984. In its 1970 amendments, Congress added that "[n]o requirement or prohibition based on smoking and health shall be imposed under State law with respect to the advertising or promotion of any cigarettes the packages of which are labeled in conformity with" the federal law. 15 U.S.C. §1334(b). The *Cipollone* decision produced plurality opinions that held warnings claims preempted but negligent-testing claims not preempted by Congress's detailed specification of smoking warnings. Medtronic, Inc., v Lohr, 518 U.S. 470 (1996), was the next significant Supreme Court decision addressing preemption. Ms. Lohr claimed a defect in her implanted pacemaker. The preamble to the federal Medical Device Amendments of 1976 stated that the amendments were "to provide for the safety and effectiveness of medical devices for human use." The amendments' preemption language stated that "no State ... may establish or continue in effect ... any requirement—(1) which is different from, or in addition to, any requirement applicable under this Act..., and (2) which relates to the safety or effectiveness of the device... ." 21 U.S.C. §360k(a). Because the agency had not approved the pacemaker under the amendments' rigorous premarket-approval process (it was equivalent to a grandfathered device), the Supreme Court held that federal law did *not* preempt state tort-law claims for the device.

Back-and-forth rulings in recent Supreme Court cases show that preemption depends on a case-by-case analysis of the choices open to the defendant under the allegedly preempting federal regulations. In Geier v. American Honda Motor Co., 529

U.S. 861 (2000), the Supreme Court found federal preemption in vehicle-airbag regulations because Congress intended to give the auto industry time to develop restraint devices while overcoming airbag safety and cost problems. The plaintiff's state-law tort action conflicted with those congressional goals, and federal law thus preempted it. *See also* Riegel v. Medtronic, Inc., 552 U.S. 312 (2008) (FDA pre-market approval of balloon catheter device preempted state-law products liability claims, where regulations established safety and effectiveness requirements). Yet in Williamson v. Mazda Motor of America, Inc., 562 U.S. 323 (2011), the Court held not preempted a state-law claim that the defendant's vehicle should have had lap-and-shoulder restraints rather than just lap belts. Federal regulations similar to those in *Geier* gave manufacturers a choice of restraints, suggesting no congressional intent to preempt state law. Similarly, in Wyeth v. Levine, 555 U.S. 555 (2009), the Court held not preempted state-law claims against drug manufacturers for failing to make warning labels stronger than FDA regulations required. Those FDA regulations did not require approval to make stronger warnings. Yet in Pliva, Inc. v Mensing, 564 U.S. 604 (2011), the Court held preempted failure-to-warn claims against generic drug manufacturers because FDA regulations required those manufacturers to use the same warnings as brand-name manufacturers. Some preemption cases, though, are easier than other cases. Consider the following case.

Bruesewitz v. Wyeth LLC,
United States Supreme Court
131 S.Ct. 1068 (2011)

Justice SCALIA delivered the opinion of the Court.

We consider whether a preemption provision enacted in the National Childhood Vaccine Injury Act of 1986 (NCVIA)[fn] bars state-law design-defect claims against vaccine manufacturers.

I
A

For the last 66 years, vaccines have been subject to the same federal premarket approval process as prescription drugs, and compensation for vaccine-related injuries has been left largely to the States.[fn] Under that regime, the elimination of communicable diseases through vaccination became "one of the greatest achievements" of public health in the 20th century.[fn] But in the 1970's and 1980's vaccines became, one might say, victims of their own success. They had been so effective in preventing infectious diseases that the public became much less alarmed at the threat of those diseases,[fn] and much more concerned with the risk of injury from the vaccines themselves.[fn]

… This led to a massive increase in vaccine-related tort litigation. Whereas between 1978 and 1981 only nine product-liability suits were filed against DTP [diphtheria-vaccine] manufacturers, by the mid–1980's the suits numbered more than 200 each year.[fn] This destabilized the DTP vaccine market, causing two of the three domestic manufacturers to withdraw; and the remaining manufacturer, Lederle Laboratories, estimated that its potential tort liability exceeded its annual sales by a factor of 200.[fn] Vaccine shortages arose when Lederle had production problems in 1984.[fn] …

To stabilize the vaccine market and facilitate compensation, Congress enacted the NCVIA in 1986. The Act establishes a[n administrative] no-fault compensation program "designed to work faster and with greater ease than the civil tort system." Shalala v. Whitecotton, 514 U.S. 268, 269[] (1995). …

Successful claimants receive compensation for medical, rehabilitation, counseling, special education, and vocational training expenses; diminished earning capacity; pain and suffering; and $250,000 for vaccine-related deaths.[fn] Attorney's fees are provided, not only for successful cases, but even for unsuccessful claims that are not frivolous.[fn] These awards are paid out of a fund created by an excise tax on each vaccine dose.[fn]

The *quid pro quo* for this, designed to stabilize the vaccine market, was the provision of significant tort-liability protections for vaccine manufacturers. … Manufacturers are generally immunized from liability for failure to warn if they have complied with all regulatory requirements (including but not limited to warning requirements).… . And most relevant to the present case, the Act expressly eliminates liability for a vaccine's unavoidable, adverse side effects: "No vaccine manufacturer shall be liable in a civil action for damages arising from a vaccine-related injury or death associated with the administration of a vaccine after October 1, 1988, if the injury or death resulted from side effects that were unavoidable even though the vaccine was properly prepared and was accompanied by proper directions and warnings."[fn]

B

… Hannah Bruesewitz was born on October 20, 1991. Her pediatrician administered doses of the DTP vaccine according to the Center for Disease Control's recommended childhood immunization schedule. Within 24 hours of her April 1992 vaccination, Hannah started to experience seizures.[fn] She suffered over 100 seizures during the next month, and her doctors eventually diagnosed her with "residual seizure disorder" and "developmental delay."[fn] Hannah, now a teenager, is still diagnosed with both conditions.

In April 1995, Hannah's parents, Russell and Robalee Bruesewitz, filed a vaccine injury petition in the United States Court of Federal Claims, alleging that Hannah suffered from on-Table residual seizure disorder and encephalopathy injuries.[fn] A Special Master denied their claims on various grounds, though they were awarded $126,800 in attorney's fees and costs. The Bruesewitzes elected to reject the unfavorable judgment, and in October 2005 filed this lawsuit in Pennsylvania state court. Their complaint alleged (as relevant here) that defective design of Lederle's DTP vaccine caused Hannah's disabilities, and that Lederle was subject to strict liability, and liability for negligent design, under Pennsylvania common law.[fn]

Wyeth removed the suit to the United States District Court for the Eastern District of Pennsylvania, which granted Wyeth summary judgment on the strict-liability and negligence design-defect claims, holding that the Pennsylvania law providing those causes of action was preempted by 42 U.S.C. § 300aa–22(b)(1).[fn] The United States Court of Appeals for the Third Circuit affirmed.[fn] We granted certiorari. [C]

II
A

The "even though" clause [of 42 U.S.C. §300aa-22(b)(1)] clarifies the word that precedes it. It delineates the preventative measures that a vaccine manufacturer *must* have taken for a side-effect to be considered "unavoidable" under the statute. Provided that there was proper manufacture and warning, any remaining side effects, including those resulting from design defects, are deemed to have been unavoidable. State-law design-defect claims are therefore preempted.

If a manufacturer could be held liable for failure to use a different design, the word "unavoidable" would do no work. A side effect of a vaccine could *always* have been avoidable by use of a differently designed vaccine not containing the harmful element. The language of the provision thus suggests that the *design* of the vaccine is a given, not subject to question in the tort action. What the statute establishes as a complete defense must be unavoidability (given safe manufacture and warning) *with respect to the particular design*. Which plainly implies that the design itself is not open to question.[fn]

B

... Petitioners and the dissent contend that the interpretation we propose would render part of §300aa–22(b)(1) superfluous: Congress could have more tersely and more clearly preempted design-defect claims by barring liability "if ... the vaccine was properly prepared and was accompanied by proper directions and warnings." The intervening passage ("the injury or death resulted from side effects that were unavoidable even though") is unnecessary. True enough. But the rule against giving a portion of text an interpretation which renders it superfluous does not prescribe that a passage which could have been more terse does not mean what it says. The rule applies only if verbosity and prolixity can be eliminated by giving the offending passage, or the remainder of the text, a competing interpretation. That is not the case here.[fn] ...

III

The structure of the NCVIA and of vaccine regulation in general reinforces what the text of §300aa–22(b)(1) suggests. ...

... Design-defect torts, broadly speaking, have two beneficial effects: (1) prompting the development of improved designs, and (2) providing compensation for inflicted injuries. The NCVIA provides other means for achieving both effects. We have already discussed the Act's generous compensation scheme. And the Act provides many means of improving vaccine design. ...

And finally, the Act's structural *quid pro quo* leads to the same conclusion: The vaccine manufacturers fund from their sales an informal, efficient compensation program for vaccine injuries;[fn] in exchange they avoid costly tort litigation and the occasional disproportionate jury verdict.[fn] But design-defect allegations are the most speculative and difficult type of products liability claim to litigate. Taxing vaccine manufacturers' product to fund the compensation program, while leaving their liability for design defect virtually unaltered, would hardly coax manufacturers back into the market. ...

For the foregoing reasons, we hold that the National Childhood Vaccine Injury Act preempts all design-defect claims against vaccine manufacturers brought by plaintiffs who seek compensation for injury or death caused by vaccine side effects. The judgment of the Court of Appeals is affirmed.

It is so ordered.

Government Specification. An issue relating to both compliance with safety statute and federal preemption is the effect of federal-government specification of design for products the government purchases. When the federal government orders a military product (a rifle or a helicopter, for example), it often does so with precise design standards and specifications, meeting national security needs that do not reflect ordinary regard for consumer safety. Where the design specifications are reasonably precise, and the product meets those specifications, the manufacturer should not be liable to a user or third-party whom a design defect injures, at least if the manufacturer warned the government about the shortcomings in the specified design. The defense applies only to federal (not state) government specifications. *Cf.* Conner v. Quality Coach, Inc., 561 Pa. 397, 750 A.2d 823 (2000) (manufacturer does not have government-contractor immunity for state-agency design in which manufacturer participated). As you read the following Supreme Court case recognizing the government-contractor defense, consider whether it should apply to non-military products and products that reached the ordinary consumer after government sale.

Boyle v. United Technologies Corp.
United States Supreme Court
487 U.S. 500 (1988)

SCALIA, J. This case requires us to decide when a contractor providing military equipment to the Federal Government can be held liable under state tort law for injury caused by a design defect.

I

On April 27, 1983, David A. Boyle, a United States Marine helicopter copilot, was killed when the CH-53D helicopter in which he was flying crashed off the coast of Virginia Beach, Virginia, during a training exercise. Although Boyle survived the impact of the crash, he was unable to escape from the helicopter and drowned. Boyle's father, petitioner here, brought this diversity action in Federal District Court against the Sikorsky Division of United Technologies Corporation (Sikorsky), which built the helicopter for the United States.

At trial, petitioner presented two theories of liability under Virginia tort law that were submitted to the jury. First, petitioner alleged that Sikorsky had defectively repaired a device called the servo in the helicopter's automatic flight control system, which allegedly malfunctioned and caused the crash. Second, petitioner alleged that Sikorsky had defectively designed the copilot's emergency escape system: the escape hatch opened out instead of in (and was therefore ineffective in a submerged craft because of water pressure), and access to the escape hatch handle was obstructed by other equipment. The jury returned a general verdict in favor of petitioner and awarded him $725,000. The District Court denied Sikorsky's motion for judgment notwithstanding the verdict.

The Court of Appeals reversed and remanded with directions that judgment be entered for Sikorsky. [C] It found, as a matter of Virginia law, that Boyle had failed to meet his burden of demonstrating that the repair work performed by Sikorsky, as opposed to work that had been done by the Navy, was responsible for the alleged malfunction of the flight control system. [C] It also found, as a matter of federal law, that Sikorsky could not be held liable for the allegedly defective design of the escape hatch because, on the evidence presented, it satisfied the requirements of the "military contractor defense," which the court had recognized the same day in *Tozer v. LTV Corp.*, 792 F.2d 403 (CA4 1986). [C] ...

II

Petitioner's broadest contention is that, in the absence of legislation specifically immunizing Government contractors from liability for design defects, there is no basis for judicial recognition of such a defense. We disagree. In most fields of activity, to be sure, this Court has refused to find federal pre-emption of state law in the absence of either a clear statutory prescription, [cc], or a direct conflict between federal and state law, [cc]. But we have held that a few areas, involving "uniquely federal interests," [c], are so committed by the Constitution and laws of the United States to federal control that state law is pre-empted and replaced, where necessary, by federal law of a content prescribed (absent explicit statutory directive) by the courts-so-called "federal common law." [Cc]

The dispute in the present case borders upon two areas that we have found to involve such "uniquely federal interests." We have held that obligations to and rights of the United States under its contracts are governed exclusively by federal law. [Cc] The present case does not involve an obligation to the United States under its contract, but rather liability to third persons. That liability may be styled one in tort, but it arises out of performance of the contract—and traditionally has been regarded as sufficiently related to the contract that until 1962 Virginia would generally allow design defect suits only by the purchaser and those in privity with the seller. [Cc].

Another area that we have found to be of peculiarly federal concern, warranting the displacement of state law, is the civil liability of federal officials for actions taken in the course of their duty. We have held in many contexts that the scope of that liability is controlled by federal law. [Cc]. The present case involves an independent contractor performing its obligation under a procurement contract, rather than an official performing his duty as a federal employee, but there is obviously implicated the same interest in getting the Government's work done.[fn]

We think the reasons for considering these closely related areas to be of "uniquely federal" interest apply as well to the civil liabilities arising out of the performance of federal procurement contracts. ...

Moreover, it is plain that the Federal Government's interest in the procurement of equipment is implicated by suits such as the present one—even though the dispute is one between private parties. ... The imposition of liability on Government contractors will directly affect the terms of Government contracts: either the contractor will decline to manufacture the design specified by the Government, or it will raise its price. Either way, the interests of the United States will be directly affected.

That the procurement of equipment by the United States is an area of uniquely federal interest does not, however, end the inquiry. That merely establishes a necessary, not a sufficient, condition for the displacement of state law.[fn] Displacement will occur only where, as we have variously described, a "significant conflict" exists between an identifiable "federal policy or interest and the [operation] of state law," *Wallis, supra,* at 68, 86 S.Ct., at 1304, or the application of state law would "frustrate specific objectives" of federal legislation, *Kimbell Foods,* 440 U.S., at 728, 99 S.Ct., at 1458. ...

... Here the state-imposed duty of care that is the asserted basis of the contractor's liability (specifically, the duty to equip helicopters with the sort of escape-hatch mechanism petitioner claims was necessary) is precisely contrary to the duty imposed by the Government contract (the duty to manufacture and deliver helicopters with the sort of escape-hatch mechanism shown by the specifications). ...

There is ... a statutory provision that demonstrates the potential for, and suggests the outlines of, "significant conflict" between federal interests and state law in the context of Government procurement. In the FTCA, Congress authorized damages to be recovered against the United States for harm caused by the negligent or wrongful conduct of Government employees, to the extent that a private person would be liable under the law of the place where the conduct occurred. 28 U.S.C. § 1346(b). It excepted from this consent to suit, however, "[a]ny claim ... based upon the exercise or performance or the failure to exercise or perform a discretionary function or duty on the part of a federal agency or an employee of the Government, whether or not the discretion involved be abused." 28 U.S.C. § 2680(a).

We think that the selection of the appropriate design for military equipment to be used by our Armed Forces is assuredly a discretionary function within the meaning of this provision. It often involves not merely engineering analysis but judgment as to the balancing of many technical, military, and even social considerations, including specifically the trade-off between greater safety and greater combat effectiveness. And we are further of the view that permitting "second-guessing" of these judgments, [c], through state tort suits against contractors would produce the same effect sought to be avoided by the FTCA exemption. ... In sum, we are of the view that state law which holds Government contractors liable for design defects in military equipment does in some circumstances present a "significant conflict" with federal policy and must be displaced.[fn]

... Liability for design defects in military equipment cannot be imposed, pursuant to state law, when (1) the United States approved reasonably precise specifications; (2) the equipment conformed to those specifications; and (3) the supplier warned the United States about the dangers in the use of the equipment that were known to the supplier but not to the United States. The first two of these conditions assure that the suit is within the area where the policy of the "discretionary function" would be frustrated—*i.e.*, they assure that the design feature in question was considered by a Government officer, and not merely by the contractor itself. The third condition is necessary because, in its absence, the displacement of state tort law would create some incentive for the manufacturer to withhold knowledge of risks, since conveying that knowledge might disrupt the contract but withholding it would produce no liability. We adopt this provision lest our effort to protect discretionary functions perversely impede them by cutting off information highly relevant to the discretionary decision. ...

Accordingly, the judgment is vacated and the case is remanded. ...

Knowledge

Tort law involves evaluating facts in light of the applicable legal theories to hold parties to objective standards of reasonable conduct. How do these fundamental constructs—fact, theory, and objectivity—affect who we are as lawyers? The word *fact* derives from the same root as to *manufacture*—to assemble within a design or pattern. Lawyers should keep in mind that their own mental processes are not distinct from the facts. Lawyers can only know facts within the mind, meaning that they select and organize them to give them pattern and meaning. The word *theory* derives from the same root as *theater*—to observe as in a play. Theater, though, is also participatory—especially the Greek theater associated with the original word "theory." The lawyer who evaluates facts in light of the applicable legal theories selects and organizes the facts, and advocates the theory, not as a cold analyst but using a creative heart, mind, and soul. Similarly, although the words "objective" and "objectivity" suggest to the scientific mind something apart from individual experience, they nonetheless denote community judgment about the wisdom and value of certain individual conduct. Legal knowledge requires sensitive thought, compassion, and care. Love—the positive

> interaction of humans for their individual and collective benefit—is the root of knowledge, not, as some suppose, curiosity and control. Tort law reflects that understanding as much or more than any other legal construct.

F. Product-Related Liability

OBJECTIVE: Given a mixed transaction involving the sale of a product combined with the provision of a service causing injury, analyze whether products liability theories will apply under the law and principles reflected in these pages of the text.

Case Study: A homeowner hired a contractor to install a new gas furnace in his house. The contractor chose, supplied, and installed a model that, although advertised to handle the house's size, was in fact inadequate to keep the house heated. As a result, the furnace ran constantly during a very cold spell when the owner was away, resulting in the furnace's complete failure and the freezing and bursting of pipes throughout the house. ***Evaluate whether the homeowner has a products-liability claim against the contractor for the property damage to the house.***

Products liability, it seems too obvious to say, reaches only product-caused injury. The Restatement (Third) of Torts: Products Liability §19(b) (1998) states simply that for products liability, "services, even when provided commercially, are not products." Explore briefly here the boundaries between products and services, real property, human and animal life, intellectual property, utilities, and other things of value that are not products for purposes of products liability. One of the simpler boundaries is between a product and real property. Products-liability law does not apply to conditions of land including artificial improvements to land. Houses and other buildings are not products, unless (possibly) manufactured off-site and shipped in a largely assembled condition to the site, as in the case of pre-fabricated housing. *See* Oliver v. Superior Court, 259 Cal. Rptr. 160 (Ct. App. 1989); Restatement (Third) of Torts: Products Liability §19(a), Comment *e* (1998). On the other hand, some states imply a warranty of habitability between the builder and buyer of a new home. *See* Schipper v. Levitt & Sons, Inc., 44 N.J. 70, 207 A.2d 314 (1965); Humber v. Morton, 426 S.W.2d 554 (Tex. 1968). How is *habitability* different, if at all, from *merchantability*? The Restatement (Third) of Torts: Products Liability §19, Comment *e* (1998) would also extend strict products liability to builders for defective appliances they supply with newly constructed homes.

Services. Another boundary of products liability has to do with product-related services. In the medical malpractice setting, for instance, a strict-products-liability theory related to the medical device used on or implanted in the plaintiff could remove substantial cost and procedural impediments to recovery. Under strict products liability, limitations periods may be longer, damages caps different or absent, and notice-of-claim requirements absent, and the claimant would not have to define the professional standard of care by expensive expert testimony. Yet the courts have generally not permitted strict-products-liability claims against defendants whose essential activity was to provide not a product but a service. *See* Madison v. American Home Prods. Corp., 358 S.C. 449, 595 S.E.2d 493 (2004) (pharmacist not strictly liable for drug sold because transaction was primarily a service); In re Breast Implant Prod. Liab. Litig., 331 S.C. 540, 503 S.E.2d 445 (1998) (surgeons not strictly liable for implanted product); Cafazzo v. Central Med. Health Services, Inc., 542 Pa. 526, 668

A.2d 521 (1995) (prosthesis defect does not give rise to physician strict liability); Hector v. Cedars-Sinai Medical Ctr., 180 Cal. App.3d 493, 225 Cal. Rptr. 595 (1986) (hospital not strictly liable for implanting defective pacemaker). The product manufacturer retains strict products liability but not the service provider who specified, used, applied, installed, or implanted the product.

Combined Sales and Services. Can you, on the other hand, envision combined sales-service transactions where the *sale* aspect predominates? *See* O'Laughlin v. Minnesota Natural Gas. Co., 253 N.W.2d 826 (Minn. 1977) (strict liability for furnace sale where installation was incidental); *see also* Schriner v. Pennsylvania Power & Light Co., 348 Pa. Super. 177, 501 A.2d 1128 (1985) (electricity is a product for strict-liability purposes after it passes through the customer's meter); Restatement (Third) of Torts: Products Liability §19, Comment *d* (1998) (a majority of courts extend strict liability to utilities only after the product passes through the meter). The case of Newmark v. Gimbel's, Inc., 54 N.J. 585, 258 A.2d 697 (1969), is representative. The plaintiff received a permanent wave at the defendant's beauty salon that required a specific product that the plaintiff could have purchased separately for home application. The appellate court extended strict products liability in that mixed sales-service setting because the sale aspect predominated. As you consider the following illustrative case, see if you can articulate the two policies on which the distinction between sales and services rests.

Ayyash v. Henry Ford Health Sys.
Michigan Court of Appeals
210 Mich. App. 142, 533 N.W.2d 353 (1995)

SAAD, J. The trial court granted summary disposition to defendants—a doctor and a hospital—because it held that, absent negligence, these health care providers should not be legally responsible, on strict liability theories, for an admittedly defective implant placed in Samira Ayyash (hereinafter plaintiff) by defendant physician at defendant hospital. For reasons articulated below, we agree with and affirm the trial court's ruling. ...

Plaintiff fell down a flight of stairs at her home and broke her lower jaw, which was repaired surgically at Henry Ford Hospital. Thereafter, Dr. Wolford, who was at the time head of oral surgery at defendant hospital, treated plaintiff.

After the initial surgery, plaintiff continued to complain of pain and discomfort in her jaw, and Dr. Wolford treated plaintiff for approximately one year. In November 1983, Dr. Wolford surgically implanted into plaintiff's temporomandibular joint a medical device known as a Vitek Proplast Silastic. It is this surgery that gave rise to this suit. After the implant surgery, plaintiff continued treating with Dr. Wolford until April 1986.

The Vitek implants were approved by the Food and Drug Administration in 1983. In June 1990, Vitek, Inc., filed for Chapter 7 bankruptcy, and, in September 1991, plaintiff received a letter from a bankruptcy court in Texas that said that Vitek had gone into bankruptcy and that she was entitled to make a claim against the bankruptcy estate. The implants were recalled in 1992 because many patients were experiencing a breakdown in the implants. In May 1993, plaintiff's implant was removed surgically.

...

II. STRICT LIABILITY OR NEGLIGENCE

... [T]he legal issue, of first impression, before this Court is whether a plaintiff, injured by an admittedly defective medical implant placed in her body during surgery by her physician (at a hospital) may maintain a strict liability claim against her doctor and the hospital for the injuries caused by the defective implant.

... Faced with this precise issue, other jurisdictions have used the "essence of the transaction" test to determine whether the appropriate theory of recovery is strict liability or negligence. [Cc] In other words, appellate courts have imposed strict liability upon sellers of defective products, but not upon providers of services.[fn] [Cc] Where, as here, the putative defendant uses a defective product in the course of providing a service, the courts must decide whether the "transaction" is primarily a sale or a service. ...

In the case of a physician or hospital rendering medical care, as here, courts typically have characterized the "transaction" as a service and, accordingly, used negligence rather than strict liability theories of recovery.[fn] [Cc] We agree with this approach and adopt it here, because there are good reasons to do so.

Because the primary function of physicians and hospitals is to provide care, not to manufacture or distribute products, those economic theories that underlie the imposition of strict liability upon makers and sellers of products do not justify the extension of strict liability to those who provide medical services. It is reasonable to conclude that the vast majority of patients would bear the increased costs associated with such an impractical imposition of liability upon the medical profession for the benefit of a few who for some reason (here bankruptcy) may not be able to obtain recovery from the manufacturer of the defective product. ...

Because imposing liability without fault in such cases would ultimately hurt rather than help patients and their doctors, we affirm the lower court's grant of summary disposition.

Human Tissue. A second boundary involves human organs, blood, and other tissue, which the law does not consider products for strict-products-liability purposes. *See* Cryolife, Inc., v. Superior Ct., 2 Cal. Rptr.3d 396 (Ct. App. 2003); Weishorn v. Miles-Cutter, 721 A.2d 811 (Pa. Super, Ct. 1998) (blood). Agencies heavily regulate human-tissue markets to the point that they do not function like an ordinary market. Blood and human-tissue suppliers are not subject to products-liability law. *See* Restatement (Third) of Torts: Products Liability §19(c). Can you articulate why legislatures would grant human-tissue suppliers immunity from strict products liability and would impose restrictions on the market-price sale of human tissue?

Animals. States disagree on whether animals, whether sold as livestock or pets, are products. *See* Worrell v. Scahs, 563 A.2d 1387 (Conn. Super. 1989) (diseased dog is a product); Beyer v. Aquarium Supply Co., 94 Misc.2d 336, 404 N.Y.S.2d 778 (1977) (hamster is a product); *but see* Blaha v. Stuard, 640 N.W.2d 85 (S.D. 2002) (biting dog not a product); Latham v. Wal-Mart Stores, Inc., 818 S.W.2d 673 (Mo. App. 1991) (parrot transmitting disease to buyer is not a product for strict-liability purposes). The Restatement (Third) of Torts: Products Liability §19, Comment *b* (1998) takes the view that a diseased animal sold commercially is a product for strict-products-liability purposes. What are the rationales either side would use to support their rule? Does a middle ground exist?

Writings. The law does not generally consider writings (books, periodicals) as products, except that charts and maps used for commercial purposes may be products. *See* Artiglio v. General Elec. Co., 71 Cal. Rptr.2d 817 (Cal. App. 1998) (pilot's map is a product); Fluor Corp. v. Jeppesen & Co., 170 Cal. App.3d 468, 216 Cal. Rptr. 68 (1985) (same) (misrepresented height of hill). What about a nature-guide book that misrepresents or omits information about poisonous mushrooms? *See* Winter v. G.P. Putnam's Sons, 938 F.2d 1033 (9th Cir. 1991) (no strict products liability). What about a travel-guide book that describes scenic grounds without alerting readers to their hidden hazards? *See* Birmingham v. Fodor's Travel Pubs., Inc., 73 Haw. 359, 833 P.2d 70 (1992) (no strict products liability). What about a diet book that leads a reader to her death? *See* Smith v. Linn, 386 Pa. Super. 392, 563 A.2d 123 (1989) (no strict products liability). How treat games that encourage unreasonably dangerous behavior? *See* James v. Meow Media, Inc., 300 F.3d 683 (6th Cir. 2002) (no strict products liability for makers of video-game that allegedly desensitized high-school student, causing him to shoot classmates); Watters v. TSR, Inc., 904 F.2d 378 (6th Cir. 1990) (no strict products liability); Wilson v. Midway Games, Inc., 198 F. Sup.2d 167 (D. Conn. 2002) (no strict products liability for killing patterned after defendant manufacturer's video game). Can you discern any circumstance under which a book should be a product for strict products liability?

Careers

Tort practice, especially on the plaintiff's side where lawyers tend to work as solo practitioners or in small firms while earning their fees on contingency, requires a greater degree of enterprise skills than some other law fields. Law practice involves more than law knowledge and advocacy skills. Lawyers who manage law firms can benefit by knowing budgeting, finance, project management, marketing, systems development, and other entrepreneurial skills. Courses in Law Office Management, bar association Practice Management Institutes, mentor relationships, professional networks, and business and management literature can all aid law students and lawyers who wish to develop and hone their enterprise skills. Even lawyers in larger firms must be responsible to their clients and firms for their productivity and efficiency. Develop your sense of entrepreneurial, practice-development, and innovation skills. Consider the book *Entrepreneurial Practice* by this text's author.

Chapter XI

Strict Liability

Strict liability occupies an uneasy place in tort law for historical, political, and analytical reasons. In its simplest modern conception, strict liability is liability without intent or fault. One pays whether one intended injury, was careless, or showed complete care without any fault. Strict liability is the third overall class of torts after intentional torts and torts of negligence. Strict liability does not depend on a standard for the defendant's conduct, but instead, on classifying the type of activity in which the defendant engaged. Strict liability is not absolute liability, although case opinions occasionally call it that. Strict liability is not absolute because if the activity that caused injury does not fit the strict-liability classification, then no strict liability exists. Strict-liability classifications substitute for fault concepts, limiting strict liability to reasonable bounds. One might even say that engaging in the classified conduct presumes responsibility if not also fault. Strict liability is also not absolute liability because certain defenses may bar or reduce strict liability even when the claim fits the strict-liability classification.

Strict liability's genesis lies in the English history of the trespass writ. Actions under the trespass writ required proof of the defendant's direct action but did not require proof of intent or fault. Hence, trespass-writ liability existed for damage done by livestock driven onto another's lands. Gradually, the law of the trespass writ extended liability to damage done by livestock that wandered onto another's land. Actions for straying livestock did not involve the defendant's direct action, as the trespass writ required, but strict liability for strays encouraged good husbandry. The common-law rules regarding animals described below are an outgrowth of these historical considerations. Consistent with what the above says about the distinction between strict liability on one hand and negligence and intentional torts on the other, animal strict-liability rules rely on classifying the defendant's activity and animal, not evaluating the quality of the defendant's conduct.

The other credit for the modern development of strict liability goes to the English case Rylands v. Fletcher, 3 H & C. 774, 159 Eng. Rep. 737 (1865), L.R. 1 Ex. 265 (1866). The *Rylands* defendants (mill owners) constructed a reservoir on their land, unwittingly, over closed mineshafts. The reservoir's water soon escaped through the mineshafts, flooding the plaintiff neighbor's land. The trial court, the Court of Exchequer, found the defendant mill owners not negligent, not in direct action as to the water's entry onto their neighbor's land, and therefore not liable under the trespass writ or otherwise. The appellate Exchequer Chamber reversed, Judge Blackburn stating that "it seems but reasonable and just that the neighbor, who has brought something on his own property that was not naturally there, … which he knows to be mischievous if it gets on his neighbor's [land], should be obliged to make good the damage which ensures if he does not succeed in confining it to his own property. … [I]t seems just that he should at his peril keep it there so that no mischief may accrue, or answer for the natural and anticipated consequences." The House of Lords affirmed the

Exchequer Chamber's holding in *Rylands* for the plaintiff, Lord Chancellor Cairns writing that "if the defendants, not stopping at the natural use of their close, had desired to use it for any purpose which I may term a non-natural use, for the purpose of introducing into the close that which in its natural condition was not in or upon it...; and if in consequence of their doing so, ... , the water came to escape and to pass off into the close of the plaintiff, then it appears to me that that which the defendants were doing they were doing at their own peril ... [and] would be liable."

Rylands does not mean that any human habitation and use of lands is "unnatural" and therefore subject to strict liability for damage caused. Rather, *Rylands* meant that the defendants' construction of a reservoir *in those mining lands* was uncommon. *Rylands*-type strict liability made its way into the Restatement (First) of Torts §§519, 520 (1938), under the formulation that a defendant would be strictly liable for harm from an "ultrahazardous activity" involving a "risk of serious harm" that "cannot be eliminated by the exercise of the utmost care" and "is not a matter of common usage." The Restatement (Second) of Torts §519 (1977) altered both strict liability's name and standard, calling it an "abnormally dangerous activity" and limiting it to harms that flow from the risk that make it abnormally dangerous. Section 520 of the Restatement (Second) listed six factors to determine whether the activity is abnormally dangerous: "a) existence of a high degree of risk of some harm to the person, land or chattels of others; b) likelihood that the harm that results from it will be great; c) inability to eliminate the risk by the exercise of reasonable care; d) extent to which the activity is not a matter of common usage; e) inappropriateness of the activity to the place where it is carried on; and f) extent to which its value to the community is outweighed by its dangerous attributes." The following two sections treat animal strict liability and strict liability for abnormally dangerous activities.

A. Animals

OBJECTIVE: Given injuries caused by various animals under various circumstances, identify those instances in which the animals' owner or keeper is strictly liable, consistent with the law reflected in this section of the text.

Case Study: A mother often visited her daughter at a stable. One evening, the mother heard whining coming from a stall at the end of the stable hallway. The mother noticed a hand-written sign tacked to the stall warning of dog bite. She could see a cute Dalmatian dog wagging its tail and acting playfully inside the stall. She reached her hand into the stall to pet the dog. The dog snapped at her hand with its mouth, tearing the mother's skin and severing tendons. The daughter later told the mother that the stable's owner had told her that the dog gets defensive when in closed areas and had snapped at others. ***Analyze the mother's strict-liability claim in a jurisdiction having no dog-bite statute but recognizing a traditional form of strict liability for animals.***

As the above discussion indicates, the common law and statutes regarding animal liability have to do with the history of the trespass writ. They also have to do with the history, agriculture, and politics of the local region. Traditional common-law rules limited strict liability to damage done by livestock of the sort that livestock usually cause, which would have included primarily property damage. *See* King v. Blue Mtn. Forest Assn, 100 N.H. 212, 123 A.2d 151 (1956); Adams Bros. v. Clark, 189 Ky. 279, 224 S.W. 1046 (1920) (property damage by chickens). Those traditional rules did not provide for strict liability for damage done by livestock wandering temporarily onto lands while being driven along a road—more good husbandry sense for getting animals to market. *See* Wood v. Snider, 187 N.Y. 28, 79 N.E. 858 (1907) (no liability to landowner adjacent to highway, but liability to second landowner not adjacent to highway). Western states, where open ranges were common, rejected traditional strict-liability rules for grazing animals. *See* Beinhorn v. Griswold, 27 Mont. 79, 69 P.557 (1902); *see also* Andersen v. Two Dot Ranch, 49 P.3d 1011 (Wyo. 2002) (summary judgment for defendant rancher on motorists' strict-liability claim involving motor vehicle collision with open-range grazing cattle). Some states adopted *fence-out* statutes providing strict liability against the grazing animal's owner only as to losses by landowner's with properly fenced lands. *See* Hart v. Meredith, 196 Ill. App.3d 367, 553 N.E.2d 782, 143 Ill. Dec. 75 (1990) (fence-out statute strict liability for bull breaking through fence to breed cows). Other more-settled states adopted *fence-in* statutes that provided for strict liability against animal owners who failed to fence their animals in. *See* Fisel v. Wynns, 667 So.2d 761 (Fla. 1996) (no animal-owner liability for animal-escape onto highway causing crash, where owner had fenced animal in). Still other states allow each individual county within the state to choose the rule.

Traditional tort law has also offered strict liability for damage done by wild animals that the defendant owned or controlled. A wild animal is one not domestic within the region. *See* Johnson v. Swain, 787 S.W.2d 36 (Tex. 1989) (strict liability for bull-elephant gore); Isaacs v. Powell, 267 So.2d 864 (Fla. App. 1972) (strict liability for injury by chimpanzee); Fraken v. Sioux Ctr., 272 N.W.2d 422 (Iowa 1978) (strict liability for injury by tiger); Briley v. Mitchell, 238 La. 551, 115 So.2d 851 (1959) (strict liability for injury by deer); *cf.* Wilhelm v. Flores, 133 S.W.3d 726 (Tex. App. 2003) (no strict liability for injury from hived bees); Marshall v. Ranne, 511 S.W.2d 255 (Tex. 1974) (no strict liability for injury from boar); Maung Kayn Dun v. Ma Kyian, 2 Upper Burma Rulings, Civ. 570 (1900) (owner of domesticated elephant in Burma not strictly liable); *but see* Ollhoff v. Peck, 177 Wis. 2d 719, 503 N.W.2d 323 (1993) (plaintiff must show defendant's negligence with respect to natural habits of musky). An interesting historical case is Filburn v. People's Palace & Aquarium, Ltd., Q.B. Div. 258 (1890), in which an elephant on exhibit unpredictably broke free on a rampage. The court granted the injured plaintiff judgment because "a man keeps at his peril" wild animals—like elephants—that are by nature capable of harm. Classification can create problems. *See* Gallick v. Barto, 828 F. Supp. 1168 (M.D. Pa. 1993) (ferret is wild animal despite pet market); *see also* Zinter v. Oswskey, 633 N.W.2d 278 (Wis. Ct. App. 2001) (jury decides whether rabbits are wild). So can issues of ownership and control. *See* Leber v. Hyatt Hotels, 124 F.2d 47 (1st Cir. 1997) (hotel not liable for injury to guest bitten by mongoose from neighboring swamp not owned or controlled by hotel). Zoos are more likely to face a negligence, not strict-liability, standard. *See* City and County of Denver v. Kennedy, 29 Colo. App. 15, 476 P.2d 762 (1970); Hansen v. Broan, 145 Mont. 224, 400 P.2d 265 (1965).

Under the common law, strict liability for injury by pets depends on a showing that the owner or keeper was aware of the pet's abnormally vicious propensities that caused the injury. *See* Walters v. Grand Teton Crest Outfitters, Inc., 804 F. Supp. 1442 (D. Wyo. 1992) (mule having thrown previous riders); Barger v. Jimerson, 130 Colo. 459, 276 P.2d 744 (1954); Olson v. Pederson, 206 Minn. 415, 288 N.W. 856 (1939) (no strict liability for pets without knowledge of propensities); Restatement (Second) of Torts §509 (1965). Given that limitation, the liability would seem to be less than strict and more likely based on an inference of fault drawn from keeping a pet with abnormally vicious propensities. This suspected justification leads us to another important point about liability related to animals generally—that whether strict liability is available or not, the owner or keeper may be liable in negligence for the same injury. *See* Duren v. Kunkel, 814 S.W.2d 935 (Mo. 1991) (no strict liability, only negligence claim, for bull having no apparent dangerous propensity). Even though strict liability is the first thought when animals injure or cause loss, do not ignore the defendant's fault supporting a negligence claim. Although strict liability may make easier the proof of the claim, it may also remove from the jury's view and consideration defendant's alarmingly negligent or reckless acts or omissions. Many states have adopted strict-liability or modified strict-liability statutes regarding the owning and keeping of animals. Consider the following case interpreting one of those statutes, and then two state statutes on dog-bite liability.

Pingaro v. Rossi
New Jersey Superior Court, Appellate Division
731 A.2d 523 (N.J. Super. App. Div. 1999)

HAVEY, J. A jury awarded $300,000 in damages to plaintiff Ellen Pingaro, a meter reader for defendant New Jersey Natural Gas Company (NJNG), for injuries she sustained as a result of a dog bite she suffered from a German Shepherd owned by defendant Joseph Rossi. By leave granted, plaintiff and NJNG appeal a post-verdict order granting a new trial as to liability. ... The new trial order permits Rossi to argue plaintiff's comparative negligence by introducing evidence of her failure to heed NJNG's employee safety manual by not taking due care in attempting to read Rossi's meter when warned that a "bad dog" may be present. ...

We reverse. Under the so-called "dog bite" statute, *N.J.S.A.* 4:19-16, Rossi was strictly liable for plaintiff's injuries. There was no evidence adduced during trial supporting a finding that plaintiff incited Rossi's dog or voluntarily and unreasonably exposed herself to a known risk. There is therefore no basis in law to submit the issue of plaintiff's negligence to the jury. ...

During trial plaintiff testified that on June 27, 1996, while performing her meter reading duties for NJNG, she was assigned a route in Beachwood, Ocean County. When she arrived at Rossi's house, her data cap, a hand-held computer, "beeped" a message: "[b]ad dog, knock." The data cap provides the meter reader with the name of the street and location of the meter and at times displays specialized messages pertaining to the customer, such as whether a "bad dog" may be present.

According to plaintiff, she had never been to Rossi's home before. She knocked on Rossi's door but received no answer. She proceeded to the fenced-in backyard, rattled the gate and her keys and yelled "gas company." There was no response. She looked around the backyard for dogs or other animals. After satisfying herself that the yard was clear, she unhooked the gate and walked towards the meter. Immediately upon entering the back yard two dogs approached her. One dog, a large German Shepard, jumped up, knocked her down and bit her on both arms, legs and head. She subdued the dog by hitting it with her flashlight, exited the yard and called for help. A nearby construction worker summoned an ambulance which took her to Community Medical Center where she received numerous stitches and was released later that afternoon. ...

Rossi testified that the dog which attacked plaintiff was kept fenced in his backyard. The only gate to the backyard was the gate utilized by plaintiff in entering the yard. He stated that a large "Beware of Dog" sign was posted on the gate.

According to Rossi, over the course of ten years he had spoken with several meter readers about his dog and told them they should not enter his yard if no one was home. The meter readers responded that they would comply with his request. Rossi noted that this arrangement had worked for over ten years, and when he was not at home the meter readers would estimate his bill, leave a card for him to mail in or come back at a later date. ...

The so-called "dog bite" statute, *N.J.S.A.* 4:19-16, reads in pertinent part: "The owner of any dog which shall bite a person while such person is on or in a public place, or lawfully on or in a private place, including the property of the owner of the dog, shall be liable for such damages as may be suffered by the person bitten, regardless of the former viciousness of such dog or the owner's knowledge of such viciousness."

There is no question that plaintiff fulfilled the three elements necessary to establish Rossi's liability under the statute. Rossi was the owner of the dog, the dog bit plaintiff and the bite occurred while plaintiff was lawfully on Rossi's property. [C] Satisfaction of the elements of the statute imposes strict liability upon Rossi for damages sustained by plaintiff. ...

Here, it is conceded that plaintiff did not provoke Rossi's dog. Further, plaintiff hardly entered the yard knowing that the "bad dog" was present and voluntarily exposed herself to the danger of being attacked by it. She did not deliberately and unreasonably encounter the dog, knowing that it was dangerous. Although she had been alerted that a "bad dog" may be present, when she arrived at the Rossi residence she saw no signs of the dog. She knocked on the door, rattled the gate and her keys and shouted "gas company." Only when there was no evidence of the presence of the "bad dog" did she enter the yard where she was suddenly attacked by it. That "encounter" was hardly deliberate or voluntary. ...

Reversed and remanded for a new trial on damages[for the erroneous admission of evidence of prior dog bites, that may have unduly prejudiced and inflamed the jury].

MICH. COMP. L §287.351. Injuries by dogs; liability of owners
(1) If a dog bites a person, without provocation while the person is on public property, or lawfully on private property, including the property of the owner of the dog, the owner of the dog shall be liable for any damages suffered by the person bitten, regardless of the former viciousness of the dog or the owner's knowledge of such viciousness.
(2) A person is lawfully on the private property of the owner of the dog within the meaning of this act if the person is on the owner's property in the performance of any duty imposed upon him or her by the laws of this state or by the laws or postal regulations of the United States, or if the person is on the owner's property as an invitee or licensee of the person lawfully in possession of the property unless said person has gained lawful entry upon the premises for the purpose of an unlawful or criminal act.

Fla. Stat. Ann. §767.04. Dog owner's liability for damages to persons bitten
The owner of any dog that bites any person while such person is on or in a public place, or lawfully on or in a private place, including the property of the owner of the dog, is

liable for damages suffered by persons bitten, regardless of the former viciousness of the dog or the owners' knowledge of such viciousness. However, any negligence on the part of the person bitten that is a proximate cause of the biting incident reduces the liability of the owner of the dog by the percentage that the bitten person's negligence contributed to the biting incident. A person is lawfully upon private property of such owner within the meaning of this act when the person is on such property in the performance of any duty imposed upon him or her by the laws of this state or by the laws or postal regulations of the United States, or when the person is on such property upon invitation, expressed or implied, of the owner. However, the owner is not liable, except as to a person under the age of 6, or unless the damages are proximately caused by a negligent act or omission of the owner, if at the time of any such injury the owner had displayed in a prominent place on his or her premises a sign easily readable including the words "Bad Dog." The remedy provided by this section is in addition to and cumulative with any other remedy provided by statute or common law.

Skills

Dog-bite claims are relatively common sources of litigation for torts practitioners. Homeowner's liability insurance is commonly the fund out of which dog-bite liability claims are paid. In which of the following cases would there be liability under the above case and statutes?

A Homeowner, when pit bull dog owned by upstairs tenant broke chain in yard, ran after mail carrier, and bit mail carrier on face and throat while mail carrier tried to hide between screen door and inside door of neighboring residence.

B Homeowner, when Rottweiler dog owned by adult daughter bit visiting five-year-old child on face after knocking over child and standing over her when she tried to pet it. Adult daughter dog-owner kept dog with homeowner on weekends when adult daughter was traveling.

C Homeowner, when Bull Mastiff dog owned by adult daughter escaped from home, ran across several yards, and bit teenage child playing in own yard while child stood still rather than run like other children. Adult daughter dog-owner kept dog with homeowner more or less permanently.

D Homeowner, when Rottweiler dog owned by homeowner's minor children bit neighbor's teenage child on leg and arm when neighbor's child rode bicycle past homeowner's residence, and dog broke free from leash held by minor child of homeowner.

E Homeowner, when Labrador Retriever dog owned by homeowner, bolted from yard to chase passing road-touring bicyclist, and dog knocked bicyclist from bike causing bicyclist to break his arm and clavicle. City has leash law.

INQUIRY

Propensities. In common-law states where plaintiff must prove the owner's knowledge of the pet animal's abnormally vicious propensities, how would you do so? *See* Zarek v. Fredericks, 138 F.2d 689 (3d Cir. 1943) (owner always accompanied dog that snarled at guests); Perkins v. Drury, 57 N.M. 269, 258 P.2d 379 (1953) (owner warned children to stay away from dog); Federickson v. Kepner, 82 Cal. App.2d 905, 187 P.2d 800 (1947) (owner used dog as watch dog and kept it tied). Is proving the animal's vicious *breed* enough to establish the owner's knowledge of the animal's vicious *propensities*? *See* Montiero v. Silver Lake, 813 A.2d 978 (R.I. 2003) (no—pit bull); Carter v. Metro North Assocs., 255 A.D.2d 251, 680 N.Y.S.2d 239 (1998) (same); *cf.* Poznanski v. Horvath, 788 N.E.2d 1255 (Ind. 2003) (although breed may be relevant, mixed-breed sheepdog is not of vicious breed). What is a vicious or dangerous propensity? *See* Bauman v. Auch, 539 N.W.2d 320 (S.D. 1995) (horse's flighty nature sufficient to take strict-liability claim to jury on dangerous propensity); Restatement (Second) of Torts §509, Comment c (1977) (dog's playfulness may constitute danger subjecting owner to strict liability). Can an animal that is naturally dangerous but no more dangerous than others of its kind, satisfy the dangerous-propensity element? The cases and secondary authorities suggest that the propensity must be abnormal to the animal's class. *See* Maura v. Randall, 705 A.2d 334 (Md. App.) (knowledge of propensity of Rottweiler breed toward violence is not sufficient to establish knowledge as to propensities of individual dog of that breed), *cert. denied*, 709 A.2d 140 (Md. 1998); Duren, *supra* (bull not within strict-liability class).

Statutes. The two dog-bite statutes shown above, and others like them, *see* Wis. Stat. §174.02(1)(a) (2001), eliminate the plaintiff's need to prove knowledge of the animal's abnormally vicious propensities. *See also* Wis. Stat. §174.02(1)(b) (2001) (doubling damages for knowledge that dog previously injured another). In those states that have no statute, courts are reluctant to alter the common-law requirement that the owner know the animal's abnormally vicious propensities. *See* Gerhtz v. Batteen, 620 N.W.2d 775 (S.D. 2001). Where strict liability is not available by common law or statute, how will the animal owner's violation of a leash or muzzling law affect the owner's liability? The statute or ordinance may establish a standard of care for a negligence action, and the violation may be negligence per se or provide a presumption or inference of negligence. *See* Wistafka v. Grotowski, 205 Ill. App. 529 (1917) (negligence per se). What if the owner violated the muzzle or leash statute or ordinance, but the violation had nothing to do with the animal-caused injury? Kennet v. Sossnitz, 260 App. Div. 759, 23 N.Y.S.2d 961 (1940) *affd.*, 286 N.Y. 623, 36 N.E.2d 459 (1941) (violation inapplicable and plaintiff must prove negligence otherwise). Can a statute that abolishes strict liability for animal injuries where the owner displays a warning sign, protect an owner who invites a person to ignore the sign? *See* Noble v. Yorke, 490 So.2d 29 (Fla. 1986) (no—statute inapplicable). Does a property owner owe a tenant the duty to warn the tenant that another tenant has a pit bull? *See* Wylie v. Gresch, 191 Cal. App.3d 12, 236 Cal. Rptr. 552 (1987) (no).

B. Abnormally Dangerous Activities

OBJECTIVE: Given various unusual activities causing injury under varying circumstances, apply the strict liability rules for abnormally dangerous activities to determine those for which there is liability, consistent with the law reflected in this section of the text.

Case Study: Over neighborhood opposition, a corporation won a court battle for the right to erect a radio tower adjacent to a subdivision. High winds one night during the tower's construction toppled a portion of the tower, damaging three residences. State safety and police investigations determined that the tower's fall was due to a combination of the high winds and vandalism, absolving the corporation and its contractors of wrongdoing. ***Discuss and evaluate the homeowners' strict-liability claims for an abnormally dangerous activity, assuming that the jurisdiction's law of strict liability is unclear.***

Most states recognize *Rylands*-style strict liability for abnormally dangerous activities, in either the natural-nonnatural Restatement (First) ultrahazardous-activity form or the Restatement (Second) factors form. *See* Klein v. Pyrodyne Corp., 117 Wash.2d 1, 810 P.2d 917 (Wash. 1991) (adopting Restatement (Second) approach to determine that fireworks show was an abnormally dangerous activity); Yukon Equipment, Inc. v. Fireman's Fund Ins. Co., 585 P.2d 1206 (Alaska 1978) (rejecting Restatement (Second) approach as too much like negligence and imposing strict liability on basis of Restatement (First) consideration of ultrahazardous nature of activity); Cities Service Co. v. State, 312 So.2d 799, 801 (Fla. App. 1975) ("The doctrine of Rylands v. Fletcher should be applied in Florida."). Where courts recognize the *Rylands* form of strict-liability, they also hold that the judge, not the jury, decides whether strict liability is available for the particular claim—whether the activity was abnormally dangerous. *See* Chambers v. City of Helena, Montana, 49 P.3d 587 (Mont. 2002); Restatement (Second) of Torts §520, Comment *l* (1965). Not all states recognize the *Rylands* form of strict liability. Some states expressly reject strict liability for abnormally dangerous activities. *See* Turner v. Big Lake Oil Co., 128 Tex. 155, 96 S.W.2d 221, (Tex. 1936); *see also* Jones v. Texaco, Inc., 945 F. Supp. 1037 (S.D. Tex. 1996) (acknowledging that Texas continues to reject the Restatement (Second) of Torts §520's strict-liability formulation). Some courts, following the Restatement (Second) of Torts §521, reject strict liability where public duty requires the abnormally dangerous activity—including for common carriers. *But see* National Steel Service Ctr., Inc. v. Gibbons, 319 N.W.2d 269 (Iowa 1982) (refusing to recognize the common-carrier exception). Consider the following case as an illustration of the strict-liability test's application and for how it explores and gives context to strict liability's justification.

Siegler v. Kuhlman
Washington Supreme Court
81 Wash.2d 448, 502 P.2d 1181 (1972)

HALE, J. Seventeen-year-old Carol J. House died in the flames of a gasoline explosion when her car encountered a pool of thousands of gallons of spilled gasoline. She was driving home from her after-school job in the early evening of November 22, 1967, along Capitol Lake Drive in Olympia.... There was a slight impact with some object, a muffled explosion, and then searing flames from gasoline pouring out of an overturned trailer tank engulfed her car. The result of the explosion is clear, but the real causes of what happened will remain something of an eternal mystery.

Aaron L. Kuhlman had been a truck driver for nearly 11 years after he completed the tenth grade in high school and after he had worked at other jobs for a few years. He had been driving for Pacific Intermountain Express for about 4 months, usually the night shift out of the Texaco bulk plant in Tumwater. That evening of November 22nd, he was scheduled to drive a gasoline truck and trailer unit, fully loaded with gasoline, from Tumwater to Port Angeles. Before leaving the Texaco plant, he inspected the trailer, checking the lights, hitch, air hoses and tires. Finding nothing wrong, he then set out, driving the fully loaded truck tank and trailer tank, stopping briefly at the Trail's End Cafe for a cup of coffee. It was just a few minutes after 6 p.m., and dark, but the roads were dry when he started the drive to deliver his cargo—3,800 gallons of gasoline in the truck tank and 4,800 gallons of gasoline in the trailer tank. With all vehicle and trailer running lights on, he drove the truck and trailer onto Interstate Highway 5, proceeded north on that freeway at about 50 miles per hour, he said, and took the offramp about 1 mile later to enter Highway 101 at the Capitol Lake interchange. Running downgrade on the offramp, he felt a jerk, looked into his left-hand mirror and then his right-hand mirror to see that the trailer lights were not in place. The trailer was still moving but leaning over hard, he observed, onto its right side. The trailer then came loose. Realizing that the tank trailer had disengaged from his tank truck, he stopped the truck without skidding its tires. He got out and ran back to see that the tank trailer had crashed through a chain-link highway fence and had come to rest upside down on Capitol Lake Drive below. He heard a sound, he said, "like somebody kicking an empty fifty-gallon drum and that is when the fire started." The fire spread, he thought, about 100 feet down the road.

... When the trailer landed upside down on Capitol Lake Drive, its lights were out, and it was unilluminated when Carol House's car in one way or another ignited the spilled gasoline.

Carol House was burned to death in the flames. There was no evidence of impact on the vehicle she had driven, Kuhlman said, except that the left front headlight was broken.

Why the tank trailer disengaged and catapulted off the freeway down through a chain-link fence to land upside down on Capitol Lake Drive below remains a mystery. What caused it to separate from the truck towing it, despite many theories offered in explanation, is still an enigma. ...

The jury apparently found that defendants had met and overcome the charges of negligence. ...

From a judgment entered upon a verdict for defendants, plaintiff appealed to the Court of Appeals which affirmed. [C] We granted review ([c]), and reverse.

In the Court of Appeals, the principal claim of error was directed to the trial court's refusal to give an instruction on res ipsa loquitur, and we think that claim of error well taken. Our reasons for ruling that an instruction on res ipsa loquitur should have been given and that an inference of negligence could have been drawn from the event are found, we believe, in our [cited case law.] We think, therefore, that plaintiff was entitled to an instruction permitting the jury to infer negligence from the occurrence.

But there exists here an even more impelling basis for liability in this case than its derivation by allowable inference of fact under the res ipsa loquitur doctrine, and that is the proposition of strict liability arising as a matter of law from all of the circumstances of the event.

Strict liablity is not a novel concept; it is at least as old as Fletcher v. Rylands, L.R. 1 Ex. 265, 278 (1866), affirmed, House of Lords, 3 H.L. 330 (1868). In that famous case, where water impounded in a reservoir on defendant's property escaped and damaged neighboring coal mines, the landowner who had impounded the water was held liable without proof of fault or negligence. Acknowledging a distinction between the natural and nonnatural use of land, and holding the maintenance of a reservoir to be a nonnatural use, the Court of Exchequer Chamber imposed a rule of strict liability on the landowner. ...

... The basic principles supporting the Fletcher doctrine, we think, control the transportation of gasoline as freight along the public highways the same as it does the impounding of waters and for largely the same reasons. [C]

In many respects, hauling gasoline as freight is no more unusual, but more dangerous, than collecting water. When gasoline is carried as cargo—as distinguished from fuel for the carrier vehicle—it takes on uniquely hazardous characteristics, as does water impounded in large quantities. Dangerous in itself, gasoline develops even greater potential for harm when carried as freight—extraordinary dangers deriving from sheer quantity, bulk and weight, which enormously multiply its hazardous properties. And the very hazards inhering from the size of the load, its bulk or quantity and its movement along the highways presents another reason for application of the Fletcher v. Rylands, Supra, rule not present in the impounding of large quantities of water—the likely destruction of cogent evidence from which negligence or want of it may be proved or disproved. It is quite probable that the most important ingredients of proof will be lost in a gasoline explosion and fire. Gasoline is always dangerous whether kept in large or small quantities because of its volatility, inflammability and explosiveness. But when several thousand gallons of it are allowed to spill across a public highway—that is, if, while in transit as freight, it is not kept impounded—the hazards to third persons are so great as to be almost beyond calculation. As a consequence of its escape from impoundment and subsequent explosion and ignition, the evidence in a very high percentage of instances will be destroyed, and the reasons for and causes contributing to its escape will quite likely be lost in the searing flames and explosions. ...

The rule of strict liability rests not only upon the ultimate idea of rectifying a wrong and putting the burden where it should belong as a matter of abstract justice, that is, upon the one of the two innocent parties whose acts instigated or made the harm possible, but it also rests on problems of proof.... .

Thus, the reasons for applying a rule of strict liability obtain in this case. We have a situation where a highly flammable, volatile and explosive substance is being carried at a comparatively high rate of speed, in great and dangerous quantities as cargo upon the public highways, subject to all of the hazards of high-speed traffic, multiplied by the great dangers inherent in the volatile and explosive nature of the substance, and multiplied again by the quantity and size of the load. Then we have the added dangers of ignition and explosion generated when a load of this size, that is, about 5,000 gallons of gasoline, breaks its container and, cascading from it, spreads over the highway so as to release an invisible but highly volatile and explosive vapor above it.

Danger from great quantities of gasoline spilled upon the public highway is extreme and extraordinary, for any spark, flame or appreciable heat is likely to ignite it. The incandescent filaments from a broken automobile headlight, a spark from the heat of a tailpipe, a lighted cigarette in the hands of a driver or passenger, the hot coals from a smoker's pipe or cigar, and the many hot and sparking spots and units of an automobile motor from exhaust to generator could readily ignite the vapor cloud gathered above a highway from 5,000 gallons of spilled gasoline. Any automobile passing through the vapors could readily have produced the flames and explosions which killed the young woman in this case and without the provable intervening negligence of those who loaded and serviced the carrier and the driver who operated it. Even the most prudent and careful motorist, coming unexpectedly and without warning upon this gasoline pool and vapor, could have driven into it and ignited a holocaust without knowledge of the danger and without leaving a trace of what happened to set off the explosion and light the searing flames. ...

The rule of strict liability, when applied to an abnormally dangerous activity, as stated in the Restatement (Second) of Torts s 519 (Tent.Draft No. 10, 1964), was adopted as the rule of decision in this state.... .

Transporting gasoline as freight by truck along the public highways and streets is obviously an activity involving a high degree of risk; it is a risk of great harm and injury; it creates dangers that cannot be eliminated by the exercise of reasonable care. That gasoline cannot be practicably transported except upon the public highways does not decrease the abnormally high risk arising from its transportation. Nor will the exercise of due and reasonable care assure protection to the public from the disastrous consequences of concealed or latent mechanical or metallurgical defects in the carrier's equipment, from the negligence of third parties, from latent defects in the highways and streets, and from all of the other hazards not generally disclosed or guarded against by reasonable care, prudence and foresight. Hauling gasoline in great quantities as freight, we think, is an activity that calls for the application of principles of strict liability.

The case is therefore reversed and remanded to the trial court for trial to the jury on the sole issue of damages.

Practice

"I'm so sorry for being here," the potential client was telling the personal-injury lawyer on the client's first visit to the lawyer's office, "My pastor says that people who sue are irresponsible money-grubbers. I don't want you to think that I'm like *those people*." The lawyer had heard the pastor tell lawyer jokes and rail against frivolous lawsuits. The lawyer felt strange that someone so committed to caring and healing would denigrate the tort-law system that peacefully promotes and achieves those purposes, while denigrating the professionals who devote their careers to care and compensation, and discourage the vulnerable injured from resorting to their aid. "But I've lost my job and marriage, am about to lose my house, and may lose my children because of my accident," the woman continued, ending, "Can't you help me?" Unfortunately, the lawyer could not help because the woman's delay had cost her the legal right to pursue first- and third-party claims relating to her motor-vehicle-accident injury. On the lawyer's drive home that evening, he pondered whether he should talk to the pastor about how his insensitivity was affecting his community and membership.

INQUIRY

Justification. The *Siegler* case represents a leading opinion on imposing strict liability under Section 520 of the Restatement (Second). As *Siegler* suggests, strict liability has both moral and economic justifications. The moral justifications begin with the understanding that preservation of human dignity is an intrinsic good—the rich basis of tort law. *Intrinsic* means that the good does not require other justification. Thus, an entity conducting an abnormally dangerous activity that destroys human life ought, as a matter of fitness and moral right, to compensate for that life's destruction. Defining inherent goods is neither subjective nor a circular proposition. Given that law evaluates human activity, law should base evaluation on human prospering. Preserving human dignity is necessary to human prospering. Defining human goods enables law to articulate successively more-detailed policies and rules consistent with those goods—as ends in themselves. In the case of strict liability, the defendant's fault is immaterial because the defendant could have avoided the activity or insured against loss. The conduct of the activity alone justifies liability because of the responsibility owed the community the endeavor adversely affects. The economic rationale supporting this moral justification has to do with internalizing enterprise costs. If markets for enterprise goods are to reflect true costs, then the enterprise, not others outside the enterprise, should bear the costs—whether the enterprise can reduce the risk of harm or not. To have the community bear the loss is to externalize the cost to a population outside of the enterprise that conducts and profits from the risk-creating activity. *See* Weston, *The Metaphysics of Modern Tort Theory*, 28 Val. U. L.Rev. 919 (1994); Epstein, *Causation and Corrective Justice: A Reply to Two Critics*, 8 J. Legal Stud. 477 (1979); Epstein, *A Theory of Strict Liability*, 2 J. Legal Stud. 151 (1973); Fletcher, *Fairness and Utility in Tort Theory*, 85 Harv. L.Rev. 537 (1972).

Utilitarianism. Scholars disagree, though, whether morality or economics justify strict liability. Judge Richard Posner, an economist, prolific legal scholar, and former judge of the United States Seventh Circuit Court of Appeals, disfavors strict liability including especially its moral aspects. Richard Posner, *Strict Liability: A Comment*, 2 J. Legal Stud. 205. Judge Posner, in his 1999 book *The Problematics of Moral and Legal Theory* and other writings, claims that the moral principles that the Declaration of Independence and Constitution reflect are useless and spurious, and have nothing to offer judges and legal scholars. He considers statements like "murder is wrong" to be tautological rather than synthetic and informative. He prefers (in his own words) a pragmatically "vague utilitarianism" and "diluted versions of moral subjectivism, moral skepticism, and noncognitivism." Thus, we should accept harms that have social benefit because they maximize overall wealth even if they destroy individual autonomy and liberty. In holding to this philosophy, Judge Posner considers economic and evolutionary-biology theory to be "beautiful and useful," that he and others may prefer Nietzsche's inegalitarian warrior society to our own "on aesthetic grounds impossible to refute"—and that lawyers have little to offer the paying public. *Id.* at xii, 12, 20, 187. Consider then another strict-liability case opinion by Judge Posner.

Indiana Harbor Belt R. Co. v. American Cyanamid Co.
United States Court of Appeals, Seventh Circuit
916 F.2d 1174 (7th Cir. 1990)

POSNER, J. American Cyanamid Company, the defendant in this diversity tort suit governed by Illinois law, is a major manufacturer of chemicals, including acrylonitrile, a chemical used in large quantities in making acrylic fibers, plastics, dyes, pharmaceutical chemicals, and other intermediate and final goods. On January 2, 1979, at its manufacturing plant in Louisiana, Cyanamid loaded 20,000 gallons of liquid acrylonitrile into a railroad tank car that it had leased from the North American Car Corporation. The next day, a train of the Missouri Pacific Railroad picked up the car at Cyanamid's siding. The car's ultimate destination was a Cyanamid plant in New Jersey served by Conrail rather than by Missouri Pacific. The Missouri Pacific train carried the car north to the Blue Island railroad yard of Indiana Harbor Belt Railroad, the plaintiff in this case, a small switching line that has a contract with Conrail to switch cars from other lines to Conrail, in this case for travel east. The Blue Island yard is in the Village of Riverdale, which is just south of Chicago and part of the Chicago metropolitan area.

The car arrived in the Blue Island yard on the morning of January 9, 1979. Several hours after it arrived, employees of the switching line noticed fluid gushing from the bottom outlet of the car. The lid on the outlet was broken. After two hours, the line's supervisor of equipment was able to stop the leak by closing a shut-off valve controlled from the top of the car. No one was sure at the time just how much of the contents of the car had leaked, but it was feared that all 20,000 gallons had, and since acrylonitrile is flammable at a temperature of 30° Fahrenheit or above, highly toxic, and possibly carcinogenic (*Acrylonitrile,* 9 International Toxicity Update, no. 3, May-June 1989, at 2, 4), the local authorities ordered the homes near the yard evacuated. The evacuation lasted only a few hours, until the car was moved to a remote part of the yard and it was discovered that only about a quarter of the acrylonitrile had leaked. Concerned nevertheless that there had been some contamination of soil and water, the Illinois Department of Environmental Protection ordered the switching line to take decontamination measures that cost the line $981,022.75, which it sought to recover by this suit.

One count ... asserts that the transportation of acrylonitrile in bulk through the Chicago metropolitan area is an abnormally dangerous activity, for the consequences of which the shipper (Cyanamid) is strictly liable to the switching line, which bore the financial brunt of those consequences because of the decontamination measures that it was forced to take. ...

The parties agree that the question whether placing acrylonitrile in a rail shipment that will pass through a metropolitan area subjects the shipper to strict liability is, as recommended in Restatement (Second) of Torts § 520, comment *l* (1977), a question of law, so that we owe no particular deference to the conclusion of the district court. They also agree ... that the Supreme Court of Illinois would treat as authoritative the provisions of the Restatement governing abnormally dangerous activities. The key provision is section 520, which sets forth six factors to be considered in deciding whether an activity is abnormally dangerous and the actor therefore strictly liable.

The roots of section 520 are in nineteenth-century cases. The most famous one is *Rylands v. Fletcher,* 1 Ex. 265, aff'd, L.R. 3 H.L. 300 (1868), but a more illuminating one in the present context is *Guille v. Swan,* 19 Johns. (N.Y.) 381 (1822). A man took off in a hot-air balloon and landed, without intending to, in a vegetable garden in New York City. A crowd that had been anxiously watching his involuntary descent trampled the vegetables in their endeavor to rescue him when he landed. The owner of the garden sued the balloonist for the resulting damage, and won. Yet the balloonist had not been careless. In the then state of ballooning it was impossible to make a pinpoint landing.

Guille is a paradigmatic case for strict liability. (a) The risk (probability) of harm was great, and (b) the harm that would ensue if the risk materialized could be, although luckily was not, great (the balloonist could have crashed into the crowd rather than into the vegetables). The confluence of these two factors established the urgency of seeking to prevent such accidents. (c) Yet such accidents could not be prevented by the exercise of due care; the technology of care in ballooning was insufficiently developed. (d) The activity was not a matter of common usage, so there was no presumption that it was a highly valuable activity despite its unavoidable riskiness. (e) The activity was inappropriate to the place in which it took place—densely populated New York City. The risk of serious harm to others (other than the balloonist himself, that is) could have been reduced by shifting the activity to the sparsely inhabited areas that surrounded the city in those days. (f) Reinforcing (d), the value to the community of the activity of recreational ballooning did not appear to be great enough to offset its unavoidable risks.

These are, of course, the six factors in section 520. ...

Against this background we turn to the particulars of acrylonitrile. Acrylonitrile is one of a large number of chemicals that are hazardous in the sense of being flammable, toxic, or both; acrylonitrile is both, as are many others. A table in the record, drawn from Glickman & Harvey, Statistical Trends in Railroad Hazardous Material Safety, 1978 to 1984, at pp. 63-65 (Draft Final Report to the Environmental & Hazardous Material Studies Division of the Association of American Railroads, April 1986) (tab. 4.1), contains a list of the 125 hazardous materials that are shipped in highest volume on the nation's railroads. Acrylonitrile is the fifty-third most hazardous on the list. ... The plaintiff's lawyer acknowledged at argument that the logic of the district court's opinion dictated strict liability for all 52 materials that rank higher than acrylonitrile on the list, and quite possibly for the 72 that rank lower as well, since all are hazardous if spilled in quantity while being shipped by rail. Every shipper of any of these materials would therefore be strictly liable for the consequences of a spill or other accident that occurred while the material was being shipped through a metropolitan area. The plaintiff's lawyer further acknowledged the irrelevance, on her view of the case, of the fact that Cyanamid had leased and filled the car that spilled the acrylonitrile; all she thought important is that Cyanamid introduced the product into the stream of commerce that happened to pass through the Chicago metropolitan area. Her concession may have been incautious. One might want to distinguish between the shipper who merely places his goods on his loading dock to be picked up by the carrier and the shipper who, as in this case, participates actively in the transportation. But the concession is illustrative of the potential scope of the district court's decision.

No cases recognize so sweeping a liability. Several reject it, though none has facts much like those of the present case. ...

Siegler v. Kuhlman, 81 Wash.2d 448, 502 P.2d 1181 (1972), also imposed strict liability on a transporter of hazardous materials, but the circumstances were again rather special. A gasoline truck blew up, obliterating the plaintiff's decedent and her car. The court emphasized that the explosion had destroyed the evidence necessary to establish whether the accident had been due to negligence; so, unless liability was strict, there would be no liability—and this as the very consequence of the defendant's hazardous activity. [C] ... We shall see that a further distinction of great importance between the present case and *Siegler* is that the defendant there was the transporter, and here it is the shipper. ...

... [T]he storer (like the transporter, as in *Siegler*) has more control than the shipper.

So we can get little help from precedent, and might as well apply section 520 to the acrylonitrile problem from the ground up. To begin with, we have been given no reason, whether the reason in *Siegler* or any other, for believing that a negligence regime is not perfectly adequate to remedy and deter, at reasonable cost, the accidental spillage of acrylonitrile from rail cars. [C] Acrylonitrile could explode and destroy evidence, but of course did not here, making imposition of strict liability on the theory of the *Siegler* decision premature. More important, although acrylonitrile is flammable even at relatively low temperatures, and toxic, it is not so corrosive or otherwise destructive that it will eat through or otherwise damage or weaken a tank car's valves although they are maintained with due (which essentially means, with average) care. No one suggests, therefore, that the leak in this case was caused by the *inherent* properties of acrylonitrile. It was caused by carelessness—whether that of the North American Car Corporation in failing to maintain or inspect the car properly, or that of Cyanamid in failing to maintain or inspect it, or that of the Missouri Pacific when it had custody of the car, or that of the switching line itself in failing to notice the ruptured lid, or some combination of these possible failures of care. Accidents that are due to a lack of care can be prevented by taking care; and when a lack of care can (unlike *Siegler*) be shown in court, such accidents are adequately deterred by the threat of liability for negligence.

It is true that the district court purported to find as a fact that there is an inevitable risk of derailment or other calamity in transporting "large quantities of anything." [C] This is not a finding of fact, but a truism: anything can happen. The question is, how likely is this type of accident if the actor uses due care? For all that appears from the record of the case or any other sources of information that we have found, if a tank car is carefully maintained the danger of a spill of acrylonitrile is negligible. If this is right, there is no compelling reason to move to a regime of strict liability, especially one that might embrace all other hazardous materials shipped by rail as well. This also means, however, that the amici curiae who have filed briefs in support of Cyanamid cry wolf in predicting "devastating" effects on the chemical industry if the district court's decision is affirmed. If the vast majority of chemical spills by railroads are preventable by due care, the imposition of strict liability should cause only a slight, not as they argue a substantial, rise in liability insurance rates, because the incremental liability should be slight. The amici have momentarily lost sight of the fact that the feasibility of avoiding accidents simply by being careful is an argument *against* strict liability.

This discussion helps to show why *Siegler* is indeed distinguishable even as interpreted in *New Meadows*. There are so many highway hazards that the transportation of gasoline by truck is, or at least might plausibly be thought, inherently dangerous in the sense that a serious danger of accident would remain even if the truckdriver used all due care (though *Hawkins* and other cases are *contra*). Which in turn means, contrary to our earlier suggestion, that the plaintiff really might have difficulty invoking res ipsa loquitur, because a gasoline truck might well blow up without negligence on the part of the driver. The plaintiff in this case has not shown that the danger of a comparable disaster to a tank car filled with acrylonitrile is as great and might have similar consequences for proof of negligence. ...

The district judge and the plaintiff's lawyer make much of the fact that the spill occurred in a densely inhabited metropolitan area. ... But this argument overlooks the fact that, like other transportation networks, the railroad network is a hub-and-spoke system. And the hubs are in metropolitan areas. Chicago is one of the nation's largest railroad hubs. ... With most hazardous chemicals (by volume of shipments) being at least as hazardous as acrylonitrile, it is unlikely—and certainly not demonstrated by the plaintiff—that they can be rerouted around all the metropolitan areas in the country, except at prohibitive cost. Even if it were feasible to reroute them one would hardly expect shippers, as distinct from carriers, to be the firms best situated to do the rerouting. ...

The difference between shipper and carrier points to a deep flaw in the plaintiff's case. Unlike *Guille,* and unlike *Siegler,* and unlike the storage cases, beginning with

Rylands itself, here it is not the actors—that is, the transporters of acrylonitrile and other chemicals—but the manufacturers, who are sought to be held strictly liable. [C] A shipper can in the bill of lading designate the route of his shipment if he likes, 49 U.S.C. § 11710(a)(1), but is it realistic to suppose that shippers will become students of railroading in order to lay out the safest route by which to ship their goods? Anyway, rerouting is no panacea. Often it will increase the length of the journey, or compel the use of poorer track, or both. When this happens, the probability of an accident is increased, even if the consequences of an accident if one occurs are reduced; so the expected accident cost, being the product of the probability of an accident and the harm if the accident occurs, may rise. [C] It is easy to see how the accident in this case might have been prevented at reasonable cost by greater care on the part of those who handled the tank car of acrylonitrile. It is difficult to see how it might have been prevented at reasonable cost by a change in the activity of transporting the chemical. This is therefore not an apt case for strict liability. ...

The relevant activity is transportation, not manufacturing and shipping. This essential distinction the plaintiff ignores. But even if the defendant is treated as a transporter and not merely a shipper, the plaintiff has not shown that the transportation of acrylonitrile in bulk by rail through populated areas is so hazardous an activity, even when due care is exercised, that the law should seek to create (perhaps quixotically) incentives to relocate the activity to nonpopulated areas, or to reduce the scale of the activity, or to switch to transporting acrylonitrile by road rather than by rail, perhaps to set the stage for a replay of *Siegler v. Kuhlman*. It is no more realistic to propose to reroute the shipment of all hazardous materials around Chicago than it is to propose the relocation of homes adjacent to the Blue Island switching yard to more distant suburbs. It may be less realistic. Brutal though it may seem to say it, the inappropriate use to which land is being put in the Blue Island yard and neighborhood may be, not the transportation of hazardous chemicals, but residential living. The analogy is to building your home between the runways at O'Hare.

The briefs hew closely to the Restatement, whose approach to the issue of strict liability is mainly *allocative* rather than *distributive*. By this we mean that the emphasis is on picking a liability regime (negligence or strict liability) that will control the particular class of accidents in question most effectively, rather than on finding the deepest pocket and placing liability there. At argument, however, the plaintiff's lawyer invoked distributive considerations by pointing out that Cyanamid is a huge firm and the Indiana Harbor Belt Railroad a fifty-mile-long switching line that almost went broke in the winter of 1979, when the accident occurred. Well, so what? A corporation is not a living person but a set of contracts the terms of which determine who will bear the brunt of liability. Tracing the incidence of a cost is a complex undertaking which the plaintiff sensibly has made no effort to assume, since its legal relevance would be dubious. We add only that however small the plaintiff may be, it has mighty parents: it is a jointly owned subsidiary of Conrail and the Soo line.

The case for strict liability has not been made. Not in this suit in any event. ...

The judgment is reversed (with no award of costs in this court) and the case remanded for further proceedings, consistent with this opinion, on the plaintiff's claim for negligence.

INQUIRY

Environmental Claims. State and federal environmental laws today govern claims for damage due to environmental hazards, like the Superfund Act, 42 U.S.C. §9607(a), providing for the strict liability of the polluter and owners of polluted lands. Setting aside statutory liability for environmental hazards, the easier cases in which to apply *Rylands* strict liability are probably those, like *Rylands*, that involve sudden escape of impounded hazardous substances. *See* Department of Environmental Protection v. Ventron Corp., 94 N.J. 473, 468 A.2d 150 (1983) (strict liability for damage due to toxic mercury waste); Cities Serice Co. v. State, 312 So.2d 799 (Fla. App. 1975) (strict liability for loss due to impoundment of phosphate slime). Should the law offer strict liability for damage due to percolation (rather than sudden escape) of toxic materials? *See* Yommer v. McKenzie, 255 Md. 220, 257 A.2d 138 (1969) (yes, for gasoline); Iverson v. Vint, 243 Iowa 949, 54 N.W.2d 494 (1952) (yes, for molasses). Should the buyer of land have a strict-liability claim against the land's seller who allowed environmental hazards to percolate into the sold land? *See* T & E Indus., Inc. v. Safety Light Corp., 123 N.J. 371, 587 A.2d 1249 (1991) (yes, strict liability not only as to adjoining landowners but to purchasers of the originating land).

Explosives. Most cases allow strict liability for the use of explosives (blasting cases). *See* Otero v. Burgess, 84 N.M. 575, 505 P.2d 1251 (1973). Should there be strict liability for the *storage* of explosives? Some courts would impose strict liability only for use, not storage, of explosives. *But see* Chavez v. Southern Pac. Transp. Co., 413 F. Supp. 1203 (E.D. Cal. 1976) (strict liability for storing bombs in railroad cars near town). What about storage of other highly combustible materials not intended for use as explosives? *See* Northglenn v. Chevron USA, Inc., 519 F. Supp. 515 (D. Colo. 1981) (strict liability for damage related to storing gasoline in underground tanks near residential area); *but see* Hudson v. Peavey Oil Co., 279 Or. 3, 566 P.2d 175 (1977) (no strict liability for gasoline storage). What about fireworks displays? *See* Klein v. Pyrodyne Corp., 117 Wash.2d 1, 810 P.2d 917 (1991) (strict liability); *but see* Cadena v. Chicago Fireworks Mfg. Co., 297 Ill. App.3d 945, 697 N.E.2d 802 (1998) (no strict liability). What about crop dusting? *See* Langan v. Valicopters, Inc., 88 Wash.2d 855, 567 P.2d 218 (1977) (strict liability); Loe v. Lenhardt, 227 Or. 242, 362 P.2d 312 (1961) (strict liability); *but see* Lawler v. Skelton, 241 Miss. 274, 130 So.2d 565 (1961) (no strict liability). Do you see any pattern here—if only in the divided cases?

Ethics

Although law practice has felt some effects of the globalization of the United States economy, tort-law practice by its nature—involving local accidents and their local effects—tends to be less global and more regional and local. Because law licensing is a state function, tort-law practice has generally been intra-state rather than inter-state. Most tort lawyers practice in a single state. Yet tort lawyers take depositions in other states. May a lawyer who has a tort case pending in one state in which the lawyer is licensed take a deposition in that case in another state in which the lawyer is *not* licensed—or is that the unauthorized practice of law? Rule 5.5(c) of the ABA Model Rules of Professional Conduct permits the lawyer to take the deposition (to "provide legal services on a temporary basis")—but not, for example, to file a new case in the state in which the lawyer holds no license. Torts lawyers who wish to file a case in a state in which they have no license may seek pro-hac-vice (one-time-only) admission, seek permanent admission (satisfying all requirements including taking the bar exam if necessary), or refer the case to a lawyer holding a license in that state.

Non-Obvious Risks. Other strict-liability cases involve somewhat less obvious risks than those connected with explosives and other hazardous materials. Should strict liability exist for injury from a stray bullet richocheting from a firearm range? *See* Miller v. Civil Constructors, Inc., 272 Ill. App.3d 263, 651 N.E.2d 239 (1995) (no—not if firearm range is near a quarry). What about strict liability for one who accidentally kills another with carbon monoxide poisoning while killing himself? *See* Laterra v. Treaster, 17 Kan. App.2d 714, 844 P.2d 724 (1992) (strict liability). For injury from not repairing or replacing a frayed electrical cord? *See* Brown v. Sears, Roebuck & Co., 136 Ariz. 556, 667 P.2d 750 (1983) (no strict liability). For ground damage from commercial-airline crashes? *See* Crosby v. Cox Aircraft Co., 109 Wash.2d 581, 746 P.2d 1198 (1987) (negligence, not strict liability). For loss and injury from the transmission of electricity and natural gas? *See* Voelker v. Delmarva Power & Light Co., 727 F. Supp. 991 (D. Md. 1989) (no strict liability as matter of common usage); *cf.* 42 U.S.C. §2210 (Price-Anderson Act providing for limited atomic-energy damages). For drunk driving? *See* Goodwin v. Reilley, 176 Cal. App.3d 86, 221 Cal. Rptr. 374 (1985) (no strict liability). Again, do you see a pattern—perhaps in the activity's commonness?

Beyond Land. The cases generally restrict strict liability to abnormally dangerous uses of land. Within that restriction, law shows considerable variety as to the activities for which strict liability may be available. *See* Koos v. Roth, 293 Or. 670, 652 P.2d 1255 (1982) (spreading field-fire of abnormal proportion); Smith v. Lockheed Propulsion Co., 247 Cal. App.2d 774, 56 Cal. Rptr. 128 (1967) (ground vibration from rocket testing); Caporale v. C.W. Blakeslee & Sons, Inc., 149 Conn. 79, 175 A.2d 561 (1961) (vibration from pile driving); Green v. General Petroleum Corp., 205 Cal. 328, 270 P. 952 (1928) (blow out of oil well). Should Restatement (Second) of Torts §520 strict liability exist for marketing abnormally dangerous products? Courts have generally rejected §520 strict-liability claims for the manufacture and marketing (as distinguished from the use) of dangerous products like guns. *See* Perkins v. F.I.E. Corp., 762 F.2d 1250 (5th Cir. 1985) (no strict liability for small-caliber handgun manufacturers); Kelley v. R.G. Indus., Inc., 304 Md. 124, 497 A.2d 1143 (1985) (no strict liability for handgun manufacturer). What if the user fires the handgun attempting to assassinate a United States president? *See* Delahanty v. Hinckley, 564 A.2d 758 (D.C. 1989) (no strict liability for maker of handgun used to shoot police officer in attempt on President Reagan's life). What about the marketer of fertilizer used to create an explosive with which to destroy a federal building? *See* Gaines-Tabb v. ICI Explosives USA, Inc., 995 F. Supp. 1304 (W.D. Okla. 1996) (no strict liability—Oklahoma City federal building bombing). In all of these cases, distinguish §520 strict liability from strict *products* liability of the kind that requires proof of product defect.

Defenses. The Restatement (Second) of Torts §524 holds that the plaintiff's voluntary and knowing encounter of the risk defends a strict-liability claim, even though under the traditional rule, contributory negligence is not a defense to a strict-liability claim. With the advent of comparative negligence, the more recent Restatement of Apportionment §8 and the Restatement (Third) of Torts: Liability for Physical Harm §25, Comment e (tentative draft no. 1, 2001), each provide that a jury may compare the defendant's strict liability to the plaintiff's comparative negligence to allocate responsibility for the plaintiff's loss. *See* Andrade v. Shiers, 564 So.2d 787

(La. App. 1990) (defendant's strict liability reduced by plaintiff's eighty-percent comparative negligence). Causation can also be an issue in strict-liability cases. *See* Golden v. Amory, 329 Mass. 484, 109 N.E.2d 131 (1952) (hurricane-induced overflow of river constitutes superseding "act of God" to strict-liability claim over maintenance of dike). Consider two cases illustrating type-of-harm and causation limits on §520 strict liability.

Foster v. Preston Mill Co.
Washington Supreme Court
44 Wash.2d 440, 268 P.2d 645 (1954)

HAMLEY, J. Blasting operations conducted by Preston Mill Company frightened mother mink owned by B. W. Foster, and caused the mink to kill their kittens. Foster brought this action against the company to recover damages. His second amended complaint, upon which the case was tried, sets forth a cause of action on the theory of absolute liability... .

After a trial to the court without a jury, judgment was rendered for plaintiff in the sum of $1,953.68. The theory adopted by the court was that, after defendant received notice of the effect which its blasting operations were having upon the mink, it was absolutely liable for all damages of that nature thereafter sustained. ...

Respondent's mink ranch is located in a rural area one and one-half miles east of North Bend, in King county, Washington. The ranch occupies seven and one half acres on which are located seven sheds for growing mink. ...

Appellant and several other companies have been engaged in logging in the adjacent area for more than fifty years. Early in May, 1951, appellant began the construction of a road to gain access to certain timber which it desired to cut. ...

It was necessary to use explosives to build the road. The customary types of explosives were used, and the customary methods of blasting were followed. The most powder used in one shooting was one hundred pounds, and usually the charge was limited to fifty pounds. The procedure used was to set off blasts twice a day—at noon and at the end of the work day.

Roy A. Peterson, the manager of the ranch in 1951, testified that the blasting resulted in "a tremendous vibration, is all. Boxes would rattle on the cages." The mother mink would then run back and forth in their cages and many of them would kill their kittens. Peterson also testified that on two occasions the blasts had broken windows. ...

The primary question presented by appellant's assignments of error is whether, on these facts, the judgment against appellant is sustainable on the theory of absolute liability. ...

There is a division of judicial opinion as to whether the doctrine of absolute liability should apply where the damage from blasting is caused, not by the casting of rocks and debris, but by concussion, vibration, or jarring. [C]

However the authorities may be divided on the point just discussed, they appear to be agreed that strict liability should be confined to consequences which lie within the extraordinary risk whose existence calls for such responsibility. [Cc] This limitation on the doctrine is indicated in the italicized portion of the rule as set forth in Restatement of Torts, supra: "Except as stated in §§ 521-4, one who carries on an ultrahazardous activity is liable to another whose person, land or chattels the actor should recognize as likely to be harmed by the unpreventable miscarringe of the activity for harm resulting thereto *from that which makes the activity ultrahazardous*, although the utmost care is exercised to prevent the harm." (Italics supplied.)

This restriction which has been placed upon the application of the doctrine of absolute liability is based upon considerations of policy. ...

Applying this principle to the case before us, the question comes down to this: Is the risk that any unusual vibration or noise may cause wild animals, which are being raised for commercial purposes, to kill their young, one of the things which make the activity of blasting ultrahazardous?

We have found nothing in the decisional law which would support an affirmative answer to this question. The decided cases, as well as common experience, indicate that the thing which makes blasting ultrahazardous is the risk that property or persons may be damaged or injured by coming into direct contact with flying debris, or by being directly affected by vibrations of the earth or concussions of the air. ...

It is our conclusion that the risk of causing harm of the kind here experienced, as a result of the relatively minor vibration, concussion, and noise from distant blasting, is not the kind of risk which makes the activity of blasting ultrahazardous. The doctrine of absolute liability is therefore inapplicable under the facts of this case, and respondent is not entitled to recover damages.

The judgment is reversed.

Pecan Shoppe of Springfield, Mo., Inc. v. Tri-State Motor Transit Co.
Missouri Court of Appeals
573 S.W.2d 431 (Mo. App. 1978)

FLANIGAN, J. Defendant Tri-State Motor Transit Co. is a motor carrier licensed by the state of Missouri and the Department of Transportation. On September 14, 1970, the union employees of Tri-State went on strike. In the early morning hours of September 30, 1970, a tractor-trailer unit, owned by Tri-State and driven by its non-striking employee John A. Galt, was transporting a load of dynamite, for shipper DuPont Company, from Joplin, Missouri, to a mining site at Boss, Missouri.

As the unit was traveling on Interstate Highway 44 in Greene County, Missouri, it approached an overpass on which stood Bobby Shuler, one of the striking employees. Using a 30-30 rifle, Shuler fired three shots at the unit, thereby causing a "tremendous" explosion which resulted in the death of Galt[fn] and the destruction of the unit. The explosion caused heavy damage to nearby improved land owned by plaintiff Pecan Shoppe of Springfield, Missouri, Inc., on which it conducted a restaurant and service station business.

Plaintiff brought this action for damages against Tri-State.... The jury returned a verdict in favor of Tri-State. Plaintiff appeals.

Plaintiff's principal "point relied on" is that the trial court erred in failing to direct a verdict for plaintiff on the issue of liability. It is plaintiff's position that the doctrine of strict liability was applicable to the admitted facts and that the sole province of the jury was to determine the extent of plaintiff's uncompensated damages and to render the appropriate award. ...

It is the position of Tri-State that the trial court did not err in the manner claimed because "the theory of strict liability does not apply to a common carrier engaged in transporting explosives," and further, that the cause of the explosion "was the intervening criminal act of convicted murderer Bobby Shuler." ...

... Tri-State points out that the Restatement of Torts, Second, ... Section 521 is to the effect that "the rules as to strict liability for abnormally dangerous activities" do not apply if the activity is carried on in pursuance of a public duty imposed upon the actor as a common carrier.[fn] Tri-State advances the alternative argument that the criminal conduct of Shuler serves to exculpate it, even assuming that liability would otherwise attach. ...

... This case, viewed in all of its aspects, seems to be one of first impression and the disposition of this appeal has not been free of difficulty. This court concludes that the trial court did not err in refusing to direct a verdict for the plaintiff. ...

Other jurisdictions have dealt with the liability of a storer or transporter of dangerous substances where the explosion was caused by the intentional misconduct of a third person. [Cc] [The opinion summarized several other opinions refusing to hold the defendant strictly liable where the abnormal danger was realized due to an intentional act.]

On the other hand, even if the immediate cause of plaintiff's injuries was the criminal act of a third person, defendant is not always relieved of liability. [The opinion summarized one case where the defendant was held strictly liable for an abnormal danger realized due to an intentional tort.]

Plaintiff made no showing that Tri-State violated any statute or regulation dealing with the transportation of dynamite. There was nothing unlawful in Tri-State's operation of the unit which exploded.

In order for this court to uphold plaintiff's contention it must adopt the minority view, ... which refuses to recognize the general rule of non-liability of common carriers for explosions occurring in the absence of negligence and elements of nuisance. Plaintiff has cited no authority to support the view that a carrier which devotes most of its business to the transportation of explosives is entitled to less favorable consideration than the ordinary common carrier. In the absence of a clear legislative intent, the granting of a specific classification to a carrier should not create a liability where otherwise none exists. Further, this court would have to take the additional step ... of invoking the doctrine of absolute liability where the undisputed evidence shows that the explosion was caused by the criminal act of a third person. This it is unwilling to do. Plaintiff's principal point has no merit. ...

The judgment is affirmed.

Knowledge

Lawyers, like physicians and other professionals, have methods of exercising their expertise—intuitive ways of drawing on their law knowledge as they encounter new situations requiring their expertise. Nowhere is this expertise more fluid, useful, and distinct than when a lawyer encounters a new client. As the lawyer listens, asks questions, and gives small bits of encouragement and advice, the lawyer is at the same time silently formulating and testing hypotheses—ideas of what the client's objective may be and whether the law will support it. Of course, the client is also thinking silently while communicating with the lawyer.

Chapter XII

Misrepresentation

OBJECTIVE: Given statements intended to induce another to take some action that results in a loss to that person, apply the law, principles, and elements reflected in these pages of the text to determine whether there is a misrepresentation claim.

Case Study: A woman crafts expensive jewelry for fine jewelers using 14-kt gold and diamonds. She also crafts much less expensive rings and bracelets for herself and friends using 14-kt gold and fake diamonds—a side-interest that she does not hide from her fine-jeweler customers. Her fine jewelry can cost from $2,000 to $20,000. She often gives away the jewelry she crafts using fake diamonds or, for more elaborate pieces, sells it for amounts generally under $200. Over the course of a year, the designer spent considerable time crafting an incredibly detailed and ornate 14-kt gold ring. It took her so much time and it was so attractive that she did not want to sell it to her fine-jeweler customers, so she set a fake diamond in the ring and wore it herself. One of those fine-jeweler customers saw the designer's ring and insisted that she sell it to him. Without saying anything to the customer about its fake diamond, the designer told him that she would have to have $3,000 for it. The customer bought it instantly, only to find out later that the diamond was fake. ***Discuss and evaluate the customer's misrepresentation claim against the designer.***

In its analytical form, the tort of misrepresentation involves a knowing, false, material statement made with the purpose and effect of inducing justifiable reliance to the hearer's loss or detriment. In its more-interesting parochial form, misrepresentation is a scam, swindle, artifice, fraud, or deceit. Human capacity for pride and self-delusion being prominent, those accused of misrepresentation may object to the more-pejorative labels *fraud* and *deceit* that misrepresentation also bears. The otherwise upstanding homeowners who check the "none" boxes on a state-law-mandated home-sale disclosure form, knowing the contrary that they have had basement or roof leaks, just as surely engage in fraud as the street-corner hustler—but would just as surely object to the characterization. The experienced tort practitioner knows that alleging fraudulent misrepresentation can carry precisely that sort of sting to the sensitive conscience. No matter which of the common phrases one uses for fraud, deceit, misrepresentation, or fraudulent misrepresentation, they all mean the same thing—a representation made knowing its falsity, to deprive another of some interest or benefit. All states recognize fraud, a tort as old as law's history.

Misrepresentation takes related forms. One form, known as *silent fraud, fraudulent concealment,* or *fraudulent omission,* involves not an affirmative false statement but an omission to disclose or active concealing of fact under circumstances where the omission or concealment have the purpose and effect of an affirmative misrepresentation. Consider the homeowner who leaves blank the "description" section on the mandated home-sale disclosure form, when the homeowner instead knows that the home has defects that the homeowner must disclose. Does that homeowner commit silent fraud upon a sale to an unsuspecting buyer who, relying on the omissions, pays more for the home than its defective condition warrants? Most jurisdictions recognize silent fraud (fraudulent omission) but only when some duty, imposed by statute or special relationship, requires disclosure. Otherwise, buyers should investigate and beware. Sellers ordinarily do not have to tell buyers everything wrong with the proposed deal.

Two other misrepresentation-type torts, *negligent misrepresentation* and *innocent misrepresentation*, fall short of misrepresentation's fraudulent form. The qualifiers *negligent* and *innocent* modify the *knowing* element of the misrepresentation tort. In other words, in the case of negligent misrepresentation, the defendant need not know that the statement the defendant makes that induces the plaintiff's reliance is false. The defendant must only act negligently with respect to the statement's falsity. Not all jurisdictions recognize the negligent misrepresentation. Courts recognizing negligent misrepresentation tend to limit recovery from the defendant to only those amounts the defendant received because of the negligent misrepresentation. In the claim of innocent misrepresentation, the defendant need not even have acted negligently with respect to the statement's falsity but may have made the false statement in the exercise of ordinary and reasonable care. Few jurisdictions recognize innocent misrepresentation. Those that do limit damages to that which the defendant gained.

Misrepresentation can be a complex subject. Its complexity arises in part because it has aspects of intentional tort law, negligence, warranty, breach of contract, and in some cases even products liability. Consumer and commercial norms peculiar to various products, services, fields, and industries further complicate the misrepresentation tort. What passes for puffing or "salesman's talk" in one field, another field may consider fraud. What may fall under "caveat emptor" or buyer beware in one field may require disclosure in another. The law of misrepresentation is not muddled or insensitive. It has a clear framework much like that of negligence law—duty (representation made with the intent to induce reliance), breach (knowledge of falsity), causation (inducing justifiable reliance), and damages (loss or detriment). Misrepresentation law's fluidity and variety ensures that it properly applies to the variety of human commerce and circumstance. Learn its elements, but appreciate that they may apply differently depending on the circumstance. Consider, then, the elements of misrepresentation.

A. Representation

Misrepresentation begins with communication. If a person intends no communication, then no misrepresentation cause of action exists. Misrepresentation involves the defendant's intention that the plaintiff form an impression that the circumstances are as they are not. Communication must take place, and it must be false. The clearest case will involve an affirmative misstatement by the defendant—whether words, writings, communicative actions (nods, gestures), or a combination. Misrepresentation, though, need not depend on writings. Statutes of "frauds," barring actions in the absence of writings, curiously enough apply to breach-of-contract claims, not to fraudulent misrepresentation. Oral statements may form the basis for a fraud claim. Indeed, misrepresentation need not depend on words but could occur with intentionally inaccurate numbers in (for instance) financial statements, with misleading diagrams or doctored photographs, and in other false depictions. Arranging physical conditions to falsely represent or to conceal can also form fraud's basis.

To qualify as a misrepresentation, the communication must also be objectively and verifiably false. Statements that a court cannot measure against some objective standard to establish their truth or falsity simply cannot form the basis for a claim of misrepresentation. Thus, opinions subjectively expressed concerning the merits of properties, business opportunities, and the like, are not actionable because they cannot be false. *Salesman's talk*, *trade talk*, and *puffing* are phrases that capture the quality of these non-actionable assertions. The context of the statements can subtly influence how the law will judge their quality, whether actionable as fraud or not. The law does not judge false what the factfinder only finds to be guess, speculation, or conjecture. The general rule that is that opinions are not actionable as fraud because one cannot prove them false, although don't let this rule mislead you. Opinions that professionals express as matters of expert judgment are certainly capable of misleading and hence may be actionable in fraud (if all other elements are satisfied) or malpractice (given other circumstances). Consider a well-known decision by the esteemed Judge Learned Hand, parsing the distinction between an actionable misrepresentation and non-actionable puffing or opinion.

Vulcan Metals Co. v. Simmons Mfg. Co.
United States Court of Appeals, Second Circuit
248 Fed. 853 (2d Cir. 1918)

Writ of error to two judgments of the District Court for the Southern District of New York, entered in the first case upon a verdict directed by the court dismissing the complaint, and in the second case, upon a verdict directed by the court in favor of the plaintiff for the sum of $43,423.04. ...

The gist of the complaint in the first action was the fraudulent procurement by the Simmons Manufacturing Company of a contract executed by the defendant Freeman on behalf of the Vulcan Metals Company, Incorporated, by which he purchased from the Simmons Company for $75,000 all the tools, dies, and equipment owned by it for the manufacture of its vacuum cleaning machines, all manufactured machines and unassembled parts, as set forth in a schedule thereto attached, and all inventions, applications, and letters patent owned by the Simmons Company in vacuum cleaners.... . The complaint further alleges that the officers and agents of the Simmons Manufacturing Company made false representations as to the character of the vacuum cleaners so sold and the extent to which they had been used upon the market, to which the Vulcan Metals Company, Incorporated, acted to its prejudice, because the machines and patents were totally inefficient and unmarketable. ...

The second class of misrepresentations was that the Simmons Manufacturing Company had not sold the machine, or made any attempt to sell it; that they had not shown it to any one; that it had never been on the market, and that no one outside of the company officials and the men in the factory knew anything about it; that they had manufactured 15,000 of them, but before making any attempt to market it they had been told by their agent that it would be a mistake for them to attempt to sell these along with their ordinary line, which was furniture; that on that account they had withdrawn them from the market and had never made any attempt to put them out. ...

There was evidence that the machines, when exploited by the Vulcan Metals Company, Incorporated, proved to be ineffective and of little or no value, and that their manufacture was discontinued by that company not very long after they had undertaken it. There was also evidence that several of the Western agents of the Simmons Manufacturing Company had had the machines in stock and had attempted to market some of them; that they had been unsuccessful in these efforts... .

HAND, J. (after stating the facts as above). The first question is of the misrepresentations touching the quality and powers of the patented machine. These were general commendations, or, in so far as they included any specific facts, were not disproved; e.g., that the cleaner would produce 18 inches of vacuum with 25 pounds water pressure. They raise, therefore, the question of law how far general "puffing" or "dealers' talk" can be the basis of an action for deceit.

The conceded exception in such cases has generally rested upon the distinction between "opinion" and "fact"... . The reason of the rule lies, we think, in this: There are some kinds of talk which no sensible man takes seriously, and if he does he suffers from his credulity. If we were all scrupulously honest, it would not be so; but, as it is, neither party usually believes what the seller says about his own opinions, and each knows it. Such statements, like the claims of campaign managers before election, are rather designed to allay the suspicion which would attend their absence than to be understood as having any relation to objective truth. It is quite true that they induce a compliant temper in the buyer, but it is by a much more subtle process than through the acceptance of his claims for his wares. ...

In the case at bar, since the buyer was allowed full opportunity to examine the cleaner and to test it out, we put the parties upon an equality. It seems to us that general statements as to what the cleaner would do, even though consciously false, were not of a kind to be taken literally by the buyer. As between manufacturer and customer, it may not be so; but this was the case of taking over a business, after ample chance to investigate. Such a buyer, who the seller rightly expects will undertake an independent and adequate inquiry into the actual merits of what he gets, has no right to treat as material in his determination statements like these. ... We therefore think that the District Court was right in disregarding all these misrepresentations.

As respects the representation that the cleaners had never been put upon the market or offered for sale, the rule does not apply; nor can we agree that such representations could not have been material to Freeman's decision to accept the contract. The actual test of experience in their sale might well be of critical consequence in his decision to buy the business, and the jury would certainly have the right to accept his statement that his reliance upon these representations was determinative of his final decision. We believe that the facts as disclosed by the depositions of the Western witnesses were sufficient to carry to the jury the question whether those statements were false. It is quite true, as the District Judge said, that the number of sales was small, perhaps not 60 in all; but they were scattered in various parts of the Mountain and Pacific States, and the jury might conclude that they were enough to contradict the detailed statements of Simmons that the machines had been kept off the market altogether. ...

It results from the foregoing that the judgment in the action for deceit must be reversed. ... [N]o representations should be allowed as to the efficiency, durability, or economy of the cleaners, and the case should be tried upon the sole issue whether the defendant, through duly authorized agents, represented to Freeman that the goods had not been put on sale when in fact they had... .

> **Practice**
> Within a year or two of starting with a law firm that did primarily insurance-defense work in torts cases, the associate, fresh out of law school, had a strong sense of his peculiar place in the world of commerce—as, he would occasionally chuckle to himself, a "master of disaster." His work exposed him to a variety of legal matters, but the immediacy, reality, and detail of the various tort claims in which his work was deeply involving him made it seem that disasters were the only thing about which he knew a lot. He did not mind—in fact, just the opposite. Practicing tort law was like pulling a curtain open on what one suspected—the foolishness, carelessness, greed, vengeance, recklessness, insensitivity, and sometimes the sheer silliness or even lunacy of the human heart and will. Truth—that which the associate was daily encountering—was indeed stranger than the fiction he had previously imagined. In this law practice that he daily gave an ever richer professional embrace, the client-tortfeasors and their opposing-party victims, the lay and expert witnesses, and the company representatives often seemed like stronger and clearer caricatures of a great drama in which he was now an actor—a strangely grateful participant trying to set aright a small corner of it.

INQUIRY

Opinions. One of the traditional rules that Judge Learned Hand stated in the above *Vulcan Metals Co.* case (omitted from the edited text) is that statements of value or worth are ordinarily not actionable. *See* Ryan v. Collins, 496 S.W.2d 205 (Tex. Civ. App. 1973) (statements that stock was "hot" and had "unlimited" potential were not actionable misrepresentations); *see also* Parker v. Arthur Murray, Inc., 10 Ill. App.3d 1000, 295 N.E.2d 487 (1973) (statements that dance-lesson customer had "exceptional potential" were not actionable misrepresentations). Can you see why? Some regard the essence of bargaining to be that sellers may express their own opinions on their property's value. Judge Hand suggests so when he writes that exaggerated statements are "designed to allay the suspicion which would attend their absence"—that the buyer expects as much. But the cases do not always grant the seller such license to exaggerate. *See* Hokanson v. Oatman, 165 Mich. 512, 131 N.W. 111 (1911) (affirming judgment in fraud for defendant agent's misrepresentation that seller principal would take no less than $1,200 when land was available for $900). For instance, the owner of real property who falsely claims to a potential lessor to have had an offer to lease it for $10,000 commits an actionable misrepresentation if not so. *See* Kabatchnick v. Hanover-Elm Bldg. Corp., 328 Mass. 341, 103 N.E.2d 692 (1952). Equally actionable would be false assertions that other nearby land had sold for certain amounts and that potential buyers made specific offers on the land for sale. *See* Brody v. Foster, 134 Minn. 91, 158 N.W. 824 (1916). How far may a seller go in estimating facts as to the property for sale, before the estimate becomes an actionable representation? *See* Saxby v. Southern Land Co., 109 Va. 196, 63 S.E. 423 (1909) (over-estimate that real property sold contained 150 acres of timber of which only 20 acres had been burned, when 60 acres had been burned and only 120 acres remained, held not actionable).

> **Ethics**
> Negotiation ethics are a significant issue for torts practitioners. What are the ethics to a plaintiff's lawyer's asserting as a negotiation tactic that the plaintiff will not take anything less than a certain dollar figure in settlement, when to the contrary the plaintiff has authorized settlement at a lower figure? Would the other side expect that kind of

> assertion? Does expectation make a difference to whether the assertion violates ethics? Rule 3.4 of the ABA Model Rules of Professional Conduct Rule require fairness to an opposing party and counsel, and Rule 4.1 prohibits lawyers from making false statements to others. Certainly, knowingly false statements regarding facts material to settlement—like past earnings, the circumstances of the tort incident, the availability of witnesses, and provable medical expense and wage loss—would be grounds on which to set aside a settlement as fraudulent. The tort lawyer would not want to commit a tort, in addition to a violation of ethics rules, when resolving a tort claim. Although significant debate exists as to what are appropriate negotiation ethics, a lawyer may wisely choose to avoid exaggerated and strategic puffing both because of its ethical implications and because it is a poor way to build the credibility necessary for optimal settlements.

Omissions. Misrepresentation does not always depend on an affirmative statement. Omitting to disclose information when the law and circumstance impose a duty to disclose can also constitute misrepresentation. For instance, a banker who answers a question about a customer's financial condition with general assurances probably implies knowledge of specific undisclosed facts that would support the general assurances—and had better have those facts. *See* Simpson v. Western Natl. Bank, 497 P.2d 878 (Wyo. 1972) (actionable implied representation). A sales agent who reassures an investor that a certain bank is sound and will keep making money probably implies knowledge of specific facts supporting the reassurance. *See* Wink Enterps. v. Dow, 491 S.W.2d (Tex. Civ. App. 1973) (actionable implied representation). Context is important in these cases. An agent who misrepresents that the builder of a certain home was one of the best in the area and reputable, when the builder was instead the agent's niece who had never built a home before (omissions the agent failed to disclose), faces a misrepresentation claim for the mixed misrepresentation and omission. *See* Oltmer v. Zamora, 94 Ill. App.3d 651, 49 Ill. Dec. 652, 418 N.E.2d 506 (1981). A disparity in expertise, or a special relation of trust, may be the critical difference. Consider the following illustrative case.

Bergen v. Baker
Michigan Court of Appeals
264 Mich. App. 376, 691 N.W.2d 770 (2004)

PER CURIAM. ... This action was filed after plaintiffs purchased a home from defendants in 2001 and then discovered a significant leak in the glass-paned roof of a sunroom, or alternately referred to as the hot tub room, that is attached to the back of the house. ...

Plaintiffs filed a complaint sounding in fraud, negligent misrepresentation, and breach of contract arising out of defendants' alleged failure to disclose the leaking roof. Before the sale was consummated, defendants executed and delivered a seller's disclosure statement that affirmatively indicated problems with a leaking roof, but also noted, in regard to the roofing, that there had been a "complete tear-off & replacement [in] June 1998." Another portion of the disclosure statement reflected that there had been evidence of water in the home's basement or crawl space, with the statement specifically providing that there had been "leaking under front porch"; however, the problem was "completely rectified w/new roof '98." There is no specific mention of leaking skylights or leaks in the sunroom roof. A reasonable interpretation of the disclosure statement is that there had once been a problem with a leaking roof, but it was rectified with a new roof in 1998.

In 1999, however, defendants had hired Gregory Glass & Maintenance, Inc., to perform repairs on leaking skylights in the sunroom. Brant Rousseaux, owner of Gregory Glass, provided a quote for the repairs, which quotation indicated that the "existing caulking has failed and is hard and dry creating many areas where water is penetrating under the flashing and around the glass to the interior of the system." Rousseaux recommended that all the old caulking be removed and replaced, and the repairs were performed in October 1999. Rousseaux testified in his deposition that he informed defendant Karen Baker that certain areas of rotting wood in the sunroom, including around the skylights, needed to be addressed by a carpenter.

Before the closing on the real estate transaction, plaintiffs had a home inspection performed... . Under the heading of "hot tub," the inspection report provided that the "glass enclosure shows heavy applications of silicone along the edge where the glass has leaked in the past." In the summary section of the inspection report, which section addressed "significant concerns and considerations," the report states that the "[h]ot tub room has experienced past leakage... ." ...

The trial court found that plaintiffs failed to create a factual issue on the matter of actual reliance. The court's ruling is necessarily predicated on its conclusory belief that the disclosure statement and the inspection report provided sufficient notice to plaintiffs that there was a problem with leakage and that such knowledge could not be overcome with an affidavit to the contrary. ...

A claim for fraudulent misrepresentation or actionable fraud generally requires a showing that "(1) the defendant made a material representation; (2) the representation was false; (3) when the defendant made the representation, the defendant knew that it was false, or made it recklessly, without knowledge of its truth as a positive assertion; (4) the defendant made the representation with the intention that the plaintiff would act upon it; (5) the plaintiff acted in reliance upon it; and (6) the plaintiff suffered damage." [*M & D, Inc. v. McConkey,* 231 Mich.App. 22, 27, 585 N.W.2d 33 (1998)[; cc.]

Furthermore, under the silent fraud doctrine, a cause of action "is established when there is a suppression of material facts and there is a legal or equitable duty of disclosure." [C] Further, "there must be some type of misrepresentation, whether by words or action, in order to establish a claim of silent fraud." [C]

Plaintiffs' claims arise out of statements or omissions in the seller's disclosure statement, which necessarily requires us to focus on the Michigan Seller Disclosure Act (SDA), MCL 565.951 *et seq.* ...

... The statutory form requires and provides, in part, that the seller answer all questions and report known conditions affecting the property. The form reads, "This statement is a disclosure of the condition and information concerning the property, known by the seller." MCL 565.957(1). The statutory form also provides that the disclosure "is not a warranty of any kind by the seller or by any agent representing the seller in [the] transaction, and is not a substitute for any inspections or warranties the buyer may wish to obtain." *Id.* The disclosure statement or form particularly requires a seller to disclose whether the roof leaks. *Id.* ...

The disclosures required by the act are to be made in "good faith," and "good faith" means "honesty in fact in the conduct of the transaction." MCL 565.960. "The specification of items for disclosure in this act does not limit or abridge any obligation for disclosure created by any other provision of law regarding fraud, misrepresentation, or deceit in transfer transactions." MCL 565.961. ...

... The SDA clearly creates a legal duty of disclosure relative to the transaction in this case. ...

The problem that arises comes from the accompanying explanatory language: "complete tear-off & replacement June 1998." Also, the disclosure statement provides, in relation to basement or crawl space evidence of water, that "leaking under front porch completely rectified w/new roof '98." When this language is taken into consideration with the indication of a leaking roof, reasonable minds could conclude that the information actually suggested a past problem, and not a current problem, with a leaking roof and that the problem had been corrected by the installation of a new roof. ... There is no specific reference in the disclosure statement to leaking skylights or a leaking sunroom roof, which compounds the possible confusion. ... It is for the trier of fact to resolve the issue of how to interpret the disclosure statement. ...

... [T]he disclosure statement can be read as suggesting that there were no existing or active problems with roof leakage, and the inspection report did not indicate that the sunroom roof was currently leaking or had lost its seal, but rather spoke of past leakage. The inspector's observation of wood rot and heavy caulking, couched in terms of past leakage, could reasonably have led plaintiffs to believe that there was no active problem with leaking and that past repairs had been successful. The trial court erred in granting summary disposition for defendants because, viewing all of the documentary evidence in a light most favorable to plaintiffs, they submitted sufficient documentary evidence to create a question of fact regarding whether they actually and reasonably relied on the seller's disclosure statement, when both the disclosure statement and the inspection report failed to identify any active leakage problem affecting the property.[fn]

Reversed and remanded for proceedings consistent with this opinion. We do not retain jurisdiction.

INQUIRY

Bare Nondisclosure. The traditional (and still correct) view, from old English cases, is that bare nondisclosure cannot support a claim for misrepresentation—a duty to disclose must exist before a failure to disclose will be actionable as the silent-fraud form of misrepresentation. *See* Peek v. Gurney, L.R. 6 H.L. 377 (1873); Keates v. Earl of Cardogan, 10 C.B. 591, 138 Eng. Rep. 234 (1851); *see also* Swinton v. Whitinsville Svgs. Bk., 311 Mass. 677, 42 N.W.2d 808 (1942) (home seller's failure to disclose termite damage does not support a fraud claim in absence of duty to disclose). Logic and common sense would tell us as much. A duty to disclose must exist before a failure in that duty would be actionable. The problem that misrepresentation law faces in drawing such a bright line between affirmative misrepresentations and silent nondisclosures is, in part, that those who are artful enough to conceive of a fraudulent scheme tend to be equally artful in their manipulation of the circumstances to conceal the fact of their misrepresentation. Misrepresentation law occasionally encounters baldface liars and readily holds them liable—although the more outrageous schemers are usually the less collectible. As the above *Bergen v. Baker* case illustrates, misrepresentation cases much more often involve arguable affirmative misstatements mixed with arguable failures to disclose.

Relationships. In this context of artful liars and arms-length buyer-beware transactions, the bare-nondisclosure limitation can appear harsh in some instances. An example is when the buyer of real property or another item of considerable value is grossly mistaken as to the property's nature and can readily prove the reasonableness of the mistake without necessarily attributing it to any duty of the seller to disclose. In those cases, some courts have been willing to rescind the sale contract as a form of equitable relief for the buyer, without allowing a misrepresentation claim for monetary damages against the innocent seller. *See* Slade v. McIntyre, 11 Mass. L. Rep. 79 (Mass. Super. 1999). Another place where an aggrieved party may find relief from the bare-nondisclosure limitation—and may be able to sue the silent misrepresenter—is where the one who failed to disclose owed a fiduciary duty to the party the nondisclosure aggrieved. Many possible fiduciary relationships exist in which a failure to disclose could be actionable as misrepresentation, including trustee and beneficiary, insurer and insured, surety and secured, attorney and client, banker and bank customer, partners or joint venturers, guardians and wards, and possibly even family members. *See* Buxcel v. First Fid. Bank, 601 N.W.2d 593 (S.D. 1999); Brasher v. First Ntl. Bank, 232 Ala. 340, 168 So. 42 (1936); Newport v. Lamon, 132 Wash. 369, 231 P. 952 (1925). What is the exception to the bare-nondisclosure limitation in the following case?

Croyle v. Moses
Pennsylvania Supreme Court
90 Pa. 250 (1879)

MERCUR, J. delivered the opinion of the court, June 23d 1879. This is an action on the case to recover damages for the fraudulent sale of a horse. The declaration contains two counts. One, charging a fraudulent warranty, the other, deceit and fraudulent representations. Two distinct questions are thus presented; the one, whether the defendant warranted the horse to be sound, the other, whether, without any warranty, he fraudulently and deceitfully practised some trick or artifice in making the sale whereby the plaintiff was deceived and injured. ...

The learned judge ... appears to have overlooked the distinction between warranty and deceitful representations. As was said in Krumbharr v. Birch, 2 Norris 426, "It needs no citation of authorities to prove that the wilful misrepresentation or concealment of a material fact by the vendor constitutes a fraud." But fraudulent representations may be as well by arts or artifices calculated to deceive, as by positive assertions[.] [Cc]

... [I]n the absence of artifice or deceitful representations, the jury was correctly told "the defendant was not bound to inform the plaintiff that the horse was a cribber. He had a right to remain silent and let the purchaser examine for himself and buy on his own judgment." ... The question presented by the points was substantially, if at the time of the sale the horse was known to the defendant to be "a cribber or windsucker," and this fact was artfully concealed by him to the injury of the plaintiff, whether it was such a concealment of a latent defect as would avoid the contract. The points submitted did not rest on the mere facts that the horse was hitched short and the reasons assigned therefor, but also on the additional facts that the defendant knew him to be a crib-biter, and resorted to this artifice to conceal it, and gave an untruthful reason to mislead and deceive the plaintiff. The complaint is not for a refusal or omission to answer, but for an evasive and artful answer. That the horse was actually a crib-biter, and so known to the defendant, was clearly proved. Whether that defect made him unsound was fairly submitted to the jury, under the evidence. That it lessened his market value seems to admit of no doubt. If the jury should believe, as the plaintiff testified, that he said to the defendant, "If there is anything wrong with the horse, I do not want him at any price," and that the defendant, with knowledge he was a crib-biter, answered the plaintiff artfully and evasively, with intent to deceive him, and did thereby deceive him to his injury, it was such a fraud on the plaintiff as would justify him in rescinding the contract. The answer of the court, blending warranty with fraudulent artifices, failed to present the latter to the mind of the jury in a proper manner. ...

Judgment reversed[trial had resulted in a defense verdict], and a *venire facias de novo* awarded.

INQUIRY

Active Concealment. The above *Croyle v. Moses* case, demonstrating that even in horse-trading misrepresentation may be actionable, is the leading American case on active concealment. Its modern incarnation, suggested by *Bergen v. Baker*, involves the concealing with paint, putty, and caulk, of defects in vehicles, *see* Kuelling v. Roderick Lean Mfg. Co., 183 N.Y. 78, 75 N.E. 1098 (1905), or buildings, *see* Reichelt v. Urban Inv. & Dev. Co., 577 F. Supp. 971 (N.D. Ill. 1984). A customer asks to see the material for sale. The seller shows the customer corded bundles of the material with undamaged pieces deliberately placed at the top of each bundle, with the customer effectively unable to inspect the damaged pieces bundled inside. Misrepresentation? *See* Salzman v. Maldaver, 315 Mich. 403, 24 N.W.2d 161 (1946) (yes—affirming denial of motion to dismiss misrepresentation claims but granting dismissal of warranty claims). What is the exception to the bare-nondisclosure limitation in the following case?

Ensminger v. Terminix Intern. Co.
United States Court of Appeals, Tenth Circuit
102 F.3d 1571 (10th Cir. 1996)

PORFILIO, J. In this appeal, Terminix International Company contends a jury's adverse verdict is infested with error which the district court failed to repair when it denied post-trial motions for judgment as a matter of law and new trial. Concluding Terminix has infused the issues with its own interpretation of the elements of a claim of fraud by silence under the structure of Kansas law, we affirm.

In purchasing a home in a Wichita suburb, Cynthia and Danny Ensminger obtained from the sellers assurance the house was free of termites. The Wood Destroying Insect Information Report which they submitted with their financing documentation indicated, "based on careful visual inspection of the readily accessible areas of the property no visible evidence of infestation from wood destroying insects was observed." Robert Stotts, a termite inspector employed by Terminix, signed the form after performing an inspection of the property. However, shortly after the Ensmingers moved in, ceramic tiles plummeted from the bathroom wall exposing catacombs of termite activity.

The Ensmingers sued Terminix[fn] alleging under Kansas law claims of actual fraud and fraud by silence. After the court exterminated their claim of actual fraud, the lack of evidence of an intent to deceive mandating partial summary judgment, a jury heard plaintiffs' evidence of Terminix's commission of fraud by silence. According to plaintiffs, the sellers contacted Terminix after a first inspection they solicited revealed the presence of termites in an unattached doghouse in the back of the house. Observing other conditions conducive to termite infestation, the house sitting in the ground, earth-wood contact in the front and rear, and the road's sloping down into the property, the first inspector advised the sellers to remove the doghouse whose infested wooden structure abutted the house and seek a second opinion to confirm his recommendation termite treatment was warranted. The seller removed the doghouse, contacted Terminix and told its agent about the first inspection, although Mr. Stotts characterized this information "kind of like water off a duck's back." However, termite damage visible in an accessible humidifier room and in three accessible attic areas remained undetected and unnoted as Mr. Stotts wrote, "no visible signs of damage, in my opinion." ...

The jury found Terminix liable and awarded $120,800 in actual damages, later reduced by $10,000. Then, providing the predicate for an award of punitive damages under Kan. Stat. Ann. § 60-3701, the jury concluded Terminix's conduct was wanton, and the court accepted that recommendation and awarded $200,000 in punitive damages. ...

Terminix uses the district court's grant of partial summary judgment on plaintiffs' actual fraud claim to attack the judgment for fraud by silence. It reasons, absent an intent to deceive or a special relationship, as a matter of law, plaintiffs could show no evidence Terminix had a duty to disclose information which they characterized as concealed. ...

... In *Wolf v. Brungardt,* 215 Kan. 272, 524 P.2d 726, 736 (1974), the Kansas Supreme Court described the claim: "Where one party to a contract or transaction has superior knowledge, or knowledge which is not within the fair and reasonable reach of the other party and which he could not discover by the exercise of reasonable diligence, or means of knowledge which are not open to both parties alike, he is under a legal obligation to speak, and his silence constitutes fraud, especially when the other party relies upon him to communicate to him the true state of facts to enable him to judge of the expedience of the bargain."

Key to this cause of action, we think, is the unequal relationship in which the claimant seeks particular information from a specialist upon which the recipient intends to rely or act. Under Kansas law, that interaction in those circumstances may create a fiduciary relationship. ... In *Denison State Bank v. Madeira,* 230 Kan. 684, 640 P.2d 1235, 1243 (1982), the court quoted from a venerable Kansas case: "A fiduciary relation does not depend upon some technical relation created by, or defined in, law. It may exist under a variety of circumstances, and does exist in cases where there has been a special confidence reposed in one who, in equity and good conscience, is bound to act in good faith and with due regard to the interests of the one reposing the confidence. ..." [C] ...

... [T]his record discloses, as the district court found, Terminix employees know that home buyers rely on the termite inspection report in making the decision whether to purchase a home. Plaintiffs had no experience or ability to detect termite activity themselves. They relied on the report supplied by the sellers and signed by Terminix. Surely, knowing the prospective purchase is termite free or poised to emit a swarm of these winged pests can fairly be characterized as material information leading a purchaser to accept the bargain or abandon the deal. [C] Here, undertaking that obligation for the *sellers* for the benefit and use of the prospective *buyers* who would have no ability to detect a problem even with the exercise of reasonable diligence creates a duty to disclose. Consequently, the essence of a fiduciary relationship under Kansas law is created mandating Terminix to disclose that information its superior position controlled or to face liability for its concealment. ...

Hence, under the law of fraud by silence in Kansas, construing the evidence and inferences in plaintiffs' favor, we cannot say the evidence was not susceptible to the inferences the jury drew. Not only do we reject Terminix's effort to insert the element of a specific intent to deceive in a cause of action for fraud by silence,[fn] but also we find its interpretation of Kansas law of what constitutes a fiduciary relationship is too wooden. ...

Given our plenary review, we **AFFIRM** the denial of the motion for judgment as a matter of law. ...

INQUIRY

Superior Capability. Do not assume from this one case that superior knowledge alone is sufficient to support a duty to disclose—and a claim for misrepresentation for failing to do so. What limitations do you see to this duty to disclose based on a party's superior knowledge and capability? The disclosure must relate to some transaction. *See* Griffith v. Byers Constr. Co., 212 Kan. 65, 510 P.2d 198 (1973) (developer liable for fraud in the concealment of lawn soil's infertility, in action by homebuyer who at time of purchase had no capability of determining soil's source or fertility). Yet as *Ensminger* makes clear, privity is not always necessary. *See* Banca Del Sempione v. Provident Bank, 75 F.3d 951 (4th Cir. 1996) (misrepresentation claim by third-party based on defendant's letter of credit). What is the critical requirement to establish the duty, then? The Restatement (Second) of Torts §531 states that a misrepresentation defendant is liable for failure to disclose when the defendant "has reason to expect" that the class of which the plaintiff is a member would be relying on the misrepresentation. Courts have interpreted the standard to be subjective, requiring the defendant's actual knowledge. *See* Ernst & Young, L.L.P. v. Pacific Mut. Life Ins. Co., 51 S.W.2d 573 (Tex. 2001). What if any conflicts of interest does the duty of an inspector, like the defendant in *Ensminger*, to disclose to third-party buyers, create, when the seller hired the inspector? What if any practical difficulties does that duty create for the inspector to get reliable information into the hands of the buyer? Is satisfying the duty as simple as ensuring that reports and opinion letters are accurate?

B. Knowledge of Falsity

The classic case of misrepresentation is, as the above study makes clear, one in which the defendant knows that the statement is false. To borrow a term more commonly associated with criminal law, fraud is a tort of *scienter*—one that requires the defendant's knowledge (in effect) of wrong. American case law traces the requirement that the defendant know that the statement is false to the House of Lords decision in Derry v. Peek, 14 App. Cas. 337 (H. L. 1889). *See* Neurosurgery and Spine Surgery, S.C. v. Goldman, 339 Ill. App.3d 177, 790 N.E.2d 925 (2003); International Prods. Co. v. Erie R.R. Co., 244 N.Y. 331, 155 N.E. 662 (Ct. App. 1927). But the English common law adopted a tort of deceit or misrepresentation independent of contract much earlier than *Derry v. Peek*. *See* Pasley v. Freeman, 100 Eng. Rep. 450 (K.B. 1789). And the tort has always borne that connotation of knowing wrong. The plaintiff in a fraudulent misrepresentation claim must prove that the defendant knew that the defendant's statement was false. The proof may be by circumstantial evidence from the unreasonableness of the defendant's denial. *See* Palmacci v. Umpierrez, 121 F.3d 781 (1st Cir. 1997). The proof need not include any showing that the defendant had any nefarious motive. Motive is not an element of the fraud claim. *See* Nielsen v. Adams, 223 Neb. 262, 388 N.W.2d 840 (1986); *cf.* Thompson v. Modern Sch. of Bus. and Corresp., 183 Cal. 112, 190 P. 451 (1920) (motive relevant to punitive damages). But the plaintiff must present evidence from which a reasonable juror could infer that the defendant knew of the statement's falsity at the time the defendant made that false statement.

The *Derry v. Peek* decision is instructive, in that it upheld the dismissal of a claim by an investor who purchased a tram company's shares based on a false statement that the company had the necessary government approval to operate. The *Derry v. Peek* defendants had published the false prospectus believing that it was true. Hence no fraud claim existed, even though the statement was indisputably false and injurious. The Restatement (Second) of Torts §526 (1965) loosens the knowledge requirement somewhat by accepting that a misrepresentation is fraudulent if the defendant "(a) knows or believes that the matter is not as he represents it to be, (b) does not have the confidence in the accuracy of his representation that he states or implies, or (c) knows that he does not have the basis for his representation that he states or implies." None of the §526 alternatives, however, would permit a finding of fraud based on an honestly believed but negligent misrepresentation.

Figure

Tort lawyer William Schultz, a partner in the Washington, D.C. law firm Zuckerman Spaeder LLP, began his law career at Public Citizen Litigation Group, trying and arguing public-interest cases in federal and state trial and appellate courts including the Supreme Court. He then served as a Deputy Assistant Attorney General in the United States Department of Justice, supervising the federal government's lawsuit against the tobacco industry—one of the largest cases the government ever brought. He also served as the Food and Drug Administration's Deputy Commissioner for Policy, where he supervised the development of FDA policies and regulations, and as counsel to the Chairman of the House Subcommittee on Health and the Environment, where he assisted with food, drug, and healthcare legislation. Mr. Schultz's government service gave him special knowledge, skill, and experience to represent individuals injured by food, drugs, medical devices, and other products.

Intentions. The *Derry v. Peek* decision suggests another situation that complicates misrepresentation law—when the actor asserts that the actor has an intention to accomplish an act material to the transaction but does not accomplish it. If the defendants in *Derry v. Peek* had merely announced that they *intended* to obtain the authority to operate a steam company (not that they already had the authority), and despite reasonable efforts they failed to do so, then no misrepresentation claim would exist, if they had the intent they claimed at the time they claimed it. Expressions of intent are often a part of negotiations and transactions. *See* Schott Motorcycle Supply v. American Honda Motor Co., 976 F.2d 58 (1st Cir. 1992) (assurance of future commitment to business was mere puffing and not actionable misrepresentation); *see also* Morgan v. Celender, 780 F. Supp. 307 (W.D. Pa. 1992) (assurance that disclosures to reporter would be "off the record" and confidential might have promised future conduct but were not actionable misrepresentations as to present facts). Yet statements of intent to engage in specific acts within a sufficiently specific period, together with evidence that the actor had no such intent at the time the actor expressed the intention, may be actionable misrepresentation when they serve to induce justifiable reliance causing a loss. *See* Charpentier v. Los Angeles Rams Football Co., 75 Cal. App.4th 301, 89 Cal. Rptr.2d 115 (1999) (ownership's representation that the team had no intent to move to another city was actionable in claim by season-ticket purchaser). Consider the following illustrative case by the inestimable Judge Learned Hand.

California Conserving Co. v. D'Avanzo
United States Court of Appeals, Second Circuit
62 F.2d 528 (2d Cir. 1933)

HAND, J. D'Avanzo, the bankrupt, owned a wholesale grocery business in New Haven and on July twenty-seventh, 1929, bought of the petitioner six hundred cases of tomato paste at ten dollars a case. ... On November sixth, the petitioner shipped three hundred and ten cases, and on November twenty-first D'Avanzo accepted a draft (trade acceptance), for $3,100, the price... . The cases reached New York on the thirtieth and D'Avanzo got possession of one hundred and twenty-five of them on December third. On the fourth, a petition was filed against him and a receiver appointed, who later took delivery of the remaining hundred and eighty-five. On December eighteenth the petitioner, learning of the bankruptcy, demanded the paste of the receiver and later filed a petition to reclaim it, which merely alleged that "the contract was entered into and the shipment made * * * as a result of untrue and fraudulent statements made by the bankrupt and his agents." ... [The bankruptcy court judge] passed an order against the bankrupt for the amount of the draft.

... From the evidence it did not indeed definitely appear that on July twenty-seventh, when the contract was made, the bankrupt was so far insolvent that he could not then have intended to pay, but we may by permissible latitude construe the word 'shipment' to include the surrender by the seller of the documents of title on November twenty-first, when the bankrupt accepted the draft; and under the actual contract of sale the buyer was bound to return the bill of lading, if he did not honor the bill of exchange. [C] Therefore, if the surrender was procured by fraud, the transaction may be avoided and the lien restored to the petitioner.

On November twenty-first, D'Avanzo was within two weeks of bankruptcy, upon which his assets were found to have a book value of $83,000 and his liabilities $140,000. ... [H]e must have known that his ability to keep going for ten weeks more was at best a forlorn hope, and his general conduct justifies the conclusion that he thought his end to be not far off. ...

Starting with Donaldson v. Farwell, 93 U. S. 631, 23 L. Ed. 993, it has been settled by a number of decisions in federal courts that it is a fraud for an insolvent, concealing his condition, to buy goods, for which he does not mean to pay. ... No difficulty in the application of this doctrine arises when it is proved that the buyer positively intends not to pay; but that is often not the case. He may mean to pay if he survives, though he knows that he is extremely unlikely to do so. If his promise declares only that he intends to pay, it would be hard in such a case to say that he has deceived the seller; and the doctrine presupposes some deceit. But promises, like other utterances, must be read with their usual implications. True, they are predictions and no one can foretell the future; the seller known this as well as the buyer. However, a man's affairs may reach such a pass that ordinarily honest persons would no longer buy, if they had no greater chance to pay; and the seller is entitled to rely upon that implication. He may assume that the buyer would not promise if the odds were so heavy against him. He may read the promise as more than the declaration of a conditional intent, as affirming that that intent had reasonable hope of fruition. In that event, if the buyer knows that it has no such hope, he deceives the seller, as much as though he intended not to pay at all. This duty does not indeed depend upon what reasonable persons would think of his chances; or of how they would interpret the implication of his promise. But if he himself believes his position to be desperate, and if he understands his promise to mean what it normally would, the seller may rescind. [Cc]

In the case at bar D'Avanzo's affairs by November twenty-first had become so precarious that the petitioner was justified in understanding his acceptance of the draft as a declaration that his ability to pay was not so far compromised as in fact it was. We do not believe that he thought his position brighter than it would have seemed to any one else; or that he supposed his acceptance of the draft to imply less than it did to the petitioner.

Order affirmed.

INQUIRY

Breach of Contract. The above *California Conserving Co.* case illustrates a common issue having to do with the remedy when in retrospect it looks like, at the time the obligor made the contract, the obligor had little hope of performing the contract. Should the resulting cause of action be in fraud or breach of contract? The answer can be important for several reasons including that a fraud claim may avoid the statute of frauds, the parol-evidence rule, an integration clause in the contract, a remedy limitation in the contract, a shorter statute of limitations, a notice-of-claim provision in the contract, and minority and failure-of-consideration defenses. *See* Pinnacle Peak Developers v. TRW Investment Corp., 129 Ariz. 385, 631 P.2d 540 (Ct. App. 1980) (affirming summary judgment on basis of parol-evidence rule and rejecting fraud claim for promise without intention to perform it) (O'Connor, Sandra, J.). Parties often do use contracts to modify their procedural and substantive rights and remedies. A fraud claim can restore the traditional, common-law rights and remedies that a party may have unwisely bargained away in the contract. Courts patrol the line between breach-of-contract and misrepresentation actions for the unjust manipulation of these distinct causes of action, using the general rule that misrepresentations claims do not arise on statements of promise or intention later broken.

Predictions. What about predictions—should they be actionable when they do not come to fruition? The usual prediction makes no representation of an existing fact and so creates little or no opportunity to claim an actionable misrepresentation. *See* Spragins v. Sunburst Bank, 605 So.2d 777 (Miss. 1992) (prediction that plaintiff will successfully purchase in foreclosure held not actionable); Kennedy v. Flo-Tronics, Inc., 274 Minn. 327, 143 N.W.2d 827 (1966) (prediction that stock would triple in value held not actionable); Trustees of Columbia Univ. v. Jacobsen, 53 N.J. Super. 574, 148 A.2d 63 (1959) (prediction that student would acquire wisdom held not actionable), cert. denied, 363 U.S. 808. Yet if a misrepresentation as to a future event is the scheme that accomplished the fraud, then courts may recognize the claim. *See* Hanks v. Hubbard Broadcasting, Inc., 493 N.W.2d 302 (Minn. App. 1992) (assertion that news anchor's role reduction was only temporary was actionable as intentional misrepresentation where it was instead intended to be permanent); Steinberg v. Chicago Med. Sch., 69 Ill.2d 320, 13 Ill. Dec. 699, 371 N.E.2d 634 (1977) (misrepresentations in school catalog as to graduate-program selection criteria held actionable). A misrepresentation as to one's present rights in anticipation of future events can be actionable, at least if the misrepresentation occurs within a professional relationship. *See* Campbell v. Bettius, 244 Va. 347, 421 S.E.2d 433 (1992) (attorney's assertion that plaintiffs had guaranteed rights was actionable misrepresentation, not prediction of future events). Commercial relationships also exist in which a prediction can come close to, and can sound to one of the contracting parties like, an assurance that the circumstances as they exist at the time of the prediction are such that the hoped-for event will in fact occur. *See* Nader v. Allegheny Airlines, Inc., 445 F. Supp. 168 (D.C. D.C. 1978) (recognizing fraud claim for airline's practice of overbooking and then bumping passengers), revd., 626 F.2d 1031 (D.C. Cir. 1980) (no reliance because passenger knew of overbooking practice). In other words, the line between a non-actionable prediction of a future event and an actionable misrepresentation of an existing fact is not as clear as it might seem—at least to those who rely on the predictions to their detriment. Consider the following illustrative case in which the defendant allegedly predicted that the plaintiff would be successful in obtaining a loan.

Birt v. Wells Fargo Home Mortgage, Inc.
Wyoming Supreme Court
75 P.3d 640 (Wyo. 2003)

VOIGT, J. ... In their complaint, the Birts allege that, from April to October 2000, Wells Fargo negligently misrepresented to them that their loan application would be approved.[fn] ...

Analysis of the negligent misrepresentation cause of action is made difficult by the fact that the Birts' argument focuses almost entirely on non-disclosure. We can, however, glean from their arguments several points properly within the realm of alleged negligent misrepresentation. Those include allegations that: Gibbs told the Birts they could afford an architect; Gibbs told the Birts that Mr. Birt's employment change would not negatively affect the loan application; Gibbs instructed the Birts to "forge on" with the construction contract; Gibbs advised the Birts to deed their property over to Carter Brothers for construction purposes; and Gibbs informed the Birts that there should be no trouble acquiring a loan in a sufficient amount. ...

The district court granted summary judgment to Wells Fargo on the issue of negligent misrepresentation, with the following explanation: "The Birts use this theory as a back up to their contention that the bank promised to lend money. A failed promise cannot be converted into a viable theory by virtue of the doctrine of negligent misrepresentation. Negligent misrepresentation requires that the wrongdoer have a pecuniary interest in the matter and supply false information for the guidance of others in their business transactions. It involves situations in which one enterprise provides information to another enterprise that in turn predicates a decision upon the information. None of the examples in Restatement (Second) of Torts §552 embody the reach for which the Birts argue. Moreover, a good faith mistake doesn't trigger this tort. This record provides no basis to allow negligent misrepresentation to go forward."

We will affirm the summary judgment entered in favor of Wells Fargo. The gist of the district court's reasoning, which is correct, is that negligent misrepresentation does not apply to misrepresentations of future intent or to statements of opinion. ... Indeed, the extension of negligent misrepresentation to situations involving future intentions would "'endow every breach of contract with a potential tort claim for negligent promise.'" *Wilkinson v. Shoney's, Inc.*, 269 Kan. 194, 4 P.3d 1149, 1167 (2000) (*quoting Eckholt v. American Business Information, Inc.*, 873 F.Supp. 526, 532 (D.Kan.1994)). The question of whether the alleged misrepresentation was one of present fact or of opinion or of future intention is a question of law. [C][fn]

The undisputed facts of this case do not support a cause of action for negligent misrepresentation because Gibbs' alleged misrepresentations may all be characterized as statements of his opinion as to the progress of the loan or statements as to his expectation that the loan would be made. The gravamen of the Birts' claim is an allegation of just the sort of "negligent promise" to which the cause of action should not be extended. ...

[Summary judgment for defendants was affirmed.]

INQUIRY

Negligent Misrepresentation. Despite the limitations suggested by the above *Birt v. Wells Fargo Home Mortgage* case, misrepresentation law continues to countenance, in at least some jurisdictions and circumstances, various forms of misrepresentation claim in which the defendant did not know that the statement was false when made. The reason for limiting fraud to knowingly false statements has a lot to do with ensuring the free exchange of information and flow of goods in commerce. On the other hand, reasons for permitting misrepresentation-type claims where the defendant was only negligent or even innocent with respect to a statement's falsity ensure some integrity to that information within certain relationships and contexts, and return undue gains to those who have suffered the concomitant loss. Thus, parties often plead and prove claims for negligent misrepresentation where, for instance, the defendant made a false statement without knowledge of its falsity but carelessly within a special relationship. The Restatement (Second) of Torts §311 (1965) recognizes negligent-misrepresentation claims resulting in physical harm to others. Section 552 recognizes negligent-misrepresentation claims involving business, professional services, employment, and other pecuniary transactions, but limits recovery to out-of-pocket loss. Even in England, the House of Lords finally relented in Hedley Byrne & Co. v. Heller & Partners [1964] A.C. 465, when it recognized liability for negligent misrepresentations within a special relationship. Consider the following case.

Martens Chevrolet, Inc. v. Seney
Maryland Supreme Court
292 Md. 328, 439 A.2d 534 (1982)

DIGGES, J. In this action we consider whether there still exists in Maryland a tort suit for negligent misrepresentation independent of one for deceit. The case arose when appellant Martens Chevrolet, Inc.[fn] instituted ... this action against the appellees, Loving Chevrolet, Inc. and its sole stockholders, Franklin Loving and Howard F. Seney, alleging in separate counts breach of contract, deceit and negligent misrepresentation arising from the sale of an automobile dealership. On the apparent belief that no such action exists in Maryland, the trial judge granted at the close of appellant's case the defendants' motion for a directed verdict on the negligent misrepresentation count; a directed verdict was also granted in favor of the defendants on the breach of contract claim.[fn] The remaining count, sounding in deceit, was, however, submitted to the jury for its consideration, but that body returned a verdict in favor of Loving, Seney and their company. ...

For reasons which we will explore presently, we conclude that the tort of negligent misrepresentation is viable in Maryland. ... In February, 1976, Imperial Investment Company through its officers, Harry J. Marten, Jr. and his son, Harry J. Marten, III, initiated negotiations for the purchase of a Chevrolet automobile dealership owned in corporate form by Franklin Loving and Howard F. Seney. Throughout the bargaining period, the Martens informed the sellers that they intended to continue the operation of the Chevrolet franchise after the sale, and therefore desired accurate information concerning the past profitability of the enterprise. When asked during the first meeting of the parties about the financial status of the dealership, Mr. Seney responded by handing the buyers a handwritten financial "trend" sheet and stating, "this pretty well depicts the trends of how we have been doing." This sheet received by the Martens contained a list of the "net profit" figures for each year the dealership had been in operation, including a figure showing $2,211 profit for the previous year, 1975. ... Since this sheet revealed the Loving operation to be mildly profitable, the buyers, in reliance on it, concluded that with their industriousness and management efficiency they could substantially improve the profitability of the business. Accordingly, acting on behalf of their corporation, the Martens entered into an agreement with the owners of Loving Chevrolet for the purchase of the dealership on May 6, 1976.

After the franchise operated as Martens Chevrolet, Inc. for six months, the accountant for the new company presented its owners with a statement revealing a $187,000 loss. The Martens were baffled as to the reason for the dealership's financial plunge until its comptroller, who had formerly worked in that capacity for the seller, divulged a 1975 year-end financial statement which he had prepared for Loving Chevrolet listing a deficit for that year of $39,153.00, instead of a $2,211 profit as reflected in the 1975 trend sheet. In addition, the comptroller gave the new owners a financial statement completed by a certified accountant, following an audit, which stated that the losses sustained by the former dealership in that year were not $39,153, but rather, $69,000. Both of these documents had been prepared well before the date of sale, but the sellers had neglected to inform the buyers of their existence. On the basis of this newly received information, the Martens brought the present action against Loving, Seney and their company. ...

With the relevant factual predicate in hand, we turn now to address the question of whether there is presently cognizable in Maryland a tort action for negligent misrepresentation. We begin our inquiry by noting that initially under the common law there existed no separate tort of negligent misrepresentation. Thus, if a party was injured by the false representations of another, his only recourse in tort, if there was one, compelled the bringing of an action for deceit and proving all the elements of that tort. [Cc]

The critical element of the tort of deceit that distinguishes it from others arising from false representation is scienter on the part of the defendant—intent to deceive the other party. In formulating the contours of this state of mind requirement, our predecessors in Cahill v. Applegarth, 98 Md. 493, 56 A. 794 (1904), essentially embraced the view established in the landmark English case, Derry v. Peek, 14 App.Cas. 337, 374 (1889).... .

Realizing the inequities stemming from the strictures imposed for recovery in a deceit action, and being cognizant of the development of this area of the law in our sister jurisdictions, this Court in 1938 recognized for the first time the existence in this State of an action for negligent misrepresentation. ...

... [W]e reaffirm that, in Maryland, there exists a cause of action for negligent misrepresentation separate from that of deceit.

We summarize and clarify. The principal elements of the tort of negligent misrepresentation, as formulated in Virginia Dare[Stores v. Schuman, 175 Md. 287, 1 A.2d 897 (1938)], and subsequent cases decided by this Court, may be outlined as follows: "(1) the defendant, owing a duty of care to the plaintiff, negligently asserts a false statement; (2) the defendant intends that his statement will be acted upon by the plaintiff; (3) the defendant has knowledge that the plaintiff will probably rely on the statement, which, if erroneous, will cause loss or injury; (4) the plaintiff, justifiably, takes action in reliance on the statement; and (5) the plaintiff suffers damage proximately caused by the defendant's negligence. ...

In the present case, the appellants, by their amended declaration, alleged in separate counts both negligent misrepresentation and deceit. Nothing prohibits a plaintiff from pleading both deceit and negligent misrepresentation in one declaration and then relying on the same nucleus of facts in an attempt to satisfy the differing burdens of proof on these alternative claims. [Cc] The trial judge, however, by directing a verdict in this case, eliminated the possibility of recovery under the negligent misrepresentation count, seemingly on the ground that the cause of action does not exist in this State. ...

JUDGMENT OF THE CIRCUIT COURT FOR MONTGOMERY COUNTY REVERSED AND CASE REMANDED TO THAT COURT FOR A NEW TRIAL. COSTS TO BE PAID BY THE APPELLEES.

INQUIRY

Scope. As suggested above, not all jurisdictions permit negligent-misrepresentation claims. Others limit the claims to circumstances where the defendant had a monetary interest in the matter about which one made the negligent misrepresentation. *See* Hawaii v. United States Steel Corp., 919 P.2d 294 (Haw. 1996). Others limit negligent-misrepresentation claims to defendants who were in the business of supplying the misrepresented information. *See* Westby v. Gorsuch, 112 Wash. App. 558, 50 P.3d 284 (2002); Fry v. Mount, 554 N.W.2d 263 (Iowa 1996). Some jurisdictions recognize negligent-misrepresentation claims involving information exchanged in negotiations occurring over whether to form an agreement, *see* Weisman v. Connors, 312 Md. 428, 540 A.2d 783 (1988), while other jurisdictions do not, instead requiring an existing professional relationship, *see* Onita Pacific Corp. v. Trustees of Bronson, 315 Or. 149, 843 P.2d 890 (1992). Although the Restatement (Second) of Torts §311 (1965) recognizes negligent misrepresentation claims, its Comment *b* would extend those claims only to "any person who, in the course of an activity which is in furtherance of his own interests, undertakes to give information to another, and knows or should realize that the safety of the person or others may depend upon the accuracy of the information." Is Comment *b*'s "in furtherance of his own interests" a substantial enough limitation on negligent-misrepresentation claims to ensure the generally free flow of information? Consider now a case discussing innocent misrepresentation including its limitations, and distinguishing other forms of misrepresentation.

M & D, Inc. v. W.B. McConkey
Michigan Court of Appeals
231 Mich App 22, 585 N.W.2d 33 (1998)

JANSEN, J. ... In the present case, plaintiff M&D purchased commercial property in January 1991 on an "as is" basis from defendant Relenco Partnership. Defendant McConkey Real Estate Company handled the sale of the property. M&D leased the property to plaintiff Donmar, Inc., for the operation of a pet supplies store. Two months after the store opened, the building flooded after a heavy rainfall. The evidence at trial showed that the property had experienced flooding problems for many years. W.B. McConkey testified at trial that he had witnessed flooding on the property. However, there was no evidence that plaintiffs asked whether the property had experienced any flooding, and defendants never made any representation concerning flooding to plaintiffs. Further, Relenco refused to prepare a seller's disclosure statement and made this refusal an explicit part of the purchase agreement. Rather, on the face of the preprinted seller's disclosure statement, the following disclaimer appears: "Owner has never occupied this property. No representations or warranties implied as to condition. Property being sold in 'as is' condition."

Plaintiffs filed suit in October 1992, raising claims of breach of contract, negligence, innocent misrepresentation, and fraud against Relenco and McConkey Real Estate.[fn] The trial court dismissed plaintiffs' claims of fraud and innocent misrepresentation... .

1. COMMON-LAW FRAUD

... In this case, the trial court ... held that ... Relenco made no material "representation" of fact to plaintiffs upon which a common-law fraud claim could rest. Indeed, plaintiffs failed to present evidence that defendant made *any* affirmative representations concerning the nature of the flooding problem on the subject property. We agree with the circuit court's reasoning that, without a *representation,* plaintiffs could not maintain an action for common-law fraud because proof of some *false representation* made with an intent to deceive was a necessary element of their prima facie case. ...

2. INNOCENT MISREPRESENTATION

A claim of innocent misrepresentation is shown if a party detrimentally relies upon a false representation in such a manner that the injury suffered by that party inures to the benefit of the party who made the representation. [C] The innocent misrepresentation rule represents a species of fraudulent misrepresentation but has, as its distinguished characteristics, the elimination of the need to prove a *fraudulent purpose* or an intent on the part of the defendant that the misrepresentation be acted upon by the plaintiff, and has, as added elements, the necessity that it be shown that an unintendedly false representation was made in connection with the making of a contract and that the injury suffered as a consequence of the misrepresentation inure to the benefit of the party making the misrepresentation. [C] Thus, the party alleging innocent misrepresentation is not required to prove that the party making the misrepresentation intended to deceive or that the other party knew the representation was false. [C] Finally, in order to prevail on an innocent misrepresentation claim, a plaintiff must also show that the plaintiff and defendant were in privity of contract. [C]

In the present case, only M&D was in privity of contract with Relenco, and, therefore, it is the only plaintiff that could raise an innocent misrepresentation claim against Relenco. Moreover, as the trial court concluded, because Relenco made no false, or other, representation regarding the condition of the property, neither corporate plaintiff could maintain a claim of innocent misrepresentation. [C]

3. "SILENT FRAUD"

"Silent fraud," also known as fraud by nondisclosure or fraudulent concealment, is a commonly asserted, but frequently misunderstood, doctrine. This is primarily because most fraud claims are based upon alleged affirmatively stated false representations of material fact. A claim of "silent fraud" requires a plaintiff to set forth a more complex set of proofs. ... Michigan courts have recognized that silence cannot constitute actionable fraud *unless* it occurred under circumstances where there was a legal duty of disclosure. [C]

M&D and Donmar argue that dismissal of their fraud and misrepresentation claims was improper because Relenco, and specifically W.B. McConkey, its managing partner, knew about the history of the flooding problem and its severity and failed to disclose its concealed condition to plaintiffs before the sale of the property. ... [P]laintiffs argue that a fraud claim can be maintained where the purchaser is able to prove that the vendor knew about a defective condition and did not disclose it to the purchaser. We do not believe that this argument is supported by existing Supreme Court precedent.

Our Supreme Court has recognized a vendor's duty to disclose material facts when the vendor and purchaser have generally discussed the condition at issue—when the purchaser has expressed some particularized concern or made a direct inquiry—and the seller fails to fully disclose the material facts within the seller's knowledge related to the condition and the buyer detrimentally relies upon the resulting *misdirection.* [C]

Accordingly, the touchstone of liability for misdirection or "silent fraud" is that *some* form of representation has been made and that it was or proved to be false. In other words, we believe that, at least as applied to fraud cases, there is no general inchoate duty to disclose all hidden defects. ...

In the present case, plaintiffs have not established the elements of silent fraud. There is no evidence of a legal or equitable duty on behalf of Relenco to disclose the history of the flooding of the subject property to plaintiffs. The documents of the sale transaction contain an "as is" clause and other statements specifically disclaimed seller representations and warranties about the condition of the property. Further, Relenco refused to prepare a seller's disclosure statement and made this refusal a part of the purchase agreement. On the face of the seller's disclosure statement, the following appears: "Owner has never occupied this property. No representations or warranties implied as to condition. Property being sold in 'as is' condition." Moreover, plaintiffs have not set forth any evidence that they inquired into any history of flooding or water problems with the property. Therefore, this is not a situation where the buyer expressed some particularized concern or made a direct inquiry and the seller failed to fully disclose the material facts within the seller's knowledge and the buyer detrimentally relied on the misimpression. [C] Accordingly, plaintiffs have not set forth any evidence that Relenco was under a legal (for example, a contractual) or equitable (for example, where the buyers express a particularized concern or directly inquire of the seller) duty to disclose the history of the flooding problem.

... Plaintiffs state that the property was "cleaned up" and "all outward traces of the flooding were removed." Plaintiffs specifically contend that the property was painted and damaged carpet was removed. The fact that the property may have been cleaned, painted, and some carpet replaced is not sufficient evidence that the seller intended to create an affirmative impression that there was no flooding problem with the building. Sellers will often take steps to improve the property in an effort to get more money from a potential buyer. This cannot automatically lead to the conclusion that the seller is perpetrating fraud against potential buyers. Therefore, we conclude that plaintiffs have not set forth sufficient evidence that Relenco engaged in misleading actions (representations) such that a claim of silent fraud can be maintained. ...

Affirmed.

INQUIRY

Scope. Although only a few states recognize innocent misrepresentation as a tort claim, the Restatement (Second) of Torts §552C (1965) adopts that minority position. Section 552C(1), eschewing the label "innocent misrepresentation" but recognizing the tort nonetheless, states, "One who, in a sale, rental or exchange transaction with another, makes a misrepresentation of a material fact for the purpose of inducing the other to act or to refrain from acting in reliance upon it, is subject to liability to the other for pecuniary loss caused to him by his justifiable reliance upon the misrepresentation, even though it is not made fraudulently or negligently." Why is the defendant in such a case not entirely innocent? Both the above case and the Restatement §552C limit the tort to (1) parties involved in a transaction (where a duty of fair dealing might naturally exist) and (2) the plaintiff's recovery of the pecuniary loss that the defendant gains by the innocent misrepresentation. The plaintiff may claim in damages only the pecuniary loss that inures to the benefit of the defendant as a consequence of the transaction. *See* United States Fid. & Guar. Co. v. Black, 412 Mich. 99, 313 N.W.2d 77 (1981).

Rescission. As you can see from these limitations of the innocent-misrepresentation tort, to recovery of pecuniary gain by a party misrepresenting a material fact in a transaction, innocent misrepresentation is an outgrowth of the contract-law right of a party to rescind an agreement. In those instances where the plaintiff does not wish to keep the property acquired in the misrepresented transaction, the plaintiff's recourse is to rescind the contract and recover the defendant's gain in restitution—a contract, not a tort, action. *See* Ross v. Harding, 64 Wash.2d 231, 391 P.2d 526 (1964). Courts that do not recognize the innocent-misrepresentation tort will still recognize the contract rights of rescission and restitution. *See* Bortz v. Noon, 556 Pa. 489, 729 A.2d 555 (1999). Is the distinction important? Do we really need an innocent-misrepresentation tort?

C. Reliance

Misrepresentation only begins with the defendant's knowledge that the defendant has made a false representation. The knowledge and false-representation elements are only the first half of the total tort. The plaintiff must also show that the defendant made the false statement with the purpose and effect of inducing the plaintiff's reliance on it. The reliance element of the misrepresentation tort is, in essence, a causation requirement. *See* McIntyre v. Lyon, 325 Mich. 167, 37 N.W.2d 903 (1949) (directing judgment for defendant where plaintiff admitted that he acted for reasons other than the alleged misrepresentations which he suspected were false). Simply because a misrepresentation occurs does not mean that it must have led to harm. Simply because some harm occurred does not mean that misrepresentation caused it. The reliance element ensures that the plaintiff makes a logical connection between the wrong and the harm, to support the demand for a legal remedy. *See* Cox v. Johnson, 227 N.C. 69,

40 S.E.2d 418 (1946) (affirming judgment for defendant sellers where evidence showed that plaintiffs knew representation as to acreage in tobacco was false).

Reliance will often be obvious, established not only by showing that the plaintiff acted on the defendant's misrepresentation but also by the plaintiff's testimony that the misrepresentation made the difference. For example, the purchaser of a boat in dry dock who writes out a check for the boat immediately after the seller falsely assures the purchaser that the boat is seaworthy, and who testifies that the assurance was a critical part of the transaction, will have established the reliance element necessary to pursue the seller in misrepresentation when the boat leaks badly and sinks immediately when placed in the water. *See* Radford v. J.J.B. Enterps., Ltd., 163 Wis.2d 534, 472 N.W.2d 790 (1991) (actionable fraud claim based on seller's assurance that hull was sound and dry rot removed). If the buyer expresses concern about possible defects in the sale property, from evidence of the need for repair, and the seller falsely assures the buyer that the seller made the repair and no defect remains, then the buyer may still establish justifiable reliance. *See* Sippy v. Cristich, 4 Kan. App.2d 511, 609 P.2d 204 (1980) (buyer's seeing water spots on carpet do not defeat claim that seller had fraudulently misrepresented that roof had been repaired). Yet a purchaser who admits that a misrepresentation before the transaction made no difference to the purchase, or only hears about a misrepresentation after the transaction, will not establish reliance. Whether the plaintiff relied is the first question to address as to the reliance element.

Claimants must also address a significant qualifier to the reliance element in many instances. Reliance must be *justifiable*. A person cannot establish reliance when the circumstances indicate that the person had no justifiable basis to rely on the misrepresentation. For example, the purchaser of a boat who acknowledges buying the boat "as is," hires an expert to inspect it for seaworthiness, puts it in the water for a trial run to investigate its seaworthiness before the purchase, and receives the expert's report that it leaks badly and will require substantial repair to be seaworthy, cannot have justifiably relied on the seller's misrepresentation that the boat is seaworthy. The terms and circumstances of a transaction (including the opportunity of inspection), the nature and timing of the misrepresentation, the knowledge and expertise of both the plaintiff and the defendant, and other factors, can all affect whether the plaintiff justifiably relied. The justifiable-reliance requirement reflects both law's logic (that redress should depend on a connection between the wrong and harm) and its equity (that the law should not protect or promote the unjustifiably ignorant in their gullibility).

On the other hand, the courts do not appear to be saying that fraud victims must prove that they acted reasonably. Defrauders should not expect such substantial protection from the requirement. *See* Adan v. Steinbrecher, 116 Minn. 174, 133 N.W. 477 (1911) (fraud recovery by "gullible young man" cheated out of retirement funds by improbable scam); Chamberlin v. Fuller, 59 Vt. 247, 9 A. 832 (1887) ("No rogue should enjoy his ill-gotten plunder for the simple reason that his victim is by chance a fool."). Misrepresenters will not find a defense in the plaintiff's comparative or contributory negligence. *See* Greycas, Inc. v. Proud, 826 F.2d 1560 (7th Cir. 1987) (alleged negligent failure to perform duplicative UCC search not a defense to fraudulent misrepresentation that one had been performed); Yorke v. Taylor, 332 Mass. 368, 124 N.E.2d 912 (1955) (fraudulent sale of land not excused by allegation of buyer's negligent failure to search the real property records). Justifiable reliance can include the victim's peculiar circumstance and vulnerability. Consider the following illustrative case.

Chicago Title & Trust Co. v. First Arlington Natl. Bank
Illinois Court of Appeals
118 Ill. App.3d 401, 454 N.E.2d 723 (1983)

LORENZ, J. Chicago Title and Trust Company (CT & T) filed a complaint against Executive Construction, Inc. (E.C.I.) [and] Dennis L. Coates ... for a misrepresentation made by E.C.I. and Coates when applying for a disbursement from the escrow. ...

Following trial by the court, judgment was entered in favor of CT & T, and against E.C.I. and Coates, in the amount of $40,662.90. ...

E.C.I. and Coates appeal, raising the ... issue[]: 1. Was the evidence sufficient to find them liable in tort for deceit? ...

Arlington Bank agreed to lend $312,000 to the Lewises so that they could build a manufacturing facility... . E.C.I. was hired as general contractor, and the Lewises, along with Arlington Bank, entered into an escrow agreement with CT & T so that the contractor could obtain progress payments as work was completed on the project.

To receive progress payments under this escrow agreement, E.C.I. was obligated to submit a sworn application detailing the work performed and materials supplied. Once the architect hired by the Lewises certified that the application was correct, Arlington Bank was to furnish CT & T with funds to pay E.C.I.

... [O]n December 13, 1977, ... CT & T mistakenly issued a $42,000 check to E.C.I. although Arlington Bank had not supplied funds to cover this payment. ...

E.C.I.'s president, Dennis Coates, testified that although he knew the $42,000 had been issued by mistake, the check was deposited in one of E.C.I.'s accounts without notifying CT & T of its error. ...

CT & T's escrow officer testified that she relied upon Coates' representation in the third application in deciding to approve the payment of $47,187 and was unaware of the $42,000 mistaken payment. Therefore, CT & T did not recoup the $42,000 overdraw from the $47,187 sought in the third application. ...

First we consider whether the evidence was sufficient to justify finding Coates and E.C.I. liable in tort for fraud. The defendants argue that CT & T was not justified in relying on the representation Coates made in the third application because it *knew or should have known* that Coates' statement was false. ...

CT & T's escrow officer testified she was unaware of the $42,000 overdraft, and that she approved the third disbursement without recouping the overdraw because she relied on the representation made by Coates concerning the amount of money which E.C.I. had already received from CT & T. As the defendants point out, however, CT & T's auditors became aware of the overdraw within a few days of when the $42,000 check was mistakenly issued, and the defendants conclude CT & T was not deceived because it had imputed knowledge that Coates' representation was false. Furthermore, the defendants contend that the escrow officer's reliance on Coates' representation was not justified because reasonably prudent investigation would have revealed the falsity of the statement.

We start with the fundamental principle that "[t]he recipient of a fraudulent misrepresentation can recover against its maker for pecuniary loss resulting from it if, but only, if (a) he relies on the misrepresentation in acting or refraining from action, and (b) his reliance is justifiable." (Restatement (Second) of Torts (1977) § 537; [c].) The first element of this two-part requirement refers to factual causation: If plaintiff knew that defendant's representation was false, he could not have relied on the misrepresentation, and was not deceived. ...

CT & T ... had imputed knowledge of what its auditors became aware of. Nevertheless, a tortfeasor does not automatically escape liability for deceit merely because a defrauded corporation had imputed knowledge of the truth. Corporations typically have a large number of employees, and it would not be reasonable to expect each of them to be aware of all the knowledge obtained by every other corporate employee. To blindly preclude recovery for deceit practiced upon a corporate agent merely because a fellow employee knew the truth would make corporations safe marks for fraud. In an action for deceit, therefore, the appropriate focus is on the knowledge of the agent who was deceived... .

In the present case, CT & T's escrow officer testified that she relied on the misrepresentation made by the defendants in their third application. This was sufficient to satisfy the "actual reliance" requirement even though CT & T had imputed knowledge of the truth through other corporate agents.

We next consider whether the escrow officer's reliance was justifiable.

The attitude of courts toward the question of justifiable reliance has almost completely changed in the last 50 years... .

... [A]ll the relevant circumstances of the particular case must be considered in determining whether plaintiff's reliance was justifiable. ... It is therefore recognized that "[a]lthough the plaintiff's reliance on the misrepresentation must be justifiable, * * * this does not mean that his conduct must conform to the standard of the reasonable man. Justification is a matter of the qualities and characteristics of the particular plaintiff, and the circumstances of the particular case rather than the application of a community standard in all cases. Negligent reliance and action sometimes will not be justifiable, and recovery will be barred; but this is not always the case." Restatement (Second) of Torts (1976), § 545A, comment *b*. ...

The third disbursement application appeared regular on its face, and plaintiff's escrow officer did not have notice of suspicious circumstances which would have triggered a duty to investigate further. Under the circumstances of this case it was not against the manifest weight of the evidence to find that plaintiff's employee acted reasonably and was thereby justified in relying upon the misrepresentation. ...

Based on the reasons given above, the judgment of the circuit court is affirmed in part, reversed in part, and remanded with directions. ...

INQUIRY

Scams. When does a fraud become so obvious that the victim cannot justifiably rely? As the two cases *Adan* and *Chamberlin*, cited above just before the principal case, suggest, the courts will protect the gullible. Those cases are hard with which to disagree, given that the greater wrong is certainly the fraud over the gullibility. Yet the cases nonetheless plumb incredulity, reaching a point where the courts are not sympathetic to the putative victim. Should, for instance, recovery be permitted for a fraud in which the buyer of eyeglasses accepts that they would over time adapt themselves to the victim's eyesight? *See* H. Hirschberg Optical Co. v. Michaelson, 1 Neb. Unof. 137, 95 N.W. 461 (1901) (affirming verdict for defendant). Another memorable fraud case involved the mystical Land of Shalam. *See* Ellis v. Newbrough, 6 N.M. 181, 27 P. 490 (1891) (affirming verdict for defendants because plaintiff, who participated in the preposterously "communistic theories and practices" did not give "evidence of such imbecility as would entitle him to maintain" his suit for deceit). Why, in the end, are cases involving outright scams no large part of tort practice? Litigation winners must collect judgments. Try to find the scammer. Should the fact that the putative victim is an otherwise highly sophisticated corporation change the relatively loose standard as to what constitutes justifiable reliance? Any practitioner who has had substantial enough experience with a broad enough population over a long enough time will recognize that you can fool all of the people (whether or not of means or educated) at least some of the time. *See* Hitachi Credit America Corp. v. Signet Bank, 166 F.3d 614 (4th Cir. 1999) (plaintiff held to have justifiably relied on scam representations regarding offshore cigarettere venture so secret as to prevent investigation).

Practice

To the lawyer, the experience felt a bit like finally meeting the devil. The lawyer had counseled any number of elderly, poor, uneducated, and unsophisticated clients against submitting to the various scam offers that they had brought to him for review. He would occasionally call the attorney general's fraud hotline just to be sure, but most of the time the scam was obvious from the face, source, and nature of the offers. The lawyer had seen such a wide array of scams—Nigerian and South African gold, other African business ventures designed to prey on a minority population's sympathies, false inheritances, fake annuities, and the ever-present "you have won" sweepstakes. Now here, right in the courthouse hallway, attending case evaluation, was a lawyer who defended one of the largest sweepstakes companies against individual and class-action fraud lawsuits. Oh yes, the sweepstakes lawyer admitted to the other lawyer, the elderly did fall prey. He had seen sad cases that made him wonder about his client's business model. Yet by and large, the sweepstakes lawyer explained, many of the claims were highly defensible. The sweepstakes—the smiling celebrity—were all that the plaintiffs had. The connection with hope and celebrity gave them something that their sorry lives lacked. The real shame, the sweepstakes lawyer felt, was on the families of these gullible individuals for not seeing that the victim had better social support. And then, the sweepstakes lawyer added, to see the family members fight over the money their gullible family member won. Many kinds of devil are out there, and the defrauder represents only one of them.

Investigation. What is the effect on the reliance element of the plaintiff's investigation before entering into the transaction? When the plaintiff goes so far as to make a thorough investigation of the circumstances before the transaction, the plaintiff will find much harder to establish that the plaintiff relied on the defendant's misrepresentation. *See* Burroughs v. Jackson Natl. Life Ins. Co., 618 So.2d 1329 (Ala. 1993) (plaintiff's investigation of terms of insurance policy defeat claim to having relied on agent's misrepresentation of terms); Savings Bank Retirement System v. Clarke, 258 Md. 501, 265 A.2d 921 (1970) (fraud plaintiff's hiring title experts for independent investigation before entering transaction demonstrates that plaintiff did not rely on the alleged misrepresentation as to title); *cf.* Fausett & Co. v. Bullard, 217 Ark. 176, 229 S.W.2d 490 (1950) (purchasing agent's living in house and making limited investigation may still prove reliance on sellers' misrepresentations). What if the plaintiff only has the ability to investigate but does not do so? Courts tend to hold that the plaintiff may justifiably rely on the defendant's misrepresentation even where the plaintiff has the ready ability to investigate. *See* Buckley v. Buckley, 230 Mich. 504, 202 N.W. 955 (1925) (plaintiff's opportunity to examine books of corporation does not defeat opportunity to rely on defendant's misrepresentation as to corporation's value). On the other hand, no justifiable reliance exists when the means of discovering the representation is exceedingly simple. *See* Williams v. Rank 7 Son Buick, Inc., 44 Wis.2d 239, 170 N.W.2d 807 (1969) (purchaser's taking vehicle for a 90-minute test drive is sufficient to destroy purchaser's ability to rely on seller's false assurance that the vehicle had air conditioning).

Context. Other reliance-element issues can arise. One has to do with the context in which the defendant made the false statement. For instance, the courts have generally not recognized misrepresentation claims against book publishers who print false information causing injury. A leading case rejecting fraudulent and negligent misrepresentation claims against a book publisher is Winter v. G.P. Putnam's Sons, 938 F.2d 1033 (9th Cir. 1991), in which wrong advice in *The Encyclopedia of Mushrooms* allegedly resulted in two mushroom eaters requiring liver transplants after they consumed poisonous mushrooms misdescribed in the guide. *See also* Smith v. Linn, 386 Pa. Super. 392, 563 A.2d 123 (1989) (no misrepresentation claim relating to death from diet book); Jones v. J.B. Lippincott, 694 F. Supp. 1216 (D. Md. 1988) (no misrepresentation claim regarding medical textbook); Alm v. Van Nostrand Reinhold Co., 134 Ill. App.3d 716, 480 N.E.2d 1263, 89 Ill. Dec. 520 (1985) (no misrepresentation claim regarding tool manual). Reliance can also be an issue regarding the role or reputation of the one making the false statement. For instance, some courts have allowed misrepresentation or even negligent-misrepresentation claims against a commercial certifier of consumer goods. *See* Hanberry v. Hearst Corp., 276 Cal. App.2d 680, 81 Cal. Rptr. 519 (1969) (negligent-misrepresentation claim against "Good Housekeeping"-seal entity permitted for slippery shoe product). Consider a related issue involving whether the one who believes the misrepresentation justifiably relied.

Williams v. Dougherty County
Georgia Court of Appeals
101 Ga. App. 193, 113 S.E.2d 168 (1960)

NICHOLS, J. As stated in the brief of the plaintiff: "There is no complaint that she [the plaintiff] did not understand the contents of the deed or understand what she was signing. This case is based on *fraud in the procurement of the deed*." Emphasis by the plaintiff. The plaintiff relies on Cline v. Nelson, 46 Ga.App. 600, 168 S.E. 70, and similar cases to support her contention that a cause of action is set forth in the petition because she was induced by fraud to part with title to her land. In that case the plaintiff sought to recover because of the fraudulent misrepresentation of a *fact*. Such is not so in the case sub judice for the alleged misrepresentation here was as to matters of law. The petition alleged that the agent seeking the right of way deed to her property told her that they, the government, wanted the property in question, that they did not pay for this type of deed and would cause her a lot of trouble if she did not sign the deed presented to her when he "well knew that in order to secure a right-of-way over the property of the plaintiff, the defendant and the State Highway Department of Georgia would have to pay the plaintiff the value of her property for such right of way." Admittedly these were misrepresentations of law and as was said in the case of Dixon v. Dixon, 211 Ga. 557, 563, 87 S.E.2d 369-373: "The general rule is well settled that fraud cannot be predicated upon misrepresentations of law or misrepresentations as to matters of law." [Cc] The basis for this generally is that everyone is presumed to know the law, and therefore cannot in legal contemplation be deceived by erroneous statements of law. ... "A misrepresentation as to a legal liability, which induces the making of a contract, does not constitute actionable fraud if the matter be open to the observation of both parties equally and there is no relation of trust or confidence between them." Salter v. Brown, 56 Ga.App. 792(1), 193 S.E. 903. In the present case no such contention is made, the plaintiff relying on the allegation that she was "an ignorant and uneducated woman, and that there is great disparity between her mental capacity and that of the said Geer, and that the said Geer, acting for the defendant and the State Highway Department of Georgia, took advantage of this disparity in mental ability in inducing the plaintiff to sign said right-of-way deed, which she would not have signed except for the fraud practiced upon her by the said Geer as aforesaid." Where there is no fiduciary relationship between the parties there can be no actionable fraud where the alleged misrepresentation is to a matter of law, and, "it is obvious that the plaintiff, by consulting an attorney at law, could have had the question determined, and that he was not obliged to rely on the representations of the agent of the defendant." Beckmann v. Atlantic Refining Co., 53 Ga.App. 671(3), 187 S.E. 158, 159. ... In the present case it cannot be said that there was any actionable fraud used on the plaintiff where she was chargeable with knowing the law and the only misrepresentation allegedly practiced upon her was as to a matter of law. Accordingly, for this reason the trial court did not err in sustaining the defendant's general demurrer and it becomes unnecessary to pass on the other grounds of demurrers successfully urged before the trial court by the defendant.

Judgment affirmed.

INQUIRY

Law. Are you uncomfortable with the above *Williams v. Doughtery County* decision? So are others. Although the rule that the above case states—that misrepresentations of law are generally not actionable—remains a reasonable starting point, *see* Gibson v. Mendenhall, 203 Okl. 558, 224 P.2d 251 (1950) (misrepresentation that plaintiff could easily obtain tavern license not actionable); Ad. Dernehl & Sons Co. v. Detert, 186 Wis. 113 , 202 N.W. 207 (1925) (misrepresentation that 18%-alcohol beverage could be legally sold is not actionable), its harshness evidently warrants exceptions. First, where the assertion of law requires the existence of certain facts to support it, the assertion of law becomes an actionable, mixed law-fact assertion (in essence, an assertion of facts). Sorenson v. Gardner, 215 Or. 255, 334 P.2d 471 (1959), is an example in which the seller of a home falsely represented that it met all code requirements. Although code-compliance is arguably a matter of law, it actually requires the existence of a substantial body of facts. The *Sorenson* appellate court held the false assertion to be actionable—outside the rule that misrepresentations of law are not actionable. The Restatement (Second) of Torts §545, "Misrepresentation of Law," agrees, allowing actionable reliance on assertions of law that imply underlying facts to substantiate them. Cases also treat as actionable assertions of fact, misrepresentations regarding the law of other jurisdictions. *See* Fireman's Ins. Co. v. Jones, 245 Ark. 179, 431 S.W.2d 728 (1968).

Materiality. Reliance can also be an issue when the alleged misrepresentations do not reasonably relate to the transaction at hand. The misrepresentation must be material to the transaction for the plaintiff to justifiably rely on it. Materiality is an objective standard (what the reasonable person would have regarded as material to the matter), except that the Restatement (Second) of Torts §538 (1965) and case authority accept that materiality exists when the defendant misrepresenter knows or should know that the plaintiff "is likely to regard the matter as important in determining his choice of action, although a reasonable man would not so regard it." *See* Haverland v. Lane, 89 Wash. 557, 154 P. 1118 (1916) (disguised identity of buyer of stock is immaterial to sale transaction); *see also* Farnsworth v. Duffner, 142 U.S. 43 (1891) (land seller's religious and political association is immaterial to sale).

Skills

An opening statement is a non-argumentative recitation of the facts relevant to each element of the case. Although an opening statement must be non-argumentative, room for advocacy exists in crafting an opening statement. The advocacy of an opening statement is not in strong adjectives or other hyperbole—that would be argument. Rather, the advocacy is in selecting and organizing the facts into a cohesive and motivating whole—an intelligible and moving true story. Misstating or overstating the evidence may lead to counsel's loss of credibility with the judge and jury, and, in the more egregious instance, litigation sanction.

Policy. Reliance can also be an issue around policy concerns. For example, several courts permit adoptive parents to rely on agency misrepresentations and omissions regarding known genetic and medical information on the adopted child. *See* Jackson v. State, 956 P.2d 35 (Mont. 1998) (common-law and statutory duties to disclose); M.H. v. Caritas Family Services, 488 N.W.2d 282 (Minn. 1992) (duty to disclose that child was product of incest); Burr v. Board of County Commrs., 23 Ohio St.3d 69, 491 N.E.2d 1101 (1986) (duty to disclose child's Huntingon's Disease risks). Others permit the agency to refuse all disclosures if the agency makes no half-truth disclosures, *see* Mallette v. Children's Friend and Service, 661 A.2d 67 (R.I. 1995), while still others refuse to impose on an agency any duty to investigate, *see* **Meracle v.**

Children's Service Society, 149 Wis.2d 19,, 437 N.W.2d 532 (1989). Similarly, some courts may permit a public employer to rely on a former public employer's recommendation of a former employee that intentionally omitted the former employee's sexual misconduct. *See* Randi W. v. Muroc Jt. Unif. Sch. Dist., 14 Cal.4th 1066, 929 P.2d 582 (1997) (misrepresentation claim on behalf of the affected child). Other courts will not. *See* Richland Sch. Dist. V. Mabton Sch. Dist. 111 Wash. App. 377, 45 P.3d 580 (2002). Each of these examples involve policy judgments by the courts as to the relative interests not only of the parties but of third-persons and society generally.

Third Persons. Reliance can also be an issue as to the conduct and claims of third persons who did not hear the false statement initially or directly. Misrepresentation liability to third parties has vexed and divided courts, especially as to accountant defendants. An accounting firm that intentionally defrauds its client is liable to the client. Equally, if the accounting firm negligently misrepresents the client's financial condition in statements that the accounting firm prepares at the request of the client for the client's own consideration, then the firm should malpractice liability for any resulting harm. But what if the accounting firm's misrepresentation reaches the client's creditors—say, a bank that extends a line of credit to the client relying on the accountant's inaccurate financial statements? Should the accounting firm be liable to the creditor for the creditor's subsequent loss in relying on the misrepresented statements? The issue is significant because third-party liability can be large. Accounting firms are not insurers of their clients' financial condition for the benefit of their clients' creditors. But they are, in a way, *assurers* of financial condition. When are they liable? The first answer is relatively simple—if the defendant acts intending to deceive the third party, then the courts grant the third party a misrepresentation claim. Consider the celebrated case that became the pivot point for the issue.

Ultramares Corp. v. Touche, Niven & Co.
New York Court of Appeals
255 N.Y. 170, 174 N.E. 441 (Ct. App. 1931)

CARDOZO, C.J. The action is in tort for damages suffered through the misrepresentations of accountants, the first cause of action being for misrepresentations that were merely negligent, and the second for misrepresentations charged to have been fraudulent.

In January, 1924, the defendants, a firm of public accountants, were employed by Fred Stern & Co., Inc., to prepare and certify a balance sheet exhibiting the condition of its business.... Fred Stern & Co., Inc., which was in substance Stern himself, was engaged in the importation and sale of rubber. To finance its operations, it required extensive credit and borrowed large sums of money from banks and other lenders. All this was known to the defendants. The defendants knew also that in the usual course of business the balance sheet when certified would be exhibited by the Stern Company to banks, creditors, stockholders, purchasers, or sellers, according to the needs of the occasion, as the basis of financial dealings. Accordingly, when the balance sheet was made up, the defendants supplied the Stern Company with thirty-two copies.... Nothing was said as to the persons to whom these counterparts would be shown or the extent or number of the transactions in which they would be used. In particular there was no mention of the plaintiff.... The range of the transactions in which a certificate of audit might be expected to play a part was as indefinite and wide as the possibilities of the business that was mirrored in the summary. ...

Capital and surplus were intact if the balance sheet was accurate. In reality both had been wiped out, and the corporation was insolvent. The books had been falsified by those in charge of the business so as to set forth accounts receivable and other assets which turned out to be fictitious. ...

The plaintiff, a corporation engaged in business as a factor, was approached by Stern in March, 1924, with a request for loans of money to finance the sales of rubber. ... As a condition of any loans the plaintiff insisted that it receive a balance sheet certified by public accountants, and in response to that demand it was given one of the certificates signed by the defendants and then in Stern's possession. On the faith of that certificate the plaintiff made a loan which was followed by many others. ... On January 2, 1925, the Stern Company was declared a bankrupt.

This action, brought against the accountants in November, 1926, to recover the loss suffered by the plaintiff in reliance upon the audit, was in its inception one for negligence. On the trial there was added a second cause of action asserting fraud also. ...

1. We think the evidence supports a finding that the audit was negligently made, though in so saying we put aside for the moment the question whether negligence, even if it existed, was a wrong to the plaintiff. ...

We begin with the item of accounts receivable. At the start of the defendant's audit, there had been no posting of the general ledger since April, 1923. Siess, a junior accountant, was assigned by the defendants to the performance of that work. ... He says that in doing this he supposed the entries to be correct, and that, his task at the moment being merely to post the books, he thought the work of audit or verification might come later, and put it off accordingly. ... Verification, however, there never was either by Siess or by his superiors, or so the triers of the facts might say. If any had been attempted, or any that was adequate, an examiner would have found that the entry in the ledger was not supported by any entry in the journal. ...

We are brought to the question of duty, its origin and measure.

The defendants owed to their employer a duty imposed by law to make their certificate without fraud, and a duty growing out of contract to make it with the care and caution proper to their calling. Fraud includes the pretense of knowledge when knowledge there is none. To creditors and investors to whom the employer exhibited the certificate, the defendants owed a like duty to make it without fraud, since there was notice in the circumstances of its making that the employer did not intend to keep it to himself. [Cc] A different question develops when we ask whether they owed a duty to these to make it without negligence. If liability for negligence exists, a thoughtless slip or blunder, the failure to detect a theft or forgery beneath the cover of deceptive entries, may expose accountants to a liability in an indeterminate amount for an indeterminate time to an indeterminate class. The hazards of a business conducted on these terms are so extreme as to enkindle doubt whether a flaw may not exist in the implication of a duty that exposes to these consequences. ...

The assault upon the citadel of privity is proceeding in these days apace. How far the inroads shall extend is now a favorite subject of juridical discussion. [Cc] ... In the field of the law of torts a manufacturer who is negligent in the manufacture of a chattel in circumstances pointing to an unreasonable risk of serious bodily harm to those using it thereafter may be liable for negligence though privity is lacking between manufacturer and user. [Cc] ... We are now asked to say that a like liability attaches to the circulation of a thought or a release of the explosive power resident in words. ...

The extension, if made, will so expand the field of liability for negligent speech as to make it nearly, if not quite, coterminous with that of liability for fraud. Again and again, in decisions of this court, the bounds of this latter liability have been set up, with futility the fate of every endeavor to dislodge them. Scienter has been declared to be an indispensable element, except where the representation has been put forward as true of one's own knowledge ([c]) or in circumstances where the expression of opinion was a dishonorable pretense ([cc]) ... This has not meant, to be sure, that negligence may not be evidence from which a trier of the facts may draw an inference of fraud ([c]), but merely that, if that inference is rejected, or, in the light of all the circumstances, is found to be unreasonable, negligence alone is not a substitute for fraud. ...

Liability for negligence if adjudged in this case will extend to many callings other than an auditor's. Lawyers who certify their opinion as to the validity of municipal or corporate bonds, with knowledge that the opinion will be brought to the notice of the public, will become liable to the investors, if they have overlooked a statute or a decision, to the same extent as if the controversy were one between client and adviser. Title companies insuring titles to a tract of land, with knowledge that at an approaching auction the fact that they have insured will be stated to the bidders, will become liable to purchasers who may wish the benefit of a policy without payment of a premium. These illustrations may seem to be extreme, but they go little, if any, farther than we are invited to go now. ...

Our holding does not emancipate accountants from the consequences of fraud. It does not relieve them if their audit has been so negligent as to justify a finding that they had no genuine belief in its adequacy, for this again is fraud. It does no more than say that, if less than this is proved, if there has been neither reckless misstatement nor insincere profession of an opinion, but only honest blunder, the ensuing liability for negligence is one that is bounded by the contract, and is to be enforced between the parties by whom the contract has been made. We doubt whether the average business man receiving a certificate without paying for it, and receiving it merely as one among a multitude of possible investors, would look for anything more.

2. The second cause of action is yet to be considered. ...

Correspondence between the balance sheet and the books imports something more, or so the triers of the facts might say, than correspondence between the balance sheet and the general ledger, unsupported or even contradicted by every other record. The correspondence to be of any moment may not unreasonably be held to signify a correspondence between the statement and the books of original entry, the books taken as a whole. If that is what the certificate means, a jury could find that the correspondence did not exist, and that the defendants signed the certificates without knowing it to exist and even without reasonable grounds for belief in its existence. The item of $706,000, representing fictitious accounts receivable, was entered in the ledger after defendant's employee Siess had posted the December sales. He knew of the interpolation, and knew that there was need to verify the entry by reference to books other than the ledger before the books could be found to be in agreement with the balance sheet. The evidence would sustain a finding that this was never done. By concession the interpolated item had no support in the journal, or in any journal voucher, or in the debit memo book, which was a summary of the invoices, or in any thing except the invoices themselves. The defendants do not say that they ever looked at the invoices, seventeen in number, representing these accounts. They profess to be unable to recall whether they did so or not. They admit, however, that, if they had looked, they would have found omissions and irregularities so many and unusual as to have called for further investigation. When we couple the refusal to say that they did look with the admission that, if they had looked, they would or could have seen, the situation is revealed as one in which a jury might reasonably find that in truth they did not look, but certified the correspondence without testing its existence.

In this connection we are to bear in mind the principle already stated in the course of this opinion that negligence or blindness, even when not equivalent to fraud, is none the less evidence to sustain an inference of fraud. …

The defendants attempt to excuse the omission of an inspection of the invoices proved to be fictitious by invoking a practice known as that of testing and sampling. A random choice of accounts is made from the total number on the books, and these, if found to be regular when inspected and investigated, are taken as a fair indication of the quality of the mass. … Verification by test and sample was very likely a sufficient audit as to accounts regularly entered upon the books in the usual course of business. It was plainly insufficient, however, as to accounts not entered upon the books where inspection of the invoices was necessary, not as a check upon accounts fair upon their face, but in order to ascertain whether there were any accounts at all. … A jury might find that, with suspicions thus awakened, they closed their eyes to the obvious, and blindly gave assent.

We conclude, to sum up the situation, that in certifying to the correspondence between balance sheet and accounts the defendants made a statement as true to their own knowledge, when they had, as a jury might find, no knowledge on the subject. If that is so, they may also be found to have acted without information leading to a sincere or genuine belief when they certified to an opinion that the balance sheet faithfully reflected the condition of the business. …

Upon the defendants' appeal as to the first cause of action, the judgment of the Appellate Division should be reversed, and that of the Trial Term affirmed, with costs in the Appellate Division and in this court.

Upon the plaintiff's appeal as to the second cause of action, the judgment of the Appellate Division and that of the Trial Term should be reversed, and a new trial granted, with costs to abide the event.

INQUIRY

Division. *Ultramares* holds that accountants have liability for fraud as to third parties. That part of Justice Cardozo's opinion produced no controversy. However, the *Ultramares* holding limiting negligent-misrepresentation claims did not meet with universal acceptance. Instead, courts divide on third-party negligent-misrepresentation rules, along a spectrum. At one end of the spectrum are cases like Credit Alliance Corp. v. Arthur Andersen & Co., 65 N.Y.2d 536, 483 N.E.2d 110, 493 N.Y.S.2d 435 (Ct. App. 1985), imposing three strict requirements before an accounting firm would be liable to a third party for negligent misrepresentation. The *Credit Alliance* opinion held that "(1) the accountants must have been aware that the financial reports were to be used for a particular purpose or purposes; (2) in the furtherance of which a known party or parties was intended to rely; and (3) there must have been some conduct on the part of the accountants linking them to that party or parties, which evinces the accountants' understanding of that party or parties' reliance." New York continues to follow the *Credit Alliance* position. *See* Security Pacific Business Credit, Inc. v. Peat Marwick Main & Co., 79 N.Y.2d 695, 597 N.E.2d 1080, 586 N.Y.S.2d 87 (1992). At the other end of the spectrum, cases like Citizens State Bank v. Timm, Schmidt & Co., 113 Wis.2d 376, 335 N.W.2d 361 (1983), reject special requirements and instead impose liability on accountants for negligent misrepresentation to third parties under accepted negligence rules. The *Citizens State Bank* opinion limited liability only by public-policy considerations having to do with whether the injury was too remote, out of proportion, or extraordinary, or the liability too burdensome, unlimited, or potentially fraudulent.

Ethics

Solicitation—popularly known as "ambulance chasing"—is the scarlet letter for the plaintiff's lawyer. Rule 7.3(a) of the ABA Model Rules of Professional Conduct prohibits lawyers from soliciting a prospective client in-person, by live telephone, or by real-time electronic contact (chat rooms) "when a significant motive for the lawyer's doing so is the lawyer's pecuniary gain," unless the potential client whom the lawyer contacts is another lawyer or a family member, close friend, or former client. Can you articulate the justifications for prohibiting lawyer soliciting of accident victims? States generally permit targeted mailings to accident victims, although Rule 7.3(c) requires that lawyers mark "Advertising Material" on the envelopes and communications. Can you discern why?

Middle Ground. The Restatement (Second) of Torts §552(2) (1965) adopts a middle ground between the purpose-person-conduct requirements at one end of the spectrum and the general-negligence rule at the other end, for professional negligent-misrepresentation liability to third parties. Section 552(2) restricts the class and transactions to which the accounting firm is liable without requiring particular conduct toward the third person—in essence, adopting a similar person-similar transaction rule. Under §552(2), if the accountant intends the information for the benefit of a person or group of persons, for influencing a certain transaction or substantially similar transaction, then the accountant is liable for loss due to negligent misrepresentation to one of that group in one of those transactions. Section 522(2)'s middle ground is probably the majority position. *See* First Ntl. Bank of Commerce v. Monco Agency, 911 F.2d 1053 (5th Cir. 1990) (Louisiana law); Nycal v. KPMG Peat Marwick LLP, 426 Mass. 491, 688 N.E.2d 1368 (1998). Consider an illustrative case taking §522(2)'s majority, middle-ground position.

Bily v. Arthur Young & Co.
California Supreme Court
3 Cal.4th 370, 834 P.2d 745, 11 Cal. Rptr.2d 51 (1992)

LUCAS, C.J. We granted review to consider whether and to what extent an accountant's duty of care in the preparation of an independent audit of a client's financial statements extends to persons other than the client.

Since Chief Judge Cardozo's seminal opinion in *Ultramares Corp. v. Touche* (1931) 255 N.Y. 170, 174 N.E. 441 (*Ultramares*), the issue before us has been frequently considered and debated by courts and commentators. Different schools of thought have emerged. At the center of the controversy are difficult questions concerning the role of the accounting profession in performing audits, the conceivably limitless scope of an accountant's liability to nonclients who may come to read and rely on audit reports, and the effect of tort liability rules on the availability, cost, and reliability of those reports. ...

This litigation emanates from the meteoric rise and equally rapid demise of Osborne Computer Corporation (hereafter the company). Founded in 1980 by entrepreneur Adam Osborne, the company manufactured the first portable personal computer for the mass market. Shipments began in 1981. By fall 1982, sales of the company's sole product, the Osborne I computer, had reached $10 million per month, making the company one of the fastest growing enterprises in the history of American business.

In late 1982, the company began planning for an early 1983 initial public offering of its stock, engaging three investment banking firms as underwriters. ... In order to obtain "bridge" financing needed to meet the company's capital requirements until the offering, the company issued warrants to investors in exchange for direct loans or letters of credit to secure bank loans to the company (the warrant transaction). The warrants entitled their holders to purchase blocks of the company's stock at favorable prices that were expected to yield a sizable profit if and when the public offering took place.

Plaintiffs in this case were investors in the company. ... Several plaintiffs purchased warrants from the company as part of the warrant transaction. ...

The company retained defendant Arthur Young & Company ... to perform audits and issue audit reports on its 1981 and 1982 financial statements. ... In its role as auditor, Arthur Young's responsibility was to review the annual financial statements prepared by the company's in-house accounting department, examine the books and records of the company, and issue an audit opinion on the financial statements.

Arthur Young issued unqualified or "clean" audit opinions on the company's 1981 and 1982 financial statements. ...

Arthur Young's audit opinion on the 1982 financial statements was issued on February 11, 1983. The Arthur Young partner in charge of the audit personally delivered 100 sets of the professionally printed opinion to the company. With one exception, plaintiffs testified that their investments were made in reliance on Arthur Young's unqualified audit opinion on the company's 1982 financial statements.[fn]

As the warrant transaction closed on April 8, 1983, the company's financial performance began to falter. ... The company filed for bankruptcy on September 13, 1983. Plaintiffs ultimately lost their investments.

... The focus of plaintiffs' claims was Arthur Young's audit and audit opinion of the company's 1982 financial statements.

Plaintiffs' principal expert witness, William J. Baedecker, reviewed the 1982 audit and offered a critique identifying more than 40 deficiencies in Arthur Young's performance amounting, in Baedecker's view, to gross professional negligence. In his opinion, Arthur Young did not perform its examination in accordance with GAAS. He found the liabilities on the company's financial statements to have been understated by approximately $3 million. As a result, the company's supposed $69,000 operating profit was, in his view, a loss of more than $3 million. ...

The case was tried to a jury for 13 weeks. At the close of the evidence and arguments, the jury received instructions and special verdict questions including three theories of recovery: fraud, negligent misrepresentation, and professional negligence.
...

The jury exonerated Arthur Young with respect to the allegations of intentional fraud and negligent misrepresentation, but returned a verdict in plaintiffs' favor based on professional negligence. ...

The complex nature of the audit function and its economic implications has resulted in different approaches to the question whether CPA auditors should be subjected to liability to third parties who read and rely on audit reports. ...

A substantial number of jurisdictions follow the lead of Chief Judge Cardozo's 1931 opinion for the New York Court of Appeals in *Ultramares, supra,* 174 N.E. 441, by denying recovery to third parties for auditor negligence in the absence of a third party relationship to the auditor that is "akin to privity." [C] In contrast, a handful of jurisdictions, spurred by law review commentary, have recently allowed recovery based on auditor negligence to third parties whose reliance on the audit report was "foreseeable." [C]

Most jurisdictions, supported by the weight of commentary and the modern English common law decisions cited by the parties, have steered a middle course based in varying degrees on Restatement Second of Torts section 552, which generally imposes liability on suppliers of commercial information to third persons who are intended beneficiaries of the information. [C] ...

Section 552 of the Restatement Second of Torts covers "Information Negligently Supplied for the Guidance of Others." It states a general principle that one who negligently supplies false information "for the guidance of others in their business transactions" is liable for economic loss suffered by the recipients in justifiable reliance on the information. [C] But the liability created by the general principle is expressly limited to loss suffered: "(a) [B]y the person or one of a limited group of persons for whose benefit and guidance he intends to supply the information or knows that the recipient intends to supply it; and (b) through reliance upon it in a transaction that he intends the information to influence or knows that the recipient so intends or in a substantially similar transaction." [C] To paraphrase, a supplier of information is liable for negligence to a third party only if he or she intends to supply the information for the benefit of one or more third parties in a specific transaction or type of transaction identified to the supplier. ...

Under the Restatement rule, an auditor retained to conduct an annual audit and to furnish an opinion for no particular purpose generally undertakes no duty to third parties. ...

Viewing the problem before us in light of the factors set forth above, we decline to permit all merely foreseeable third party users of audit reports to sue the auditor on a theory of professional negligence. Our holding is premised on three central concerns: (1) Given the secondary "watchdog" role of the auditor, the complexity of the professional opinions rendered in audit reports, and the difficult and potentially tenuous causal relationships between audit reports and economic losses from investment and credit decisions, the auditor exposed to negligence claims from all foreseeable third parties faces potential liability far out of proportion to its fault; (2) the generally more sophisticated class of plaintiffs in auditor liability cases (e.g., business lenders and investors) permits the effective use of contract rather than tort liability to control and adjust the relevant risks through "private ordering"; and (3) the asserted advantages of more accurate auditing and more efficient loss spreading relied upon by those who advocate a pure foreseeability approach are unlikely to occur; indeed, dislocations of resources, including increased expense and decreased availability of auditing services in some sectors of the economy, are more probable consequences of expanded liability. ...

There is, however, a further narrow class of persons who, although not clients, may reasonably come to receive and rely on an audit report and whose existence constitutes a risk of audit reporting that may fairly be imposed on the auditor. Such persons are specifically intended beneficiaries of the audit report who are known to the auditor and for whose benefit it renders the audit report. While such persons may not recover on a general negligence theory, we hold they may, for the reasons stated in part IV(B) *post*, recover on a theory of negligent misrepresentation.

The sole client of Arthur Young in the audit engagements involved in this case was the company. None of the plaintiffs qualify as clients.[fn] Under the rule we adopt, they are not entitled to recover on a pure negligence theory. Therefore, the verdict and judgment in their favor based on that theory are reversed. ...

[Then considering the negligent-misrepresentation claims:] Of the approaches we have reviewed, Restatement Second of Torts section 552, subdivision (b) is most consistent with the elements and policy foundations of the tort of negligent misrepresentation. The rule expressed there attempts to define a narrow and circumscribed class of persons to whom or for whom representations are made. In this way, it recognizes commercial realities by avoiding both unlimited and uncertain liability for economic losses in cases of professional mistake and exoneration of the auditor in situations where it clearly intended to undertake the responsibility of influencing particular business transactions involving third persons. The Restatement rule thus appears to be a sensible and moderate approach to the potential consequences of imposing unlimited negligence liability which we have identified. ...

For the reasons stated above, the judgment of the Court of Appeal is reversed and this case is remanded with instructions to: (1) direct judgment in favor of defendant Arthur Young and against plaintiff Bily; and (2) decide the cross-appeal of the Shea plaintiffs and then to direct judgment or further proceedings as appropriate, consistent with our opinion.

INQUIRY

Lawyers. Although the leading cases addressing third-party liability for negligent misrepresentation have involved accounting firms, courts may apply the same rules to claims against other professionals, including lawyers. *See* Vereins-Und Westbank, AG v. Carter, 691 F. Supp. 704 (S.D. N.Y. 1988) (*Ultramares*-type liability of lawyer to third party for misrepresentations in opinion letter); Prudential Ins. Co. v. Dewey, Ballantine, et al., 80 N.Y.2d 377, 605 N.E.2d 318, 590 N.Y.S.2d 831 (1992) (lawyer subject to misrepresentation liability for opinion letter written to client's lender); *cf.* Robinson v. Omer, 952 S.W.2d 423 (Tenn. 1997) (no third-party liability for lawyer's bad advice that secret taping of sexual encounters would be legal because it did not involve a commercial transaction); *but see* Ackerman v. Schwartz, 733 F. Supp. 1231 (N.D. Ind. 1989) (no third-party liability for lawyer's opinion letter). Attorneys in transactional settings commonly author opinion letters. Even litigators may opine for the benefit of their clients' creditors on probable litigation outcomes (recovery and exposure). Knowing what you do about the above third-party liability rules, what practices would you adopt to minimize your own exposure when writing an opinion letter to a client's lender, investor, or potential purchaser? What difference would it make to your practices to know that your state had adopted one of the above three alternatives—(1) the *Credit Alliance* purpose-person-conduct standard, (2) Restatement (Second) of Torts §522(2)'s similar person-similar transaction standard, or (3) the broader negligence-foreseeability formulation? Can you find a safe harbor (adopt clear practices to avoid third-party liability) under all three standards?

> **Ethics**
> The above opinions do not explore the conflicts of interest that a professional can have when stating opinions about a client's matters for the benefit of a third party. The ABA's Model Rule of Professional Conduct 1.7 prohibits a lawyer from engaging in a concurrent conflict of interest. Rule 1.7(a)(2) defines a concurrent conflict of interest to include those instances when "there is a significant risk that" the client's representation "will be materially limited by the lawyer's responsibilities to ... a third person... ." If a corporate client asks you to write an opinion letter to the client's bank evaluating the client's exposure in litigation in which you are defending the corporate client, then your advocate's role in the litigation may compromise your objectivity in writing that opinion. The safe practice may be to advise the client to retain independent counsel to make that evaluation.
> A simpler example would be if you tried to represent both a motor-vehicle driver and passenger from the same vehicle, in a tort claim against the driver of another vehicle whose negligence allegedly injured both of your clients in the motor-vehicle collision. If the defendant driver proves that your client driver was comparatively negligent in causing the accident, then your other client—the passenger—may have a claim against your driver client. Plaintiff's lawyers in that situation tend to avoid representing both the driver and passenger, because doing so may lead to the lawyer's disqualification from representing either.

Other Professionals. Can you envision other professions to which the alternative rules for third-party negligent-misrepresentation liability may apply? What about contractors and inspectors who give opinions on the condition of homes for sale? *See*

Barrie v. V.P. Exterminators, Inc., 625 So.2d 1007 (La. 1993) (termite inspector owes duty to third party). What about engineers who prepare site and soils analyses for job bids? *See* M. Miller Co. v. Contra Costa Sanitary Dist., 198 Cal. App.2d 305, 18 Cal. Rptr. 13 (1961) (engineers owe duty to third party); *but see* Marcellus Constr. Co. v. Village of Broadalbin, 302 A.D.2d 640, 755 N.Y.S.2d 474 (2003) (engineers owe no duty to third party, applying *Credit Alliance* test).

Indirect Reliance. What if the plaintiff cannot prove that the plaintiff relied on the misrepresentation but can prove that the plaintiff relied on others who relied on the misrepresentation? Some cases allow proof of indirect reliance ("fraud on the market") for claims involving personal injuries. *See* City of New York v. Lead Indus. Assn., 241 A.D.2d 387, 660 N.Y.S.2d 422 (1997) (personal-injury claim against entity misrepresenting safety of lead pigment allowed on basis of indirect reliance). Courts reject the concept outside of the personal-injury context. *See* Mirkin v. Wasserman, 5 Cal.4th 1082, 858 P.2d 568, 23 Cal. Rptr.2d 101 (1993); Kaufman v. i-Stat Corp., 165 N.J. 94, 754 A.2d 1188 (2000). Why the difference?

D. Loss

Finally, misrepresentation requires proof of loss or detriment. Tort law does not presume damages for fraud, even though fraud can produce the embarrassment, offense, humiliation, and other burdens of the dignitary torts like assault or intentional infliction of emotional distress. As shown repeatedly above, lawyers often plead fraud as an alternative liability theory to these torts, negligence and professional malpractice, property torts like conversion, business torts like interference with prospective economic advantage, and to breach of contract. Indeed, claimants sometimes too readily allege fraud. After all, the factual basis for the tort takes little more than the putative victim's claim that the victim subjectively relied on something that the defendant said or did in a way that led to some loss of expectation or advantage. The courts have dealt with the concern over fraudulent or frivolous claims of fraud in two ways. One is to raise the burden of proof from the usual preponderance of the evidence to the higher clear-and-convincing-evidence standard for fraudulent (as compared to negligent) misrepresentation. The traditional rule is that the plaintiff must prove fraud by clear and convincing evidence. The other way that the courts ensure that fraud claims are more than window-dressing to some other tort or strategic ploys pled for bargaining advantage is to require proof of loss.

The majority of courts employ a *benefit-of-the-bargain* measure for fraud damages, in which the plaintiff recovers loss based on the difference between what the plaintiff would have received if the transaction had been as the defendant represented and that which the plaintiff received in the transaction. A minority of courts restrict the plaintiff to proving *out-of-pocket* damages measured by the difference between what the plaintiff paid and what the plaintiff received—ignoring the (presumably higher) value of what the defendant misrepresented. Benefit-of-the-bargain damages will usually be higher than out-of-pocket measures. The defendant who misrepresents that a property having a $50,000 value but sold to the plaintiff for $75,000 has qualities and is in a condition that would warrant a $90,000 market value causes the plaintiff $25,000 in out-of-pocket loss but $40,000 in benefit-of-the-bargain damages. The Restatement (Second) of Torts §549 (1965) follows a compromise that allows an aggrieved party to recover out-of-pocket loss but also, in a business transaction, to attempt to prove benefit-of-the-bargain loss if shown with reasonable certainty.

Importantly, fraud permits recovery of compensatory damages in cases where no property has exchanged hands but the fraud affected other interests, where the benefit-of-the-bargain and out-of-pocket-loss rules do not work well. For example, in Brooks v. Doherty, Rumble & Butler, 481 N.E.2d 120 (Minn. Ct. App. 1992), the court allowed the plaintiff attorney to recover emotional-distress damages from the defendant law firm, when the plaintiff was able to show that the defendant fraudulently induced the plaintiff to accept an employment contract. Tort practitioners recognize these broader damages implications of fraud claims and advise their clients accordingly. Punitive damages may even be available, depending on the jurisdiction, especially with proof of intent to injure. *See* Roboserve, Inc. v. Kato Kagaku Co., 78 F.3d 266 (7th Cir. 1996); Warner Communics., Inc. v Keller, 888 S.W.2d 586 (Tex. App. 1994).

Chapter XIII

Defamation

The law of defamation has two major parts. The common-law elements of a defamation claim are the first part. You are quite familiar by now with learning and applying the elements of another tort. The elements of defamation are, like the elements of negligence and misrepresentation, actually overlapping conditions reflecting the policy concerns and interests that underlie the tort—not quite the analytically discrete aspects that one might, for learning purposes, wish them to be. You can still readily understand and apply them. What is distinct about defamation from other torts is the extent to which the United States Supreme Court has constitutionalized defamation law. The second part of defamation law involves understanding and applying a substantial body of First Amendment case law having its own analytical framework quite unlike the common-law elements of defamation. Thus, lawyers must analyze defamation claims in two parts—first to satisfy the common-law elements and then to determine whether the defendant's constitutional rights protect against the common-law claim. A third but quite subsidiary concern is whether common-law privileges also protect against the claim. Constitutional rights make the common-law privileges less significant in many cases. This chapter treats defamation in that order—the common-law elements, the constitutional framework, and the remaining consequences of the common-law privileges.

Defamation is a fascinating and highly specialized field of tort practice. Defamation is an ancient tort. It is the first tort listed in the torts section of the Roman Twelve Tables (449 B.C.)—that "[i]f any person had sung or composed a song, which caused slander or insult to another person ..., he should be clubbed to death." Defamation has an interesting, more-recent history in the English Court of Star Chamber's attempts to suppress seditious libel. It has an equally interesting (and equally political) history around the founding and early governance of the United States and a recent history touching on World War II, the McCarthy Era, the Civil Rights Movement, the Vietnam War, Watergate, and other national epochs and events. Defamation law has had to adapt to meet the rise and proliferation of the news and entertainment media. The internet now challenges it once again. Defamation law may seem antiquated in an information age and strained to respond appropriately to big government and omnipresent media, yet somehow it continues to provide a framework for the just redress of important personal rights and interests. You will soon see just how important and personal those interests can be. First gain a clear sense of its common-law elements, before appreciating the challenges defamation law faces to serve individual liberty, privacy, and property interests while accommodating the interests of the government, public, and electorate.

A. Common Law

OBJECTIVE: Given fact patterns involving communications over which a person desires to sue for damages, apply the common-law elements of defamation to determine which of those communications are actionable consistent with this section of the text.

Case Study: An academy had a financial audit every school year as required by state and federal law. The 2006 audit report showed that the academy complied with generally accepted accounting practices and had adequate cash reserves but that the academy should install a time clock to reduce the probability of over- or under-payment of three part-time, hourly employees. The academy board treasurer, a respected local accountant, moved to adopt the audit report, and it was unanimously. One week later, the local newspaper ran an editorial titled, "Where's the money?" The editorial stated that the academy board was "siphoning off" and "misusing" funding once reserved for traditional public schools. The editorial stated that the academy was "cash rich" and had inadequate financial controls, that employees were overpaid, and that there was "missing money." The editorial did not name any academy board members but did refer repeatedly to the academy board. The newspaper published the editorial during the academy's enrollment period, and enrollment dropped off. The academy's treasurer has said that she needs to resign to protect her professional practice. ***Identify, discuss, and evaluate the common-law elements of the academy's defamation claims and claims of any board members against the newspaper.***

Defamation involves false communication published of and concerning another that, together with extrinsic facts, carries a meaning tending to hold that other up to ridicule or contempt, resulting in special damages unless an exception exists where law presumes damages. Notice that no malice, explicit intent, or even negligence requirement exists among the common-law elements. A false publication that adversely affects the plaintiff's reputation in a manner that the defendant did not expect and need not have reasonably foreseen can constitute defamation under its common-law elements—a form, in a sense, of strict liability. *See* Cassidy v. Daily Mirror Newsp., Ltd., [1929] 2 K.B. 331. The definition just given includes several terms of art, as the unusual nature of some of the language implies. The element of "publication," the "of and concerning" requirement (traditionally known as the "colloquium"), the "extrinsic facts" aspect (traditionally known as the "inducement"), the defamatory meaning requirement (traditionally known as the "innuendo"), and "special damages" all have their own meanings defined by case law and their own rules, categories, and contexts. The subsections below treat each requirement in turn. To complete the framework before beginning, though, know that defamation is generally of two types—libel and slander. Libel is generally of the written form, while slander is generally of the oral form. Libel is one of the exceptions where the law presumes damages—where the plaintiff need not prove "special damages." Although claimants must ordinarily prove special damages for slander, exceptions exist if the defendant's statements are slanderous per se—typically including assertions that the plaintiff has a loathsome disease, has committed crimes of moral turpitude, has engaged in sexual misconduct, or is incompetent in business, profession, or trade. Consider each element.

1. Defamatory Meaning

The defendant's statement must carry a defamatory meaning. An old case Riley v. Lee, 11 Ky. Rptr. 586, 11 S.W. 713 (Ky. App. 1889), does a good job of collecting even older phrases that capture what the law means by a "defamatory meaning." To defame another means to "induce... an ill opinion to be had of the plaintiff, or [to] make him contemptible and ridiculous," "to hinder mankind from associating or having intercourse with him," "to disgrace," "to degrade him in society," or "to injure the reputation of another by exposing him to hatred, contempt, or ridicule...." Others trace the meaning to Parmiter v. Coupland, 6 Mees & W. 105 (1840) (Parke, Baron), defining it as "any imputation of wicked or corrupt motives...." The Restatement (Second) of Torts §559 (1977) defines a defamatory statement as one that "tends so to harm the reputation of another as to lower him in the estimation of the community or to deter third persons from associating or dealing with him." No matter the precise verbal formulation, just what carries a defamatory meaning depends on time and circumstance. What was defamatory fifty years ago might seem trite today—and what was trite fifty years ago might well be defamatory today. The statement need not be defamatory in the eyes of everyone or among "right-thinking" people. The plaintiff must only show that the statement would lower the plaintiff's reputation among "a substantial and respected minority" of people. Restatement (Second) of Torts §559, Comment *c* (1977); *cf.* Agnant v. Shakur, 30 F. Supp.2d 420 (S.D. N.Y. 1998) (song whose lyrics falsely identified plaintiff as a federal informant not defamatory even among a respectable minority). Would the defamatory statements in these cases still be defamatory today?

Grant v. Reader's Digest Assn.
United States Court of Appeals, Second Circuit
151 F.2d 733 (2d Cir. 1945)

HAND, J. This is an appeal from a judgment dismissing a complaint in libel for insufficiency in law upon its face. The complaint alleged that the plaintiff was a Massachusetts lawyer, living in that state; that the defendant, a New York corporation, published a periodical of general circulation, read by lawyers, judges and the general public; and that one issue of the periodical contained an article entitled 'I Object To My Union in Politics,' in which the following passage appeared: "And another thing. In my state the Political Action Committee has hired as its legislative agent one, Sidney S. Grant, who but recently was a legislative representative for the Massachusetts Communist Party."

The innuendo then alleged that this passage charged the plaintiff with having represented the Communist Party in Massachusetts as its legislative agent, which was untrue and malicious. Two questions arise: (1) What meaning the jury might attribute to the words; (2) whether the meaning so attributed was libellous. ... [A]lthough the words did not say that the plaintiff was a member of the Communist Party, they did say that he had acted on its behalf, and we think that a jury might in addition find that they implied that he was in general sympathy with its objects and methods. ... The case therefore turns upon whether it is libellous in New York to write of a lawyer that he has acted as agent of the Communist Party, and is a believer in its aims and methods.

The interest at stake in all defamation is concededly the reputation of the person assailed; and any moral obliquity of the opinions of those in whose minds the words might lessen that reputation, would normally be relevant only in mitigation of damages. A man may value his reputation even among those who do not embrace the prevailing moral standards; and it would seem that the jury should be allowed to appraise how far he should be indemnified for the disesteem of such persons. That is the usual rule. [Cc] The New York decisions define libel, in accordance with the usual rubric, as consisting of utterances which arouse "hatred, contempt, scorn, obloquy or shame," and the like. [Cc] However, the opinions at times seem to make it a condition that to be actionable the words must be such as would so affect "right-thinking" people.... . As was said in Mawe v. Piggott, Irish rep. 4 Comm.Law, 54, 62, among those "who were themselves criminal or sympathized with crime," it would expose one "to great odium to represent him as an informer or prosecutor or otherwise aiding in the detection of crime"; yet certainly the words would not be actionable. Be that as it may, in New York if the exception covers more than such a case, it does not go far enough to excuse the utterance at bar. Katapodis v. Brooklyn Spectator, Inc., supra (287 N.Y. 17, 38 N.E.2d 112), ... held that the imputation of extreme poverty might be actionable; although certainly "right-thinking" people ought not shun, or despise, or otherwise condemn one because he is poor. Indeed, the only declaration of the Court of Appeals ([c]) leaves it still open whether it is not libellous to say that a man is insane. ... We do not believe, therefore, that we need say whether "right-thinking" people would harbor similar feelings toward a lawyer, because he had been an agent for the Communist Party, or was a sympathizer with its aims and means. It is enough if there be some, as there certainly are, who would feel so, even though they would be "wrong-thinking" people if they did. ...

... [The authorities are] conclusive upon us, unless there is a difference between saying that a man is a Communist and saying that he is an agent for the Party or sympathizes with its objects and methods. Any difference is one of degree only: those who would take it ill of a lawyer that he was a member of the Party, might no doubt take it less so if he were only what is called a "fellow-traveler"; but, since the basis for the reproach ordinarily lies in some supposed threat to our institutions, those who fear that threat are not likely to believe that it is limited to party members. Indeed, it is not uncommon for them to feel less concern at avowed propaganda than at what they regard as the insidious spread of the dreaded doctrines by those who only dally and coquette with them, and have not the courage openly to proclaim themselves.

Judgment reversed; cause remanded.

Gersten v. Newark Morning Ledger Co.
New Jersey Superior Court
52 N.J. Super. 152, 145 A.2d 56 (1958)

FULOP, J.C.C. (temporarily assigned). The plaintiffs move for a summary judgment as to liability alone in an action for libel.

The plaintiff husband is an attorney at law of this State and has held the position of township attorney of the Township of Hillside. He has been a candidate for elective office. The plaintiffs allege that they have been "happily married since July 9, 1933" and the plaintiff husband verifies this by affidavit. There is no contradictory verification.

On December 18, 1957, defendant corporation published in its newspaper the following article:

> Wife Trouble Holds up Jobs.
> Hillside-A divorce suit upset the political applecart at last night's Township Committee meeting.
> Three top appointments were shelved at least temporarily, because of Township Attorney Emanuel Gersten's pending divorce trial.
> Before the session began, Gersten was slated to be named assistant attorney for 1958 with Magistrate Sidney Birnbaum taking the top attorney post. Former Mayor Henry Goldhor was to succeed Birnbaum as Magistrate.
> On the positive side, Adolph A. Winston was announced as successor to Mayor V. William Di Buono, effective Jan. 1.

Plaintiffs allege and it is admitted that plaintiffs were not involved in a divorce trial or "wife trouble," and the fact is orally conceded that the plaintiff husband's name was erroneously given in place of that of another person who was involved in a divorce proceeding. Defendant alleges that it published a complete retraction and apology on the following day.

Both sides concede that the publication complained of did not result in the loss of the appointment referred to therein. Plaintiffs contend that the publication is libelous per se and injured their general reputation and injured the plaintiff husband in his professional reputation as a lawyer and public official.

Defendants in their answer admit the publication and allege lack of knowledge and deny most of the other allegations of the complaint. They also assert the following affirmative defenses: 1. The words published do not have the defamatory sense averred and are not defamatory. 2. Absence of malice. 3. Absence of damages. 4. Privilege. 5. Publication of retraction. 6. Reasonable care. 7. Unavoidable mistake.

Truth is not pleaded and, in view of the retraction, is obviously not a defense.

It seems clear that none of the affirmative defenses pleaded are valid legal defenses as to liability except the denial of defamatory meaning. ...

" * * * [W]hen the words used are unambiguous in meaning but would be taken by some but not all persons in a given community to disparage the reputation of the plaintiff because of differing attitudes as to whether the conduct or character imputed to the plaintiff was reprehensible * * * the most authoritative viewpoint is that the words are actionable if the plaintiff would be demeaned thereby in the eyes of a substantial number of respectable people in the community, whether or not all so-called 'right thinking' people woud take the same view." Herrmann v. Newark Morning Ledger Co., 48 N.J.Super. 420, 439, 138 A.2d 61, 71 (App.Div.1958).

Thus the question is whether the plaintiff would be demeaned by the false statements in the eyes of a substantial number of respectable people.

It is common knowledge that a very substantial segment of the respectable population deem it disgraceful and even sinful to procure a divorce. To be sued for divorce in this State involves a charge of one of three wrongful courses of conduct, namely, adultery, extreme cruelty or desertion. There seems no escaping the conclusion that to be a party to a divorce proceeding suggests conduct disapproved by many respectable people. It does not establish guilt. Neither does an indictment. Yet, who can say that it is not injurious to reputation to be indicted?

Reputation is a fragile flower. A breath of unfounded scandal is often sufficient to wither it. Many may fail to read the retraction. Many may forget the details of the incident, but nevertheless long remember that there was once something derogatory in the press about an individual.

The injury may well be aggravated in the case of the plaintiff husband who is an attorney and who was a public official. Impeccable character is an essential ingredient of professional fitness for an attorney. His livelihood depends upon the degree to which he is trusted in the community. However, that may well go to the question of damages rather than to liability in this case, since the words published, if untrue, would be libelous with respect to any one. ...

Under N.J.S. 2A:43-2, N.J.S.A., the retraction excludes punitive damages. It has no affect on liability. Both general and special damages may be recovered. [Cc] ...

The motion for interlocutory summary judgment is ... granted as against the defendant Newark Morning Ledger Co.

INQUIRY

Time and Place. Would a false publication that a person is a liberal rather than a conservative, or a conservative rather than a liberal, be defamatory—subject the person to ridicule or contempt? *See* Steinman v. Di Roberts, 23 A.D.2d 693, 257 N.Y.S.2d 695 (1965) ("liberal" not libel); Haas v. Evening Democrat Co., 252 Iowa 517, 107 N.W.2d 444 (1961) ("conservative" not libel). Would the implication that a person was a member of a minority group be defamatory? *See* Natchez Times Pub. Co. v. Dunigan, 221 Miss. 320, 72 So.2d 681 (1954) (telephone listing indicating plaintiff was "negro" held defamatory). Would the false publication that a person had a certain sexual orientation be defamatory? *Contrast* Yonaty v. Mincolla, __ N.Y.S.2d __, 2012 WL 1948006 (N.Y. App. Div. May 31, 2012) (statements falsely imputing homosexuality are as a matter of law not actionable as defamation); Hayes v. Smith, 832 P.2d 1022 (Colo. App. 1991) (statement that plaintiff had proposed a homosexual relationship not slander per se); Boehm v. American Bankers Ins. Group, 557 So.2d 91 (Fla. Dist. Ct. App. 1990) (describing the "modern view" that statements regarding sexual preference are not slander per se), *with* Matherson v. Marchello, 100 A.D.2d 233, 473 N.Y.S.2d 998 (N.Y. App. Div. 1984) (defendant subject to defamation liability for mischaracterizing plaintiff's sexual orientation); Manale v. New Orleans, 673 F.2d 122 (5th Cir. 1982) (reference to plaintiff as "ya little fruit" slander per se); Mazart v. State, 109 Misc.2d 1092, 441 N.Y.S.2d 600 (1981) (reference to plaintiffs as members of gay community held slander per se). Cases have held that a false publication that a person had informed the police—perhaps a "jailhouse snitch," or a "rat"—is not defamatory. *See* Byrne v. Deane, [1937] 1 K.B. 818 (publication that plaintiff had informed police of illegal gambling at club of which plaintiff was a member held not defamatory). Can you articulate why? The law has supported efforts to protect racial minorities and members of faiths from hate speech, women from sexual harassment, children from pornography, and members of other classes from social stigma and marginalization. *See* Beauharnais v. Illinois, 343 U.S. 250 (1952). How should defamation law treat these efforts in the context of free-speech rights today? *See* R.A.V. v. City of St. Paul, 505 U.S. 377 (1992) (hate-speech legislation held unconstitutional in challenge by cross-burners).

> **Figure**
> Civil litigator Pamela Bresnahan is a partner at the Washington, D.C. office of the law firm Vorys, Sater, Seymour and Pease LLP, where she concentrates her law practice on the defense of professional-liability claims and insurance-coverage actions. She also chairs the law firm's Washington and Alexandria offices' litigation-practice group and advises law firms and lawyers on management and discipline issues. Ms. Bresnahan has chaired the ABA's Standing Committee on Lawyers' Professional Liability. She was also an ABA representative before the United States Senate for the confirmation hearings for Supreme Court Chief Justice John Roberts, and is a member of the American Law Institute. She is also a frequent speaker on professional liability and responsibility issues when not defending individuals, firms, insurers, financial institutions, and others relating to professional malpractice and other liability issues.

Innuendo. The defamatory meaning need not be in the words themselves but may arise from a combination of words, omissions, and accompanying materials or circumstances—traditionally known as the "innuendo." *See* Restatement (Second) of Torts §563, Comment c (1977). The plaintiff must plead the words and innuendo so that the factfinder may reasonably infer defamatory meaning, or the plaintiff will have failed in pleading. *See* Grice v. Holk, 268 Ala. 500, 108 So.2d 359 (1959). Defamation law looks to the circumstances surrounding the communication because of the artfulness that publishers may employ to avoid defamation but attempt to communicate its salacious or ridiculing effect. Perfectly innocuous statements and images can, when combined out of their innocent context, create defamatory content. *See* Geary v. Goldstein, 831 F. Supp. 269 (S.D. N.Y. 1993) (juxtaposing commercial actress's promotion of bread product with sexually explicit scenes created libelous implications of pornographic activity). On the other hand, some statements that might be clearly defamatory in one context may in another have no such sting. *See* Greenbelt Coop. Pub. Assn. v. Bresler, 398 U.S. 6 (1970) ("blackmailer" in bargaining context has no defamatory sting).

Truth. Truth, lawyers sometimes say, is a defense to a claim of defamation. *See* Newberry v. Allied Stores, Inc., 108 N.M. 424, 773 P.2d 1231 (1989), citing, N.M. Stat. Ann. §38-2-9 (1978). Stated properly, though, to be defamatory (to carry a ridiculing meaning on which the plaintiff may sue for defamation), the publication must be false. Yet several states retain a common-law presumption that defamatory speech is false, shifting to the defendant the burden to prove truth. In the constitutional context of speech on public issues, the Supreme Court has held that the plaintiff must have the burden to prove falsity as part of the plaintiff's case rather than that the defendant prove truth. *See* Philadelphia Newspapers, Inc. v. Hepps, 475 U.S. 767 (1986). Statutes authorizing actions for true statements made with unjustifiable motives may be unconstitutional. *See* Farnsworth v. Tribune Co., 43 Ill.2d 286, 253 N.E.2d 408 (1969). One might think that a plaintiff could hardly complain that the truth about the plaintiff was in itself demeaning—although some have tried. *See* Hutchins v. Page, 75 N.H. 215, 72 A. 689 (1909). Invasion-of-privacy claims may exist for unjustifiable public disclosures of private matters. Early in the nation's history and in the early common law, prosecutions for criminal libel (seditious libel or sedition) were possible even as to, and perhaps especially as to, true statements undermining of public authority. *See* Franklin's Case, 9 Hargrave St. Trials 255, 269 (1731). But Jefferson freed those convicted under the Sedition Law and remitted their fines with interest, and the Supreme Court has much more recently held any such criminal statute to be unconstitutional. *See* Garrison v. Louisiana, 379 U.S. 64 (1964). And so because a statement cannot be defamatory but true, and because the plaintiff has the burden of proving a defamatory meaning, better to say that the defamatory-meaning element requires falsehood than to say that "truth is a defense." Consider the following illustrative case.

St. Surin v. Virgin Islands Daily News
United States Court of Appeals, Third Circuit
21 F.3d 1309 (3d Cir. 1994)

HUTCHINSON, J. Appellant, Gabriel St. Surin ("St. Surin"), appeals an order of the District Court of the Virgin Islands granting summary judgment for ... the Virgin Islands Daily News, Inc. ("Daily News") ... in a defamation action involving articles the defendants published about St. Surin's activities at the Department of Public Works ("DPW"). The Daily News story inaccurately quoted a federal prosecutor as saying charges would be filed shortly against St. Surin. In fact, no federal criminal charges were ever filed against St. Surin. ...

St. Surin filed this defamation action on October 24, 1989, alleging two Virgin Islands newspapers published defamatory statements about him. In his claim against the Daily News, he contends that an article which appeared in that paper's Thursday, July 27, 1989, edition was false and defamed him. That edition carried a front-page story, headlined "Charges near against DPW official—prosecutor," under the byline of reporter Abu Bakr. The body of the article stated "[a] federal prosecutor says charges are expected to be filed next week against a Public Works Department official" and named Assistant U.S. Attorney James Hurd as its source. According to the story, Hurd had confirmed a suspicion that St. Surin was the target of a federal investigation. The article states Hurd and current and former DPW officials would not discuss the investigation's focus but refers to another law enforcement source as saying it centers on allegations St. Surin had granted government contracts in exchange for favors when St. Surin was head of the DPW's engineering division.

On the day the article was published, Hurd contacted the Daily News and told it his conversation with Bakr had been inaccurately reported. ... St. Surin was, however, the subject of an investigation by the Environmental Protection Agency ("EPA") for improper activity on an EPA grant. ...

... [W]e hold the district court erred in granting summary judgment on the merits. ...

One who publishes a defamatory statement of fact is not subject to liability for defamation if the statement is true. [Cc] The truth required is not complete truth but rather substantial truth. Minor inaccuracies regarding factual information will not make an article untrue and libelous so long as the statement would not materially mislead the reader. [Cc]

In a libel trial, the burden rests with the public-figure plaintiff[fn] to prove falsity. [Cc] [In] *Schiavone Constr. Co. v. Time, Inc.*, 847 F.2d 1069, 1083 (3d Cir.1988)[,] ... we held "the truth must be as broad as the defamatory imputation or 'sting' of the statement." [C] Therefore, it is necessary to determine the sting of the offending article before we can assess its truth. [C] We start with the headline over the Daily News article: "Charges near against DPW official—prosecutor." [C] It states a "prosecutor" has announced charges will soon be filed against St. Surin. The body of the article reinforces the statement. It says: "A federal prosecutor says charges are expected to be filed next week against a Public Works Department official." [C]

It is undisputed that the Environmental Protection Agency was engaged in an investigation of St. Surin at the time the article was published and that Hurd was aware of the investigation. In the affidavit he submitted with the Daily News' motion for summary judgment, Hurd stated he had told Bakr "an investigation was ongoing" at the time of the article. [C] In that respect, the article is true. It also appears St. Surin was the subject of an investigation concerning improprieties in performance of his public office with DPW. The article is also truthful in that respect.

Nevertheless, given the headline's reference to a "prosecutor" and the body's reference to the U.S. Attorney's office, the next sentence clearly implies to the ordinary reader that these charges will be criminal. It states: "Assistant U.S. Attorney James Hurd Jr. confirmed that the target of the allegations is Gabriel St. Surin, coordinator for special projects." [C] Later in the article, readers learn that the substance of the investigation, and presumably the charges, is the allegation that St. Surin "granted contracts and sought favors in return." [C]

The most troubling aspects of the article are its statement that federal charges are "expected to be filed next week," and the headline implying that they would be criminal in nature. [C] ... Hurd's affidavit expressly says he never indicated the action would be the filing of charges. St. Surin was never charged with a federal crime, though the EPA later proposed administrative sanctions against him. Nothing in the record shows any federal prosecutor anticipated charges, criminal or administrative, were imminent; and Hurd's quick request for a retraction strongly indicates the article did not accurately reflect either what Hurd said or the intentions of the United States Attorney's office. ...

The fact that a governmental entity was considering administrative sanctions when the Daily News published the article is not equivalent to the article's "sting." Public knowledge that one is the subject of an administrative investigation does not harm one's reputation as much as public knowledge that one is about to be charged with a crime. The "sting" of the article is the intention of the United States Attorney to file criminal charges against St. Surin within a week. The article does not mention any potential EPA sanctions but focuses instead on statements about "charges" falsely attributed to Hurd in his capacity as "prosecutor."

The Daily News' argument that the word "charges" could include any sanction from the government does not remove the sting of the article. Words take on meaning in the company of other words. They are gregarious. They take on tone and color from syntax and context. In defamation actions, words should be construed as they would be understood by the average reader. [C] So construed, we think the Daily News' article falsely implies that a federal prosecutor said the government will soon bring criminal charges against St. Surin. The record, as it now exists, is sufficient to survive summary judgment on the issue of falsity.[fn] ...

Accordingly, we will reverse the order of the district court granting summary judgment for the defendants and remand for further proceedings consistent with this opinion.

INQUIRY

Sting. The above *St. Surin* case illustrates that a statement with some truth in it may yet form the basis for a defamation claim if a reasonable interpretation is that the "sting" of the statement is not substantially true. Under this standard, would a report that prosecutors charged the plaintiff with one crime be substantially true if the plaintif was in fact charged with a lesser crime? *See* Sun Printing & Pubg. Assn. v. Schenck, 938 Fed. 925 (2d Cir. 1900) (no). Would a publication that a witness had observed a colonel's mistreatment of wounded soldiers in certain particulars be substantially true on evidence of the colonel's mistreatment of soldiers in other particulars? *See* Kilian v. Doubleday & Co., 367 Pa. 117, 79 A.2d 657 (1951) (no—publication could be false). Would a statement that the plaintiff was a "whore" be substantially true if she had once worked in a dance hall where she earned a percentage of the drinks she helped sell to men with whom she danced and who had the opportunity to consort with other women serving as prostitutes? *See* Crellin v. Thomas, 122 Utah 122, 247 P.2d 264 (1952) (no—statement could be false). An analytically true but commonly misleading statement, such as those occasionally employed in tabloid headlines, can have sufficient sting to the mind of the average reader to make it actionable. *See* Kaelin v. Globe Communs. Corp., 162 F.3d 1036 (9th Cir. 1998) (headline's sting not removed by clarification in body of article). On the other hand, some false statements simply do not have any sting—do not lower the person's reputation in a way that would make them actionable in defamation. *See* Tatur v. Solsrud, 174 Wis.2d 735, 498 N.W.2d 232 (Wis. 1993) (false report of plaintiff legislator's votes on legislation not defamatory); Decker v. Princeton Packet, Inc., 116 N.J. 418, 561 A.2d 1122 (N.J. 1989) (false obituary not defamation without proof that it was harmful to plaintiff's reputation).

2. Publication

A statement that carries a defamatory meaning but reaches no one, or reaches only the person who would have suffered lowered reputation had the speaker published it to others, is not actionable in defamation. *Publication*—a term of art having a meaning defined by substantial case law—is an element of every defamation claim. Publication does not require printing and distribution in the ordinary sense of "a publication." Indeed, it does not require any formality beyond that the statement reached someone other than the person defamed by it, and that the other person understood it. If the statement reaches others who do not understand the statement, such as when the statement is in another language the hearer does not understand, then no publication occurs—not to mention no ridicule or other harm to reputation. *See* Economopoulos v. A.G. Pollard Co., 218 Mass. 294, 105 N.E. 896 (1914) (no publication where words spoken in presence of others were Greek—a language not understood by those others); *cf.* Kimm v. Steketee, 48 Mich. 322, 12 N.W. 177 (1882) (German-language newspaper circulated among German-speaking population presumed to have been read and understood—and therefore been published). Publication can be either intentional or negligent. One who intends that a defamatory statement reach someone other than the person whom it would defame will have published the statement when it is does reach another person. A person who does not intend but reasonably should have expected a defamatory statement to reach another will also have published the statement when it does reach another. *See* Restatement (Second) of Torts §577 (1977). If the statement does not reach another person other than the person whom it would have defamed, or if it reaches others only through means the utterer should not reasonably have foreseen, then there will have been no publication, as the following case illustrates.

Morrow v. II Morrow, Inc.
Oregon Court of Appeals
139 Or. App. 212, 911 P.2d 964 (1996)

EDMONDS, J. Plaintiff appeals a summary judgment for defendants.[fn] [C] The judgment dismisses claims for wrongful discharge from employment, publishing a memo that purportedly cast plaintiff in a false light, and libel. We affirm. …

In January 1991, Piedra became the general manager of II Morrow. Plaintiff worked under Piedra's supervision. … In March 1993, plaintiff received an anonymous phone call on his voice mail at work. The caller advised plaintiff to look on the "O" drive on his personal work computer. Plaintiff found a file entitled "Jim" on that drive. He opened the file and discovered that it was a memo written by Piedra describing a meeting that he had had with plaintiff in December 1992. In the memo, Piedra [criticized plaintiff's work performance and noted that plaintiff had admitted that the criticism was correct.] …

… In his affidavit Piedra said, in part: "7. I began drafting the memorandum after receiving Mr. Hughes' directive. As I was drafting the memorandum, I saved it in a file labeled 'Jim.' I believed that I was saving the memorandum on my terminal only. I believed also that no one else on the network could access the file while as [*sic*] I was working on it. 8. After I completed the memorandum, I printed two copies of it. I sent one copy to Mr. Hughes, as he had requested. I placed the other copy in a confidential file. No one had access to the file. 9. I then took steps to delete the file labeled 'Jim.' After I did this, I believed that the file no longer existed. I believed also that the only two copies of the memorandum were the copies I printed for Mr. Hughes and myself. 10. After [plaintiff] resigned in April 1993, I learned that I had failed to delete the file labeled 'Jim' from the network. …"

Shortly after plaintiff discovered the memorandum on the "O" drive, he submitted his resignation to Hughes. In his affidavit, Hughes testified[that he implored plaintiff not to resign and told him that he was going to move Piedra soon and would find an acceptable place for plaintiff in the meantime.] … Hughes' imploration did not succeed. Plaintiff quit and filed this action. …

… [P]laintiff argues that "the trial court erred in dismissing [his] claims for false light and libel on the grounds that there had been no adequate publication." Initially, we address plaintiff's claim of libel. … The *Restatement (Second) of Torts* § 577 defines what constitutes publication: "(1) Publication of defamatory matter is its communication intentionally or by a negligent act to one other than the person defamed."

In this case, the evidence is uncontroverted that defendants did not intentionally or negligently publish the memorandum on the "O" drive. The only evidence is that publication, other than to Hughes, was inadvertent.[fn] *Restatement* § 577, *comment*

O, discusses the effect of an accidental communication: "The accidental communication of matter defamatory of another to a third person is not a publication if there was no negligence. Thus, an act that is not intended to communicate to a third person matter that is defamatory and which does not create an unreasonable risk of the communication is not a publication." ...

Plaintiff did not offer any evidence in the summary judgment record from which an objectively reasonable juror could infer that Piedra acted negligently. The only evidence is that Piedra believed that he had deleted the "Jim" file and that it no longer existed on the data base. We conclude that the trial court properly granted summary judgment on plaintiff's claim for libel because there is no evidence that defendants intentionally or negligently communicated the contents of the memorandum to a third party. ...

Affirmed.

INQUIRY

Negligence. What evidence might the plaintiff's attorney in the above *Morrow* case have been able to marshall and present to the court to prove that saving a potentially defamatory statement on a shared drive was negligence? Can a person safely send a letter to another person if the letter would, in the hands of a third person, be defamatory? *See* Barnes v. Clayton House Motel, 435 S.W.2d 616 (Tex. Civ. App. 1968) (yes, so long as the sender does not know that the plaintiff is married and that the plaintiff's wife might open and read the letter); *cf.* Roberts v. English Mfg. Co., 155 Ala. 414, 46 So. 752 (1908) (publication if sender should know that a third person may read letter). Would the reasonable person expect others to read a note posted on a bulletin board even though directed to just one individual? *See* Abofreka v. Alston Tobacco Co., 288 S.C. 122, 341 S.E.2d 622 (1986) (yes—presumption that it would be read by others); *but see* McKeel v. Latham, 202 N.C. 318, 162 S.E. 747 (1932) (declining to allow presumption and instead requiring proof that someone actually read it).

Internal Communications. Does a person who uses a stenographer to record internal communications publish them to the stenographer, or is the stenographer merely a cipher? *See* Rickbeil v. Grafton Deaconess Hosp., 74 N.D. 525, 23 N.W.2d 247 (1946) (publication, but possibly privileged); *but see* Watson v. Wanamaker, 216 S.C. 295, 57 S.E.2d 477 (1950) (no publication). How should the law treat necessary communications within an organization—as publication, no publication, or privileged? Cases reach all three conclusions. *See* Hagebak v. Stone, 133 N.M. 75, 61 P.3d 201 (App. 2002) (qualified privilege to make internal communications); Perez v. Boatmen's Natl. Bank, 788 S.W.2d 296 (Mo. App. 1990) (employee communications between branches not a publication); Jerolamon v. Fairleigh Dickinson Univ., 199 N.J. Super. 179, 488 A.2d 1064 (App. Div. 1985) (report of guards to director is publication).

Republication. How does one treat the liability of the original defamer (the one who originally spoke or wrote the defamatory communication, also known as the *primary publisher*), when the harm is not through the original statement by the defamer but through the statement's media republication? What, for example, does one do about the defamation liability of a person who only speaks the defamatory statement to a news reporter and no one else? The cases generally hold that the primary publisher is liable for the harm from natural and probable republications of the original defamation—that the primary publisher should reasonably have anticipated republication. *See* Moore v. Allied Chem. Co., 480 F. Supp. 364 (E.D. Va. 1979) (employer liable for *60 Minutes* republication of employer's defamatory statements concerning plaintiff's chemical affecting employees); Brown v. First Natl. Bank, 193 N.W.2d 547 (Iowa 1972) (bank liable for republication of missing-funds story told only to reporter). The one who repeats a defamatory statement made by another is also liable—even if truthfully attributing the statement to another, *see* Flowers v. Carville, 310 F.3d 1118 (9th Cir. 2002), and even if purporting not to be believe it, *see* Cobbs v. Chicago Defender, 308 Ill. App. 55, 31 N.E.2d 323 (1941). Can you articulate why the repeater—the gossip or newspaper reporter—should also be liable? Although the common law of defamation has its own conceptual framework and verbal formulations that do not explicitly include negligence-type language and elements, recognize in defamation's republication rule both the foreseeable-consequences principle and proximate-cause element of an ordinary negligence claim. Consider the following illustrative case.

Tuman v. Genesis Assocs.
United States District Court
894 F. Supp. 183 (E.D. Pa. 1995)

PADOVA, J. This case, apparently the first of its kind in Pennsylvania, is a "false memory" lawsuit[fn] by parents against their daughter's former mental health counselors.[fn] Plaintiffs, Kenneth J. Tuman and Joan E. Tuman, allege that while treating the Tuman's only child, Diane, for bulimia, Defendants implanted false memories that Plaintiffs murdered numerous children, sexually assaulted Diane, and routinely performed bizarre satanic rituals. …

Plaintiffs also allege that on numerous occasions during group therapy sessions, Defendants stated that Diane was the victim of incest and ritual satanic abuse, and then invited Diane to tell group members the identity of her abusers. With this encouragement, Diane falsely stated that Plaintiffs committed incest and murder, and lead a satanic cult. …

… Defendants assert that Plaintiffs' defamation claim must be dismissed because the Complaint fails to allege that Defendants published any defamatory communication. I disagree.

To state a claim for defamation, a plaintiff must allege (1) a defamatory communication; (2) pertaining to the plaintiff; (3) published by the defendant to a third party; (4) who understood that the communication pertained to the plaintiff and had a defamatory meaning; and (5) that resulted in plaintiff's injury. [Cc] Although Plaintiffs have not alleged that Defendants specifically stated that Plaintiffs committed incest and murder, Plaintiffs have alleged that Defendants implanted in Diane false memories of severe childhood abuse, and in this way induced and encouraged Diane to publish Defendants' defamatory statements about her parents. *See* Restatement (Second) of Torts § 577 cmt. f (1977) ("One is liable for publication of defamation by a third person whom as his servant, agent, or otherwise he directs or procures to publish defamatory matter."). … Accordingly, I shall not dismiss the defamation claim at this time. …

An appropriate order follows. …

INQUIRY

Republishers. If (as the above case shows) the one who originally makes the defamatory statement is liable for its foreseeable republication by another, what of the liability of the republisher? Obviously, certain entities traditionally called *conduits* like the postal service, telephone companies, and email service providers do not have defamation liability for unknowingly facilitating the transmission of defamatory communications. *See* Lunney v. Prodigy Services Co., 94 N.Y.2d 242, 723 N.E.2d 539 (1999) (no internet-service-provider liability for defamatory customer emails), cert. denied, 529 U.S. 1098 (2000); Anderson v. New York Tel. Co., 35 N.Y.2d 746, 320 N.E.2d 647 (1974) (same for telephone company transmissions). What may not be so obvious is that media republishers—newspaper, magazine, book publisher, radio, television, and film companies, for example, traditionally called *secondary publishers*—can share the defamation liability of the original defamer, again, traditionally called the *primary publisher*. We explore the subject further in the constitutional discussion in the section below. Can you articulate the different treatment of media secondary publishers and conduit communications companies?

Landowners. On a related but subsidiary issue, some courts have held liable for the republication or ratification of defamation the landowner on whose premises others post defamatory material, when the landowner fails to remove it after learning of its presence and defamatory nature. *See* Hellar v. Bianco, 111 Cal. App.2d 424, 244 P.2d 757 (1952); Tidmore v. Mills, 33 Ala. App. 243, 32 So.2d 769 (1947); *but see* Scott v. Hull, 22 Ohio App.2d 141, 259 N.E.2d 160 (1970) (rejecting defamation liability for failure to remove graffiti). The Restatement (Second) of Torts §577(2) agrees that "[o]ne who intentionally and unreasonably fails to remove defamatory matter that he knows to be exhibited on land or chattels in his possession or under his control is subject to liability for its continued publication."

Immunity. Congress granted internet service providers immunity from defamation liability, with the Communications Decency Act of 1996. Courts draw that immunity from the act's provision stating, "No provider or user of an interactive computer service shall be treated as the publisher or speaker of any information provided by another information content provider." 47 U.S.C. §230(c)(1). As this provision states, the immunity is for service providers (or, as the act also labels it, "interactive computer services"), not for content providers. One who creates and posts internet content retains defamation liability. *See* Hawbecker v. Hall, 276 F.Supp.3d 681 ((W.D. Tex. 2017) ($443,000 damages award for defamatory Facebook postings falsely asserting that plaintiff martial-arts instructor was a child molester). Service providers who enable the posting but do not create its content are immune. Some courts have treated the immunity broadly, following Congress's expressed intent to promote internet development to preserve a free market—even under aggravating circumstances involving highly threatening posts. *See* Carafano v. Metrosplash.com, Inc., 339 F.3d 119 (2003) (immunity for defamatory, pornographic post leading to disclosure of actress's contact information and sexually explicit threats to her and her son, requiring that they vacate home for several months); Zeran v. America Online, Inc., 129 F.3d 327 (4th Cir. 1997) (immunity for defamatory post disclosing plaintiff's home telephone, leading to death and other threats reaching a volume of one every two minutes, even after notice of defamatory content). One decision has applied the immunity not only to internet service providers but to anyone using an interactive computer service, expressly rejecting a notice-liability formulation that would have held liable users who post but did not originate the defamatory material, after given notice of the defamatory content. *See* Barrett v. Rosenthal, 40 Cal.4th 33, 146 P.3d 510, 51 Cal. Rptr.3d 55 (2006). Other decisions read the act more narrowly to allow claims where the service provider itself created the objectionable content, *see* Doe v. GTE Corp., 347 F.3d 655 (7th Cir. 2003), or where the service provider had no reason to believe that the objectionable content was for dissemination, *see* Batzel v. Smith, 333 F.3d 1018 (9th Cir. 2003).

Figure

Whistleblower advocate John Phillips, a partner at the Washington, D.C. law firm Phillips & Cohen, helped legislators modernize qui tam measures in the federal False Claims Act and since then has obtained over $2 billion in qui tam recoveries on the federal government's behalf from private companies defrauding the government. He also obtained a settlement for whistleblowers in their $160 million claim against a money manager alleged to have used sham companies for government licenses and discounts. Mr. Phillips founded the public-interest group Taxpayers Against Fraud Education Fund, to represent whistleblowers who file under the False Claims Act.

Self-Publication. What if the person (the plaintiff) whom the statement impugns is the only one to have repeated it—is the statement *published*? A good starting point is to recognize that the person who unnecessarily repeats a statement that has the effect of defaming the person may not complain of the effects of the repetition. *See* Lyle v. Waddle, 144 Tex. 90, 188 S.W.2d 770 (1945). Yet some statements simply must bear repeating. The classic case of compelled self-publication involves the employee dismissed on a false charge that would, if published, be defamatory. Although employees in this situation would have no interest in repeating such statements, subsequent applications for employment may require that they disclose the basis on which they left their former employments and the reasons for their termination, as legitimate subjects of inquiry for prospective employers. The former employer who made the false statement should foresee compelled self-publication in certain circumstances. Yet given the contrary interest and privilege that employers have in sharing frank evaluations with employees on their discharge, courts have not agreed on whether to recognize compelled self-publication as grounds to support a defamation claim. *Contrast* Cweklinsky v. Mobil Chem. Co., 267 Conn. 210, 837 A.2d 759 (2004) (self-publication does not satisfy defamation's publication element); Sullivan v. Baptist Mem. Hosp., 995 S.W.2d 569 (Tenn. 1999) (same); *with* Van-Go Transport Co. v New York City Bd. of Educ., 971 F. Supp. 90 (E.D. N.Y. 1997) (defamation liability for foreseeable self-publication). Some courts have followed a middle ground permitting self-publication claims but requiring that defendant know the statement was false or seriously doubt its truth, and intend or know of a high likelihood that plaintiff would have to repeat it. Arthaud v. Mutual of Omaha Ins. Co., 170 F.3d 860 (8th Cir. 1999).

Single-Publication Rule. How should defamation law treat, for statute-of-limitation purposes, the publication and sale of written materials—with a single cause of action arising only at the first publication or with new causes of action arising at each publication? The English common-law rule was that each new publication (each new delivery and sale) gave rise to a new cause of action. The majority of American states take the opposite, single-publication approach, since the advent in 1952 of the Uniform Single Publications Act. *See* Ogden v. Association of the United States Army, 177 F. Supp. 498 (D.C. D.C. 1959); Backus v. Look, Inc., 39 F. Supp. 662 (S.D. N.Y. 1941). Can you foresee any circumstance under which a second cause of action should arise after the initial publication? Restatement (Second) of Torts §577A, Comment *d* (1977) (printing of subsequent editions, rebroadcast of television or radio shows, and subsequent showings of films are separate publications from the original publication). Should the single-publication rule apply to the internet, just as it does to publication of books and magazines, broadcast of television and radio, and showing of films? Consider the following case holding that it does apply.

Firth v. State
Court of Appeals of New York
98 N.Y.2d 365, 775 N.E.2d 463 (2002)

LEVINE, J. This appeal presents the first occasion for us to determine how our defamation jurisprudence, developed in connection with traditional mass media communications, applies to communications in a new medium—cyberspace—in the modern Information Age. Specifically, we must resolve the question whether, for statute of limitations purposes, the single publication rule is applicable to allegedly defamatory statements that are posted on an Internet site and, if so, whether an unrelated modification to a different portion of the Web site constitutes a republication.

Claimant George Firth was formerly employed by the Department of Environmental Conservation as Director of the Division of Law Enforcement. His responsibilities included weapons acquisition. At a press conference held on December 16, 1996, the Office of the State Inspector General issued a report entitled "The Best Bang for Their Buck," which was critical of claimant's managerial style and procurement of weapons. On the same day, the State Education Department posted an executive summary with links to the full text of the report on its Government Information Locator Service Internet site.

On March 18, 1998, more than one year after the report was first released and posted on the Internet, claimant filed a claim against the State alleging that the report defamed him. The State moved to dismiss on the ground that the claim was time-barred under the one-year statute of limitations for defamation ([c]). ...

The State proffered an affidavit from Thomas Ruller, a State Education Department associate programmer analyst, stating that on December 16, 1996, at the request of the Inspector General, he placed an executive summary of the report on the Internet and made links to enable users to download or view the text of the report. Ruller further averred that no subsequent modifications to the text were made. In response, claimant's attorney submitted a letter indicating that neither he nor his client knew of any posting of the report on the Internet other than that described in Ruller's affidavit. The letter also noted that the State had modified the Web site by posting a report of the Inspector General regarding the Department of Motor Vehicles (DMV), which previously had been submitted to the court. Claimant asserted that a modification of a Web site should be considered a republication of information previously contained on that site. ...

[The trial court dismissed, and the appellate court affirmed.]

In *Gregoire v. Putnam's Sons,* we adopted the single publication rule, namely that "the publication of a defamatory statement in a single issue of a newspaper, or a single issue of a magazine, although such publication consists of thousands of copies widely distributed, is, in legal effect, one publication which gives rise to one cause of action and that the applicable [s]tatute of [l]imitation[s] runs from the date of that publication" (298 N.Y. 119, 123 [81 N.E.2d 45] [1948]; *see* Restatement [Second] of Torts § 577A [3]).

Claimant argues that the single publication rule should not be applied verbatim to defamatory publications posted on the Internet in light of significant differences between Internet publications and traditional mass media. Instead, claimant maintains that because a Web site may be altered at any time by its publisher or owner and because publications on the Internet are available only to those who seek them, each "hit" or viewing of the report should be considered a new publication that retriggers the statute of limitations. We disagree. ...

The policies impelling the original adoption of the single publication rule support its application to the posting of the Inspector General's report regarding claimant on the State's Web site. Communications accessible over a public Web site resemble those contained in traditional mass media, only on a far grander scale. Those policies are even more cogent when considered in connection with the exponential growth of the instantaneous, worldwide ability to communicate through the Internet. ... Communications posted on Web sites may be viewed by thousands, if not millions, over an expansive geographic area for an indefinite period of time.

Thus, a multiple publication rule would implicate an even greater potential for endless retriggering of the statute of limitations, multiplicity of suits and harassment of defendants. Inevitably, there would be a serious inhibitory effect on the open, pervasive dissemination of information and ideas over the Internet, which is, of course, its greatest beneficial promise ([cc]). Thus, we hold that the single publication rule applies in this case.

Claimant alternatively argues that if the single publication rule governs, the State should be deemed to have republished the report within one year of the filing of the claim when it added an unrelated report of the Inspector General on the DMV to the Education Department's Web site in May 1997.[fn] We conclude as a matter of law that this modification of the State's Web site did not constitute a republication of the allegedly defamatory report at issue here.

Republication, retriggering the period of limitations, occurs upon a separate aggregate publication from the original, on a different occasion, which is not merely "a delayed circulation of the original edition"). The justification for this exception to the single publication rule is that the subsequent publication is intended to and actually reaches a new audience ([cc]). Thus, for example, repetition of a defamatory statement in a later edition of a book, magazine or newspaper may give rise to a new cause of action ([cc]).

... The justification for the republication exception has no application at all to the addition of unrelated material on a Web site, for it is not reasonably inferable that the addition was made either with the intent or the result of communicating the earlier and separate defamatory information to a new audience.

We observe that many Web sites are in a constant state of change, with information posted sequentially on a frequent basis. ... A rule applying the republication exception under the circumstances here would either discourage the placement of information on the Internet or slow the exchange of such information, reducing the Internet's unique advantages. ... These policy concerns militate against a holding that any modification to a Web site constitutes a republication of the defamatory communication itself. ...

Accordingly, the order of the Appellate Division should be affirmed, with costs.

INQUIRY

Worldwide Communications. Social-media posts and other unfiltered and convenient use of the internet give individuals an unprecedented opportunity to air private and public grievances, whether true, false, or defamatory. *See* Chastain v. Hodgdon, 202 F.Supp.3d 1216 (D.Kan. 2016) (denying motion to dismiss political figure's defamation claim over private individual's Facebook post alleging twenty-year-old sexual assault). The international nature of the internet's worldwide web creates other challenges for defamation law—namely, at what distance a plaintiff may claim its protection and what defamation law the courts will apply. Courts in Australia and England have recognized defamation claims under law different from that of the United States, for defamation that originated on the internet in the United States. *See* Lewis v. King [2004] E.W.C.A. Civ. 1329 (C.A. 2004) (English court applying English law that does not follow the American single-publication rule); Dow Jones & Co. v. Gutnick, 210 C.L.R. 575 (Austl. 2002) (applying Victoria law that does not recognize *New York Times v. Sullivan* First Amendment protections); *see also* Berezovsky v. Michaels [2000] 1 W.L.R. 1004 (English House of Lords applying English law to Russian's claim against American publication). The worldwide web challenges not only substantive law on the publication element of defamation but also related jurisdiction and choice-of-law principles.

3. Of and Concerning

To be defamatory, a publication must identify the claimant. The identification ("of and concerning" or "colloquium") element of defamation requires evidence that the defendant's communication would lead the reasonable person who knows the plaintiff to believe that the defendant intended to identify the plaintiff. A reputation-lowering statement that does not identify any person is not actionable. *See* Brunner v Holloway, 235 So.3d 1153 (La. Ct. App. 2017) (fraternity director's social-media post not actionable as defamation when not identifying plaintiff expelled fraternity members); Weidman v. Ketcham, 278 N.Y. 129, 15 N.E.2d 426 (1938) (postcard shown to postmaster without identifying plaintiff, and then, given its defamatory nature, placed in envelope and marked with plaintiff's name outside postmaster's presence, has not sufficiently connected the plaintiff to the defamatory statement to be actionable). Defamatory communications that name the plaintiff clearly satisfy the of-and-concerning element. Publications that do not use the plaintiff's name but instead identify the plaintiff's role ("the agent for the company"), title ("the Attorney General"), or office ("the president of the board of directors of the corporation"), also satisfy the of-and-concerning element, if someone who knows the plaintiff and the plaintiff's role, title, or office would believe that the publication referred to the plaintiff. *Contrast* Peagler v. Phoenix Newspapers, Inc., 114 Ariz. 309, 560 P.2d 1216 (1977) (identification as owner of business defamed by publication), *with* Arnold v. Sharpe, 296 N.C. 533, 251 S.E.2d 452 (1979) (reference to an employee, without specifying the plaintiff, held not identifying of plaintiff); Sims v. Kiro, Inc., 20 Wash. App. 229, 580 P.2d 642 (1978) (depicting defamed store without identifying owner does not satisfy identification element as to owner). The defamatory communication and its context may certainly help in establishing the of-and-concerning element. Problems applying the of-and-concerning element arise in at least two contexts—purportedly fictional accounts that the person who knows the plaintiff would understand to be about the plaintiff, or when the statement identifies only a group of which the plaintiff is a member. Consider the following illustrative case.

Bindrim v. Mitchell
Supreme Court of California
92 Cal. App.3d 61, 155 Cal. Rptr. 29 (1979),
cert. denied, 444 U.S. 1040 (1980)

KINGSLEY, J. This is an appeal taken by Doubleday and Gwen Davis Mitchell from a judgment for damages in favor of plaintiff-respondent Paul Bindrim, Ph.D. The jury returned verdicts on the libel counts against Doubleday and Mitchell and on the contract count against Mitchell. ...

Plaintiff is a licensed clinical psychologist and defendant is an author. Plaintiff used the so-called "Nude Marathon" in group therapy as a means of helping people to shed their psychological inhibitions with the removal of their clothes.

Defendant Mitchell had written a successful best seller in 1969 and had set out to write a novel about women of the leisure class. Mitchell attempted to register in plaintiff's nude therapy but he told her he would not permit her to do so if she was going to write about it in a novel. Plaintiff said she was attending the marathon solely for therapeutic reasons and had no intention of writing about the nude marathon. Plaintiff brought to Mitchell's attention paragraph B of the written contract which reads as follows: "The participant agrees that he will not take photographs, write articles, or in any manner disclose who has attended the workshop or what has transpired. If he fails to do so he releases all parties from this contract, but remains legally liable for damages sustained by the leaders and participants."

Mitchell reassured plaintiff again she would not write about the session, she paid her money and the next day she executed the agreement and attended the nude marathon.

Mitchell entered into a contract with Doubleday two months later and was to receive $150,000 advance royalties for her novel.

Mitchell met Eleanor Hoover for lunch and said she was worried because she had signed a contract and painted a devastating portrait of Bindrim.

Mitchell told Doubleday executive McCormick that she had attended a marathon session and it was quite a psychological jolt. The novel was published under the name "Touching" and it depicted a nude encounter session in Southern California led by "Dr. Simon Herford."

Plaintiff first saw the book after its publication and his attorneys sent letters to Doubleday and Mitchell. Nine months later the New American Library published the book in paperback. ...

Plaintiff asserts that he was libeled by the suggestion that he used obscene language which he did not in fact use. Plaintiff also alleges various other libels due to Mitchell's inaccurate portrayal of what actually happened at the marathon. Plaintiff alleges that he was injured in his profession and expert testimony was introduced showing that Mitchell's portrayal of plaintiff was injurious and that plaintiff was identified by certain colleagues as the character in the book, Simon Herford. ...

Appellants claim that, even if there are untrue statements, there is no showing that plaintiff was identified as the character, Simon Herford, in the novel "Touching."

Appellants allege that plaintiff failed to show he was identifiable as Simon Herford, relying on the fact that the character in "Touching" was described in the book as a "fat Santa Claus type with long white hair, white sideburns, a cherubic rosy face and rosy forearms" and that Bindrim was clean shaven and had short hair. ...

... [T]he only differences between plaintiff and the Herford character in "Touching" were physical appearance and that Herford was a psychiatrist rather than psychologist. Otherwise, the character Simon Herford was very similar to the actual plaintiff. We cannot say ... that no one who knew plaintiff Bindrim could reasonably identify him with the fictional character. Plaintiff was identified as Herford by several witnesses and plaintiff's own tape recordings of the marathon sessions show that the novel was based substantially on plaintiff's conduct in the nude marathon. ...

... [A]part from some of those episodes allegedly constituting the libelous matter itself, and apart from the physical difference and the fact that plaintiff had a Ph.D., and not an M.D., the similarities between Herford and Bindrim are clear, and the transcripts of the actual encounter weekend show a close parallel between the narrative of plaintiff's novel and the actual real life events. Here, there were many similarities between the character, Herford, and the plaintiff Bindrim... . There is overwhelming evidence that plaintiff and "Herford" were one.

... Defendants contend that the fact that the book was labeled as being a "novel" bars any claim that the writer or publisher could be found to have implied that the characters in the book were factual representations not of the fictional characters but of an actual non-fictional person. That contention, thus broadly stated, is unsupported by the cases. The test is whether a reasonable person, reading the book, would understand that the fictional character therein pictured was, in actual fact, the plaintiff acting as described. [C] Each case must stand on its own facts. [C] In some cases, ... an appellate court can, on examination of the entire work, find that no reasonable person would have regarded the episodes in the book as being other than the fictional imaginings of the author about how the character he had created would have acted. ... Whether a reader, identifying plaintiff with the "Dr. Herford" of the book, would regard the passages herein complained of as mere fictional embroidering or as reporting actual language and conduct, was for the jury. Its verdict adverse to the defendants cannot be overturned by this court. ...

Defendants raise the question of whether there is "publication" for libel where the communication is to only one person or a small group of persons rather than to the public at large. Publication for purposes of defamation is sufficient when the publication is to only one person other than the person defamed. [C] Therefore, [it is] irrelevant whether all readers realized plaintiff and Herford were identical. ...

The judgment, as modified on the motion for a new trial, is further modified as follows: (1) By substituting for separate judgments against defendants Mitchell and Doubleday a joint and several judgment against both of said defendants in the amount of $50,000; and (2) By including in said judgment a separate judgment against Doubleday of $25,000 for punitive damages.

Otherwise the judgment is affirmed. Neither party shall recover costs on appeal.

INQUIRY

Fictional Accounts. As the above *Bindrim* case suggests, the outcome of defamation claims involving fictional accounts can be uncertain, depending on the degree of similarity and the person's knowledge of the plaintiff. The topic has produced voluminous case law and academic study. To appreciate the variety and subtlety of the cases, contrast Pring v. Penthouse Intl., 695 F.2d 438 (10th Cir. 1982), cert. denied, 462 U.S. 1132 (1983) (Miss Wyoming pageant winner not defamed by account of a fictional Miss Wyoming performing sexual feats at a Miss America pageant); Flip Side, Inc. v. Chicago Tribune Co., 206 Ill. App.3d 641, 564 N.E.2d 1244 (1990) (business not defamed by Dick Tracy cartoon character of same name); and Springer v. Viking Press, 60 N.Y.2d 916, 458 N.E.2d 1256, 470 N.Y.S.2d 579 (1983) (former girlfriend of author not defamed by fiction using girlfriend's name), with Bryson v. News America Pubs., 672 N.E.2d (Ill. 1996) (fictional account using plaintiff's name and locale was sufficiently identifying); Geisler v. Petrocelli, 616 F.2d 636 (2d Cir. 1980) (fiction regarding a transsexual tennis player defames real tennis player having same name); and Middlebrooks v. Curtis Pubg. Co., 413 F.2d 141 (4th Cir. 1969) (obvious work of fiction that would be defamatory as to fictional character is not defamatory to author's boyhood friend whose identity bore some resemblances). Consider then a case illustrating the problem of identifying the plaintiff in a group-libel claim.

Fawcett Pubs., Inc., v. Morris
Supreme Court of Oklahoma
377 P.2d 42 (Okla. 1962), cert. denied, 376 U.S. 513 (1964)

JACKSON, J. In the trial court, plaintiff Dennit Morris sued Fawcett Publications, Inc., the publisher of "True" Magazine ... for damages for libel. The suit grew out of an article in a 1958 issue of "True" Magazine entitled "The Pill That Can Kill Sports," concerning the use of amphetamine and other similar drugs by athletes throughout the country.

Plaintiff alleged in his petition that he was a member of the 1956 Oklahoma University football team; that the article imputed to him a crime against the laws of the state of Oklahoma and was libelous per se; and asked for general damages in the amount of $100,000, and punitive damages in the amount of $50,000.

At the conclusion of the evidence, the trial court instructed the jury to return a verdict against Fawcett, leaving only the amount of the damages for jury determination. ...

The jury returned a verdict for plaintiff and against Fawcett in the amount of $75,000 for actual damages. ...

... The article is approximately seven full pages in length; was studiously prepared after what purports to be painstaking research; and starts at pages 44 and 45 of the magazine. Across the center of pages 44 and 45, we find in large letters and bold type the following: "THE PILL that can KILL SPORTS." In the upper left hand corner of page 44 are these words: "Simply by using a phony letterhead, the author purchased by mail enough drugs to hop up over 100 football teams." Immediately under this statement is the following: "A SHOCKING REPORT:," which is emphasized by a red line underneath. In the middle of pages 44 and 45 is a picture of five bottles of pills; the sixth bottle is of the shape and type commonly used for hypodermic needle injections; and there are two hypodermic needles. In the upper right hand corner of page 44 is found the following: "You can go to jail for selling amphetamine to a truck driver or injecting it into a racehorse, yet this same drug is being handed out to high school and college athletes all over the country."

In the lower half of page 45, and flowing over onto page 44, is pictured a heavily loaded dual-wheeled truck bearing the sign or label on its side, "DOPE." In the body of the truck are two individuals labeled 'Avarice' and 'Ignorance' shovelling out dope to athletes, including football players, who are running behind the truck and catching the pills. Another person is handing out pills to a football player from the cab of the truck. Above the engine of the truck are these words: "Victory at any Cost." ...

While the article is too lengthy to be quoted, a few excerpts which appear to be fairly representative of the entire article are quoted as follows: ... "*Speaking of football teams*, during the 1956 season, *while Oklahoma was increasing its sensational victory streak*, several *physicians observed Oklahoma players being sprayed in the nostrils with an atomizer. And during a televised game, a close-up showed Oklahoma spray jobs to the nation.* 'Ten years ago,' Dr. Howe observed acidly, 'when that was done to a horse, the case went to court. Medically, there is no reason for such treatment. If *players* need therapy, they shouldn't be on the field.'" [Emphasis in original.] ...

The article refers to several nationally known brutal crimes as being committed by users of amphetamine.

Plaintiff's evidence at the trial shows that the substance administered to Oklahoma players and members of the 1956 football team was "spirits of peppermint," a harmless substance used for the relief of "cotton mouth," or dryness of mouth, resulting from prolonged or extreme physical exertion; that plaintiff did not use amphetamine or any other narcotic drug, and there was no evidence that any other member of the team used amphetamine or narcotic drugs.

Plaintiff's evidence further shows that ... there were sixty or seventy members of the team in 1956.

Plaintiff's evidence further shows that many people asked plaintiff about the article in True, beginning shortly after its publication, and continuing until shortly before trial. ...

After reading the entire article and considering its effect upon the mind of the average lay reader, we are convinced that the article is clearly defamatory on its face and does expose the entire O. U. team to public hatred and contempt and tends to deprive the team and its membership of public confidence. The reader was unequivocally informed that the members of the team illegally used amphetamine; the article explained that amphetamine could be administered with a nasal spray and that for 95 cents one could purchase "enough to hop up an entire football team." The use of the phrase "hop up" negates any implication that the amphetamine was legally administered under the direction of a physician for medical purposes. The reference to the 1956 O. U. football team is so well tied into, or interwoven, into the article that the full weight and import of the article falls upon the O. U. team. ...

The additional and final legal argument presented under Fawcett's second proposition is that a defamatory publication concerning a large group is not libelous per se as to an unnamed member of that group. In this connection it appears that the courts have generally held that defamatory words used broadly in respect to a large class or group will not support a libel action by an individual member of the group. [C] ...

While there is substantial precedent from other jurisdictions to the effect that a member of a "large group" may not recover in an individual action for a libelous publication unless he is referred to personally, we have found no substantial reason why *size* alone should be conclusive. We are not inclined to follow such a rule where, as here, the complaining member of the group is as well known and identified in connection with the group as was the plaintiff in this case. ...

We hold, in answer to Fawcett's second proposition, that since the article is libelous on its face without the aid of extrinsic facts to make it so, it is libelous per se; that the article libels every member of the team, including the plaintiff, although he was not specifically named therein; that the average lay reader who was familiar with the team, and its members, would necessarily believe that the regular players, including the plaintiff, were using an amphetamine spray as set forth in the article; that the article strongly suggests that the use of amphetamine was criminal; and that plaintiff has sufficiently established his identity as one of those libeled by the publication.

In reaching the conclusion that plaintiff has established his identity in the mind of the average lay reader as one of those libeled, we are mindful that a full-back on the alternate squad of a university team who has played in nine out of eleven all victorious games in one season will not be overlooked by those who were familiar with the team, and the contribution made by its regular players. It should be remembered that plaintiff was a constant player, and not a part of the "changing" element of that group. ...

The judgment in favor of plaintiff and against Fawcett Publications, Inc., is affirmed... .

INQUIRY

Numerical Rule. Other courts have followed an intensity-of-suspicion test somewhat like the reasonable-identification analysis employed by *Fawcett Publications* above. *See* Brady v. Ottaway Newspapers, Inc., 84 A.D.2d 226, 445 N.Y.S.2d 786 (2d Dept. 1981) (plaintiff held to have been identified by defamatory remark made about a force of 53 police officers). These modern approaches contrast with the traditional numerical approach in which the courts consider only the size of the group and specificity of the remark made about it. *See* Restatement (Second) of Torts §564A, Comment *b* (1977) (members of groups of 25 or less are generally successful). Under the numerical approach, group size is only one of two important considerations. The other important consideration is whether the defamatory publication stated that it applied to all, some, or only one of the group. Thus, a letter that defamed "some of your workmen" adequately identified the five plaintiffs who sued, when they were the only five workmen. *See* Ball v. White, 3 Mich. App. 579, 143 N.W.2d 188 (1966). A report that defamed eleven workmen "or some of them" identified the one who sued. *See* Hardy v. Williamson, 86 Ga. 551, 12 S.E. 874 (1891). A publication that made a defamatory remark about "most of the sales staff" of twenty-five men defamed all fifteen plaintiffs of that group who sued. *See* Neiman-Marcus v. Lait, 13 F.R.D. 311 (S.D. N.Y. 1952). Yet an otherwise defamatory remark as to "the salesgirls" who numbered 382 was not actionable because not identifying of the thirty of that group who sued. Neiman-Marcus, *supra*. An otherwise defamatory remark as to ranchers in the United States did not identify Texas Panhandle ranchers. *See* Texas Beef Group v. Winfrey, 11 F. Supp.2d 858 (N.D. Tex. 1998). A defamatory remark that one of three persons was a thief was not actionable. *See* Cohn v. Brecher, 20 Misc.2d 329, 192 N.Y.S.2d 877 (1959).

Permissible Plaintiffs. The living may suffer defamation but not the dead, as to who remains (it is said) no personal reputation to impugn. *See* Gruschus v. Curtis Pub. Co., 342 F.2d 775 (10th Cir. 1965); Bello v. Random House, Inc., 422 S.W.2d 339 (Mo. 1967). What if the publication impugns the dead in a way that affects the reputation of surviving relatives? *See* Merrill v. Post Pub. Co., 197 Mass. 185, 83 N.E. 419 (1908) (allowing claim). Corporate entities can be defamed as to their reputation for fair-dealing and their business character, *see* Brown & Williamson Tobacco Corp. v. Jacobson, 713 F.2d 262 (7th Cir. 1983), but not as to matters, like chastity and disease, that are wholly personal, *see* Gilbert v. Crystal Ftn. Lodge, 80 Ga. 284, 4 S.E. 905 (1887). The harm to a tax-exempt nonprofit organization from defamatory remarks regarding the character and efficiency of its operations can be substantial. *See* R.H. Bouligny, Inc. v. United Steelworkers of America, 270 N.C. 160, 154 S.E.2d 344 (1967); Boston Nutrition Society v. Stare, 342 Mass. 439, 173 N.E.2d 812 (1961). Governmental entities, by contrast, are not afforded the right to maintain defamation actions. *See* City of Chicago v. The Tribune Co., 307 Ill. 595, 139 N.E. 86 (1923). Can you articulate why?

4. Special Damages

As the above introduction states, defamation takes two forms—libel (generally written) and slander (generally oral). The difference becomes important as to the *special-damages* element required only of slander (unless an exception applies) and not of libel. Although history explains the difference between libel and slander, the difference survives not as a relic of history but for its function—just as law likely first adopted it for functional purposes. The special-damages element addresses the concern that, without it, persons might sue for all kinds of unpleasant but otherwise innocuous comments that have no substantial reputation-lowering effect. Special damages require proof that the defamatory publication led to a pecuniary loss on the plaintiff's part—with *pecuniary loss* having its own defining cases and concepts but most obviously meaning a loss of employment, trade, or earnings, or other losses readily measured in monetary terms. Slander claims ordinarily require special damages, and not libel claims, because the spoken word is temporal, transient, ephemeral, and therefore less likely harmful than the written word. The written word can last, if not forever then a long time, on bookshelves, in magazine racks, and in files and papers. The spoken word vanishes with its hearer's memory. The special-damages element has the functional purpose of ensuring that plaintiffs bring slander claims only when loss is more certain than the spoken word's often-transitory effects.

The law patrols the line between libel and slander using the same functional interest. One would think that the distinction between libel and slander would be easy. Libel obviously includes newspaper, magazine, book, flyer, leaflet, sign, and other written publications. Slander obviously includes verbal remarks spoken between gossips, neighbors, acquaintances, and others, published and republished by word of mouth about the town, damaging the victim's reputation. Yet what of television, radio, and film? What of the republication by print and other news media of oral defamatory statements (that is, of slander)? Does the original speaker's slander spoken to the newspaper reporter become libel when it appears in the newspaper? The courts tend to use the functional purpose of the distinction—to ensure the reliability of damages proofs—to define the libel and slander categories. The Restatement (Second) of Torts §568 (1977) states that libel "consists of the publication of defamatory matter by written or printed words, or by its embodiment in physical form, *or by any other form of communication which has the potentially harmful qualities characteristic of written or printed words*" (emphasis added). Section 568 likewise defines slander as "consist[ing] of the publication of defamatory matter by spoken words, transitory gestures," or what is left outside its libel definition. Section 568 then adds, "The area of dissemination, the deliberate and premeditated character of its publication, and the persistence of the defamation are factors to be considered in determining whether a publication is a libel rather than a slander." Statutes today (following the Supreme Court's development of the constitutional principles) typically require treatment of defamatory statements in radio, film, and television after the fashion of slander—imposing additional requirements like demand for retraction and proof of special damages or actual malice—even though the common law would probably treat media like radio, film, and television as libel. *See* Shor v. Billingsley, 4 Misc.2d. 857, 158 N.Y.S.2d 476 (1956), affd., 4 A.D.2d 1017, 169 N.Y.S.2d 416 (1957). Consider the following illustrative statute.

KENTUCKY REV. STAT. §411.061 Actions against a radio or television broadcasting station for damages for publication of a defamatory statement; definitions

(1) In any action against a radio or television broadcasting station for damages for the publication of a defamatory statement by a visual or sound radio broadcast, the plaintiff shall recover no more than special damages unless he shall allege and prove that he made a sufficient demand for correction and that the radio or television broadcasting station failed to make conspicuous and timely publication of said correction.

(2) A "sufficient demand for correction" is a demand for correction which is in writing; which is signed by the plaintiff or his duly authorized attorney or agent; which specifies the statement or statements claimed to be false and defamatory, states wherein they are false, and sets forth the true facts; and which is delivered to the defendant prior to the commencement of the action.

(3) A "correction" is either (a) the publication of an acknowledgment that the statement or statements specified as false and defamatory in the plaintiff's demand for correction are erroneous, or (b) the publication of the plaintiff's statement of the true facts (as set forth in his demand for correction) or a fair summary thereof, exclusive of any portions thereof which are defamatory of another, obscene, or otherwise improper

for publication. If the demand for correction has specified two or more statements as false and defamatory, the correction may deal with some of such statements pursuant to (a) above and with other of such statements pursuant to (b) above.

(4) A "conspicuous publication" in a visual or sound radio broadcast is a publication which is broadcast at substantially the same time of day, and with the same sending power, as the statement or statements specified as false and defamatory in the demand for correction. A publication in a particular manner which is agreeable to the plaintiff shall in any event be deemed "conspicuous."

(5) A "timely publication" in a visual or sound radio broadcast is a publication within one business day after the day on which a sufficient demand for correction is received by the defendant. A "business day" is any day other than a Sunday or legal holiday. A publication on a particular day which is agreeable to the plaintiff shall in any event be deemed "timely."

(6) "Special damages" are pecuniary damages which the plaintiff alleges and proves that he has suffered in respect to his property, business, trade, profession, or occupation (including such amounts of money as the plaintiff alleges and proves he has expended as a proximate result of the alleged defamation), and no other.

INQUIRY

Boundary. What if personnel at a retail store stop a customer and search her bag without making any verbal accusations—libel or slander? *See* Bennett v. Norban, 396 Pa. 94, 151 A.2d 476 (1959) (slander—transitory act). What if a speaker reads aloud a defamatory writing? *See* Bander v. Metropolitan Life Ins. Co., 313 Mass. 337, 47 N.E.2d 595 (1943) (libel). What if the defamation defendant speaks in a setting where the defendant knows a transcriptionist records the speaking? *See* Ostrowe v. Lee, 256 N.Y. 36, 175 N.E. 505 (1931) (libel). Courts have held that the person who speaks defamatory statements to a newspaper reporter in a setting in which the person should reasonably expect that a written story commits libel. *See* Valentine v. Gonzalez, 190 App. Div. 490, 179 N.Y.S. 711 (1920). Historically, some confusion exists whether certain libel actions (those requiring proof of extrinsic facts beyond the statement to show the statements defamatory nature—and labeled "libel per quod") would still require proof of special damages. But the confusion seems to have abated, *see* Hinsdale v. Orange County Pubs., Inc., 17 N.Y.2d 284, 217 N.E.2d 650, 270 N.Y.S.2d 592 (1966), and the Restatement (Second) of Torts §569 (1977) does not require special damages, or "special harm" as the Restatement prefers to call it, in any libel action.

Figure

Mass-tort lawyer Michael Ciresi, a partner in the Minneapolis law firm Robins, Kaplan, Miller & Ciresi, represented the state of Minnesota and Blue Cross and Blue Shield of Minnesota in the tobacco-industry litigation. His work led to a $6.5 billion settlement and the release of millions of pages of industry documents. Mr. Ciresi used $30 million of the legal fees he earned from that case to fund a foundation supporting indigent civil legal services and other charitable causes. Among his other well-known credits was a $40 million verdict in a lawsuit involving anti-aging technology and for his work as chief counsel to the government of India in its claim against Union Carbide Corp. for the Bhopal disaster.

Proof. The difference between libel and slander—the imposition of the special-damages requirement for slander—can be significant in practice. From a practical standpoint, special damages are harder to prove than they might first appear. The plaintiff must find a witness who will testify that the witness heard the defamatory publication and believed it enough to let it affect the witness's assessment of the plaintiff's character or reputation in a way that led to the plaintiff's pecuniary loss. One must find a witness who is at once both friendly or sympathetic enough to the plaintiff in order to step forward and admit the necessary state of mind to support the claim, and at the same time unfriendly or unsympathetic enough to the plaintiff to have believed the scurrilous falsehood and have let it affect the witness's assessment of the plaintiff. The cases do not always adequately reflect this practical difficulty. The following case shows that the courts will dismiss slander cases in which proof of special damages are absent. It also recites some of the *slander per se* exceptions not requiring special damages even though the remark is only slander and not libel.

Scott v. Harrison
Supreme Court of North Carolina
215 N.C. 427, 2 S.E.2d 1 (1939)

This is an action to recover damages for an alleged slander of plaintiff by the defendant. The slander charged is that the defendant falsely and maliciously uttered concerning the plaintiff: "That the plaintiff while her husband, B. A. Scott, was the principal of the public schools in Northampton County, North Carolina, was forbidden by the authorities in charge from going upon the school grounds or premises of the Jackson High School at Jackson, North Carolina, for a period of six months." The charge is further supplemented by an allegation that the defendant stated that "the reason he was not reelecting Mr. B. A. Scott was due to the character and reputation of his wife." Plaintiff's husband was at the time of the alleged slanderous utterance, or immediately preceding that time, principal of the Dabney High School, which position he had held for ten years, and to which he had not been reelected; the defendant Harrison was Chairman of the County Board of Education of Vance County, having something to do with the selection of principals and teachers in Dabney District. ...

The plaintiff alleges that because of the slanderous remarks of the defendant, her husband was required to accept as a condition to his reelection that he would not seek reelection to his present position of principal.

No special damage is alleged other than the above, and the slander was not laid with an "innuendo", attaching a special meaning to the words "character" and "reputation" used concerning the plaintiff. ...

SEAWELL, J. ... Where slanderous words or accusations are not actionable per se so that general damages may be awarded therefor, the courts will not sustain a complaint as sufficiently setting up a cause of action which does not allege some special damage sustained by the plaintiff by reason of the slanderous remarks. In this respect the courts of this State adhere to the common law doctrine pertaining to libel and slander. The distinction between slanderous utterances actionable per se and those in which special damage must be alleged is traditional and does not always appear to be philosophical. The standards employed and the sense of moral values implied belong, perhaps, to a more practical age, and the rationale of some of the classifications is weakened or destroyed by changes which have come about through the years in the subjects to which they apply. It has been surmised that it was intended to confine actions of that sort to the graver accusations and those obviously calculated to result in damage. ...

Whatever may have been the origin, the courts are not permitted to go outside of the categories established by long usage to hold words, which to the layman may appear equally malicious and harmful, as actionable per se. Under this rule, false and slanderous utterances affecting one's business or occupation ([c]), false and malicious accusations of crime calculated to expose the person accused to public hatred or contempt ([cc]), and slanders of like kind, are actionable per se, and on account of their nature and relation, when properly charged, the law will presume that injury or compensable general damage has resulted, without allegation of special damage. [Cc] When the words do not come within this category, special damages must be alleged and proved. In the complaint under consideration none of the charges of slander is laid with an "innuendo" attaching any special meaning to the words used other than that which is obvious, and under the ordinary meaning they are not actionable per se. ...

Embarrassment, humiliation, and mental suffering, caused by the defamation, may be considered in connection with slanders which are actionable per se, [cc,] but, standing alone, will not be sufficient as an allegation of special damage. The injury must be material and pecuniary. "It is not usually enough for the plaintiff to plead that the publication of the slander has humiliated or embarrassed him or has been productive of mental anguish." McCormick on Damages, Hornbook Series, Section 114, p. 419. Perhaps because humiliation and the poignancy of mental distress are not easily measured in money values, they have been, at least in slander cases, considered in aggravation of damages. [C]

It is suggested that the condition imposed upon plaintiff's husband at the time of his reelection might eventually lead to his unemployment and result in damage to her. This, we think, is too remote and speculative for present consideration. [Cc] ...

The judgment overruling the demurrer is reversed.

INQUIRY

Exceptions. The above *Scott v. Harrison* case mentions some of the common-law exceptions to special damages—where even though the defamatory remark was only slander, the law considers it slander per se and recognizes a claim even without proof of pecuniary loss. Four common exceptions recognize where reputational harm would be so probable as not to require proof of pecuniary loss—defamatory accusations of (1) crimes of moral turpitude, (2) loathsome disease, (3) incompetence in trade or profession, or (4) sexual misconduct. Each, of course, has its defining limitations. The category for crimes of moral turpitude probably includes only major crimes with an implication of vileness or dishonesty, not merely minor assaults. *Cf.* Sipp v. Coleman, 19 Fed. 997 (D.N.J. 1910) (accusation that the plaintiff beat his mother would, though mere accusation of an assault, imply vileness sufficient to qualify for the slander-per-se exception). "Loathsome" disease probably includes the more serious venereal diseases but not a common cold or chicken pox. Incompetence in trade or profession certainly includes false accusations that an attorney is a "shyster," *see* Nolan v. Standard Pub. Co., 67 Mont. 212, 216 P. 571 (1923), a teacher is a molester of students, *see* Thompson v. Bridges, 209 Ky. 710, 273 S.W. 529 (1925), or a driver is a drunk, *see*

Louisville Taxicab & Transfer Co. v. Ingle, 229 Ky. 578, 17 S.W.2d 709 (1929); *but see* Bedford v. Spassoff, 520 S.W.3d 901 (Tex. Sup. Ct. 2017) (social-media post that baseball coach was a home wrecker not related to profession). Must the plaintiff still be employed in the profession to claim the harm? *See* Bassim v. Howlett, 191 A.D.2d 760, 594 N.Y.S.2d 381 (3d Dept. 1993) (physician who lost professional license has no cause for defamatory statement regarding his incompetence made near the time of the license revocation). Traditionally, the sexual-misconduct exception meant imputing unchastity to a woman, *see* Gnapinsky v. Goldyn, 23 N.J. 243, 128 A.2d 697 (1957), but the exception probably would now apply equally to men and women, *see* Wardlaw v. Peck, 282 S.C. 199, 318 S.E.2d 270 (Ct. App. 1984). Whether it continues to include false imputation of homosexuality is open to question. *Contrast* Donovan v. Fiumara, 114 N.C. App. 524, 442 S.E.2d 572 (1994) (false accusations that plaintiff is "gay" and "bisexual" are not actionable without proof of special damages), *with* Nazeri v. Missouri Valley College, 860 S.W.2d 303 (Mo. 1993) (false imputation of homosexuality remains actionable).

B. Constitution

OBJECTIVE: **Given a claim satisfying the elements of defamation, determine whether the plaintiff may maintain that claim under the First Amendment cases reflected in this section.**

Case Study: A newspaper's readers are college students who rent housing in a city where property owners are not popular. The student union distributed flyers objecting to high rents and poor living conditions. One property owner is particularly unpopular for renting subsistence housing at high prices close to campus. The newspaper ran an article calling the property owner a "slumlord" who makes "outrageous profits," and that he had been "convicted of rental housing crimes" for bad plumbing, roof leaks, non-working smoke detectors, and other safety and use issues. The article pondered whether he might have "done hard time" had he not "made friends in high places," and asked whether he had "paid the right people off." Public records show that city officials cited the property owner less often than other rental property owners, who constantly repaired his dilapidated properties. He had a heart for students, was charging just enough rent to cover the costs of his expensive and declining properties, lived frugally, and took enforcement action only because he had to and did not want paying students to subsidize deadbeats. The city treats rental housing violations as a civil infraction rather than a crime. The property owner's default rates skyrocketed after the newspaper article, requiring that he exhaust his modest cash savings, and he had several anonymous telephone threats and could not go anywhere without embarrassment. The newspaper's only "source" for its article was the student union flyer and interviews with student union representatives. ***Discuss and evaluate the newspaper's constitutional defenses to the property owner's defamation claim.***

As the above treatment of the common-law elements of a defamation claim suggests, defamation ordinarily does not require scienter. The defendant who publishes a defamatory statement need not have known that it was false. Law implies from the defamatory nature of the statement itself the knowledge, scienter, or malice that one might have expected the defamation tort required. Perhaps too charitably, the law presumes that we do not speak ill of one another without knowing the ill that we speak. From an instrumental standpoint, we cannot know with any certainty how strong of an impetus defamation law provides to truthful and civil discourse. Nonetheless, whether instrumentally or simply from the standpoint of right, the common law of defamation encourages that we speak only truth when lowering the reputation of another, causing pecuniary loss—whether in the public or private sphere.

The Supreme Court changed defamation's truthful-negative-discourse rule for the public sphere, in a series of First Amendment decisions spanning a little more than two decades from the mid-1960s to the mid-1980s. As the law now stands, defamation's common-law elements apply as above only when the defamatory statement is about a private figure on an issue of private concern. *See* Dun & Bradstreet v. Greenmoss Builders, Inc., 472 U.S. 749 (1985). When, instead, the defamatory statement is about a public official—elected or appointed, or any other government employee about whose qualifications the public would have an interest beyond the general interest (including, for instance, police chiefs, school superintendents, city managers)—the plaintiff must prove that the defendant made the statement with *actual malice* in addition to satisfying the common-law elements. *See* New York Times v. Sullivan, 376 U.S. 254 (1964); *see also* Monitor Patriot Co. v. Roy, 401 U.S. 265 (1971) (constitutional protection extends to defamatory statement "former small-time bootlegger" made about candidate for public office). A plaintiff must also prove actual malice when the plaintiff is a public figure, meaning someone universally famous or who voluntarily injects him- or herself into an issue of public concern to which the defamatory statement related, giving the person media access. *See* Curtis Pub. Co. v. Butts, 388 U.S. 130 (1967). A plaintiff who does not voluntarily inject him- or herself into a public issue but about whom, as a private figure, the defendant makes a defamatory statement on an issue of public concern, must prove the defendant's fault in making the defamatory statement and must prove actual malice to recover presumed or punitive damages. *See* Gertz v. Robert Welch, Inc., 418 U.S. 323 (1974).

When applying these constitutional rules, the Supreme Court defines *actual malice* not as the common law defines it (hatred, ill will, or the desire to see the plaintiff harmed) but as knowledge or reckless disregard of the truth when making the false and defamatory statement. *See* New York Times v. Sullivan, supra. The Supreme Court further defines a reckless disregard of the truth to mean a false and defamatory statement made with a high degree of awareness of the truth, *see* Garrison v. State of Louisiana, 379 U.S. 64 (1964), or with subjective serious doubt of the truth, *see* St. Amant v. Thompson, 390 U.S. 727 (1968), or while purposefully avoiding the truth, *see* Harte-Hanks Communs., Inc. v. Connaughton, 491 U.S. 657 (1989), or by materially changing the meaning by a deliberate misquote, *see* Masson v. New Yorker Magazine, Inc., 501 U.S. 496 (1991). The Supreme Court requires clear and convincing evidence meeting the constitutional standard and that the summary judgment standard for the defamation defendant reflect plaintiff's higher burden of proof. *See* Anderson v. Liberty Lobby, 477 U.S. 242 (1986). What constitutes actual malice is clearly a question of law for the judge to decide, not a question of fact. *See* Bose Corp. v. Consumers Union of United States, Inc., 466 U.S. 485 (1984). Consider, then, the progenitor *New York Times v. Sullivan* case, followed by more-detailed discussion of these rules.

New York Times v. Sullivan
Supreme Court of the United States
376 U.S. 254 (1964)

BRENNAN, J. We are required in this case to determine for the first time the extent to which the constitutional protections for speech and press limit a State's power to award damages in a libel action brought by a public official against critics of his official conduct.

Respondent L. B. Sullivan is one of the three elected Commissioners of the City of Montgomery, Alabama. He testified that he was "Commissioner of Public Affairs and the duties are supervision of the Police Department, Fire Department, Department of Cemetery and Department of Scales." He brought this civil libel action against the four individual petitioners, who are Negroes and Alabama clergymen, and against petitioner the New York Times Company, a New York corporation which publishes the New York Times, a daily newspaper. A jury in the Circuit Court of Montgomery County awarded him damages of $500,000, the full amount claimed, against all the petitioners, and the Supreme Court of Alabama affirmed. [C]

Respondent's complaint alleged that he had been libeled by statements in a full-page advertisement that was carried in the New York Times on March 29, 1960.[fn] Entitled "Heed Their Rising Voices," the advertisement began by stating that "As the whole world knows by now, thousands of Southern Negro students are engaged in widespread non-violent demonstrations in positive affirmation of the right to live in human dignity as guaranteed by the U.S. Constitution and the Bill of Rights." It went on to charge that "in their efforts to uphold these guarantees, they are being met by an unprecedented wave of terror by those who would deny and negate that document which the whole world looks upon as setting the pattern for modern freedom. * * *" Succeeding paragraphs purported to illustrate the "wave of terror" by describing certain alleged events. …

The text appeared over the names of 64 persons, many widely known for their activities in public affairs, religion, trade unions, and the performing arts. Below these names, and under a line reading "We in the south who are struggling daily for dignity and freedom warmly endorse this appeal," appeared the names of the four individual petitioners and of 16 other persons, all but two of whom were identified as clergymen in various Southern cities. The advertisement was signed at the bottom of the page by the "Committee to Defend Martin Luther King and the Struggle for Freedom in the South," and the officers of the Committee were listed. …

It is uncontroverted that some of the statements contained in the two paragraphs were not accurate descriptions of events which occurred in Montgomery. Although Negro students staged a demonstration on the State Capital steps, they sang the National Anthem and not "My Country, 'Tis of Thee." Although nine students were expelled by the State Board of Education, this was not for leading the demonstration at the Capitol, but for demanding service at a lunch counter in the Montgomery County Courthouse on another day. Not the entire student body, but most of it, had protested the expulsion, not by refusing to register, but by boycotting classes on a single day; virtually all the students did register for the ensuing semester. The campus dining hall was not padlocked on any occasion, and the only students who may have been barred from eating there were the few who had neither signed a preregistration application nor requested temporary meal tickets. Although the police were deployed near the campus in large numbers on three occasions, they did not at any time "ring" the campus, and they were not called to the campus in connection with the demonstration on the State Capitol steps, as the third paragraph implied. Dr. King had not been arrested seven times, but only four; and although he claimed to have been assaulted some years earlier in connection with his arrest for loitering outside a courtroom, one of the officers who made the arrest denied that there was such an assault. ...

The trial judge submitted the case to the jury under instructions that the statements in the advertisement were "libelous per se" and were not privileged, so that petitioners might be held liable if the jury found that they had published the advertisement and that the statements were made "of and concerning" respondent. ...

... We hold that the rule of law applied by the Alabama courts is constitutionally deficient for failure to provide the safeguards for freedom of speech and of the press that are required by the First and Fourteenth Amendments in a libel action brought by a public official against critics of his official conduct.[fn] We further hold that under the proper safeguards the evidence presented in this case is constitutionally insufficient to support the judgment for respondent. ...

The general proposition that freedom of expression upon public questions is secured by the First Amendment has long been settled by our decisions. The constitutional safeguard, we have said, "was fashioned to assure unfettered interchange of ideas for the bringing about of political and social changes desired by the people." [C] "The maintenance of the opportunity for free political discussion to the end that government may be responsive to the will of the people and that changes may be obtained by lawful means, an opportunity essential to the security of the Republic, is a fundamental principle of our constitutional system." [C] "(I)t is a prized American privilege to speak one's mind, although not always with perfect good taste, on all public institutions," [c], and this opportunity is to be afforded for "vigorous advocacy" no less than "abstract discussion." [C] The First Amendment, said Judge Learned Hand, "presupposes that right conclusions are more likely to be gathered out of a multitude of tongues, than through any kind of authoritative selection. To many this is, and always will be, folly; but we have staked upon it our all." United States v. Associated Press, 52 F.Supp. 362, 372 (D.C.S.D.N.Y.1943). ...

Thus we consider this case against the background of a profound national commitment to the principle that debate on public issues should be uninhibited, robust, and wide-open, and that it may well include vehement, caustic, and sometimes unpleasantly sharp attacks on government and public officials. [Cc] The present advertisement, as an expression of grievance and protest on one of the major public issues of our time, would seem clearly to qualify for the constitutional protection. The question is whether it forfeits that protection by the falsity of some of its factual statements and by its alleged defamation of respondent.

If neither factual error nor defamatory content suffices to remove the constitutional shield from criticism of official conduct, the combination of the two elements is no less inadequate. This is the lesson to be drawn from the great controversy over the Sedition Act of 1798, 1 Stat. 596, which first crystallized a national awareness of the central meaning of the First Amendment. ...

Although the Sedition Act was never tested in this Court,[fn] the attack upon its validity has carried the day in the court of history. ... These views reflect a broad consensus that the Act, because of the restraint it imposed upon criticism of government and public officials, was inconsistent with the First Amendment. ...

What a State may not constitutionally bring about by means of a criminal statute is likewise beyond the reach of its civil law of libel.[fn] The fear of damage awards under a rule such as that invoked by the Alabama courts here may be markedly more inhibiting than the fear of prosecution under a criminal statute. …

The state rule of law is not saved by its allowance of the defense of truth. … A rule compelling the critic of official conduct to guarantee the truth of all his factual assertions—and to do so on pain of libel judgments virtually unlimited in amount—leads to a comparable "self-censorship." … The rule thus dampens the vigor and limits the variety of public debate. It is inconsistent with the First and Fourteenth Amendments.

The constitutional guarantees require, we think, a federal rule that prohibits a public official from recovering damages for a defamatory falsehood relating to his official conduct unless he proves that the statement was made with "actual malice"—that is, with knowledge that it was false or with reckless disregard of whether it was false or not. …

We hold today that the Constitution delimits a State's power to award damages for libel in actions brought by public officials against critics of their official conduct. Since this is such an action,[fn] the rule requiring proof of actual malice is applicable. While Alabama law apparently requires proof of actual malice for an award of punitive damages,[fn] where general damages are concerned malice is "presumed." Such a presumption is inconsistent with the federal rule. …

Applying these standards, we consider that the proof presented to show actual malice lacks the convincing clarity which the constitutional standard demands, and hence that it would not constitutionally sustain the judgment for respondent under the proper rule of law. The case of the individual petitioners requires little discussion. Even assuming that they could constitutionally be found to have authorized the use of their names on the advertisement, there was no evidence whatever that they were aware of any erroneous statements or were in any way reckless in that regard. The judgment against them is thus without constitutional support.

As to the Times, we similarly conclude that the facts do not support a finding of actual malice. The statement by the Times' Secretary that, apart from the padlocking allegation, he thought the advertisement was "substantially correct," affords no constitutional warrant for the Alabama Supreme Court's conclusion that it was a "cavalier ignoring of the falsity of the advertisement (from which), the jury could not have but been impressed with the bad faith of The Times, and its maliciousness inferable therefrom." The statement does not indicate malice at the time of the publication; even if the advertisement was not "substantially correct"—although respondent's own proofs tend to show that it was—that opinion was at least a reasonable one, and there was no evidence to impeach the witness' good faith in holding it. …

Finally, there is evidence that the Times published the advertisement without checking its accuracy against the news stories in the Times' own files. The mere presence of the stories in the files does not, of course, establish that the Times "knew" the advertisement was false, since the state of mind required for actual malice would have to be brought home to the persons in the Times' organization having responsibility for the publication of the advertisement. With respect to the failure of those persons to make the check, the record shows that they relied upon their knowledge of the good reputation of many of those whose names were listed as sponsors of the advertisement, and upon the letter from A. Philip Randolph, known to them as a responsible individual, certifying that the use of the names was authorized. ... We think the evidence against the Times supports at most a finding of negligence in failing to discover the misstatements, and is constitutionally insufficient to show the recklessness that is required for a finding of actual malice. [Cc] ...

The judgment of the Supreme Court of Alabama is reversed and the case is remanded to that court for further proceedings not inconsistent with this opinion. ...

INQUIRY

Actual Malice. With the new constitutional, *actual-malice* standard in place to protect those who publish what the common law would consider to be defamatory statements against public officials, the Supreme Court then further defined actual malice through a series of subsequent cases. The *New York Times v. Sullivan* decision defined actual malice as (1) "knowledge that it was false or with reckless disregard of whether it was false or not." *See* Henry v. Collins, 380 U.S. 356 (1965) (repeating standard). As stated in the introduction above, the Supreme Court's decisions in the *Garrison, St. Amant, Harte-Hankes Communications,* and *Masson* cases resulted in the current understanding that actual malice also includes defamatory statements made with (2) a high degree of awareness of its falsity or (3) subjective serious doubt of its truth, or while (4) purposefully avoiding the truth, or by (5) materially changing the defamation target's meaning by a deliberate misquote. Each of these further definitions was necessary because of the different factual circumstances the Supreme Court and lower courts were facing for various defamatory statements against public officials. Although we state these further definitions in the disjunctive (as if any one alone would satisfy the standard), courts do not always read them independent of one another. *See* Tavoulareas v. Piro, 817 F.2d 762 (D.C. Cir. 1987) (purposefully not investigating is not alone enough), cert. denied, 484 U.S. 870 (1987). Can you hypothesize fact scenarios in which each of these further definitions would be more helpful than the *New York Times* decision's original *knowledge-or-reckless-disregard* standard? When, for instance, might the *purposeful-avoidance-of-the-truth* definition help establish the defaming publisher's actual malice?

Subjectivity. Each of the Supreme Court's definitions of actual malice involves a subjective, rather than objective, evaluation. Why are journalists not held to a negligence (professional malpractice) standard like doctors, lawyers, and other professionals? Does giving journalists the freedom to publish without professional-liability standards make the journalism profession any more or less competent? Any more or less respected? Any more or less trustworthy? Are public understanding of the political process and participation in it better served by increasing protection for falsehoods? Would truth and democracy be better served by allowing tort law to deter falsehood in the way that it deters unreasonably dangerous products, premises, and driving? Do you think that protecting "vehement, caustic, and sometimes unpleasantly sharp" false attacks on public officials elevates public discourse or lowers it? Is public discourse of a better or worse quality today than it was in 1964 on the eve of the *New York Times* decision? How would we even measure the answers to these questions? By the qualities and commitments of those who are willing to participate in such a process? Is politics today as honorable and desirable of a profession as it was in 1964?

See Post Pub. Co. v. Hallam, 59 Fed. 530 (6th Cir. 1893). Is the media more or less helpful to our understanding of the important issues? Are elections won and lost more so today based on truth than they were in 1964—or based on who can smear the other candidate more successfully? Does the *New York Times* standard promote the competition to climb to the shining city on the hill or to slide to the bottom of it?

Discovery. The actual-malice standard presents some interesting challenges—and opportunities—for the practitioner. How is the defamation plaintiff's lawyer to prove what the publisher knew or did not know—in essence, the publisher's state of mind? In Herbert v. Lando, 441 U.S. 153 (1968), the Supreme Court recognized that under its *New York Times v. Sullivan* standard, the plaintiff who must prove knowledge or reckless disregard that a defamatory statement is false should have discovery on the publisher's knowledge. The plaintiff has a right to discover from the defendant and others evidence that would support the plaintiff's claim that the defendant knew or recklessly disregarded that the published statement was false—although the justices in *Herbert v. Lando* did not all agree on the extent to which plaintiffs could compel disclosure. It does appear that courts would ordinarily permit the plaintiff to conduct depositions of the journalist writing the story and the editor reading and approving it, as well as to obtain interview notes, recordings of interviews, and other source material from the defendant's file. Should the reporter and publisher have any privileges—for instance, to protect journalistic sources? *See* Southwell v. The Southern Poverty Law Ctr., 949 F. Supp. 1303 (W.D. Mich. 1996) (source remains confidential).

Public Officials. The Supreme Court intended the *New York Times* decision to promote open criticism of public officials in the belief that it would lead to right conclusions and stronger government. Who, then, is a public official the robust and occasionally defamatory criticism of whom helps the public? Begin with elected and appointed officials who make policy decisions—like Commissioner Sullivan. Yet what of the hundreds of thousands of other public employees—like school teachers, housing inspectors, and bus drivers? In Rosenblatt v. Baer, 383 U.S. 75 (1966), a case involving false statements regarding the supervisor of a county recreation area, the Supreme Court held that a public official is one who has "substantial responsibility for or control over the conduct of governmental affairs." Remanding the case for determination of the supervisor's status, the *Rosenblatt* decision added that the First Amendment protects defamatory criticism of public officials "[w]here a position in government has such apparent importance that the public has an independent interest in the qualifications and performance of the person who holds it, beyond the general public interest in the qualifications and performance of all government employees...." So where would you draw the line? *See* Kassel v. Gannett Co., 875 F.2d 935 (1st Cir. 1989) (Veterans Affairs psychologist is not a public official for defamation-suit purposes); Staheli v. Smith, 548 So.2d 1299 (Miss. 1989) (state college professor not a public official for purposes of defamation suit against dean for statements contributing to denial of tenure); Krutech v. Schimmel, 50 MiSc.2d 1052, 272 N.Y.S.2d 261 (1966) (public-works accountant not a public official).

Public Figures. Before long, the Supreme Court found necessary recognizing another category to which to apply the *New York Times* actual-malice standard—public figures. *See* Curtis Pub. Co. v. Butts, 388 U.S. 130 (1967). The *Butts* decision involved two cases, one plaintiff the football coach Wally Butts and the other well-known retired Army general Edwin Walker, both of whom the Supreme Court held to be public figures. How the Supreme Court would treat a situation of obvious public interest and concern but that did not involve a government official remained uncertain until the following case.

Gertz v. Robert Welch, Inc.
Supreme Court of the United States
418 U.S. 323 (1974)

POWELL, J. This Court has struggled for nearly a decade to define the proper accommodation between the law of defamation and the freedoms of speech and press protected by the First Amendment. With this decision we return to that effort. We granted certiorari to reconsider the extent of a publisher's constitutional privilege against liability for defamation of a private citizen. [C] …

In 1968 a Chicago policeman named Nuccio shot and killed a youth named Nelson. The state authorities prosecuted Nuccio for the homicide and ultimately obtained a conviction for murder in the second degree. The Nelson family retained petitioner Elmer Gertz, a reputable attorney, to represent them in civil litigation against Nuccio.

Respondent publishes American Opinion, a monthly outlet for the views of the John Birch Society. Early in the 1960's the magazine began to warn of a nationwide conspiracy to discredit local law enforcement agencies and create in their stead a national police force capable of supporting a Communist dictatorship. As part of the continuing effort to alert the public to this assumed danger, the managing editor of American Opinion commissioned an article on the murder trial of Officer Nuccio. For this purpose he engaged a regular contributor to the magazine. In March 1969 respondent published the resulting article under the title "FRAME-UP: Richard Nuccio And The War On Police." The article purports to demonstrate that the testimony against Nuccio at his criminal trial was false and that his prosecution was part of the Communist campaign against the police.

In his capacity as counsel for the Nelson family in the civil litigation, petitioner attended the coroner's inquest into the boy's death and initiated actions for damages, but he neither discussed Officer Nuccio with the press nor played any part in the criminal proceeding. Notwithstanding petitioner's remote connection with the prosecution of Nuccio, respondent's magazine portrayed him as an architect of the "frame-up." According to the article, the police file on petitioner took "a big, Irish cop to lift." The article stated that petitioner had been an official of the "Marxist League for Industrial Democracy, originally known as the Intercollegiate Socialist Society, which has advocated the violent seizure of our government." It labeled Gertz a "Leninist" and a "Communist-fronter." It also stated that Gertz had been an officer of the National Lawyers Guild, described as a Communist organization that "probably did more than any other outfit to plan the Communist attack on the Chicago police during the 1968 Democratic Convention."

These statements contained serious inaccuracies. The implication that petitioner had a criminal record was false. Petitioner had been a member and officer of the National Lawyers Guild some 15 years earlier, but there was no evidence that he or that organization had taken any part in planning the 1968 demonstrations in Chicago. There was also no basis for the charge that petitioner was a "Leninist" or a "Communist-fronter." And he had never been a member of the "Marxist League for Industrial Democracy" or the "Intercollegiate Socialist Society."

The managing editor of American Opinion made no effort to verify or substantiate the charges against petitioner. Instead, he appended an editorial introduction stating that the author had "conducted extensive research into the Richard Nuccio Case." And he included in the article a photograph of petitioner and wrote the caption that appeared under it: "Elmer Gertz of Red Guild harasses Nuccio." Respondent placed the issue of American Opinion containing the article on sale at newsstands throughout the country and distributed reprints of the article on the streets of Chicago. ...

... After all the evidence had been presented but before submission of the case to the jury, the court ruled in effect that petitioner was neither a public official nor a public figure. It added that, if he were, the resulting application of the New York Times standard would require a directed verdict for respondent. Because some statements in the article constituted libel per se under Illinois law, the court submitted the case to the jury under instructions that withdrew from its consideration all issues save the measure of damages. The jury awarded $50,000 to petitioner.

Following the jury verdict and on further reflection, the District Court concluded that the New York Times standard should govern this case even though petitioner was not a public official or public figure. ... Accordingly, the court entered judgment for respondent notwithstanding the jury's verdict.[fn] ...

The Court of Appeals ... affirmed, [c]. For the reasons stated below, we reverse. ...

The principal issue in this case is whether a newspaper or broadcaster that publishes defamatory falsehoods about an individual who is neither a public official nor a public figure may claim a constitutional privilege against liability for the injury inflicted by those statements. ...

We begin with the common ground. Under the First Amendment there is no such thing as a false idea. However pernicious an opinion may seem, we depend for its correction not on the conscience of judges and juries but on the competition of other ideas.[fn] But there is no constitutional value in false statements of fact. Neither the intentional lie nor the careless error materially advances society's interest in "uninhibited, robust, and wide-open" debate on public issues. New York Times Co. v. Sullivan, 376 U.S., at 270, 84 S.Ct., at 721. They belong to that category of utterances which "are no essential part of any exposition of ideas, and are of such slight social value as a step to truth that any benefit that may be derived from them is clearly outweighed by the social interest in order and morality." [C]

Although the erroneous statement of fact is not worthy of constitutional protection, it is nevertheless inevitable in free debate. As James Madison pointed out in the Report on the Virginia Resolutions of 1798: "Some degree of abuse is inseparable from the proper use of every thing; and in no instance is this more true than in that of the press." 4 J. Elliot, Debates on the Federal Constitution of 1787, p. 571 (1876). And punishment of error runs the risk of inducing a cautious and restrictive exercise of the constitutionally guaranteed freedoms of speech and press. Our decisions recognize that a rule of strict liability that compels a publisher or broadcaster to guarantee the accuracy of his factual assertions may lead to intolerable self-censorship. ...

The need to avoid self-censorship by the news media is, however, not the only societal value at issue. ...

The legitimate state interest underlying the law of libel is the compensation of individuals for the harm inflicted on them by defamatory falsehood. We would not lightly require the State to abandon this purpose, for, as Mr. Justice Stewart has reminded us, the individual's right to the protection of his own good name "reflects no more than our basic concept of the essential dignity and worth of every human being—a concept at the root of any decent system of ordered liberty. The protection of private personality, like the protection of life itself, is left primarily to the individual States under the Ninth and Tenth Amendments. But this does not mean that the right is entitled to any less recognition by this Court as a basic of our constitutional system." [C]

Some tension necessarily exists between the need for a vigorous and uninhibited press and the legitimate interest in redressing wrongful injury. ... In our continuing effort to define the proper accommodation between these competing concerns, we have been especially anxious to assure to the freedoms of speech and press that "breathing space" essential to their fruitful exercise. [C] To that end this Court has extended a measure of strategic protection to defamatory falsehood.

The New York Times standard defines the level of constitutional protection appropriate to the context of defamation of a public person. Those who, by reason of the notoriety of their achievements or the vigor and success with which they seek the public's attention, are properly classed as public figures and those who hold governmental office may recover for injury to reputation only on clear and convincing proof that the defamatory falsehood was made with knowledge of its falsity or with reckless disregard for the truth. This standard administers an extremely powerful antidote to the inducement to media self-censorship of the common-law rule of strict liability for libel and slander. And it exacts a correspondingly high price from the victims of defamatory falsehood. Plainly many deserving plaintiffs, including some intentionally subjected to injury, will be unable to surmount the barrier of the New York Times test. ... For the reasons stated below, we conclude that the state interest in compensating injury to the reputation of private individuals requires that a different rule should obtain with respect to them. ...

... [W]e have no difficulty in distinguishing among defamation plaintiffs. The first remedy of any victim of defamation is self-help—using available opportunities to contradict the lie or correct the error and thereby to minimize its adverse impact on reputation. Public officials and public figures usually enjoy significantly greater access to the channels of effective communication and hence have a more realistic opportunity to counteract false statements then private individuals normally enjoy.[fn] Private individuals are therefore more vulnerable to injury, and the state interest in protecting them is correstpondingly greater.

More important than the likelihood that private individuals will lack effective opportunities for rebuttal, there is a compelling normative consideration underlying the distinction between public and private defamation plaintiffs. An individual who decides to seek governmental office must accept certain necessary consequences of that involvement in public affairs. ...

Those classed as public figures stand in a similar position. Hypothetically, it may be possible for someone to become a public figure through no purposeful action of his own, but the instances of truly involuntary public figures must be exceedingly rare. For the most part those who attain this status have assumed roles of especial prominence in the affairs of society. Some occupy positions of such persuasive power and influence that they are deemed public figures for all purposes. More commonly, those classed as public figures have thrust themselves to the forefront of particular public controversies in order to influence the resolution of the issues involved. In either event, they invite attention and comment.

Even if the foregoing generalities do not obtain in every instance, the communications media are entitled to act on the assumption that public officials and public figures have voluntarily exposed themselves to increased risk of injury from defamatory falsehood concerning them. No such assumption is justified with respect to a private individual. He has not accepted public office or assumed an "influential role in ordering society." [C] He has relinquished no part of his interest in the protection of his own good name, and consequently he has a more compelling call on the courts for redress of injury inflicted by defamatory falsehood. Thus, private individuals are not only more vulnerable to injury than public officials and public figures; they are also more deserving of recovery.

For these reasons we conclude that the States should retain substantial latitude in their efforts to enforce a legal remedy for defamatory falsehood injurious to the reputation of a private individual. ...

We hold that, so long as they do not impose liability without fault, the States may define for themselves the appropriate standard of liability for a publisher or broadcaster of defamatory falsehood injurious to a private individual.[fn] ...

Our accommodation of the competing values at stake in defamation suits by private individuals allows the States to impose liability on the publisher or broadcaster of defamatory falsehood on a less demanding showing than that required by New York Times. ... [W]e endorse this approach in recognition of the strong and legitimate state interest in compensating private individuals for injury to reputation. But this countervailing state interest extends no further than compensation for actual injury. For the reasons stated below, we hold that the States may not permit recovery of presumed or punitive damages, at least when liability is not based on a showing of knowledge of falsity or reckless disregard for the truth.

The common law of defamation is an oddity of tort law, for it allows recovery of purportedly compensatory damages without evidence of actual loss. Under the traditional rules pertaining to actions for libel, the existence of injury is presumed from the fact of publication. Juries may award substantial sums as compensation for supposed damage to reputation without any proof that such harm actually occurred. The largely uncontrolled discretion of juries to award damages where there is no loss unnecessarily compounds the potential of any system of liability for defamatory falsehood to inhibit the vigorous exercise of First Amendment freedoms. ...

We would not, of course, invalidate state law simply because we doubt its wisdom, but here we are attempting to reconcile state law with a competing interest grounded in the constitutional command of the First Amendment. It is therefore appropriate to require that state remedies for defamatory falsehood reach no farther than is necessary to protect the legitimate interest involved. It is necessary to restrict defamation plaintiffs who do not prove knowledge of falsity or reckless disregard for the truth to compensation for actual injury. We need not define "actual injury," as trial courts have wide experience in framing appropriate jury instructions in tort actions. Suffice it to say that actual injury is not limited to out-of-pocket loss. Indeed, the more customary types of actual harm inflicted by defamatory falsehood include impairment of reputation and standing in the community, personal humiliation, and mental anguish and suffering. ...

We also find no justification for allowing awards of punitive damages against publishers and broadcasters held liable under state-defined standards of liability for defamation. ... In short, the private defamation plaintiff who establishes liability under a less demanding standard than that stated by New York Times may recover only such damages as are sufficient to compensate him for actual injury. ...

Respondent's characterization of petitioner as a public figure raises a different question. That designation may rest on either of two alternative bases. In some instances an individual may achieve such pervasive fame or notoriety that he becomes a public figure for all purposes and in all contexts. More commonly, an individual voluntarily injects himself or is drawn into a particular public controversy and thereby becomes a public figure for a limited range of issues. In either case such persons assume special prominence in the resolution of public questions.

Petitioner has long been active in community and professional affairs. He has served as an officer of local civic groups and of various professional organizations, and he has published several books and articles on legal subjects. Although petitioner was consequently well known in some circles, he had achieved no general fame or notoriety in the community. ... It is preferable to reduce the public-figure question to a more meaningful context by looking to the nature and extent of an individual's participation in the particular controversy giving rise to the defamation.

In this context it is plain that petitioner was not a public figure. He played a minimal role at the coroner's inquest, and his participation related solely to his representation of a private client. He took no part in the criminal prosecution of Officer Nuccio. Moreover, he never discussed either the criminal or civil litigation with the press and was never quoted as having done so. He plainly did not thrust himself into the vortex of this public issue, nor did he engage the public's attention in an attempt to influence its outcome. We are persuaded that the trial court did not err in refusing to characterize petitioner as a public figure for the purpose of this litigation.

We therefore conclude that the New York Times standard is inapplicable to this case and that the trial court erred in entering judgment for respondent. Because the jury was allowed to impose liability without fault and was permitted to presume damages without proof of injury, a new trial is necessary. We reverse and remand for further proceedings in accord with this opinion.

It is ordered.

Reversed and remanded.

Practice

The tort practitioner realized one retrospective afternoon that she just loved people—loved hearing the odd things that their job demanded of them, how they did it, what it meant to them, what they expected it do for others. She never tired of learning from a client or, for that matter, an opposing party or expert witness, about a profession that was new to her. She had represented, consulted, retained, or deposed real-estate agents and their brokers, mechanical, electrical, and civil engineers, plant-, product-, and vehicle-safety experts, bus and truck drivers, school teachers and administrators, college professors, plumbers and carpenters, police officers and detectives, architects and planners, orthopedists, neurosurgeons, cardiologists, pediatricians, and podiatrists, oral surgeons and dentists, nurses, office and human-resource managers, pilots and flight engineers, vehicle and aircraft mechanics, labor economists, nurse life-care planners, physical and occupational therapists,

> rehabilitation counselors, publishers and journalists, homemakers, dog and horse owners and breeders, children of all ages, nursing-home aides and residents, court administrators and reporters, and, of course, lawyers in so many different fields. She knew that every one of them had a story to tell and purpose to fulfill, and that she had become a part of their story just as they had become a part of hers within her professional practice. The variety of their experiences and the richness of their stories was a big part of what she loved about tort practice.

INQUIRY

Universal Public Figures. The *Gertz* decision adopted two classifications for public figures—(1) universal public figures and (2) limited public figures. As the *Gertz* opinion states, universal public figures are those who have "assumed roles of especial prominence in the affairs of society," occupying "positions of such persuasive power and influence that they are deemed public figures for all purposes." Can you name some examples? *See* Hustler Magazine v. Falwell, 485 U.S. 486 (1988) (televangelist the Reverend Jerry Falwell a universal public figure). Whether a person is a public figure is a law question for the court. *See* Neely v. Wilson, 418 S.W.3d 52, 70 (Tex. Sup. Ct. 2013) (neurosurgeon not a public figure on television broadcast negatively portraying neurosurgeon's work).

Limited Public Figures. As *Gertz* indicates, the Supreme Court uses two main criteria—(1) the plaintiff's media access and (2) whether the plaintiff voluntarily assumed the risk of publicity in a public controversy—to determine whether the plaintiff is a limited public figure. Is a football coach a public figure? *See* Brewer v. Rogers, 211 Ga. App. 343, 439 S.E.2d 77 (1993) (yes—on alleged grade-changing scandal). Is a restaurant a public figure, when claiming that critical reviews were defamatory? *See* Mr. Chow of New York v. Ste. Jour Azur S.A., 759 F.2d 219 (2d Cir. 1985). Is a person who takes the stage for a photograph near a famous political candidate—just at the moment, coincidentally, when the candidate suffers assassination? *See* Khawar v. Globe Intl., Inc., 19 Cal.4th 254, 79 Cal. Rptr.2d 178 (1998) (no—no media access). A former E.P.A. official who becomes an officer of a corporation contracted to haul hazardous waste? *See* White v. Mobile Press Register, Inc., 514 So.2d 902 (Ala. 1987) (yes—limited public figure). Note that the Supreme Court assesses the plaintiff's media access and publicity seeking just before, not after, the defamatory statement thrusts the plaintiff into the limelight. The media cannot turn a private figure into a public figure simply by intense scrutiny. For example, shortly after *Gertz v. Robert Welch, Inc.*, the Supreme Court decided in Time, Inc. v. Firestone, 424 U.S. 448 (1976), that the plaintiff Palm Beach heiress was a private figure—notwithstanding that she was going through a very public divorce—because she had not thrust herself into the public eye. Then in Hutchinson v. Proxmire, 443 U.S. 111 (1979), the Supreme Court held that a mental-health research director who had received a federal grant to study aggression by observing animals, and who had received Senator Proxmire's Golden Fleece Award, was nonetheless a private figure. He had not assumed the risk of exposure and had no media access until after the award. Also, in Wolston v. Reader's Digest Assn., 443 U.S. 157 (1979), the Supreme Court held that the plaintiff was a private figure, although convicted of contempt of court years earlier during investigation of espionage. In each of those cases, the defendant's publication had given the plaintiff a certain amount of notoriety that probably would have given the plaintiff ready access to the media, if the plaintiff had wanted it.

Involuntary Public Figures. On the other hand, some cases that involve persons drawn quite unwillingly into public controversy do nonetheless find them to be public figures—presumably because of their media access (the other factor next to voluntariness). Those involuntary public figues include: one of the first female Navy combat pilots, *see* Lohrenz v. Donnelly, 350 F.3d 1272 (D.C. Cir. 2003); an unwitting suspect in the bomb blast at the Atlanta Olympics, *see* Atlanta Journal-Constitution v. Jewell, 251 Ga. App. 808, 555 S.E.2d 175 (2002); an air-traffic controller working during an airliner crash, *see* Dameron v. Washington Magazine, Inc., 779 F.2d 736 (D.C. Cir. 1985), cert. denied, 476 U.S. 1141 (1986); a prosecution witness in an infamous trial, *see* Street v. N.B.C., 645 F.2d 1227 (6th Cir. 1981); and the wife of entertainer Johnny Carson, *see* Carson v. Allied News Co., 529 F.2d 206 (7th Cir. 1976). A case in which a secretary to one of the Watergate figures G. Gordon Liddy was held not to be an involuntary public figure, Wells v. Liddy, 186 F.3d 505 (4th Cir. 1999), suggested that the involuntary public figure standard is whether the person engaged in conduct from which the reasonable person would foresee public interest.

Public Issues. As the full opinion in *Gertz v. Robert Welch, Inc.* shows, for a time up until the *Gertz* decision, the Supreme Court appeared to have given *New York Times v. Sullivan* protection not only to public officials and figures but also to defamatory statements against private figures, if the statements were on matters of public concern. A plurality of Supreme Court justices in Rosenbloom v. Metromedia, Inc., 403 U.S. 29 (1971), affirmed the appellate courts application of the *New York Times* standard to a private-figure publisher's claim against a radio station that had newscast that the police had seized obscene materials from the publisher's "smut literature racket" and "girlie-book peddlers." Because no majority of Supreme Court justices agreed on the *Rosenbloom* decision's controlling rationale, the justices in *Gertz* had little trouble rejecting its implication. *Gertz* firmly established that whether the *New York Times* standard applies depends on whether the plaintiff is a public official/public figure or private figure—not on whether the issue is one of public concern. The *Gertz* decision also held that the plaintiff must show actual malice for presumed or punitive damages on issues of public concern. What is a matter of public concern? Indications are that the term of art gets very broad construction. *See* Cox Enterps., Inc. v. Thrasher, 264 Ga. 235, 442 S.E.2d 740 (1994) (newspaper article that married woman contracted venereal disease raises issue of public concern); Shaari v. Harvard Student Agencies, Inc., 427 Mass. 129, 691 N.W.2d 925 (1998) (guidebook's statement that hostel owner had been sued frequently for sexual harassment states matter of public concern).

Fault. The *Gertz* decision also held that even in the case of a private figure like the attorney Gertz, if the matter involved a public issue (an issue of public concern), then the plaintiff would have to prove fault. *See also* Philadelphia Newspapers, Inc. v. Hepps, 475 U.S. 767 (1986) (private plaintiff allegedly bribing a public official is involved in a public issue, requiring plaintiff to prove defendant's fault). This ruling requires the states to impose at least a negligence standard for defamation liability for false reports on public issues. The vast majority of states have done so—rejected the actual-malice standard and adopted a negligence standard for private-figure plaintiffs on public issues. *See* Mead Corp. v. Hicks, 448 So.2d 308 (Ala. 1983); Taskett v. KING Broadcasting Co., 86 Wash.2d 439, 546 P.2d 81 (1976). A very few states impose the higher actual-malice standard as to all public issues, whether the defamatory statement is about a public official or figure, or a private figure. *See* Journal-Gazette Co. v. Bandido's, Inc., 712 N.E.2d 446 (Ind.), cert. denied, 528 U.S.

1005 (1999); Walker v. Colorado Springs Sun, Inc., 188 Colo. 86, 538 P.2d 450 (1975). As a result, some think that the Supreme Court may have effectively federalized the practice of journalism after all, at least when it involves public issues.

Falsity. As briefly mentioned above in the section on the common-law elements of defamation, a little more than a decade after *Gertz* the Supreme Court extended constitutional protection to one other aspect of a defamation claim—the plaintiff must have the burden of proof to show that the defamatory statement was false. Several states had retained a common-law presumption that a defamatory statement (one that lowered the reputation of the person it identified) is false, shifting to the defendant the burden to prove truth. The major circumstance under which this presumption made a difference was when neither party could prove the statement *true or false*. In those cases where the defamatory statement was, for instance, a collection of epithets difficult to prove true, the defendant would lose in a jurisdiction retaining the presumption. In Philadelphia Newspapers, Inc. v. Hepps, 475 U.S. 767 (1986), the Supreme Court held that for a defamatory statement involving a public issue, the plaintiff—whether a public or private figure—must retain the burden of proof that the statement was false. The four dissenting justices in *Hepps* wrote that requiring a private plaintiff to bear the burden of proving false a statement deliberately published to assassinate the plaintiff's character was a "pernicious result." Reserve judgment as you read the *Hepps* decision below, until you have read the case that follows it—and then decide what you think.

Philadelphia Newspapers, Inc. v. Hepps
United States Supreme Court
475 U.S. 767 (1986)

O'CONNOR, J. This case requires us once more to "struggl[e] ... to define the proper accommodation between the law of defamation and the freedoms of speech and press protected by the First Amendment." *Gertz v. Robert Welch, Inc.,* 418 U.S. 323, 325, 94 S.Ct. 2997, 3000, 41 L.Ed.2d 789 (1974). In *Gertz,* the Court held that a private figure who brings a suit for defamation cannot recover without some showing that the media defendant was at fault in publishing the statements at issue. *Id.,* at 347, 94 S.Ct., at 3010. Here, we hold that, at least where a newspaper publishes speech of public concern, a private-figure plaintiff cannot recover damages without also showing that the statements at issue are false.

I

[Appellee] Maurice S. Hepps is the principal stockholder of General Programming, Inc. (GPI), a corporation that franchises ... "Thrifty" stores—selling beer, soft drinks, and snacks. ... Appellant Philadelphia Newspapers, Inc., owns the Philadelphia Inquirer (Inquirer). The Inquirer published a series of articles ... that appellees had links to organized crime and used some of those links to influence the State's governmental processes, both legislative and administrative. ... The stories reported that federal "investigators have found connections between Thrifty and underworld figures," [c]; that "the Thrifty Beverage beer chain ... had connections ... with organized crime," [c]; and that Thrifty had "won a series of competitive advantages through rulings by the State Liquor Control Board," [c]. A grand jury was said to be investigating the "alleged relationship between the Thrifty chain and known

Mafia figures," and "[w]hether the chain received special treatment from the [state Governor's] administration and the Liquor Control Board." [c]

Appellees brought suit for defamation against appellants in a Pennsylvania state court. Consistent with *Gertz, supra,* Pennsylvania requires a private figure who brings a suit for defamation to bear the burden of proving negligence or malice by the defendant in publishing the statements at issue. [C] As to falsity, Pennsylvania follows the common law's presumption that an individual's reputation is a good one. Statements defaming that person are therefore presumptively false, although a publisher who bears the burden of proving the truth of the statements has an absolute defense. [Cc]

... After all the evidence had been presented by both sides, the trial court concluded that Pennsylvania's statute giving the defendant the burden of proving the truth of the statements violated the Federal Constitution. [C] The trial court therefore instructed the jury that the plaintiffs bore the burden of proving falsity. [C]

... [T]he appellees here brought an appeal directly to the Pennsylvania Supreme Court. That court viewed *Gertz* as simply requiring the plaintiff to show fault in actions for defamation. It concluded that a showing of fault did not require a showing of falsity, held that to place the burden of showing truth on the defendant did not unconstitutionally inhibit free debate, and remanded the case for a new trial.[fn] ... We noted probable jurisdiction, [c], and now reverse.

II

[The Court reviewed its First Amendment-defamation case law beginning with *New York Times v. Sullivan.*]

One can discern in these decisions two forces that may reshape the common-law landscape to conform to the First Amendment. The first is whether the plaintiff is a public official or figure, or is instead a private figure. The second is whether the speech at issue is of public concern. When the speech is of public concern and the plaintiff is a public official or public figure, the Constitution clearly requires the plaintiff to surmount a much higher barrier before recovering damages from a media defendant than is raised by the common law. When the speech is of public concern but the plaintiff is a private figure, as in *Gertz,* the Constitution still supplants the standards of the common law, but the constitutional requirements are, in at least some of their range, less forbidding than when the plaintiff is a public figure and the speech is of public concern. When the speech is of exclusively private concern and the plaintiff is a private figure, as in *Dun & Bradstreet,* the constitutional requirements do not necessarily force any change in at least some of the features of the common-law landscape.

Our opinions to date have chiefly treated the necessary showings of fault rather than of falsity. Nonetheless, as one might expect given the language of the Court in *New York Times,* [c], a public-figure plaintiff must show the falsity of the statements at issue in order to prevail in a suit for defamation. [Cc]

Here, as in *Gertz,* the plaintiff is a private figure and the newspaper articles are of public concern. In *Gertz,* as in *New York Times,* the common-law rule was superseded by a constitutional rule. We believe that the common law's rule on falsity—that the defendant must bear the burden of proving truth—must similarly fall here to a constitutional requirement that the plaintiff bear the burden of showing falsity, as well as fault, before recovering damages.

There will always be instances when the factfinding process will be unable to resolve conclusively whether the speech is true or false; it is in those cases that the burden of proof is dispositive. Under a rule forcing the plaintiff to bear the burden of showing falsity, there will be some cases in which plaintiffs cannot meet their burden despite the fact that the speech is in fact false. The plaintiff's suit will fail despite the fact that, in some abstract sense, the suit is meritorious. ...

... In a case presenting a configuration of speech and plaintiff like the one we face here, and where the scales are in such an uncertain balance, we believe that the Constitution requires us to tip them in favor of protecting true speech. To ensure that true speech on matters of public concern is not deterred, we hold that the common-law presumption that defamatory speech is false cannot stand when a plaintiff seeks damages against a media defendant for speech of public concern.

In the context of governmental restriction of speech, it has long been established that the government cannot limit speech protected by the First Amendment without bearing the burden of showing that its restriction is justified. [c] It is not immediately apparent from the text of the First Amendment, which by its terms applies only to governmental action, that a similar result should obtain here: a suit by a private party is obviously quite different from the government's direct enforcement of its own laws. Nonetheless, the need to encourage debate on public issues that concerned the Court in the governmental-restriction cases is of concern in a similar manner in this case involving a private suit for damages: placement by state law of the burden of proving truth upon media defendants who publish speech of public concern deters such speech because of the fear that liability will unjustifiably result. [C] Because such a "chilling" effect would be antithetical to the First Amendment's protection of true speech on matters of public concern, we believe that a private-figure plaintiff must bear the burden of showing that the speech at issue is false before recovering damages for defamation from a media defendant. To do otherwise could "only result in a deterrence of speech which the Constitution makes free." [C]

We recognize that requiring the plaintiff to show falsity will insulate from liability some speech that is false, but unprovably so. ... In attempting to resolve related issues in the defamation context, the Court has affirmed that "[t]he First Amendment requires that we protect some falsehood in order to protect speech that matters." *Gertz,* 418 U.S., at 341, 94 S.Ct., at 3007. ... To provide "'breathing space,'" [cc], for true speech on matters of public concern, the Court has been willing to insulate even *demonstrably* false speech from liability, and has imposed additional requirements of fault upon the plaintiff in a suit for defamation. [Cc] We therefore do not break new ground here in insulating speech that is not even demonstrably false.

We note that our decision adds only marginally to the burdens that the plaintiff must already bear as a result of our earlier decisions in the law of defamation. The plaintiff must show fault. ...

For the reasons stated above, the judgment of the Pennsylvania Supreme Court is reversed, and the case is remanded for further proceedings not inconsistent with this opinion. ...

Cox Enterprises, Inc. v. Thrasher
Georgia Supreme Court
264 Ga. 235, 442 S.E.2d 740 (1994)

HUNSTEIN, J. Corlis Thrasher brought a defamation suit against Cox Enterprises and two of its employees, an editor and a writer, for the publication of a newspaper article which she alleged implied that she, a married woman, had contracted chlamydia, a sexually transmitted disease, and that such was due to her promiscuity. The trial court held that although the article could reasonably be read to imply Thrasher had suffered from chlamydia, she had failed to meet her burden of proving the falsity of the statements in the article and granted summary judgment to defendants. The Court of Appeals reversed, [c], and we granted certiorari to consider this case in light of *Philadelphia Newspapers v. Hepps*, 475 U.S. 767, 106 S.Ct. 1558, 89 L.Ed.2d 783 (1986). We find *Hepps* controls and reverse the Court of Appeals.

1. The U.S. Supreme Court in *Hepps*, supra, held that where a newspaper publishes speech of public concern, a private-figure plaintiff cannot recover damages without also showing that the statements at issue are false. [C] The *Hepps* court held it to be a "constitutional requirement that the plaintiff bear the burden of showing falsity, as well as fault, before recovering damages." [C] … While the U.S. Supreme Court recognized that "requiring the plaintiff to show falsity will insulate from liability some speech that is false, but unprovably so," [c], it concluded that the policy behind the First Amendment's protection of true speech on matters of public concern compelled its decision. [C]

2. Thrasher is a private-figure citizen; the newspaper article was of public concern.[fn] The evidence in the instant case is uncontroverted that Thrasher was infected with a bacteria that was treated with a drug used to cure chlamydia. As the trial court noted, because the bacteria was not identified before it was treated, whether Thrasher in fact had chlamydia is and will remain unknown. Because the factfinding process will be unable to resolve conclusively whether the speech at issue was true or false, the burden of proof is dispositive and the trial court properly granted summary judgment to defendants on Thrasher's claim that she was defamed by the publication intimating she had contracted chlamydia. *Hepps*, supra.

3. Because a plaintiff must show both falsity and fault before recovering damages, *Hepps*, supra [c], Thrasher's inability to carry her burden on the issue of falsity renders it unnecessary for us to determine whether the defendants were at fault in the publication of the article.

4. As to the remaining basis for Thrasher's defamation claim, our review and construction of the publication at issue reveals that the trial court properly concluded that the publication was not defamatory because no reasonable reader could have inferred from it that Thrasher had engaged in promiscuous or adulterous sexual behavior. [Cc]

Judgment reversed.

INQUIRY

Private Figures and Issues. What, then, is left? Where has the Supreme Court not constitutionalized defamation law? The answer—only for private figures on private issues—was not entirely clear until the following *Dun & Bradstreet* decision. The *Dun & Bradstreet* decision permits states to treat defamation claims by private figures on private issues according to the common law or the dictates of their legislatures. Not every state has maintained the common law's strict-liability-like elements for private figure/private issue defamation. *See* Newberry v. Allied Stores, Inc., 108 N.M. 424, 773 P.2d 1231 (1989) (negligence standard applies to private figure/private issue defamation). As you read the *Dun & Bradstreet* decision, consider whether you favor the common-law formulation it permits or some higher standard influenced by the constitutional cases.

Dun & Bradstreet v. Greenmoss Builders, Inc.
Supreme Court of the United States
472 U.S. 749 (1985)

POWELL, J. announced the judgment of the Court and delivered an opinion, in which REHNQUIST, J. and O'CONNOR, J. joined.

In *Gertz v. Robert Welch, Inc.*, 418 U.S. 323, 94 S.Ct. 2997, 41 L.Ed.2d 789 (1974), we held that the First Amendment restricted the damages that a private individual could obtain from a publisher for a libel that involved a matter of public concern. More specifically, we held that in these circumstances the First Amendment prohibited awards of presumed and punitive damages for false and defamatory statements unless the plaintiff shows "actual malice," that is, knowledge of falsity or reckless disregard for the truth. The question presented in this case is whether this rule of *Gertz* applies when the false and defamatory statements do not involve matters of public concern. …

Petitioner Dun & Bradstreet, a credit reporting agency, provides subscribers with financial and related information about businesses. All the information is confidential; under the terms of the subscription agreement the subscribers may not reveal it to anyone else. On July 26, 1976, petitioner sent a report to five subscribers indicating that respondent, a construction contractor, had filed a voluntary petition for bankruptcy. This report was false and grossly misrepresented respondent's assets and liabilities. That same day, while discussing the possibility of future financing with its bank, respondent's president was told that the bank had received the defamatory report. He immediately called petitioner's regional office, explained the error, and asked for a correction. In addition, he requested the names of the firms that had received the false report in order to assure them that the company was solvent. Petitioner promised to look into the matter but refused to divulge the names of those who had received the report.

After determining that its report was indeed false, petitioner issued a corrective notice on or about August 3, 1976, to the five subscribers who had received the initial report. The notice stated that one of respondent's former employees, not respondent itself, had filed for bankruptcy and that respondent "continued in business as usual." Respondent told petitioner that it was dissatisfied with the notice, and it again asked for a list of subscribers who had seen the initial report. Again petitioner refused to divulge their names.

Respondent then brought this defamation action in Vermont state court. It alleged that the false report had injured its reputation and sought both compensatory and punitive damages. The trial established that the error in petitioner's report had been caused when one of its employees, a 17-year-old high school student paid to review Vermont bankruptcy pleadings, had inadvertently attributed to respondent a bankruptcy petition filed by one of respondent's former employees. Although petitioner's representative testified that it was routine practice to check the accuracy of such reports with the businesses themselves, it did not try to verify the information about respondent before reporting it.

After trial, the jury returned a verdict in favor of respondent and awarded $50,000 in compensatory or presumed damages and $300,000 in punitive damages. Petitioner moved for a new trial. It argued that in *Gertz v. Robert Welch, Inc., supra,* at 349, 94 S.Ct., at 3011, this Court had ruled broadly that "the States may not permit recovery of presumed or punitive damages, at least when liability is not based on a showing of knowledge of falsity or reckless disregard for the truth," and it argued that the judge's instructions in this case permitted the jury to award such damages on a lesser showing. ...

In *New York Times Co. v. Sullivan, supra,* the Court for the first time held that the First Amendment limits the reach of state defamation laws. That case concerned a public official's recovery of damages for the publication of an advertisement criticizing police conduct in a civil rights demonstration. ... [T]he Court held that a public official cannot recover damages for defamatory falsehood unless he proves that the false statement was made with " 'actual malice'—that is, with knowledge that it was false or with reckless disregard of whether it was false or not," *id.,* at 280, 84 S.Ct., at 726. In later cases, all involving public issues, the Court extended this same constitutional protection to libels of public figures, [c], and in one case suggested in a plurality opinion that this constitutional rule should extend to libels of any individual so long as the defamatory statements involved a "matter of public or general interest," [c]. ...

In *Gertz [v. Robert Welch, Inc.,* 418 U.S. 323 (1974)], we held that the fact that expression concerned a public issue did not by itself entitle the libel defendant to the constitutional protections of *New York Times.* ... [W]e held that a State could not allow recovery of presumed and punitive damages absent a showing of "actual malice." Nothing in our opinion, however, indicated that this same balance would be struck regardless of the type of speech involved.[fn] ...

We have never considered whether the *Gertz* balance obtains when the defamatory statements involve no issue of public concern. To make this determination, we must employ the approach approved in *Gertz* and balance the State's interest in compensating private individuals for injury to their reputation against the First Amendment interest in protecting this type of expression. This state interest is identical to the one weighed in *Gertz.* ...

The First Amendment interest, on the other hand, is less important than the one weighed in *Gertz.* We have long recognized that not all speech is of equal First Amendment importance.[fn] It is speech on "'matters of public concern'" that is "at the heart of the First Amendment's protection." [Cc] ...

In contrast, speech on matters of purely private concern is of less First Amendment concern. [C] As a number of state courts, including the court below, have recognized, the role of the Constitution in regulating state libel law is far more limited when the concerns that activated *New York Times* and *Gertz* are absent.[fn] In such a case, "[t]here is no threat to the free and robust debate of public issues; there is no potential interference with a meaningful dialogue of ideas concerning self-government; and there is no threat of liability causing a reaction of self-censorship by the press. The facts of the present case are wholly without the First Amendment concerns with which the Supreme Court of the United States has been struggling." [C]

... In light of the reduced constitutional value of speech involving no matters of public concern, we hold that the state interest adequately supports awards of presumed and punitive damages—even absent a showing of "actual malice." [fn]

The only remaining issue is whether petitioner's credit report involved a matter of public concern. In a related context, we have held that "[w]hether ... speech addresses a matter of public concern must be determined by [the expression's] content, form, and context ... as revealed by the whole record." [C] These factors indicate that petitioner's credit report concerns no public issue.[fn] It was speech solely in the individual interest of the speaker and its specific business audience. [C] This particular interest warrants no special protection when—as in this case—the speech is wholly false and clearly damaging to the victim's business reputation. [Cc] Moreover, since the credit report was made available to only five subscribers, who, under the terms of the subscription agreement, could not disseminate it further, it cannot be said that the report involves any "strong interest in the free flow of commercial information." [C] There is simply no credible argument that this type of credit reporting requires special protection to ensure that "debate on public issues [will] be uninhibited, robust, and wide-open." *New York Times Co. v. Sullivan,* 376 U.S., at 270, 84 S.Ct., at 720.

In addition, the speech here, like advertising, is hardy and unlikely to be deterred by incidental state regulation. [C] It is solely motivated by the desire for profit, which, we have noted, is a force less likely to be deterred than others. [C] Arguably, the reporting here was also more objectively verifiable than speech deserving of greater protection. [C] In any case, the market provides a powerful incentive to a credit reporting agency to be accurate, since false credit reporting is of no use to creditors. Thus, any incremental "chilling" effect of libel suits would be of decreased significance.[fn] ...

We conclude that permitting recovery of presumed and punitive damages in defamation cases absent a showing of "actual malice" does not violate the First Amendment when the defamatory statements do not involve matters of public concern. Accordingly, we affirm the judgment of the Vermont Supreme Court. ...

INQUIRY

Opinion. The Supreme Court also declined (in a case decided not long after *Dun & Bradstreet*) to extend constitutional protection to matters of opinion. *See* Milkovich v. Lorain Journal Co., 497 U.S. 1 (1990). The reader should not misinterpret the Supreme Court's action in *Milkovich* as a reversal of fortune for publishers and an undermining of First Amendment protection. Readers better understand the *Milkovich* decision, along with *Dun & Bradstreet*, as the end of an arc in which the Supreme Court first boldly created First Amendment protections in *New York Times v. Sullivan*, then extended and refined those protections to the point of *Gertz* and *Hepps*, until the Court could confirm the outer boundaries of the doctrine in *Dun & Bradstreet* and *Milkovich*. *Hepps*, Chief Justice Rehnquist's *Milkovich* opinion took pains to note, still requires defamation plaintiffs on public issues to prove falsity and fault. Thus, public-issue opinions having no factual content—those that parties cannot prove true or false—still should lead to no defamation liability, even after *Milkovich*. As you read the *Milkovich* excerpts below, consider whether they convince you that additional constitutional protection for opinions was unnecessary. Only Justice Brennan (the author of the *New York Times v. Sullivan* opinion) and Justice Marshall dissented in *Milkovich*.

Milkovich v. Lorain Journal Co.
United States Supreme Court
497 U.S. 1 (1990)

REHNQUIST, C.J. Respondent J. Theodore Diadiun authored an article in an Ohio newspaper implying that petitioner Michael Milkovich, a local high school wrestling coach, lied under oath in a judicial proceeding about an incident involving petitioner and his team which occurred at a wrestling match. Petitioner sued Diadiun and the newspaper for libel, and the Ohio Court of Appeals affirmed a lower court entry of summary judgment against petitioner. This judgment was based in part on the grounds that the article constituted an "opinion" protected from the reach of state defamation law by the First Amendment to the United States Constitution. We hold that the First Amendment does not prohibit the application of Ohio's libel laws to the alleged defamations contained in the article.

... Petitioner Milkovich, now retired, was the wrestling coach at Maple Heights High School in Maple Heights, Ohio. In 1974, his team was involved in an altercation at a home wrestling match with a team from Mentor High School. Several people were injured. In response to the incident, the Ohio High School Athletic Association (OHSAA) held a hearing at which Milkovich and H. Don Scott, the Superintendent of Maple Heights Public Schools, testified. Following the hearing, OHSAA placed the Maple Heights team on probation for a year and declared the team ineligible for the 1975 state tournament. OHSAA also censured Milkovich for his actions during the altercation. Thereafter, several parents and wrestlers sued OHSAA in the Court of Common Pleas of Franklin County, Ohio, seeking a restraining order against OHSAA's ruling on the grounds that they had been denied due process in the OHSAA proceeding. Both Milkovich and Scott testified in that proceeding. The court overturned OHSAA's probation and ineligibility orders on due process grounds.

The day after the court rendered its decision, respondent Diadiun's column appeared in the News-Herald, a newspaper which circulates in Lake County, Ohio, and is owned by respondent Lorain Journal Co. The column bore the heading "Maple beat the law with the 'big lie,'" beneath which appeared Diadiun's photograph and the words "TD Says." The carryover page headline announced "... Diadiun says Maple told a lie." The column contained the following passages:

> ... [A] lesson was learned (or relearned) yesterday by the student body of Maple Heights High School, and by anyone who attended the Maple-Mentor wrestling meet of last Feb. 8.
>
>> A lesson which, sadly, in view of the events of the past year, is well they learned early. It is simply this: If you get in a jam, lie your way out.
>>
>> If you're successful enough, and powerful enough, and can sound sincere enough, you stand an excellent chance of making the lie stand up, regardless of what really happened.
>>
>> The teachers responsible were mainly head Maple wrestling coach, Mike Milkovich, and former superintendent of schools H. Donald Scott. ...

Anyone who attended the meet, whether he be from Maple Heights, Mentor, or impartial observer, knows in his heart that Milkovich and Scott lied at the hearing after each having given his solemn oath to tell the truth.

But they got away with it.

Is that the kind of lesson we want our young people learning from their high school administrators and coaches?

'I think not.' [C][fn]

Petitioner commenced a defamation action against respondents in the Court of Common Pleas of Lake County, Ohio, alleging that the headline of Diadiun's article and the nine passages quoted above "accused plaintiff of committing the crime of perjury, an indictable offense in the State of Ohio, and damaged plaintiff directly in his life-time occupation of coach and teacher, and constituted libel per se." [C] ...

[The opinion summarized defamation law and its treatment by the Court.]

Respondents would have us recognize, in addition to the established safeguards discussed above, still another First-Amendment-based protection for defamatory statements which are categorized as "opinion" as opposed to "fact." For this proposition they rely principally on the following dictum from our opinion in Gertz: "Under the First Amendment there is no such thing as a false idea. However pernicious an opinion may seem, we depend for its correction not on the conscience of judges and juries but on the competition of other ideas. But there is no constitutional value in false statements of fact." [C]

Judge Friendly appropriately observed that this passage "has become the opening salvo in all arguments for protection from defamation actions on the ground of opinion, even though the case did not remotely concern the question." Cianci v. New Times Publishing Co., 639 F.2d 54, 61 (CA2 1980). Read in context, though, the fair meaning of the passage is to equate the word "opinion" in the second sentence with the word "idea" in the first sentence. Under this view, the language was merely a reiteration of Justice Holmes' classic "marketplace of ideas" concept. ...

Thus, we do not think this passage from Gertz was intended to create a wholesale defamation exemption for anything that might be labeled "opinion." ... Not only would such an interpretation be contrary to the tenor and context of the passage, but it would also ignore the fact that expressions of "opinion" may often imply an assertion of objective fact. ...

Apart from their reliance on the Gertz dictum, respondents ... contend that in every defamation case the First Amendment mandates an inquiry into whether a statement is "opinion" or "fact," and that only the latter statements may be actionable. They propose that a number of factors developed by the lower courts (in what we hold was a mistaken reliance on the Gertz dictum) be considered in deciding which is which. But we think the " 'breathing space' " which " [f]reedoms of expression require in order to survive,' " Hepps, 475 U.S., at 772, 106 S.Ct., at 1561 (quoting New York Times, supra, 376 U.S., at 272, 84 S.Ct., at 721), is adequately secured by existing constitutional doctrine without the creation of an artificial dichotomy between "opinion" and fact.

Foremost, we think Hepps stands for the proposition that a statement on matters of public concern must be provable as false before there can be liability under state defamation law, at least in situations, like the present, where a media defendant is involved.[fn] ... Hepps ensures that a statement of opinion relating to matters of public concern which does not contain a provably false factual connotation will receive full constitutional protection.[fn] ...

We are not persuaded that, in addition to these protections, an additional separate constitutional privilege for "opinion" is required to ensure the freedom of expression guaranteed by the First Amendment. The dispositive question in the present case then becomes whether a reasonable factfinder could conclude that the statements in the Diadiun column imply an assertion that petitioner Milkovich perjured himself in a judicial proceeding. We think this question must be answered in the affirmative. As the Ohio Supreme Court itself observed: "[T]he clear impact in some nine sentences and a caption is that [Milkovich] 'lied at the hearing after ... having given his solemn oath to tell the truth.'" [C] This is not the sort of loose, figurative, or hyperbolic language which would negate the impression that the writer was seriously maintaining that petitioner committed the crime of perjury. Nor does the general tenor of the article negate this impression.

We also think the connotation that petitioner committed perjury is sufficiently factual to be susceptible of being proved true or false. A determination whether petitioner lied in this instance can be made on a core of objective evidence by comparing, inter alia, petitioner's testimony before the OHSAA board with his subsequent testimony before the trial court. ...

The numerous decisions discussed above establishing First Amendment protection for defendants in defamation actions surely demonstrate the Court's recognition of the Amendment's vital guarantee of free and uninhibited discussion of public issues. But there is also another side to the equation; we have regularly acknowledged the "important social values which underlie the law of defamation," and recognized that "[s]ociety has a pervasive and strong interest in preventing and redressing attacks upon reputation." Rosenblatt v. Baer, 383 U.S. 75, 86, 86 S.Ct. 669, 676, 15 L.Ed.2d 597 (1966). Justice Stewart in that case put it with his customary clarity: "The right of a man to the protection of his own reputation from unjustified invasion and wrongful hurt reflects no more than our basic concept of the essential dignity and worth of every human being-a concept at the root of any decent system of ordered liberty. ..... The destruction that defamatory falsehood can bring is, to be sure, often beyond the capacity of the law to redeem. Yet, imperfect though it is, an action for damages is the only hope for vindication or redress the law gives to a man whose reputation has been falsely dishonored." Id., at 92-93, 86 S.Ct., at 679-680 (concurring opinion).

We believe our decision in the present case holds the balance true. The judgment of the Ohio Court of Appeals is reversed, and the case is remanded for further proceedings not inconsistent with this opinion.

Reversed.

INQUIRY

Epithets. Are publishers still free after *Milkovich* to cast vilifying (but non-factual) epithets at persons involved in public issues? Is calling someone a "communist" a factual assertion or a non-factual epithet? *See* Yetman v. English, 168 Ariz. 71, 811 P.2d 323 (1991) (factual assertion—actionable). Is asserting that a woman supported with "doctored" tapes her story that she had an affair with the president? *See* Flowers v. Carville, 310 F.3d 1118 (9th Cir. 2002) (factual assertion—

actionable). Is saying that someone used "blackmail"? *See* Greenbelt Pub. Assn. v. Bresler, 398 U.S. 6 (1970) (rhetorical hyperbole—not actionable). Is televising that a museum paid a "grossly inflated price" for an antique candelabra? *See* Weller v. American Broadcasting Corp., 232 Cal. App.3d 1991, 283 Cal. Rptr. 644 (1991) (provably false—actionable). Calling someone a "sexual harasser"? *See* Williams v. Garraghty, 249 Va. 224, 455 S.E.2d 209 (1995) (factual assertion—actionable). Is saying that the plaintiff was responsible for "outrageous overhead and unrelated business expense"? *See* Wachtel v. Storm, 796 F. Supp. 114 (S.D. N.Y. 1992) (actionable—implied facts). Is calling someone "a very poor lawyer? *See* Sullivan v. Conway, 157 F.3d 1092 (7th Cir. 1998) (non-factual assertion—not actionable). Is saying that an attorney is "an ambulance chaser" and only takes "slam dunk cases"? *See* Flamm v. American Assn. of Univ. Women, 201 F.3d 144 (2d Cir. 2000) (actionable—factual assertions). Who makes the decision—judge or jury? *See* Williams, *supra* (judge). Should the law permit a plaintiff to call a linguistics expert to help determine an allegedly defamatory statement's intended meaning? *See* Weller, *supra* (yes—on context, juxtaposition, word choice, tone, and inflection). That a comedian speaks the statement in a humorous context will not make everything the speaker says a joke or opinion, if the statement contains a factual assertion. *See* Unelko v. Rooney, 912 F.2d 1049 (9th Cir. 1990) (Andy Rooney on *60 Minutes* calling a windshield product "junk" is a factual assertion).

C. Privileges

OBJECTIVE: **Given a claim satisfying the elements of defamation, evaluate that claim to determine whether the claim is barred by a common-law privilege reflected in this section.**

Case Study: A staffing company provided personnel to an industrial concern on a contract basis. The industrial concern terminated the temporary contract with respect to one employee's services. The staffing company requested that the industrial concern complete its questionnaire on the employee's performance. The industrial concern indicated that on two occasions tools were found missing in the employee's area during her shift and that surveillance tapes indicated suspicious behavior supporting that she may have stolen the tools. As a result, the staffing company removed the employee from its approved-employee list and refused to offer her further employment. ***Evaluate the industrial concern's defense of qualified privilege in the employee's defamation suit against it.***

Privilege raises the question of whether the common law will, for policy reasons, protect a person or entity from a defamation action notwithstanding that the publication was defamatory. Unlike the constitutional protections, which look to the status of the *plaintiff* as a public official or figure and the content of the communication as a public issue, privileges look to the *defendant's* role and interests to determine whether policy supports the right to make the defamatory statement. Privileges were quite important before the *New York Times v. Sullivan* decision created the constitutional protections. The question of privilege is significantly less important today when the matter involves a public official or figure, or a public issue, given the constitutional protections that serve the same or similar role and largely subsume or displace the privileges in the public context. But the common-law privilege continues to play a significant role in defamation actions involving communications between private parties on matters not of public concern. Analysis of a defamation action should include consideration of common-law privileges. Two general classes of privileges exist—absolute and qualified. Absolute privileges have primarily to do with ensuring that public officials and those involved in public proceedings can perform their functions. Qualified privileges have primarily to do with protecting private interests. Consider each in turn.

1. Absolute Privileges

Absolute privileges are those that do not depend on the good or bad faith—or actual malice or negligence—of the one making the defamatory statement. If the defendant invoking the absolute privilege has the protected status, made the statement in the protected forum, and made the statement related to a matter relevant within that forum, then the privilege bars the plaintiff's defamation action against the defendant notwithstanding that the defendant may have made the statement in bad faith, negligently, or with actual malice. Three absolute privileges exist, one privilege protecting participants in each branch of government—judicial, legislative, and executive.

Judicial Privilege. The judicial privilege extends not only to statements made by judges within and relating to judicial proceedings but also to other participants in the judicial process—lawyers, prosecutors, public defenders, parties, and witnesses. The core of the privilege is the right to speak, argue, and testify in court relating to a pending matter, whether voluntarily or under compulsion, free of the threat of a defamation action. Those statements are privileged even if the one who speaks, argues, or testifies does so in bad faith, negligently, or maliciously. The judicial privilege has broader scope than open-court statements, also protecting pleadings, court papers, and affidavits filed with the court. *See* Di Blasio v. Kolodner, 233 Md. 512, 197 A.2d 245 (1964); Fleming v. McRae Pub. Co., 113 Ky. 383, 68 S.W. 457 (1902). The privilege does not protect out-of-court statements—to the press for instance. *See* Kennedy v. Cannon, 229 Md. 92, 182 A.2d 54 (1962). To acquire the privilege's protection, the statement must relate in some reasonable fashion to the pending matter, *see* Stahl v. Kincade, 135 Ind. App. 699, 192 N.E.2d 493 (1963), even if only under a mistaken belief, *see* Johnson v. Dover, 201 Ark. 175, 143 S.W.2d 1112 (1940). The judicial privilege means that parties have no civil remedy for perjured testimony, *see* Ginsburg v. Halpern, 383 Pa. 178, 118 A.2d 201 (1955), although law may offer a civil remedy for suborning (procuring) the perjury of another, *see* Bailey v. McGill, 247 N.C. 286, 100 S.E.2d 860 (1957). Consider the following two cases illustrating the judicial privilege and its limits.

Wiener v. Weintraub
New York Court of Appeals
292 N.Y.S.2d 667, 239 N.E.2d 540 (1968)

FULD, C.J. In this action for libel, the plaintiff, a member of the New York Bar, alleges in his complaint that the defendants falsely and maliciously charged him, in a letter addressed to the Grievance Committee of the Association of the Bar of the City of New York, with dishonesty and fraud. The defendants moved, [c], to dismiss the complaint on the ground that it fails to state a cause of action in that the letter to the Grievance Committee was absolutely privileged. The court at Special Term granted the motion, dismissing the complaint. The Appellate Division unanimously affirmed the resulting order and granted leave to appeal to us.

There can, of course, be no doubt that statements made by counsel and parties in the course of "judicial proceedings" and privileged as long as such statements "are material and pertinent to the questions involved * * * irrespective of the motive" with which they are made. ([Cc]) Petitions or complaints charging professional misconduct of an attorney which, in the past, were presented to the General Term of the Supreme Court ([c]) are now usually filed with the Grievance Committee of a bar association. ([Cc]) And, it has been observed, a proceeding before such a committee constitutes a "judicial proceeding." ([C]) In the investigation of such complaints and in the conduct of such proceedings, then, the bar association's Grievance Committee acts as a quasi-judicial body and, as such, is an arm of the Appellate Division. Quite clearly, the filing of the complaint in the present case initiated a judicial proceeding.

It follows, therefore, that the defendants' letter to the Grievance Committee was absolutely privileged. ([Cc])

Assuredly, it is in the public interest to encourage those who have knowledge of dishonest or unethical conduct on the part of lawyers to impart that knowledge to a Grievance Committee or some other body designated for investigation. If a complainant were to be subject to a libel action by the accused attorney, the effect in many instances might well be to deter the filing of legitimate charges. We may assume that on occasion false and malicious complaints will be made. But, whatever the hardship on a particular attorney, the necessity of maintaining the high standards of our bar—indeed, the proper administration of justice requires that there be a forum in which clients or other persons, unlearned in the law, may state their complaints, have them examined and, if necessary, judicially determined. A lawyer against whom an unwarranted complaint has been lodged will surely not suffer injury to his reputation among the members of the Grievance Committee since it is their function to determine whether or not the charges are supportable. Any other risk of prejudice is eliminated by the provision of the Judiciary Law (s 90, subd. 10) which declares that "all papers * * * upon any complaint, inquiry, investigation or proceeding relating to the conduct or discipline of an attorney * * * shall * * * be deemed private and confidential."

In sum, then, since the statement to the Grievance Committee was material and pertinent to the matter in issue, the defendants were protected by an absolute privilege and the courts below had no alternative but to grant the motion dismissing the complaint.

The order appealed from should be affirmed, with costs.

Stahl v. Kincade

Indiana Court of Appeals
135 Ind. App. 699, 192 N.E.2d 493 (1963)

PFAFF, J. ... The complaint in the injunction action alleged that the defendants owned property which adjoined plaintiff's property at the rear thereof and that they erected a basketball court thereon; ... that the use of the basketball court was an abuse of the residential private property rights of plaintiff; that the defendants' back yard was converted from a private and residential use to a public use; that defendants encouraged the use of their back yard as a public basketball playground, which was unsupervised, unfenced and unguarded. Further allegations were made as to the noise, annoyance and disturbance as constituting a nuisance and as to trespasses by the players upon plaintiff's property, and the use of vulgar and profane language. The prayer was for an injunction enjoining the defendants from permitting their residential property from being used as a public playground, and from permitting the basketball players to trespass upon plaintiff's property.

... It is alleged that the appellee lawyers, with the consent and approval of the [defendants in the injunction action] "contriving and wantonly and maliciously intending to besmirch and injure the plaintiff in her good name, reputation and credit, and to bring her in public scandal, infamy and disgrace and low repute, infamy and disgrace with and among her good neighbors and other good and worthy citizens, and to cause it to be suspected and believed by these neighbors and citizens that the plaintiff had been and was guilty of the offenses * * * set forth in (the) counterclaim" did not file the same in due course of law and that it was not pertinent, relevant or germane to the issues in the injunction suit; that after the counterclaim was stricken from the record the defendants to further malign, blaspheme and maliciously attack and deprive plaintiff of her good name and character, filed the second purported counterclaim which was entirely foreign and irrelevant to the issues involved, alleging maliciously and falsely that plaintiff was openly and notoriously guilty of adultery; that the besmirching and blasphemous charge was made for the sole purpose of injuring and damaging plaintiff's character and reputation among her neighbors and friends and other citizens; that her character was besmirched and her health impaired; that the second purported counterclaim was not filed in due course of law as it was neither pertinent nor relevant to the issues involved. It is further alleged that all charges made in the purported counterclaim were wholly false and designed to besmirch and ruin plaintiff's character and good name; that the charges were framed and conspired in malice; that the repetition of the charge of open and notorious adultery in the verified purported counterclaim was knowingly, wantonly and falsely made in malice. A judgment for damages was prayed for. ...

The principal argument by the parties in this case concerns whether or not the matters set forth in the purported counterclaims were privileged.

As this court said in Cadle v. McIntosh (1912), 51 Ind.App. 365, 370, 99 N.E. 779, 781: "The law of libel and slander recognizes two classes of privileged communication, absolute and qualified. If the communication is made under such circumstances as to constitute an absolute privilege, no right of action accrues, even though the words, spoken or written, would otherwise be actionable." [Cc]

It is said in 33 Am. Jur., Libel and Slander, § 149, p. 144: "In England the rule obtains that any statement contained in a pleading is absolutely privileged irrespective of its relevancy to the issues. This rule is followed in a few American jurisdictions. The prevailing rule in the United States is that such statements are privileged when pertinent and relevant to the subject under inquiry, however false and malicious such statements may be. But statements in pleadings are not privileged if they are not relevant or pertinent to the subject matter of the action. * * *." ...

We are inclined that the rule presently followed in England should not be adopted here without the qualification generally adhered to in other jurisdictions throughout the United States that the statements in order to be privileged must be pertinent or relevant to the litigation or bear some relation thereto.

As stated in 33 Am. Jur., Libel and Slander, § 150, p. 146: "The question of the relevancy or pertinency of matters contained in the pleadings, when in issue, is never left to the jury, but is a question of law for the court. As to the degree of relevancy or pertinency necessary to make alleged defamatory matter privileged, the courts favor a liberal rule. The matter to which the privilege does not extend must be so palpably irrelevant to the subject matter of the controversy that no reasonable man can doubt its irrelevancy and impropriety. In order that matter alleged in a pleading may be privileged, it need not be in every case material to the issues presented by the pleadings. It must, however, be legitimately related thereto, or so pertinent to the subject of the controversy that it may become the subject of inquiry in the course of the trial." [Cc] ...

In the present case the matter alleged in the purported counterclaims was not relevant or pertinent to the matter in controversy and had no relation thereto. It may be reasonably inferred from the facts pleaded that appellees did not have reasonable or probable cause to believe the matter to be relevant or pertinent.

The demurrers should have been overruled.

Judgment reversed with instructions to overrule the demurrers, and for further proceedings not inconsistent with this opinion.

INQUIRY

Legislative Privilege. The legislative privilege has both a common-law and constitutional basis, unlike the judicial privilege above that courts base solely on the common law. *See* U.S. Const. Art. I, §6, cl. 1 (speech-and-debate clause); Cochran v. Couzens, 42 F.2d 783 (D.C. Cir. 1930). Courts have interpreted the additional, constitutional basis for the legislative privilege to mean that not only is the privilege absolute (notwithstanding the speaker's bad faith, malice, or negligence) but that the privilege extends to *any* statements made within a legislative proceeding, not only those statements that relate to the proceeding. *See* Kilbourn v. Thompson, 103 U.S. 168 (1880); Cole v. Richards, 108 N.J.L. 356, 158 A. 466 (1932); *but see* Logan's Super Markets v. McCalla, 208 Tenn. 68, 343 S.W.2d 892 (1961). In that respect, the legislative privilege is broader than the judicial privilege that, as shown in the *Stahl* case above, conditions the privilege on the statement relating to the proceeding. The legislative privilege may be absolute but has its limit. The legislative privilege remains, like the judicial privilege, one that applies only to statements made within the proceeding. Legislators and public advocates who speak to the legislative body on the chamber floor have the privilege to speak on any subject they wish but lose the privilege when they speak outside the legislative forum to the press or distribute press releases and newsletters to constituents. *See* Hutchinson v. Proxmire, 443 U.S. 111 (1979) (senator's allegedly defamatory publications awarding "Golden Fleece of the Month Award" are not privileged outside Senate chamber). In that respect, the legislative privilege is a deliberative rather than diplomatic privilege. It rests on the presumed contribution of the statements to the legislative proceeding, not on the speaker's special status.

Figure

> Plaintiff's mass-tort lawyer Elizabeth Cabraser, a partner in the San Francisco law firm Lieff, Cabraser, Heimann & Bernstein, LLP, may be best known for her lead-counsel role in the $80 million class-action settlement of the Tri-State Crematorium cases involving the desecration of human remains—or for her co-class counsel role in the federal and state Exxon Valdez litigation. Yet she has other high-profile credits to her name, including federal multidistrict products-liability litigation over VIOXX, Bextra/Celebrex, and human-heart defibrillators. Ms. Cabraser has many public-interest honors and awards for her mass-tort work that helped to turn her small law firm into a national presence. She has many publications and speaking credits, is a member of the Council of the American Law Institute, and has co-chaired the ABA's Committee on Mass Torts.

Executive Privilege. The Supreme Court in Barr v. Mateo, 360 U.S. 564 (1959), extended the federal form of the executive privilege against defamation actions to federal administrative officials of all ranks. The Supreme Court had previously applied it only to Cabinet-level officials. *See* Spalding v. Vilas, 161 U.S. 483 (1896). The executive privilege is, like the judicial and executive privileges, absolute notwithstanding the speaker's malice or negligence. The executive privilege protects statements made within the scope of the official's duties—a scope that narrows with the lower rank of the official. *See* Doe v. MacMillan, 412 U.S. 306 (1973). State courts have also recognized the executive privilege as to higher state executive-branch officials. *See* Blair v. Walker, 64 Ill.2d 1, 349 N.E.2d 385 (1976). State courts disagree on whether lower executive officials should have absolute or only qualified immunity. *Contrast* McNayr v. Kelly, 184 So.2d 428 (Fla. 1966) (absolute immunity applies to lower-level administrative-branch officials); Sheridan v. Crisona, 14 N.Y.2d 108, 198 N.E.2d 359, 249 N.Y.S.2d 161 (1964) (same), *with* Chamberlain v. Mathis, 151 Ariz. 551, 729 P.2d 905 (1986) (recommending qualified immunity); Gardner v. Hollifields, 96 Idaho 609, 533 P.2d 730 (1975) (qualified privilege). Because the executive privilege includes administrative (not merely deliberative or judicial) actions, the scope of the executive privilege can include the right to inform the public in press releases. *See* Hackworth v. Larson, 83 S.D. 674, 165 N.W.2d 705 (1969).

2. Qualified Privileges

Law recognizes five common-law qualified privileges against defamation actions—(1) to speak to protect one's own interest, (2) to speak to protect a common interest with another, (3) to speak to protect the interests of a third person, (4) the fair-reporting privilege, and (5) the fair-comment privilege. The first three of these five qualified privileges protect communications made in good faith for lawful purposes but as to which the speaker may occasionally be mistaken. The first three qualified privileges, unlike the absolute privileges, depend on the good faith of the person making the allegedly defamatory statement. If the person making the statement does so in bad faith or with actual malice, then the privilege will not apply. Because the qualified privilege depends on the common law of each state rather than the United States Constitution, and there are no controlling Supreme Court cases, a variety of rules and formulations exist defining bad faith or actual malice. Some courts hold that the privilege depends on whether the publication is in a reasonable manner and for a proper purpose. Other factors may include whether the defamer volunteered the statement (in which case it is more likely with actual malice) or made the statement in response to a reasonable request for necessary information (in which case it is less likely with actual malice), and whether the speaker made the statement with ulterior motive—one that unrelated to the reason for the request or to the content of the statement. The fair-reporting and fair-comment privileges have their own formulations. The following section treat each of the five qualified privileges.

Self-Interest. The common law of privilege recognizes that certain occasions exist on which persons should have the liberty to speak, even in error, to protect their own interests—if they do not speak with actual malice. Think, for example, of the report and recovery of stolen property, *see* Montgomery Ward & Co. v. Watson, 55 F.2d 184 (4th Cir. 1932) (store manager has qualified privilege to report suspected employee theft), recovery and defense of alleged debt, *see* Teichner v. Bellan, 7 A.D.2d 247, 181 N.Y.S.2d 842 (1959) (qualified privilege to dispute bill), and protection of financial and corporate interests under threat by the mismanagement or malfeasance of others, *see* Gardner v. Standard Oil Co., 179 Miss. 176, 175 So. 203 (1937) (plant manager has qualified privilege to warn employees that individual had stolen plant gasoline). Self-interest warranting the qualified privilege can include statements made on both offense and defense—to protect person and recover property or to dispute charges by others. *See* Mencher v. Chesley, 193 Misc. 829, 85 N.Y.S.2d 431 (1948) (qualified privilege to attack another's motives in making allegations).

Common Interests. The common law of privilege also recognizes a privilege to speak, even in defamation if not with malice, to protect and promote common interests between two or more persons. *See* Restatement (Second) of Torts §596. Knowledge that a statement is false, like other forms of actual malice, destroys the common-interest privilege. Russell v. Geis, 251 Cal. App.2d 560, 59 Cal. Rptr. 569 (1967). Common interests may be found among members of a family, *see* Kroger Co. v. Young, 210 Va. 564, 172 S.E.2d 720 (1970), a labor union, *see* Bereman v. Power Pub. Co., 93 Colo. 581, 27 P.2d 749 (1933), a church, Slocinski v. Radwan, 83 N.H. 501, 144 A. 787 (1929), or a social club, *see* Hayden v. Hasbrouck, 34 R.I. 556, 84 A. 1087 (1912). One place, though, where potentially defamatory communications can be quite common is between employers regarding the qualifications of employees who seek to change employers. Consider one of those cases below.

Sindorf v. Jacron Sales Co.
Maryland Court of Special Appeals
27 Md. App. 53, 341 A.2d 856 (1975),
affd., 276 Md. 751, 350 A.2d 688 (1976)

ORTH, C.J. "The security of his reputation or good name from the arts[fn] of detraction and slander, are rights to which every man is entitled by reason and natural justice; since, without these, it is impossible to have the perfect enjoyment of any other advantage or right." 1 W. Blackstone, Commentaries 134.

Jack Sindorf felt that his right to personal security had been violated by the defamation of his reputation and good name by a corporation upon the spoken words of one of its employees, Robert Fridkis. Seeking balm for his hurt, he instituted an action ... for the tort of slander.... He did not prevail. Fridkis was dismissed from the action prior to trial and a judgment was entered in his favor for costs.[fn] A verdict in favor of the corporation, which went to trial on a plea of the general issue, was directed by the trial judge at the close of all the evidence. Sindorf appealed from the judgment entered thereon in favor of the corporation for costs.[fn] ...

... Sindorf was employed by the Pennsylvania Jacron for 18 months as a salesman. He resigned ... because of a dispute over certain sales made by him and commissions he believed due him. ...

A few days after his association with the Pennsylvania corporation terminated, Sindorf was hired by the Tool Box Corporation of Maryland... . When [Jacon president] Langton learned that Sindorf was working for Tool Box, he called Fridkis, Vice President of the Virginia Jacron. He asked Fridkis to verify Sindorf's current employment and to ascertain whether Sindorf had been working for Tool Box at the same time he had been working for the Pennsylvania Jacron. Langton told Fridkis why Sindorf left the Pennsylvania corporation: "We had mentioned that we had discrepancies with him, the sales picture, and the policy of how he would sell against company policies and do whatever he pleased, and that he had left us and in his possession he had taken with him his complete inventory and wouldn't return it to us. He claimed that he would return it when he would get his commission money." ...

... Although the Virginia Jacron and Tool Box were competitors, they would, at times, exchange goods and information and buy from and sell to each other. Brose said that if a former employee was employed or was about to be employed by Jacron, he would call Fridkis, discuss the employee and apprise Fridkis of any problems. ...

In the posture in which the case is presented, we are not concerned with the nature of the slanderous publication uttered by Fridkis and imputed to Jacron. Jacron does not dispute that the words were slanderous per se, that is, such words as "apparently and on the face of them, import such defamation as will of course be injurious." Jacron ... maintained, however, that it had a conditional privilege to defame. ...

Privilege to Defame

... [T]he law of this State is that a defamatory publication is conditionally privileged when the occasion shows that the communicating party and the recipient have a mutual interest in the subject matter, or some duty with respect thereto. [Cc] Over seventy-five years ago the Court of Appeals established that where an employer gives a character of an employee the communication is conditionally privileged under the principle that the party communicating has a duty owed, even though such duty is not a legal one, but only a moral or social duty of imperfect obligation. This is so even though the defamatory information was given voluntarily rather than upon request. [C][fn] ... [Q]ualified privilege arising by reason of common interest in the subject matter can inhere in business dealings between the publisher and the recipient... . The authorities are in general agreement that where a former employer communicates with a new or prospective employer about a former employee, a conditional privilege arises from a discharge of duty owed to the new or prospective employer. [Cc] ...

... The basis for the privilege depends upon the particular circumstances of the communication. Other persons may have a bona fide belief that they owe a moral or social duty to inform a new or prospective employer about an employee. This is not to say that anyone is privileged to communicate adverse information to an employer. In many instance a reasonable man would conclude that to communicate with an employer would be "officious intermeddling," [c], and therefore the communication would not be privileged. The circumstances here, however, were that the defamer was the vice-president of the subsidiary of the corporation which was Sindorf's former employer, and that the communicator and recipient, even though competitors, had a close personal and business relationship. Whether based on a duty owed or a common interest, we think that a qualified privilege arose. ...

Loss of a Conditional Privilege to Defame

Because a conditional or qualified privilege is conditioned upon publication in a reasonable manner and for a proper purpose, it is defeasible. "A finding of conditional privilege conditionally negates the presumption of malice and shifts the burden to the plaintiff to show actual malice." [Cc] The Court of Appeals said in Orrison v. Vance, supra, 262 Md. at 295, 277 A.2d at 578: "(M)alice means 'a reckless disregard of truth, the use of unnecessarily abusive language, or other circumstances which would support a conclusion that the defendant acted in an ill-tempered manner or was motivated by ill-will." [C] In determining an abuse of privilege all relevant circumstances are admissible, [c], including the defendant's reasonable belief in the truth of his statements, [c], the excessive nature of the language used, [cc], whether the disclosures were unsolicited, [c], and whether the communication was made in a proper manner and only to proper parties, [c].[fn]

... The motion for a directed verdict was primarily based on the theory that there was no sufficient showing by Sindorf of malice within the meaning of that word as defeating a conditional privilege. It appears that the grant of the motion was substantially bottomed on that reason. We think that the grant of the motion was wrong. We believe that the evidence, when viewed as required by the rule pertaining to the grant vel non of a directed verdict, led to conclusions from which reasonable minds could differ. We start with the rule that the publisher's motive will be more carefully scrutinized if his statements are volunteered than if they are in response to an inquiry, in which latter instance, greater latitude is permitted. We observe that Fridkis clearly indicated that Sindorf had been fired, whereas, as far as the record shows, he resigned. ... We observe that the publisher will be liable if he publishes his statement to accomplish a distinct objective, which may be legitimate enough in itself but is not within the privilege. [C] We think that a reasonable person could conclude from the evidence that Fridkis's communication to Brose was an effort to pressure Sindorf into returning the material he was holding, or, perhaps, simply to ascertain, as Langton requested, the date of employment of Sindorf by Tool Box. Neither would be within the privilege. The short of it is that we cannot find, assuming the truth of all credible evidence on the issue of malice and of all inferences fairly deducible therefrom, and considering them in the light most favorable to Sindorf, that they lead to the conclusions, from which reasonable minds could not differ, that Fridkis, and through him, Jacron, did not abuse the privilege to defame by excessive publication or by use of the occasion for an improper purpose, or by lack of grounds for belief in the truth of what was said. Therefore, the question of malice was properly for the jury and the trial judge erred in granting the motion for a directed verdict. The issue of malice should have gone to the jury with appropriate instructions. We reverse the judgment and remand the case for a new trial. ...

Judgment reversed; case remanded for a new trial; costs to be paid by appellee.

INQUIRY

Protecting Others. A third form of qualified privilege involves the right to make communications, even defamatory ones if without malice, to protect third persons and the public. *See* Restatement (Second) of Torts §595. The difference between the self-interest and common-interest privileges, and this privilege to protect others, is that the speaker has no interest but speaks to benefit another. Common enough circumstances exist, especially in commercial and employment settings, where a third person must seek information from another who has no personal interest in sharing it—such as a creditor obtaining information about a debtor from a bank, creating for the bank a qualified privilege to share it. *See* Melcher v. Beeler, 48 Colo. 233, 110 P. 181 (1910). One can see that an important factor in creating the privilege can be the presence of an information request, although circumstances exist where the law protects even volunteered information. *See* De Van Rose v. Tholborn, 153 Mo. App. 408, 134 S.W. 1093 (1911) (qualified privilege to volunteer notice regarding undesirable tenant). In the above *Sindorf* case, the former employer had a self-interest in sharing information with the plaintiff's current and prospective employer—one that ultimately led to the appellate court's finding an ulterior motive capable of defeating the qualified privilege. In the more-common situation, like the one illustrated in the case below, a former employer has no interest in speaking about a former employee but does have a qualified privilege (one more easily sustained) to do so in the interests of the prospective employer.

Wynn v. Cole
Michigan Court of Appeals
91 Mich. App. 517, 284 N.W.2d 144 (1979)

CYNAR, J. Plaintiffs appeal as of right from a directed verdict entered against them at the close of their proofs.

... The substance of this claim was that Victoria Wynn's prospective employer, the Red Cross, had requested information concerning her abilities as a nurse from previous employers, including the Flint Department of Public Health (hereinafter FDPH). Plaintiffs alleged that defendant, in her capacity as Director of the FDPH, had maliciously published to the Red Cross false and defamatory statements regarding plaintiff's previous employment with the FDPH (references to "plaintiff" hereinafter refer to plaintiff Victoria Wynn). The allegedly libelous publication consisted of a form sent out by the Red Cross requesting evaluation of various qualities and abilities of plaintiff. This form also indicated the information would be held in strict confidence. The form was completed and returned to the Red Cross... . The evaluation of ability as fair was made by Shirley Collins. Ability to work in a group was evaluated by Shirley Collins as fair. Intelligence and ability to grasp ideas was evaluated as fair by Shirley Collins. Personality was evaluated by Verna Cole as poor. Stability and dependability was evaluated as fair by Shirley Collins. Character, integrity and honesty was marked fair. Personal appearance was marked average. Under personal handicaps, Shirley Collins wrote "disgruntled about something most of the time." Attendance record is indicated as good. Under the item "would you hire this person into your organization", is "no", and Shirley Collins would not give this evaluation. The reason for leaving was "resignation sick" and may have been written by Shirley Collins. The additional words "Felt Vicki did not really apply herself to the best of her ability. Eager to get on the bandwagon if trouble existed" were the observations of Shirley Collins. ...

Plaintiff was working in a private nursing home in Flint when she applied for a position as a nurse with the Red Cross and had an interview about the first week of February, 1973. Plaintiff left the interview with a feeling she was hired subject to work recommendations being received from past employers. She submitted her resignation to the nursing home. One day before her last day at the nursing home, plaintiff received a call from the director of nursing at the Red Cross, stating she was not fit for work with the Red Cross because she received an unsatisfactory work rating from an undisclosed party. ...

According to Carol Krumbach, who was a director at the American National Red Cross at the time plaintiff sought employment as a nurse, it was standard procedure to send out reference forms to former employers. A response was received from the FDPH and it was a factor in the decision not to employ the plaintiff. ...

On appeal, plaintiff correctly concedes that defendant's publication of the allegedly defamatory statements were clothed with a qualified privilege[fn] which can only be overcome by a showing of "actual malice." [Cc] However, there is a split among the panels of this Court as to what is meant by "actual malice." Some cases define "malice" as some species of ill will or bad faith. [Cc] Others have adopted the definition set forth in New York Times v. Sullivan, 376 U.S. 254, 280, 84 S.Ct. 710, 11 L.Ed.2d 686 (1964), and have concluded that malice is established by proof that the defamatory statement was made "with knowledge that it was false or with reckless disregard of whether it was false or not." [Cc] Although previous decisions of the Michigan Supreme Court have employed the former definition, [c], in the most recent pronouncement from that Court on the subject it appears to have adopted the New York Times definition. [C] ... [W]e will apply the New York Times standard to the case at bar. ...

We conclude that a directed verdict was properly entered in this case.[fn] Plaintiff offered no evidence of defendant's state of mind at the time the allegedly defamatory statement was made. Although plaintiff did testify as to several incidents which tend to indicate that defendant did not particularly like her, this, without more, is insufficient to raise the inference that defendant committed the alleged libel with knowledge that the statements were false or with reckless disregard for their truth. In the absence of any evidence of malice, defendant's statements are protected by her qualified privilege and the case was properly taken from the jury's consideration.

Affirmed. Costs to defendant.

INQUIRY

Fair Reporting. The common law also recognizes a privilege of *fair reporting*, or *reporter's privilege*. The privilege permits publication of verbatim records or fair and accurate summaries of matters others allege in official proceedings and reports, at public meetings, and, in at least some states, court papers and pleadings. *See* Humperdinck v. National Enquirer, Inc., 973 F.2d 1431 (9th Cir. 1992) (privilege to report contents of affidavit filed in family-court matter). The underlying allegations may have been defamatory, but the privilege permits the reporter to report the allegations. In Time, Inc. v. Pape, 401 U.S. 279 (1971), the Supreme Court effectively constitutionalized the privilege. The case involved Time's publication of an article that, by omitting the word "alleged," stated as fact that the plaintiff had engaged in police brutality when, to the contrary, the federal Commission of Civil Rights report on which Time had relied had only been repeating allegations in civil-rights complaints. The Supreme Court decided that the omission could not constitute actual malice, effectively giving constitutional protection to reporters' judgments when repeating and summarizing what others allege. Even without the constitutional protection, the fair-reporting privilege would protect a verbatim report or fair and accurate summary of what others falsely allege. A minority of courts extend the privilege to include neutral reporting of charges made by public officials, public figures, and prominent organizations, on current public controversies. *See* Cianci v. New Times Pub. Co., 639 F.2d 54 (2d Cir. 1980); Edwards v. Natl. Audubon Socy., Inc., 556 F.2d 113 (2d Cir. 1977), cert. denied, 434 U.S. 1002 (1977).

Fair Comment. The common-law privilege of *fair comment*, as its name implies, protects the expression of *opinion* ("comment") when criticizing public officials but does not, in its majority form, protect false statements of *fact*. *See* Post Pub. Co. v. Hallam, 59 Fed. 530 (6th Cir. 1893). Although about three-fourths of the states follow that majority form, the remaining one-fourth minority extend the fair-comment privilege to protect false statements of fact, if made in good faith. *See* Coleman v. MacLennan, 78 Kan. 711, 98 P. 281 (1908). Obviously, the First Amendment is now the primary source of protection for criticism of public officials. The fair-comment privilege still has its place protecting criticism of private figures on private issues. *See* Magnusson v. New York Times, 98 P.3d 1070 (Okl. 2004) (Kansas law offers qualified fair-comment privilege to plastic surgeon criticized in consumer reporting).

D. Remedies

OBJECTIVE: Given a compensable defamation claim, describe the damages and other remedies available to the plaintiff as reflected in this section.

Case Study: A restaurant critic published in the local newspaper that the local truckstop diner was not the sort of place to which one would want to go "if the customer had a clean premises, safe food, and good health in mind." Diner receipts declined following the publication, with the wait-staff noticing a big dropoff in local customers. In the diner's defamation suit, the trial-court judge denied the newspaper's motion for summary judgment, holding that the quoted material and other like criticism, juxtaposed against false factual references to the diner having failed health-department inspections, could constitute a false and defamatory publication, and that there was also supporting evidence of actual malice. ***Describe the defamation damages the diner could pursue under the common law and the evidence it might offer to prove them.***

Unlike the typical personal-injury claim, as to which the sole remedy is monetary compensation, several possible remedies exist for defamation claims. Nominal, compensatory, and punitive damages may be available when the evidence satisfies the elements and overcomes constitutional protections and common-law privileges. The text below addresses the types of damages, the legal rules that support or limit them, and some ways in which parties prove them. Yet first consider some other important options. The experienced practitioner knows well that pursuing damages for some defamation claims in a court proceeding can be the worst of options—especially for the client who wishes to forestall further disclosure. The lawsuit's filing may engender the very public attention that the client most wishes to avoid. The fair-reporting and fair-comment privileges alone—the right of the media to reproduce verbatim, accurately summarize, and even comment upon court filings—should give the defamation client and practitioner pause before making those court filings.

Retraction. Probably the most commonly exercised remedy option is to make a confidential demand to cease, desist, and retract the defamation. Retraction statutes in about 30 states, some of them requiring a demand for retraction before allowing certain forms of damages, reinforce the wisdom of making and complying with a demand for retraction before embarking on litigation. *See* Mich. Comp. L. §600.2911(2)(b) ("Exemplary and punitive damages shall not be recovered in actions for libel unless the plaintiff, before instituting his or her action, gives notice to the defendant to publish a retraction and allows a reasonable time to do so... ."); Or. Rev. Stat. §31.210 (no general damages without demand for retraction); *see also* The Uniform Correction or Clarification of Defamation Act of 1993 (National Conf. of Commnrs. on Uniform State Laws). Although a retraction will not necessarily defeat the entire defamation claim, it may certainly help in defense of the claim. *See* Mich. Comp. L. §600.2911(2)(b) ("proof of the publication or correction shall be admissible in evidence under a denial on the question of the good faith of the defendant, and in mitigation and reduction of exemplary or punitive damages"). Or it may not. *See* Burnett v. National Enquirer, Inc., 144 Cal. App.3d 991, 193 Cal. Rptr. 206 (1983), appeal dismissed, 465 U.S. 1014 (1984). In the *Burnett* case, the defendant tabloid's evasive and incomplete retraction aided the plaintiff-entertainer Carol Burnett's claim. *See also* Morgan v. Dun & Bradstreet, Inc, 421 F.2d 1241 (5th Cir. 1970) (refusal to retract may be evidence of malice). Not only the content but the notoriety of the retraction may also be in dispute. *See* Mich. Comp. L. §600.2911(2)(b) ("For libel based on a radio or television broadcast, the retraction shall be made in the same manner and at the same time of the day as the original libel; for libel based on a publication, the retraction shall be published in the same size type, in the same editions and as far as practicable, in substantially the same position as the original libel... .").

Response. Another option the Supreme Court highlighted in *Gertz v. Robert Welch, Inc.*, is for the defamed person to resort to self-help "to contradict the lie or correct the error and thereby to minimize its adverse impact on reputation." 418 U.S. at 344. Media responses and campaigns may, in the court of public opinion, be more effective than legal ones. Turnabout is fair play. A defamed person will likely have the same constitutional protections that the publisher had in making the defamatory statement, to make a public response and may even have a qualified privilege of self-interest. *See* Phifer v. Foe, 443 P.2d 870 (Wyo. 1968).

Declaratory Actions. Defamation cases exist in which money is a lesser object than informing the public of the truth. Two famous cases of that type involved American General William Westmoreland and Israeli General Ariel Sharon's efforts to preserve and restore their reputations after media criticism. *See* Westmoreland v. CBS, Inc., 596 F. Supp. 1170 (S.D. N.Y. 1984); Sharon v. Time, Inc., 575 F. Supp. 1162 (S.D. N.Y. 1983). A defamation plaintiff may simply want a judicial forum in which to establish what is true and false—and what a publisher did with actual malice. Note the question that arises here, whether nominal damages are enough, after *Gertz* required that the plaintiff complaining of a defamatory statement on an issue of public concern prove "actual injury." Law would still seem to offer actions to vindicate a name, in the nature of an action for declaratory relief, even if the plaintiff suffered only nominal damages. *See* Hearst Corp. v. Hughes, 297 Md. 112, 466 A.2d 486 (1983).

Damages. Defamation damages begin with the injury to the plaintiff's reputation but also include the humiliation, embarrassment, and other forms of mental suffering the plaintiff can show attendant on the defamatory publication. *See* Gertz v. Robert Welch, Inc., 418 U.S. 323 (1974) ("the more customary types of actual harm inflicted by defamatory falsehood include impairment of reputation and standing in the community, personal humiliation, and mental anguish and suffering"); Restatement (Second) of Torts §621 ("One who is liable for a defamatory communication is liable for the proved, actual harm caused to the reputation of the person defamed."). Defamation cases for lowered reputation and mental distress compound the problem that practitioners have in helping juries translate pain, suffering, and other non-economic loss in cases of physical injury into monetary amounts. Defamation cases do not involve physical injury, usually no medical expense, and often even no economic loss against which to gauge the reputational injury. Of course, the defamation plaintiff does well to prove any economic (pecuniary) loss, whether in the form of a lost job, lost sales, other lost income, and medical expense. That proof may be through business, employment, and income records and with expert testimony. *See* Dun & Bradstreet v. Greenmoss Builders, Inc., 472 U.S. 749 (1985) ($50,000 in compensatory damages). But some of the larger awards, including the $500,000 awarded but reversed on constitutional grounds in *New York Times Co. v. Sullivan*, appear to be made without clear basis. *See* Restatement (Second) of Torts §621, Comment *a* ("At common law general damages have traditionally been awarded not only for harm to reputation that is proved to have occurred, but also, in the absence of this proof, for harm to reputation that would normally be assumed to flow from a defamatory publication of the nature involved."). Beyond the *Gertz* decision's warning that damages, including distress damages, depends on "actual injury," the Supreme Court is unclear whether it will eventually address in greater detail the constitutional standard for awarding and evaluating awards of defamation damages.

Punitive Damages. A later chapter on damages discusses punitive damages and the constitutional limits on the size of a punitive-damage award generally (established outside of the defamation context). As shown above, the *Gertz* decision requires that the plaintiff prove actual malice to support an award of presumed or punitive damages in a case involving an issue of publc concern. The common law generally required proof of actual malice to support a punitive damage award but did not require actual malice to award presumed damages—although some states did not even require actual malice for a punitive-damage award. The *Dun & Bradstreet* decision confirmed that the Supreme Court will not require proof of actual malice for punitive damages in a case brought by a private figure and not involving an issue of public concern—although again, few states authorize such an award, instead ordinarily requiring actual malice. The damages chapter below discusses measures of punitive damages.

Already-Bad Reputations. Some authority exists that in rare cases, the plaintiff's reputation with respect to a certain matter may already be so bad that defaming the plaintiff on that matter cannot make the plaintiff's reputation any worse—that the alleged defamation lacks of possible damage. *See* Logan v. District of Columbia, 447 F. Supp. 1328 (D.C. D.C. 1978). After professional-association representatives called assisted-suicide proponent Dr. Jack Kevorkian "a reckless instrument of death," "a great threat to the public," and "a killer" who was engaging in "criminal practices," the court held that the complained-of implication that he was a murderer could cause his reputation no damage. *See* Kevorkian v. American Medical Assn., 237 Mich. App. 1, 602 N.W.2d 233 (1999); *see also* Cerasani v. Sony Corp., 991 F. Supp. 343 (S.D. N. Y. 1998) (plaintiff, a "convicted racketeer, Mafia associate, bank robber, and drug dealer," is libel proof). Where, as will ordinarily be the case, the plaintiff's bad reputation is not so bad as to make the plaintiff "libel proof," the defendant may nevertheless offer evidence of the plaintiff's bad reputation to reduce the plaintiff's damages—if the bad-reputation evidence relates to the defamatory matter. *See* Towle v. St. Albans Pub. Co., 122 Vt. 134, 165 A.2d 363 (1960). Evidence rules also require that bad-reputation evidence be as to character rather than specific matters. *See* Small v. Chronicle & Gazette Pub. Co., 96 N.H. 265, 74 A.2d 544 (1950).

Incremental Harm. Authority also exists recognizing that in some cases, when the speaker places a minor defamatory statement next to substantially greater reputation-harming *true* statements, the defamatory harm may be so small as to be incremental and therefore nonactionable. See Sharon v. Time, Inc., *supra*; Tonnessen v. The Denver Pub. Co., 5 P.3d 959 (Colo. Ct. App. 2000). The incremental-harm doctrine is disfavored. *See* Liberty Lobby, Inc. v. Anderson, 746 F.2d 1563 (D.C. Cir. 1984) ("The law ... proceeds upon the optimistic premise that there is a little bit of good in all of us—or perhaps the pessimistic assumption that no matter how bad someone is, he can always be worse."), vacated, Anderson v. Liberty Lobby, Inc., 477 U.S. 242 (1986); *see also* Masson v. The New Yorker Magazine, Inc., 960 F.2d 896 (1992) (rejecting doctrine), on remand from, 501 U.S. 496 (1991). Then-Judge and later Supreme Court Justice Antonin Scalia wrote the *Liberty Lobby* opinion just quoted. The law disfavors the incremental-harm doctrine. Although juries have made and appellate courts have affirmed substantial defamation awards without considerable proof of general or punitive damages, the law nonetheless allows the defendant many opportunities to present reputation evidence reducing the plaintiff's damages. Consider a case illustrating the factfinder's latitude to award—or not to award—general and punitive damages depending on the proof of harm to the plaintiff's reputation.

Walkon Carpet Corp. v. Klapprodt
South Dakota Supreme Court
89 S.D. 172, 231 N.W.2d 370 (1975)

COLER, J. This action, brought by Walkon Carpet Corporation and W. P. Larson, sought recovery of a note due from defendant in the sum of $2826.29; the recovery of a Ford Econoline van which the defendant was to have contributed to the capital of the corporation; and the value of other property allegedly misappropriated by the defendant. The defendant ... counterclaimed ... for slander by W. P. Larson.

The trial to the court resulted in a verdict ... [in] the sum of $1.00 against W. P. Larson because of his slanderous statements. Defendant appeals claiming the court erred in ... awarding inadequate damages for slander.

We affirm. ...

The record in this case exemplifies a not unusual but unfortunate failure of the individuals going into a joint venture to document by books and records in the nature of inventory of stock, fixtures and equipment, profit and loss statements and balance sheets, and the assets and liabilities of the sole proprietorship being assimilated into a corporation in which the two of them were to be equal shareholders. ... The incorporators were W. P. Larson, Paul Klapprodt and Curtis Larson, a son of W. P. Larson. W. P. Larson was elected president and Paul Klapprodt secretary. ...

[Klapprodt, the defendant, served the venture as its general manager.] ... The record here supports the trial court's finding that the defendant was discharged as general manager without malice, oppression or fraud and the judgment against the defendant for property wrongfully withheld from the corporation furnishes justification for the employer's retention of the salary.

The defendant's final assertion is that he should be entitled to an award of substantial compensatory and punitive damages in the absence of proof of special damages when he was found to be the victim of slander per se, actuated by malice. [C] The trial court found that "Plaintiff Larson on several occasions told others that defendant was a crook, that he stole carpet and that he belonged in the penitentiary" and further that the remarks were actuated by malice. The charging of a person with a crime is slander per se under SDCL 20-11-4(1), [c]. No proof of actual harm to reputation or any other damage is required to recover for slander per se, [c], and plaintiff is entitled to at least nominal damages. [Cc]

In his counterclaim defendant alleged that the plaintiff Larson had slandered him in telling certain persons that he both drank to excess and was sexually promiscuous. The trial court may properly have considered from the development of the evidence on that count and from other evidence in the record that the reputation of the defendant was not such, in its tarnished state, as to have been materially damaged by the slander of the plaintiff. Since damage to reputation was at least part of Klapprodt's claim, evidence of his reputation or past misdeeds was admissible both in establishing truth, [c], and in mitigating damages. [C] The Restatement of Torts, Explanatory Notes §621, comment d, at 287 (Tent.Draft No. 20, 1974), supports this view. "In determining the amount of an award of general damages, the jury or other trier of fact may consider the character of the plaintiff and his general standing in the community as affecting the loss which he has sustained or will sustain."

Our review of the entire record does not leave us with the requisite definite and firm conviction that the award of $1.00 to Klapprodt was such a mistake as to justify reversal as clearly erroneous. [Cc]

SDCL 21-3-2 provides that the trial judge may award punitive damages because the slanderous statement was actuated by malice. In his discretion he elected to not make such an award and we find nothing in the record to indicate an abuse of this discretion.

Judgment is affirmed.

All the Justices concur.

Skills

The conclusion of a torts trial involves several important activities. (1) The trial lawyers must evaluate and may make directed-verdict motions, at the close of the other side's proofs, if the other side has failed to produce evidence supporting or opposing one or more of the elements of the case. (2) The lawyers must plan closing-argument themes. (3) The lawyers must choose standard jury instructions approved for the jurisdiction. The lawyers may also draft and propose special jury instructions on peculiar issues that arise during trial. (4) Lawyers often review a case for appeal issues before they know the outcome at trial because they may have to preserve appeal issues by offers of proof or by request for or objection to certain jury instructions. (5) Settlement talks occasionally continue during and immediately after trial, and during an appeal. The parties may agree on a "high-low" settlement during trial or even while the jury deliberates. In a high-low, the parties agree that if the verdict is below the low figure on which the parties agree, the low figure will be paid rather than the lower verdict—and if the verdict exceeds the high figure on which the parties agree, that the high figure will be paid rather than the higher verdict. The parties may also waive appeals, interest, and costs, and make other agreements.

CHAPTER XIV

INVASION OF PRIVACY

OBJECTIVE: Given fact patterns implicating rights of privacy, apply the definitions of each of the four forms of privacy reflected in this chapter to determine whether there is a compensable privacy tort claim.

Case Study: A woman was horrified to learn from an acquaintance that a national comedy magazine had used one of her wedding photographs to depict her as participating in and winning an "ugliest bride" contest. She had never participated in any such contest and had not given anyone consent to use her photograph. She was aware that the photography service that had taken her wedding pictures had for a brief time displayed some of them on its website and guessed that the magazine had taken the photograph from there. ***What form of tort action does the woman have against the magazine, if any? Analyze and evaluate her likelihood of prevailing.***

Invasion of privacy is a tort by one who exposes another to public scrutiny under circumstances that warrant liability for the harm caused. Proving the tort does not ordinarily depend on showing any misrepresentation or falsehood by the defendant as to the plaintiff's private activity. Just the opposite—invasion of privacy's harm arises from the public exposure of the plaintiff's true, but intensely private, circumstance. In that public-invasion-of-private-rights respect, invasion of privacy differs from other dignitary torts like intentional infliction of emotional distress. Those other torts need not involve any public exposure and indeed often remain intensely private. Defamation differs from invasion of privacy in that it requires falsehood. The varying forms of the invasion-of-privacy tort, and the cases recognizing those forms, show the rationales for protecting privacy. Law links privacy not so much to a need for secrecy to conceal wrongs but instead to human dignity—the personal liberty, recovery, growth, and maturity from preserving a sphere of serenity in solitude. Living under the prying and scrutiny of others distorts the psyche and heart—especially when the scrutiny is against one's will, trades on one's persona, and disrupts one's relationships.

> **Practice**
> The lawyer silently groaned as his wife recounted the sordid details of the breakup of her friend's marriage. Their conversation was not gossip. The lawyer and his wife knew better than that. Her friend needed counsel and guidance. Her husband had hidden a voice-activated tape-recorder under the bed when he left for a business trip. She knew he had been cheating on her, but now he knew... well, things that she had wanted to keep private. "Better tell her to stop in or call, or let me know if she would like the name of a woman lawyer" the lawyer told his wife, feeling a vague sense of shame at the human race as he mulled to himself the state's eavesdropping statute, invasion of privacy, and divorce laws.

While the right of a person to be let alone has probably existed from time immemorial, several developments have led states to recognize various forms of an invasion-of-privacy tort. An advertising industry capable of commercially exploiting personal identities, an entertainment media with ubiquitous paparazzi, and the ever-greater technological capabilities available for observing, tracking, and recording personal activity each make the protection of privacy an increasing concern. Nearly all states now recognize at least one invasion-of-privacy form, although some states limit by statute or case law the recognized types. Like other areas within tort law, invasion-of-privacy law is not monolithic but instead involves various forms and rules fitting the variety of activities disrupting the personal lives and interests of one another. Law in any one state may recognize any one or more of four forms of invasion of privacy—(1) commercial exploitation of likeness, also known as appropriation or the right of publicity, (2) intrusion on another's seclusion, (3) public disclosure of private facts, and (4) false light. Consider each form in turn.

A. Appropriation

The commercial-exploitation, appropriation, or right-of-publicity form of invasion of privacy is the easiest to recognize and define. In appropriation's case, the tort has less to do with privacy and more to do with the unfairness of allowing one to make a profit from another's name. The appropriation tort arises when the defendant uses the plaintiff's name, likeness, or persona, ordinarily for commercial but possibly for other advantageous purpose, without the plaintiff's permission. The Restatement (Second) of Torts §652C (1977) states simply, "One who appropriates to his own use or benefit the name or likeness of another is subject to liability to the other for invasion of privacy." Property and personal forms of the appropriation tort exist in different states. Under the property or commercial form, reflected by the just-quoted Restatement, the plaintiff must show (1) defendant's use of plaintiff's likeness (2) in a manner that trades on its value (3) for the defendant's advantage, (4) causing (5) loss. Some statutes limit the tort to its commercial form—misuse for trade or advertising. *See* N.Y. McKinney's Civil Rts. Laws §51. In the personal form, the plaintiff need not show a value to the plaintiff's image or that defendant had a commercial purpose. Mental anguish, humiliation, embarrassment, and outrage—or the simple right not to have one's image publicized for defendant's purposes—are enough. *See* Hinish v. Meier & Frank Co., 166 Or. 482, 113 P.2d 438 (1941) (publicity right not to have name used on telegram urging governor's veto); Goodyear Tire & Rubber Co. v. Vandergriff, 52 Fa. App. 662, 184 S.E. 452 (1936) (publicity right against impersonation to steal trade secrets); Vanderbilt v. Mitchell, 72 N.J. Eq. 910, 67 A. 97 (1907) (publicity right not to shown as father on birth certificate); *but see* Cox v. Hatch, 761 P.2d 556 (Utah 1988) (political officeholder has right to use for campaign purposes photographs of persons who voluntarily posed with officeholder). Some cases implicate both a commercial and personal right. *See* Michaels v. Internet Entertainment Group, Inc., 5 F. Supp.2d 823 (C.D. Cal. 1998) (publicity right of couple not to have sex tape exploited commercially on internet). Consider a first case illustrative of the property form followed by a second case that may have had (you decide) both property and personal consequences for the well-known plaintiff.

Edison v. Edison Polyform Mfg. Co.
Chancery Court of New Jersey
73 N.J. Eq. 136, 67 A. 392 (1907)

STEVENS, V.C. The complainant, who is an inventor of electrical instruments and processes, and enjoys in this regard a wordwide reputation, early in his career compounded a medicinal preparation [called Polyform] intended to relieve neuralgic pains by external application. … [A] New Jersey company, the present defendant, … is now carrying on the business of making and selling Polyform in that city. …

The prayer of the bill is that the defendant company may be restrained from using the name 'Edison' as a part of its corporate title or in connection with its business, or in connection with any advertisements circulated or published by it, and from holding out that complainant is the inventor or manufacturer or seller of the preparation sold by defendant. What the defendant company is doing is to manufacture and sell a liquid preparation containing apparently all but one of the drugs (viz., morphine) mentioned in Mr. Edison's formula. On each bottle is a label, containing on the one side directions for use, and on the other a picture of Mr. Edison and the following words: "Edison's Polyform. I certify that this preparation is compounded according to the formula devised and used by myself. Thos. A. Edison." Mr. Edison testifies that he has never authorized the use of his picture and that he has never made or authorized this certificate. As to the present defendant, there is absolutely no pretense that he has. …

There must be limits to the so-called right of privacy. … And as far as my researches have extended I do not find that it has yet been decided that injury to property in some form is not an essential element to relief. … I think that under the above authorities the complainant in the present case is clearly entitled to an injunction to restrain the unauthorized use of his name, his picture, and his certificate. …

It is difficult to imagine a case in which preventive relief would be more appropriate than the present. In a perfectly unauthorized way a certificate falsely purporting to be made by Mr. Edison, and also false in fact, because the preparation is not compounded with all the ingredients of the formula, is put by a company bearing Edison's name upon every bottle of Polyform which it sells. That there may be no mistake as to who is intended, the certificate is accompanied with a likeness.

I think an injunction should be granted restraining the defendant company from holding out, either in the name of the company, or by certificate, or by pictorial representation, that Mr. Edison has any connection with or part in the complainant's business. I cannot divorce the company's name from the other parts of the representation. It is, as the evidence stands, part of the fraudulent contrivance. The abstract question whether a company can innocently use, as a part of its title, the name of a distinguished living character, is not before me for decision, and no opinion is expressed about it.

Carson v. Here's Johnny Portable Toilets, Inc.
United States Court of Appeals, Sixth Circuit
698 F.2d 831 (6th Cir. 1983)

BROWN, J. This case involves claims of unfair competition and invasion of the right of privacy and the right of publicity arising from appellee's adoption of a phrase generally associated with a popular entertainer.

Appellant, John W. Carson (Carson), is the host and star of "The Tonight Show," a well-known television program broadcast five nights a week by the National Broadcasting Company. Carson also appears as an entertainer in night clubs and theaters around the country. From the time he began hosting "The Tonight Show" in 1962, he has been introduced on the show each night with the phrase "Here's Johnny." ... In 1967, Carson first authorized use of this phrase by an outside business venture, permitting it to be used by a chain of restaurants called "Here's Johnny Restaurants."

Appellant Johnny Carson Apparel, Inc. (Apparel), formed in 1970, manufactures and markets men's clothing to retail stores. Carson, the president of Apparel and owner of 20% of its stock, has licensed Apparel to use his name and picture, which appear on virtually all of Apparel's products and promotional material. Apparel has also used, with Carson's consent, the phrase "Here's Johnny" on labels for clothing and in advertising campaigns. ... The phrase "Here's Johnny" has never been registered by appellants as a trademark or service mark.

Appellee, Here's Johnny Portable Toilets, Inc., is a Michigan corporation engaged in the business of renting and selling "Here's Johnny" portable toilets. Appellee's founder was aware at the time he formed the corporation that "Here's Johnny" was the introductory slogan for Carson on "The Tonight Show." He indicated that he coupled the phrase with a second one, "The World's Foremost Commodian," to make "a good play on a phrase." ...

Shortly after appellee went into business in 1976, appellants brought this action alleging unfair competition, trademark infringement under federal and state law, and invasion of privacy and publicity rights. They sought damages and an injunction prohibiting appellee's further use of the phrase "Here's Johnny" as a corporate name or in connection with the sale or rental of its portable toilets.

After a bench trial, the district court issued a memorandum opinion and order, [c], which ... ordered the dismissal of the appellants' complaint. ... On the right of privacy and right of publicity theories, the court held that these rights extend only to a "name or likeness," and "Here's Johnny" did not qualify. ...

In an influential article, Dean Prosser delineated four distinct types of the right of privacy: (1) intrusion upon one's seclusion or solitude, (2) public disclosure of embarrassing private facts, (3) publicity which places one in a false light, and (4) appropriation of one's name or likeness for the defendant's advantage. Prosser, *Privacy*, 48 Calif.L.Rev. 383, 389 (1960). This fourth type has become known as the "right of publicity." [Cc] ...

... The right of publicity, as we have stated, is that a celebrity has a protected pecuniary interest in the commercial exploitation of his identity. If the celebrity's identity is commercially exploited, there has been an invasion of his right whether or not his "name or likeness" is used. Carson's identity may be exploited even if his name, John W. Carson, or his picture is not used. ...

In this case, Earl Braxton, president and owner of Here's Johnny Portable Toilets, Inc., admitted that he knew that the phrase "Here's Johnny" had been used for years to introduce Carson. Moreover, in the opening statement in the district court, appellee's counsel stated: "Now, we've stipulated in this case that the public tends to associate the words 'Johnny Carson,' the words 'Here's Johnny' with plaintiff, John Carson and, Mr. Braxton, in his deposition, admitted that he knew that and probably absent that identification, he would not have chosen it." [C] That the "Here's Johnny" name was selected by Braxton because of its identification with Carson was the clear inference from Braxton's testimony irrespective of such admission in the opening statement.

We therefore conclude that, applying the correct legal standards, appellants are entitled to judgment. The proof showed without question that appellee had appropriated Carson's identity in connection with its corporate name and its product.[fn]

... It is not fatal to appellant's claim that appellee did not use his "name." Indeed, there would have been no violation of his right of publicity even if appellee had used his name, such as "J. William Carson Portable Toilet" or the "John William Carson Portable Toilet" or the "J.W. Carson Portable Toilet." The reason is that, though literally using appellant's "name," the appellee would not have appropriated Carson's identity as a celebrity. Here there was an appropriation of Carson's identity without using his "name." ...

The judgment of the district court is vacated and the case remanded for further proceedings consistent with this opinion.

INQUIRY

Celebrity. As the above *Edison* and *Carson* cases suggest, trading on the celebrity of another is a common pattern for the publicity-right form of the invasion-of-privacy tort. *See* White v. Samsung Electronics America, Inc., 971 F.2d 1395 (9th Cir. 1992) (game-show figure Vanna White); Midler v. Ford Motor Co., 849 F.2d 460 (9th Cir. 1988) (singer-actress Bette Midler); Eastwood v. Superior Ct., 149 Cal. App.3d 409, 198 Cal. Rptr. 342 (1983) (film star Clint Eastwood); Lugosi v. Universal Pictures, 25 Cal.3d 813, 603 P.2d 425 (1979) (film star Bella Lugosi); Ali v. Playgirl, Inc., 447 F. Supp. 723 (S.D. N.Y. 1978) (fighter Muhammad Ali); Onassis v. Christian Dior-New York, Inc., 472 N.Y.S.2d 254, affd. 110 A.D.2d 1095 (1985) (assassinated president's widow). Celebrity, though, is not an element of the tort. Appropriation can occur without the person who suffers appropriation being famous. *See* Joe Dickerson & Assocs., LLC v. Dittmar, 34 P.3d 995 (Colo. 2001) (private figure convicted of felony has publicity right against use of name in newsletter advertising detective services); Slocum v. Sears Roebuck & Co., 542 So.2d 777 (La App. 1989) (infant has publicity right against use of photograph in advertising).

Relief. What remedies should be available? The above *Edison* and *Carson* cases show that the courts will grant injunction against defendant's continued use of plaintiff's identity. The defendant's unjust enrichment may be a damages measure, as may the economic loss to plaintiff from the misappropriated use. What about non-economic damages? *See* Abdul-Jabbar v. General Motors Corp., 85 F.3d 407 (9th Cir. 1996) (allowing mental-distress damages in connection with publicity-right claim). Should the law presume damages? *See* Petty v. Chrysler Corp., 343 Ill. App.3d 815, 799 N.E.2d 432 (2003) (allowing presumed damages for misappropriation claim).

Survivability. Whether a state recognizes the commercial or personal form of the appropriation form of the invasion-of-privacy tort may determine whether a cause of action survives the appropriated figure's death. If the only concern is the figure's privacy, then law has no purpose recognizing the tort after the figure's death. If, on the other hand, the appropriation form reflects a property right, then the appropriated figure's estate should have a continuing cause of action to enforce the right. All but two states (New York and Wisconsin) appear to accept that the tort survives the appropriated figure's death. *See* Herman Miller v. Pelazzetti Imports & Exports, 270 F.3d 298 (6th Cir. 2001). Tennessee law at one time did not recognize appropriation claims after death. *See* Memphis Development Fdn. v. Factors Etc., Inc., 616 F.2d 956 (6th Cir. 1980), cert. denied, 449 U.S. 953 (1980). Yet the Tennessee courts stepped in to protect an especially famous deceased figure's privacy rights. *See* Elvis Presley Enterprises, Inc. v. Elvisly Yours, Inc., 817 F.2d 104 (6th Cir. 1987). Elvis lives? The appropriation tort protects the continuing right of a deceased figure's heirs to benefit from controlling the commercial use of the decedent's identity. *See* Martin Luther King, J., Center for Social Change v. American Heritage Prds., Inc., 250 Ga. 135, 296 S.E.2d 697 (1982) (enjoining sale of busts of deceased civil-rights leader).

The First Amendment. As the chapter on defamation shows, substantial constitutional protections surround public statements about public and even private figures, on public issues. One fine line that the First Amendment requires litigants draw is that between artistic expression happening to involve a famous figure and the commercial exploitation of that figure's image. Should a songwriter have the artistic license to use a famous figure's name in a song title even if the name has no bearing on the song's subject—or is that commercial exploitation? *See* Parks v. LaFace Records, 329 F.3d 437 (6th Cir. 2003) (actionable appropriation of civil-rights leader's name). If a celebrity golfer wins a tournament, may an artist interpret the event on canvas and license prints of it? *See* ETW Corp. v. Jireh Pub., Inc., 332 F.3d 915 (6th Cir. 2003) (publicity right bows to public interest in artistic expression); *see also* Montana v. San Jose Mercury-News, Inc., 34 Cal. App.4th 790, 40 Cal. Rptr.2d 639 (Cal. Ct. App. 1995) (newspaper has First Amendment right to sell poster-format pictures of football star reprinted from newspaper issues); Namath v. Sports Illustrated, 39 N.Y.2d 897, 386 N.Y.S.2d 397, 352 N.E.2d 584 (N.Y. 1976) (magazine has right to use football star's image in magazine advertising). The standard may involve a determination of the degree to which the use involves the artist's expression, *see* Winter v. DC Comics, 30 Cal.4th 881, 69 P.3d 473 (2003) ("significant expressive content"), and the extent to which the artist's work transforms the person's image into an independent creative expression, *see* Comedy III Prods. V. Gary Saderup, 106 Cal. Rptr.2d 126, 21 P.3d 797 (2001) (challenging use of Three Stooges lithographs). What steps would you advise that a client take before making use of another's image? What if the person whose image your client wishes to use is dead? Recognize that First Amendment protections extend to the invasion-of-privacy realm, although (given the absence of a falsehood) not under the same actual-malice test the Supreme Court employs to protect defamation. *See* Joe Dickerson & Assocs., LLC v. Dittmar, 34 P.3d 995 (Colo. 2001) (public right to know defeats publicity right not to have newsletter advertising detective services use convicted plaintiff's name). Consider the following illustrative Supreme Court case.

Zacchini v. Scripps-Howard Broadcasting Co.
United States Supreme Court
433 U.S. 562 (1977)

WHITE, J. Petitioner, Hugo Zacchini, is an entertainer. He performs a 'human cannonball' act in which he is shot from a cannon into a net some 200 feet away. Each performance occupies some 15 seconds. In August and September 1972, petitioner was engaged to perform his act on a regular basis at the Geauga County Fair in Burton, Ohio. He performed in a fenced area, surrounded by grandstands, at the fair grounds. Members of the public attending the fair were not charged a separate admission fee to observe his act.

On August 30, a freelance reporter for Scripps-Howard Broadcasting Co., the operator of a television broadcasting station and respondent in this case, attended the fair. He carried a small movie camera. Petitioner noticed the reporter and asked him not to film the performance. The reporter did not do so on that day; but on the instructions of the producer of respondent's daily newscast, he returned the following day and videotaped the entire act. This film clip approximately 15 seconds in length, was shown on the 11 o'clock news program that night, together with favorable commentary.[fn]

Petitioner then brought this action for damages, alleging that ... such conduct was an "unlawful appropriation of plaintiff's professional property." [C] Respondent answered and moved for summary judgment, which was granted by the trial court. ...

We granted certiorari, [c], to consider an issue unresolved by this Court: whether the First and Fourteenth Amendments immunized respondent from damages for its alleged infringement of petitioner's statelaw "right of publicity." [C] Insofar as the Ohio Supreme Court held that the First and Fourteenth Amendments of the United States Constitution required judgment for respondent, we reverse the judgment of that court. ...

The Ohio Supreme Court held that respondent is constitutionally privileged to include in its newscasts matters of public interest that would otherwise be protected by the right of publicity, absent an intent to injure or to appropriate for some nonprivileged purpose. If under this standard respondent had merely reported that petitioner was performing at the fair and described or commented on his act, with or without showing his picture on television, we would have a very different case. But petitioner is not contending that his appearance at the fair and his performance could not be reported by the press as newsworthy items. His complaint is that respondent filmed his entire act and displayed that film on television for the public to see and enjoy. This, he claimed, was an appropriation of his professional property. The Ohio Supreme Court agreed that petitioner had "a right of publicity" that gave him "personal control over commercial display and exploitation of his personality and the exercise of his talents."[fn] ...

The broadcast of a film of petitioner's entire act poses a substantial threat to the economic value of that performance. As the Ohio court recognized, this act is the product of petitioner's own talents and energy, the end result of much time, effort, and expense. Much of its economic value lies in the "right of exclusive control over the publicity given to his performance"; if the public can see the act free on television, it will be less willing to pay to see it at the fair.[fn] The effect of a public broadcast of the performance is similar to preventing petitioner from charging an admission fee. ... Moreover, the broadcast of petitioner's entire performance, unlike the unauthorized use of another's name for purposes of trade or the incidental use of a name or picture by the press, goes to the heart of petitioner's ability to earn a living as an entertainer. Thus, in this case, Ohio has recognized what may be the strongest case for a "right of publicity" involving, not the appropriation of an entertainer's reputation to enhance the attractiveness of a commercial product, but the appropriation of the very activity by which the entertainer acquired his reputation in the first place.

There is no doubt that entertainment, as well as news, enjoys First Amendment protection. It is also true that entertainment itself can be important news. [C] But it is important to note that neither the public nor respondent will be deprived of the benefit of petitioner's performance as long as his commercial stake in his act is appropriately recognized. Petitioner does not seek to enjoin the broadcast of his performance; he simply wants to be paid for it. Nor do we think that a state-law damages remedy against respondent would represent a species of liability without fault contrary to the letter or spirit of Gertz v. Robert Welch, Inc., 418 U.S. 323, 94 S.Ct. 2997, 41 L.Ed.2d 789 (1974). Respondent knew that petitioner objected to televising his act, but nevertheless displayed the entire film.

We conclude that although the State of Ohio may as a matter of its own law privilege the press in the circumstances of this case, the First and Fourteenth Amendments do not require it to do so.

Reversed.

B. Intrusion

The second form of invasion-of-privacy tort is one that does not involve commercial exploitation and instead more clearly involves the plaintiff's interest to be left alone. The intrusion form of invasion of privacy requires that plaintiff show defendant's unauthorized instrusion into plaintiff's reasonable expectation of privacy in a way that would be highly offensive to a reasonable person and did so offend the plaintiff. *See* Restatement (Second) of Torts §652B (1977). Notice the definition's objective standards. Unless the plaintiff can show the reasonableness of the plaintiff's expectation of privacy *and* offense, the facts do not satisfy intrusion's elements. But the intrusion need not be a physical entry into a physical place. An intrusion may instead include the defendant's using photography, recording devices, or other secret and even electronic means of access to the plaintiff's private place. *See* Roach v. Harper, 143 W. Va. 869, 105 S.E.2d 564 (1958) (hidden microphone). No publication of the observed matters is necessary. The intrusion itself is sufficient. *See* Dietemann v. Time, Inc., 449 F.2d 245 (9th Cir. 1971) (actionable intrusion by reporters posing as patient and spouse, making video and audio recordings inside plaintiff's home); Pearson v. Dodd, 410 F.2d 701 (1969) (actionable intrusion into senator's office and papers). Also, intrusion addresses not only the plaintiff's private *place* but also the plaintiff's private *matter*. Intrusion may thus include gathering plaintiff's confidential data—any matter in which the plaintiff had a reasonable expectation of privacy the violation of which would highly offend the reasonable person. *See* Zimmermann v. Wilson, 81 F.2d 847 (3d Cir. 1936) (intrusion claim regarding secret inspection of bank accounts); *see also* Josh Blackman, *Omniveillance, Google, Privacy in Public, and the Right to Your Digital Identity*, 49 Santa Clara L.Rev. 313 (2009).

The privacy necessary to support the intrusion tort need not necessarily be complete. Others may have access to the private place, as in the oft-cited, progenitor case of De May v. Roberts, 46 Mich. 160, 9 N.W. 146 (1881), recognizing a claim on behalf of a woman delivering a child at home. The delivering physician had the right to be present, given the woman's consent, but his putative assistant who had no medical training or qualification did not have such a right. Sanders v. American Broadcasting Cos., 20 Cal.4th 907, 978 P.2d 67, 85 Cal. Rptr.2d 909 (1999), is a modern case in which the court recognized a privacy right in the workplace (a "telepsychic" boutique) even where others expecting the same right could overhear the private conversations. *See also* Doe v. B.P.S. Guard Services, Inc., 945 F.2d 1422 (8th Cir. 1991) (intrusion claim for models changing in back-stage dressing area, when guards observed using surveillance cameras). Consider the following case illustrative of several of the above points.

Hamberger v. Eastman
New Hampshire Supreme Court
106 N.H. 107, 206 A.2d 239 (1964)

The plaintiffs, husband and wife, brought companion suits for invasion of their privacy against the defendant who owned and rented a dwelling house to the plaintiffs. The plaintiffs allege that the defendant installed and concealed "a listening and recording device" in their bedroom... .

The declaration in the suit by the husband reads as follows: ... "That... plaintiff discovered the listening and recording device which defendant had willfully and maliciously concealed in his bedroom, and the plaintiff, ever since that time and as a direct result of the actions of the defendant, has been greatly distressed, humiliated, and embarrassed and has sustained and is now sustaining, intense and severe mental suffering and distress, and has been rendered extremely nervous and upset, seriously impairing both his mental and physical condition, and that the plaintiff has sought, and still is under, the care of a physician; that large sums have been, and will be in the future, expended for medical care and attention; that because of his impaired mental and physical condition, the plaintiff has been and still is unable to properly perform his normal and ordinary duties as a father and as a husband, and has been unable to properly perform his duties at his place of employment, and has been otherwise greatly injured."

The declaration in the suit by the wife is identical, with appropriate substitutes of the personal pronoun, and omission of the allegation of inability to perform duties at her place of employment. ...

KENISON, C.J. The question presented is whether the right of privacy is recognized in this state. There is no controlling statute and no previous decision in this jurisdiction which decides the question. Inasmuch as invasion of the right of privacy is not a single tort but consists of four distinct torts, it is probably more concrete and accurate to state the issue in the present case to be whether this state recognizes that intrusion upon one's physical and mental solitude or seclusion is a tort. ...

The tort of intrusion upon the plaintiff's solitude or seclusion is not limited to a physical invasion of his home or his room or his quarters. ... The right of privacy has been upheld in situations where microphones have been planted to overhear private conversations. ...

We have not searched for cases where the bedroom of husband and wife has been "bugged" but it should not be necessary—by way of understatement—to observe that this is the type of intrusion that would be offensive to any person of ordinary sensibilities. What married "people do in the privacy of their bedroom is their own business so long as they are not hurting anyone else." Ernst and Loth, For Better or Worse, 79 (1952). The Restatement, Torts §867 provides that "a person who unreasonably and seriously interferes with another's interest in not having his affairs known to others * * * is liable to the other." As is pointed out in *comment* d "liability exists only if the defendant's conduct was such that he should have realized that it would be offensive to persons of ordinary sensibilities. It is only where the intrusion has gone beyond the limits of decency that liability accrues. These limits are exceeded where intimate details of the life of one who has never manifested a desire to have publicity are exposed to the public * * *."

The defendant contends that the right of privacy should not be recognized on the facts of the present case as they appear in the pleadings because there are no allegations that anyone listened or overheard any sounds or voices originating from the plaintiffs' bedroom. The tort of intrusion on the plaintiffs' solitude or seclusion does not require publicity and communication to third persons although this would affect the amount of damages... . The defendant also contends that the right of privacy is not violated unless something has been published, written or printed and that oral publicity is not sufficient. Recent cases make it clear that this is not a requirement. [Cc]

If the peeping Tom, the big ear and the electronic eavesdropper (whether ingenious or ingenuous) have a place in the hierarchy of social values, it ought not to be at the expense of a married couple minding their own business in the seclusion of their bedroom who have never asked for or by their conduct deserved a potential projection of their private conversations and actions to their landlord or to others. Whether actual or potential such "publicity with respect to private matters of purely personal concern is an injury to personality. It impairs the mental peace and comfort of the individual and may produce suffering more acute than that produced by a mere bodily injury." III Pound, Jurisprudence 58 (1959). The use of parabolic microphones and sonic wave devices designed to pick up conversations in a room without entering it and at a considerable distance away makes the problem far from fanciful. [C] ...

The motion to dismiss should be denied.

Remanded.

INQUIRY

The Press. Because the intrusion form of the invasion-of-privacy tort is complete without publication, First Amendment rights and interests are minimal. The press occasionally attempts intrusive forms of information gathering. While the information the intrusion generates may be important to the public, its importance does not justify the intrusion, which remains actionable even if the information's publication is not. The intrusion form of the tort does not address the information's *publication* but instead the *means* by which the defendant obtained the information in violation of privacy rights. *See* Food Lion v. Capital Cities/ABC, Inc., 194 F.3d 505 (4th Cir. 1999) (grocer has action against television company for taping private areas of business by fraudulent means). The First Amendment still has influence. The fact that the intrusion was for newsgathering purposes may make it less offensive to the reasonable person and, therefore, less likely actionable as an intrusion. *See* Deteresa

v. American Broadcasting Cos., 121 F.3d 460 (9th Cir. 1997) (no intrusion for television reporter secretly taping on the street a flight attendant from O.J. Simpson's flight from Los Angeles after wife's murder); Desnick v. American Broadcasting Cos., 44 F.3d 1345 (7th Cir. 1995) (no intrusion for secret taping of physician by investigators posing as patients); *but see* Shulman v. Group W Prods., Inc., 18 Cal.4th 200, 74 Cal. Rptr.2d 843 (1998) (emergency technician's secret taping of accident victim for television may be an intrusion). On the other hand, the Supreme Court held in Wilson v. Layne, 526 U.S. 603 (1999), that police who execute a search warrant bringing ride-along media into the searched home violate Fourth Amendment protection against unreasonable searches, where the media did not aid the warrant's execution.

C. Public Disclosure

The third form of the invasion-of-privacy tort involves the public disclosure of private facts. Its four elements include (1) publication to more than a few persons of (2) private facts that would be (3) highly offensive to the reasonable person, coupled with (4) an absence of any legitimate public interest in the disclosure. *See* Restatement (Second) of Torts §652D (1977); *see also* McSurely v. McClellan, 753 F.2d 88 (D.C. Cir. 1985) (publication of details of plaintiff's pre-marital affair to plaintiff's husband was sufficient publicity even though only to one person because that one person was the most significant audience); Hawkins v. Multimedia, Inc., 288 S.C. 569, 344 S.E.2d 145 (public disclosure that minor was father of illegitimate child is actionable), cert. denied, 479 U.S. 1012 (1986). The public-disclosure form does not involve an intrusion into the plaintiff's private place. The information that the defendant makes public may have been accessible without intrusion. Nor does the public-disclosure form of the tort require any commercial exploitation of, or any falsehood in, the publication. Rather, the offensiveness arises from the defendant making publicly known what the reasonable person would consider a private matter—according to the Restatement (Second) of Torts §652D, reflecting community mores as to standards of common decency. "The line is to be drawn when the publicity ceases to be the giving of information to which the public is entitled, and becomes a morbid and sensational prying into private lives for its own sake, with which a reasonable member of the public, with decent standards, would say that he had no concern." *Id.* at Comment *h*; *see also* Johnson v. Harcourt, Brace, Jovanovich, Inc., 43 Cal. App.3d 880, 118 Cal. Rptr. 370 (Ct. App. 1974) (publication that plaintiff had returned money lost by armored truck not a highly offensive disclosure). Because the public-disclosure form of the tort has as its functional definition the public's interest in knowing, it obviously implicates First Amendment interests. *See* Sipple v. Chronicle Pub. Co., 154 Cal. App.3d 1040, 201 Cal. Rptr. 665 (1984) (public disclosure of plaintiff's participation in homosexual parades and campaigns not actionable because not of private facts, and protected where plaintiff was an involuntary public figure).

Figure
Trial lawyer Prince Chambliss Jr. is a partner at the Memphis, Tennessee law firm Stokes, Bartholomew, Evans & Petree. He has been a civil litigator and mediator of personal-injury, class-action, insurance-coverage, securities-fraud, and other tort cases for over three decades. He also gets credit as the first African-American partner at a

non-minority law firm in the state of Tennessee and the first African-American president of the Memphis Bar Association.

The Supreme Court. The Supreme Court broadly interpreted and constitutionalized the no-public-interest element of the public-disclosure tort, in a series of five cases. In Cox Broadcasting Corp. v. Cohn, 420 U.S. 469 (1975), the Court held unconstitutional on First Amendment grounds a statute that, as applied, prohibited the television broadcast of a rape victim's name. In Smith v. Daily Mail Pub Co., 443 U.S. 97 (1979), the Court held unconstitutional on First Amendment grounds a statute that prohibited publication of the names of juvenile delinquents. In Landmark Communs., Inc. v. Virginia, 435 U.S. 829 (1978), the Court held unconstitutional on First Amendment grounds a statute prohibiting disclosure of judicial-review commission action. In The Florida Star v. B.J.F., 491 U.S. 524 (1989), the Court held protected by the First Amendment a newspaper's publication of the name of a rape victim obtained from a police report mistakenly released with the name disclosed. The plaintiff endured calls and threats, suffered distress, and had to move from her home. The *Florida Star* dissent noted "the trend in 'modern' jurisprudence to eclipse an individual's right to maintain private any truthful information that the press wished to publish," and added, "Today, we hit the bottom of the slope." Not quite. In Bartnicki v. Vopper, 532 U.S. 514 (2001), the Court held protected by the First Amendment the playing of an audiotape secretly recorded in violation of federal and state law, on a radio talk show, again resulting in threats of violence against the plaintiff. The following case illustrates the poignancy of these cases.

Hall v. Post
North Carolina Supreme Court
323 N.C. 259, 372 S.E.2d 711 (1988)

MITCHELL, J. In the present case, this Court must decide whether claims for tortious invasion of privacy by truthful public disclosure of "private" facts concerning the plaintiffs are cognizable at law in North Carolina. We hold that they are not and reverse the decision of the Court of Appeals.

The plaintiffs, Susie Hall and her adoptive mother, Mary Hall, brought separate civil actions against the defendants for invasion of privacy. The actions were based upon two articles printed in The Salisbury Post and written by its special assignment reporter, Rose Post. …

… [O]n 18 July 1984, The Salisbury Post published an article by Rose Post which bore the headline "Ex-Carny Seeks Baby Abandoned 17 Years Ago." The article concerned the search by Lee and Aledith Gottschalk for Aledith's daughter by a previous marriage, whom she and her former husband had abandoned in Rowan County in September of 1967. The article told of Aledith's former marriage to a carnival barker named Clarence Maxson, the birth of their daughter in 1967, their abandonment of the child at the age of four months, events in Aledith's life thereafter, and her return to Rowan County after seventeen years to look for the child. The article indicated that Clarence Maxson had made arrangements in 1967 for a babysitter named Mary Hall to keep the child for a few weeks. Clarence and Aledith then moved on with the carnival, and Clarence later told Aledith that he had signed papers authorizing the baby's adoption.

Aledith was married to Lee Gottschalk in 1984, and they decided to travel to Rowan County to look for Aledith's child. The newspaper article of 18 July 1984 related the details of their unsuccessful search and then stated: "If anyone, they say, knows anything about a little blonde baby left here when the county fair closed and the carnies moved on in September 1967, Lee and Aledith Gottschalk can be reached in Room 173 at the Econo Motel."

Shortly after the article was published, the Gottschalks were called at the motel and informed of the child's identity and whereabouts.

The defendants published a second article on 20 July 1984 reporting that the Gottschalks had located the child with the aid of responses to the earlier article. The second article identified the child as Susie Hall and identified her adoptive mother as Mary Hall. The article related the details of a telephone encounter between the Gottschalks and Mrs. Hall and described the emotions of both families.

The plaintiffs alleged that they fled their home in order to avoid public attention resulting from the articles. Each plaintiff alleged that she sought and received psychiatric care for the emotional and mental distress caused by the incident. ...

In the present case, we consider for the first time that branch of the invasion of privacy tort which is most commonly referred to as the "public disclosure of private facts." The plaintiffs have at all times acknowledged that the facts published about them by the defendants were true and accurate in every respect, but they contend, nevertheless, that they are entitled to recover. ...

The private facts branch of the invasion of privacy tort was not recognized at common law in 1776 or at the times of adoption of either the Constitution or the Bill of Rights. It has never been recognized in England, Australia, New Zealand, Canada, or other jurisdictions sharing the heritage of the English common law. [C] After an extensive study, the British Committee on Privacy recommended that the invasion of privacy tort not be adopted in Great Britain, because its application would be too difficult and time consuming and would unnecessarily threaten free speech. [Cc] ...

The same two basic concerns which prevented our adoption of the tort of false light invasion of privacy strongly favor our rejecting the tort of invasion of privacy by publishing private facts, as to which not even truth is a defense. First, decisions of the Supreme Court of the United States, scholarly articles and the Restatement make it clear that the private facts branch of the invasion of privacy tort is, at the very best, constitutionally suspect. [Cc] ... Second, the constitutionally suspect private facts branch of the invasion of privacy tort will almost never provide a plaintiff with any advantage not duplicated or overlapped by the tort of intentional infliction of emotional distress and possibly by other torts such as trespass or intrusive invasion of privacy. ...

We conclude that any possible benefits which might accrue to plaintiffs are entirely insufficient to justify adoption of the constitutionally suspect private facts invasion of privacy tort which punishes defendants for the typically American act of broadly proclaiming the truth by speech or writing. Accordingly, we reject the notion of a claim for relief for invasion of privacy by public disclosure of true but "private" facts.

For the foregoing reasons, the decision of the Court of Appeals is reversed.
REVERSED.

INQUIRY

The Famous. Courts have held those individuals already well known in the locale of the public disclosure to have no right to complain of the public disclosure of private facts. *See* Martin v. Dorton, 210 Miss. 668, 50 So.2d 391 (1951) (sheriff); Cohen v. Marx, 94 Cal. App.2d 704, 211 P.2d 320 (1949) (prize fighter). Does a private figure who involuntarily becomes well known have the right to maintain a claim for the public disclosure of private facts? The courts permit greater public disclosure and scrutiny even of the involuntarily well known. *See* Elmhurst v. Pearson, 153 F.2d 467 (D.C. Cir. 1946) (sedition-trial defendant); Stryker v. Republic Pictures Corp., 108 Cal. App.2d 191, 238 P.2d 670 (1951) (war hero). The courts also do not protect the private figure publicly portrayed as background to other newsworthy events. *See* Mark v. King Broadcasting, 27 Wash. App. 344, 618 P.2d 512 (1980) (no public-disclosure claim for television report using plaintiff as background); Jacova v. Southern Radio and Television Co., 83 So.2d 34 (Fla. 1955) (same). The possibility of a claim exists if the defendant exploits the plaintiff's image to promote the news programming. *See* Anderson v. Fisher Broadcasting Co., 300 Or. 452, 712 P.2d 803 (1986) (dicta). Can you articulate why?

Confidentiality. What remedy exists when the defendant obtains private information under confidential circumstances—as, for instance, in medical treatment—before disclosing it? Courts have recognized as a basis for liability both the public-disclosure form of the invasion-of-privacy tort and a separate theory for breach of confidence. *See* Cohen v. Cowles Media Co., 501 U.S. 663 (1991) (reporter's breach of promise of confidentiality, made to source, is actionable); Ruzicka v. Conde Nast Pubs., Inc., 999 F.2d 1319 (8th Cir. 1993) (same); Bullion v. Gadaleto, 872 F. Supp. 303 (W.D. Va. 1995) (psychiatrist's actionable disclosure of patient's information to solicit wife's sexual liaison); Estate of Behringer v. Medical Ctr. at Princeton, 249 N.J. Super. 597, 592 A.2d 1251 (1991) (actionable disclosure of HIV status); Urbaniak v. Newton, 226 Cal. App.3d 1128, 277 Cal. Rptr. 354 (1991) (same); Doe v. Roe, 93 Misc.2d 201, 400 N.Y.S.2d 668 (1977) (tort liability for psychiatrist's publication of book disclosing plaintiff's fantasies). Breach of confidentiality has been the basis for liability in other settings beyond medical care, where a special relationship exists between the person requiring confidentiality and the one who breaches it. *See* Humphers v. First Interstate Bank, 298 Or. 706, 696 P.2d 527 (1985) (actionable claim for birth mother against estate of physician who delivered adopted-out infant); *see also* Copley v. Northwestern Mut. Life Ins. Co., 295 F. Supp. 93 (S.D. W. Va. 1968) (insurance company's actionable disclosure of insured's business information to competitors). Of course, if the information claimed confidential is in fact not—is already available to the public—then one cannot establish the public-disclosure or breach-of-confidence tort. *See* Messinger v. United States, 769 F. Supp. 935 (D. Md. 1991); Meetze v. Associated Press, 230 S.C. 330, 95 S.E.2d 606 (1956) (marriage and birth dates). Extenuating circumstances may also warrant disclosure and defeat the tort. *See* Bryson v. Tillinghast, 749 P.2d 110 (Okla. 1988) (physician's disclosure of rape perpetrator's identity is protected).

D. False Light

The false-light form of the invasion-of-privacy tort fills a gap left by the other three forms of invasion-of-privacy tort, as many (but less than a majority of) courts find it. *See* Godbehere v. Phoenix Newspapers, Inc., 162 Ariz. 335, 783 P.2d 781 (1989). Other courts find the false-light form an unnecessary duplication of those other invasion-of-privacy torts and of defamation. *See* Denver Pub. Co. v. Bueno, 54 P.3d 893 (Colo. 2002); Lake v. Wal-Mart Stores, Inc., 582 N.W.2d 231 (Minn. 1998); Cain v. Hearst Corp., 878 S.W.2d 577 (Tex. 1994). To state a claim for false-light invasion of privacy, the plaintiff must show that the defendant publicly depicted the plaintiff in a false manner that would be highly offensive to the reasonable person. *See* Restatement (Second) of Torts § 652E (1976). In one of the earlier English cases recognizing it, Byron v. Johnston, 2 Mer. 29, 35 Eng. Rep. 851 (1816), the Chancery Division enjoined the publication of a poorly written poem falsely attributed to Lord Byron. The misattribution was not defamation, appropriation, intrusion, or a public disclosure of private facts, but had the effect of tarnishing Lord Byron's reputation. Another example of false light would be to misuse an innocent taxi driver's photograph as a convenient illustration for an article on the graft committed by taxi drivers in general. *See* Peay v. Curtis Pub. Co., 78 F. Supp. 305 (D. D.C. 1948). Or to misuse the 95-year-old plaintiff's photograph to illustrate a tabloid story of a 101-year-old working woman whose affair with a millionaire resulted in her pregnancy. *See* Peoples Bank and Trust Co. v. Globe Intl. Pub. Co., 978 F.2d 1065 (8th Cir. 1992) (affirming $850,000 award of punitive damages but reversing $650,000 compensatory-damages award). The defendant makes no explicit assertion but only implies facts, and their implication has a highly offensive, denigrating effect. As in the case of the intrusion form of the tort, the offensiveness element depends on an objective standard tied to how the reasonable person would feel about the false depiction. *See* Douglass v. Hustler Magazine, 769 F.2d 1128, 1136 (7th Cir. 1985) (false suggestion that plaintiff had posed nude for magazine "is unquestionably degrading to a normal person") ; *see also* Solano v. Playgirl, Inc., 292 F.3d 1078 (9th Cir. 2002) (same).

Because it involves the publication of (albeit false) information often regarding public figures, the false-light form of the invasion-of-privacy tort also implicates First Amendment rights and interests. *See* Bridgman v. New Trier High Sch. Dist., 128 F.3d 1146 (7th Cir. 1997) (false-light claim fails where high-school student cannot show actual malice in school official's decision to search student for drugs). The Supreme Court applied the *New York Times v. Sullivan* rule of actual malice to a false-light claim brought by a private figure in Time, Inc. v. Hill, 385 U.S. 374 (1967), requiring the private-figure plaintiff to show that the defendant publisher made the false implication knowingly or recklessly. But *Time, Inc. v. Hill* came before the Court's decision in Gertz v. Robert Welch, Inc., 418 U.S. 323 (1974), repudiating Rosenbloom v. Metromedia, Inc., 402 U.S. 29 (1971), while holding that the actual-malice standard applies only to public officials and public figures, with a fault standard applying to private figures on public issues. Courts have since then assumed that the Supreme Court would in false-light cases follow the framework it applies in defamation cases, in which actual malice is necessary for cases brought by public officials and public figures but that only fault is necessary in cases involving private figures on public issues. *See* Wood v. Hustler Magazine, Inc., 736 F.2d 1084 (5th Cir. 1984); Jones v. Communications, Inc., 440 N.W.2d 884 (Iowa 1989). Consider how the Supreme Court treated the distinction between common-law malice and *New York*

Times v. Sullivan malice in the following false-light case, in which it skirted the issue of whether to apply a lower standard.

Cantrell v. Forest City Pub. Co.
United States Supreme Court
419 U.S. 245 (1974)

STEWART, J. Margaret Cantrell and four of her minor children brought this diversity action in a Federal District Court for invasion of privacy against the Forest City Publishing Co., publisher of a Cleveland newspaper, the Plain Dealer, and against Joseph Eszterhas, a reporter formerly employed by the Plain Dealer, and Richard Conway, a Plain Dealer photographer. The Cantrells alleged that an article published in the Plain Dealer Sunday Magazine unreasonably placed their family in a false light before the public through its many inaccuracies and untruths. The District Judge struck the claims relating to punitive damages as to all the plaintiffs and dismissed the actions of three of the Cantrell children in their entirety, but allowed the case to go to the jury as to Mrs. Cantrell and her oldest son, William. The jury returned a verdict against all three of the respondents for compensatory money damages in favor of these two plaintiffs.

The Court of Appeals for the Sixth Circuit reversed, holding that, in the light of the First and Fourteenth Amendments, the District Judge should have granted the respondents' motion for a directed verdict as to all the Cantrells' claims. [C] We granted certiorari, [c].

I

In December 1967, Margaret Cantrell's husband Melvin was killed along with 43 other people when the Silver Bridge across the Ohio River at Point Pleasant, W.Va., collapsed. The respondent Eszterhas was assigned by the Plain Dealer to cover the story of the disaster. He wrote a "news feature" story focusing on the funeral of Melvin Cantrell and the impact of his death on the Cantrell family.

Five months later, after conferring with the Sunday Magazine editor of the Plain Dealer, Eszterhas and photographer Conway returned to the Point Pleasant area to write a follow-up feature. The two men went to the Cantrell residence, where Eszterhas talked with the children and Conway took 50 pictures. Mrs. Cantrell was not at home at any time during the 60 to 90 minutes that the men were at the Cantrell residence.

Eszterhas' story appeared as the lead feature in the August 4, 1968, edition of the Plain Dealer Sunday Magazine. The article stressed the family's abject poverty; the children's old, ill-fitting clothes and the deteriorating condition of their home were detailed in both the text and accompanying photographs. As he had done in his original, prize-winning article on the Silver Bridge disaster, Eszterhas used the Cantrell family to illustrate the impact of the bridge collapse on the lives of the people in the Point Pleasant area.

It is conceded that the story contained a number of inaccuracies and false statements. Most conspicuously, although Mrs. Cantrell was not present at any time during the reporter's visit to her home, Eszterhas wrote, "Margaret Cantrell will talk neither about what happened nor about how they are doing. She wears the same mask of non-expression she wore at the funeral. She is a proud woman. Her world has changed. She says that after it happened, the people in town offered to help them out with money and they refused to take it."[fn] Other significant misrepresentations were contained in details of Eszterhas' descriptions of the poverty in which the Cantrells were living and the dirty and dilapidated conditions of the Cantrell home.

The case went to the jury on a so-called "false light" theory of invasion of privacy. In essence, the theory of the case was that by publishing the false feature story about the Cantrells and thereby making them the objects of pity and ridicule, the respondents damaged Mrs. Cantrell and her son William by causing them to suffer outrage, mental distress, shame, and humiliation.[fn]

II

In Time, Inc. v. Hill, 385 U.S. 374, 87 S.Ct. 534, 17 L.Ed.2d 456, the Court considered a similar false-light, invasion-of-privacy action. The New York Court of Appeals had interpreted New York Civil Rights Law, [c], to give a "newsworthy person" a right of action when his or her name, picture or portrait was the subject of a "fictitious" report or article. Material and substantial falsification was the test for recovery. [C] Under this doctrine the New York courts awarded the plaintiff James Hill compensatory damages based on his complaint that Life Magazine had falsely reported that a new Broadway play portrayed the Hill family's experience in being held hostage by three escaped convicts. This Court, guided by its decision in New York Times Co. v. Sullivan, 376 U.S. 254, 84 S.Ct. 710, 11 L.Ed.2d 686, which recognized constitutional limits on a State's power to award damages for libel in actions brought by public officials, held that the constitutional protections for speech and press precluded the application of the New York statute to allow recovery for "false reports of matters of public interest in the absence of proof that the defendant published the report with knowledge of its falsity or in reckless disregard of the truth." [C] Although the jury could have reasonably concluded from the evidence in the Hill case that Life had engaged in knowing falsehood or had recklessly disregarded the truth in stating in the article that "the story re-enacted" the Hill family's experience, the Court concluded that the trial judge's instructions had not confined the jury to such a finding as a predicate for liability as required by the Constitution. [C]

The District Judge in the case before us, in contrast to the trial judge in Time, Inc. v. Hill, did instruct the jury that liability could be imposed only if it concluded that the false statements in the Sunday Magazine feature article on the Cantrells had been made with knowledge of their falsity or in reckless disregard of the truth.[fn] …

III

At the close of the petitioners' case-in-chief, the District Judge struck the demand for punitive damages. He found that Mrs. Cantrell had failed to present any evidence to support the charges that the invasion of privacy "was done maliciously within the legal definition of that term." The Court of Appeals interpreted this finding to be a determination by the District Judge that there was no evidence of knowing falsity or reckless disregard of the truth introduced at the trial. Having made such a determination, the Court of Appeals held that the District Judge should have granted the motion for a directed verdict for respondents as to all the Cantrells' claims. [C]

The Court of Appeals appears to have assumed that the District Judge's finding of no malice "within the legal definition of that term" was a finding based on the definition of "actual malice" established by this Court in New York Times Co. v. Sullivan, [c]: "with knowledge that (a defamatory statement) was false or with reckless disregard of whether it was false or not." As so defined, of course, "actual malice" is a term of art, created to provide a convenient shorthand expression for the standard of liability that must be established before a State may constitutionally permit public officials to recover for libel in actions brought against publishers.[fn] As such, it is quite different from the common-law standard of "malice" generally required under state tort law to support an award of punitive damages. In a false-light case, common-law malice—frequently expressed in terms of either personal ill will toward the plaintiff or reckless or wanton disregard of the plaintiff's rights—would focus on the defendant's attitude toward the plaintiff's privacy, not toward the truth or falsity of the material published. [Cc]

Although the verbal record of the District Court proceedings is not entirely unambiguous, the conclusion is inescapable that the District Judge was referring to the common-law standard of malice rather than to the New York Times "actual malice" standard when he dismissed the punitive damages claims. For at the same time that he dismissed the demands for punitive damages, the District Judge refused to grant the respondents' motion for directed verdicts as to Mrs. Cantrell's and William's claims for compensatory damages. And, as his instructions to the jury made clear, the District Judge was fully aware that the Time, Inc. v. Hill meaning of the New York Times "actual malice" standard had to be satisfied for the Cantrells to recover actual damages. Thus, the only way to harmonize these two virtually simultaneous rulings by the District Judge is to conclude, contrary to the decision of the Court of Appeals, that in dismissing the punitive damages claims he was not determining that Mrs. Cantrell had failed to introduce any evidence of knowing falsity or reckless disregard of the truth. This conclusion is further fortified by the District Judge's subsequent denial of the respondents' motion for judgment n.o.v. and alternative motion for a new trial.

Moreover, the District Judge was clearly correct in believing that the evidence introduced at trial was sufficient to support a jury finding that the respondents Joseph Eszterhas and Forest City Publishing Co. had published knowing or reckless falsehoods about the Cantrells.[fn] There was no dispute during the trial that Eszterhas, who did not testify, must have known that a number of the statements in the feature story were untrue. In particular, his article plainly implied that Mrs. Cantrell had been present during his visit to her home and that Eszterhas had observed her "wear(ing) the same mask of nonexpression she wore (at her husband's) funeral." These were "calculated falsehoods," and the jury was plainly justified in finding that Eszterhas had portrayed the Cantrells in a false light through knowing or reckless untruth.

The Court of Appeals concluded that there was no evidence that Forest City Publishing Co. had knowledge of any of the inaccuracies contained in Eszterhas' article. However, these was sufficient evidence for the jury to find that Eszterhas' writing of the feature was within the scope of his employment at the Plain Dealer and that Forest City Publishing Co. was therefore liable under traditional doctrines of respondeat superior.[fn] Although Eszterhas was not regularly assigned by the Plain Dealer to write for the Sunday Magazine, the editor of the magazine testified that as a staff writer for the Plain Dealer, Eszterhas frequently suggested stories he would like to write for the magazine. When Eszterhas suggested the follow-up article on the Silver Bridge disaster, the editor approved the idea and told Eszterhas the magazine would publish the feature if it was good. From this evidence, the jury could reasonably conclude that Forest City Publishing Co., publisher of the Plain Dealer, should be held vicariously liable for the damage caused by the knowing falsehoods contained in Eszterhas' story.

For the foregoing reasons, the judgment of the Court of Appeals is reversed and the case is remanded to that court with directions to enter a judgment affirming the judgment of the District Court as to the respondents Forest City Publishing Co. and Joseph Eszterhas. ...

Reversed and remanded.

Inquiry

Intentional Infliction. Law could instead treat invasion of privacy in its most flagrant and offensive instances as intentional infliction of emotional distress. The intentional-infliction tort requires intent to harm, knowledge of substantial certainty of harm, or recklessness (knowledge of a high probability of harm), while invasion of privacy most likely imposes a similar requirement (actual malice) only when constitutional protection exists. The intentional-infliction tort also requires that the conduct be beyond all bounds of decency, whereas invasion of privacy in most forms requires conduct highly offensive to the reasonable person—both of which standards some conduct may well satisfy. One might thus expect the two torts to overlap, which they occasionally do. One might also expect that the intentional-infliction tort would have no constitutional protection. After all, intentional infliction's intent element should satisfy the highest constitutional standard of actual malice. Yet the Supreme Court held to the contrary in the cases below that in some instances, the First Amendment protects even a purposeful effort to destroy another's character and inflict severe emotional distress. Can you discern the limits of this First Amendment protection to purposefully destroy another? What makes these cases different from ordinary invasion of privacy and intentional infliction of emotional distress?

Hustler Magazine v. Falwell
United States Supreme Court
485 U.S. 46 (1988)

REHNQUIST, C.J. Petitioner Hustler Magazine, Inc., is a magazine of nationwide circulation. Respondent Jerry Falwell, a nationally known minister who has been active as a commentator on politics and public affairs, sued petitioner and its publisher, petitioner Larry Flynt, to recover damages for invasion of privacy, libel, and intentional infliction of emotional distress. The District Court directed a verdict against respondent on the privacy claim, and submitted the other two claims to a jury. The jury found for petitioners on the defamation claim, but found for respondent on the claim for intentional infliction of emotional distress and awarded damages. We now consider whether this award is consistent with the First and Fourteenth Amendments of the United States Constitution.

The inside front cover of the November 1983 issue of Hustler Magazine featured a "parody" of an advertisement for Campari Liqueur that contained the name and picture of respondent and was entitled "Jerry Falwell talks about his first time." This parody was modeled after actual Campari ads that included interviews with various celebrities about their "first times." Although it was apparent by the end of each interview that this meant the first time they sampled Campari, the ads clearly played on the sexual double entendre of the general subject of "first times." Copying the form and layout of these Campari ads, Hustler's editors chose respondent as the featured celebrity and drafted an alleged "interview" with him in which he states that his "first time" was during a drunken incestuous rendezvous with his mother in an outhouse. The Hustler parody portrays respondent and his mother as drunk and immoral, and suggests that respondent is a hypocrite who preaches only when he is drunk. In small print at the bottom of the page, the ad contains the disclaimer, "ad parody—not to be taken seriously." The magazine's table of contents also lists the ad as "Fiction; Ad and Personality Parody." ...

On appeal, the United States Court of Appeals for the Fourth Circuit affirmed the judgment against petitioners. [C] The court rejected petitioners' argument that the "actual malice" standard of *New York Times Co. v. Sullivan,* 376 U.S. 254[] (1964), must be met before respondent can recover for emotional distress. ... In the court's view, the *New York Times* decision emphasized the constitutional importance not of the falsity of the statement or the defendant's disregard for the truth, but of the heightened level of culpability embodied in the requirement of "knowing ... or reckless" conduct. Here, the *New York Times* standard is satisfied by the state-law requirement, and the jury's finding, that the defendants have acted intentionally or recklessly.[fn] The Court of Appeals then went on to reject the contention that because the jury found that the ad parody did not describe actual facts about respondent, the ad was an opinion that is protected by the First Amendment. As the court put it, this was "irrelevant," as the issue is "whether [the ad's] publication was sufficiently outrageous to constitute intentional infliction of emotional distress." [C][fn] ...

This case presents us with a novel question involving First Amendment limitations upon a State's authority to protect its citizens from the intentional infliction of emotional distress. We must decide whether a public figure may recover damages for emotional harm caused by the publication of an ad parody offensive to him, and doubtless gross and repugnant in the eyes of most. Respondent would have us find that a State's interest in protecting public figures from emotional distress is sufficient to deny First Amendment protection to speech that is patently offensive and is intended to inflict emotional injury, even when that speech could not reasonably have been interpreted as stating actual facts about the public figure involved. This we decline to do.

At the heart of the First Amendment is the recognition of the fundamental importance of the free flow of ideas and opinions on matters of public interest and concern. "[T]he freedom to speak one's mind is not only an aspect of individual liberty—and thus a good unto itself—but also is essential to the common quest for truth and the vitality of society as a whole." *Bose Corp. v. Consumers Union of United States, Inc.,* 466 U.S. 485, 503-504[] (1984). We have therefore been particularly vigilant to ensure that individual expressions of ideas remain free from governmentally imposed sanctions. The First Amendment recognizes no such thing as a "false" idea. [C] As Justice Holmes wrote, "when men have realized that time has upset many fighting faiths, they may come to believe even more than they believe the very foundations of their own conduct that the ultimate good desired is better reached by free trade in ideas—that the best test of truth is the power of the thought to get itself accepted in the competition of the market...." *Abrams v. United States,* 250 U.S. 616, 630 [] (1919) (dissenting opinion). ...

Of course, this does not mean that *any* speech about a public figure is immune from sanction in the form of damages. Since *New York Times Co. v. Sullivan,* [*supra*], we have consistently ruled that a public figure may hold a speaker liable for the damage to reputation caused by publication of a defamatory falsehood, but only if the statement was made "with knowledge that it was false or with reckless disregard of whether it was false or not." [C] False statements of fact are particularly valueless; they interfere with the truth-seeking function of the marketplace of ideas, and they cause damage to an individual's reputation that cannot easily be repaired by counterspeech, however persuasive or effective. [C] But even though falsehoods have little value in and of themselves, they are "nevertheless inevitable in free debate," [c], and a rule that would impose strict liability on a publisher for false factual assertions would have an undoubted "chilling" effect on speech relating to public figures that does have constitutional value. "Freedoms of expression require 'breathing space.' " *Philadelphia Newspapers, Inc. v. Hepps,* 475 U.S. 767, 772[] (1986) ([c]). This breathing space is provided by a constitutional rule that allows public figures to recover for libel or defamation only when they can prove *both* that the statement was false and that the statement was made with the requisite level of culpability.

Respondent argues, however, that a different standard should apply in this case because here the State seeks to prevent not reputational damage, but the severe emotional distress suffered by the person who is the subject of an offensive publication. [C] In respondent's view, and in the view of the Court of Appeals, so long as the utterance was intended to inflict emotional distress, was outrageous, and did in fact inflict serious emotional distress, it is of no constitutional import whether the statement was a fact or an opinion, or whether it was true or false. It is the intent to cause injury that is the gravamen of the tort, and the State's interest in preventing emotional harm simply outweighs whatever interest a speaker may have in speech of this type.

Generally speaking the law does not regard the intent to inflict emotional distress as one which should receive much solicitude, and it is quite understandable that most if not all jurisdictions have chosen to make it civilly culpable where the conduct in question is sufficiently "outrageous." But in the world of debate about public affairs, many things done with motives that are less than admirable are protected by the First Amendment. In *Garrison v. Louisiana,* 379 U.S. 64[] (1964), we held that even when a speaker or writer is motivated by hatred or illwill his expression was protected by the First Amendment: "Debate on public issues will not be uninhibited if the speaker must run the risk that it will be proved in court that he spoke out of hatred; even if he did speak out of hatred, utterances honestly believed contribute to the free interchange of ideas and the ascertainment of truth." [C]

Thus while such a bad motive may be deemed controlling for purposes of tort liability in other areas of the law, we think the First Amendment prohibits such a result in the area of public debate about public figures.

Were we to hold otherwise, there can be little doubt that political cartoonists and satirists would be subjected to damages awards without any showing that their work falsely defamed its subject. …

Respondent contends, however, that the caricature in question here was so "outrageous" as to distinguish it from more traditional political cartoons. There is no doubt that the caricature of respondent and his mother published in Hustler is at best a distant cousin of the political cartoons described above, and a rather poor relation at that. If it were possible by laying down a principled standard to separate the one from the other, public discourse would probably suffer little or no harm. But we doubt that there is any such standard, and we are quite sure that the pejorative description "outrageous" does not supply one. "Outrageousness" in the area of political and social discourse has an inherent subjectiveness about it which would allow a jury to impose liability on the basis of the jurors' tastes or views, or perhaps on the basis of their dislike of a particular expression. An "outrageousness" standard thus runs afoul of our longstanding refusal to allow damages to be awarded because the speech in question may have an adverse emotional impact on the audience. [C] ...

We conclude that public figures and public officials may not recover for the tort of intentional infliction of emotional distress by reason of publications such as the one here at issue without showing in addition that the publication contains a false statement of fact which was made with "actual malice," *i.e.*, with knowledge that the statement was false or with reckless disregard as to whether or not it was true. This is not merely a "blind application" of the *New York Times* standard, see *Time, Inc. v. Hill,* 385 U.S. 374, 390[] (1967), it reflects our considered judgment that such a standard is necessary to give adequate "breathing space" to the freedoms protected by the First Amendment.

Here it is clear that respondent Falwell is a "public figure" for purposes of First Amendment law.[fn] The jury found against respondent on his libel claim... . Respondent is thus relegated to his claim for damages awarded by the jury for the intentional infliction of emotional distress by "outrageous" conduct. But for reasons heretofore stated this claim cannot, consistently with the First Amendment, form a basis for the award of damages when the conduct in question is the publication of a caricature such as the ad parody involved here. The judgment of the Court of Appeals is accordingly

Reversed.

Snyder v. Phelps,
United States Supreme Court
562 U.S. 443 (2011)

Chief Justice ROBERTS delivered the opinion of the Court.

A jury held members of the Westboro Baptist Church liable for millions of dollars in damages for picketing near a soldier's funeral service. The picket signs reflected the church's view that the United States is overly tolerant of sin and that God kills American soldiers as punishment. The question presented is whether the First Amendment shields the church members from tort liability for their speech in this case.

I
A

Fred Phelps founded the Westboro Baptist Church in Topeka, Kansas, in 1955. The church's congregation believes that God hates and punishes the United States for its tolerance of homosexuality, particularly in America's military. The church frequently communicates its views by picketing, often at military funerals. In the more than 20 years that the members of Westboro Baptist have publicized their message, they have picketed nearly 600 funerals. [C]

Marine Lance Corporal Matthew Snyder was killed in Iraq in the line of duty. Lance Corporal Snyder's father selected the Catholic church in the Snyders' hometown of Westminster, Maryland, as the site for his son's funeral. Local newspapers provided notice of the time and location of the service.

Phelps became aware of Matthew Snyder's funeral and decided to travel to Maryland with six other Westboro Baptist parishioners (two of his daughters and four of his grandchildren) to picket. On the day of the memorial service, the Westboro congregation members picketed on public land adjacent to public streets near the Maryland State House, the United States Naval Academy, and Matthew Snyder's funeral. The Westboro picketers carried signs that were largely the same at all three locations. They stated, for instance: "God Hates the USA/Thank God for 9/11," "America is Doomed," "Don't Pray for the USA," "Thank God for IEDs," "Thank God for Dead Soldiers," "Pope in Hell," "Priests Rape Boys," "God Hates Fags," "You're Going to Hell," and "God Hates You."

The church had notified the authorities in advance of its intent to picket at the time of the funeral, and the picketers complied with police instructions in staging their demonstration. The picketing took place within a 10-by 25-foot plot of public land adjacent to a public street, behind a temporary fence. [C] That plot was approximately 1,000 feet from the church where the funeral was held. Several buildings separated the picket site from the church. [C] The Westboro picketers displayed their signs for about 30 minutes before the funeral began and sang hymns and recited Bible verses. None of the picketers entered church property or went to the cemetery. They did not yell or use profanity, and there was no violence associated with the picketing. [C]

The funeral procession passed within 200 to 300 feet of the picket site. Although Snyder testified that he could see the tops of the picket signs as he drove to the funeral, he did not see what was written on the signs until later that night, while watching a news broadcast covering the event. [C][fn]

B

Snyder filed suit against Phelps, Phelps's daughters, and the Westboro Baptist Church (collectively Westboro or the church) ... . Snyder alleged five state tort law claims: defamation, publicity given to private life, intentional infliction of emotional distress, intrusion upon seclusion, and civil conspiracy. Westboro moved for summary judgment contending, in part, that the church's speech was insulated from liability by the First Amendment. [C]

The District Court awarded Westboro summary judgment on Snyder's claims for defamation and publicity given to private life, concluding that Snyder could not prove the necessary elements of those torts. [C] A trial was held on the remaining claims. At trial, Snyder described the severity of his emotional injuries. He testified that he is unable to separate the thought of his dead son from his thoughts of Westboro's picketing, and that he often becomes tearful, angry, and physically ill when he thinks about it. [C] Expert witnesses testified that Snyder's emotional anguish had resulted in severe depression and had exacerbated pre-existing health conditions.

A jury found for Snyder on the intentional infliction of emotional distress, intrusion upon seclusion, and civil conspiracy claims, and held Westboro liable for $2.9 million in compensatory damages and $8 million in punitive damages. ... The District Court remitted the punitive damages award to $2.1 million, but left the jury verdict otherwise intact. [C]

In the Court of Appeals, Westboro's primary argument was that the church was entitled to judgment as a matter of law because the First Amendment fully protected Westboro's speech. The Court of Appeals agreed. [C] ...

II

... The Free Speech Clause of the First Amendment—"Congress shall make no law ... abridging the freedom of speech"—can serve as a defense in state tort suits.... See, *e.g.*, *Hustler Magazine, Inc. v. Falwell*, 485 U.S. 46, 50-51, 108 S.Ct. 876, 99 L.Ed.2d 41 (1988).[fn]

Whether the First Amendment prohibits holding Westboro liable for its speech in this case turns largely on whether that speech is of public or private concern, as determined by all the circumstances of the case. "[S]peech on 'matters of public concern' ... is 'at the heart of the First Amendment's protection.'" *Dun & Bradstreet, Inc. v. Greenmoss Builders, Inc.*, 472 U.S. 749, 758-759[] (1985) (opinion of Powell, J.) (quoting *First Nat. Bank of Boston v. Bellotti*, 435 U.S. 765, 776[] (1978)). The First Amendment reflects "a profound national commitment to the principle that debate on public issues should be uninhibited, robust, and wide-open." *New York Times Co. v. Sullivan*, 376 U.S. 254, 270[] (1964). That is because "speech concerning public affairs is more than self-expression; it is the essence of self-government." *Garrison v. Louisiana*, 379 U.S. 64, 74-75[] (1964). Accordingly, "speech on public issues occupies the highest rung of the hierarchy of First Amendment values, and is entitled to special protection." *Connick v. Myers*, 461 U.S. 138, 145[] (1983) (internal quotation marks omitted).

"'[N]ot all speech is of equal First Amendment importance,'" however, and where matters of purely private significance are at issue, First Amendment protections are often less rigorous. *Hustler, supra,* at 56[] (quoting *Dun & Bradstreet, supra,* at 758[]); see *Connick, supra,* at 145-147[]. That is because restricting speech on purely private matters does not implicate the same constitutional concerns as limiting speech on matters of public interest: "[T]here is no threat to the free and robust debate of public issues; there is no potential interference with a meaningful dialogue of ideas"; and the "threat of liability" does not pose the risk of "a reaction of self-censorship" on matters of public import. *Dun & Bradstreet, supra,* at 760[] (internal quotation marks omitted). ...

Speech deals with matters of public concern when it can "be fairly considered as relating to any matter of political, social, or other concern to the community," *Connick, supra,* at 146[], or when it "is a subject of legitimate news interest; that is, a subject of general interest and of value and concern to the public," *San Diego[v. Roe,* 543 U.S. 77,] 83-84[(2004)]. [Cc] The arguably "inappropriate or controversial character of a statement is irrelevant to the question whether it deals with a matter of public concern." *Rankin v. McPherson,* 483 U.S. 378, 387[] (1987).

Our opinion in *Dun & Bradstreet,* on the other hand, provides an example of speech of only private concern. ...

Deciding whether speech is of public or private concern requires us to examine the "'content, form, and context'" of that speech, "'as revealed by the whole record.'" *Dun & Bradstreet, supra,* at 761[] (quoting *Connick, supra,* at 147-148[]). ... In considering content, form, and context, no factor is dispositive, and it is necessary to evaluate all the circumstances of the speech, including what was said, where it was said, and how it was said.

The "content" of Westboro's signs plainly relates to broad issues of interest to society at large, rather than matters of "purely private concern." *Dun & Bradstreet, supra,* at 759[]. The placards ... may fall short of refined social or political commentary, [but] the issues they highlight—the political and moral conduct of the United States and its citizens, the fate of our Nation, homosexuality in the military, and scandals involving the Catholic clergy—are matters of public import. The signs certainly convey Westboro's position on those issues, in a manner designed, unlike the private speech in *Dun & Bradstreet,* to reach as broad a public audience as possible. And even if a few of the signs—such as "You're Going to Hell" and "God Hates You"—were viewed as containing messages related to Matthew Snyder or the Snyders specifically, that would not change the fact that the overall thrust and dominant theme of Westboro's demonstration spoke to broader public issues.

Apart from the content of Westboro's signs, Snyder contends that the "context" of the speech—its connection with his son's funeral—makes the speech a matter of private rather than public concern. The fact that Westboro spoke in connection with a funeral, however, cannot by itself transform the nature of Westboro's speech. ...

Westboro's choice to convey its views in conjunction with Matthew Snyder's funeral made the expression of those views particularly hurtful to many, especially to Matthew's father. ... But Westboro conducted its picketing peacefully on matters of public concern at a public place adjacent to a public street. ...

Simply put, the church members had the right to be where they were. Westboro alerted local authorities to its funeral protest and fully complied with police guidance on where the picketing could be staged. The picketing was conducted under police supervision some 1,000 feet from the church, out of the sight of those at the church. The protest was not unruly; there was no shouting, profanity, or violence. ...

... What Westboro said, in the whole context of how and where it chose to say it, is entitled to "special protection" under the First Amendment, and that protection cannot be overcome by a jury finding that the picketing was outrageous.

For all these reasons, the jury verdict imposing tort liability on Westboro for intentional infliction of emotional distress must be set aside.

III

The jury also found Westboro liable for the state law torts of intrusion upon seclusion and civil conspiracy. The Court of Appeals did not examine these torts independently of the intentional infliction of emotional distress tort. ...

Snyder argues that even assuming Westboro's speech is entitled to First Amendment protection generally, the church is not immunized from liability for intrusion upon seclusion because Snyder was a member of a captive audience at his son's funeral. [C] We do not agree. ...

As a general matter, we have applied the captive audience doctrine only sparingly to protect unwilling listeners from protected speech. For example, we have upheld a statute allowing a homeowner to restrict the delivery of offensive mail to his home, see *Rowan v. Post Office Dept.,* 397 U.S. 728, 736-738[] (1970).... .

Here, Westboro stayed well away from the memorial service. Snyder could see no more than the tops of the signs when driving to the funeral. And there is no indication that the picketing in any way interfered with the funeral service itself. We decline to expand the captive audience doctrine to the circumstances presented here.

Because we find that the First Amendment bars Snyder from recovery for intentional infliction of emotional distress or intrusion upon seclusion—the alleged unlawful activity Westboro conspired to accomplish—we must likewise hold that Snyder cannot recover for civil conspiracy based on those torts. ...

The judgment of the United States Court of Appeals for the Fourth Circuit is affirmed.

It is so ordered.

Justice BREYER, concurring[, omitted].

Justice ALITO, dissenting.

Our profound national commitment to free and open debate is not a license for the vicious verbal assault that occurred in this case.

Petitioner Albert Snyder is not a public figure. He is simply a parent whose son, Marine Lance Corporal Matthew Snyder, was killed in Iraq. Mr. Snyder wanted what is surely the right of any parent who experiences such an incalculable loss: to bury his son in peace. But respondents, members of the Westboro Baptist Church, deprived him of that elementary right. They first issued a press release and thus turned Matthew's funeral into a tumultuous media event. They then appeared at the church, approached as closely as they could without trespassing, and launched a malevolent verbal attack on Matthew and his family at a time of acute emotional vulnerability. As a result, Albert Snyder suffered severe and lasting emotional injury.[fn] ...

... When grave injury is intentionally inflicted by means of an attack like the one at issue here, the First Amendment should not interfere with recovery. ...

In this case, respondents brutally attacked Matthew Snyder, and this attack, which was almost certain to inflict injury, was central to respondents' well-practiced strategy for attracting public attention. ...

This strategy works because it is expected that respondents' verbal assaults will wound the family and friends of the deceased and because the media is irresistibly drawn to the sight of persons who are visibly in grief. The more outrageous the funeral protest, the more publicity the Westboro Baptist Church is able to obtain. Thus, when the church recently announced its intention to picket the funeral of a 9-year-old girl killed in the shooting spree in Tucson—proclaiming that she was "better off dead"[fn]—their announcement was national news,[fn] and the church was able to obtain free air time on the radio in exchange for canceling its protest.[fn] Similarly, in 2006, the church got air time on a talk radio show in exchange for canceling its threatened protest at the funeral of five Amish girls killed by a crazed gunman.[fn]

In this case, respondents implemented the Westboro Baptist Church's publicity-seeking strategy. Their press release ... guaranteed that Matthew's funeral would be transformed into a raucous media event and began the wounding process. ...

In light of this evidence, it is abundantly clear that respondents, going far beyond commentary on matters of public concern, specifically attacked Matthew Snyder because (1) he was a Catholic and (2) he was a member of the United States military. Both Matthew and petitioner were private figures,[fn] and this attack was not speech on a matter of public concern. While commentary on the Catholic Church or the United States military constitutes speech on matters of public concern, speech regarding Matthew Snyder's purely private conduct does not. ...

... [F]unerals are unique events at which special protection against emotional assaults is in order. At funerals, the emotional well-being of bereaved relatives is particularly vulnerable. ... Allowing family members to have a few hours of peace without harassment does not undermine public debate. I would therefore hold that, in this setting, the First Amendment permits a private figure to recover for the intentional infliction of emotional distress caused by speech on a matter of private concern.

Respondents' outrageous conduct caused petitioner great injury, and the Court now compounds that injury by depriving petitioner of a judgment that acknowledges the wrong he suffered.

In order to have a society in which public issues can be openly and vigorously debated, it is not necessary to allow the brutalization of innocent victims like petitioner. I therefore respectfully dissent.

INQUIRY

Perspectives. What perspective is the *Hustler Magazine v. Falwell* opinion reflecting when it states that "[t]he freedom to speak one's mind" is "a good unto itself"? Societies define themselves by what they identify as intrinsic goods. Moses and Jesus defined love for God and others as intrinsic goods. Immanuel Kant likewise defined considering the other as a "categorical imperative" or intrinsic good—that we must treat others as ends and not means, and that any action must be one that we can accept as universal for all. How does the Supreme Court defining self-expression—instead of love for others—as the intrinsic good establish or change the character of society and relationship? Is self-expression good unto itself or only good to the extent that it furthers some other goal? Would a lawyer's professional career dedicated to the lawyer's own self-expression be satisfying, meaningful, or even possible—no less good for clients? *Hustler Magazine* publisher Larry Flynt admitted on deposition in the case that his purpose in running the parody was to assassinate the character of Reverend Falwell. Given Flynt's admission, was his parody of Reverend Falwell either for the purpose of self-expression or to promote truth in a marketplace of ideas? Although the jury had evidence to support its conclusion that the parody distressed Reverend Falwell severely, he subsequently used it in a fund-raising campaign. Mr. Flynt, apparently, is an equal-opportunity offender. One court used the *Hustler Magazine v. Falwell* decision to protect his magazine's violent sexual parody of a feminist law-scholar advocating against pornography, one that had severely distressed the scholar. *See* Dworkin v. Hustler Magazine Inc., 867 F.2d 1188 (9th Cir. 1989).

Career

Service can make a difference in finding employment and succeeding in tort practice. Volunteer for pro-bono service and other legal-services or law-related activities. Doing so improves your interpersonal skills, exposing you to a variety of individuals with different communications styles and preferences. It builds your confidence. It builds your knowledge base. It helps you see how lawyers use your classroom and casebook knowledge. In that respect, it can improve your academics. Volunteering can also lend balance to your law studies, giving you appropriate outlets from the mental challenge of continual study. It is also the right thing to do, even when you have obligations as substantial as those required by law school. Then list your volunteering and pro-bono service on your resume. Draw on the lawyers and law professors with whom you volunteer for references and letters of recommendation. Let prospective employers know the value of your volunteer and pro-bono work to improving your skill and competence. Firms and other employers of lawyers value community and professional service. See the book *Building Your Practice with Pro Bono for Lawyers* for further inspiration.

Chapter XV

Damages

A. Personal Injury

OBJECTIVE: Given tort claims involving various personal injuries, identify the categories of recoverable damages and the proofs in support consistent with this section of the text.

Case Study: A college student suffered a closed-head injury and ruptured spleen in a motor vehicle accident caused by a motorist's negligence. An ambulance took the student to the hospital, where surgeons performed exploratory abdominal and removed the student's spleen. There is little empirical evidence that the removal of the spleen has any adverse impact on life span, wellness, or capacity. The student's closed-head injury resulted in frequent headaches, sleep disruption, emotional volatility, and an inability to concentrate on his college studies. As a result, the student's roommate and significant other ended their relationship, and the student had to withdraw from college and move back in with his parents. ***Identify the categories of recoverable damages and the proofs in support.***

Do not think of liability as the engine of tort law and damages as the caboose. The reverse might well be true. Tort law without remedy would be sickly sweet and sentimental. Damages awards—genuine compensation as a make-whole remedy—keep tort law meaningful and robust. Yet damages law is not a favorite topic for tort law professors. Damages are too personal and contextual to conceptualize easily. *See* Louis L. Jaffe, *Damages for Personal Injury: The Impact of Insurance*, 18 LAW & CONTEMP. PROBS. 219, 221-222 (1953) (the "crucial controversy in personal injury torts" is damages, notwithstanding the difficulty lawyers face in their conceptualization). Thus, this chapter relies less on cases and more on prosaic discussion. Consider the following outline of damages issues.

The greatest practical challenge to personal-injury damages (other than finding an insured or collectible defendant) is quantifying them. How much is enough—and too much? Plaintiffs' lawyers, insurance-defense lawyers, insurance claim representatives, judges, juries, and parties answer that question various ways. The primary approach is to categorize injury and loss. Yet quantification is not the only challenge a tort lawyer faces in addressing damages. Proving damages is another issue. What investigation must a tort lawyer (plaintiff's or defense counsel) make to determine how the liability incident changed the course of the plaintiff's life? How will the lawyers prove those damages facts at trial? Tort practitioners must have good investigation and presentation skills. Knowing how to prove damages requires not only knowing damages rules but also proof conventions. Proving damages involves habits and practices that the bench and tort bar accept. Finally, damages involve outcomes—treating winners and losers, requiring further rules and additional conventions, not to mention substantial practical skill in the management of cases and clients.

Begin your study of personal-injury damages with the categories. Personal-injury damages divide into two main categories, sometimes expressed as *economic* versus *non-economic* damages but also expressed within the insurance industry as *special* versus *general* damages. Practitioners place within the category of economic or special damages all of those readily quantifiable monetary *out-of-pocket* losses like lost income and incurred expenses. In the usual case, these economic losses are primarily medical expense and wage loss—the two big-ticket items present in many if not most personal injury cases. But economic damages may also include related costs and losses like mileage to and from medical treatment, medical monitoring for developing conditions, in-home attendant care and medical equipment, lost vacation and retirement benefits, lost bonuses and commissions, required home modification, vocational rehabilitation, replacement-service expense, and more—especially as the injury severity increases. In the most severe cases, one may prove economic-loss claims for college education to retrain the physically impaired and the cost of a nurse life-care planner or similar medical administrator to manage medical care and costs.

Figure

Tort lawyer Lawrence Charfoos of the Detroit law firm Charfoos & Christensen, P.C., rose to acclaim during the 1970s while representing women who claimed increased cancer risk from their mothers having taken diethylstilbestrol (DES) during pregnancy. Doubleday published his history of the DES litigation. He also has had medical-malpractice and personal-injury-practice handbooks published by Prentice Hall and Lawyers Co-Operative. Although lawyers know Mr. Charfoos nationally for his drug and medical-malpractice litigation, he has also handled airliner-crash cases, consumer-tort class actions, and complex commercial litigation, and spoken worldwide on tort-law issues. Mr. Charfoos' law partner David Christensen has had an equally distinguished tort-law career, representing and obtaining substantial verdicts or settlements on behalf of birth-trauma victims, the family of a person crushed at a *Who* rock concert, an early Pinto-vehicle-defect claimant, and a seatbelt-defect claimant, among many others.

Non-economic or general damages are all of those other injuries to the claimant's physical, mental, and relational capacities outside of direct monetary loss. Although "pain and suffering" is the traditional formulation, model jury instructions may include other descriptions including humiliation, embarrassment, shock, fright, mortification, mental or emotional distress, depression, disability, scarring, disfigurement, and loss of the enjoyment of life. *See* MICH. MODEL CIV. JURY INSTR. 50.01 et seq. The last general category of lost enjoyment of life, sometimes called *hedonic* damages, includes the inability to engage in physical and mental recreation and social relationships including, for instance, intimate relations with one's spouse. Indeed, the spouse of an injured plaintiff has a derivative claim for what law calls *consortium loss*—the loss of the injured spouse's household services, emotional support, social companionship, and physical touch. With a married injured plaintiff, the non-injured spouse often maintains a loss-of-consortium claim in the same case, represented by the same counsel. Husband-and-wife plaintiffs commonly plead tort claims together, even though only one of the two suffered direct physical injury. The plaintiff's lawyer who fails to advise a married injured plaintiff of the non-injured spouse's right to maintain a consortium loss claim runs the risk of committing legal malpractice.

Non-economic damages are obviously more difficult to quantify—and thus more controversial, especially in attempts to use expert testimony to establish hedonic losses. In part because of that difficulty, the insurance industry commonly uses economic loss as a rough measure of non-economic loss—not directly, one-to-one, but by a multiplier depending on other factors such as the reprehensibility of the misconduct. Insurance claim representatives often estimate that general (non-economic) damages are "two to three times specials" (economic loss). And so, a personal injury that results in medical expense and wage loss totaling $25,000 may have a $75,000 total value—doubling the economic loss to account for non-economic loss and then adding the two figures together for the total case value. This rule of thumb, based on substantial verdict and settlement experience, is not a rule of law but only approximates case values. Many cases have small economic loss but much higher non-economic loss. Can you think of one? Now consider a case highlighting some of these difficulties in quantifying damages.

Kenton v. Hyatt Hotels Corp.
Missouri Supreme Court
693 S.W.2d 83 (Mo. 1985)

DOWD, J. Plaintiff, Kay Kenton, who had completed two years of law school obtained a jury verdict of $4,000,000 as compensatory damages for injuries sustained by the collapse of the suspended skywalks in the Hyatt Regency Hotel lobby, in Kansas City, Missouri, on July 17, 1981. On after-trial motions, the trial court concluded that the verdict was excessive and entered an order sustaining a motion for a new trial unless the plaintiff filed a remittitur of $250,000. ...

... We affirm the judgment of the trial court, in all respects, except remittitur; we reverse that part of the trial court's order granting a remittitur, and ... remand the cause with directions to set aside the order of remittitur, reinstate the verdict and enter judgment for plaintiff for the verdict sum of $4,000,000. ....

Respondent's sister, Ann Kenton, who was with her on the evening of the disaster, testified as to her observations of that occurrence. She and respondent arrived at the Hyatt about 6:15 p.m. on July 17, 1981. At the time of the collapse, Ann was not beneath the skywalks, but was in an area east of the dance floor. Respondent was beneath the area of the second and fourth floor skywalks which fell about her near the south end of the lobby. Ann, Captain Olds, and respondent all indicated the area (encircled) on Plaintiff's Exhibit 2, where respondent was situated, which was beneath the southern portions of the fallen second and fourth floor walkways. Ann described the sounds she heard coming from people in and around the skywalks after the collapse: "A. It was hysterical, hysteria. There were grown men crying for help and there was nothing I could do for them. There were people crushed everywhere, blood, and I looked in the area where she had been and there was rubble and bodies and I couldn't pick her out of the bodies. And the moans and screams." Ann later found respondent slumped in a chair to the west of the skywalks, and respondent was carried outside and placed on a gurney or a stretcher.

Still photographs of the scene were admitted into evidence, some in color and some in black and white. Ann Kenton identified Exhibit 4K as the area where respondent had been and described it thus: "A. There were people sticking halfway out from under the skywalk, from here up there were grown men screaming for help, moaning and I walked through the blood, or there was blood everywhere. And the rescue people were pulling out whoever was more alive than others, I suppose." None of the admitted photographs show any dead or injured persons.

... Appellants argue that the testimony concerning the events of July 17, 1981, was neither probative nor material to the issue of respondent's compensation; it was an attempt to incite the jury with evidence of how she was injured; and that the "slight probative value the testimony may have had concerning the nature of Ms. Kenton's injuries was outweighed completely by the gruesome and highly inflammatory nature of the evidence." ....

The trial court, in ruling on the motion for new trial, expressed some concern about the testimony and photographic displays of the conditions immediately following the collapse of the skywalks, saying, "It was that part of the testimony presented by the plaintiff that *while relevant and appropriate* could not help but have evoked a great deal of sympathy for the plaintiff." The key words are here "relevant and appropriate," which under the above cited cases make the testimony and photographs admissible. The element of sympathy for this respondent and all the other injured and dead, and the relatives of everyone involved in the accident, is inherent in this case and could not be avoided by the triers of fact, or even this court, given the wide knowledge of this horrible tragedy.

The evidence of respondent's injuries is that she suffered a cervical fracture which produced an initial paralysis of her body. In addition, Dr. Walter Menninger stated that she was subjected to the most severe psychosocial stressor imaginable, Grade 7, and the traumatic event and the crippling effects it produced caused a dramatic and profound psychic trauma which is continuing in nature. Dr. Francisco Gomez, respondent's treating psychiatrist, and Dr. Menninger classified her psychiatric injury as post-traumatic stress disorder, chronic and severe. Dr. Menninger testified further that she exhibited symptoms characteristic of a post-traumatic stress disorder: re-experiencing the trauma by either recurrent recollections, recurrent dreams, or suddenly acting or feeling as if the event was happening; and a numbing of responsiveness or reduced involvement with the external world sometime afterward. Certainly, the jury was entitled to consider the evidence of the scene of the collapse, the utter chaos that prevailed, and the effect upon respondent of being pinned beneath the debris, amidst blood, dead and injured bodies, and the sheer terror of the voices around her, in evaluating her physical and mental injuries for the purpose of fixing her compensation. The evidence was relevant, material, and appropriate. Its probative value far outweighed any prejudicial effect it might have had on the jury. There was no error in admitting the evidence, and Point I is overruled. ....

In Point III, appellants contend both in the Court of Appeals and in this court that the trial court erred in refusing to exclude the testimony of two law school professors that respondent was unable to return to law school or to practice law. ...

Professor James W. Jeans, of the University of Missouri at Kansas City, Missouri, was called as a witness for respondent. He has been licensed as an attorney since 1951, having prior to that time attended Washington University Law School at St. Louis for three years. He practiced civil trial and appellate work for about 14 years, and had been a law school professor for 18 years, during which time he continued to represent clients. He was familiar with the work habits and hours required of law students in and out of the classroom—on an average 16 hours a week is spent in class, and about 48 hours a week is spent outside of class in preparation. Extra-curricular activities such as moot court require extra time. Professor Jeans was provided respondent's hospital and medical reports, which had been admitted into evidence without objection, and which he reviewed. ... Professor Jeans gave his opinion that respondent could not succeed as a law student. He also opined that the psychological and the emotional injuries that she suffered would keep her from being effective in other types of law that would deal with counseling and advocacy.

[There was similar testimony from a second law professor.]

[Defendants rebutted the testimony with testimony from a disabled lawyer.]

The trial court properly determined that expert testimony was needed to inform the jury as to the physical and mental rigors of a person attending law school and practicing law. Members of the jury would not ordinarily have knowledge of that subject, and certainly the two professors, being actively engaged in that field would have superior knowledge and expertise thereof by reason of their education and experience. ... It seems clear that these professors' opinions would aid the trier of the fact in determining the effect of respondent's injuries and disabilities. ....

Appellants' Point VI contends that the trial court erred in refusing to grant a remittitur of $2,000,000. They contend that as a matter of law the jury's verdict greatly exceeded the upper limits of "fair and reasonable compensation," the proper measure of damages, and that the verdict was, as the trial court itself recognized, the erroneous product of a mistaken evaluation of highly incendiary evidence and [was] improperly disproportionate to awards for comparable or more severe injuries.

Taking respondent's evidence in the light most favorable to her, as this court must do, her loss of income and the reasonably anticipated future loss of income because of the injuries sustained was testified to be $1,869,433 to $2,164,642; assuming she should complete law school and be employed as a lawyer on a part-time basis, her economic loss ranged from $1,605,846 to $2,018,316; [by comparison, appellants' expert placed her economic losses as high as $1,371,065]. Respondent's evidence shows her economic losses to have been between $1,605,846 as a low, to a high of $2,164,642.

The evidence shows that, to the time of trial, respondent's hospital, medical and therapy expenses incurred amounted to at least $80,000; her future physical therapy and cost of an electronic device (T.E.N.S.) was from $189,759 to $250,000; her homemaking assistance and care, $307,228 to $614,457; her future medical and supplemental insurance, $100,679. This evidence places the low of these items at $677,666, and the high at $1,045,136.

The economic loss, present and future medical, and therapy expenses thus shows a range of between $2,283,512 to $3,209,778.

Respondent's age was 28 years at the time of trial. She has a life expectancy of 51.8 years.

The nature and extent of respondent's injuries, is shown by the following evidence, all shown to have been permanent. She suffered a broken neck with permanent spinal cord damage [with miraculous surgical treatment, she avoided becoming a permanent quadriplegic] [sic]; she has spasticity and weakness in all four limbs, inability to walk without crutches, and must wear a knee cage to prevent buckling of the left knee; lack of endurance and easy fatigability; reduced vital capacity and impaired breathing muscles; sensory loss of much of her body below her neck, including female parts. She will not enjoy a normal sexual life or have children normally; she has impaired bladder and bowel function with periods of incontinence. Her bladder condition causes her to retain urine which will eventually produce renal or kidney damage; psychic and emotional trauma diagnosed as chronic and severe post-traumatic stress syndrome, which will require continued psychiatric care; destruction of her athletic lifestyle which will prevent her from ever again playing tennis, skiing, running, jogging, playing softball, raquetball, hiking, backpacking and riding horses; and a commitment to 2 to 4 hours a day to maintain her present limited muscle function.

There was some evidence that respondent's cost of therapy and the T.E.N.S. unit would increase over her lifetime, and her income would also increase should she be employed as a lawyer, these being the effects of inflation.

The jury was entitled to consider the intangibles of the evidence of respondent's past and future pain and suffering, the destruction of her previous lifestyle, along with the evidence of economic loss. All of the matters going to the nature and extent of respondent's injuries were primarily for the jury's consideration because it is in a far better position to appraise them for the assessment of damages which would fairly and reasonably compensate her. ...

In most litigation, and particularly in personal injury actions, there is a large range between the damage extremes of inadequacy and excessiveness. Within that range a jury has virtually unfettered discretion to determine the damages incurred and is under no obligation to, and is in fact prohibited from, specifying what amounts have been attributed to each of the various elements of damage. Past and future pain and suffering, embarrassment and humiliation, future care and medical treatment, loss of or reduction in employment opportunities and many other factors, do not lend themselves to precise calculation.

There is no exact formula to determine whether a verdict is excessive; each case is considered on its own facts. The ultimate test is what fairly and reasonably compensates plaintiff for the injuries sustained. In making this determination consideration is given to the nature and extent of the injuries, diminished earning capacity, economic conditions, plaintiff's age, and a comparison of the compensation awarded and permitted in cases of comparable injuries. ... This case is not out of line with others... on the tangible damages shown to cause this court to take corrective action. ...

Turning to the merits of this case, we believe that the trial court abused its discretion in ordering a remittitur of $250,000 after a verdict of $4,000,000 under the circumstances of this case. This amount represents a miniscule percentage (6.25%) of the total verdict which demonstrates judicial hairsplitting and shows the extremes to which the remittitur practice has fallen. The order of remittitur here is set aside in accordance with the holding in *Firestone v. Crown Center Redevelopment Corporation,* 693 S.W.2d 99 (1985), which "concludes that remittitur shall no longer be employed in Missouri."

What we said in *Firestone, supra,* as to the power and discretion of trial courts to control jury verdicts is equally applicable here.

Accordingly, the verdict of the jury is affirmed and the cause is remanded with directions to set aside the order of remittitur and to reinstate the verdict and enter judgment for the plaintiff, Kay Kenton, in the sum of $4,000,000.00.

INQUIRY

Categories. Just because law usually quantifies damages by categorizing losses does not mean that one must always do so. In some tort cases, such as for the rape of a young woman, the attempt to itemize damages may distract from and diminish the overall harm. A plaintiff lawyer's laborious itemization of damages for a jury's benefit may produce a surer verdict, but it won't necessarily produce a larger or just verdict. Yet then again, juries may punish damages exaggeration and overreaching. The same is true for the defense lawyer—that the defense lawyer must take care in advocating on the damages issue. Defense lawyers often plan and offer virtually no damages proofs, instead restricting their efforts to scrutinizing plaintiff's damages claims for dishonesty and overreaching. Yet too close of a scrutiny can make the defense appear callous. The impressions jurors draw regarding the conduct of counsel with respect to proof and challenge of damages, although not strictly relevant to quantifying compensatory damages, may influence verdicts especially when quantifying non-economic losses where the measures are less clear and more subject to juror impressions.

Investigation. Investigating and proving the categorized economic and non-economic losses is a second important damages topic. The plaintiff lawyer's investigation usually begins with sensitive fact gathering through the injured client—interviews not only of the client but also of family members and employer, and perhaps a home or hospital visit. Defense counsel ordinarily serves extensive written discovery requests for the plaintiff to answer and deposes the plaintiff and, depending on the injury severity, the plaintiff's spouse or other key lay witnesses to the plaintiff's injury, capabilities, and condition. Of equal or greater significance to both plaintiff's and defense counsel is investigating the plaintiff's medical condition. The lawyers obtain, scrutinize, compare, and summarize medical records from before and after the injury. The lawyers interview or depose physicians and other treating and examining medical care providers. Defense counsel may require the plaintiff to attend a medical examination—typically called an "independent medical examination" or IME but one in which the defendant chooses and pays the examiner. The parties may hotly contest the examiner's opinions and credibility. Both sides also investigate the plaintiff's work history and wage and benefits losses, often obtaining Social Security earnings records, tax returns, and payroll records.

Knowledge

Lawyers analyze both deductively and inductively—top-down from fundamental principles and bottom-up from observed data. Yet lawyers also use abductive reasoning. Abduction is the process of asking relevant questions—usefully conjecturing or speculating—in a way that leads the lawyer to discover claims, theories, and evidence. Abductive reasoning precedes deductive and inductive reasoning, generating the data on which the usual forms of analysis can take place. Cases do not arrive in a lawyer's office ready made. Lawyers discover, develop, and assemble cases in a process that differs from the formal analysis (deductive and inductive) mastered in law school. Indeed, the tort lawyer survives and thrives using abductive skills more so than formal deductive and inductive analysis. Recognize and practice your abductive skills. Tort lawyers need not be conspiracy theorists. They certainly do not manufacture evidence or plead imaginary and frivolous claims. Yet they do need to generate and explore reasonable possibilities—a process that begins with controlled imagination leading to hard evidence.

Proofs. Presenting damages proofs involves a somewhat different skill from investigating and determining the losses. Lawyers may use admission requests to gain admission of foundational facts and records. They may ask the judge to take judicial notice of government labor statistics. Yet the primary skill is one of identifying, retaining, and preparing qualified damages experts. The plaintiff's lawyer who expects the client's treating physician alone to provide the necessary testimony to establish damages may have problems. Physicians often do not know and cannot testify to the cost of past and future medical treatment—not to mention home treatment and assistance, and wage and benefits losses. In cases involving more-serious injuries, the plaintiff's lawyer may need to locate, retain, and prepare to testify a range of damages experts including medical account managers and administrators, life care planners, labor economists, and rehabilitation specialists. *See* Delong v. Erie County, 455 N.Y.S.2d 887 (App. Div. 1982) (expert testimony as to $527,659 value of 28-year-old decedent homemaker's services). The plaintiff's lawyer prepares demonstrative exhibits, summaries, and damages calculations. To give the jury the broadest picture of an injury's effect on the plaintiff's life, the plaintiff's lawyer may call family member, friend, or pastor witnesses, and may prepare a day-in-the-life video. The better plaintiff's lawyers preparing the larger cases for trial exercise the skills of a manager for a dramatic production—not to suggest any distortion of the facts. The opposite is true—that fair depiction of a serious injury's effect can involve more-elaborate communication than simply calling the plaintiff and the plaintiff's doctor as witnesses.

Collateral-Source Rule. The above text outlines the categories, investigation, and proof of damages. Now consider some legal rules that govern this context. Tort claim recoveries are not the only source that injured claimants may have to protect against losses. Health, disability, or worker's compensation insurance may also apply. Gratuitous employer payments and family services may occur, along with Social Security disability benefits (about which plaintiff's counsel should advise the client who has a long-term work disability). The common-law collateral-source rule—both a substantive damages rule and a rule of evidence—provides that these other sources do not reduce the injured plaintiff's recovery and are not admissible as evidence. *See* McKinney v. California Portland Cement Co., 117 Cal. Rptr.2d 849 (Cal. App. 2002); Cox v. Spangler, 5 P.3d 1265 (Wash. 2000); *see also* Montgomery Ward & Co. v. Anderson, 976 S.W.2d 382 (Ark. 1998) (collateral-source rule bars evidence that medical-care provider was willing to cut bills in half); *but see* Coyne v. Campbell, 183 N.E.2d 891 (N.Y. 1962) (rejecting collateral-source rule as allowing for windfall recoveries). The collateral-source rule finds its rationale in that the plaintiff has, in one way or another, paid for those benefits and that the defendant ought not to have the advantage of plaintiff's labor. The rule also serves an important tacit function in that the double, windfall recovery it creates for some plaintiffs softens for them the impact of having to pay their attorneys a contingency fee in the neighborhood of one-third of the total recovery. Notwithstanding these justifications, some states have recently modified or eliminated the rule for some or all tort cases, as part of tort reform. *See* N.Y. C.P.L.R. §4545 (2003) (no collateral-source rule for medical malpractice cases); N.J. Stat. §2A:15-97 (2002) (no collateral-source rule in personal-injury cases for certain payments); *but see* Thompson v. KFB Ins. Co., 850 P.2d 773 (Kan. 1993) (statute altering collateral-source rule is unconstitutional). Consider the rule's defense in the following case.

Helfend v. Southern California Rapid Transit Dist.
California Supreme Court
2 Cal.3d 1, 84 Cal.. Rptr. 173, 465 P.2d 61 (1970)

TOBRINER, A.C.J. Defendants appeal from a judgment of the Los Angeles Superior Court entered on a verdict in favor of plaintiff, Julius J. Helfend, for $16,400 in general and special damages for injuries sustained in a bus-auto collision that occurred on July 19, 1965, in the City of Los Angeles.

We have concluded that the judgment for plaintiff in this tort action against the defendant governmental entity should be affirmed. The trial court properly followed the collateral source rule in excluding evidence that a portion of plaintiff's medical bills had been paid through a medical insurance plan that requires the refund of benefits from tort recoveries. ….

Plaintiff filed a tort action against the Southern California Rapid Transit District, a public entity, and Mitchell, an employee of the transit district. At trial plaintiff claimed slightly more than $2,700 in special damages, including $921 in doctor's bills, a $336.99 hospital bill, and about $45 for medicines.[fn omitted] Defendant requested permission to show that about 80 percent of the plaintiff's hospital bill had been paid by plaintiff's Blue Cross insurance carrier and that some of his other medical expenses may have been paid by other insurance. …. The court ruled that defendants should not be permitted to show that plaintiff had received medical coverage from any collateral source.

After the jury verdict in favor of plaintiff in the sum of $16,300, defendants appealed, raising only two contentions: (1) The trial court committed prejudicial error in refusing to allow the introduction of evidence to the effect that a portion of the plaintiff's medical bills had been paid from a collateral source. (2) The trial court erred in denying defendant the opportunity to determine if plaintiff had been compensated from more than one collateral source for damages sustained in the accident.

We must decide whether the collateral source rule applies to tort actions involving public entities and public employees in which the plaintiff has received benefits from his medical insurance coverage.

2. The collateral source rule.

The Supreme Court of California has long adhered to the doctrine that if an injured party receives some compensation for his injuries from a source wholly independent of the tortfeasor, such payment should not be deducted from the damages which the plaintiff would otherwise collect from the tortfeasor. … As recently as August 1968 we unanimously reaffirmed our adherence to this doctrine, which is known as the 'collateral source rule.' …

Although the collateral source rule remains generally accepted in the United States,[fns omitted here and following] nevertheless many other jurisdictions have restricted or repealed it. In this country most commentators have criticized the rule and called for its early demise. …

The collateral source rule as applied here embodies the venerable concept that a person who has invested years of insurance premiums to assure his medical care should receive the benefits of his thrift.[fn omitted] The tortfeasor should not garner the benefits of his victim's providence.

The collateral source rule expresses a policy judgment in favor of encouraging citizens to purchase and maintain insurance for personal injuries and for other eventualities. Courts consider insurance a form of investment, the benefits of which become payable without respect to any other possible source of funds. If we were to permit a tortfeasor to mitigate damages with payments from plaintiff's insurance, plaintiff would be in a position inferior to that of having bought no insurance, because his payment of premiums would have earned no benefit. Defendant should not be able to avoid payment of full compensation for the injury inflicted merely because the victim has had the foresight to provide himself with insurance.

Some commentators object that the above approach to the collateral source rule provides plaintiff with a "double recovery," rewards him for the injury, and defeats the principle that damages should compensate the victim but not punish the tortfeasor. We agree with Professor Fleming's observation, however, that "double recovery is justified only in the face of some exceptional, supervening reason, as in the case of accident or life insurance, where it is felt unjust that the tortfeasor should take advantage of the thrift and prescience of the victim in having paid the premiums." (Fleming, Introduction to the Law of Torts (1967) p. 131.) As we point out Infra, recovery in a wrongful death action is not defeated by the payment of the benefit on a life insurance policy.

Furthermore, insurance policies increasingly provide for either subrogation or refund of benefits upon a tort recovery, and such refund is indeed called for in the present case. ... Hence, the plaintiff receives no double recovery;[fn omitted] the collateral source rule simply serves as a means of by-passing the antiquated doctrine of non-assignment of tortious actions and permits a proper transfer of risk from the plaintiff's insurer to the tortfeasor by way of the victim's tort recovery. The double shift from the tortfeasor to the victim and then from the victim to his insurance carrier can normally occur with little cost in that the insurance carrier is often intimately involved in the initial litigation and quite automatically receives its part of the tort settlement or verdict.[fn omitted]

Even in case in which the contract or the law precludes subrogation or refund of benefits,[fn omitted] or in situations in which the collateral source waives such subrogation or refund, the rule performs entirely necessary functions in the computation of damages. For example, the cost of medical care often provides both attorneys and juries in tort cases with an important measure for assessing the plaintiff's general damages. ... To permit the defendant to tell the jury that the plaintiff has been recompensed by a collateral source for his medical costs might irretrievably upset the complex, delicate, and somewhat indefinable calculations which result in the normal jury verdict. ...

We also note that generally the jury is not informed that plaintiff's attorney will receive a large portion of the plaintiff's recovery in contingent fees or that personal injury damages are not taxable to the plaintiff and are normally deductible by the defendant.[fn omitted] Hence, the plaintiff rarely actually receives full compensation for his injuries as computed by the jury. The collateral source rule partially serves to compensate for the attorney's share and does not actually render 'double recovery' for the plaintiff. Indeed, many jurisdictions that have abolished or limited the collateral source rule have also established a means for assessing the plaintiff's costs for counsel directly against the defendant rather than imposing the contingent fee system.[fn omitted] In sum, the plaintiff's recovery for his medical expenses from both the tortfeasor and his medical insurance program will not usually give him "double recovery," but partially provides a somewhat closer approximation to full compensation for his injuries.[fn omitted]

If we consider the collateral source rule as applied here in the context of the entire American approach to the law of torts and damages, we find that the rule presently performs a number of legitimate and even indispensible functions. Without a thorough revolution in the American approach to torts and the consequent damages, the rule at least with respect to medical insurance benefits has become so integrated within our present system that its precipitous judicial nullification would work hardship. In this case the collateral source rule lies between two systems for the compensation of accident victims: the traditional tort recovery based on fault and the increasingly prevalent coverage based on non-fault insurance. Neither system possesses such universality of coverage or completeness of compensation that we can easily dispense with the collateral source rule's approach to meshing the two systems. ... The reforms which many academicians propose cannot easily be achieved through piecemeal common law development; the proposed changes, if desirable, would be more effectively accomplished through legislative reform. In any case, we cannot believe that the judicial repeal of the collateral source rule, as applied in the present case, would be the place to begin the needed changes. ...

The judgment is affirmed.

INQUIRY

Subrogation. Note the *Helfend* opinion's discussion of the potential subrogation rights of a nonparty who pays all or some of the plaintiff's damages. Health-insurance policies, for example, routinely have reimbursement and subrogation clauses. A reimbursement clause permits the health insurer to recover from the insured plaintiff any health-care expense the plaintiff recovers in the plaintiff's personal-injury lawsuit. If the insured does not pursue a tort recovery, then the subrogation clause permits the insurer to pursue it by "standing in the shoes" (exercising the legal rights) of the insured. *See* Perreira v. Rediger, 778 A.2d 429 (N.J. 2001); Shumpert v. Time Ins. Co., 496 S.E.2d 653 (S.C. 1998). Some courts imply a right of subrogation where the insuring agreement does not state it. *See* Cunningham v. Metropolitan Life Ins. Co., 360 N.W.2d 33 (Wis. 1985). When the plaintiff weighs settlement offers, the plaintiff's lawyer must advise the client of the right or potential right of health insurers, disability insurers, and others who have paid for losses the plaintiff suffered as a consequence of the tort, to seek reimbursement. Otherwise, the plaintiff may make an ill-informed decision, with a net recovery significantly less than the plaintiff expects. Settlement money that the plaintiff expected to keep may go to insurers or others, and the plaintiff may have a malpractice cause of action against the plaintiff's lawyer.

Duty to Mitigate. A second common legal issue on damages has to do with the plaintiff's duty to mitigate tort-claim damages. Tort claims are not vacations from the basic responsibility to care for oneself. The plaintiff who fails to follow a physician's reasonable treatment orders, or who violates temporary work restrictions causing further injury, or who in other ways acts unreasonably in not trying to recover from the tort-accident injuries, faces a defense of failure to mitigate. Failure to mitigate, like contributory or comparative negligence, is an affirmative defense on which the defendant has the burden of proof. Distinguish it from contributory or comparative negligence in that the conduct of the plaintiff that failure-to-mitigate examines is conduct occurring *after* the original injury, not leading up to and contributing to the original injury. Courts, though, would not ordinarily hold a plaintiff to have failed to mitigate damages if the plaintiff's refusal to accept medical treatment for the tort-caused injury was due to a sincerely held religious belief. *See* Munn v. Algee, 924 F.2d 568 (5th Cir. 1991).

Practice

Trial was only three weeks away, but the attorney was still without a clue as to how to conduct his tort-plaintiff client's direct examination. No matter what the attorney asked the client as they worked through the client's direct examination in the office—even something as simple as the client's name and address—the client would look away, duck his head, roll his neck, and shift uncomfortably as if he were lying. When not under examination, the client was a likable young man who was increasingly at ease with himself and his very obvious and serious amputation injury. But when under examination, he looked and acted as if he was guilty of a heinous crime—even though the accident and his awful injury were not his fault. Then the attorney thought of something. "Remember your Marine service?" the attorney asked, adding, "Then just pretend for a moment that I am your commanding officer." Instantly, the client looked the attorney straight back in the eye, sat up in his seat, and stopped fidgeting. Two more questions—with firm "yessir" and "nosir" answers from the client—and the attorney knew they were ready. No more practice. The client testified perfectly at trial—attentive, confident, and respectful. Finally, the attorney asked the last question on direct examination: "How has your amputation injury affected your relationship with your teenage son?" The client stared back at the attorney without so much as a blink, while one large tear slowly rolled down his cheek—not a stain of self-pity but a proud mark of intensely controlled emotion. "He's a ballplayer like I was, sir, but we can't play catch anymore. Can't grip a bat. Can't throw a ball. Can't put on a glove. He says it's alright. But I know it bothers him—I know it does from the way he won't look at me anymore. That hurts, sir. That hurts."

Aggravation of Pre-Existing Conditions. Another common legal issue on damages has to do with how the law treats claims in which the plaintiff had a condition that pre-existed the liability incident that aggravated the condition. A classic example is a minor motor-vehicle accident in which mild trauma to the plaintiff's neck or back produces severe disability because of a pre-existing severe degenerative condition of the plaintiff's spine. In those cases, pleading rules require plaintiff's counsel to plead the aggravation of the plaintiff's pre-existing injury—to put the defense on reasonable notice that worsening of the plaintiff's condition is part of the tort claim. Another issue arises when the plaintiff and defendant are unable to distinguish between what constitutes the continuation or natural and progressive worsening of the plaintiff's original condition, and the tort incident's aggravation of that condition. Medical evidence distinguishing aggravation from progression can be notoriously difficult to obtain. Medical care providers are often nonplussed when lawyers ask them to make that distinction. They devote their training, actions, and record keeping to healing, not forensics. In those cases where the parties cannot distinguish condition from aggravation of condition, the traditional rule is that the defendant pays for all of the worsening (whether aggravation or progression). Better (the thought may be) that the defendant pay for all of what might be the result of defendant's wrong, than that plaintiff go uncompensated in part.

Inflamed Passion and Prejudice. The peculiar nature of tort claims can test and alter other rules. Ordinarily, law entitles a party to attend the party's own trial. Indeed, the defendant in criminal cases has a constitutional, confrontation-clause right to do so. But the tort case involving an egregious injury to the plaintiff can create the concern that the sympathy, passion, and prejudice produced by the jury's observation of the plaintiff's injury may influence the verdict. For instance, the constant care a paraplegic plaintiff requires (wiping the mouth and tears, offering sips of water) every few minutes can distract from the legal claims and issues. Judges have the right and duty to control proceedings to ensure a verdict of integrity. At a minimum, judges will place some limits on what injuries (including video and photographs) the plaintiff displays, to minimize the influence of passion and sympathy. Indeed, a traditional rule bars what lawyers know as "Golden Rule" arguments. Plaintiff's counsel must not make a closing argument to the jury that urges jurors to put themselves in plaintiff's position when considering what damages to award. On the other hand, a majority of jurisdictions accepts *per-diem arguments* that jurors should award a certain amount for every day the plaintiff suffers with a tort-related condition. *See* Beagle v. Vasold, 417 P.2d 673 (Cal. 1966) (approving of per-diem arguments); *but see* Caley v. Manicke, 182 N.E.2d 206 (Ill. 1962) (disallowing per-diem arguments).

Outcomes. The outcomes of tort claims implicate other important issues with which tort practitioners must be familiar. In some jurisdictions, statutory tort reforms require that the trial judge apportion the verdict between past and future damages, apportion future damages year to year, and reduce the verdict to present value. The concept of present value can be significant in larger cases. The amount awarded today to compensate for one dollar of loss that the plaintiff will not suffer or incur until 20 years from now, is much less than one dollar. The plaintiff could invest amounts awarded today for future losses, producing returns that pay for part of the loss. Parties to tort actions have always had the opportunity to argue and offer evidence as to the effect of present valuing. Present value figures have been a routine part of case presentation, and standard jury instructions support present-value arguments. Counsel will sometimes trade an instruction on present value (favoring the defendant) for an instruction on the effect of inflation (favoring the plaintiff) to simplify proofs and argument. Yet in some states today, statute requires that the verdict form reflect the apportionment of damages necessary for the court to reduce the verdict to present value after the verdict. *See* Mich. Comp. Laws 600.6306; MICH. MODEL CIV. JURY INSTR. 50.21.

Damages Caps. Statutory damages caps also now exist in many states, again as a part of the wave of tort reform. Some caps limit damages overall. *See* Va. Code Ann. §8.01-581-15 ($1.5 million cap on medical malpractice awards). Others limit only non-economic damages. *See* Cal. Civ. Code §3333.2 ($250,000 cap on non-economic damages in medical malpractice cases). Some caps apply only to certain forms of action—the typical example being medical malpractice. *See* Butler v. Flint Goodrich Hosp., 607 So.2d 517 (La. 1992) (upholding $500,000 medical-malpractice cap); Fein v. Permanente Med. Group, 695 P.2d 665 (Cal. 1985) (upholding $250,000 medical-malpractice cap). Some remove or raise the cap in cases involving certain types of more serious injuries. Others lift the cap for more-culpable conduct such as gross negligence or recklessness. Constitutional challenges to damages caps have been successful in some states, on jury-trial and due-process grounds. *See* Carson v. Maurer, 424 A.2d 825 (N.H. 1980); Arneson v. Olson, 270 N.W.2d 125 (N.D. 1978).

Caps do constrain the right to a jury trial in that they limit, and in that sense frustrate, jury awards. Yet the majority of states to consider the question have held damages caps constitutional. *See* Pulliam v. Coastal Emerg. Servs., Inc., 509 S.E.2d 307 (Va. 1999).

Income Taxes. The tax treatment of damage awards is another important outcome consideration. The federal income tax code currently does not tax damages awards "on account of personal physical injuries or physical sickness." 26 U.S.C. §104. The usual personal-injury recovery is not subject to federal (and by extension, most state) income tax—even as to that part of the settlement or judgment that compensates for lost income or goes to the attorneys for fees. (The law taxes attorneys on the fees as income.) On the other hand, the code does tax punitive-damage awards and awards for cases in which the plaintiff suffers no physical injury or sickness and, instead, only mental or emotional distress. Thus, a recovery in a case for fraud, defamation, or violation of civil rights is subject to income tax. Reducing a recovery by income tax can have huge implications for the plaintiff entitled to the recovery. Accordingly, personal-injury lawyers must advise their clients regarding the tax implications of settlements before a client accepts one. The customary rule is that juries are not to learn of the tax-free or taxable status of an award, when evaluating and determining damages. Federal courts do not follow that general rule. *See* Norfolk & Western Ry. v. Liepelt, 444 U.S. 490 (1980) (Federal Employers' Liability Act actions); Fannetti v. Helenic Lines, Ltd., 678 F.2d 424 (2d Cir. 1982) (all federal-law actions), *cert. denied*, 463 U.S. 1206 (1983).

Structured Settlements. The federal tax code has another important effect on tort recoveries about which plaintiff's lawyers must be aware and as to which they must advise their clients, in cases involving larger recoveries. No federal income tax accrues on the earnings of tort recoveries if properly structured as payment of an income stream over time. A *structured settlement* is one in which the plaintiff negotiates to receive not a single lump sum recovery but a smaller lump-sum payment up front followed by monthly, yearly, or other periodic payments over time—often for life, with a period of years guaranteed against the plaintiff's early death. The tax savings on the earnings of funds set aside for future payments provides a potentially large investment advantage. In effect, the structuring investment company has the advantage of tax-free investing without the usual restrictions to municipal bonds and the like. Given the investment advantage, the total after-tax payments that the plaintiff receives by structuring a settlement should be significantly larger than if the plaintiff takes all of the recovery in a single up-front payment. Plaintiff's and their lawyers turn to structured settlement companies in these circumstances because the plaintiff must follow the tax code's special rules—including that the plaintiff not take possession of the settlement funds before structuring—in order to gain this tax advantage. Structuring recoveries can be especially wise for plaintiffs who are incapable of prudent financial management. Claimants have lost many recoveries to imprudent management and overreaching family and friends.

Contingency Fees. The plaintiff lawyer's treatment of the recovery also implicates important rules. The contingency-fee agreement controls the plaintiff lawyer's disposition of recovered funds, but the fee agreement is itself subject to ethics rules. First, fees must be reasonable. The plaintiff's lawyer may be required to reduce an unreasonably high fee for a tort case settled quickly without substantial legal work—even if the fee agreement provides for the fee and the client agrees to pay it.

Clients change their minds. A lawyer must be able to justify a fee to the bar's grievance administrator. Second, lawyers must not commingle client funds with funds belonging to the attorney or law firm. The plaintiff's lawyer must place tort recoveries in a trust account until dividing the funds according to the fee agreement. Third, a plaintiff's lawyer may reimburse the firm out of the recovered funds not only for the fee but also for expenses stated in the fee agreement. Yet those expenses must also be reasonable and actually incurred, and the fee agreement must also properly disclose them. Fourth, although expert-witness fees are a substantial part of reimbursed expenses in many tort cases, a lawyer must not reimburse an expert witness on a contingency basis. A party must pay an expert witness whether the party wins or loses the case. The expert's fee must not depend on the case's outcome. Finally, in the event of a lost case, the plaintiff's lawyer must ordinarily retain the right to pursue the client for recovery of those advanced expenses. To do otherwise—for the lawyer to pay expenses without obligating the client for reimbursement, and effectively to support the client during the litigation, known as champerty and maintenance—law has traditionally viewed as unwisely running the risk of drumming up frivolous litigation.

Skills

Choose four other students with whom to work. In ten minutes, working as a team, plan the proof of damages for the following client maintaining a personal injury claim. In the first five minutes, one student outline the damages categories, another plan the necessary investigation, another plan the damages experts, another plan the trial exhibits, and another plan the trial and settlement figures. In the second five minutes, spend one minute reviewing and improving each of those five assignments as a team. *Facts.* Your client is a 40-year-old, self-employed, married homemaker and mother of two teenage children. She suffered a disabling back injury in a motor vehicle accident caused by the negligence of a truck driver. The trucking company liable for your client's damages has a primary insurance policy with $100,000 limits and an umbrella policy with $1,000,000 limits. Your client suffered lumbar-spine fractures in the accident. She required hospitalization for three weeks during which she had two surgeries in which plates and cement were used to stabilize her spine. She was then restricted to bed at home for an additional 12 weeks. Her total medical expense has been $86,000. She will require future medical examination and physical and occupational therapy at a cost she does not know. Nine months have passed since the accident, and she still ambulates stooped and painfully. She does not know her prognosis. She is unable to perform the household chores she habitually did for her family. She has not worked at her home bookkeeping business since her injury. She has not yet estimated her income loss. She has engaged in no substantial recreational activities since her injury, even though she exercised regularly before the accident by walking, jogging, and doing yard work. She and her husband have not been intimate since the accident, and she has not played tennis with her daughter, gone for hikes with her son and daughter, or played catch with her son as she occasionally did before the accident.

INQUIRY

Motions in Limine. What relief, before suffering an adverse verdict, might defense counsel appropriately seek in the event that the plaintiff's damages are so emotive of sympathy, passion, and prejudice as to affect the liability portion of the trial? *See* Witherbee v. Honeywell, Inc., 151 F.R.D. 27 (N.D. N.Y. 1993) (bifurcation of liability and damages portions of trial, under authority of Fed. R. Civ. P. 42(b)). A motion in limine asks the trial judge to prevent the admission of certain evidence and any related statement or argument to the jury. Trial judges usually hear motions in limine shortly before trial. Motions to bifurcate proceedings into liability and damages phases can also have a significant impact on trial preparation and outcomes. Which party do you think is the one usually filing these motions? Why?

Comparable Awards. Should the law permit or encourage trial and appellate judges to review comparative jury awards, when evaluating whether damages are excessive? *Compare* Meyers v. Wal-Mart Stores, East, Inc., 257 F.3d 625 (6th Cir. 2001) (correct to consider comparable award); Donlon v. City of New York, 284 A.D.2d 13, 727 N.Y.S.2d 94 (2001) (comparable awards set standard); and Martell v. Boardwalk Enters. Inc., 748 F.2d 740 (2d Cir. 1984) (take caution in ensuring similarity of cases when comparing awards), *with* Ritter v. Stanton, 745 N.E.2d 828 (Ind. App. 2001) (comparable awards not ordinarily to be considered); Barry v. Owens-Corning Fiberglas Corp., 668 N.E.2d 8 (Ill. App. 1996) (evidence of other awards is irrelevant). Are there any circumstances in which an award of, say, $10,000 per day for pain and suffering would be warranted? *See* Surrette v. Islamic Republic of Iran, 231 F. Supp.2d 260 (D. D.C. 2002) (death-inducing torture of hostage, encouraged by Republic of Iran) ("this Court typically has awarded former hostages or their estates roughly $10,000 for each day of captivity"). Consider the following case exploring the basis for noneconomic-loss damages—what law popularly knows as "pain and suffering" and sometimes now refers to as "hedonic damages" from the Greek word for "pleasure."

McDougald v. Garber
New York Court of Appeals
73 N.Y.2d 246, 536 N.E.2d 372 (1989)

WACHTLER, C.J. This appeal raises fundamental questions about the nature and role of nonpecuniary damages in personal injury litigation. By nonpecuniary damages, we mean those damages awarded to compensate an injured person for the physical and emotional consequences of the injury, such as pain and suffering and the loss of the ability to engage in certain activities. Pecuniary damages, on the other hand, compensate the victim for the economic consequences of the injury, such as medical expenses, lost earnings and the cost of custodial care.

The specific questions raised here deal with assessment of nonpecuniary damages and are (1) whether some degree of cognitive awareness is a prerequisite to recovery for loss of enjoyment of life and (2) whether a jury should be instructed to consider and award damages for loss of enjoyment of life separately from damages for pain and suffering. We answer the first question in the affirmative and the second question in the negative.

I.

On September 7, 1978, plaintiff Emma McDougald, then 31 years old, underwent a Caesarean section and tubal ligation at New York Infirmary. Defendant Garber performed the surgery; defendants Armengol and Kulkarni provided anesthesia. During the surgery, Mrs. McDougald suffered oxygen deprivation which resulted in severe brain damage and left her in a permanent comatose condition. This action was brought by Mrs. McDougald and her husband, suing derivatively, alleging that the injuries were caused by the defendants' acts of malpractice.

A jury found all defendants liable and awarded Emma McDougald a total of $9,650,102 in damages, including $1,000,000 for conscious pain and suffering and a separate award of $3,500,000 for loss of the pleasures and pursuits of life. The balance of the damages awarded to her were for pecuniary damages—lost earnings and the cost of custodial and nursing care. Her husband was awarded $1,500,000 on his derivative claim for the loss of his wife's services. On defendants' posttrial motions, the Trial Judge reduced the total award to Emma McDougald to $4,796,728 by striking the entire award for future nursing care ($2,353,374) and by reducing the separate awards for conscious pain and suffering and loss of the pleasures and pursuits of life to a single award of $2,000,000 ([c]). Her husband's award was left intact. On cross appeals, the Appellate Division affirmed ([c]) and later granted defendants leave to appeal to this court.

II.

... Also unchallenged are the awards in the amount of $770,978 for loss of earnings and $2,025,750 for future custodial care—that is, the pecuniary damage awards that survived defendants' posttrial motions.

What remains in dispute, primarily, is the award to Emma McDougald for nonpecuniary damages. At trial, defendants sought to show that Mrs. McDougald's injuries were so severe that she was incapable of either experiencing pain or appreciating her condition. Plaintiffs, on the other hand, introduced proof that Mrs. McDougald responded to certain stimuli to a sufficient extent to indicate that she was aware of her circumstances. Thus, the extent of Mrs. McDougald's cognitive abilities, if any, was sharply disputed.

The parties and the trial court agreed that Mrs. McDougald could not recover for pain and suffering unless she were conscious of the pain. Defendants maintained that such consciousness was also required to support an award for loss of enjoyment of life. The court, however, accepted plaintiffs' view that loss of enjoyment of life was compensable without regard to whether the plaintiff was aware of the loss. Accordingly, because the level of Mrs. McDougald's cognitive abilities was in dispute, the court instructed the jury to consider loss of enjoyment of life as an element of nonpecuniary damages separate from pain and suffering. ...

We conclude that the court erred, both in instructing the jury that Mrs. McDougald's awareness was irrelevant to their consideration of damages for loss of enjoyment of life and in directing the jury to consider that aspect of damages separately from pain and suffering.

III.

We begin with the familiar proposition that an award of damages to a person injured by the negligence of another is to compensate the victim, not to punish the wrongdoer ([cc]). The goal is to restore the injured party, to the extent possible, to the position that would have been occupied had the wrong not occurred ([c]). To be sure, placing the burden of compensation on the negligent party also serves as a deterrent, but purely punitive damages—that is, those which have no compensatory purpose—are prohibited unless the harmful conduct is intentional, malicious, outrageous, or otherwise aggravated beyond mere negligence ([cc]).

Damages for nonpecuniary losses are, of course, among those that can be awarded as compensation to the victim. This aspect of damages, however, stands on less certain ground than does an award for pecuniary damages. An economic loss can be compensated in kind by an economic gain; but recovery for noneconomic losses such as pain and suffering and loss of enjoyment of life rests on "the legal fiction that money damages can compensate for a victim's injury" ([c]). We accept this fiction, knowing that although money will neither ease the pain nor restore the victim's abilities, this device is as close as the law can come in its effort to right the wrong. We have no hope of evaluating what has been lost, but a monetary award may provide a measure of solace for the condition created ([c]).

Our willingness to indulge this fiction comes to an end, however, when it ceases to serve the compensatory goals of tort recovery. When that limit is met, further indulgence can only result in assessing damages that are punitive. The question posed by this case, then, is whether an award of damages for loss of enjoyment of life to a person whose injuries preclude any awareness of the loss serves a compensatory purpose. We conclude that it does not.

Simply put, an award of money damages in such circumstances has no meaning or utility to the injured person. ...

We recognize that, as the trial court noted, requiring some cognitive awareness as a prerequisite to recovery for loss of enjoyment of life will result in some cases "in the paradoxical situation that the greater the degree of brain injury inflicted by a negligent defendant, the smaller the award the plaintiff can recover in general damages" ([c]). The force of this argument, however—the temptation to achieve a balance between injury and damages—has nothing to do with meaningful compensation for the victim. Instead, the temptation is rooted in a desire to punish the defendant in proportion to the harm inflicted. However relevant such retributive symmetry may be in the criminal law, it has no place in the law of civil damages, at least in the absence of culpability beyond mere negligence.

Accordingly, we conclude that cognitive awareness is a prerequisite to recovery for loss of enjoyment of life. We do not go so far, however, as to require the fact finder to sort out varying degrees of cognition and determine at what level a particular deprivation can be fully appreciated. With respect to pain and suffering, the trial court charged simply that there must be "some level of awareness" in order for plaintiff to recover. We think that this is an appropriate standard for all aspects of nonpecuniary loss. No doubt the standard ignores analytically relevant levels of cognition, but we resist the desire for analytical purity in favor of simplicity. A more complex instruction might give the appearance of greater precision but, given the limits of our understanding of the human mind, it would in reality lead only to greater speculation.

We turn next to the question whether loss of enjoyment of life should be considered a category of damages separate from pain and suffering.

IV.

There is no dispute here that the fact finder may, in assessing nonpecuniary damages, consider the effect of the injuries on the plaintiff's capacity to lead a normal life. Traditionally, in this State and elsewhere, this aspect of suffering has not been treated as a separate category of damages; instead, the plaintiff's inability to enjoy life to its fullest has been considered one type of suffering to be factored into a general award for nonpecuniary damages, commonly known as pain and suffering.

Recently, however, there has been an attempt to segregate the suffering associated with physical pain from the mental anguish that stems from the inability to engage in certain activities, and to have juries provide a separate award for each ([cc]). ...

The advocates of separate awards contend that because pain and suffering and loss of enjoyment of life can be distinguished, they must be treated separately if the plaintiff is to be compensated fully for each distinct injury suffered. We disagree. Such an analytical approach may have its place when the subject is pecuniary damages, which can be calculated with some precision. But the estimation of nonpecuniary damages is not amenable to such analytical precision and may, in fact, suffer from its application. Translating human suffering into dollars and cents involves no mathematical formula; it rests, as we have said, on a legal fiction. The figure that emerges is unavoidably distorted by the translation. Application of this murky process to the component parts of nonpecuniary injuries (however analytically distinguishable they may be) cannot make it more accurate. If anything, the distortion will be amplified by repetition.

Thus, we are not persuaded that any salutary purpose would be served by having the jury make separate awards for pain and suffering and loss of enjoyment of life. We are confident, furthermore, that the trial advocate's art is a sufficient guarantee that none of the plaintiff's losses will be ignored by the jury.

The errors in the instructions given to the jury require a new trial on the issue of nonpecuniary damages to be awarded to plaintiff Emma McDougald. …

Accordingly, the order of the Appellate Division, insofar as appealed from, should be modified, with costs to defendants, by granting a new trial on the issue of nonpecuniary damages of plaintiff Emma McDougald, and as so modified, affirmed.

INQUIRY

More Categories. Not all courts follow the *McDougald* approach to noneconomic damages. Some hold that loss of enjoyment of life differs from pain and suffering as a damages category. *See* Fantozzi v. Sandusky Cement Prods. Co., 597 N.E.2d 474 (Ohio 1992). Courts have recognized as compensable many other forms or items of non-economic damages. *See* Braud v. Painter, 730 F. Supp. 1 (M.D. La. 1990) (loss of smell and memory); Ramos v. Kuzas, 600 N.E.2d 241 (Ohio 1992) (inability to drive a vehicle); Guilbeaux v. Lafayette Gen. Hosp., 589 So.2d 629 (La. Ct. App. 1991) (impotence); Curtiss v. YMCA, 511 P.2d 991 (Wash. 1973) (incontinence).

Appellate Review. Given the trial judge's opportunity to observe first-hand the proofs and plaintiff, what is the appropriate standard for appellate review of a trial judge's determination to remit or not to remit a damages award? *See* Kessel v. Leavitt, 511 S.E. 2d 720 (W. Va. 1998) (deferential review of jury verdict, without reference to trial court analysis); Thrailkill v. Patterson, 879 S.W.2d 836 (Tenn. 1994) (abuse of discretion); *see also* Gasperini v. Center for Humanities, Inc., 518 U.S. 415 (1996) (Seventh Amendment's reexamination clause requires federal appellate courts to follow abuse-of-discretion standard).

Additur. A motion for remittitur tests whether the jury's award was too high. What if the jury's damage award is too *low*? *See* Southern v. Lyons, 696 So.2d 129 (La. Ct. App. 1997) (appellate court increases jury-awarded damages from $14,000 to $85,000 and reduces comparative negligence from 50% to 20%). Motions for additur to increase a verdict, though exceedingly rare, are in theory available when the proofs demand more in damages than the jury awarded. Why are they so rare? Can you think of some instances where a jury, having found liability, must award a certain amount in damages at a minimum?

Loss of Consortium. Loss of consortium is the claim of a spouse for the lost services, society, and companionship caused by the tortious injury of the other spouse. Should the law permit loss of consortium only in favor of a spouse, or should parents and children be allowed loss of consortium claims as well? *See* Borer v. American Airlines, Inc., 19 Cal.3d 441, 138 Cal. Rptr. 302, 563 P.2d 858 (1977) (spouses only) (majority rule); Hutchinson v. Broadlawns Medical Ctr., 459 N.W.2d 273 (Iowa 1990) (no consortium loss claim for caretaker grandfather). Must the plaintiff be physically injured for the spouse to bring a loss-of-consortium claim? *See* Molien v. Kaiser Fdn. Hosps., 27 Cal.3d 916, 167 Cal. Rptr. 831, 616 P.2d 813 (Cal. 1980) (wife's loss-of-consortium claim allowed against defendant physician for misdiagnosing husband as having syphilis, upon which wife reasonably assumed husband had committed adultery).

B. Wrongful Death

OBJECTIVE: Given a tort claim involving survival for a limited time followed by death caused by the tort, itemize the damages typically recoverable, list the typical beneficiaries, and describe the principal procedural issues consistent with this section of the text and the discussion in class.

Case Study: The estate of a 55-year-old married woman maintains a wrongful-death claim against the manufacturer of an allegedly defective product. The woman suffered severe electrical shock from the product's use, suffered cardiac arrest, and, though hospitalized for ten days, never regained consciousness. The woman had been separated from her husband for five years up to the time of her injury and death. A 30-year-old son and 16-year-old daughter survived her. The woman had not seen the son since her separation but cared for the daughter at home while the daughter attended high school. The woman's husband paid her child support. The woman worked part-time as a bookkeeper for a local business. ***Itemize the estate's wrongful-death claim damages.***

When a tort causes the death of a person, the law treats the tort claim in a different fashion both from a procedural and substantive standpoint. The procedural differences have to do with who maintains the claim, when they must maintain it, and how they may resolve it. The substantive differences have to do with damages—what loss law compensates and who receives that compensation. One might think that the decedent's tort claim disappears with the death of the injured person who would have maintained it. After all, who remains to compensate? And if the person who caused the death did so intentionally or in another manner that would subject the person to severe criminal sanction, then who would pay the compensation? The old English felony-merger doctrine held the civil claim subsumed into the criminal felony and thus barred it. The criminal would in any event have forfeited all property to the Crown. Thus, there existed a common-law bar to recovery for wrongful death, *see* Baker v. Bolton, 1 Camp. 493, 170 Eng. Rep. 1033 (1808), likely due to the felony-merger doctrine, *see* Moragne v. States Marine Lines, Inc., 398 U.S. 375 (1970).

But of course, even after the putative claimant's death, or especially in the case of the putative claimant's death, family members would remain who had suffered the loss of the decedent's love, services, and financial support to compensate. Deterring the defendant would be another interest. As the United States Supreme Court held in *Moragne, supra,* in finally recognizing a wrongful death claim under American admiralty law (the last bastion against it) for unseaworthiness, not recognizing a tort claim where the conduct is so reprehensible as to cause a person's death violates elementary tort-law principles and ordinary notions of justice. *See also* Norfolk Shipbuilding & Drydock Corp. v. Garris, 532 U.S. 811 (2001) (extending maritime wrongful-death actions to include negligence theories). Thus it was not too long after the *Baker v. Bolton* decision cited above, that in 1846 Parliament enacted Lord Campbell's Act, which quickly became the model for many American wrongful death statutes.

Today, all fifty states have wrongful-death statutes. The statutes do not provide that death alone creates the cause of action. Rather, a liability theory such as negligence or one of its variants (medical malpractice, premises liability, products liability, etc.), or an intentional tort, must first exist for the wrongful-death action to proceed. Labeling a claim a *wrongful-death action* is in that respect a slight misnomer. The liability portion of the claim remains one for negligence, battery, or some other recognized tort. But the peculiar procedural and substantive-law rules for wrongful-death actions require lawyers to label and address them as such—while still proving or disproving the liability portion of the claim as in personal-injury cases. Consider the following two wrongful-death acts.

MICH. COMP. L. ANN. §600.2922. Wrongful death
(1) Whenever the death of a person, injuries resulting in death, or death as described in section 2922a shall be caused by wrongful act, neglect, or fault of another, and the act, neglect, or fault is such as would, if death had not ensued, have entitled the party injured to maintain an action and recover damages, the person who or the corporation that would have been liable, if death had not ensued, shall be liable to an action for damages, notwithstanding the death of the person injured or death as described in section 2922a, and although the death was caused under circumstances that constitute a felony.
(2) Every action under this section shall be brought by, and in the name of, the personal representative of the estate of the deceased. Within 30 days after the commencement of an action, the personal representative shall serve a copy of the complaint and notice as prescribed in subsection (4) upon the person or persons who may be entitled to damages under subsection (3) in the manner and method provided in the rules applicable to probate court proceedings.
(3) Subject to sections 2802 to 2805 of the estates and protected individuals code, 1998 PA 386, MCL 700.2802 to 700.2805, the person or persons who may be entitled to damages under this section shall be limited to any of the following who suffer damages and survive the deceased:
(a) The deceased's spouse, children, descendants, parents, grandparents, brothers and sisters, and, if none of these persons survive the deceased, then those persons to whom the estate of the deceased would pass under the laws of intestate succession determined as of the date of death of the deceased.
(b) The children of the deceased's spouse.
(c) Those persons who are devisees under the will of the deceased, except those whose relationship with the decedent violated Michigan law, including beneficiaries of a trust under the will, those persons who are designated in the will as persons who may be entitled to damages under this section, and the beneficiaries of a living trust of the deceased if there is a devise to that trust in the will of the deceased. ...
(5) If, for the purpose of settling a claim for damages for wrongful death where an action for those damages is pending, a motion is filed in the court where the action is pending by the personal representative asking leave of the court to settle the claim, the

court shall, with or without notice, conduct a hearing and approve or reject the proposed settlement.

(6) In every action under this section, the court or jury may award damages as the court or jury shall consider fair and equitable, under all the circumstances including reasonable medical, hospital, funeral, and burial expenses for which the estate is liable; reasonable compensation for the pain and suffering, while conscious, undergone by the deceased during the period intervening between the time of the injury and death; and damages for the loss of financial support and the loss of the society and companionship of the deceased. ...

BALDWIN'S OHIO REV. CODE ANN. §2125.01. Civil action for wrongful death.
When the death of a person is caused by wrongful act, neglect, or default which would have entitled the party injured to maintain an action and recover damages if death had not ensued, the person who would have been liable if death had not ensued, or the administrator or executor of the estate of such person, as such administrator or executor, shall be liable to an action for damages, notwithstanding the death of the person injured and although the death was caused under circumstances which make it aggravated murder, murder, or manslaughter. When the action is against such administrator or executor, the damages recovered shall be a valid claim against the estate of such deceased person. ...

BALDWIN'S OHIO REV. CODE ANN. §2125.02 Proceedings; damages allowable; limitation of actions; statute of repose for product liability claims; abandonment of deceased child; definitions
(A)(1) Except as provided in this division, a civil action for wrongful death shall be brought in the name of the personal representative of the decedent for the exclusive benefit of the surviving spouse, the children, and the parents of the decedent, all of whom are rebuttably presumed to have suffered damages by reason of the wrongful death, and for the exclusive benefit of the other next of kin of the decedent. A parent who abandoned a minor child who is the decedent shall not receive a benefit in a civil action for wrongful death brought under this division.
(2) The jury, or the court if the civil action for wrongful death is not tried to a jury, may award damages authorized by division (B) of this section, as it determines are proportioned to the injury and loss resulting to the beneficiaries described in division (A)(1) of this section by reason of the wrongful death and may award the reasonable funeral and burial expenses incurred as a result of the wrongful death. In its verdict, the jury or court shall set forth separately the amount, if any, awarded for the reasonable funeral and burial expenses incurred as a result of the wrongful death.
(3)(a) The date of the decedent's death fixes, subject to division (A)(3)(b)(iii) of this section, the status of all beneficiaries of the civil action for wrongful death for purposes of determining the damages suffered by them and the amount of damages to be awarded. A person who is conceived prior to the decedent's death and who is born alive after the decedent's death is a beneficiary of the action. ...
(b)(iii) Consistent with the Rules of Evidence, a party to a civil action for wrongful death may present evidence that the surviving spouse of the decedent is remarried. If that evidence is presented, then, in addition to the factors described in divisions (A)(3)(b)(i) and (ii) of this section, the jury or court may consider that evidence in determining the damages suffered by the surviving spouse by reason of the wrongful death.
(B) Compensatory damages may be awarded in a civil action for wrongful death and may include damages for the following:
(1) Loss of support from the reasonably expected earning capacity of the decedent;

(2) Loss of services of the decedent;
(3) Loss of the society of the decedent, including loss of companionship, consortium, care, assistance, attention, protection, advice, guidance, counsel, instruction, training, and education, suffered by the surviving spouse, dependent children, parents, or next of kin of the decedent;
(4) Loss of prospective inheritance to the decedent's heirs at law at the time of the decedent's death;
(5) The mental anguish incurred by the surviving spouse, dependent children, parents, or next of kin of the decedent. ...
(E)(1) If the personal representative of a deceased minor has actual knowledge or reasonable cause to believe that the minor was abandoned by a parent seeking to benefit from a civil action for wrongful death or if any person listed in division (A)(1) of this section who is permitted to benefit from a civil action for wrongful death commenced in relation to a deceased minor has actual knowledge or reasonable cause to believe that the minor was abandoned by a parent seeking to benefit from the action, the personal representative or the person may file a motion in the court in which the action is commenced requesting the court to issue an order finding that the parent abandoned the minor and is not entitled to recover damages in the action based on the death of the minor. ...

BALDWIN'S OHIO REV. CODE ANN. §2125.03 Distribution of award
(A)(1) The amount received by a personal representative in an action for wrongful death under sections 2125.01 and 2125.02 of the Revised Code, whether by settlement or otherwise, shall be distributed to the beneficiaries or any one or more of them. The court that appointed the personal representative, except when all of the beneficiaries are on an equal degree of consanguinity to the deceased person, shall adjust the share of each beneficiary in a manner that is equitable, having due regard for the injury and loss to each beneficiary resulting from the death and for the age and condition of the beneficiaries. If all of the beneficiaries are on an equal degree of consanguinity to the deceased person, the beneficiaries may adjust the share of each beneficiary among themselves. If the beneficiaries do not adjust their shares among themselves, the court shall adjust the share of each beneficiary in the same manner as the court adjusts the shares of beneficiaries who are not on an equal degree of consanguinity to the deceased person. ...

INQUIRY

Personal Representatives. As to the preliminary question of who may bring a wrongful-death action, the statutes typically provide that the decedent's personal representative (an executor or administrator) bring such actions in the name of the decedent's estate. Determining the appropriate personal representative can itself be a significant issue. The decedent may not have left a will designating a qualified personal representative. Two or more family members may have the same statutory priority to serve. Each potential representative may have retained a different personal-injury lawyer. The representative typically files a separate probate court case coincident with the wrongful-death action, establishing the decedent's estate and confirming the representative's authority. The personal representative then typically formally retains the personal-injury lawyer (who may have filed the probate case as well, if the family has no probate lawyer who has already done so) and works closely with the lawyer to determine claim, trial, and settlement strategy, while communicating with the interested family members about the proceeding's course. Settlements require approval of the court of general jurisdiction in which the wrongful-death action pends, the probate court, or both. Distribution of the settlement proceeds typically occurs through the probate court, with that court deciding disputes among the interested beneficiaries.

> **Figure**
> Plaintiff's lawyer Salvador Liccardo limits his highly successful, San Jose, California tort-law practice to representing the severely injured in catastrophic-injury cases. For more than 20 years, he has been a fellow of the International Academy of Trial Lawyers, an organization for which he was a faculty member on its China Project, educating Chinese government lawyers on the rule of law in America. He was a founder and has been president of Public Justice, a national public-interest law firm that seeks to protect the rights of Americans against environmental damage and corporate and governmental wrongdoing. Mr. Liccardo has had many multi-million-dollar verdicts and settlements in tort cases involving such matters as motor-vehicle accidents, an Olympic bobsledder, and product defects in breast implants, pharmaceuticals, infant seats, and industrial equipment. He is also a sports enthusiast and pianist.

Beneficiaries. The next question involves identifying interested beneficiaries. The wrongful-death statutes always provide for the decedent's spouse, routinely provide for the decedent's children (especially when dependent on the decedent at the time of death, and especially in the absence of a spouse), and occasionally provide for the decedent's parents (especially when dependent on the decedent at the time of death). Beyond that, the statutes may provide for other next of kin including grandparents, siblings, grandchildren, and other lineal descendants—especially in the absence of closer family members. They may also provide for those beneficiaries whom the decedent designated in a will. This last possibility raises an important point. Wrongful-death recoveries are not, strictly speaking, part of the decedent's estate. Wrongful-death statutes provide for distribution outside of any will the decedent may have left and outside of the estate. By contrast, real and personal property that the decedent owns at the time of death (that which has nothing directly to do with the wrongful-death action) distributes through the estate, according to the decedent's expressed wishes in a will or other testamentary instrument, or by intestate succession. The wrongful-death statutes often do not follow precisely the state's priorities for intestate succession. Thus, wrongful-death recoveries are likely to distribute at least somewhat differently, and possibly very differently, than other property distributed through the estate.

> **Ethics**
> The personal-injury lawyer who handles the wrongful-death action does not take sides in distribution disputes between family members or other interested parties because to do so would implicate a conflict of interest. The lawyer represents the estate—construed to mean all beneficiaries of the estate and no one beneficiary over another. The lawyer who represents the estate may well, in the course of the underlying liability litigation, have made estimates of each interested party's loss, as a basis for the damages claim made in that underlying case. These estimates may become the basis for agreements on distributions when the liability case resolves. When disputes arise that the interested parties cannot resolve without assistance, the lawyer who represents the estate will advise the interested parties to seek other counsel. When substantial sums

> are at stake and several family members claim entitlement to distribution, each of several interested parties may bring their own lawyer to the distribution hearing.

Measures of Loss. The next significant question is just what the wrongful-death action compensates. Under Lord Campbell's Act and the similar American wrongful-death statutes, damages are only the "pecuniary loss" associated with the decedent's death. The law typically treats pecuniary loss as monetary contributions the decedent would have made to the beneficiaries' support and possibly also the value of the decedent's services to the beneficiaries—but not loss of the decedent's love, society, and companionship. Because fact-finders tend to measure the latter non-economic losses as equal to or even a multiple of the economic losses, this historical restriction to pecuniary losses is significant. As the following case and a second opinion in the same case after remand show, this historical restriction has gradually eroded to the point that a number of jurisdictions allow beneficiaries to recover for non-economic loss of the decedent's society and companionship.

Selders v. Armentrout
Nebraska Supreme Court
190 Neb. 275, 207 N.W.2d 686 (1973)

McCOWN, J. This is an action by Earl and Ila Selders to recover damages for the wrongful deaths of three of their minor children. The children were killed in an automobile accident. The jury found the defendants Charles and William Armentrout negligent and returned a verdict against them for the exact amount of the medical and funeral expenses of the three children. The parents have appealed.

The sole issue on this appeal involves the proper elements and measure of damages in a tort action in Nebraska for the wrongful death of a minor child. The court essentially instructed the jury that except for medical and funeral expenses, the damages should be the monetary value of the contributions and services which the parents could reasonably have expected to receive from the children less the reasonable cost to the parents of supporting the children.

The defendants contend that the measure of damages is limited to pecuniary loss and that the instructions to the jury correctly reflect the measure and elements of damage. The plaintiffs assert that the loss of the society, comfort, and companionship of the children are proper and compensable elements of damage.... .

It is quite apparent from an examination of the judicial decisions and the legal literature in the field, that a broadening concept of the measure and elements of damages for the wrongful death of a minor child has been in the development stage for many years. ...

The original pecuniary loss concept and its restrictive application arose in a day when children during minority were generally regarded as an economic asset to parents. Children went to work on farms and in factories at age 10 and even earlier. This was before the day of child labor laws and long before the day of extended higher education for the general population. A child's earnings and services could be generally established and the financial or pecuniary loss which could be proved became the measure of damages for the wrongful death of a child. Virtually all other damages were disallowed as speculative or as sentimental.

The damages involved in a wrongful death case even today must of necessity deal primarily with a fictitious or speculative future life, as it might have been had the wrongful death not occurred. For that reason, virtually all evidence of future damage is necessarily speculative to a degree. The measure and elements of damage involved in a wrongful death case, however, have been excessively restrictive as applied to a minor child in contrast to an adult. Modern economic reality emphasizes the gulf between the old concepts of a child's economic value and the new facts of modern family life. To limit damages for the death of a child to the monetary value of the services which the next of kin could reasonably have expected to receive during his minority less the reasonable expense of maintaining and educating him stamps almost all modern children as worthless in the eyes of the law. In fact, if the rule was literally followed, the average child would have a negative worth. This court has already held that contributions reasonably to be expected from a minor, not only during his minority but afterwards, may be allowed on evidence justifying a reasonable expectation of pecuniary benefit. Draper v. Tucker, 69 Neb. 434, 95 N.W. 1026; Fisher v. Trester, 119 Neb. 529, 229 N.W. 901. Even with that modification, the wrongful death of a child results in no monetary loss, except in the rare case, and the assumption that the traditional measure of damages is compensatory is a pure legal fiction.

Particularly in the last decade, a growing number of courts have extended the measure of damages to include the loss of society and companionship of the minor child, even under statutes limiting recovery to pecuniary loss or pecuniary value of services less the cost of support and maintenance, or similar limitations. ...

In this state, the statute has not limited damages for wrongful death to pecuniary loss but this court has imposed that restriction. For an injury to the marital relationship, the law allows recovery for the loss of the society, comfort, and companionship of a spouse. This court has allowed such a recovery for the wrongful death of a wife. See Ensor v. Compton, 110 Neb. 522, 194 N.W. 458. There is no logical reason for treating an injury to the family relationship resulting from the wrongful death of a child more restrictively. It is no more difficult for juries and courts to measure damages for the loss of the life of a child than many other abstract concepts with which they are required to deal. We hold that the measure of damages for the wrongful death of a minor child should be extended to include the loss of the society, comfort, and companionship of the child. To the extent this holding is in conflict with prior decisions of this court, they are overruled. ...

The judgment of the trial court as to liability is affirmed, the judgment as to damages is reversed and the cause remanded for trial on the issue of damages only, consistent with our holding in this opinion.

Affirmed in part, and in part reversed and remanded with directions.

Selders v. Armentrout
Nebraska Supreme Court
192 Neb. 291, 220 N.W.2d 222 (1974)

BOSLAUGH, J. This is an action for damages for the wrongful death of Marcella Selders, Doureen Selders, and Gary Selders, minor children of Earl Selders and Ila Selders. The children died as a result of injuries sustained in an automobile accident on February 3, 1967.

The issue of the defendants' liability was determined in a previous trial. See Selders v. Armentrout, 190 Neb. 275, 207 N.W.2d 686. The sole issue tried in the lower court was the amount of damages which the plaintiffs should recover. The jury returned verdicts for the plaintiffs in the amount of $1,500 on each cause of action. The plaintiffs appeal, contending the verdicts were inadequate... .

At the time of the accident which resulted in the death of the children the plaintiffs were separated. A decree of divorce had been entered on October 10, 1966. The custody of the children had been awarded to Mrs. Selders, and they were living with her.

The verdicts included all pecuniary loss sustained by the plaintiffs including medical, hospital, and funeral expenses. Doureen was killed instantly in the accident. The medical and hospital expenses for Marcella and Gary amounted to $297.10. The funeral expenses for the three children amounted to $3,395. It was a question for the jury whether the funeral expense was reasonable in view of the ages of the children and all the facts and circumstances.

Marcella was 15 years of age, Doureen was 13, and Gary was 9. The evidence showed the deceased children had made no contribution of earnings other than to their own support. The evidence concerning the two other children in the family who were not involved in the accident showed they had left home when they became self-supporting and had contributed very little of a pecuniary nature to their parents.

The amount which should be awarded in any wrongful death case is incapable of computation and is largely a matter for the jury. As stated in Dorsey v. Yost, 151 Nev. 66, 36 N.W.2d 574, 14 A.L.R.2d 544: "The amount to which a parent is entitled cannot be accurately determined because of the numerous contingencies involved. The amount being very problematical, it is peculiarly for the jury to determine, after hearing all the evidence bearing upon the situation, including the parent's position in life, the physical and mental condition of the child, his surroundings and prospects, and any other matter that sheds light upon the subject. Members of juries generally have children of their own and have information as to the pecuniary value of children's services and the expense involved in their care and education. A jury is peculiarly fitted to determine the loss sustained by a parent in such a case. At best, the verdict can only be an approximation as no yardstick exists by which the correct answer can be found with exactness."

The evidence in this case was such that the jury could have concluded the pecuniary loss to the parents, including the value of society and companionship, was relatively small. We are unable to say under all the facts and circumstances the verdicts were inadequate. ...

The judgment of the District Court is affirmed.

INQUIRY

Damages Caps. While a trend has existed to allow wrongful-death recovery for loss of society and companionship, either by reinterpreting "pecuniary loss" to include lost society and companionship, *see* Hancock v. Chattanooga-Hamilton Cty. Hosp. Auth. 54 S.W.3d 234 (Tenn. 2001), or by amending the wrongful-death statute, *see* Hawaii Rev. Stat. §663-3 (2003), an opposite trend has existed toward capping wrongful-death damages. *See* Kan. Stat. Ann. §60-1903 (2003) ($250,000); Me. Rev.

Stat. Ann. 18A §2-804 (2003) ($400,000). The Warsaw Convention limits personal-injury and wrongful-death negligence liability relating to international-air travel to $75,000. Zicherman v. Korean Air Lines Co., 516 U.S. 217 (1996). Interestingly, caps were present in many of the original wrongful-death statutes but gradually abandoned as their amounts became incommensurate.

Loss to the Estate. Some states take a simpler approach and measure the loss not to the beneficiaries but to the estate. This approach simplifies the proofs in that the monetary-loss question becomes what the decedent would have earned. If, for instance, the decedent had worked another twenty years at $50,000 per year, the wage loss to the estate would be $1 million (ignoring issues of inflation, present value, bonuses, raises, benefits, and so on). Whether the court should reduce those lost earnings by what the decedent would have consumed in the decedent's own support complicates this approach. Most, but not all, jurisdictions require consumption reduction. Parties usually base loss calculations in wrongful-death cases on the decedent's life expectancy—typically proven by mortality table. *See* Zimmerman v. Ausland, 513 P.2d 1167 (Or. 1973) (affirming award based on statutory mortality tables).

Survival Actions. When the decedent survives for some period (short or long) before dying from the tort's injuries, tort law today typically treats the decedent's damages for the period of survival as if the decedent had survived to bring the claim for that period—and assigns any recovery to the decedent's estate. Damages for the decedent's conscious pain and suffering before death are thus an asset of the decedent's estate that the probate court distributes with other assets of the estate—unlike the wrongful death recovery that distributes according to the wrongful death statute, typically to beneficiaries without passing through the estate (and thus not subject to estate creditors). Consider the following case.

Murphy v. Martin Oil Co.
Illinois Supreme Court
56 Ill.2d 423, 308 N.E.2d 583 (1974)

WARD, J. The plaintiff, Charryl Murphy, as administratrix of her late husband, Jack Raymond Murphy, and individually, and as next friend of Debbie Ann Murphy, Jack Kenneth Murphy and Carrie Lynn Murphy, their children, filed a complaint in the circuit court of Cook County against the defendants, Martin Oil Company and James Hocker. Count I of the complaint claimed damages for wrongful death under the Illinois Wrongful Death Act and count II sought damages for conscious pain and suffering, loss of wages and property damage. The circuit court allowed the defendants' motion to strike the second count of the complaint on the ground that it failed to state a cause of action. When the court further ordered that there was no just reason for delaying enforcement or appeal from this order the plaintiffs then appealed the dismissal under Rule 304 (50 Ill.2d R. 304) to the appellate court. That court affirmed the dismissal of count II of the complaint as to its allegations of pain and suffering and reversed the judgment as to its allegations of loss of wages and property damage. The cause was remanded with directions to reinstate as much of count II as related to loss of wages and property damage. (4 Ill.App.3d 1015, 283 N.E.2d 243.) We granted the plaintiff's petition for leave to appeal.

The first count set out the factual background for the complaint. It alleged that on June 11, 1968, the defendants owned and operated a gasoline station in Oak Lawn, Cook County, and that on that date the plaintiff's decedent, Jack Raymond Murphy, while having his truck filled with gasoline, was injured through the defendants' negligence in a fire on the defendants' premises. Nine days later he died from the injuries. Damages for wrongful death were claimed under the Illinois Wrongful Death Act. ...

The second count of the complaint asked for damages for the decedent's physical and mental suffering, for loss of wages for the nine-day period following his injury and for the loss of his clothing worn at the time of injury. These damages were claimed under the common law and under our survival statute, which provides that certain rights of action survive the death of the person with the right of action. (Ill.Rev.Stat.1971, ch. 3, par. 339.) The statute states: "In addition to the actions which survive by the common law, the following also survive: actions of replevin, actions to recover damages for an injury to the person (except slander and libel), actions to recover damages for an injury to real or personal property or for the detention or conversion of personal property, actions against officers for misfeasance, malfeasance, or nonfeasance of themselves or their deputies, actions for fraud or deceit, and actions provided in Section 14 of Article VI of 'An Act relating to alcoholic liquors,' approved January 31, 1934, as amended."

On this appeal we shall consider: (1) whether the plaintiff can recover for the loss of wages which her decedent would have earned during the interval between his injury and death; (2) whether the plaintiff can recover for the destruction of the decedent's personal property (clothing) at the time of the injury; (3) whether the plaintiff can recover damages for conscious pain and suffering of the decedent from the time of his injuries to the time of death.

This State in 1853 enacted the Wrongful Death Act and in 1872 enacted the so-called Survival Act (now section 339 of the Probate Act). This court first had occasion to consider the statutes in combination in 1882 in Holton v. Daly, 106 Ill. 131. The court declared that the effect of the Wrongful Death Act was that a cause of action for personal injuries, which would have abated under the common law upon the death of the injured party from those injuries, would continue on behalf of the spouse or the next of kin and would be "enlarged to embrace the injury resulting from the death." (106 Ill. 131, 140.) In other words, it was held that the Wrongful Death Act provided the exclusive remedy available when death came as a result of given tortious conduct. In considering the Survival Act the court stated that it was intended to allow for the survival of a cause of action only when the injured party died from a cause other than that which caused the injuries which created the cause of action. Thus, the court said, an action for personal injury would not survive death if death resulted from the tortious conduct which caused the injury.

This construction of the two statutes persisted for over 70 years. ... Damages, therefore, under the Wrongful Death Act were limited to pecuniary losses, as from loss of support, to the surviving spouse and next of kin as a result of the death. ... Under the survival statute damages recoverable in a personal injury action, as for conscious pain and suffering, loss of earnings, medical expenses and physical disability, could be had only if death resulted from a cause other than the one which gave rise to the personal injury action. ...

This disfavoring of abatement and enlarging of survival statutes has been general. In Prosser, Handbook of the Law of Torts (4th ed. 1971), at page 901, it is said: "(T)he modern trend is definitely toward the view that tort causes of action and liabilities are as fairly a part of the estate of either plaintiff or defendant as contract debts, and that the question is rather one of why a fortuitous event such as death should extinguish a valid action. Accordingly, survival statutes gradually are being extended; and it may be expected that ultimately all tort actions will survive to the same extent as those founded on contract." And at page 906 Prosser observes that where there have been wrongful death and survival statutes the usual holding has been that actions may be concurrently maintained under those statutes. The usual method of dealing with the two causes of action, he notes, is to allocate conscious pain and suffering, expenses and loss of earnings of the decedent up to the date of death to the survival statute, and to allocate the loss of benefits of the survivors to the action for wrongful death.

As the cited comments of Prosser indicate, the majority of jurisdictions which have considered the question allow an action for personal injuries in addition to an action under the wrongful death statute, though death is attributable to the injuries. Recovery for conscious pain and suffering is permitted in most of these jurisdictions. ...

We consider that those decisions which allow an action for fatal injuries as well as for wrongful death are to be preferred to this court's holding in Holton v. Daly that the Wrongful Death Act was the only remedy available when injury resulted in death.

The holding in Holton was not compelled, we judge, by the language or the nature of the statutes examined. The statutes were conceptually separable and different. The one related to an action arising upon wrongful death; the other related to a right of action for personal injury arising during the life of the injured person.

The remedy available under Holton will often be grievously incomplete. There may be a substantial loss of earnings, medical expenses, prolonged pain and suffering, as well as property damage sustained, before an injured person may succumb to his injuries. To say that there can be recovery only for his wrongful death is to provide an obviously inadequate justice. Too, the result in such a case is that the wrongdoer will have to answer for only a portion of the damages he caused. Incongruously, if the injury caused is so severe that death results, the wrongdoer's liability for the damages before death will be extinguished. It is obvious that in order to have a full liability and a full recovery there must be an action allowed for damages up to the time of death, as well as thereafter. Considering "It is more important that the court should be right upon later and more elaborate consideration of the cases than consistent with previous declarations" (Barden v. Northern Pacific R.R. Co. (1894), 154 U.S. 288, 322, 14 S.Ct. 1030, 1036, 38 L.Ed. 992, 1000), we declare Holton and the cases which have followed it overruled. What this court observed in Molitor v. Kaneland Community Unit Dist. No. 302 (1959), 18 Ill.2d 11, 26, 163 N.E.2d 89, 96, may appropriately be said again: "We have repeatedly held that the doctrine of Stare decisis is not an inflexible rule requiring this court to blindly follow precedents and adhere to prior decisions, and that when it appears that public policy and social needs require a departure from prior decisions, it is our duty as a court of last resort to overrule those decisions and establish a rule consonant with out present day concepts of right and justice. (Bradley v. Fox, 7 Ill.2d 106, 111, 129 N.E.2d 699; Nudd v. Matsoukas, 7 Ill.2d 608, 615, 131 N.E.2d 525; Amann v. Faidy, 415 Ill. 422, 114 N.E.2d 412.)."

For the reasons given, the judgment of the appellate court is affirmed insofar as it held that an action may be maintained by the plaintiff for loss of property and loss of wages during the interval between injury and death, and that judgment is reversed insofar as it held that the plaintiff cannot maintain an action for her decedent's pain and suffering.

Affirmed in part; reversed in part.

INQUIRY

Other Dependents. Given that wrongful-death statutes make spouses beneficiaries of wrongful-death claims, how should law treat former spouses who remain close to, and perhaps dependent on, the decedent? *See* Lewis v. Allis-Chalmers Corp., 615 F.2d 1129 (5th Cir. 1980) (no, applying Louisiana law). What about unmarried cohabiting couples? *See* Holguin v. Flores, 122 Cal. App.4th 428, 18 Cal. Rptr.3d 749 (2004) (no); Raum v. Restaurant Assocs., Inc., 252 A.D.2d 369, 675 N.Y.S.2d 343 (1998) (no). What about unmarried domestic partners who have complied with statutory formalities recognizing that status? *See* Cal. Code Civ. Proc. §377.60 (2004) (granting wrongful-death beneficiary status to domestic partners); 15 Vt. Stat. Ann. §1204(e)(2) (2004) (granting status to civil-union parties); Haw. Rev. Stat. 66303(b)(3) (2003) (granting status to reciprocal beneficiaries); *see also* Langan v. St. Vincent's Hosp., 196 Misc.2d 440, 765 N.Y.S.2d 411 (2003) (granting New York wrongful-death beneficiary status to Vermont civil union partner); *but see* Littleton v. Prange, 9 S.W.3d 223 (Tex. App. 1999) (denying wrongful-death beneficiary status to person born male but having undergone surgical sex reassignment and having putatively married a male).

Children. Given that wrongful-death statutes typically list children as wrongful-death action beneficiaries, what about stepchildren—should they be beneficiaries, too? *See* Klossner v. San Juan County, 93 Wash.2d 42, 605 P.2d 330 (1980) (not unless adopted or where statute grants status to those to whom decedent stood "in *loco parentis*"); Steed v. Imperial Airlines, 12 Cal.3d 115, 524 P.2d 801, 115 Cal. Rptr. 329 (1974) (no, but statute subsequently amended to include dependent step-children). What about children born out of wedlock? *See* Glona v. American Guarantee & Liab. Ins. Co., 391 U.S. 73 (1968) (discrimination in parent's wrongful-death beneficiary status, on the basis of out-of-wedlock birth of decedent child, denies equal protection); Levy v. Louisiana, 391 U.S. 68 (1968) (discrimination in child's wrongful-death beneficiary status, on the basis of out-of-wedlock birth status as to decedent parent, denies constitutional equal protection). What about natural children of the decedent whom the decedent adopted out? *See* Phraner v. Cote Mart, Inc., 55 Cal. App.4th 166, 63 Cal. Rptr.2d 740 (Cal. Ct. App. 1997) (no recovery); *but see* Estate of Jones v. Howell, 687 So.2d 1171 (Miss. 1996) (yes, though damages might be difficult to establish). And what about the claim to wrongful-death beneficiary status of a decedent's parent whom law had not yet legally recognized as the decedent's parent during the decedent's lifetime? *See* Brookbank v. Gray, 74 Ohio St.3d 279, 658 N.E.2d 724 (1996) (beneficiary may prove parentage after child's wrongful death); *see also* Guard v. Jackson, 132 Wash.2d 660, 940 P.2d 642 (1997) (requiring father to prove financial support of child before child's wrongful death, to qualify as wrongful-death beneficiary, denies equal protection where there was no similar requirement of mother). Should a wrongful-death action exist for the death of an unborn child? *See* Aka v. Jefferson Hosp. Assn., 344 Ark. 627, 42 S.W.3d 508 (2001) (yes); Connor v.

Monkem Co., 898 S.W.2d 89 (Mo. 1995) (yes); Farley v. Sartin, 195 W. Va. 671, 466 S.W.2d 522 (1995) (yes); *but see* Tanner v. Hartog, 696 So.2d 705 (Fla. 1997) (no, unless the child was born alive); Kandel v. White, 339 Md. 432, 663 A.2d 1264 (1995) (same); Miller v. Kirk, 120 N.M. 654, 905 P.2d 194 (1995) (no, if the child was not viable at the time of injury).

Predeceasing the Decedent. Must at least one beneficiary exist to file a wrongful-death action? The statutory answer in most jurisdictions is yes—the cause of action fails without a beneficiary. *See* Murrell v. Springdale Memorial Hosp., 330 Ark. 121, 952 S.W.2d 153 (1997); Thomas v. Eads, 400 N.E.2d (Ind. App. 1980). Does that rule mean that the person whose tort kills an utter loner gets off free? What if a beneficiary living when the wrongful death occurred, dies before results in the wrongful-death action? *See* McDaniel v. Bullard, 34 Ill.2d 487, 216 N.E.2d 140 (1966) (wrongful-death claim survives with the beneficiary's estate as the beneficiary); Gray v. Goodson, 61 Wash.2d 319, 378 P.2d 413 (1963) (same).

Comparative Negligence. The law typically holds the decedent's comparative negligence to reduce wrongful-death beneficiaries' recovery by the decedent's percentage fault. *See* Horwich v. Superior Court, 21 Cal.3th 272, 980 P.2d 927, 87 Cal. Rptr.2d 222 (1999); Adamy v. Ziriakus, 92 N.Y.2d 396, 704 N.E.2d 216, 681 N.Y.S.2d 463 (1998). What about fault by the beneficiary contributing to the decedent's death? Although authority is inconsistent on this point, a beneficiary's fault most likely reduces the beneficiary's recovery but not the recovery of other beneficiaries. *See* Restatement (Third) of Torts: Apportionment of Liability §6 (2000).

Statutes of Limitations. What statute of limitations governs a wrongful-death action? Where the wrongful-death statute has its own limitations period, that period obviously governs—but do not assume that tolling provisions apply. *See* Moreno v. Sterling Drug, Inc., 787 S.W.2d 348 (Tex. 1990) (most jurisdictions do not apply tolling provisions to wrongful-death limitations periods); Taylor v. Black & Decker Mfg. Co., 21 Ohio App.3d 186, 486 N.E.2d 1173 (1984) (minority-tolling provision does not apply); *see also* Ortiz v. Gavenda, 590 N.W.2d 119, 590 N.W.2d 119 (Minn. 1999) (relation-back rule regarding pleading amendments, does not apply); *but see* LaFage v. Jani, 166 N.J. 412, 766 A.2d 1066 (2001) (tolling for beneficiary minors does apply).

C. Property Damage

OBJECTIVE: **Given various tort claims involving damage to property, identify the measure of recoverable damages and the proofs in support consistent with this section of the text.**

Case Study: A small-business owner owned stock she pledged to a bank to secure a short-term loan. The loan agreement permitted her to prepay the loan at any time through any means including by her sale of the pledged stock. When the small-business owner saw that her stock had risen to new highs, she directed the bank's loan agent to sell her stock to prepay the loan and to release the remaining funds to her. The agent wrongfully refused. In the 60 days that it took the small-business owner to convince the bank that she had the right to sell her stock to prepay the loan, the stock crashed to no value. ***Identify the measure of damages in the small-business owner's conversion action against the bank.***

The usual damages measure for tort claims involving destroyed personal property is the fair market value of the property at the time of its destruction. Most property has a market for its sale or exchange. Several sell and buy similar goods at prices that establish the market value of the destroyed good. The challenges in such cases can be to determine what constitutes a similar good and whether to adjust the sale prices of other similar goods to reflect dissimilarities in the goods or anomalies in the market. Buyers and sellers adjust vehicle values, for instance, for mileage, accidents, and condition. Buyers and sellers adjust equipment values for usage and age, reflecting depreciation in the equipments' useful life. A *fair market* sale is one in the ordinary course of business, not under cloud of title, undue time constraint, or other circumstances that distort the market. Indeed from the tort-law perspective, fair market value is typically the highest value that a seller could obtain in a market sale, not the lowest price that a buyer might pay—assuming any difference. Note that the price the owner paid for the property before its destruction or at which the owner listed the property for sale (if listed before destruction) is not the determining factor. While list prices are unreliable, a purchase price might be relevant evidence if the purchase was in a market sale close enough in time to the property's destruction to be material as to its market value when destroyed.

This process of determining comparable sales and adjusting pricing to reflect market anomalies or peculiar qualities of the destroyed good, lawyers usually perform with the assistance of a qualified appraisal professional. That is, lawyers for the parties must locate, retain, prepare, and qualify appraisal experts. An expert's licensure or certification, experience, and frequency and terms of retainer, can influence the expert's credibility. Factfinders may reasonably assume that an expert who works solely or primarily for the party who advocates the appraised value tends to favor the retaining party due to the retainer and relationship. Yet in the case of property values based on comparable sales, the main point of contention usually has less to do with the appraiser's credibility than the quality of the appraiser's work in finding and adjusting the comparable sales.

If the plaintiff property owner had purchased the destroyed property at wholesale and held it in bulk or otherwise for wholesale distribution, before its destruction, then it is the property's wholesale price that is the damages measure. If instead the owner purchased at retail, then the property's retail market value is the damages measure. If the owner held the property for use, and no local market offers a replacement for the destroyed property, then the parties must take a value from the nearest market, adding the property's transportation cost to its value. Value to the owner of property held for use tends to represent the cost of the property's replacement. On the other hand, if the property was for sale, then transportation cost to market may reduce the value. The selling owner would necessarily have incurred those costs, reducing the owner's sale profit. If the property was for speculative sale, such as a grain commodity or security, then some courts follow a highest-intermediate-sale rule allowing the plaintiff the commodity's peak value between the time of its destruction and the last possible sale date—up to the trial of the action. For instance, a bank that converts a customer's security by refusing to release it on the customer's authorized demand may have to pay the security's peak price after the date of the bank's first unauthorized refusal. Other courts follow New York's lead and follow a highest-replacement-value rule that grants the plaintiff the highest value between the destruction date and a reasonable time within which a diligent plaintiff would have replaced the property. *See* Restatement (Second) of Torts §927.

In rare cases, particularly where no market exists for the property or where the market does not reflect the property's value to the plaintiff, the courts will allow the plaintiff the property's personal value to the plaintiff. *See* Gasperini v. Center for Humanities, 66 F.3d 427 (2nd. Cir. 1995), *vacated,* 518 U.S. 415 (1996) (allowing award of up to $100,000 for lost photographic slides of war zone despite that plaintiff had earned only just over $10,000 from photography over a ten-year period). One might think of this situation as the *heirloom rule*. An old family photograph, wedding album, or piece of furniture may have only nominal value on a garage-sale market but, if representing treasured family events and history, may have substantial value to its owner. The criteria for establishing value in these cases might include the original cost, nature, and prospect for replacing the item, its use by the owner, and the reasons for its sentimental value. It would not include the owner's emotional distress over the loss. *See* White Consolid. Indus., Inc. v. Wilkerson, 737 So.2d 447 (Ala. 1999) (reversing award for mental anguish for fire loss of family photographs and heirlooms).

The measure of damages for property not destroyed but only damaged is the reduction in fair market value of the damaged property—that is, the difference in its value before and after damage. Again, the usual means of establishing reduction in value is by appraisal based on comparable values established by sales of similar property—in this case, two values, the first being the value of the property before its damage and the second being its value after its damage. Reduction-in-value cases are frankly more complex. Repair cost does not help because repair cost is not the damages measure. Certain damaged items may be inexpensive to repair but suffer substantial reduction in value because of the fact of repair. Collector-quality motor vehicles come to mind—that appraisal usually takes into account the fact of damage, reducing the vehicle value by more than the cost of repair. *See* BMW of North America, Inc. v. Gore, 517 U.S. 559 (1996) (unnoticed repainting of vehicle's hood reduced its value). Other damaged items may be expensive to repair but yet suffer little reduction in value if not repaired. Junker-quality motor vehicles come to mind—that appraisal takes little account of the fact of body damage (for instance), not reducing the vehicle value by as much as it would cost to repair. Repair cost may yet be admissible evidence in some cases, as indicative of the reduction in fair market value. Can you think of an example?

When the plaintiff property-owner suffers only a temporary deprivation of the property or its use, with the property neither destroyed nor damaged, the measure of damages is the property's rental value during the lost use. Think of rental value as the lost revenue the owner might have received by not being able to rent the property or as the cost of the owner's renting replacement property for the period of deprivation. In some cases where the damage is permanent or temporary deprivation, the plaintiff property owner may also be able to claim expenses related to attempts to locate and recover the property.

D. Punitive Damages

OBJECTIVE: Given various tort claims, identify which are likely to qualify for an award of punitive damages under the standards enunciated in this section of the text, and then articulate the constitutional limitations on such an award consistent with the Supreme Court case law in the text.

Case Study: A young woman suffered severe depression, post-traumatic stress, and mental and emotional disability causing wage loss, after a repairman attempted a sexual assault on her at her home. There is evidence to support that the repair service knew when it hired the repairman and assigned him to the work order that the repairman presented a sexual assault risk to its customers. Assuming that punitive damages are available in the jurisdiction in which the young woman's tort claims will be tried against the repair service, ***identify the criteria on which punitive damages may be awarded, in order that punitive damages may be investigated and the trial proofs and arguments planned.***

The above two sections address the compensatory damages available for personal injury and property damage—the remedy to restore the plaintiff to the position the plaintiff was in before the tort and to make the plaintiff whole. Punitive damages are a separate form of damages available in some (but not in other) jurisdictions. Their function is not to compensate for the plaintiff's harm but to punish the defendant—to make an example of the defendant to satisfy the plaintiff and public while deterring the defendant and others. Punitive damages are, in that sense, a civil justice system equivalent to punishments for crime. An actor who commits criminal misconduct that also causes injury or loss can be subject to both the civil and criminal justice systems. But in the more usual civil case for punitive damages, no prosecutor has charged the defendant with a crime for the civil wrong. The reasons have to do with the nature of both the civil and criminal justice systems. One finds little point to maintaining a civil action against a person who has committed an egregious crime for which the person will suffer long-term incarceration. If the defendant had any available financial resources at the time of the crime (which in itself would be unusual), then the defendant likely either exhausted those resources in the crime's defense or secreted them the reach of creditors. When, on the other hand, the injury-causing crime is of the more minor type that only the tort system redresses, prosecutors are often reluctant to spend their own scarce resources on what they may feel is only a civil matter.

Jurisdictions allowing punitive damages tend to require proof of a greater degree of culpability than mere negligence, such as malice, recklessness, or willful and wanton misconduct. *See In re Air Crash Disaster Near Chicago*, 644 F.2d 594 (7th Cir. 1981), cert. denied, 454 U.S. 878 (1981); *Owens-Illinois, Inc. v. Zenobia*, 325 Md. 420, 601 A.2d 633 (1992); *Allman v. Bird*, 186 Kan. 802, 353 P.2d 216 (1960). Gross negligence is a closer call, with some jurisdictions recognizing the right to punitive damages in such cases, *see Williams v Wilson*, 972 S.W.2d 260 (Ky. 1998), and others not, *Doe v. Isaacs*, 265 Va. 531, 579 S.E.2d 174 (2003). Of course, the commission of an intentional tort will usually qualify, provided that it evokes some sense of outrage and is not merely of the *Garratt v Dailey*, knowledge-of-a-substantial-certainty type. *See Jones v. Fisher*, 42 Wis.2d 209, 166 N.W.2d 175 (1969). Most jurisdictions also impose the higher, clear-and-convincing-evidence proof burden for an award of punitive damages. *See Rodriguez v. Suzuki Motor Corp.*, 936 S.W.2d 104 (Mo. 1996). Many state legislatures have acted to regulate punitive-damage awards. *See* Fla. Stat.

§768.73(1)(a) (three times compensatory damages); N.J. Stat. §2A:15-5.14 (greater of $350,000 or five times compensatory damages).

In those jurisdictions in which they are available, punitive damages can be controversial but can also serve important purposes. The controversy usually has to do with the seemingly arbitrary size of the punitive-damage award, at least when compared to the plaintiff's harm. When, for instance, the punitive award is one-hundred times the plaintiff's actual damages, the award can appear arbitrary, vindictive, and a windfall to the plaintiff. The United States Supreme Court has, in a series of recent cases, imposed increasingly strict standards for punitive damages awards, to a large degree federalizing their scrutiny under constitutional due-process standards. Criteria have always existed against which to measure punitive-damage awards. Those criteria include the reprehensibility of the defendant's harm, the defendant's profit from it, the defendant's wealth, the amount necessary to deter the defendant and others, and whether other fines or penalties are available for that purpose, and if so, their amount. Study shows that punitive awards are actually relatively rare and usually modest—within the reach or realm of the accompanying compensatory award. Why do you think that punitive damages, which have been around for hundreds of years, have recently become so controversial? Consider the following case.

Mathias v. Accor Econ. Lodging, Inc.
United States Court of Appeals, Seventh Circuit
347 F.3d 672 (7th Cir. 2003)

POSNER, J. The plaintiffs brought this diversity suit governed by Illinois law against affiliated entities (which the parties treat as a single entity, as shall we) that own and operate the "Motel 6" chain of hotels and motels. One of these hotels (now a "Red Roof Inn," though still owned by the defendant) is in downtown Chicago. The plaintiffs, a brother and sister, were guests there and were bitten by bedbugs, which are making a comeback in the U.S. as a consequence of more conservative use of pesticides. ... The plaintiffs claim that in allowing guests to be attacked by bedbugs in a motel that charges upwards of $100 a day for a room and would not like to be mistaken for a flophouse, the defendant was guilty of "willful and wanton conduct" and thus under Illinois law is liable for punitive as well as compensatory damages. ... The jury agreed and awarded each plaintiff $186,000 in punitive damages though only $5,000 in compensatory damages. The defendant appeals, complaining primarily about the punitive-damages award. It also complains about some of the judge's evidentiary rulings, but these complaints are frivolous and require no discussion. ...

The defendant argues that at worst it is guilty of simple negligence, and if this is right the plaintiffs were not entitled by Illinois law to any award of punitive damages. It also complains that the award was excessive—indeed that any award in excess of $20,000 to each plaintiff would deprive the defendant of its property without due process of law. The first complaint has no possible merit, as the evidence of gross negligence, indeed of recklessness in the strong sense of an unjustifiable failure to avoid a *known* risk... was amply shown. In 1998, EcoLab, the extermination service that the motel used, discovered bedbugs in several rooms in the motel and recommended that it be hired to spray every room, for which it would charge the motel only $500; the motel refused. The next year, bedbugs were again discovered in a room but EcoLab was asked to spray just that room. The motel tried to negotiate "a building sweep [by EcoLab] free of charge," but, not surprisingly, the negotiation failed. By the spring of 2000, the motel's manager "started noticing that there were refunds being given by my desk clerks and reports coming back from the guests that there were ticks in the rooms and bugs in the rooms that were biting." She looked in some of the rooms and discovered bedbugs. The defendant asks us to disregard her testimony as that of a disgruntled ex-employee, but of course her credibility was for the jury, not the defendant, to determine.

Further incidents of guests being bitten by insects and demanding and receiving refunds led the manager to recommend to her superior in the company that the motel be closed while every room was sprayed, but this was refused. ...

The infestation continued and began to reach farcical proportions, as when a guest, after complaining of having been bitten repeatedly by insects while asleep in his room in the hotel, was moved to another room only to discover insects there; and within 18 minutes of being moved to a third room he discovered insects in that room as well and had to be moved still again. (Odd that at that point he didn't flee the motel.) By July, the motel's management was acknowledging to EcoLab that there was a "major problem with bed bugs" and that all that was being done about it was "chasing them from room to room." Desk clerks were instructed to call the "bedbugs" "ticks," apparently on the theory that customers would be less alarmed, though in fact ticks are more dangerous than bedbugs because they spread Lyme Disease and Rocky Mountain Spotted Fever. Rooms that the motel had placed on "Do not rent, bugs in room" status nevertheless were rented.

It was in November that the plaintiffs checked into the motel. They were given Room 504, even though the motel had classified the room as "DO NOT RENT UNTIL TREATED," and it had not been treated. Indeed, that night 190 of the hotel's 191 rooms were occupied, even though a number of them had been placed on the same don't-rent status as Room 504. ...

Although bedbug bites are not as serious as the bites of some other insects, they are painful and unsightly. Motel 6 could not have rented any rooms at the prices it charged had it informed guests that the risk of being bitten by bedbugs was appreciable. Its failure either to warn guests or to take effective measures to eliminate the bedbugs amounted to fraud and probably to battery as well.... . There was, in short, sufficient evidence of "willful and wanton conduct" within the meaning that the Illinois courts assign to the term to permit an award of punitive damages in this case.

But in what amount? In arguing that $20,000 was the maximum amount of punitive damages that a jury could constitutionally have awarded each plaintiff, the defendant points to the U.S. Supreme Court's recent statement that "few awards [of punitive damages] exceeding a single-digit ratio between punitive and compensatory damages, to a significant degree, will satisfy due process." *State Farm Mutual Automobile Ins. Co. v. Campbell,* 538 U.S. 408, 123 S.Ct. 1513, 1524, 155 L.Ed.2d 585 (2003). The Court went on to suggest that "four times the amount of compensatory damages might be close to the line of constitutional impropriety." *Id.,* citing *Pacific Mutual Life Ins. Co. v. Haslip,* 499 U.S. 1, 23-24, 111 S.Ct. 1032, 113 L.Ed.2d 1 (1991), and *BMW of North America, Inc. v. Gore,* 517 U.S. 559, 581, 116 S.Ct. 1589, 134 L.Ed.2d 809 (1996). Hence the defendant's proposed ceiling in this case of $20,000, four times the compensatory damages awarded to each plaintiff. The ratio of punitive to compensatory damages determined by the jury was, in contrast, 37.2 to 1.

The Supreme Court did not, however, lay down a 4-to-1 or single-digit-ratio rule—it said merely that "there is a presumption against an award that has a 145-to-1 ratio," *State Farm Mutual Automobile Ins. Co. v. Campbell, supra,* 123 S.Ct. at 1524—and it would be unreasonable to do so. We must consider why punitive damages are awarded and why the Court has decided that due process requires that such awards be limited. The second question is easier to answer than the first. The term "punitive damages" implies punishment, and a standard principle of penal theory is that "the punishment should fit the crime" in the sense of being proportional to the wrongfulness of the defendant's action, though the principle is modified when the probability of detection is very low (a familiar example is the heavy fines for littering) or the crime is potentially lucrative (as in the case of trafficking in illegal drugs). Hence, with these qualifications, which in fact will figure in our analysis of this case, punitive damages should be proportional to the wrongfulness of the defendant's actions.

Another penal precept is that a defendant should have reasonable notice of the sanction for unlawful acts, so that he can make a rational determination of how to act; and so there have to be reasonably clear standards for determining the amount of punitive damages for particular wrongs.

And a third precept, the core of the Aristotelian notion of corrective justice, and more broadly of the principle of the rule of law, is that sanctions should be based on the wrong done rather than on the status of the defendant; a person is punished for what he does, not for who he is, even if the who is a huge corporation.

What follows from these principles, however, is that punitive damages should be admeasured by standards or rules rather than in a completely ad hoc manner, and this does not tell us what the maximum ratio of punitive to compensatory damages should be in a particular case. To determine that, we have to consider why punitive damages are awarded in the first place. See *Kemezy v. Peters,* 79 F.3d 33, 34-35 (7th Cir.1996).

England's common law courts first confirmed their authority to award punitive damages in the eighteenth century, ... at a time when the institutional structure of criminal law enforcement was primitive and it made sense to leave certain minor crimes to be dealt with by the civil law. And still today one function of punitive-damages awards is to relieve the pressures on an overloaded system of criminal justice by providing a civil alternative to criminal prosecution of minor crimes. An example is deliberately spitting in a person's face, a criminal assault but because minor readily deterrable by the levying of what amounts to a civil fine through a suit for damages for the tort of battery. Compensatory damages would not do the trick in such a case, and this for three reasons: because they are difficult to determine in the case of acts that inflict largely dignitary harms; because in the spitting case they would be too slight to give the victim an incentive to sue, and he might decide instead to respond with violence—and an age—old purpose of the law of torts is to provide a substitute for violent retaliation against wrongful injury—and because to limit the plaintiff to compensatory damages would enable the defendant to commit the offensive act with impunity provided that he was willing to pay, and again there would be a danger that his act would incite a breach of the peace by his victim.

When punitive damages are sought for billion-dollar oil spills and other huge economic injuries, the considerations that we have just canvassed fade. As the Court emphasized in *Campbell,* the fact that the plaintiffs in that case had been awarded very substantial compensatory damages—$1 million for a dispute over insurance coverage—greatly reduced the need for giving them a huge award of punitive damages ($145 million) as well in order to provide an effective remedy. Our case is closer to the spitting case. The defendant's behavior was outrageous but the compensable harm done was slight and at the same time difficult to quantify because a large element of it was emotional. And the defendant may well have profited from its misconduct because by concealing the infestation it was able to keep renting rooms. Refunds were frequent but may have cost less than the cost of closing the hotel for a thorough fumigation. The hotel's attempt to pass off the bedbugs as ticks, which some guests might ignorantly have thought less unhealthful, may have postponed the instituting of litigation to rectify the hotel's misconduct. The award of punitive damages in this case thus serves the additional purpose of limiting the defendant's ability to profit from its fraud by escaping detection and (private) prosecution. If a tortfeasor is "caught" only half the time he commits torts, then when he is caught he should be punished twice as heavily in order to make up for the times he gets away.

Finally, if the total stakes in the case were capped at $50,000 (2 x [$5,000 + $20,000]), the plaintiffs might well have had difficulty financing this lawsuit. It is here that the defendant's aggregate net worth of $1.6 billion becomes relevant. A defendant's wealth is not a sufficient basis for awarding punitive damages. ... That would be discriminatory and would violate the rule of law, as we explained earlier, by making punishment depend on status rather than conduct. Where wealth in the sense of resources enters is in enabling the defendant to mount an extremely aggressive defense against suits such as this and by doing so to make litigating against it very costly, which in turn may make it difficult for the plaintiffs to find a lawyer willing to handle their case, involving as it does only modest stakes, for the usual 33-40 percent contingent fee.

In other words, the defendant is investing in developing a reputation intended to deter plaintiffs. It is difficult otherwise to explain the great stubbornness with which it has defended this case, making a host of frivolous evidentiary arguments despite the very modest stakes even when the punitive damages awarded by the jury are included.
...

All things considered, we cannot say that the award of punitive damages was excessive, albeit the precise number chosen by the jury was arbitrary. It is probably not a coincidence that $5,000 + $186,000 = $191,000/191 = $1,000: i.e., $1,000 per room in the hotel. ...

But it would have been helpful had the parties presented evidence concerning the regulatory or criminal penalties to which the defendant exposed itself by deliberately exposing its customers to a substantial risk of being bitten by bedbugs. That is an inquiry recommended by the Supreme Court. See *State Farm Mutual Automobile Ins. Co. v. Campbell, supra,* 123 S.Ct. at 1520, 1526; *BMW of North America, Inc. v. Gore, supra,* 517 U.S. at 583-85, 116 S.Ct. 1589. But we do not think its omission invalidates the award. We can take judicial notice that deliberate exposure of hotel guests to the health risks created by insect infestations exposes the hotel's owner to sanctions under Illinois and Chicago law that in the aggregate are comparable in severity to the punitive damage award in this case.

"A person who causes bodily harm to or endangers the bodily safety of an individual by any means, commits reckless conduct if he performs recklessly the acts which cause the harm or endanger safety, whether they otherwise are lawful or unlawful." 720 ILCS 5/12-5(a). This is a misdemeanor, punishable by up to a year's imprisonment or a fine of $2,500, or both. ... Of course a corporation cannot be sent to prison, and $2,500 is obviously much less than the $186,000 awarded to each plaintiff in this case as punitive damages. But this is just the beginning. Other guests of the hotel were endangered besides these two plaintiffs. And, what is much more important, a Chicago hotel that permits unsanitary conditions to exist is subject to revocation of its license, without which it cannot operate. [C] We are sure that the defendant would prefer to pay the punitive damages assessed in this case than to lose its license.

AFFIRMED.

INQUIRY

Constitutional Limits. What are the constitutional limits on punitive damages? The above case provides a recent summary of the United States Supreme Court's punitive-damages jurisprudence. As the above case suggests, State Farm Mutual Auto. Ins. Co. v. Campbell, 538 U.S. 408 (2003), is the Supreme Court's lead opinion. In that case, a State Farm-insured motorist's attempt to pass six vans traveling ahead of him on a two-lane highway resulted in the death of an oncoming motorist who had swerved to avoid a head-on collision, and the serious injury of another motorist with whom the swerving motorist collided. State Farm refused to settle the resulting claims even though it could have done so for its $50,000 policy limits. When State Farm's insured suffered a verdict substantially in excess of those policy limits, he and his wife sued State Farm for bad faith, fraud, and intentional infliction of emotional distress for acts relating to its refusal to settle. A jury awarded them $2.6 million in compensatory and $145 million in punitive damages. The trial court reduced those amounts to $1 million and $25 million, respectively, but the Utah Supreme Court reinstated the $145 million punitive-damages award. The United States Supreme Court reversed and remanded the case, reiterating and elaborating the standard it had adopted in BMW of North America, Inc. v. Gore, 517 U.S. 559 (1996), under which the courts are to consider the reprehensibility of the defendant's conduct, the ratio between the harm and punitive damages (not as a bright-line rule but as a factor), and the ratio between the punitive damages and other civil or criminal penalties for the same or similar misconduct. On remand, the Utah Supreme Court imposed punitive damages of approximately $9 million on the basis of a 9-to-1 ratio. Campbell v. State Farm Mutual Auto. Ins. Co., 2004 UT. 34, 98 P.3d 409, 418, *cert. denied*, 125 S. Ct. 114 (2004).

After *State Farm,* the Supreme Court held constitutionally excessive $79.5 million in punitive damages, about one-hundred times the $821,000 compensatory award, in a smoking-death case Philip Morris, USA v. Williams, 549 U.S. 346 (2007). The jury had based the award in part on harm to nonparties, which the Supreme Court had previously rejected as unconstitutional in *BMW of North America.* In previously approving the $79.5 million in punitive damages, the Oregon Supreme Court had pointed out that harm to nonparties can look a lot like reprehensibility, which is a constitutionally permissible consideration. In reversing, the United States Supreme Court ruled that the state courts must ensure that juries distinguish between harm to nonparties (not a permissible consideration) and reprehensibility (still permissible).

The Supreme Court again addressed punitive damages in Exxon Shipping Co. v. Baker, 128 S.Ct. 2605 (2008), not under the constitutional due-process standard but as a matter of federal maritime law. There, it reduced the trial court's $4.5-billion punitive-damages award, which the appellate court had already reduced to $2.5-billion, to the $507.5-million amount of the compensatory damages, consistent with its *State Farm* case.

Defendant's Wealth. Of what relevance is the defendant's wealth? Although Judge Posner suggests in the case above that law considers the defendant's conduct rather than the defendant's status, and that to consider status is discriminatory, it is clear that wealth, or the ability to pay, is a factor commonly considered in justifying punitive damage awards. *See* Ore. Rev. Stat. §30.925 (2003) (defendant's financial condition is a permissible measure of punitive damages); Atlas Food Sys. and Svcs., Inc. v. Crane Nat. Vendors, Inc., 99 F.3d 587 (4th Cir. 1996) (defendant's ability to pay); Coats v. Construction & Gen. Laborers Local No. 185, 15 Cal. App.3d 908, 93 Cal. Rptr. 639 (1971) ("the wealth of the defendant"). What policy or rationale justifies considering the defendant's wealth? What evidence may the plaintiff discover and offer as to the defendant's wealth? *See* Corbetta v. Albertson's, Inc., 975 P.2d 718 (Colo. 1999) (no discovery of defendant's financial records permitted where punitive damages are tied to amount of compensatory damages). As defense counsel, what procedural protection would you request that the trial court afford your client against the bias evidence of wealth might engender among jurors who have not yet decided the liability issue? *See* Cal. Civ. Code Ann. §3295(d) (2004) (bifurcation of punitive-damages issue required on defendant's request); *see also* Kan. Stat. Ann. §60-3701(a)-(b) (2003) (jury determines punitive-damages liability but judge determines amount).

Relationship to Compensatory Damages. Must the defendant cause the plaintiff at least some compensable harm to uphold an award of punitive damages? *Compare* Cheatham v Pohle, 789 N.E.2d 467 (2003) ("A claim for punitive damages can be sustained only if it is accompanied by a viable claim for compensatory damages."); *with* Jacque v. Steenberg Homes, Inc., 209 Wis.2d 605, 563 N.W.2d 154 (1997) (allowing punitive damages for trespass that caused only nominal damages, against the contrary general rule); Clark v McClurg, 215 Cal. 279, 9 P.2d 505 (1932) (punitive damages allowed without award of compensatory damages). What if the defendant's malicious intent had no direct relationship to the compensatory harm but only occurred after it? *See* Moskovitz v. Mt. Sinai Medical Ctr., 69 Ohio St.3d 638, 635 N.E.2d 331 (1994) (punitive damages allowed for defendant's altering plaintiff's medical records to frustrate medical malpractice claim); *cf.* Ferguson v. Lieff, Cabraser, Heimann & Bernstein, 135 Cal. Rptr.2d 46, 30 Cal.4th 1037, 69 P.3d 965 (2003) (no punitive damages allowed against attorney in legal malpractice claim, where attorney's negligence resulted in potential loss of punitive-damages award in underlying case-within-a-case).

Practice

The lawyer promised his severely injured client that the lawyer would attend the defendant's sentencing in the related criminal action for negligent maiming with a watercraft, and report the sentence to the client. After all, the client had a huge and quite legitimate grievance against the defendant who had recklessly run over him with a boat. The client's life would never be the same, given the injury's severity. But at the hearing, the sentencing judge was apologetic to the defendant. "You look to me like a decent man who was caught in a bad situation," the judge opined, adding, "It could

> have happened to any of us." The sentence amounted to a very small fine, some community service, and to pay for the victim's eyeglasses and clothing the defendant had ruined. The sentence did not include paying for the tens of thousands of dollars in medical expense or for the victim's fractured, disfigured, and permanently scarred face, head, and neck, severe depression and headaches, and emotional outbursts related to the victim's serious closed-head injury. "Good thing," the lawyer thought to himself, "that the client wasn't here."

Discretion. Should law require punitive damages in the most egregious of cases? *See* Luke v. Mercantile Acceptance Corp., 111 Cal. App.2d 431, 244 P.2d 764 (1952) (jury has discretion to refuse to make punitive-damage award). Should law allow punitive-damages awards against an estate, where the wrongdoer is no longer around to be punished and deterred? *See* G.J.D. v. Johnson, 552 Pa. 169, 713 A.2d 1127 (1998) (ex-boyfriend distributes sexually explicit photographs of plaintiff before committing suicide) (punitive damages allowed despite that majority of jurisdictions would not). What if the defendant has already paid punitive damages in a case involving related or similar misconduct? *See* Ore. Rev. Stat. §30.925(2)(g) (2003) (paid punitive damages are admissible in mitigation); Owens-Corning Fiberglas Corp. v. Malone, 972 S.W.2d 35 (Tex. 1998) (same). What if criminal conviction has already punished the defendant? *See* Hanover Ins. Co. v. Hayward, 464 A.2d 156 (Me. 1983) (criminal penalties already imposed may be considered in determining whether to award punitive damages as an additional deterrent); *but see* Owens-Illinois, Inc. v. Zenobia, 325 Md. 420, 601 A.2d 633 (1992) (criminal penalties not admissible). As defense counsel, would you recommend that your client offer evidence of its prior punishment for the misconduct presently under consideration?

Recovery of Punitive Damages. If the purpose of punitive damages is to punish rather than to compensate, should the defendant pay all or some of the punitive damages award to a state fund rather than to the plaintiff? *See* Ore. Rev. Stat. §31.735 (2003) (60% of punitive damages are to be paid into a state crime victims compensation fund); In. Code §34-51-3-6(b)(2) (1995) (75% of punitive damages are to be paid into a state crime victims compensation fund). Must legislation require punitive damages paid to the state, or may a court make that order on its own? *See* Dardinger v. Anthem Blue Cross & Blue Shield, 98 Ohio St.3d 77, 781 N.E.2d 121 (2002) (order to pay part of $30 million punitive award to state university research fund). Should the judge tell the jury where the funds would go? *See* Ford v. Uniroyal Goodrich Tire Co., 267 Ga. 226, 476 S.E.2d 565 (1996) (no—not relevant).

Insurance Coverage. Should liability insurance cover punitive damages? One would think at first blush that the issue would be one of interpretation of the insurance contract language—and it is in one respect, that if the insurance policy does not arguably provide for payment of punitive damages, then no basis exists for that payment. But even when the policy language does permit an inference of punitive-damages coverage, courts split on whether public policy would permit or bar enforcement of such a contract. *Compare* Allen v. Simmons, 533 A.2d 541 (R.I. 1987) (wrongdoer, not insurer, pays punitive damages); Guardianship of Est. of Smith, 507 P.2d 189 (Kan. 1973) (same), *with* Whalen v. On-Deck, Inc., 514 A.2d 1072 (Del. 1986) (insurer pays because wrongdoer would be deterred by higher premium payments); Greenwood Cemetery, Inc. v. Travelers Indemn. Co., 232 S.E.2d 910 (Ga. 1977) (same).

> **Careers**
> Some lawyers begin their law careers doing tort-litigation work, joining defense firms whose clients include major liability insurers. Other lawyers who start in solo practice or small general-practice law firms may gradually begin to take simpler tort cases (perhaps motor-vehicle-accident cases) to augment their transactional and other practice. Over time, those lawyers may develop gradually more sophisticated, risky, and expensive tort-practices including products-liability, medical-malpractice, and other complex claims and even class actions. Some tort lawyers also practice employment and civil-rights litigation, which are liability cases of another complex type drawing on similar investigation, evaluation, and advocacy skills. If you have an interest in tort practice, then explore these practice-development questions with experienced lawyers. Doing so will help you discern your path into a rewarding practice field.

TORTS I—PRACTICING TORT LAW

CHAPTER XVI

MULTIPLE PARTIES

Wrongs can involve multiple human agents—understood from the cautionary aphorisms that bad company corrupts good character and that two walking together agree. Single, indivisible injuries or losses can arise from concerted, coincident, or consecutive action by two or more potentially liable defendants. Injury or loss can also arise from the failure of two or more persons to execute a duty that they each owe to the person they harmed. Law recognizes several ways in which two or more persons or entities must pay for the same harm. The liability of one person or entity does not preclude the liability of another. Because multiple defendants may all be liable for the same harm, law has rules for distributing and adjusting the liability among them. Law traditionally treats the liability of multiple defendants under rules for satisfaction and release, joint and several liability, vicarious liability, contribution, and indemnity. This chapter treats each of these rules in turn—recognizing that any one case may implicate two, several, or all of these rules. In studying multiple-parties rules, keep in mind again that tort reform, by statute and case law, has made substantial changes to the traditional rules stated here. Learn the traditional rules first, though, to better understand the changes.

A. Satisfaction and Release

OBJECTIVE: Given the payment of all or part of a tort claim by one defendant under various circumstances including settlement agreements and judgments, analyze and determine the obligation of remaining defendants to the plaintiff consistent with the law and principles stated in this section of the text.

The vast majority of tort cases settle before trial. *Settlement* of a tort case refers to an agreement eliminating or *releasing* the liability of the settling defendants in exchange for their payment of a certain amount within a reasonable time after the parties document the settlement. *Satisfaction* refers to a different means by which the parties resolve tort cases after (much less frequent) trial and court judgment. When a jury returns a verdict, read in court and written on verdict form, the lawyers reduce the verdict to a judgment that the judge signs and the court enters. If the judgment stands after any appeal or other post-trial challenges to it, and the defendants convey to the plaintiff the amount owed under the judgment or the plaintiff otherwise collects by garnishment or execution, then plaintiff's counsel prepares, signs, and files with the court a paper titled "satisfaction of judgment."

Skills
Although customs vary in how to execute a settlement, and the method can depend on both local convention and the attorneys' professional relationship, the lawyers typically exchange drafts of the settlement agreement until both sides accept its form. The plaintiff then signs it, and the plaintiff's lawyer conveys the signed original to

> the defense lawyer with a cover letter indicating to hold it in escrow until the defense lawyer conveys the settlement funds. The defense lawyer obtains the settlement check from the insurance company and, with the plaintiff's signed release already in hand, conveys the check to the plaintiff's lawyer who, after obtaining any needed endorsements on the check, immediately places the settlement funds in the law firm's trust account until the funds clear. *See* ABA Model Rules of Professional Conduct, Rule 1.15. While awaiting the funds, the plaintiff's lawyer presents the plaintiff with a settlement statement itemizing the expenses, fees, and proposed disbursement, which the plaintiff approves and signs. The plaintiff's lawyer then presents the client with a trust-account check for the net proceeds. If the plaintiff had already filed the case, then simultaneous with the preparation and execution of the settlement agreement, the lawyers execute a voluntary dismissal with prejudice of the court case, which the defense lawyer holds in escrow until supplying the settlement check. How would the procedure be different in the case of the satisfaction of a judgment?

When but a single liable or potentially liable party exists, the settlement of liability and release of the defendant, or satisfaction of judgment, is relatively simple. In the case of a single defendant, the central considerations involve what liability the parties settle (for which injuries and torts occurring over what period), how much the defendant pays for the settlement, and when the defendant will make the payment (if not immediately, meaning within a reasonable time of when the parties agree to settle). Although the parties' intent ordinarily controls in construing a settlement agreement, unintentionally overbroad descriptions of the released rights and claims can result in the loss of those rights and claims. Other common issues involve whether the amount of the settlement remains confidential (given advantages and disadvantages to both plaintiff and defendant in its disclosure) and whether plaintiff agrees to indemnify defendant against claims others bring against the defendant for the settled liability. Another less-common issue involves whether defendant may discharge in bankruptcy any financial obligations undertaken in the settlement agreement. Counsel for all parties must certainly take care to anticipate and document these matters. A plaintiff may ordinarily set aside a release only for fraud, duress, or undue influence, or on the grounds of mutual mistake, meaning that the plaintiff who assumes that an injury is less severe than it really is, does so at the plaintiff's own peril. *See* Mack v. Albee Press, 32, N.Y.S.2d 231, *affd.*, 288 N.Y. 623, 42 N.W.2d 617 (1942) (bruised-toe settlement bars recovery for eventual amputation of leg). Consider the following illustrative case involving a state statute meant to give plaintiffs a limited procedural remedy for improvident settlements.

Maglin v. Tschannerl
Vermont Supreme Court
174 Vt. 39, 800 A.2d 486 (2002)

JOHNSON, J. Plaintiff Beth Maglin appeals a Windham Superior Court order granting defendant Janaki Tschannerl's motion for summary judgment on plaintiff's personal injury claim for harm suffered in an automobile accident. The court held that a release signed by plaintiff after the accident barred her from seeking further relief. Plaintiff claims that the release should be voided because 1) the release violates the legislative remedy for rush releases, 12 V.S.A. § 1076; 2) there was a mutual mistake of fact concerning her injury; and 3) it is unconscionable to enforce the release. We affirm.

Defendant's car hit plaintiff's car from behind in a two-car accident on March 12, 1996. Plaintiff's car did not sustain major damage, but plaintiff suffered from whiplash. Ten days after the accident, an agent from defendant's insurance company, State Farm Insurance, visited plaintiff at her home. Plaintiff told the insurance agent she incurred "minor whiplash" from the accident. Plaintiff accepted the insurance agent's $500 as compensation for the accident in exchange for her agreeing to release defendant from all possible future claims. The release stated: "For the sole consideration of $500.00 the receipt and sufficiency is hereby acknowledged, the undersigned hereby releases and forever discharges [defendant] from any and all claims ... causes of action or suits of any kind or nature whatsoever, and particularly on account of *all injuries, known and unknown, both to the person and the property, which have resulted or may in the future develop* from an accident which occurred on or about the 12th day of March, 1996." (Emphasis added.) At the time, plaintiff knew she sustained injury, but believed the $500 to be reasonable compensation for what she viewed as a minor accident with minor injuries. Plaintiff did not consult a physician about her injuries or an attorney about possible claims against defendant. Nevertheless, she signed the release.

Shortly after signing the release, plaintiff's symptoms worsened. She experienced significant neck pain, headaches, nausea, pain in her arms, numbness in her hands, and she could not stand, sit, or lie down comfortably. Plaintiff's chiropractor subsequently diagnosed her symptoms as stemming from whiplash. Her chiropractor explained to her that whiplash injuries are commonly misunderstood and underestimated until serious symptoms occur. Plaintiff incurred medical expenses in excess of $10,000 for treatment for her whiplash injury and other symptoms. ...

Plaintiff filed a complaint for personal injury damages alleging that defendant's negligence resulted in severe personal injuries to plaintiff. ... In granting defendant summary judgment, the court concluded that the release is valid and enforceable. ... This appeal followed. ...

Before we turn to the specific claims of plaintiff, we note that there is a substantial body of case law with facts similar to those presented here, and that plaintiff is correct that the trend is to avoid releases on the various legal grounds plaintiff has raised here. [Cc] Apparently, it is quite common for people to enter into early releases without fully considering the consequences. Because of the unjust results in many of these cases, courts have responded by avoiding releases between injured parties and insurance companies. [C] An examination of those numerous decisions reveals at least one truth—that the greater the disparity in the actual damages that manifested themselves after the signing of a release, and the amount paid in the early settlement, the more likely it is that the court will find some manner of voiding the release. The grounds for decision vary, but include avoidance of the release on mutual mistake of fact, or on what courts have found to be a more "objective" view of the parties' intent, or because the surrounding circumstances were considered unconscionable. [Cc] To be sure, there are contrary decisions that reject the distortion of mistake of fact doctrine and contract interpretation, and that hold to the competing policies that underlie the validity of releases voluntarily and knowingly given. [Cc]

... We turn first, then, to the application of the statute and the impact of legislative policy on plaintiff's claims.

Section 1076 governs disavowal of releases for claims of personal injury or death. The statute provides in part that: "[a]n agreement entered into by a person or his legal representative within fifteen days after personal injury to him ... may be disavowed by such person or his legal representative within three years after making the agreement." *Id.* In addition, 12 V.S.A. § 1077 further requires that to disavow the release plaintiff must return "any consideration received to the person who paid or delivered the same."

Plaintiff failed to comply with either of the requirements imposed by the statutes to disavow the release. She did not meet the three-year limitation period, nor did she return the consideration received for the release. ...

Moreover, in view of the statute, we are constrained, in the absence of extraordinary facts, to find a common law remedy for plaintiff. Plaintiff argues that the release should be avoided on the basis of mutual mistake of fact, because she was mistaken as to the extent of her injuries. ... But plaintiff showed only that *she* was mistaken as to her injuries. Without a mutual mistake of fact "one of the parties can no more rescind the contract without the other's express or implied assent, than he alone could have made it." *Enequist v. Bemis*, 115 Vt. 209, 212, 55 A.2d 617, 619 (1947) (internal quotations omitted). In any event, the release signed by plaintiff explicitly covered "all injuries, known and unknown, both to the person and the property, which have resulted or may in the future develop." ...

Plaintiff complains that defendant's insurance agent was in a more powerful bargaining position based on his greater experience with whiplash injuries. Even if this allegation were true, this power differential is not enough to void the release-the power imbalance must have been used to coerce the weaker party. Here, the contract is not unconscionable because there is nothing in the record to indicate that the insurance agent coerced plaintiff into signing the release, or that plaintiff believed that she had no choice but to sign the release. Plaintiff produced no evidence showing any other circumstances, other than her desire to receive $500 for what she considered a minor injury, that compelled her *to* sign it. ... Because she had an opportunity for meaningful choice when the release was presented to her, any differential in bargaining power was not critical to the contract's formation and not enough to void the release as unconscionable.

In sum, plaintiff produced no evidence of extraordinary circumstances that would compel us to overcome, on common law grounds, the effect of the release entered into by the parties. Summary judgment was properly granted. [C]

Affirmed.

INQUIRY

Options. What is the better rule in these cases? Some courts follow a rule that enforces a release as to unknown consequences of known injuries but not for unknown injuries. *See* Neuve v. Close, 123 Wash.2d 253, 867 P.2d 635 (1994) (alleging neck sprain, settled for $150, was known but back injury unknown). Others analyze whether the plaintiff was mistaken in the plaintiff's understanding of the nature of the injury. *See* Gleason v. Guzman, 623 P.2d 378 (Colo. 1981) (remand to determine whether plaintiff guardian was mistaken on nature of head injury to minor). Both of these rules create greater opportunity to have a release set aside than the rule of mutual mistake discussed in the *Maglin* case above. *See also* Bernstein v. Kapneck, 290 Md. 452, 430 A.2d 602 (1981).

Drafting. What language might you draft when representing a defendant obtaining the plaintiff's release? Should the law always enforce a release that explicitly states that the plaintiff assumes the risk of unknown injuries, when the plaintiff realizes that risk? *See* Smothers v. Richland Mem. Hosp., 328 S.C. 566, 493 S.W.2d 107 (1997) (release language that plaintiff assumed risk bars claim for unknown injuries); *cf.* Williams v. Glash, 789 S.W.2d 261 (Tex. 1990) (parties' intent controls, but evidence of intent can go beyond the release's language). Should a release of personal-injury claims bar a wrongful-death claim brought after the person signing the release has died from tort injuries? The majority rule bars wrongful-death actions after settlement of personal-injury claims. *See* Varelis v. Northwestern Mem. Hosp., 167 Ill.2d 449, 212 Ill. Dec. 652, 657 N.E.2d 997 (1995); *but see* Sea-Land Services v. Gaudet, 414 U.S. 573 (1974) (for some admiralty cases); Alfonev v. Sarno, 87 N.J. 99, 432 A.2d 857 (1981) (not necessarily barred, but duplication of damages not allowed).

Improvident Settlement. The *Maglin* case above shows one legislature's attempt to address the problem of improvident settlements. *See also* Md. Cts. & Jud. Proc. Code §5-401.1 (plaintiff signing release within five days of injury may void it within 60 days). Can you think of any other alternatives? *See* N.Y. Judic. L. §480 (unlawful in most cases to enter hospital with purpose of obtaining release through settlement).

Ethics

The client, not the lawyer, decides whether to settle. The ABA Model Rules of Professional Conduct admonish in Rule 1.2(a) that "[a] lawyer shall abide by a client's decision whether to settle a matter." Rule 1.4(a) also requires that lawyers "promptly inform a client of any decision or circumstance with respect to which the client's informed consent ... is required" and to "keep the client reasonably informed about the status of the matter... ." To comply with these rules, tort lawyers immediately convey settlement offers as soon as received, in writing to their clients. When several defendants make a global settlement favoring multiple plaintiffs, how and when may the lawyers address the settlement's benefits and obligations? Rule 1.8(g) of the ABA Model Rules of Professional Conduct admonishes attorneys who represent two or more clients in the same matter not to "participate in making an aggregate settlement of the claims of or against the clients" unless each client gives written, informed consent. Informed consent requires that the attorney disclose "the existence and nature of all claims" and "the participation of each person in the settlement." Routinely, every party knows what they must pay and what they will receive before they finalize a settlement. An exception is an estate's settlement of a wrongful-death claim, in which determining the portion each beneficiary receives occurs after the settlement in a probate proceeding.

Single-Satisfaction Rule. The tort claim involving only a single liable or potentially liable person or entity is the exception rather than the rule. Law must have rules for when multiple parties have joint-and-several liability, and one or more but not all parties settle. A first rule is that plaintiffs get only a single satisfaction of their damages, no matter how many defendants may be liable. *See* Saichek v. Lupa, 204 Ill.2d 127, 787 N.E.2d 827, 272 Ill. Dec. 641 (2003); Bundt v. Embro, 48 Misc.2d 802, 265 N.Y.S.2d 872 (1965). Increasing the number of defendants who are liable for the plaintiff's loss does not increase the amount of plaintiff's recovery, which tort law instead measures by plaintiff's provable damages. Indeed, once trial determines plaintiff's damages, the verdict and judgment may collaterally estop the plaintiff from seeking a greater amount of damages in a second trial against other defendants who shared the same liability. *See* Nielson v. Spanaway General Med. Clinic, Inc., 135 Wash.2d 255, 956 P.2d 312 (1998); *but cf.* Kirkpatrick v. Chrysler Corp. (920 P.2d 122 (Okla. 1996) (treat satisfaction of consent judgments as only partial satisfaction if plaintiff is able to prove consent judgment represented only partial damages).

Partial-Satisfaction Rule. The single-satisfaction rule has a corollary partial-satisfaction rule that a defendant who has not yet paid its liability gets credit for amounts paid by other defendants for the same injury. Non-settling defendants get a credit for settling defendants' payments either dollar-for-dollar, *see* Va. Code Ann. §8.01-35.1 (2004), or by the percentage of fault of the settling defendant, *see* Jones v. Ahlberg, 49 N.W.2d 576 (N.D. 1992)—the latter being the approach the Restatement (Third) of Torts: Apportionment of Liability §26 (2000) favors. The order of granting credits and making other adjustments to the verdict can change the outcome. A current trend favors the plaintiff, deducting settlements from the verdict amount before reducing the verdict by the plaintiff's comparative negligence. *See* Whalen v. Kawasaki Motors Corp., 680 N.Y.S.2d 435, 92 N.Y.2d 288, 703 N.E.2d 246 (1998). States split on whether to apply damages caps before or after deducting settlements. *See* Fairfax Hosp. Sys., Inc. v Nevitt, 249 Va. 591, 457 S.E.2d 10 (1995) (cap first, then settlement credit); *but see* Teeter v. Missouri Hwy. & Transp. Comn., 891 S.W.2d 817 (Mo. 1995) (settlement credit, then cap). In states eliminating joint-and-several liability, setoffs and credits for settlements are unnecessary because each defendant presumably pays only its own pro-rata liability. *See* Neil v. Kavena, 176 Ariz. 93, 859 P.2d 203 (App. 1993).

Release Rules. Settlement with one out of a number of potentially liable defendants also raises the question of the form and effect of the settling defendant's release. Traditionally, the release of one defendant was a release of all defendants who would have been jointly and severally liable—no matter the intent of the settling parties or the language of their release. The traditional rule made some conceptual sense and eliminated the credit issues seen just above, but it also discouraged prompt settlement and encouraged unreasonable holdouts. Some jurisdictions recognized an exception for covenants not to sue—an artificial contrivance in which the plaintiff only promised not to sue but did not technically release the defendant. Today, states divide in the way they treat the effect on other parties of the release of one. Some hold to the traditional distinction that a release of one releases all, while a covenant not to sue releases only the covenanting defendant. Others hold (by case law or statute) that releases expressly reserving rights against non-settling defendants release only the settling defendant but that releases without a reservation release all. Still others construe a release as its parties intended, to release only those whom the agreement so indicates, not requiring any magic language. The Uniform Contribution Among Tortfeasors Act §4 (1955) follows the last approach to the release of joint tortfeasors.

SETTLEMENT AGREEMENT AND RELEASE

In consideration for the payment to them of the amount of _____ dollars ($_____), receipt of which they acknowledge, **CLAIMANTS** release and forever discharge **RESPONDENT**, and its agents, employees, attorneys, insurers, representatives, officers, directors, predecessors, successors, and assigns, from all claims, demands, and causes of action for loss, damages, injuries, claims, and liability, whether known or unknown, and whether past or present, arising out of the fire incident on **INCIDENT DATE**, involving **CLAIMANTS** and their residence at **ADDRESS**, and further release these entities from all other liability which was alleged or which could have been alleged in the case entitled **CLAIMANTS** v **RESPONDENT**, **COUNTY** Circuit Court No. **CASE NUMBER**. **CLAIMANTS** further agree to promptly dismiss with prejudice and without costs that pending case and any other case or legal proceeding against the released entities and to forebear from filing or causing to be filed any other legal claim or proceeding to enforce the rights, claims, and interests released by this agreement.

The parties expressly understand and agree that they enter into this settlement agreement and release as a compromise and resolution of disputed claims. This settlement agreement and release is not an admission of liability or of the validity of any of the claims, which **RESPONDENT** instead expressly denies.

Any persons signing this agreement on behalf of any other individuals or corporate entities represent and warrant that they have obtained all authorizations, resolutions, and approvals, have met the requirements for any insurance or bond, and have otherwise met all other rules and legal requirements necessary to their binding and effective release of the above persons and entities. They further represent and warrant that in signing this agreement they have relied on themselves or on the advice of their own chosen representatives and counsel and not on any representation or omission made by the opposing parties or their representatives and counsel. This paper contains all the terms of the settlement agreement and release between these parties. The parties make no representation beyond the scope of this writing, on which the opposing party may rely for entering into this agreement. This agreement is voluntary.

CLAIMANT HUSBAND   **CLAIMANT WIFE**

Signed: _____   Signed: _____

Related Parties. Tort practitioners must take care to identify exactly whom their documents release. Defendants are reasonable in their concern that they not pay for their torts twice by obtaining their own release, only to have the plaintiff sue a related party (perhaps an employee, agent, director, officer, or representative) whom counsel did not expressly identify in the release but whom the same defendants owe indemnity. The temptation arises for defendants to demand a release of "any and all persons or entities having any connection whatsoever with the matter alleged." Courts continue to reasonably construe a general release of that nature, entered into only between the plaintiff and one defendant who pays only for that defendant's liability, as a release of all persons and entities—including those whose liability remains unpaid and owing. *See* Enos v. Key Pharmaceuticals, Inc., 106 F.3d 838 (8th Cir. 1997) (general release obtained by physician releases claims against drug manufacturers); Collas v. Garnick, 425 Pa. Super. 8, 624 A.2d 117 (1993) (malpractice claim allowed for lawyer's having advised general release when unpaid claims remained). The plaintiff may have to prove mutual mistake to proceed against defendants whose liability the parties to the general release did not intend to extinguish. *See* Hess v. Ford Motor Co., 117 Cal. Rptr.2d 220, 27 Cal.4th 516, 41 P.3d 46 (2002).

Release of Agents. Legal rules similarly vary as to the effects of releasing an employee or agent for whose tortious acts an employer or principal has vicarious liability. In some jurisdictions, the release of the agent employee releases the employer principal. *See* Williams v. Vandeberg, 620 N.W.2d 187 (S.D. 2000) (agent driver's release discharges principal); Anne Arundel Med. Ctr., Inc. v. Condon, 102 Md. App.

408, 649 A.2d 1189 (1994) (doctor's release discharges employer hospital). In others, it does not. *See* JFK Med. Ctr. v. Price, 647 So.2d 833 (Fla. 1994) (doctor's release does not discharge employer hospital). The following case on *Mary Carter* agreements illustrates the concerns and strategies regarding settlement by fewer than all potentially liable defendants. As the case indicates, states take a variety of approaches to these agreements, either allowing them, allowing them only if not secret, or holding them void. You may never encounter a *Mary Carter* agreement, but notice from the following case how parties change positions as their financial interests change.

Elbaor v. Smith
Texas Supreme Court
845 S.W.2d 240 (1992)

GONZALEZ, J. In this medical malpractice case we consider... whether Mary Carter agreements are void as contrary to public policy. The trial court rendered judgment in favor of the plaintiff, and the court of appeals affirmed. 845 S.W.2d 282. We hold that ... Mary Carter agreements are void as against public policy.[fn] We thus reverse the judgment of the court of appeals and remand this cause to the trial court for a new trial.

I.

At 2:00 a.m. on May 8, 1985, Carole Smith was seriously injured in a single-vehicle accident when the Corvette she was driving left the highway and collided with a tree. She received emergency treatment at the Dallas/Fort Worth Medical Center-Grand Prairie ("D/FW Medical Center") from Dr. Abraham Syrquin for multiple injuries including a compound fracture of her left ankle. ...

While Ms. Smith was at ACH, she was treated by a team of physicians including Dr. Elbaor, Dr. Joseph Stephens, a plastic surgeon, and Dr. Bienvenido Gatmaitan, an infectious disease specialist. ... On June 3, Ms. Smith was transferred to the care of Dr. Wayne Burkhead at Baylor University Medical Center ("Baylor"). Four days after admission, Dr. Burkhead removed a two inch section of bone from Ms. Smith's ankle. Ms. Smith received treatment from several orthopedic specialists over the next three years which ultimately led to the fusion of her ankle joint.

Ms. Smith filed suit against D/FW Medical Center, ACH, Drs. Syrquin, Elbaor, Stephens, and Gatmaitan. Sometime before trial, Ms. Smith entered into Mary Carter agreements with Dr. Syrquin, Dr. Stephens, and ACH.[fn] The Mary Carter agreements provided for payments to Ms. Smith of $350,000 from Dr. Syrquin, $75,000 from ACH, and $10 from Dr. Stephens. Under the terms of each agreement, the settling defendants were required to participate in the trial of the case. The agreements also contained pay-back provisions whereby Dr. Syrquin and ACH would be reimbursed all or part of the settlement money paid to Ms. Smith out of the recovery against Dr. Elbaor. ...

At trial, the jury found that Ms. Smith's damages totalled $2,253,237.07, of which Dr. Elbaor was responsible for eighty-eight percent, and Dr. Syrquin for twelve percent. After deducting all credits for Dr. Syrquin's percentage of causation and settlements with other defendants, the trial court rendered judgment against Dr. Elbaor for $1,872,848.62. ...

III.

... Although the Mary Carter agreements were not entered into evidence, the trial judge was troubled by them and he took remedial measures to mitigate their harmful effects by reapportioning the peremptory challenges, changing the order of proceedings to favor Dr. Elbaor, allowing counsel to explain the agreements to the jury, and instructing the jury regarding the agreements.[fn]

During the trial, the settling defendants' attorneys, who sat at the table with Dr. Elbaor's attorneys, vigorously assisted Ms. Smith in pointing the finger of culpability at Dr. Elbaor. This created some odd conflicts of interest and some questionable representations of fact. For example, although Ms. Smith's own experts testified that Dr. Syrquin committed malpractice, her attorney stated during voir dire and in her opening statement that Dr. Syrquin's conduct was "heroic" and that Dr. Elbaor's negligence caused Ms. Smith's damages. And during her closing argument, Ms. Smith's attorney urged the jury to find that Dr. Syrquin had not caused Ms. Smith's damages. This is hardly the kind of statement expected from a plaintiff's lawyer regarding a named defendant. ACH and Drs. Syrquin and Stephens had remained defendants of record, but their attorneys asserted during voir dire that Ms. Smith's damages were "devastating," "astoundingly high," and "astronomical." Furthermore, on cross examination they elicited testimony from Ms. Smith favorable to her and requested recovery for pain and mental anguish. The settling defendants' attorneys also abandoned their pleadings on Ms. Smith's contributory negligence, argued that Ms. Smith should be awarded all of her alleged damages, and urged that Dr. Elbaor was 100 percent liable.

A.

... A Mary Carter agreement exists when the settling defendant retains a financial stake in the plaintiff's recovery and remains a party at the trial of the case.[fn] This definition comports with both the present majority view[fn] and the original understanding of the term.[16] [FN16. The first case to utilize the term "Mary Carter agreement" was Ward v. Ochoa, 284 So.2d 385, 386 (Fla.1973). The Florida Supreme Court defined a Mary Carter agreement as "a contract by which one co-defendant secretly agrees with the plaintiff that, if such defendant will proceed to defend himself in court, his own maximum liability will be diminished proportionately by increasing the liability of the other co-defendants." Id. at 387.]

A Mary Carter agreement exists, under our definition, when the plaintiff enters into a settlement agreement with one defendant and goes to trial against the remaining defendant(s). The settling defendant, who remains a party, guarantees the plaintiff a minimum payment, which may be offset in whole or in part by an excess judgment recovered at trial. [Cc] This creates a tremendous incentive for the settling defendant to ensure that the plaintiff succeeds in obtaining a sizable recovery, and thus motivates the defendant to assist greatly in the plaintiff's presentation of the case (as occurred here). Indeed, Mary Carter agreements generally, but not always, contain a clause requiring the settling defendant to participate in the trial on the plaintiff's behalf.

Given this Mary Carter scenario, it is difficult to surmise how these agreements promote settlement. Although the agreements do secure the partial settlement of a lawsuit, they nevertheless nearly always ensure a trial against the non-settling defendant. [C] Mary Carter agreements frequently make litigation inevitable, because they grant the settling defendant veto power over any proposed settlement between the plaintiff and any remaining defendant. [C] Thus, "[o]nly a mechanical jurisprudence could characterize Mary Carter arrangements as promoting compromise and discouraging litigation-they plainly do just the opposite." Stein v. American Residential Mgmt., 781 S.W.2d 385, 389 (Tex.App.-Houston [14th Dist.] 1989), writ denied per curiam, 793 S.W.2d 1 (Tex.1990). ...

The case before us reveals yet another jury trial and verdict distorted by a Mary Carter agreement. The trial judge, who fully grasped the detrimental effect these agreements could have on the outcome, attempted to monitor the lawsuit by assiduously applying the guidelines suggested in the Smithwick concurrence[,724 S.W.2d at 8-12]. The conduct of this trial, however, confirms the apprehension expressed by Justice Spears in Smithwick: that these remedial measures would only mitigate and not eliminate the unjust influences exerted on a trial by Mary Carter agreements. Equalizing peremptory strikes, reordering proceedings, thoroughly disclosing the true alignment of the parties, and revealing the agreement's substance cannot overcome collusion between the plaintiff and settling defendants who retain a financial interest in the plaintiff's success. ...

This case typifies the kind of procedural and substantive damage Mary Carter agreements can inflict upon our adversarial system. Thus, we declare them void as violative of sound public policy. ...

... Accordingly, we reverse the judgment of the court of appeals and remand this cause to the trial court for further proceedings consistent with this opinion.

DOGGETT, J., dissenting. Today a medical doctor is prohibited from participating in the trial of a lawsuit in which he is a defendant. This extraordinary and unprecedented maneuver is rooted in the majority's growing distrust of our jury system—its unfounded belief that twelve ordinary citizens are incapable of assessing facts after full disclosure of all the surrounding circumstances. Plunging helter-skelter into uncharted territory to save another medical doctor that a jury found to have committed malpractice, the majority writes without regard to the chaotic effect of its ruling on both the retrial of this action and other complex litigation pending across Texas. Because today's decision only serves to inject uncertainty and unfairness into trials, I dissent. ...

The chief problem associated with a Mary Carter agreement is that a hidden alteration of the relationship of some of the parties will give the jury a misleading and incomplete basis for evaluating the evidence. As is true in so many areas of jurisprudence, secrecy is the first enemy of justice. To address this concern, trial judges have appropriately implemented several procedural safeguards that remove the veil of secrecy from such settlements. Accordingly, we have emphasized the importance of complete disclosure of these arrangements. [Cc] A concurrence to Smithwick suggested a number of specific protections regarding such agreements: discovery of them by the non-settling parties; their pretrial disclosure to the court; thorough explanation of the nature of their terms to the jury at the beginning of the trial; and restriction of a settling defendant's leading questions of the plaintiff's witnesses. 724 S.W.2d at 9-11 (Spears and Gonzalez, JJ., concurring).[fn]

In the instant case the trial court took great care to safeguard procedurally the adversarial nature and fairness of its proceedings. Nothing about the agreements now under attack was hidden from anyone.[fn] The court appropriately solicited and welcomed suggestions from Elbaor and the other parties as to what and when to tell the jury about the Mary Carter agreements.[fn] At voir dire, the court informed prospective jury members that ACH and Syrquin, by participating in the trial, could recover all or a portion of the amounts paid in settlement to Smith, depending on the size of the verdict.[fn] An additional warning was extended regarding the possibility of witness bias arising from the agreements.f[fn] The implications of the agreements were also explored by various counsel during voir dire.[fn]

To offset any disadvantage to Elbaor resulting from the agreements, the trial court gave him the same number of peremptory challenges as those of Smith and the three settling defendants together. Recognizing that these settling parties effectively were no longer aligned against one another, the trial court denied them the customary right of an opponent to lead each other's witnesses. Finally, the order of presentation was changed to guarantee that Elbaor always had the final opportunity to present evidence and examine witnesses. ... Despite Elbaor's concession that "[t]he trial court [correctly] followed Texas law when it disclosed the Mary Carter agreements and implemented the other procedures to protect [him],"[fn] the majority rejects these procedures as "miss[ing] the point," [c], thereby renewing its commitment to limit the role of the jury in the truth-seeking process. [C] Simply because jurors may initially expect the plaintiff to have interests adverse to all defendants does not mean that they are incapable of understanding that certain defendants have an incentive for the plaintiff to succeed. Indeed the same may occur in some multiparty litigation where no Mary Carter agreement is involved. The trial cannot be a "sham of adversity," [c], when the jury, as here, is fully aware of this shift in alliances. Nor does the trial become less adversarial merely because some of the parties have switched sides-the names may have changed but the struggle is left intact. So long as at least two parties with antagonistic interests remain, the likelihood that the truth will emerge is not diminished.[fn]

Accordingly, most jurisdictions allow Mary Carter agreements when trial courts implement similar procedural safeguards to those adopted here. [Cc] In rejecting the full disclosure approach, today's opinion embraces a decidedly minority view accepted in only "a couple of states" that have previously chosen to prohibit such agreements. [C][fn] Indeed, the majority cannot point to a single case in any jurisdiction that has ever approved today's prohibition of a named party from participating at trial because of a disclosed pretrial agreement. ...

Texas has today become the first state in the nation to lock the courthouse door on a party solely because of a pretrial contract involving a partial settlement which the majority dislikes. The elitist view that ordinary people acting as jurors are incapable of determining the facts after full disclosure has once again prevailed. While protecting the litigation process from deleterious agreements, this court should avoid precipitous action with uncertain consequences for so many litigants, particularly when, as here, the parties have exercised considerable care and the trial court has conscientiously monitored the proceedings.

Practice

The lawyer's co-counsel calmly reassured the husband-and-wife clients, "Please understand that whether you want to settle for what they are offering is your decision. We've talked about the pros and cons. Whatever you decide, I want you to know that we are behind you—that we will take this case to trial and do our best for you, or we will support you if you want to settle. That is our obligation, and we will live up to it. We are perfectly comfortable with whatever decision you make. Okay?" The clients took a

> deep breath and relaxed—especially the wife, whose permanently disabled husband now had at best a couple years to live because of the tort matter over which they had filed the case. A hard afternoon in settlement talks with the facilitator had gotten them nowhere. The lawyers were risking tens of thousands of dollars and hundreds of hours of time on a case that now seemed to be going nowhere. Just that morning, the lawyer had seen another lawyer yelling at his client in the courthouse hallway that the client had to settle or the lawyer would withdraw. In this case, though, nine months later, shortly before trial, the husband-and-wife clients settled—for significantly more than defendants had offered at the facilitation. The lawyer and co-counsel had two very appreciative clients.

B. Joint-and-Several Liability

OBJECTIVE: Given descriptions of torts involving two or more culpable parties one or more of who are not collectible, apply the joint tortfeasor rules stated in this section of the text to determine which party is responsible for what portion of the damages.

The traditional tort-law rule of joint-and-several liability means that a plaintiff may require any one of multiple liable defendants to pay for the entire harm or may require that any number of them pay portions adding up to the entire harm. The rule of joint-and-several liability gives the plaintiff the option from whom to collect an award. In that sense, joint-and-several liability treats plaintiffs better than alternative modern rules—or at least gives them more options where the options may mean the difference among full recovery, partial recovery, or no recovery. If, for instance, one defendant is uncollectible, under joint-and-several liability the plaintiff may turn to any other liable defendant to pay the full award. Under joint-and-several liability, the plaintiff need not have a reason for collecting all or a portion of the award from one defendant instead of another. The plaintiff's reason might be that one defendant is uninsured and uncollectible, but the reason could just as well be a matter of the plaintiff's principle or convenience. Defendants who pay more than their fair share of an award may then attempt to recover the excess they paid by a contribution claim (discussed below) against the laggard defendant—but without other recourse if that defendant is uncollectible. Joint-and-several liability thus places the burden of an uncollectible defendant on the other defendants, not the plaintiff. The rule's rationale is that the defendants all committed wrong, dividing responsibility and dividing harm are only tenuous concepts, and better the culpable defendants than innocent plaintiff bear the burden of uncollectible defendants.

> **Skills**
> Just because two or more persons or entities are potentially liable does not mean that the plaintiff names them all as defendants in the same lawsuit. Plaintiffs and their lawyers make strategic decisions whether to name a person or entity as a defendant, including based on whether the plaintiff can collect a judgment against the person or entity. Other criteria include the relationship of the plaintiff to that person or entity (good or bad), the relative degree of their culpability, and the effect of adding them or leaving them out on the claims against the other defendants. Is an empty chair (one that the unnamed party would have occupied) better for the plaintiff or defendant? Another consideration is which collection of defendants have sufficient resources to pay

plaintiff's full recovery. Some plaintiff's lawyers would also consider the effect of having additional defense lawyers on the other side. Any other criteria? What would you need to know to advise a plaintiff which of the following defendants to name in a products-liability case—the product's designer, manufacturer, component-part supplier, distributor, retailer, customer who first purchased the product, person to whom the customer resold it and who owned it when the plaintiff was injured by it, or person who was using it when plaintiff suffered injury? When a plaintiff does not name a culpable person or entity as a defendant, the named defendant may be able to add that person or entity as a third-party defendant. What would you, as defense counsel, want to know about each of the above persons or entities to decide whether to do so, if you represented the person who was using the product when plaintiff suffered injury?

Actions in Concert. With that understanding of how joint-and-several liability operates, consider how it arises. Joint-and-several liability can arise in several ways. The first, and conceptually the easiest to grasp, involves concerted action of two or more culpable parties. When two or more act together with intention toward some end—whether productive, recreational, beneficial, or harmful—and do so in a way that results in an intentional tort or negligence claim, they are jointly and severally liable. Their concerted action may be in the manufacture of a product, the planning of an event, the competition of a race, or any other joint action. *See* Herman v. Wesgate, 464 N.Y.S.2d 315 (App. Div. 1983) (defendant groom and barge owners may be liable in concert for injury at stag party due to negligence involved in throwing party-goers into shallow water from barge). They may intend the injury. *See* Thompson v. Johnson, 180 F.2d 431 (5th Cir. 1950) (one defendant beats plaintiff while two others restrain defendant's wife from coming to plaintiff's aid—all three defendants liable for acting in concert); Garrett v. Garrett, 228 N.C. 530, 46 S.2d 2d 302 (1948) (two defendants drag plaintiff from her home and beat her in the street, acting in concert). Or one defendant may instead act negligently but have the substantial assistance of the other who either knows of the other's negligence or is negligent in providing the assistance. *See* Restatement (Second) of Torts §876 (1965); Bierczynski v. Rogers, 239 A.2d 218 (1968) (two negligent defendant drivers race, one colliding with plaintiffs' vehicle—both liable for acting in concert). Consider the following case.

Ravo v. Rogatnick
New York Court of Appeals
514 N.E.2d 1104 (N.Y. 1987)

ALEXANDER, J. In this medical malpractice action, defendant, Dr. Irwin L. Harris, appeals from an order of the Appellate Division, 121 A.D.2d 705, 503 N.Y.S.2d 890, unanimously affirming an amended judgment of Supreme Court, entered on a jury verdict, finding him jointly and severally liable with Dr. Sol Rogatnick for injuries negligently inflicted upon plaintiff, Josephine Ravo, and resulting in brain damage that has rendered her severely and permanently retarded. The issue presented is whether joint and several liability was properly imposed upon defendant under the circumstances of this case where, notwithstanding that the defendants neither acted in concert nor concurrently, a single indivisible injury—brain damage—was negligently inflicted. For the reasons that follow, we affirm.

I.

Uncontroverted expert medical evidence established that plaintiff, Josephine Ravo, who at the time of trial was 14 years of age, was severely and permanently retarded as a result of brain damage she suffered at birth. The evidence demonstrated that the child was born an unusually large baby whose mother suffered from gestational diabetes which contributed to difficulties during delivery. The evidence further established that Dr. Rogatnick, the obstetrician who had charge of the ante partum care of Josephine's mother and who delivered Josephine, failed to ascertain pertinent medical information about the mother, incorrectly estimated the size of the infant, and employed improper surgical procedures during the delivery. It was shown that Dr. Harris, the pediatrician under whose care Josephine came following birth, misdiagnosed and improperly treated the infant's condition after birth. Based upon this evidence, the jury concluded that Dr. Rogatnick committed eight separate acts of medical malpractice, and Dr. Harris committed three separate acts of medical malpractice.

Although Dr. Rogatnick's negligence contributed to Josephine's brain damage, the medical testimony demonstrated that Dr. Harris' negligence was also a substantial contributing cause of the injury. No testimony was adduced, however, from which the jury could delineate which aspects of the injury were caused by the respective negligence of the individual doctors. ...

The trial court instructed the jury that if they found that both defendants were negligent, and that their separate and independent acts of negligence were direct causes of a single injury to the plaintiff, but that it was not possible to determine what proportion each contributed to the injury, they could find each responsible for the entire injury even though the act of one may not have caused the entire injury, and even though the acts of negligence were not equal in degree. The court further instructed the jury that if they found that both defendants were negligent, they would have "to compare their negligence on the basis of 100 percent." The court also instructed the jury that if they found both defendants responsible for the plaintiff's injury "then you will evaluate their respective faults in contributing to the infant's condition."

... [T]he jury returned a verdict for plaintiff in the total amount of $2,750,000 attributing 80% of the "fault" to Dr. Rogatnick and 20% of the "fault" to Dr. Harris.

In a postverdict motion, Dr. Harris sought an order directing entry of judgment limiting the plaintiff's recovery against him to $450,000 (20% of the $2,250,000 base recovery-the court having setoff $500,000 received by plaintiff in settlement of claims against other defendants) based upon his contention that his liability was not joint and several, but rather was independent and successive. This motion was denied. The Appellate Division dismissed Harris' appeal from the order denying the postverdict motion and affirmed the amended judgment entered on the jury's verdict.

II.

When two or more tort-feasors act concurrently or in concert to produce a single injury, they may be held jointly and severally liable ([cc]). This is so because such concerted wrongdoers are considered "joint tort-feasors" and in legal contemplation, there is a joint enterprise and a mutual agency, such that the act of one is the act of all and liability for all that is done is visited upon each ([c]). On the other hand, where multiple tort-feasors "neither act in concert nor contribute concurrently to the same wrong, they are not joint tort-feasors; rather, their wrongs are independent and successive" ([c]). Under successive and independent liability, of course, the initial tort-feasor may well be liable to the plaintiff for the entire damage proximately resulting from his own wrongful acts ([c]) including aggravation of injuries by a successive tort-feasor ([cc]). The successive tort-feasor, however, is liable only for the separate injury or the aggravation his conduct has caused ([cc]).

It is sometimes the case that tort-feasors who neither act in concert nor concurrently may nevertheless be considered jointly and severally liable. This may occur in the instance of certain injuries which, because of their nature, are incapable of any reasonable or practicable division or allocation among multiple tort-feasors ([cc]).

...

... [H]ere the jury was unable to determine from the evidence adduced at trial the degree to which the defendants' separate acts of negligence contributed to the brain damage sustained by Josephine at birth. Certainly, a subsequent tort-feasor is not to be held jointly and severally liable for the acts of the initial tort-feasor with whom he is not acting in concert in every case where it is difficult, because of the nature of the injury, to separate the harm done by each tort-feasor from the others ([cc]). Here, however, the evidence established that plaintiff's brain damage was a single indivisible injury, and defendant failed to submit any evidence upon which the jury could base an apportionment of damage.

Harris argues, however, that since the jury ascribed only 20% of the fault to him, this was in reality an apportionment of damage, demonstrating that the injury was divisible. This argument must fail. Clearly, the court's instruction, and the interrogatory submitted in amplification thereof, called upon the jury to determine the respective responsibility in negligence of the defendants so as to establish a basis for an apportionment between them, by way of contribution, for the total damages awarded to plaintiff ([cc]). In that respect, the jury's apportionment of fault is unrelated to the nature of defendants' liability (i.e., whether it was joint and several or independent and successive).

Here, the jury determined that the defendants breached duties owed to Josephine Ravo, and that these breaches contributed to her brain injury. The jury's apportionment of fault, however, does not alter the joint and several liability of defendants for the single indivisible injury. Rather, that aspect of the jury's determination of culpability merely defines the amount of contribution defendants may claim from each other, and does not impinge upon plaintiff's right to collect the entire judgment award from either defendant (CPLR 1402). As we stated in *Graphic Arts Mut. Ins. Co. v. Bakers Mut. Ins. Co.,* 45 N.Y.2d 551, 557, 410 N.Y.S.2d 571, 382 N.E.2d 1347: "The right under the *Dole-Dow* doctrine to seek equitable apportionment based on relative culpability is not one intended for the benefit of the injured claimant. It is a right affecting the distributive responsibilities of tort-feasors *inter sese* ... It is elementary that injured claimants may still choose which joint tort-feasors to include as defendants in an action and, regardless of the concurrent negligence of others, recover the whole of their damages from any of the particular tort-feasors sued ([c])." This being so, in light of the evidence establishing the indivisibility of the brain injury and the contributing negligence of Dr. Harris, and of the manner in which the case was tried and submitted to the jury, we conclude that joint and several liability was properly imposed.

Accordingly, the order of the Appellate Division should be affirmed.

INQUIRY

Indivisible Injuries. Another way in which joint-and-several liability arises involves independent action by two or more parties each of whom owes the plaintiff duties, their breaches of which result in an *indivisible injury*. One culpable party creates a risk of harm that the other culpable party's actions will cause the plaintiff an injury that no one can separate as to the two parties' independent actions. An indivisible injury might be something like the trauma caused to a passenger in a single car crash. If a mechanic's negligent repair was a cause of the crash, but so was the driver's negligence, then those independent careless acts (repair and driving) will have produced an indivisible injury (the passenger's trauma from the car crash), so that mechanic and driver are jointly and severally liable. If the injuries from the independent actions are divisible (perhaps injury to the arm by one and to the leg by another), then the plaintiff has only separate tort claims, not claims for joint-and-several liability. Consider the following case.

Coney v. J.L.G. Indus., Inc.
Illinois Supreme Court
97 Ill.2d 104, 454 N.E.2d 197, 73 Ill. Dec. 337 (1983)

MORAN, J. Clifford M. Jasper died as a result of injuries sustained on January 24, 1978, while operating a hydraulic aerial work platform manufactured by defendant, J.L.G. Industries, Inc. Plaintiff, Jack A. Coney, administrator of Jasper's estate, filed a two-count complaint in the circuit court of Peoria County under the wrongful death and survival acts [c] based on a strict products liability theory. Defendant filed two affirmative defenses. The first asserted that Jasper was guilty of comparative negligence or fault in his operation of the platform. The second contended that Jasper's employer, V. Jobst & Sons, Inc., was also guilty of comparative negligence in failing to instruct and train Jasper on the operation of the platform and by failing to provide a "groundman." In these defenses, defendant requested that its fault, if any, be compared to the total fault of all parties and any judgment against defendant reflect only its percentage of the overall liability, i.e., that defendant not be held jointly and severally liable. …

[The court asked:] Whether the doctrine of comparative negligence or fault eliminates joint and several liability? …

The common law doctrine of joint and several liability holds joint tortfeasors responsible for the plaintiff's entire injury, allowing plaintiff to pursue all, some, or one of the tortfeasors responsible for his injury for the full amount of the damages. [Cc]

Defendant asserts joint and several liability is a corollary of the contributory negligence doctrine. Prior to Alvis[v. Ribar, 85 Ill.2d 1, 52 Ill. Dec. 23, 421 N.W.2d 886 (1981)], a plaintiff who was guilty of even slight contributory negligence was barred from recovery. Defendant maintains that joint and several liability balanced this inequity by permitting a faultless plaintiff to collect his entire judgment from any defendant who was guilty of even slight negligence. With the adoption of comparative negligence where damages are apportioned according to each party's fault, defendant argues it is no longer rational to hold a defendant liable beyond his share of the total damages. Defendant relies primarily on a line of cases where joint and several liability was abolished or limited in the course of construing a statutory scheme of liability. [Cc]

The vast majority of jurisdictions, however, which have adopted comparative negligence have retained joint and several liability as a part of their comparative negligence doctrine: [cc].

Generally, four reasons have been advanced for retaining joint and several liability:

(1) The feasibility of apportioning fault on a comparative basis does not render an indivisible injury "divisible" for purposes of the joint and several liability rule. A concurrent tortfeasor is liable for the whole of an indivisible injury when his negligence is a proximate cause of that damage. In many instances, the negligence of a concurrent tortfeasor may be sufficient by itself to cause the entire loss. The mere fact that it may be possible to assign some percentage figure to the relative culpability of one negligent defendant as compared to another does not in any way suggest that each defendant's negligence is not a proximate cause of the entire indivisible injury.

(2) In those instances where the plaintiff is not guilty of negligence, he would be forced to bear a portion of the loss should one of the tortfeasors prove financially unable to satisfy his share of the damages.

(3) Even in cases where a plaintiff is partially at fault, his culpability is not equivalent to that of a defendant. The plaintiff's negligence relates only to a lack of due care for his own safety while the defendant's negligence relates to a lack of due care for the safety of others; the latter is tortious, but the former is not.

(4) Elimination of joint and several liability would work a serious and unwarranted deleterious effect on the ability of an injured plaintiff to obtain adequate compensation for his injuries. [Cc]

In adopting comparative negligence, this court eliminated the total bar to recovery which a plaintiff had faced under contributory negligence. In return for allowing a negligent plaintiff to recover, this court said fairness requires that a plaintiff's damages be "reduced by the percentage of fault attributable to him." (Emphasis added.) (Alvis v. Ribar (1981), 85 Ill.2d 1, 25, 52 Ill.Dec. 23, 421 N.E.2d 886.) Were we to eliminate joint and several liability as the defendant advocates, the burden of the insolvent or immune defendant would fall on the plaintiff; in that circumstance, plaintiff's damages would be reduced beyond the percentage of fault attributable to him. We do not believe the doctrine of comparative negligence requires this further reduction. Nor do we believe this burden is the price plaintiffs must pay for being relieved of the contributory negligence bar. The quid pro quo is the reduction of plaintiff's damages. What was said in American Motorcycle Association v. Superior Court (1978), 20 Cal.3d 578, 590, 578 P.2d 899, 906, 146 Cal.Rptr. 182, 189, is applicable here: "[F]airness dictates that the 'wronged party should not be deprived of his right to redress,' … '[t]he wrongdoers should be left to work out between themselves any apportionment.' " …

Defendant concedes that where the plaintiff is free from fault each defendant should still be held jointly and severally liable. It also admits in its reply brief that the Act leaves unaffected the common law doctrine of joint and several liability. Defendant points out, however, that it was subsequent to the enactment of the Act that this court adopted comparative negligence. Now, under Alvis, damages are allocated according to fault. As such, defendant argues, Alvis mandates that a tortfeasor should be liable only to the extent that his negligent acts or omissions produced the damages.

We find nothing in Alvis which mandates either a shift in who shall bear the risk of the insolvent defendant or the elimination of joint and several liability. Defendant has not cited nor have we found persuasive judicial authority for the proposition that comparative negligence compels the abolition of joint and several liability. On the contrary, most jurisdictions which have adopted comparative negligence have retained the doctrine. Therefore, we hold that our adoption of comparative negligence in Alvis does not change the long-standing doctrine of joint and several liability. ...

Therefore, in response to the questions posed, we conclude that (1) comparative fault is applicable to strict products liability actions; (2) comparative fault does not eliminate joint and several liability; and (3) retention of joint and several liability does not deny defendants equal protection of the laws. ...

Affirmed and remanded, with directions.

INQUIRY

Failure in Common Duties. Another way in which joint-and-several liability arises is when two or more parties each owe and each fail in the same or similar duties to the plaintiff, resulting in the plaintiff's loss or injury. The parties may have a relationship to one another. For example, a hotel and security company may both owe a hotel patron a duty of reasonable care with respect to the security of the premises. If both fail in that duty in a way that causes the patron loss or injury, then they may be jointly and severally liable—along with the criminal or other person who directly caused the loss or injury. *See* Nallan v. Helmsley-Spear, Inc., 50 N.Y.2d 507, 429 N.Y.S.2d 606, 407 N.E.2d 451 (1980) (building owner and manager each liable for failing to protect patron from gunman who shot patron while patron was signing guest register). Or a manufacturer and retailer may be jointly and severally liable for failure to warn against injury caused by a defective product. *See* Marcon v. Kmart Corp., 573 N.W.2d 728 (Minn. App. 1998) (Kmart to pay full $8 million award where defendant manufacturer was bankrupt). In another common instance, one of the defendants may be jointly and severally liable to the plaintiff because of the defendant's vicarious liability for the wrong of another defendant who is directly liable—as in the case of employer vicarious liability for harm caused by the negligent actions of an employee within the course and scope of employment (see below). Both the employer and employee would be jointly and severally liable.

Abolition of Joint-and-Several Liability. The section well above on comparative negligence intimated that most states have altered or supplanted joint-and-several liability. Increased confidence in comparing fault between plaintiff and defendant led to willingness to allocate fault among defendants—which, in turn, led to questioning joint-and-several liability. Fifteen states retain traditional joint-and-several liability— Pennsylvania, Maryland, and Massachusetts among them. Sixteen states abolish joint-and-several liability—Arizona, Indiana, Michigan, and Tennessee among them. Beyond that, permutations proliferate. California, Connecticut, Florida, New York, and Ohio (among eight states) abolish joint-and-several liability for non-economic damages (pain and suffering) only but not for economic damages (wage loss, medical expense, etc.). Four states, Georgia and Missouri among them, abolish joint-and-several liability in cases where the plaintiff is at least partly at fault. Colorado abolishes joint-and-several liability for personal injury and wrongful death unless the defendants "consciously conspire and deliberately pursue a common plan or design to commit a tortious act...." Colo. Rev. Stat. §13-21-111.5(1), (4). Idaho has abolished it for all torts other than intentional torts and those relating to hazardous waste and medical and pharmaceutical products (surely an interesting combination). Hawaii has abolished it for governmental entities. Iowa, New Hampshire, Texas, New Jersey, and Wisconsin have abolished joint-and-several liability for defendants whose fault is less than a certain percentage—for example, 50 percent in New Hampshire, *see* N.H. Rev. Stat. §507:7-e(b) (West 1997). Other states combine certain of the above options, as in New Jersey where joint-and-several liability no longer exists for tort cases as to defendants whose fault is less than 60% of the total, except for environmental torts where the state preserves the doctrine. N.J. Stat. §2A:15-5-5.3. Recognizing no real consensus, the Restatement (Third) of Torts: Apportionment of Liability §27 (2000) takes no position on which to prefer but instead suggests what to do when a state has chosen a certain option.

> **Figure**
> Trial attorney Judith Livingston, a senior partner in the New York law firm of Kramer, Dillof, Livingston & Moore, claims credit as the youngest lawyer and first female advocate to enter the Inner Circle of Advocates—the top 100 plaintiff's trial lawyers in the country. She gained that credit with over 100 successful trials and settlements in personal-injury, medical-malpractice, and other tort cases. She is a fellow of the International Academy of Trial Lawyers, a member of the International Society of Barristers and several other professional organizations, and lectures frequently both nationally and in New York on medical malpractice, courtroom conduct, and women as trial lawyers.

Allocation of Fault. One common modification replaces joint-and-several liability with allocating fault by percentages among the defendants and apportioning damages by those percentages. *See* Restatement (Second) of Torts §433A (1965) (apportionment when reasonable basis exists for determining relative responsibility). In this system, each defendant pays only the apportioned share. If a defendant is uncollectible, then that defendant's pro rata share goes unpaid, and the plaintiff makes less than a full recovery. Abrogating joint-and-several liability undermines the rationale that culpable defendants should bear the burden of uncollectible loss and departs at least in part from tort law's twin policies of compensating the injured and deterring misconduct. *See* American Motorcycle Assn. v. Superior Ct., 20 Cal.3d 578, 578 P.2d 899, 146 Cal. Rptr. 182 (1978); Kaeo v. Davis, 68 Haw. 447, 719 P.2d 387 (1986). An alternative system that does not entirely supplant but only modifies joint-and-several liability is one that allocates fault and apportions damages, but if any defendant is uncollectible, the collectible defendants pay the uncollected portion based on their relative percentage liability. In this system, each defendant initially pays only its share and then pays a percentage share of uncollected portions. The plaintiff receives a full recovery if collectible defendants are capable of paying the full award. The Uniform Comparative Fault Act and several states including Connecticut, Michigan, Minnesota, and Missouri, follow this modified approach.

Disclosure to the Jury. How much of the consequences of an allocation system should a jury learn, before making its decision? That is, should the jury know what the effects of its allocation would be, or should the jury just make the allocation, the judge provide for the apportionment of damages, and the parties bear the consequences? *See*

Kaeo v. Davis, 68 Haw. 447, 719 P.2d 387 (1986) (city granted request to have jury told that it will pay whole award if found as little as one percent at fault, under joint-and-several liability).

Uncollectible Defendants. What happens under these modified systems when a party is immune from suit, has unknown identity, is uncollectible, or is for some other reason not a named defendant, but is responsible in part for the plaintiff's injury or loss? That situation presents no difficulty for traditional tort law. The plaintiff cannot sue immune persons or entities, or the unidentified, and would not sue the uncollectible. The plaintiff would hold liable only the named defendants, each jointly and severally liable for plaintiff's full injury or loss. Yet with increased experience allocating fault and apportioning damages among parties, increased confidence in the wisdom of doing so, and increased lobbying for change in tort laws, some states have provided for the allocation of fault to non-parties. *See* Joseph v. Broussard Rice Mill, Inc., 772 So.2d 94 (La. 2000); *see also* Ind. Code §§34-51-2-7 & 2-15 (defendant has burden of proof on non-party fault, and notice of non-party fault must identify non-party by name). Of course, the non-party pays no damages. Rather, the plaintiff goes uncompensated for that portion of the plaintiff's loss that the court allocates to the non-party. Some states recognizing non-party fault allow for allocation of fault to a non-party immune from suit. *See* Mack Trucks, Inc. v. Tackett, 841 So.2d 1107 (Miss. 2003); Dotson v. Blake, 29 S.W.2d 26 (Tenn. 2000); *but see* Snyder v. LTG Lufttechnische GmbH, 955 S.W.2d 252 (Tenn. 1997) (court cannot assess fault against immune employer). Allocation to an uncollectible non-party seems less troubling because not every loss receives compensation. Allocation to an unidentified person or entity seems more troubling, not knowing whom one blames. *See* Bencivenga v. J.J.A.M.M., Inc., 609 A.2d 1299 (N.J. Super. App. Div. 1992) (holding that apportionment statute did not provide for allocation to fictitious non-party). But allocation to an immune party seems to contradict the purpose of the immunity, while burdening the plaintiff.

Intentional-Tort Liability. What if one or more of the tortfeasors (parties or non-parties) committed an intentional tort while others were merely negligent? Should law allocate percentages between intentional and negligent acts that differ fundamentally in their culpability? *See* Brandon v. County of Richardson, 261 Neb. 636, 624 N.W.2d 604 (2001) (no allocation to killer non-parties in suit against county for failure to protect); Welch v. Southland Corp., 134 Wash.2d 629, 952 P.2d 162 (1998) (statute does not permit comparison of intentional shooting to negligent protection); *but see* Hutcherson v. City of Phoenix, 192 Ariz. 51, 961 P.2d 449 (1998) (allocation of 25% to killer and 75% to city that negligently handled 911 call that would have saved life).

C. Vicarious Liability

OBJECTIVE: Given evidence that one person or entity was acting for another person or entity in the course of which a tort occurred, apply the rules articulated in this section to determine whether there is vicarious liability.

Case Study: A man operated a car-detailing business out of the back of Jerry's do-it-yourself carwash. The man and one employee would spend all day picking up corporate and rental cars for hand cleaning. Throughout the day, they would also check the do-it-yourself car wash for its owner to be sure that the garbage pails were empty, the stalls clean of debris, and the coin- and bill-changers operating. They would also take complaints and give refunds for the owner. In return, the owner charged the man no rent for the use of the back area on the premises, although the man gave the owner some cash now and then to help with the water and electric bills. They had only one sign out front for both the owner's do-it-yourself carwash and the man's detailing service. Most people thought that they were partners, and they did not discourage the impression, although they kept their own books and filed their own tax returns. The owner paid the man's helper to mow the grass. A customer of the owner's lost an eye using one of the carwash wands and sued both the owner and the man who ran the detailing service. ***Discuss and evaluate the vicarious liability of the man who owned the detailing service.***

Vicarious liability is the liability of a party that is not at fault, for the torts of another person or entity. In that sense, vicarious liability is a form of strict liability. The party liable for the other's tort need not have done anything wrong in the usual sense associated with tort claims. Instead, the law holds the party liable based on their relationship to the wrongdoer, who also remains liable for the harm. The policy behind vicarious liability involves a judgment that the enterprise that engages in the activity that brought about the loss should compensate for that loss, internalizing and thus deterring the enterprise from risk while expanding the prospects for compensating the loss. The plaintiff must still prove that the person or entity who directly caused the harm committed a tort (typically negligence) but need only show that the vicariously liable party had a recognized relationship with the direct tortfeasor.

Respondeat-Superior Liability. The first of the vicarious liabilities is that of an employer for the tortious acts of an employee committed within the course of the employment—what law sometimes calls *respondeat-superior* liability. The issues in employer vicarious liability include who is an employee (versus an independent contractor), what is the course of employment, and what acts within the course of employment give rise to employer vicarious liability. The cases and inquiry below explore each of these issues. In broad outline, an employer is liable only for the torts of an employee but not an independent contractor. *See* Leaf River Forest Prods., Inc. v. Harrison, 392 So.2d 1138 (Miss. 1981) (employer sawmill not liable for independent contractor's tort while on job). An employee is one who is subject to employer control as to the means by which the employer brings about the desired work result. A tortfeasor who pursues an employer's ends but has full choice of the means is an independent contractor rather than employee. The control test is so general that courts will look to other factors to determine whether a tortfeasor is an employee, including whether the tortfeasor worked at the times dictated by the employer, used the employer's tools, and followed the employer's methods. *See* Restatement of Agency §220 (consider, among other factors, control, skills, tools, time, place, and payment method). An employee acts within the course of employment if the employee is furthering the employer's interests when the tort occurs, rather than engaging in a substantial detour or frolic. Consider, then, a case addressing whether the tortfeasor was an employee of the defendant and indicating what vicarious liability might exist even absent an employer-employee relationship.

Mavrikidis v. Petullo
New Jersey Supreme Court
153 N.J. 117, 707 A.2d 977 (1998)

GARIBALDI, J. In this case, we revisit the parameters of the vicarious liability doctrine as it pertains to whether a contractee may be vicariously liable for the negligence of its independent contractor.... .

I

This case arose from an automobile accident that resulted in severe injury to plaintiff Alice Mavrikidis[fn].... . On September 11, 1990, the intersection collision occurred after defendant Gerald Petullo,[fn] operating a dump truck registered to Petullo Brothers, Inc. (Petullo Brothers), drove through a red light, struck plaintiff's car, hit a telephone pole, and then overturned, spilling the truck's contents onto Mavrikidis's car. At the time of the accident, Gerald was transporting 10.99 tons of hot asphalt, which had been loaded onto the truck by Newark Asphalt Corporation (Newark Asphalt), to his job site at Clar Pine Servicenter (Clar Pine), a retail gasoline and automotive repair shop in Montclair.

Prior to the accident, Clar Pine's owner, Karl Pascarello (Pascarello), decided to renovate the station because he was switching gasoline brands from Getty to Gulf Oil. ...

Because Pascarello had no experience in the construction or paving business, he hired Gerald's father, Angelo Petullo, to perform the asphalt and concrete work as part of the renovation of his service station. ... Pascarello hired Angelo by verbal agreement to participate in the station's renovations based on Angelo's reputation as an excellent mason and, to a lesser extent, the debt owed Clar Pine under the Petullo Brothers' account. Over the years, Angelo and Gerald had charged gas and small repairs to their company account. In exchange for the asphalt work, both parties orally agreed that the Petullos would receive a $6,800 credit toward a $12,000 to $20,000 debt that Petullo Brothers had accumulated. ...

The Petullos supplied the labor, equipment, concrete, and most of the asphalt needed for the job, until Angelo "ran out of money" in the midst of the renovations. ... Other than general supervision and periodic consultation, Pascarello's limited participation in the asphalt work consisted of payment for three loads of asphalt, including the one involved in this accident, as well as his direction to lay the asphalt in front of the service station's bay doors first to enable him to continue his automotive repairs while the gas station was out of service. ...

II

The first question is whether Clar Pine is vicariously liable for plaintiff's injuries. As we explained in Majestic[Realty Assocs., Inc. v Toti Contracting Co., 30 N.J. 425, 153 A.2d 321 (1959)], the resolution of this issue "must be approached with an awareness of the long settled doctrine that ordinarily where a person engages a contractor, who conducts an independent business by means of his own employees, to do work not in itself a nuisance (as our cases put it), he is not liable for the negligent acts of the contractor in the performance of the contract." [30 N.J. at 430-31, 153 A.2d 321.] ...

The initial inquiry in our analysis is to examine the status of the Petullos in relation to Clar Pine. Despite plaintiff's alternate theories to the contrary, the Petullos were independent contractors rather than servants of Clar Pine. "The important difference between an employee and an independent contractor is that one who hires an independent contractor 'has no right of control over the manner in which the work is to be done, it is to be regarded as the contractor's own enterprise, and he, rather than the employer is the proper party to be charged with the responsibility for preventing the risk, and administering and distributing it.'" [Baldasarre, supra, 132 N.J. at 291, 625 A.2d 458 ([c]).]

In contrast, a servant is traditionally one who is "employed to perform services in the affairs of another, whose physical conduct in the performance of the service is controlled, or is subject to a right of control, by the other." W. Page Keeton, Prosser & Keeton, supra, § 70 at 501.

In determining whether a contractee maintains the right of control, several factors are to be considered. The Restatement (Second) of Agency sets forth these factors, including: "(a) the extent of control which, by the agreement, the master may exercise over the details of the work; (b) whether or not the one employed is engaged in a distinct occupation or business; ... (d) the skill required in the particular occupation; (e) whether the employer or the workman supplies the instrumentalities, tools, and the place of work for the person doing the work; (f) the length of time for which the person is employed; (g) the method of payment, whether by the time or by the job; (h) whether or not the work is a part of the regular business of the employer; [and] (i) whether or not the parties believe they are creating the relation of master and servant... . [Restatement (Second) of Agency § 220(2) (1958).]

Applying those Restatement factors, it is evident that neither Angelo nor Gerald was a servant of Clar Pine. The masonry work required a skilled individual. Although Pascarello paid for three loads of asphalt, the Petullos provided their own tools and the remainder of the needed materials, other than bolts and plywood supplied by Pascarello to install the canopies. Their work did not involve the regular business of Clar Pine. In addition, the period of employment spanned only the time it took to lay the asphalt and concrete. Following the accident, the Petullos continued the job for which they were hired, which was approved by the Building Inspector of Montclair. In exchange for their services, the Petullos were not paid by the hour or month; instead, they received a discharge of the portion of their debt.

Based on that threshold determination, we now must determine whether this case falls within any exceptions to the general rule of nonliability of principals/contractees for the negligence of their independent contractors. There are three such exceptions, as delineated by the Majestic Court: "(a) where the landowner [or principal] retains control of the manner and means of the doing of the work which is the subject of the contract; (b) where he engages an incompetent contractor; or (c) where ... the activity contracted for constitutes a nuisance per se." Majestic, supra, 30 N.J. at 431, 153 A.2d 321. ...

III

We now discuss each of the Majestic exceptions in turn. Under the first Majestic exception, the reservation of control "of the manner and means" of the contracted work by the principal permits the imposition of vicarious liability. [C] ... Under that test, the reservation of control over the equipment to be used, the manner or method of doing the work, or direction of the employees of the independent contractor may permit vicarious liability. [C]

However, supervisory acts performed by the contractee will not give rise to vicarious liability under that exception. As indicated by the language of the exception, application of principles of respondeat superior are not warranted where the contractee's "supervisory interest relates [only] to the result to be accomplished, not to the means of accomplishing it." Majestic, supra, 30 N.J. at 431, 153 A.2d 321; [cc].

Pascarello's actions did not exceed the scope of general supervisory powers so as to subject Clar Pine to vicarious liability for Gerald's negligence. Providing blueprints, paying for some of the asphalt, and directing that a portion of the concrete be completed first are clearly within the scope of a contractee's broad supervisory powers. ... Pascarello's actions related to the overall renovations of the station and not to the specific work for which the Petullos were engaged. ... The Appellate Division, therefore, correctly determined that there was insufficient evidence to present this issue to the jury. ...

IV

Under the second Majestic exception, a principal may be held liable for injury caused by its independent contractor where the principal hires an incompetent contractor. As the Appellate Division explained in this case, "[t]he gravamen of th[is] exception is selection of a contractor who is incompetent. The selection of a competent contractor who negligently causes injury, does not render a [principal] liable." ...

Because the second Majestic prong may include causes of action for both direct and vicarious liability, there is no reason to set out a separate tort for negligently hiring an independent contractor. To hold an employer liable under the second Majestic exception to the general rule of nonliability of principals for the negligence of their independent contractors, it is necessary to show both (1) that the contractor was incompetent or unskilled to perform the job for which he was hired, and (2) that the principal knew or had reason to know of the contractor's incompetence. The Petullos were skilled and experienced paving contractors. There is no evidence that the Petullos were unqualified to perform the masonry work for which they were hired. In fact, Pascarello visited other job sites that Angelo had paved in order to check the quality of his work. Viewing the evidence most favorably to plaintiffs, we find that the evidence does not support a finding that the Petullos were incompetent to perform the paving work for which they were engaged; hence, there is no basis for holding Clar Pine liable, either vicariously or directly, for plaintiff's injuries. ...

V

Next, we consider the application of the third Majestic exception—whether the work engaged in by Petullo Brothers was inherently dangerous. In formulating this exception, the Majestic Court explained, "where work is to be done that may endanger others, there is no real hardship in holding the party for whom it is done responsible for neglect in doing it. Though he may not be able to do it himself, or intelligently supervise it, he will nevertheless be the more careful in selecting an agent to act for him." [Majestic, supra, 30 N.J. at 440, 153 A.2d 321 ([c]).] We observed that "nuisance per se" could be equated with "inherently dangerous." [c] Namely, work can be considered to be inherently dangerous if it is "an activity which can be carried on safely only by the exercise of special skill and care, and which involves grave risk of danger to persons or property if negligently done. The term signifies that danger inheres in the activity itself at all times, so as to require special precautions to be taken with regard to it to avoid injury. It means more than simply danger arising from the casual or collateral negligence of persons engaged in it under particular circumstances." [Ibid. (citations omitted) (emphasis added).] ...

Poor driving, faulty brakes, and overloading are ordinary risks associated with motor vehicles and the transport of materials, and as such, are the responsibility of the contractor. Clar Pine did not have a nondelegable duty to take special precautions to prevent those risks. Absent proof that the contractee was aware of an enhanced risk that Petullo Brothers would drive negligently or would overload their vehicles, Clar Pine will not be held vicariously or independently liable for the ordinary dangers that arise from normal human activity, in this case, driving. Plaintiff's injuries in this case resulted "from the casual or collateral negligence," Majestic, supra, 30 N.J. at 435, 153 A.2d 321, of the Petullos, which is not normal or inherent in paving. ...

We affirm the Appellate Division's judgment ....

INQUIRY

Course of Employment. Determining that a tortfeasor was an employee does not alone make the employer vicariously liable. One must still ask whether the employee committed the tort within the course of employment. Some instances involve conduct so clearly for the employee's personal gratification that the conduct is beyond the scope of employment. *See* Stropes v. Heirtage House Children's Ctr., 547 N.E.2d 244 (Ind. 1989) (employee of children's home not acting with the course of employment when sexually abusing children). Other cases do not resolve so readily. Consider two cases illustrating the difficulty of drawing a line between an employee acting within or outside of the course of employment.

Dias v. Brigham Med. Assocs., Inc.
Massachusetts Supreme Court
438 Mass. 317, 780 N.E.2d 447 (2002)

IRELAND, J. The plaintiffs, Stella and Luis Dias, administrators of the estate of their son, Ethan Dias, claim that defendant Brigham Medical Associates, Inc. (BMA), is vicariously liable under the theory of respondeat superior for the alleged medical malpractice of one of its physician practice group members, Dr. Daniel Schlitzer. Dr. Schlitzer was the on-call obstetrician at St. Luke's Hospital who treated the pregnant Stella Dias (plaintiff), following a motor vehicle accident. A Superior Court judge granted summary judgment for BMA, concluding that to hold BMA vicariously liable for Dr. Schlitzer's negligence, the plaintiffs would have to show that the corporation exercised, or had the right to exercise, direction and control over his treatment decisions. The judge found that BMA did not and could not exercise such control over Dr. Schlitzer. The plaintiffs appealed....

Because we conclude that traditional respondeat superior liability applies to the employer of a physician, and that to establish such liability it is not necessary that the employer have the right or ability to control the specific treatment decisions of a physician-employee, we vacate the judgment and remand the case for further proceedings consistent with this opinion.

... On May 19, 1995, the plaintiff, at the time thirty-two weeks pregnant, was involved in a motor vehicle accident that resulted in her emergency treatment at St. Luke's Hospital in New Bedford. After being examined in the emergency room, she was transferred to the labor and delivery department, where she was treated by Dr. Schlitzer. The plaintiffs contend that the care rendered by him was negligent and resulted in the stillbirth of their son.[fn]

BMA, a Massachusetts corporation, a so-called "medical practice group," was comprised entirely of physicians specializing in obstetrical medicine. The record is undisputed that Dr. Schlitzer, at the time of the incident, was an employee and officer of BMA. In fact, both Dr. Schlitzer and BMA admitted in their respective interrogatory answers that Dr. Schlitzer was an employee of BMA "during the period in question," and that Dr. Schlitzer was on staff at BMA "all times relevant hereto."[fn] The judge found that, "[a]s a member of BMA, [Dr.] Schlitzer had been assigned by BMA to, and was then responsible for 'on-call' coverage at St. Luke's Hospital, and was in fact working a conventional [twenty-four]-hour shift at the [h]ospital." As to this latter point, however, the record contains ambiguities regarding Dr. Schlitzer's on-call coverage obligations on the night in question, as more fully discussed below. ...

Broadly speaking, respondeat superior is the proposition that an employer, or master, should be held vicariously liable for the torts of its employee, or servant, committed within the scope of employment. [Cc] ...

In 1969, ... this court broadened the scope of liability under the theory of respondeat superior, and held that an employer need not control the details of an employee's tasks in order to be held liable for the employee's tortious acts. [C]

To prevail against BMA, the plaintiffs need only establish that (1) at the time of the alleged negligence Dr. Schlitzer was an employee of BMA, and (2) the alleged negligent treatment of the plaintiff occurred within the scope of Dr. Schlitzer's employment by BMA. Once employment is established, the only remaining issue is whether he was working for BMA at the time of the alleged negligent treatment, i.e., whether his treatment of the plaintiff was within the scope of his employment by BMA. This comports with traditional agency law that "[a]n employer is liable for torts committed by employees while acting in the scope of their employment." Restatement (Third) of Agency § 2.04 (Tent. Draft No. 2 2001).

In order to determine whether an employer-employee relationship actually exists, a judge may consider a number of factors. [C] These factors may include, but are not limited to, the method of payment (e.g., whether the employee receives a W-2 form from the employer), and whether the parties themselves believe they have created an employer-employee relationship. While the point is not of import in this case where both BMA and Dr. Schlitzer admit the existence of the employer-employee relationship, we recognize that the task of determining what constitutes an employer-employee relationship is fact dependent, and that in cases where there is no clear admission of employment, a direction and control analysis may be useful to determine whether the relationship is that of employer-employee as opposed to that of an independent contractor.[fn] The right to direct and control the details of an alleged employee's actions "may be very attenuated," but remains an important factor that should be examined when the employer-employee relationship is contested. [C] Once an employer-employee relationship is established, however, any further analysis of the employer's right to direct and control is unnecessary. [C] All that remains to be determined is whether the tort occurred within the scope of employment. [C] ...

Because BMA admitted that Dr. Schlitzer is its employee, the judge erred in holding that, as a matter of law, BMA could not be held liable for his alleged negligent acts because of BMA's inability to exert direction and control over his clinical decisions. The judge's rationale, that such control is presumed absent unless there is evidence to the contrary, undercuts the evolved purpose of respondeat superior liability, and would create an exception for physicians not recognized for any other profession.[fn]

There remains one point that requires further comment. Dr. Schlitzer was the employee of BMA on the date of the alleged negligent treatment, but the record is ambiguous as to whether he was acting as BMA's employee at the time he treated the plaintiff. Asked at his deposition for which practice group he was covering when he treated her, Dr. Schlitzer was unable to answer. Dr. Schlitzer did testify that he covered the labor and delivery department on behalf of BMA on a rotating basis, and that at least part of his twenty-four hour shift on May 19 was in fulfilment of his obligation as a BMA employee. Dr. Schlitzer also testified, however, that he had been asked to assume coverage for additional practice groups at some point during his twenty-four hour shift. If Dr. Schlitzer was under an obligation to BMA to be present at the hospital at the time he treated the plaintiff, his treatment of her would be within the scope of his employment by BMA, regardless of whether he had agreed to take on additional coverage shifts for other groups. If, however, he was providing coverage for some other group, under an arrangement independent of his relationship with BMA, at the time he treated the plaintiff, that treatment would not have been rendered within the scope of his BMA employment. Thus, while the record conclusively establishes that Dr. Schlitzer was an employee of BMA, the record before us is inadequate for any definitive determination whether Dr. Schlitzer's treatment of the plaintiff was within the scope of his employment by BMA.

We vacate the judgment entered in the Superior Court, and remand this case for further proceedings consistent with this opinion.

O'Shea v. Welch
United States Court of Appeals, Tenth Circuit
350 F.3d 1101 (10th Cir. 2003)

McKAY, J. Appellant filed a claim in the district court for damages against Defendant Welch[fn] based on negligence after Appellant sustained injuries when the car that he was driving was struck by a car driven by Mr. Welch. In his complaint, Appellant alleged that Mr. Welch, an Osco employee, was acting within the scope of his employment at the time of the accident. Appellant sought to hold Osco liable for damages under a theory of *respondeat superior.*

... At the time of the accident, Mr. Welch was an Osco store manager. He was driving from his store to the Osco District Office to deliver football tickets for that weekend which were obtained from a vendor for distribution among Osco managers. Mr. Welch frequently made trips for Osco using his own vehicle. During his drive, Mr. Welch remembered that he needed to have some routine maintenance done on his car. He made a spur of the moment decision to pull into a service station for an estimate. Mr. Welch allegedly failed to yield in making a left turn and struck Appellant's car.

... [T]the district court granted Osco's motion and denied Appellant's motion, holding that no reasonable jury could conclude that Mr. Welch was acting within the scope of his employment. The district court did not specifically decide whether the trip to the District Office was within Mr. Welch's scope of employment. Instead, the district court held that it did not matter because, even if the trip had been within the

scope of Mr. Welch's employment, the attempted stop at the service station was not.
...

After Osco was dismissed from the case, a bench trial was held on the issue of damages. Defendant Welch did not present evidence or cross-examine witnesses. The court entered judgment against Mr. Welch in the amount of $1,014,503.70, "question[ing] whether it would arrive at the same result in a true adversary proceeding...." [C] ...

Pursuant to Kansas law, an employer is only liable for injuries caused by an employee acting within the scope of his employment. [C] The following Kansas jury instruction is an accurate illustration of Kansas scope of employment law: "An employee is acting within the scope of [his employment] when [he] is performing services for which [he] has been [employed], or when [he] is doing anything which is reasonably incidental to [his employment]. The test is not necessarily whether this specific conduct was expressly authorized or forbidden by the employer[ ], but whether such conduct should have been fairly foreseen from the nature of the [employment] and the duties relating to it." [Cc] ...

Due to the absence of binding authority, Appellant urges us to decide that Kansas would adopt the "slight deviation" rule which it already follows in worker's compensation cases. ... Pursuant to this analysis, "it must be determined whether the employee was on a frolic or a detour; the latter is a deviation that is sufficiently related to the employment to fall within its scope, while the former is the pursuit of the employee's personal business as a substantial deviation from or an abandonment of the employment. If an employee wholly abandons, even temporarily, the employer's business for personal reasons, the act is not within the scope of employment, and the employer is not liable under respondeat superior for the employee's conduct during that lapse. A diversion from the strict performance of a task is not an abandonment of responsibility and service to an employer, unless the very character of the diversion severs the employment relationship. Acts that are necessary to the comfort, convenience, health, and welfare of the employee while at work are not outside the scope of employment, if the conduct is not a substantial deviation from the duties of employment." [*See* 27 Am.Jur.2d Employment Relationship § 466 (2000).] Personal acts that are not far removed in time, distance, or purpose are deemed to be incidental to the employment. *See, e.g.,* Restatement (Second) of Agency § 237 (1958). Our research has not revealed a single jurisdiction that has considered and rejected slight deviation analysis in third-party liability cases. ...

Applying slight deviation analysis to our case, we think that the question of whether the turn was within Mr. Welch's scope of employment is for the jury to decide. ...

Appellant argues that Mr. Welch was acting within the scope of his employment and made only a slight deviation from his business-related trip at the time the accident occurred. Several factors have been identified as helpful in determining whether an employee has embarked on a slight or substantial deviation. They include: (1) the employee's intent; (2) the nature, time, and place of the deviation; (3) the time consumed in the deviation; (4) the work for which the employee was hired; (5) the incidental acts reasonably expected by the employer; and (6) the freedom allowed the employee in performing his job responsibilities. [C]

Applying these factors to our case, and viewing the facts in a light most favorable to Appellant, Mr. Welch intended to get an estimate for non-emergency maintenance on a car used for business. In terms of purpose, it was maintenance to a vehicle used regularly in performing his job duties for Osco. While his stop was not for emergency maintenance for his car, his stop for routine maintenance on a car used for business purposes could be considered enough of a mixed purpose by a jury to keep him within the scope of his employment with Osco.

In terms of time and place, the accident occurred minutes and feet from the direct route to Osco's District Office. Mr. Welch was simply attempting to turn from the most direct route into a service station right off the main road. At the time of the accident, he had not entered the service station. He was technically still on the road en route to the District Office. Because the accident occurred on this road, not at the service station, a jury could decide that Mr. Welch had not yet abandoned his employment for a personal errand at the time of the accident. It is unclear how long the estimate would have taken. However, we do know that if he had deviated at the time of the accident, the length of the deviation was only a few minutes or less.

Mr. Welch was an Osco store manager. A jury could find that an employee in a managerial position was given some freedom to attend to certain personal needs throughout the day. It is possible that Osco reasonably expected certain incidental acts to take place, especially when a store manager was en route from one store to another or from a store to the District Office.

Assuming without deciding that Mr. Welch was acting within the scope of his employment in delivering the tickets to the District Office, we hold that a reasonable jury could conclude that he was acting within the scope of his employment when he attempted to turn into the service station. ...

The district court did not specifically decide whether Mr. Welch was in the scope of his employment in making the trip from his store to the District Office. It stated: "[W]hile the court would conclude from the record that genuine issues of material fact exist with respect to whether defendant Welch's delivery of the Chiefs tickets was within the scope of his employment, the court need not address this issue because it concludes that, as a matter of law, defendant Welch's attempted stop at the service station for routine vehicle maintenance was outside the scope of his employment." [C] We agree with the district court that summary judgment is inappropriate on this issue. Therefore, this issue must be remanded for trial as well.

We further hold that, in the event that Appellee is found liable by a jury, it will have the opportunity to contest damages as it was not involved in the damages hearing.

Reversed and remanded.

INQUIRY

Commuting. In the above case, the employee attempted a largely personal but arguably also employment-related errand while on what one could construe as a job errand having a distinctly personal flavor. Cases of this mixed type are relatively common. *See* Fruit v. Scheiner, 502 P.2d 133 (Alaska 1972) (employer subject to vicarious liability for injury caused by salesman on his way back at 2:00 a.m. from searching for other conventioneers with whom to socialize off-site from the conference). What about commuting from the employee's home to work and back? The accepted rule is that employers are not liable for their employees' torts while commuting to and from work. Yet as the above case illustrates, just as employees on employer business may readily detour for personal errands, an employee's commute could also involve employer business. *See* Bussard v. Minimed, Inc., 129 Cal. Rptr.2d 675, 105 Cal. App. 4th 798 (2003) (fact issue as to whether employee sent home early due to work illness is traveling within the course of employment). Work and play can easily mix, making more difficult judgments as to employer vicarious liability.

Employer Errands. Another accepted rule is that an employee going on a special errand or mission for the employer, or traveling from one job site to another job site for the same employer, remains within the course of employment. *Compare* Harvey v. D. & L. Constr. Co., 251 Cal.App.2d 48, 59 Cal. Rptr. 255 (1967) (employer's request that employee give another employee a ride home made it within the course of employment when rides home were part of the employee's job duties); *with* Caldwell v. A.R.B., Inc., 176 Cal. App.3d 1028, 222 Cal Rptr. 494 (1986) (giving another employee a ride home is not within the course of employment absent employer involvement); *see also* Fiocco v. Carver, 137 N.E. 309 (N.Y. 1922) (Cardozo, J.) (employer not vicariously liable for employee's deviating from route to stop employer's truck to let children play on it). What if the employee is not going home when the accident happens but is on the way from one job to another job (for a different employer)? *See* O'Toole v. Carr, 175 N.J. 421, 815 A.2d 471 (2003) (lawyer traveling to part-time judicial role not within the course of law-firm employment).

Employer Recreation. Another area that raises frequent issues as to employer vicarious liability is when an employee causes injury in connection with some pastime the employer permits or encourages. *See* Taber v. Maine, 67 F.3d 1029 (2nd Cir. 1995) (federal government vicariously liable for injuries caused by military serviceman driving off-base to get fresh air after consuming cocktails in enlisted men's club and beers in a barracks party); Harris v. Trojan Fireworks Co., 155 Cal. App.3d 830, 202 Cal. Rptr. 440 (1984) (employer's office Christmas party results in accident caused by intoxicated employee). Does a claimant raise a jury issue even when the employer does not provide the pastime but only allows it during a temporary hiatus from a restrictive work environment (the "bunkhouse rule")? *See* Rodgers v. Kemper Constr. Co., 50 Cal. App.3d 608 (1975) (contractor liable for assaults occurring among employees intoxicated during down-time in job-site "dry house"); Mauk v. Wright, 367 F. Supp. 961 (M.D. Pa. 1973) (football player's training-camp "free time" may still be within the course of employment); *but see* Valdiviez v. United States, 884 F.2d 196 (5th Cir. 1989) (federal government not liable for serviceman's donating AIDS-infected blood while on duty because he was not acting within the course of employment).

Intentional Torts. The bulk of employer vicarious-liability cases involve negligent rather than intentional acts of employees because purposeful misconduct is not ordinarily within an enterprise's mission. When might an employer be liable for an employee's intentional torts? Whether these vicarious-liability claims make it to a jury tends to turn on whether the intentional act bore some relationship to the employer's mission. *Compare* Rodebush v. Oklahoma Nursing Homes, Lrd., 867 P.2d 1241 (Okla. 1993) (home vicariously liable for intoxicated aide's slapping resident in misguided discipline); Manning v. Grimsley, 643 F.2d 20 (1st Cir. 1981) (team subject to vicarious liability if pitcher assaults heckling fan to deter fan from interfering with job performance); Chuy v. Philadelphia Eagles Football Club, 595 F.2d 1265 (3d Cir. 1979) (team subject to vicarious liability for team doctor's intentionally distressing statement to the press); Jefferson v. Rose Oil Co., 232 So.2d 895 (La. App. 1970) (gas station vicariously liable for attendant's shooting delinquent customer because it was an attempt to get station paid), *with* Gibson v. Brewer, 952 S.W.2d 239 (Mo. 1997) no employer vicarious liability for minister's sexual assault of parishioner); Porter v. Harshfield, 329 Ark. 130, 948 S.W.2d 83 (1997) (no employer vicarious liability when medical-care provider sexually assaults patient); Copeland v. Samford Univ., 686 So.2d 190 (Ala. 1996) (no employer vicarious liability for debate coach's murder of student team member); *but see* Lourim v. Swenson, 328 Or. 380, 977 P.2d 1157 (1999) (Boy Scouts vicariously liable for local leader's sexual abuse of minor member). Bars hire and train bouncers, for instance, to intentionally quell unruly customers and remove them from the scene—a role that can lead to intentional-tort liability for the over-aggressive bouncer and vicarious liability for the employer. An employer will also have vicarious liability for an employee's intentional torts when the employer authorized or ratified those torts.

Employer Direct Negligence. Distinguish vicarious-liability cases from claims involving the employer's direct negligence—in, for instance, retaining the errant employee. *See* Glomb v. Ginosky, 366 Pa. Super. 206, 530 A.2d 1362 (1987) (negligent retention of babysitter who was already feared by bruised children); F. & T. Co. v. Woods, 92 N.M. 697, 594 P.2d 745 (1979) (employer subject to rape victim's direct-liability claim for negligently retaining rapist to repair home appliances). Negligent entrustment is a second theory on which employers and others are occasionally held directly liable for the torts of another. *See* Hickle v. Whitney Farms, Inc., 148 Wash.2d 911, 64 P.3d 1244 (2003) (defendants subject to negligent entrustment claim for putting hazardous substance in hands of irresponsible disposal contractors). See also the description of apparent-agency and corporate-negligence claims in the chapter on professional negligence. Federal and state civil-rights laws prohibiting racially and sexually hostile work environments create another important direct-liability consideration in this area. *See* Farragher v. City of Boca Raton, 524 U.S. 775 (1998) (employer liability for employee harassment depends on reasonableness of employer's prevention system). Will an employer be directly or vicariously liable for punitive damages awarded for misconduct of an employee? The majority of states require the employer to have authorized, assented to, or ratified the employee's misconduct, to hold the employer liable for punitive damages based on the employee's misconduct. *See* Partington v. Metallic Eng. Co., 792 So.2d 498 (Fla. 2001); Ex parte Henry, 770 So.2d 76 (Ala. 2000); *but see* College Hosp. v. Superior Court, 8 Cal.4th 704, 882 P.2d 894, 34 Cal. Rptr.2d 898 (1994) (not unless the employer was itself at fault); *see also* Restatement (Second) of Torts §909 (1965) (vicarious liability for punitive damages only if employer authorized or ratified the employee's misconduct, the employee was acting as a manager, or there is evidence of the employer's direct fault).

Independent Contractors. A second area where vicarious liability may exist involves the torts of independent contractors. As the *Mavrikidis* case above shows, the traditional formulation that employers are liable for employee torts but not the torts of independent contractors only begins the analysis. Just because a tortfeasor is *not* an employee does not necessarily absolve the party with whom the tortfeasor had some relationship, of vicarious liability for the tortfeasor's torts. Law instead offers a list of exceptions to the independent-contractor rule, where vicarious liability may still exist.

Indeed, so many exceptions to employer non-liability for independent contractors' torts exist that the exceptions may swallow the rule. The exceptions (where vicarious liability exists) include:

(1) retained control, *see* Fisher v. Townsends, Inc., 695 A.2d 53 (Del. 1997) (jury question of retained control over independent-contractor driver);

(2) nondelegable duties, *see* Rizzuto v. L.A. Wnger Contracting Co., 91 N.Y.2d 343, 670 N.Y.S.2d 816, 693 N.E.2d 1068 (N.Y. 1998) (non-delegable statutory duty of owners for safety around worksites); Maloney v. Rath, 69 Cal.2d 442, 445 P.2d 513, 71 Cal. Rptr. 897 (1968) (non-delegable statutory duty to maintain vehicle brakes, holding vehicle owner liable for mechanic's negligent repair); Alabama Power Co. v. Pierre, 236 Ala. 521, 183 So. 665 (Ala. 1938) (non-delegable duty arising by contract to install);

(3) inherently dangerous activities creating a peculiar risk of harm, *see* Wilson v. Good Humor Corp., 757 F.2d 1293 (D.C. Cir. 1985) (vicarious liability for injury from vending-truck ice-cream sales to small children); Pusey v. Bator, 94 Ohio St.3d 275, 762 N.E.2d 968 (2002) (landowner vicariously liable for inherently dangerous defense of property by contracted armed-security guards); Huddleston v. Union Rural Elec. Assn., 841 P.2d 282 (Colo. 1992) (vicarious liability for flying small plane around mountains); Rohlfs v. Weil, 271 N.Y. 444, 3 N.E.2d 588 (N.Y. 1936) (building owner vicariously liable for inherently dangerous scaffold over sidewalk); Restatement (Second) of Torts §427 ("peculiar risk"); *but see* Waite v. American Airlines, Inc., 73 F. Supp.2d 349 (S.D. N.Y. 1999) (baggage conveyor not an inherently dangerous piece of equipment in airport context); Privette v. Superior Court, 5 Cal.4th 689, 854 P.2d 721, 21 Cal. Rptr.2d 72 (1993) (employer engaging contractor to repair utilities not vicariously liable to contractor's employees for contractor's negligence); Clausen v. R.W. Gilbert Constr. Co., 309 N.W.2d 462 (Iowa 1981) (employer not liable for contractor's tort collateral to the inherent risk of the activity);

(4) maintaining the safety of land and premises, *see* Valenti v. Net Props. Mgt., Inc., 142 N.H. 633, 710 A.2d 399 (1998) (mall owner subject to vicarious liability for contractor's negligent maintenance of entrance-safety maps); Otero v. Jordon Restaurant Enterp., 119 N.M. 721, 895 P.2d 243 (App. 1995), *affd.*, 122 N.M. 187, 922 P.2d 569 (1996) (landowner vicariously liable for contractor's negligent installation of bleachers, on duty to maintain safe lands); Strayer v. Lindeman, 427 N.E.2d 781 (Ohio 1981) (landlord vicariously liable for negligence of contractor hired to satisfy landlord's legal obligation to maintain premises); Restatement (Second) of Torts §422;

(5) illegal activities, *see* Hester v. Bandy, 627 So.2d 833 (Miss. 1993) (dealer subject to vicarious liability for contractor's trespass to repossess vehicle); King v. Loessin, 572 S.W.2d 87 (Tex. Civ. App. 1978) (company vicariously liable for contractor-private investigator's break-in to competitor's office); Nelson v. Nason, 343 Mass. 220, 177 N.E.2d 887 (1961) (illegal street racing) and

(6) agents with apparent authority, *see* Wood v. Holiday Inns, Inc, 508 F.2d 167 (5th Cir. 1975) (franchisor vicariously liable for franchisee's negligent acts within scope of agency relationship); O'Banner v. McDonald's Corp., 173 Ill.2d 208, 218 Ill. Dec. 910, 670 N.E.2d (1996) (franchisor subject to vicarious liability on

apparent-agency theory for direct liability of franchisee only if plaintiff shows justifiable reliance on franchisor); Restatement (Second) of Agency §§228, 229.

Exceptions to the employer non-liability rule for the torts of independent contractors are so numerous and various that they are hard to illustrate. Parties retaining independent contractors are relatively likely to be liable for the torts of independent contractors under one of the many exceptions. Consider one such case involving an intentional tort committed by an independent contractor in execution of the defendant's non-delegable statutory duty not to breach the peace.

MBank El Paso v. Sanchez
Texas Supreme Court
836 S.W.2d 151 (Tex. 1992)

MAUZY, J. Section 9.503 of the Texas Business and Commerce Code allows a secured creditor to use nonjudicial repossession "if this can be done without breach of the peace." The issue in this case is whether a secured creditor may avoid liability for breaches of the peace by using an independent contractor to carry out repossession. The court of appeals, applying section 9.503, held that a creditor cannot delegate the duty of peaceable repossession to an independent contractor. 792 S.W.2d 530. We agree, and therefore affirm.

MBank El Paso hired El Paso Recovery Service to repossess Yvonne Sanchez's automobile because of her default on a note. Two men dispatched to Sanchez's home found the car parked in the driveway, and hooked it to a tow truck. Sanchez demanded that they cease their efforts and leave the premises; but the men nonetheless continued with the repossession. Before the men could tow the automobile into the street, Sanchez jumped into the car, locked the doors, and refused to leave. The men then towed the car at a high rate of speed, with Sanchez inside, to the repossession yard. They parked the car in the fenced repossession yard and padlocked the gate. Sanchez was left in the repossession lot, with a Doberman pinscher guard dog loose in the yard, until later rescued by her husband and police.[fn]

Sanchez filed suit against MBank, alleging that it was liable for the tortious acts of El Paso Recovery Service. ...

MBank acknowledges that section 9.503 imposes a duty on a secured party not to breach the peace, but argues that the secured party may delegate that duty to an independent contractor. We disagree. ...

As a general rule, when a duty is imposed by law on the basis of concerns for public safety, the party bearing the duty cannot escape it by delegating it to an independent contractor. Section 424 of the Restatement (Second) of Torts (1965) provides: "One who by statute or by administrative regulation is under a duty to provide specified safeguards or precautions for the safety of others is subject to liability to the others for whose protection the duty is imposed for harm caused by the failure of a contractor employed by him to provide such safeguards or precautions." Comment a to section 424 further explains that a duty to take safety precautions cannot be delegated to an independent contractor: "The rule stated in this Section applies whenever a statute or an administrative regulation imposes a duty upon one doing particular work to provide safeguards or precautions for the safety of others. In such a case the employer cannot delegate his duty to provide such safeguards or precautions to an independent contractor." ...

We believe that section 9-503 of the UCC imposes a duty on secured creditors pursuing nonjudicial repossession to take precautions for public safety. [Cc] Applying section 424 of the Restatement, a secured creditor is prohibited from delegating this duty to an independent contractor. ...

A secured creditor certainly has a strong interest in obtaining collateral from a defaulting debtor. That interest, however, must be balanced against society's interest in the public peace. If a creditor chooses to pursue self-help, it must be expected to take precautions in doing so. If this burden is too heavy, the creditor may seek relief by turning to the courts. [Cc]

Because the Bank chose to pursue nonjudicial repossession, it assumed the risk that a breach of the peace might occur. ... We therefore affirm the judgment of the court of appeals.

Joint Enterprises. A third area in which vicarious liability may arise involves torts committed in the course of a joint enterprise. The basic vicarious-liability rule is that all joint venturers are liable even if only one joint venturer committed the tort in the course of the joint enterprise. *Joint enterprise* has a functional definition, going beyond activities undertaken by groups formed and operating under written agreements. When a tort occurs during some joint undertaking, questions may arise whether a joint enterprise existed and whether the tort occurred within its course and scope. The test for a joint enterprise, set forth in the Restatement (Second) of Torts §491, Comment c, requires that the parties have a common purpose and agreement in pursuit of a pecuniary interest, under circumstances where they share direction over the enterprise—purpose, agreement, interest, and direction. Business pursuits taken together are the most obvious examples of joint enterprises. *See* Shell Oil Co. v. Prestidge, 249 F.2d 413 (9th Cir. 1957) (oil prospecting). A common form of injury is the motor-vehicle accident taken in such pursuits. Pleasure trips taken together do not ordinarily qualify as joint enterprises for vicarious-liability purposes, *see* Lovell v. Brock, 330 Ark. 206, 952 S.W.2d 161 (1997) (hunting), although a party or other pleasure outing connected in some way with pecuniary interests may qualify, *see* Cullinan v. Tretrault, 123 Me. 302, 122 A. 770 (1923) (purchasing liquor for a party). Courts have also sometimes applied the theory in the context of a criminal enterprise where pecuniary interests are not obviously present. *See* Courtney v. Courtney, 186 W. Va. 597, 413 S.E.2d 418 (1991) (mother's enterprise liability for supplying son with drugs and alcohol resulting in beating of family members). The following case illustrates the application of the four elements for a joint enterprise.

Popejoy v. Steinle
Wyoming Supreme Court
820 P.2d 545 (Wyo. 1991)

GOLDEN, J. Appellants Ronald L. and Doris J. Popejoy (Popejoys) appeal the trial court's order granting summary judgment to appellees Carl Steinle and the Converse County Bank as personal representatives of the William E. Steinle Estate (Estate). Claiming that a joint venture relationship existed between William and his wife Constance E. (Connie) Steinle, the Popejoys seek to hold William's estate vicariously liable for Connie's alleged negligence in causing a traffic accident in which Ronald Popejoy was injured. ...

We affirm the trial court's order granting summary judgment.

FACTS

On the morning of May 8, 1986, Connie Steinle, accompanied by her seven-year-old daughter and a niece, left the family ranch for Douglas, Wyoming. The purpose of the trip was to purchase a calf for the daughter to raise on the ranch. While en route to Douglas, the truck Connie was driving collided with a vehicle driven by Ronald Popejoy. Connie died as a result of the accident and Ronald sustained injuries initially diagnosed as a muscle strain. As a result of his injuries, Ronald received outpatient medical treatment at a local hospital. One week after the accident William Steinle completed the calf purchase for his daughter. The calf was raised on the Steinle ranch and sold the following year. The daughter received the proceeds from the sale.

... [Mr. and Mrs. Popejoy] filed a complaint against the personal representatives of William's estate. The complaint was premised on the theory that William and Connie Steinle were engaged in a joint venture when Connie embarked on her May 8, 1986 "business trip" to pick up the daughter's calf. ...

DISCUSSION

The Popejoys seek to impute Connie Steinle's alleged negligence to her husband William's estate by claiming that the Steinles were engaged in a joint venture relationship at the time of the accident. "The burden of establishing the existence of a joint venture is upon the party asserting that the relationship exists." *Stone v. First Wyoming Bank N.A., Lusk*, 625 F.2d 332, 341, n. 12 (10th Cir.1980). [C] Consequently, the Popejoys are required to demonstrate each of the elements of a joint venture relationship in order to prevail. They must also show that the joint venture relationship existed at the time of Connie's alleged negligent conduct. ...

... Although the Restatement [(Second) of Torts § 491 comment c at 548 (1965)] does not define elements of a joint venture, it does define the four elements of a joint enterprise as: "(1) an agreement, express or implied, among the members of the group; (2) a common purpose to be carried out by the group; (3) a community of pecuniary interest in that purpose, among the members; and (4) an equal right to a voice in the direction of the enterprise, which gives an equal right of control." ...

The Popejoys' claim in this case is premised on a theory of joint venture and the contention that William and Connie Steinle were engaged in securing an appreciable business asset for their family business at the time of the accident. ...

In support of its second motion for summary judgment, the Estate submitted several affidavits, depositions and other materials. The Steinle daughter who was accompanying her mother at the time of the accident and who was the intended recipient of the calf they were on their way to buy submitted an affidavit stating that her father did not ordinarily have any ownership interest in the cattle that she, her sisters and mother raised and owned. She also stated that she, her mother and sisters were primarily responsible for caring for the "pets" and other domestic animals raised on the ranch.

Carl Steinle, William's brother and one of two personal representatives of the Estate, submitted an affidavit indicating that Connie and the Steinle daughters regularly kept numerous farm animals as their own and that William would not have had any interest in the calf that was to be purchased. Further, he stated that the purpose of the trip was to purchase a calf for the daughter to raise as her own. A second Steinle daughter also submitted an affidavit confirming the purpose of the trip.

Other materials submitted with the motion supplemented the affidavits described above and included the affidavit and deposition of Roger Wesnitzer, a certified public accountant. After reviewing Steinle tax records, ranch journal books, bank records, livestock sales receipts and the other affidavits and depositions, Wesnitzer stated that other livestock raised by the Steinle daughters in the past had been given directly to the children by the parents. Further, he stated that while William Steinle bore the costs of raising such livestock on his ranch, sale proceeds went directly to the children. Similar "nonranch" cattle owned by the Steinle daughters in the past had been separately identified by brands owned by the daughters and sale proceeds had gone directly to the children. He stated that William and Connie did not share in any portion of livestock sale proceeds of their daughters' cattle. He concluded that it was his professional opinion that the trip in which Connie was killed and Ronald was injured did not involve a joint venture between William and Connie Steinle.

... [E]vidence exists that the calf in question would have been purchased, branded, raised and sold in identical fashion to other similar "nonranch" livestock. In other words, the calf that Connie was on her way to purchase at the time of the accident would have been paid for by the parents; it would have been branded with a brand registered and owned by one of the daughter's older sisters; it would have been raised with other livestock on the family ranch; and any profits from the eventual sale of the animal would have gone directly to the daughter. Neither side submitted any evidence or argument to the contrary.

Taken as a whole, this evidence satisfied the threshold requirement of establishing the nonexistence of any genuine issue of material fact as to whether William and Connie Steinle were engaged in a joint venture at the time of Connie's accident. ...

In attempting to demonstrate existence of a joint venture relationship, the Popejoys relied extensively on the affidavits provided by Ted Grooms, a certified public accountant. Grooms stated in his first affidavit that William and Connie Steinle did not separate their income and expenses with respect to their ranching activities and that Connie did much of the work around the ranch because of William's poor health. In his second affidavit, Grooms maintained that after reviewing all the depositions, affidavits, business and tax records submitted by the Steinles for the years 1982-1986 he was convinced that William and Connie were involved in a joint venture at the time of Connie's trip on May 8, 1986. Grooms stated that William's eventual purchase of the calf for his daughter a week after the accident, his efforts in raising and selling the calf, and the fact that the calf bore the brand of the daughter's older sister led him to the conclusion that a joint venture relationship existed between Connie and William. Finally, and significantly, he stated that it was his understanding that only a pecuniary interest and not an interest in profit was needed to show existence of a joint venture.

Noticeably missing from Grooms' testimony is any evidence that proceeds from the sale of the calf that Connie and the daughter were on their way to purchase on May 8, 1986, would not have gone solely to the daughter. Along the same lines, he found no evidence that proceeds from the actual sale of the calf that was eventually purchased for the daughter following the accident went to anyone other than the daughter. Thus, it appears that only the daughter had an actual pecuniary or financial interest in the profits of the sale of the calf that was to be purchased at the time of the accident. ...

Thus, though three of the four essential elements of a joint venture may have been present at the time of the accident, the record in this case does not demonstrate that William and Connie Steinle shared the requisite financial, pecuniary or profit motive interest in this particular calf. The Popejoys failed to refute evidence that the parents intended for the calf to belong to the daughter and that although the daughter would raise the calf on the family ranch, it would still be her own and she would enjoy all proceeds from the eventual sale of the calf. This example of parental nurturing, familial accommodation and generosity does not justify imputing negligence from one parent to the other.

Regardless of whether or not William and Connie were engaged in a joint venture in the course of their other ranching activities, Connie's trip to purchase a calf for their daughter was a separate, distinguishable event and not a part of the general course of the commercial ranching business in which William and Connie were otherwise associated. ...

CONCLUSION

... After a careful review of the record, we hold that the Popejoys failed to demonstrate the existence of a genuine issue of material fact which would preclude summary judgment as a matter of law. William and Connie Steinle were not engaged in a joint venture when Connie attempted to drive to Douglas to purchase the calf for their daughter.

The decision of the trial court is affirmed.

Ethics

When the client loses a tort case at the trial-court level, must the attorney take an appeal? Rule 1.2(c) of the ABA Model Rules of Professional Conduct permit a lawyer to limit the scope of the representation "if the limitation is reasonable and the client gives informed consent." Tort lawyers representing plaintiffs typically do not promise in their contingency-fee agreements to pursue an appeal of a lost case and instead limit the representation to the trial court. That limitation would not prevent the plaintiff's lawyer from later agreeing to pursue a meritorious appeal. The plaintiff's lawyer faces a practical, economic judgment if the appeal, like the trial-court representation, is on a contingency-fee basis, as would be the usual case. The client may also seek other appellate counsel.

Bailments. A final area in which vicarious liability may arise has to do with bailments. A bailment occurs when a person voluntarily conveys personal property to another for that other to hold (and perhaps use) until the property's return. Checking a coat or hat at a restaurant, leaving a vehicle with a valet, and checking a gun at the entrance to a hunting-resort lodge, are examples of bailments. The traditional rule that the common law of most states once recognized is that the bailor is not vicariously liable for the torts of the bailee while holding the bailor's personal property. One large inroad on the traditional rule of bailor non-liability has been by motor-vehicle owner-consent statutes. Many states have enacted legislation under which the owners of a vehicle (not including long-term commercial lessors) is vicariously liable for torts caused by another's use of the vehicle, if the owner consented to the other's use. *See* N.Y. Veh. & Traf. L. §388. Portions of one such statute appear below. The statute below and others like it create presumptions that family members of the vehicle owner have the owner's consent. Those provisions recognize the common law's family-purpose doctrine under which some courts, in states not having owner-consent statutes, find vicarious liability by presuming that family members using a vehicle were doing so for the family's benefit—even if also for the family member's pleasure. *See* McPhee v. Tufty, 623 N.W.2d 390 (N.D. 2001); *see also* Stewart v. Stephens, 225 Ga. 185, 166 S.E.2d 890 (1969) (extending family-purpose doctrine to family member's use of motorboat).

> **MICH. COMP. L. ANN. §257.401. Civil actions for injuries to person or property resulting from operation of motor vehicle; liability of owners or operators, lessors or lessees, dealers**
> (1) This section shall not be construed to limit the right of a person to bring a civil action for damages for injuries to either person or property resulting from a violation of this act by the owner or operator of a motor vehicle or his or her agent or servant. The owner of a motor vehicle is liable for an injury caused by the negligent operation of the motor vehicle whether the negligence consists of a violation of a statute of this state or the ordinary care standard required by common law. The owner is not liable unless the motor vehicle is being driven with his or her express or implied consent or knowledge. It is presumed that the motor vehicle is being driven with the knowledge and consent of the owner if it is driven at the time of the injury by his or her spouse, father, mother, brother, sister, son, daughter, or other immediate member of the family.
> (2) A person engaged in the business of leasing motor vehicles who is the lessor of a motor vehicle under a lease providing for the use of the motor vehicle by the lessee for a period that is greater than 30 days, or a dealer acting as agent for that lessor, is not liable at common law for damages for injuries to either person or property resulting from the operation of the leased motor vehicle, including damages occurring after the expiration of the lease if the vehicle is in the possession of the lessee. ...

INQUIRY

Owner-Consent Statutes. Under owner-consent statutes (or in their absence, the family-purpose doctrine), the liability of a vehicle owner for negligent injury caused by a driver to whom the owner loans the vehicle is clear enough. Clear also should be that an owner will not ordinarily have vicarious liability for injuries caused by a vehicle thief. But what if a vehicle owner consents to another's use of the vehicle, that person consents to a third person's use of the vehicle, and the third person negligently injures another using the vehicle? A general rule is that the owner remains liable for the negligence of the subpermittee (the third person). *See* Shuck v. Means, 302 Minn. 93, 226 N.W.2d 285 (1974). Note the language of the above statute that the owner must only have consented to the vehicle "being driven"—leaving (as the *Shuck* case held) the implication that the specific driver matters less than the owner having consented to the vehicle's use by others. Who drives may not matter if the owner consents to driving. Vicarious liability may well arise with any scope or line of consent from owner to negligent driver.

Subpermittees. What about the liability of those who consent to the use of other persons' vehicles, where owner-liability statutes would not directly apply? Courts recognize negligent-entrustment theories involving the use of motor vehicles, as a form of direct rather than vicarious liability. *See* Vince v. Wilson, 151 Vt. 425, 561 A.2d 103 (1989) (defendant who helped buy vehicle for alcoholic and drug-abusing family member who had no license, subject to negligent-entrustment liability); Kahlenberg v.

Goldstein, 290 Md. 477, 431 A.2d 76 (1981) (defendant who helped buy vehicle for irresponsible driver family member subject to negligent-entrustment liability). The negligent-entrustment theory applies with equal force to other items of personal property. *See* McBerry v. Ivie, 116 Ga. App. 80-8, 159 S.E.2d 109 (1967) (shotgun in hands of child); Miles v. Harrison, 223 Ga. 352, 155 S.E.2d 6 (1967) (mower); LaFaso v. LaFaso, 126 Vt. 90, 223 A.2d 814 (1966) (lighter).

Families. Should parents be vicariously liable for the torts of their children? The common-law rule is that parents are not liable. *See* Moore v. Waitt, 157 Ind. App. 1, 298 N.E.2d 456 (1973). Statutes in many states create parental vicarious liability for their children's torts but limit liability to a few thousand dollars. *See* Ind. Code §34-4-31-1 ($3,000 limit). Keep in mind, again, that direct-liability claims against parents may exist for torts committed by their children (without the statutory-damages limits) based on negligent-entrustment, respondeat-superior, and ratification theories. *See* Wells v. Hickman, 657 N.E.2d 172 (1995) (parent and grandparent liable for child beating to death another child, under circumstances where they knew or should have known of that risk of injury).

D. Contribution and Indemnity

OBJECTIVE: Given the tort liability of a defendant under various circumstances, apply the rules of contribution and indemnity stated in this section of the text to analyze and determine the obligation of other defendants or non-parties to share in, or indemnify and defend against, that liability.

Case Study: A plumber and electrician worked on a construction project. Through a combination of negligent errors by each during the course of their work on a construction project, a carpenter suffered severe electric shock and associated burns. The carpenter sued the electrician, whose insurer negotiated a settlement figure on the electrician's behalf with the carpenter. ***What terms would you include on the electrician's and his insurer's behalf in the settlement agreement with the carpenter to ensure the greatest rights and greatest protections with respect to the joint liability of the plumber? Explain your answer.***

Contribution and indemnity are, like satisfaction and release, distinct concepts often applying in the same circumstance—and so treated together here. Contribution is the claim of a defendant who is subject to liability, to require another person or entity who as a joint tortfeasor, is subject to the same liability, to pay a fair share. *See* Uniform Contribution Among Tortfeasors Act §§1, 2 (1955); *see also* National Health Labs, Inc. v. Ahmadi, 596 A.2d 555 (D.C. 1991) (defendant paying more than fair share may collect proportionate shares from other jointly and severally liable defendants). Contribution is a right. It is also the title of the cause of action that a defendant would maintain—often in a third-party complaint but occasionally in a separate action—to enforce that right. Indemnity is a separate right, claim, and title of a cause of action that a defendant may wish to maintain as a third-party claim in the same action in which the plaintiff alleges the defendant's liability. Indemnity differs from contribution in two respects. First, indemnity is a defendant's right to full reimbursement for a liability—not merely that another pay a fair share. Second, indemnity's basis is not that a joint tortfeasor owes a fair share (as to which a defendant would have contribution) but that the defendant asserting the right to indemnity has only a derivative liability based on the misconduct of the one from whom defendant seeks indemnity (in the case of common-law indemnity) or has a contractual right that another pay for it (contractual indemnity). Contribution and indemnity both rely on the fundamental equity that parties should pay compensation in proportion to their responsibility—although in contribution the responsibility is to share in paying, while in indemnity the responsibility is to make good for payment another makes on account of one's own misconduct. Consider the following illustrative case adjuciating both rights while granting neither.

Slocum v. Donahue
Massachusetts Court of Appeals
44 Mass. App. Ct. 937, 693 N.E.2d 179 (1998)

After Robert Donahue pleaded guilty to motor vehicle homicide in the death of their eighteen month old son, the Slocums filed a civil action against the Donahues alleging negligence and gross negligence. The Donahues then filed a third-party complaint against Ford Motor Company (Ford), denying negligence and alleging that Ford was negligent and was in breach of warranties of merchantability and fitness for a particular use. The Donahues claim that, when Robert Donahue was in the car prior to the accident, he inadvertently pushed the floor mat on the driver's side, under the throttle. When he later started to back the car down his driveway, the engine began to race and, although he repeatedly stepped on the brakes, his car continued to accelerate. The car's rear wheels hit the curb across the street from his house, became airborne, turned, and then hit a fence. When he got out of the car, he saw Todd Slocum lying on the lawn. The Donahues' expert would testify at trial that the floor mat was defective, permitting it to interfere with the operation of the vacuum booster which caused the power brakes to fail to function.[fn]

Prior to trial, the Slocums and Ford signed a settlement agreement providing that Ford would pay $150,000 to the Slocums in exchange for a release of any claim. Ford then moved for summary judgment as to the Donahues' claims and on the grounds that the settlement was made in good faith and ... that all claims for contribution were thereby extinguished, and that there was no basis for the Donahues' claims for indemnity. ... The Donahues appeal from the final judgment dismissing their third-party complaint against Ford.[fn] We affirm.

1. *Right to contribution.* Under G.L. c. 231B, § 4, as inserted by St.1962, c. 730, § 1, "When a release ... is given in good faith to one of two or more persons liable in tort for the same injury: ... (b) It shall discharge the tortfeasor to whom it is given from all liability for contribution to any other tortfeasor." The Donahues argue on appeal that the settlement between Ford and the Slocums was not made in good faith and was collusive both because the amount of the settlement was for less than the value of the case and because Ford allegedly told the Slocums that Ford would allow them to use its experts so that the Donahues' attempt to attribute liability to Ford at trial would be unsuccessful. ...

... [T]here were facts before the judge showing that the settlement between Ford and the Slocums was fair and reasonable. It was reasonably predictable that damages would be high and that a jury would find liability on the part of Robert Donahue, in view of the fact that he pleaded guilty in the criminal case and on the basis of his admission in his deposition that, prior to the accident, he was drinking from a bottle of vodka that he kept under the driver's seat in a brown bag. Given these facts, it was not unreasonable to think that a jury might not find any liability on the part of Ford.

According to the Donahues' attorney, in February of 1995, counsel for Ford notified the Donahues' attorney that Ford was proposing a settlement offer totaling $300,000 with $150,000 to be contributed by Ford, $125,000 by Liberty Mutual Insurance Company (the policy limits of the Donahues' insurance carrier), and $25,000 by the Donahues personally.[fn] The Donahues' attorney responded that she would discuss the matter with her clients, but that $25,000 was not an amount that her clients would be financially able to contribute to the settlement. Apparently the subsequent negotiations between the Slocums and Ford occurred without the Donahues' participation. In May, 1995, the Slocums settled with Ford for $150,000. *Noyes* [v. Raymond, 28 Mass. App. Ct. 186, 548 N.E.2d 196 (1990)] instructs that the purpose of the contribution statute is to promote settlement, that a low settlement figure *alone* is not evidence of "bad faith," and that settlements should be routinely approved without extended hearings if the purpose of the statute is to be served. Further, the court in *Noyes* observed that lack of good faith was evidenced by "collusion, fraud, dishonesty, and other wrongful conduct." *Id.* at 190, 548 N.E.2d 196. In these circumstances Ford's settlement with the Slocums for an amount contemplated as its contribution to a total settlement package does not indicate bad faith or collusion.

As to the Donahues' contention that the Slocums' use of experts originally retained by Ford is evidence of collusion, we disagree.[fn] In *Commercial Union Ins. Co. v. Ford Motor Co.*, 640 F.2d 210 (9th Cir.), cert. denied, 454 U.S. 858, 102 S.Ct. 310, 70 L.Ed.2d 154 (1981), cited by the Donahues, the court found that the settlement was collusive because, to some extent, it was "dictated by the tactical advantage of removing a deep-pocket defendant because of the experts it could produce" and, therefore, "[was] not made in 'good faith' consideration of the relevant liability of all parties." *Id.* at 214.[fn] The Donahues' argument suggests that there was bad faith here because the Slocums were not interested in the deep pocket of Ford, but settled with Ford because they believed that Ford was not responsible for the death of their son. Such a speculation does not trigger the necessity for a more extensive hearing on the issue of good faith. [C] ...

2. *Right to indemnity.* "Under G.L. c. 231B, contribution is allowed between joint tortfeasors who cause another, by reason of their wrongdoing, to incur injury or damage. In addition, ... the statute permits a plaintiff to settle with one joint tortfeasor and still have recourse against remaining tortfeasors (subject to the limitations stated in the statute). The right to contribution, unlike the right to indemnity, is based on the shared fault of the joint tortfeasors. Indemnity, on the other hand, allows someone who is without fault, compelled by operation of law to defend himself against the wrongful act of another, to recover from the wrongdoer the entire amount of his loss, including reasonable attorney's fees." *Elias v. Unisys Corp.*, 410 Mass. 479, 482, 573 N.E.2d 946 (1991). "[I]ndemnity is permitted only when the would-be indemnitee does not join in the negligent act." *Decker v. Black & Decker Mfg. Co.*, 389 Mass. 35, 40, 449 N.E.2d 641 (1983), citing *Afienko v. Harvard Club*, 365 Mass. 320, 336, 312 N.E.2d 196 (1974). "This right to indemnity is limited to those cases in which the would-be indemnitee is held derivatively or vicariously liable for the wrongful act of another." *Decker v. Black & Decker Mfg. Co.*, 389 Mass. at 40, 449 N.E.2d 641.

If the claim against Ford had gone to trial and Ford had been found liable to the Donahues,[fn] it would have been as a result of its negligence or breach of warranty.[fn] "Such liability will not be derivative or vicarious in nature, nor will it be constructive rather than actual. Accordingly, the third-party plaintiffs are not entitled to indemnification...." *Id.* at 41, 449 N.E.2d 641.

Once Ford settled with the Slocums, the sole question for the fact finder was whether Todd Slocum's death was caused by defendant Robert Donahue's negligence.[fn] Robert Donahue was free to claim that he was not negligent and that Todd Slocum's death was caused by Ford's negligence in selling a defective product. Under no set of circumstances could the jury properly have held the Donahues liable to the Slocums for the conduct of Ford. Further, in holding Robert Donahue negligent (as they did; see note 5, *supra*) the jury concluded that he was solely negligent (or was a joint tortfeasor with Ford). His liability is not vicarious and he is not entitled to indemnification from Ford. If Ford had remained in the case, any liability on its part would have been as a joint tortfeasor, and contribution would have been required. Indemnity would not have been appropriate.[fn] "Contribution and indemnity are mutually exclusive remedies." *Callahan v. A.J. Welch Equip. Corp.*, 36 Mass.App.Ct. 608, 613, 634 N.E.2d 134 (1994). Summary judgment on the issue of indemnification was appropriate. …

Judgment affirmed.

Practice

Even though the vast majority of tort cases settle rather than go to trial for verdict and judgment, a combination of factors including "tort reform," budgetary and other pressure on court dockets, and an alternative-dispute-resolution movement have resulted in measures to encourage the settlement of even more tort cases. Court rules require that parties submit all tort cases to panels for case evaluation and authorize sanctions against parties who reject the evaluated settlement figure but fail to improve their position after trial. See Mich. Court Rule 2.403. Offer-of-judgment rules permit a party to make a settlement offer and then have the court sanction the other party if its rejection of the offer fails to improve its position after trial. N.Y. McKinney's Civ. Prac. L. §3221; Cal. Code Civ. Proc. §998. Courts frequently invite—and occasionally order—parties to participate in mediations that trained mediators conduct with parties paying the mediator's fee. The efficacy of these procedures varies from case to case and jurisdiction to jurisdiction, always depending in part on the procedures' quality and the litigants' good faith and financial interests. Tort practitioners must know these procedures and develop expertise in their choice and conduct.

INQUIRY

Good Faith. As *Slocum* indicates, the law usually protects the settling defendant from a contribution claim—if the settlement was in good faith. How does the law determine good faith in the settlement context? Should the court look only for collusion, or should the court also consider the amount of the settlement? Courts divide on that question. Whatever the factors courts use in deciding good faith, the non-settling defendant who challenges a settlement to pursue contribution has an uphill battle, given the favor courts generally give to settlement. *See* Cardio Systems, Inc. v. Superior Court, 122 Cal. App.3d 880, 176 Cal. Rptr. 254 (1981) (settlement with one defendant in exchange for the defendant's agreement not to pursue costs, made in good faith as to challenge of remaining defendant seeking contribution or equitable indemnity). On the other hand, a few jurisdictions permit non-settling defendants to pursue contribution from settling defendants, even without having to show collusion. *See* Lavoie v. Celotex Corp., 505 A.2d 481 (Me. 1986). Would you advise a client defendant to settle a tort case if the client would remain subject to contribution claims from non-settling defendants in the same case?

Release. One way for the settling defendant to avoid the risk of contribution claims from other defendants is to obtain their release in the settlement. The settling party would then have no concern that the plaintiff would sue other defendants who would seek contribution from the settling defendant. In most states, a defendant who settles and obtains a release of other potentially liable persons or entities may seek contribution from those persons or entities. *See* Ariz. Rev. Stat. §12-2501(D) (West 1994); Iowa Code §668.5(2) (West 1998); Mass. Ann. Laws Ch. 231B, §1(c) (2000). Must a settling defendant obtain a nonsettling defendant's release in order for the settling defendant to obtain contribution? *See* Fetick v. American Cyanamid Co., 38 S.W.3d 415 (Mo. 2001) ("A settling defendant is barred from seeking contribution against another defendant unless the settling defendant has discharged the liability of that defendant."). Some states, on the other hand, do not allow a settling defendant to obtain contribution from others. *See* N.Y. Gen. Oblig. Law §15-108(c) (2001).

Intentional Torts. Should law grant an intentional tortfeasor a contribution claim against one whose negligence contributed to the tort? The majority rule is that intentional wrongdoers have no contribution claim because the law ought not to support or protect them in their intentional torts. *Cf.* Southern Pacific Transp. Co. v State of California, 115 Cal. App.3d 116, 171 Cal. Rptr. 187 (App. 1981) (those engaging in willful misconduct still have contribution claims); Restatement (Third) of Torts, Apportionment of Liability §16 (1999) (intentional tortfeasors should have contribution rights). Should law require contribution from one whose liability to the plaintiff arises not from liability as a joint tortfeasor but by relationship? *See* Dunn v. Praiss, 139 N.J. 564, 656 A.2d 413 (1995) (HMO subject to contribution claim of physician held liable for malpractice in wrongful death action, on basis of HMO's contract responsibility to have provided decedent with health care); *but see* Ascheman v. Village of Hancock, 254 N.W.2d 382 (Minn. 1977) (bar liable in tort to plaintiff wife and daughter, for loss of support due to injury of intoxicated husband-father, is not entitled to contribution from husband-father based on common-law duty to provide support).

Immunity. Should law require contribution when the person or entity from whom a defendant seeks contribution would be immune if plaintiff had sued? Most states follow the rule that a party immune from plaintiff's suit is also immune from a contribution action by the defendant for the same liability. *See* Crotta v. Home Depot, Inc., 249 Conn. 634, 732 A.2d 767 (1999) (parent's immunity from suit with respect to child's injury bars joint tortfeasor's contribution claim against parent). Some states permit the defendant to pursue contribution from the immune party up to the amount the immune party would have to pay under a no-fault system such as worker's compensation. *See* Kotecki v. Cyclops Welding Corp., 585 N.E.2d 1023 (Ill. 1991).

Indemnity. Contribution is unnecessary and unavailable in jurisdictions abolishing joint-and-several liability. By contrast, the abolition of joint-and-several liability does not affect indemnity, which remains an important consideration in tort cases in all jurisdictions. The right to common-law indemnity in the tort context can arise in the employment settings. When an employer has only respondeat-superior liability for the misconduct of an employee, the employer has a right of indemnity from the employee. Depending on the value of the employee and the employee's financial solvency, though, employers often forgo pursuing the right. On the other hand, law sometimes grants employees a common-law right of indemnity from the employer in circumstances when the employee's liability depends on the employee having acted on behalf of a negligent employer. Another area where common-law indemnity applies involves claims for the manufacture, distribution, and sale of injury-causing, defective products. The product's distributor and retailer may have had no direct responsibility for the product's defect and no opportunity to inspect, test for, and discover it—their products liability instead based on their having been in the chain of distribution. In that case, the manufacturer often indemnifies distributors and retailers. Indeed, the prudent distributor and retailer will have ensured their indemnity by including a *hold-harmless* clause in their contracts up the chain of distribution to the manufacturer. The primary area, though, in which indemnity arises in tort cases is through insurance policies, which are fundamentally agreements for indemnity. Consider the following case, though, showing indemnity's limits.

Interinsurance Exch. of the Auto. Club v. Flores
California Court of Appeals
53 Cal. Rptr.2d 18 (Ct. App. 1996)

GILBERT, J. An insured drives his van to a location to allow his passenger to shoot someone from the van. The driver has a standard auto insurance policy that provides coverage for injuries caused by an accident. Does the policy provide the driver with coverage for injuries to the victim? No.

Rosemary and David Flores (Flores) appeal from the judgment in favor of respondent, Interinsurance Exchange of the Automobile Club of Southern California (Automobile Club) in this declaratory relief action. We affirm the judgment.

FACTS

The facts are stipulated. An unknown pedestrian punched Eric Michael Sanders in the face while Sanders sat in his van waiting for a traffic light to change at State Street and Figueroa in Santa Barbara. Sanders told Roger Perez of the incident. Perez suggested they return to the scene, locate the assailant and seek retribution. Perez told Sanders he was armed with a handgun before he and others got into the van. Sanders knew that someone was likely to get shot. He drove Perez and the others back to the intersection where Sanders had been punched. David Flores stood on the corner of the intersection. While Sanders drove by, Perez intentionally shot and injured Flores from the van. The van itself did not inflict any injury on Flores, nor was it used to block or pin down Flores.

After his arrest for his involvement in the shooting, Sanders admitted that he knew someone was likely to be shot. In the criminal action Sanders pled nolo contendere to the felony of aiding and abetting the shooting of Flores ([c]). [C]

Rosemary Flores, individually, and as guardian ad litem for David Flores, filed the underlying civil suit against Sanders and others for conspiracy, battery and negligence. The Flores' suit alleged, inter alia, that Sanders and Perez "agreed to hunt down, shoot, and either kill or maim the perpetrator of the Sanders' attack, using Roger Perez' .22 caliber handgun." ...

Sanders owns the van involved and his parents insured it for him under an automobile insurance policy issued by the Automobile Club. The Automobile Club reserved its rights to deny coverage and filed the instant declaratory relief action to determine whether or not it had a duty to defend or indemnify Sanders for liability in the underlying Flores' action under the policy.

The trial court denied summary judgment to the Automobile Club and the parties proceeded to trial by the court on the stipulated facts. After trial, the trial court found that the shooting was not an accident, that Sanders acted intentionally in aiding and abetting the shooting and that the injuries inflicted on the Flores family were not covered by the instant policy. In its judgment, the trial court ruled that the Automobile Club is not obligated to indemnify Sanders for liability he may have to the Flores. This appeal ensued from the judgment. ...

COVERAGE

Use of the vehicle

In an insurance policy, the phrase "arising out of the use" has broad and comprehensive application. [C] It affords coverage for injuries where the insured vehicle bears "almost *any* causal relation" to the accident at issue, however minimal. [C] Here, Sanders drove to the scene for the purpose of seeking retaliation and left the scene of the shooting by use of the van. The insurer admits that the van "was passing through the intersection" when Perez shot Flores. We agree with the trial court that the Sanders' van was being used at all pertinent times within the meaning of the instant policy language.

Occurrence

The instant policy promises to "pay damages for which any person insured is legally liable because of bodily injury ... *caused by an occurrence* arising out of the ownership, maintenance or use" of the insured vehicle. (Italics added.) "Occurrence" is defined to mean "an *accident* ..., including injurious exposure to conditions, which results in bodily injury...." (Italics added.) Therefore, the instant policy provides coverage to Sanders only if he accidentally caused the injury to Flores. ...

When an injury is an unexpected or unintended consequence of the insured's conduct, it may be characterized as an accident for which coverage exists. When the injury suffered is *expected* or *intended,* coverage is denied. When one expects or intends an injury to occur, there is no "accident." [C]

Flores argues that Sanders' acts were not intended or expected because he did not shoot Flores himself or direct that he be shot. Therefore, his conduct was, at most, reckless. [Cc] We disagree. ...

Here, ... the underlying complaint and the stipulated facts establish that the instant shooting was no accident. It was planned. Sanders knew Perez was armed with a deadly weapon. He drove Perez to the place where he thought they might find the person who had punched him. Sanders knew that someone was likely to be shot. Sanders therefore intended and expected injury to result from his acts. The Flores have not borne their burden to show that Sanders' conduct was accidental within the meaning of the instant insurance policy. Accordingly, Flores did not establish potential coverage for the shooting incident.

EXCLUSIONS

Insurance Code Section 533

Coverage is also excluded because the acts were willful within the meaning of section 533, which provides a statutory exclusion in every insurance policy. [C] Section 533 states, "*An insurer is not liable for* a loss caused by the *wilful act of the insured; but* he is *not exonerated by the negligence* of the insured, or of the insured's agents or others." (Emphasis added.) ...

Because a negligent act may be done "wilfully"—the act is volitional—the term "wilful act" in section 533 means something more than performing a voluntary act which constitutes negligence. [C]

Our Supreme Court has explained that "section 533 does not preclude coverage for acts that are negligent or reckless." (*J.C. Penney Casualty Ins. Co. v. M.K., supra,* 52 Cal.3d at p. 1021, 278 Cal.Rptr. 64, 804 P.2d 689.) Where application of section 533 becomes an issue, the insurance company must establish that the insured acted with intent to harm or that the insured committed an inherently wrongful act. (*Id.* at pp. 1021-1027, 278 Cal.Rptr. 64, 804 P.2d 689.)

But, the general rule of strict construction against the insurer regarding exclusions does not apply to section 533 because it is a statutory exclusion evincing a fundamental public policy. [C] If coverage is excluded under section 533, we may not consider whether there may be coverage under any express exclusions stated in the insurance policy. [C] Whether there may be coverage due to section 533 depends upon the facts of the case.

There may be coverage under section 533 for an accident caused by drunk driving because drunk driving, per se, is reckless conduct. [C] There may not be coverage for an act such as child molestation because that act is deemed to be inherently wrongful or harmful in itself. [C] ...

Here, Sanders pled nolo contendere to the felony criminal charge of aiding and abetting an assault with a deadly weapon. "The legal effect of such a [nolo] plea, ... shall be the same as that of a plea of guilty for all purposes." (Pen.Code, § 1016, subd. 3.) Guilty and nolo pleas are admissible in a subsequent civil action, such as the underlying action, as an admission of the crime. Therefore, Sanders admitted committing the crime of aiding and abetting an assault with a deadly weapon. ...

Under section 533, the question here is whether Sanders' admission of the crime of aiding and abetting assault with a deadly weapon, together with the other stipulated or pleaded facts, constitute acts which are either inherently harmful or which evince an intent to harm.

The stipulated facts establish that Sanders drove Perez back to the intersection where Sanders had been punched in order to retaliate. Sanders knew someone was likely to get shot. When an offense includes the intent to do some act beyond the actus reus of the crime, one who aids and abets the crime *must share the specific intent of its perpetrator.* [C] Although the stipulated facts do not state the crime for which Perez was charged and convicted, they do state that "Roger Perez intentionally shot David Flores with a .22 caliber revolver while Roger Perez was inside the van."

By aiding and abetting the intentional shooting, Sanders is a principal to it and he is equally guilty for that act. (CALJIC No. 3.00) Under these facts, we conclude that Sanders harbored intent to harm within the meaning of section 533. [C]

The underlying complaint also supports our conclusion that Sanders evinced an intent to harm another. Each of its causes of action incorporate by reference the allegation that Sanders and Perez "agreed to hunt down, shoot, and either kill or maim the perpetrator of the Sanders' attack, using Roger Perez' .22 caliber handgun."

The Automobile Club has established that it may deny coverage under the implied exclusion set forth in section 533. ...

CONCLUSION

"The concept of 'fortuity' is basic to insurance law. Insurance typically is designed to protect [against] contingent or unknown risks of harm [citations], not to protect against harm which is certain or expected. [Citation.]" (*Chu v. Canadian Indemnity Co., supra,* 224 Cal.App.3d at pp. 94-95, 274 Cal.Rptr. 20; *Waller v. Truck Ins. Exchange, Inc., supra,* 11 Cal.4th at pp. 16-17, 44 Cal.Rptr.2d 370, 900 P.2d 619.) Sanders expected harm to occur here and he acted deliberately to help bring it about. Under the stipulated facts and allegations in the underlying complaint, the Automobile Club need not defend or indemnify the Flores' claims against Sanders.

The judgment is affirmed. Each party to bear their own costs.

INQUIRY

Scope of Indemnity. The *Flores* case represents the treatment of insurance-indemnity claims when the defendant seeks indemnity for injuries caused by an intentional act. Insurance ordinarily offers indemnity for harm caused by negligent rather than intentional acts. What does indemnity include? Claims for indemnity are only partly over paying settlement or judgment amounts for the liability incurred. They are also for the associated litigation costs—especially defense costs (attorney's fees and litigation costs) but also interest and costs or attorney's fees paid to the prevailing party. The costs of defense can be substantial even when the liability is not. Insurance policies typically provide for indemnity and defense. Why would an insurance company agree, indeed insist, that it provide the defense? Who decides when to settle—the insurer or the insured? Insurance policies pay only up to pre-determined figures—what insurers call *policy limits*. What happens when an insurer refuses to settle a case within the policy limits and a jury returns a verdict that subjects the insured to a judgment well in excess of those policy limits?

Ethics

The insurer's contractual right to retain, pay, and to some extent control the activities of defense counsel, through litigation budgets and review and approval procedures, raises significant ethical issues for defense counsel. When an insurer retains defense counsel to defend an insured in litigation, the formal understanding is that the insured is defense counsel's client—not the insurer who selected, retained, and pays defense counsel. Defense counsel appears in the litigation on behalf of the defendant insured. Defense counsel treats and describes the defendant insured as defense counsel's client. But in effect, defense counsel has two clients—both the insurer and the insured. Not only does the insurer select and retain defense counsel, but defense counsel reports to the insurer, and the insurer usually (although less often in professional-malpractice cases) has the contractual right to settle the case within policy limits. The ethical peril in what some call this "infernal triangle" or "eternal triangle" arises when the insured's interests depart from the insurer's—as when the insurer could settle the case within policy limits but refuses, and the insured faces a judgment in excess of those policy limits. *See Crisci v. The Security Ins. Co.,* 426 P.2d 173 (Cal. 1967) (insurer subject to insured's bad-faith claim for insurer's refusal to settle for its $10,000 policy limits, a claim that resulted in a $101,000 verdict). Because of the conflict of interest, defense counsel

> must avoid advising the insurer or insured regarding the conflicting rights of one another. Insurers and insureds typically retain other counsel to negotiate and litigate coverage disputes while defense counsel conducts the defense of the underlying tort litigation.

E. Apportionment of Damages

OBJECTIVE: Given a plaintiff who was injured at more than one different time under circumstances where a party is liable for one or more of the injuries, sort the injuries for which the party is liable from those for which the party is not liable under the apportionment rules stated in this section of the text.

Case Study: A teen seriously injured his elbow in a skating-boarding accident on a public sidewalk outside of his home. His mother got him in the family vehicle to drive him to the emergency room. On the way, as the teen's mother was driving through an intersection, a motorist ran a stop sign in another vehicle and collided with the passenger side of the vehicle in which the teen was riding. The accident aggravated the teen's elbow injury from the skating-boarding incident. The teen also suffered a serious leg injury. An ambulance took the teen to the emergency room, where a physician negligently treated the teen's leg, considerably worsening the leg injury. ***Describe the motorist's and physician's relative liability for the teen's elbow and leg injuries.***

Many states abolishing joint-and-several liability apportion damages through a system of comparative fault that assigns percentages of fault to two or more defendants and then apportions the damages according to those percentages. Other apportionment issues can arise. One other issue is when the plaintiff has a pre-existing injury and condition that defendant's tort aggravates. In that case where the tort follows and aggravates an earlier injury, the rule is that defendant pays only for the aggravation. If the factfinder cannot distinguish aggravation from the underlying condition, then courts have held the defendant liable for the entire condition. *See* Lovely v. Allstate Ins. Co., 658 A.2d 1091 (Me. 1995) (defendant who was responsible for second of two motor-vehicle accidents that injured the plaintiff's elbow, was liable for entire elbow condition where parties could not distinguish first and second injuries); *cf.* Loui v. Oakley, 50 Haw. 260, 438 P.2d 393 (1968) (instruct jury to make "rough estimate" as to which of four accidents caused which injuries, failing which to apportion damages equally among the accidents).

What happens with two or more successive torts, and when no basis exists for allocating fault among the two or more defendants because their liability is not joint but rather as successive tortfeasors? Ordinarily, each defendant who successively injures a plaintiff pays only for the injury each defendant caused. Yet parties cannot in all cases distinguish among successive injuries. Often enough, one tortfeasor will aggravate an injury that another tortfeasor initially caused, where the factfinder cannot distinguish the extent of the aggravation from the underlying injury. Where states have abolished joint-and-several liability, courts may be willing to apportion fault not merely among joint tortfeasors (as required by the abolition of joint-and-several liability) but also among *successive* tortfeasors, if the factfinder cannot distinguish the injuries they cause. *See* Piner v. Superior Court, 192 Ariz. 182, 962 P.2d 909 (1998) (if damages are indivisible among successive injuries from successively liable defendants in one lawsuit, then apportion damages by comparative fault); *see also*

Restatement (Third) of Torts: Apportionment of Liability §50 (2000) (first divide damages as possible, then apportion indivisible damages according to fault allocation).

What of the situation where an injury follows the tort for which the defendants are liable? As the following case and figure illustrate, courts may apportion damages in those cases under the rule that defendants bear no liability for damages for a successive injury when the factfinder cannot separate their portion of the damages from successive injury.

Bruckman v. Pena
Colorado Court of Appeals
29 Colo. App. 357, 487 P.2d 566 (1971)

DWYER, J. ... Plaintiff William Pena, a minor, brought this action by his mother, as next friend, against the defendants to recover damages for personal injuries sustained in an automobile collision. Plaintiff's parents, Marie Pena and Frank Pena, in a separate claim for relief, sought to recover medical expenses incurred by them for the treatment of their son's injuries. They also sought to recover for loss of earnings of their son, who was sixteen years old at the time he was injured.

The case was tried to the jury. Verdicts were returned in favor of William Pena in the sum of $50,000, and in favor of his parents in the sum of $8,063. Defendants, appearing here as plaintiffs in error, seek reversal of the judgments entered on the verdicts.

Plaintiff was injured on July 21, 1964, when the car in which he was riding collided with a truck driven by the defendant Bruckman and owned by the defendant Armored Motors Service. On June 11, 1965, plaintiff was injured in a second collision and certain injuries he had sustained in the first collision were aggravated. ... [T]he only defendants named in the action are the owner and driver of the truck involved in the first collision. ...

The [jury] instruction complained of concerns the amount of damages recoverable from the defendants. The first part of the instruction, which is a proper statement of the law applicable to the case, is as follows: "If you find that after the collision complained of Plaintiff, William Pena, had an injury which aggravated the ailment or disability received in the collision complained of, the Plaintiff is entitled to recover for the injury or pain received in the collision complained of; but he is not entitled to recover for any physical ailment or disability which he may have incurred subsequent to the collision. Where a subsequent injury occurs which aggravated the condition caused by the collision, it is your duty, if possible, to apportion the amount of disability and pain between that caused by the subsequent injury and that caused by the collision."

In addition to this correct statement of the law, the court further instructed the jury: "But if you find that the evidence does not permit such an apportionment, then the Defendants are liable for the entire disability."

It is the general rule that one injured by the negligence of another is entitled to recover the damages proximately caused by the act of the tort-feasor, and the burden of proof is upon the plaintiff to establish that the damages he seeks were proximately caused by the negligence of the defendant. In accordance with this general rule, we hold that the instruction is in error because it permits the plaintiffs to recover damages against the defendants for injuries which the plaintiff received subsequent to any act of negligence on the part of the defendants and from causes for which the defendants were in no way responsible. The instruction erroneously places upon the defendants the burden of proving that plaintiff's disability can be apportioned between that caused by the collision here involved and that caused by the subsequent injury in order to limit their liability to the damages proximately caused by their negligence. Counsel for plaintiffs argues that the rules concerning apportionment of disability announced by our Supreme Court in Newbury v. Vogel, 151 Colo. 520, 379 P.2d 811, should also apply here. In Newbury, the Court stated:

"We find the law to be that where a pre-existing diseased condition exists, and where after trauma aggravating the condition disability and pain result, and no apportionment of the disability between that caused by the pre-existing condition and that caused by the trauma can be made, in such case, even though a portion of the present and future disability is directly attributable to the pre-existing condition, the defendant, whose act of negligence was the cause of the trauma, is responsible for the entire damage."

The pre-existing condition in the Newbury case was of nontraumatic origin, but the rules there announced also apply where the pre-existing condition was caused by trauma. [C] The reasons for the adoption of the Newbury rules are not present here. It is one thing to hold a tort-feasor who injures one suffering from a pre-existing condition liable for the entire damage when no apportionment between the pre-existing condition and the damage caused by the defendant can be made, but it is quite another thing to say that a tort-feasor is liable, not only for the damage which he caused, but also for injuries subsequently suffered by the injured person. We hold that the defendants here cannot be held liable for the plaintiff's subsequent injury and this is so whether or not such damage can be apportioned between the two injuries.

The plaintiffs also rely on the case of Maddux v. Donaldson, 362 Mich. 425, 108 N.W.2d 33, 100 A.L.R.2d 1. This case involved a chain-type collision, and plaintiff's injuries resulted from successive impacts which to all intents and purposes were concurrent. The court there held that where independent concurring negligent acts have proximately caused injury and damage which cannot be apportioned between the tort-feasors, each tort-feasor is jointly and severally liable for all of the injury and damage. This rule is not applicable where, as here, the second injury or aggravation of the first injury is attributable to a distinct intervening cause without which the second injury or aggravation would not have occurred. ...

Judgments reversed and cause remanded for a new trial on the issues of damages alone.

Career

Soloing in tort practice can make a rewarding and satisfying career. Solo practitioners and lawyers in firms of just two to five members maintain plaintiff's and defense practices in torts. Insurance carriers may approve a solo practitioner or small firm as assigned counsel. A solo practitioner or small firm can base much of its work on assignments from just a single insurance company. On the plaintiff's side, solo practitioners and small firms may do nothing other than represent tort victims. They often develop specialty areas, although they just as often serve clients in a variety of torts cases. Law students can prepare for solo or small-firm torts practices by taking courses like Law Office Management and taking academic credits in clinics set up like small firms. New solo practitioners often find office-sharing relationships with other lawyers to provide a referral network and mentors, and to reduce start-up costs.

> Working for yourself has its benefits, especially when you have entrepreneurial skills, good sense, and strong work habits.

Chapter XVII

No-Fault Systems

Commentators expect a reinvigoration of no-fault systems. Modern society's speed and complexity, and its unusually pervasive technology and commercial interests, contribute to the seeming pervasiveness of tort law today. Yet we have seen that the earliest recorded laws—the ancient Laws of Ur-Nammu, Code of Lipit-Ishtar, Laws of Eshnunna, and Code of Hammurabi (all around 4,000 years old)—contain fault-based liability provisions. The ancient Roman laws, including the famous Twelve Tables of 433 A.D., were replete with detailed fault-based tort liability provisions. Of course, the Torah, which for millennia has been the foundational legal text for Jews, Christians, and Muslims alike, contains fault-based rules for compensation. Even the earliest of recorded old English cases, I de S et ux. v. W de S, [1348] Y. B. Lib. Ass. folio 99, placitum 60, had in it a rule of fault-based liability. Taking as an example the most historic and general of admonitions, to love God and your neighbor as you love yourself, one sees that tort law's care is hardly a recent invention. The social Darwinist view of tort law as having evolved out of a "medieval chrysalis" of amoral early law, *see* Wex S. Malone, *Ruminations on the Role of Fault in the History of the Common Law of Torts*, 31 La. L. Rev. 1, 9 (1970), is incorrect. *See* George P. Fletcher, *Fairness and Utility in Tort Theory*, 85 Harv. L. Rev. 537, 539 (1972) ("These beliefs about tort history are ubiquitously held, but to varying degrees they are all false or at best superficial."). Instead, the recent invention is that law does better without a fault moral.

History aside, recent experience suggests what tort law without fault looks like. Every state has a worker's compensation system that removes fault as an employer-employee issue for most workplace injuries. The worker's compensation no-fault system is expensive. The American Law Institute Reporters' Study *Enterprise Responsibility for Personal Injury* estimates worker's compensation payments made by employers to have risen from $2 billion in 1960 to nearly $35 billion in 1985 and $62 billion in 1992. Relative costs may have fallen since then. No-fault schemes are not always workable. Although approximately half of states adopted motor-vehicle no-fault schemes in the 1970s and 1980s, several have since repealed them, and only twelve states retain substantial no-fault schemes—with every one of those twelve states also retaining a fault-based compensation system for more serious injuries. Other recent experiences? In 1972, New Zealand's labor government abolished tort law based on collective rather than individual responsibility and adopted in its place a general no-fault remedy for accidental injury, administered by the government and financed by vehicle, employer, and general taxation. Query whether a tax-based, government-administered, collectivist program like New Zealand's, that largely eliminated compensation for pain and suffering and shifted the burden of uninsured loss to the poorest—especially women with children—would be consistent with the American understanding of individual independence, responsibility, accountability, and compassion. Australia introduced but rejected legislation similar to that adopted in New Zealand. No other nation has adopted such comprehensive no-fault legislation.

The New Zealand plan remains in effect today in a modified form in which risk-insurance premiums have replaced social-welfare levies as the system's revenue.

A perceived tort-litigation explosion, coupled with higher insurance costs especially in a few medical specialties, fueled scrutiny of the fault-based tort system. However, the American Law Institute's reporters' study mentioned above concluded from systematic analysis of claims trends "that there never was a true general explosion in tort litigation, or at least that any incipient trend has definitely subsided." In 1991, Rand's Institute for Civil Justice published an empirical study on the effects of shifting from fault to no-fault in motor vehicle liability. *See* Stephen J. Carroll, James S. Kakalik, Nicholas M. Pace, & John L. Adams, *No-Fault Approaches to Compensating People Injured in Automobile Accidents*, 1991 Institute for Civil Justice R-4019-ICJ. The report deduced that the total amount spent on compensating those injured by motor vehicle accidents indeed went down by twenty-two percent in no-fault versus fault states— from $3,645 to $3,182. The report also showed that the reduction occurred partly by eliminating the injured person's non-economic recovery and partly by reducing the payment lawyers receive, serving the injured. Insurance rates go down by eliminating recoveries and requiring the injured to forgo an advocate and bear the costs. Yet the report also concluded that a too-generous no-fault system can have the opposite effect of increasing total injury coverage costs. The determinative question appears not to be fault but the allowed recovery—the extent to which the injured should pay the price.

Scholars dispute whether adopting no-fault systems removes a deterrent to negligent conduct and increases accident rates. *Contrast* Elizabeth Landes, *Insurance Liability and Accidents: A Theoretical and Empirical Investigation of the Effect of No-Fault Accidents*, 25 J.L. & Econ. 49 (1982) (removes some deterrent), *with* Jeffery O'Connell & Saul Levmore, *A Reply to Landes: A Faulty Study of No-Fault's Effect on Fault?*, 48 Mo. L. Rev. 649, 652 (1983) (to be effective, empirical studies must be "awesomely complicated"). Insurance premiums have their own deterrent effect— safer drivers should pay lower premiums. Yet insurers' inability to discriminate between high and low risks, and the litigation system's limited ability to distinguish inexpensively between meritorious and non-meritorious claims, complicate the empirical questions. Whether no-fault systems make for more dangerous workplaces and interstates is unclear, but they will in at least some cases make the non-negligent pay for the negligent. *See* Keith N. Hylton & Steven E. Laymon, *The Internalization Paradox and Workers' Compensation*, 21 HOFSTRA L. REV. 109, 112 (1992) ("[e]fforts to reform the tort system by reforming the litigation process may have the unintended consequence of exacerbating the externalization problem"). Even under no-fault, the business of adjusting claims and rates remains hard and expensive work.

The current debate over fault versus no-fault systems may be shifting to individual choice—in motor-vehicle insurance, what the public knows as the "tort option." *See* Ky. Rev. Stat. Ann. §304.39-060(4) ("Any person may refuse to consent to the limitations of his tort rights and liabilities as contained in this section."); N.J. Stat. Ann. § 39:6A-1; 75 Pa. Cons. Stat. Ann. § 1705. Studies suggest that choice reduces insurance premiums for those who choose no-fault (thereby losing their traditional tort-law rights). *See* Allan Abrahamse & Stephen Carroll, *The Effects of a Choice Automobile Insurance Plan Under Consideration by the Joint Economic Committee of the United States Congress*, 1997 Institute for Civil Justice DRU-1609-ICJ. The no-fault option appears not to influence other rates for those who stick with the traditional fault system. *See* Allan F. Abrahamse & Stephen J. Carroll, *The Effects of a Choice Auto Insurance Plan on Insurance Costs*, 1995 Institute for Civil Justice MR-540-ICJ. Kentucky, New Jersey, and Pennsylvania have adopted choice plans.

The victim-compensation legislation Congress enacted in the wake of the September 11th terrorist attacks was a tort-option system. It allowed 2,680 injured persons and surviving family members of 2,880 persons killed to collect about $7 billion in compensation (an average of $2 million per family and $400,000 per injured person) in both economic and non-economic damages—unusual (in the latter respect) for a no-fault system. Taxpayers funded the payments, also serving to preserve an ailing airline industry. A minority of qualifying beneficiaries opted out to pursue common-law rights. Though reluctant to create other administrative-compensation schemes, Congress has done so on rare occasions. *See* National Childhood Vaccine Injury Act of 1986, 42 U.S.C. §§300aa-10 to 300aa-33; Black Lung Act of 1969, 30 U.S.C. §§901 et seq. Virginia and Florida have also enacted limited administrative schemes regulating medical-malpractice claims alleging neurological injuries during the delivery of infants. Fla. Stat. ch. 766.301-.316; Va. Code §§38.2-5000 to 38.2-5021.

What cannot occur without tort law itself becoming something twisted and losing justification and form is to divorce care—the fundamental concept that we owe one another some regard—from tort law. As Justice Potter Stewart put it with what another United States Supreme Court justice labeled his "customary clarity," "The right of a man to the protection of his own reputation from unjustified invasion and wrongful hurt reflects no more than our basic concept of the essential dignity and worth of every human being—a concept at the root of any decent system of ordered liberty." Rosenblatt v. Baer, 383 U.S. 75, 92 (1966) (Stewart, J., concurring), *quoted in* Milkovich v. Lorain Journal Co., 497 U.S. 1, 22 (1990) (Rehnquist, C.J.). Law cannot divorce care (including its absence fault) from tort law any more than from the law profession—cannot, at least, without cutting off law's root and the profession's reason for existing. As one high court concluded, "[i]n the field of tort law, the most equitable result that can ever be reached by a court is the equation of liability with fault." Blackburn v. Dorta, 348 So. 2d 287, 293 (Fla. 1977) (quoting Hoffman v. Jones, 280 So. 2d 431, 438 (Fla. 1973)).

A. Motor Vehicle

OBJECTIVE: Given an injury or loss arising out of the operation, use, or maintenance of a motor vehicle, identify and evaluate the motor-vehicle no-fault scheme issues that would arise with respect to claims for the injury or loss.

Case Study: A motorist's vehicle ran a red light colliding violently with a woman's 2002 Ford Pinto. The collision totaled the Pinto. The collision also required emergency and follow-up treatment of the woman's fractures. The motorist's vehicle was uninsured. The motorist had lost his job recently and not paid the premium. The injured woman maintained motor vehicle insurance but had opted for no collision coverage. The injured woman's husband from whom the woman had separated also had coverage. The woman was living at the time with her mother who also had coverage. The mother had to help the injured woman with bathing, dressing, and walking for several weeks. The mother's husband (the injured woman's stepfather) did errands for the injured woman. The injured woman had health insurance, but it only covered 80% of her medical care. The injured woman was self-employed and could not work for 12 weeks. Her income fell drastically. The motorist who caused the collision also had significant medical expense related to his accident injuries. ***Identify and evaluate the motorist's and injured woman's first- and third-party motor-vehicle no-fault rights and claims.***

The costs of motor vehicle accidents in general are large—approaching $100 billion annually by one estimate. *See* Roberta F. Mann, *On the Road Again: How Tax Policy Drives Transportation Choice*, 24 Va. Tax Rev. 587, 606 (2005). The physical hazards created when large numbers of relatively inexpert drivers accelerate themselves and their passengers and cargo to considerable speed across varied terrain under all weather conditions are extraordinary. Federal and state governments attempt to reduce and redistribute motor-vehicle-accident costs through a complex variety of criminal and civil laws and administrative regulations. The primary compulsory legal regime found in every state and the District of Columbia is one that mandates motorists' "financial responsibility," satisfied by carrying bodily injury and property-damage insurance coverage. *See* D.C. Code Ann. §50-1301.34 et seq.; Fl. Stat. Ann. §324.021; Ga. Code Ann. §33-34-4; W. Va. Code §17D-2A-3(a). The Illinois Vehicle Code has a typical provision stating:

> Proof of ability to respond in damages for any liability thereafter incurred resulting from the ownership, maintenance, use or operation of a motor vehicle for bodily injury to or death of any person in the amount of $20,000, and subject to this limit for any one person injured or killed, in the amount of $40,000 for bodily injury to or death of 2 or more persons in any one accident, and for damage to property in the amount of $15,000 resulting from any one accident. This proof in these amounts shall be furnished for each motor vehicle registered by every person required to furnish this proof. [625 ILL. COMP. STAT. ANN. §5/1-164.5 (eff. Jan. 1, 1998).]

The amounts of these minimum limits vary from state to state. The lowest minimum insurance requirements are Florida's at $10,000 per person, $20,000 per occurrence, and $10,000 for property damage. Fl. Stat. Ann. §324.021(7). The highest requirements are Alaska's and Maine's at $50,000 per person, $100,000 per occurrence, and $25,000 for property damage. Ak. Stat. §§28.20.440(2), 21.89.020; 29 Me. Rev. Stat. Ann. §1605.1.C (eff. Jan. 1, 1995).

Largely to attempt to control the growing cost of motor-vehicle accidents and the compulsory insurance covering them, legislatures adopted motor-vehicle no-fault systems in about half of the United States and the District of Columbia beginning in the early 1970s as part of the response to the expansion of tort law that had occurred over the previous half-century. Experience with the no-fault acts over the next two decades gradually led several states to abandon the experiment and return to a pure or modified common-law negligence system. Depending on how one classifies the variety of no-fault systems that remain, about twelve states (Florida, Hawaii, Kansas, Kentucky, Massachusetts, Michigan, Minnesota, New Jersey, New York, North Dakota, Pennsylvania, and Utah) have no-fault systems. Three other states, New Jersey, Pennsylvania, and Kentucky, permit a choice of fault or no-fault systems. Nine states (Arkansas, Delaware, Maryland, Oregon, South Carolina, South Dakota, Texas, Virginia, and Washington) follow fault systems but grant a choice of add-on no-fault insurance coverage. The remaining states treat motor-vehicle accident injuries under the common law of negligence.

No-Fault. Although the systems show substantial variety, the basic structure of no-fault acts is to eliminate negligence recoveries for mild to moderate injuries—effectively granting immunity to negligent drivers—in exchange for a guarantee of first-party insurance benefits without regard to fault. Whether a negligent driver causes the injuries or not, each injured person looks to their own insurer, or if they own no vehicle to insure, then to a priority scheme of insurers, for medical expense, wage loss, replacement-service, and rehabilitation expenses. In theory, the first-party coverage and benefits are generous, assured to all, and promptly paid, in a legislative exchange barring the injured person's right to recover for pain, suffering, and other non-economic loss from at-fault drivers. However, no-fault systems preserve the right of a seriously injured person to pursue a negligence action against at-fault drivers (and vehicle owners vicariously liable under state law) who cause the serious injury—in no-fault parlance a "third-party claim." In a third-party no-fault claim, a person who has a motor-vehicle-accident injury sufficiently serious to meet the no-fault act's liability threshold may hold liable an at-fault driver.

Tort Threshold. Some no-fault systems establish the threshold for a liability action using verbal formulations ("serious injury," "serious impairment of body function," etc.) and others by monetary amount in medical expense or other economic loss. The challenge in these systems is to draw the line between serious and non-serious injuries, meaning those that qualify for a liability action and those that do not qualify. Line drawing is difficult for courts in tort cases. As cases approach the line from either direction, the decision to award or not award looks increasingly arbitrary. Considering that the majority of state-law tort cases are motor-vehicle accident cases, how courts draw the line between what is a threshold injury and what is not has enormous consequences for tort practice in no-fault states. Practitioners follow closely the decisions, trends, and tendencies of the courts on the no-fault threshold issue. The threshold can also be a political issue, as the recent history of Michigan's threshold well demonstrates. Political parties nominate Michigan Supreme Court justices, even though the justices run on a non-partisan ballot. As the court's political majorities have tipped back and forth over the past decade, so have the court's threshold decisions. Consider the following case that represents a fifth successive major effort—either legislative or judicial—at clarifying Michigan's no-fault threshold since its adoption of a no-fault act.

McCormick v. Carrier,
Michigan Supreme Court
795 N.W.2d 517 (2010)

CAVANAGH, J. The issue in this case is the proper interpretation of the "serious impairment of body function" threshold for non-economic tort liability under MCL 500.3135. We hold that *Kreiner v. Fischer*, 471 Mich. 109, 683 N.W.2d 611 (2004), was wrongly decided because it departed from the plain language of MCL 500.3135, and is therefore overruled. We further hold that, in this case, as a matter of law, plaintiff suffered a serious impairment of a body function. Accordingly, we reverse and remand the case to the trial court for proceedings consistent with this opinion.

I. FACTS AND PROCEEDINGS

This case arises out of an injury that plaintiff, Rodney McCormick, suffered while working as a medium truck loader at a General Motors Corporation (GM) plant.[fn] Plaintiff's job mainly consisted of assisting in the loading of trucks, which required climbing up and around trucks and trailers, standing, walking, and heavy lifting. He generally worked nine- to ten-hour shifts, six days a week.

On January 17, 2005, a coworker backed a truck into plaintiff, knocking him over, and then drove over plaintiff's left ankle. Plaintiff was immediately taken to the hospital, and x-rays showed a fracture of his left medial malleolus.[fn] Plaintiff was released from the hospital that day, and two days later metal hardware was surgically inserted into his ankle to stabilize plaintiff's bone fragments. Plaintiff was restricted from weight-bearing activities for one month after the surgery and then underwent multiple months of physical therapy. The metal hardware was removed in a second surgery on October 21, 2005.

At defendant's request, plaintiff underwent a medical evaluation with Dr. Paul Drouillard in November 2005. He indicated that plaintiff could return to work but was restricted from prolonged standing or walking. On January 12, 2006, the specialist who performed plaintiff's surgeries cleared him to return to work without restrictions. The specialist's report noted that plaintiff had an "excellent range of motion," and an x-ray showed "solid healing with on [sic] degenerative joint disease of his ankle."

Beginning on January 16, 2006, plaintiff returned to work as a medium truck loader for several days, but he had difficulty walking, climbing, and crouching because of continuing ankle pain. He requested that his job duties be restricted to driving, but defendant directed him to cease work.

Defendant required plaintiff to undergo a functional capacity evaluation (FCE) in March 2006. The FCE determined that plaintiff was unable to perform the range of tasks his job required, including stooping, crouching, climbing, sustained standing, and heavy lifting. This was due to ankle and shoulder pain,[fn] a moderate limp, and difficulty bearing weight on his left ankle. The report stated that plaintiff's range of motion in his left ankle was not within normal limits and that difficulty climbing and lifting weights had been reported and observed.

... At plaintiff's request, another FCE was performed on August 1, 2006, which affirmed that plaintiff could return to work without restriction and was capable of performing the tasks required for his job. The report stated that plaintiff complained of "occasional aching" and tightness in his ankle, but it did not appear to be aggravated by activities such as prolonged standing or walking. It also noted that plaintiff's range of motion in his left ankle was still not within normal limits, although it had improved since the March 2006 FCE.

Plaintiff returned to work on August 16, 2006, 19 months after he suffered his injury. He volunteered to be assigned to a different job, and his pay was not reduced. He has been able to perform his new job since that time.

On March 24, 2006, plaintiff filed suit, seeking recovery for his injuries under MCL 500.3135. In his October 2006 deposition, plaintiff testified that at the time of the incident, he was a 49-year-old man and his normal life before the incident mostly consisted of working 60 hours a week as a medium-duty truck loader. He stated that he also was a "weekend golfer" and frequently fished in the spring and summer from a boat that he owns. He testified that he was fishing at pre-incident levels by the spring and summer of 2006, but he has only golfed once since he returned to work.[fn] He stated that he can drive and take care of his personal needs without assistance and that his relationship with his wife has not been affected. He stated that he has not sought medical treatment for his ankle since January 2006, when he was approved to return to work without restriction. He further testified that his life is "painful, but normal," although it is "limited," and he continues to experience ankle pain.

The trial court granted defendant's motion for summary disposition on the basis that plaintiff had recovered relatively well and could not meet the serious impairment threshold provided in MCL 500.3135(1). The Court of Appeals affirmed, with one judge dissenting. [C] ...

After initially denying leave to appeal, this Court granted plaintiff's motion for reconsideration, vacated its prior order, and granted the application for leave to appeal. *McCormick v. Carrier,* 485 Mich. 851 (2009). ...

II. STANDARD OF REVIEW

This Court reviews a motion for summary disposition de novo. [C] The proper interpretation of a statute is a legal question that this Court also reviews de novo. [C]

III. ANALYSIS

The issue presented in this case is the proper interpretation of MCL 500.3135. We hold that *Kreiner* incorrectly interpreted MCL 500.3135 and is overruled because it is inconsistent with the statute's plain language and this opinion. Further, under the proper interpretation of the statute, plaintiff has demonstrated that, as a matter of law, he suffered a serious impairment of body function. ...

In 1973, the Michigan Legislature adopted the no-fault insurance act, MCL 500.3101 et seq. The act created a compulsory motor vehicle insurance program under which insureds may recover directly from their insurers, without regard to fault, for qualifying economic losses arising from motor vehicle incidents. [Cc] In exchange for ensuring certain and prompt recovery for economic loss, the act also limited tort liability. [Cc] The act was designed to remedy problems with the traditional tort system as it relates to automobile accidents. These included that "[the contributory negligence liability scheme] denied benefits to a high percentage of motor vehicle accident victims, minor injuries were overcompensated, serious injuries were undercompensated, long payment delays were commonplace, the court system was overburdened, and those with low income and little education suffered discrimination." Shavers v. Attorney General, 402 Mich. 554, 579, 267 N.W.2d 72 (1978).

Under the act, tort liability for non-economic loss arising out of the ownership, maintenance, or use of a qualifying motor vehicle is limited to a list of enumerated circumstances. MCL 500.3135(3). The act creates threshold requirements in MCL 500.3135(1), which has remained unchanged in all key aspects since the act was adopted. That subsection currently provides that "[a] person remains subject to tort liability for noneconomic loss caused by his or her ownership, maintenance, or use of a motor vehicle only if the injured person has suffered death, serious impairment of body function, or permanent serious disfigurement."

The threshold requirement at issue in this case is whether plaintiff has suffered "serious impairment of body function." The act did not originally define this phrase. ...

In 1995, however, the Legislature intervened. It amended MCL 500.3135 to define a "serious impairment of body function" as "an objectively manifested impairment of an important body function that affects the person's general ability to lead his or her normal life." MCL 500.3135(7). The Legislature also expressly provided that whether a serious impairment of body function has occurred is a "question[ ] of law" for the court to decide unless there is a factual dispute regarding the nature and extent of injury and the dispute is relevant to deciding whether the standard is met. MCL 500.3135(2)(a). ...

This Court interpreted the amended provisions in 2004, in *Kreiner.* The question before this Court is whether the *Kreiner* majority properly interpreted the statute, and, if not, whether its interpretation should be overruled. ...

... [The] issue is the proper interpretation of MCL 500.3135(7). It provides that, for purposes of the section, a "serious impairment of body function" is "an objectively manifested impairment of an important body function that affects the person's general ability to lead his or her normal life." On its face, the statutory language provides three prongs that are necessary to establish a "serious impairment of body function": (1) an objectively manifested impairment (2) of an important body function that (3) affects the person's general ability to lead his or her normal life.[fn]

Overall, because we conclude that each of these prongs' meaning is clear from the plain and unambiguous statutory language, judicial construction is neither required nor permitted. [C] Notably, however, a dictionary may aid the Court in giving the words and phrases in MCL 500.3135(7) their common meaning... . As will be discussed within, where the *Kreiner* majority's interpretation of these prongs is inconsistent with the clear language of the statute, we hold that *Kreiner* was wrongly decided. Most significantly, its interpretation of the third prong deviates dramatically from the statute's text.

a. AN OBJECTIVELY MANIFESTED IMPAIRMENT

Under the first prong, it must be established that the injured person has suffered an objectively manifested impairment of body function. The common meaning of "an objectively manifested impairment" is apparent from the unambiguous statutory language, with aid from a dictionary... . To the extent that the *Kreiner* majority's interpretation of this prong differs from this approach, it was wrongly decided.

To begin with, the adverb "objectively" is defined as "in an objective manner," Webster's Third New International Dictionary (1966), and the adjective "objective" is defined as "1. Of or having to do with a material object as distinguished from a mental concept. 2. Having actual existence or reality. 3. a. Uninfluenced by emotion, surmise, or personal prejudice. b. Based on observable phenomena; presented factually...." The American Heritage Dictionary, Second College Edition (1982). It is defined specifically in the medical context as "[i]ndicating a symptom or condition perceived as a sign of disease by someone other than the person afflicted." *Id*.[fn] The verb "manifest" is defined as "1. To show or demonstrate plainly; reveal. 2. To be evidence of; prove." *Id*. Overall, these definitions suggest that the common meaning of "objectively manifested" in MCL 500.3135(7) is an impairment that is evidenced by actual symptoms or conditions that someone other than the injured person would observe or perceive as impairing a body function. In other words, an "objectively manifested" impairment is commonly understood as one observable or perceivable from actual symptoms or conditions. ...

The *Kreiner* majority's interpretation of this language was only partially consistent with the plain language of the statute. It addressed this issue briefly, stating that "[s]ubjective complaints that are not medically documented are insufficient [to establish that an impairment is objectively manifested]." Kreiner, 471 Mich. at 132, 683 N.W.2d 611. ... [T]o the extent that *Kreiner* could be read to *always* require medical documentation, it goes beyond the legislative intent expressed in the plain statutory text, and was wrongly decided.

b. OF AN IMPORTANT BODY FUNCTION

If there is an objectively manifested impairment of body function, the next question is whether the impaired body function is "important." The common meaning of this phrase is expressed in the unambiguous statutory language, although reference to a dictionary and limited reference to *Cassidy* is helpful.

The relevant definition of the adjective "important" is "[m]arked by or having great value, significance, or consequence." The American Heritage Dictionary, Second College Edition (1982). See also Random House Webster's Unabridged Dictionary (1998), defining "important" in relevant part as "of much or great significance or consequence," "mattering much," or "prominent or large." Whether a body function has great "value," "significance," or "consequence" will vary depending on the person. Therefore, this prong is an inherently subjective inquiry that must be decided on a case-by-case basis, because what may seem to be a trivial body function for most people may be subjectively important to some, depending on the relationship of that function to the person's life. ...

c. THAT AFFECTS THE PERSON'S GENERAL ABILITY TO LEAD HIS OR HER NORMAL LIFE

Finally, if the injured person has suffered an objectively manifested impairment of body function, and that body function is important to that person, then the court must determine whether the impairment "affects the person's general ability to lead his or her normal life." The common meaning of this phrase is expressed by the unambiguous statutory language, and its interpretation is aided by reference to a dictionary, reading the phrase within its statutory context.... .

To begin with, the verb "affect" is defined as "[t]o have an influence on; bring about a change in." The American Heritage Dictionary, Second College Edition (1982). An "ability" is "[t]he quality of being able to do something," *id.,* and "able" is defined as "having sufficient power, skill, or resources to accomplish an object." Merriam-Webster Online Dictionary, (accessed May 27, 2010). The adjective "general" means:

> 1. Relating to, concerned with, or applicable to the whole or every member of a class or category. 2. Affecting or characteristic of the majority of those involved; prevalent: *a general discontent* . 3. Being usually the case; true or applicable in most instances but not all. 4. a. Not limited in scope, area, or application: *as a general rule.* b. Not limited to one class of things: *general studies.* 5. Involving only the main features of something rather than details or particulars. ..." [The American Heritage Dictionary, Second College Edition (1982).]

... "[G]eneral" does not refer to only one specific detail or particular part of a thing, but, at least some parts of it. Thus, these definitions illustrate that to "affect" the person's "general ability" to lead his or her normal life is to influence some of the person's power or skill, i.e., the person's capacity, to lead a normal life.

The next question is the meaning of "to lead his or her normal life." The verb "lead," in this context, is best defined as "[t]o pass or go through; live." The American Heritage Dictionary, Second College Edition (1982). Although the verb "lead" has many definitions, some of which have similar nuances, this definition is the most relevant because it expressly applies in the context of leading a certain type of life. ...

Therefore, the plain text of the statute and these definitions demonstrate that the common understanding of to "affect the person's ability to lead his or her normal life" is to have an influence on some of the person's capacity to live in his or her normal manner of living. By modifying "normal life" with "his or her," the Legislature indicated that this requires a subjective, person- and fact-specific inquiry that must be decided on a case-by-case basis. Determining the effect or influence that the impairment has had on a plaintiff's ability to lead a normal life necessarily requires a comparison of the plaintiff's life before and after the incident.

There are several important points to note, however, with regard to this comparison. First, the statute merely requires that a person's general ability to lead his or her normal life has been *affected,* not destroyed. Thus, courts should consider not only whether the impairment has led the person to completely cease a pre-incident activity or lifestyle element, but also whether, although a person is able to lead his or her pre-incident normal life, the person's general ability to do so was nonetheless affected.

Second, and relatedly, "general" modifies *"ability,"* not "affect" or "normal life." Thus, the plain language of the statute only requires that some of the person's *ability* to live in his or her normal manner of living has been affected, not that some of the person's normal manner of living has itself been affected. Thus, while the extent to which a person's general ability to live his or her normal life is affected by an impairment is undoubtedly related to what the person's normal manner of living is, there is no quantitative minimum as to the percentage of a person's normal manner of living that must be affected.

Third, and finally, the statute does not create an express temporal requirement as to how long an impairment must last in order to have an effect on "the person's general ability to live his or her normal life." [T]here is no such requirement in the plain language of the statute. ...

Despite the fact that the language of the statute was plain, the *Kreiner* majority deviated significantly from the statutory text in its interpretation of this prong. To begin with, the *Kreiner* majority erred in its interpretation of the phrase "that affects the person's general ability" for two reasons. First, it selectively quoted only the dictionary definitions of "general" that best supported its conclusions. It gave one definition for this word, "'the whole; the total; that which comprehends or relates to all, or the chief part; a general proposition, fact, principle, etc.; opposed to particular; that is, opposed to special,'" and then relied on definitions of "in general" and "generally" to conclude that "general" means "'for the most part.'" Kreiner, []683 N.W.2d 611, quoting Webster's New International Dictionary. Webster's, however, offers *10* definitions of the adjective "general," many of which are similar to definitions quoted above from The American Heritage Dictionary. Moreover, of these 10 definitions, the majority chose the most restrictive, even though, as discussed above, it does not make the most sense in this context. And, even then, the *Kreiner* majority looked to other forms of the word. ...

Further, the *Kreiner* majority significantly erred in its interpretation of "to lead his or her normal life."

... [T]he *Kreiner* majority went astray and gave the statute a labored interpretation inconsistent with common meanings and common sense. Applying its chosen definition of "lead," the majority concluded that "the effect of the impairment on the course of a plaintiff's entire normal life must be considered," and if "the course or trajectory of the plaintiff's normal life has not been affected, then the plaintiff's 'general ability' to lead his normal life has not been affected...." Kreiner, []683 N.W.2d 611. In other words, the *Kreiner* majority held that the "common meaning" of whether an impairment has affected "the person's general ability to lead his or her normal life" is whether it has affected the person's general ability to conduct the course or trajectory of his or her entire normal life. This "common meaning" is quite different from the actual statutory text in form and substance. Significantly, the *Kreiner* majority's interpretation of the statute interjects two terms that are not included in the statute *or* the dictionary definitions of the relevant statutory language: *"trajectory"* and *"entire."* Both terms create ambiguity where the original statutory text had none, and the *Kreiner* majority thus erred by selectively defining the words used in definitions of statutory terms in order to shift away from the common meaning that the words have in the context of MCL 500.3135(7). ...

The *Kreiner* majority aggravated this error, and departed even more dramatically from the statutory text, by providing an extra-textual "nonexhaustive list of objective factors" to be used to compare the plaintiff's pre-and post-incident lifestyle. ...

... Therefore, we hold that the *Kreiner* majority's interpretation of this prong, including the list of non-exhaustive factors, is not based in the statute's text and is incorrect. ...

Under the facts of this case, we hold that plaintiff has met the serious impairment threshold as a matter of law.

To begin with, there is no factual dispute that is material to determining whether the serious impairment threshold is met. The parties do not dispute that plaintiff suffered a broken ankle, was completely restricted from bearing weight on his ankle for a month, and underwent two surgeries over a 10-month period and multiple months of physical therapy. ...

The other facts material to determining whether the serious impairment threshold is met are also undisputed.[fn] Before the incident, plaintiff's "normal life" consisted primarily of working 60 hours a week as a medium truck loader. Plaintiff also frequently fished in the spring and summer and was a weekend golfer. After the incident, plaintiff was unable to return to work for at least 14 months and did not return for 19 months. ...

Next, in light of the lack of a factual dispute that is material to determining whether the threshold is met, under MCL 500.3135(2)(a), this Court should decide as a matter of law whether plaintiff suffered a serious impairment of body function under the three prongs in MCL 500.3135(7).

With regard to the first prong, plaintiff has shown an objectively manifested impairment of body function. There is no dispute that plaintiff has presented evidence that he suffered a broken ankle and actual symptoms or conditions that someone else would perceive as impairing body functions, such as walking, crouching, climbing, and lifting weight. Even 14 months after the incident, an FCE report observed that ankle pain and a reduced range of motion inhibited these body functions. Thus, plaintiff has satisfied this prong.

With regard to the second prong, the impaired body functions were important to plaintiff. His testimony establishes that being unable to walk and perform other functions were of consequence to his ability to work. Thus, the second prong of MCL 500.3135(7) is met.

The next question in this case is whether the third prong is met, but we hold that plaintiff has shown that the impairment affected his general ability to lead his normal life because it influenced some of his capacity to live in his normal, pre-incident manner of living. Before the incident, plaintiff's normal manner of living consisted primarily of working, for 60 hours a week, and secondarily his hobbies of fishing and golfing. After the incident, at least some of plaintiff's capacity to live in this manner was affected. Specifically, for a month after the incident, plaintiff could not bear weight on his left ankle. He underwent two surgeries over a period of 10 months and multiple months of physical therapy. Moreover, his capacity to work, the central part of his pre-incident "normal life," was affected.[fn] Whereas before the incident he spent most of his time working, after the incident he was unable to perform functions necessary for his job for at least 14 months, and he did not return to work for 19 months.[fn] On the basis of these facts, we conclude that some of plaintiff's capacity to live in his pre-incident manner of living was affected, and the third prong of MCL 500.3135(7) is satisfied.[fn]

Because all three prongs of MCL 500.3135(7) are satisfied, we hold, as a matter of law, that plaintiff has met the serious impairment threshold requirement under MCL 500.3135(1). ...

IV. CONCLUSION

We hold that *Kreiner* should be overruled because the *Kreiner* majority's interpretation of MCL 500.3135 departed from the statute's clear and unambiguous text. Applying the unambiguous statutory language, we hold that as a question of law, in this case, plaintiff established that he suffered a serious impairment of body function. Thus, we reverse the Court of Appeals and remand the case to the trial court for proceedings consistent with this opinion.

KELLY, C.J., and WEAVER (except for the part entitled "Stare Decisis"), and HATHAWAY, JJ., concurred with CAVANAGH, J.

WEAVER, J. (concurring)[omitted].

HATHAWAY, J. (concurring)[omitted].

MARKMAN, J. (dissenting).

I respectfully dissent from the majority's decision to overrule *Kreiner v. Fischer*, 471 Mich. 109, 683 N.W.2d 611 (2004). ...

The majority overrules *Kreiner*, rejecting these factors and holding that temporal considerations are wholly or largely irrelevant in determining whether an impairment affects the plaintiff's general ability to lead his normal life. The majority instead holds that, as long as the plaintiff's general ability to lead his normal life has been affected, apparently for even a single moment in time, the plaintiff has suffered a "serious impairment of body function." This conclusion is at odds with the actual language of the no-fault automobile act and nullifies the legislative compromise embodied in that act. I continue to believe that *Kreiner* was correctly decided, and that temporal considerations are highly relevant-indeed necessary-in determining whether an impairment affects the plaintiff's general ability to lead his normal life. By nullifying the legislative compromise, which was grounded in concerns over excessive litigation, the overcompensation of minor injuries, and the availability of affordable insurance, the Court's decision today will resurrect a legal environment in which each of these hazards reappear and threaten the continued fiscal integrity of our no-fault system.

Because I do not believe that the lower courts erred in concluding that plaintiff in this case has not suffered a serious impairment of body function, I would affirm the judgment of the Court of Appeals. ...

In *Kreiner*, this Court for the first time interpreted the Legislature's definition of "serious impairment of body function." Because "generally" means "'for the most part,'" *Kreiner* held that "determining whether a plaintiff is 'generally able' to lead his normal life requires considering whether the plaintiff is, 'for the most part' able to lead his normal life." Kreiner, []683 N.W.2d 611, quoting Random House Webster's

College Dictionary (1991). In addition, because "lead" means " 'to conduct or bring in a particular course,' " *Kreiner* held that "the effect of the impairment on the course of a plaintiff's entire normal life must be considered." *Id.*[], quoting Random House Webster's Unabridged Dictionary (2001). Therefore, *Kreiner* concluded, "[a]lthough some aspects of a plaintiff's entire normal life may be interrupted by the impairment, if, despite those impingements, the course or trajectory of the plaintiff's normal life has not been affected, then the plaintiff's 'general ability' to lead his normal life has not been affected and he does not meet the 'serious impairment of body function' threshold." *Id.*[] ...

The majority overrules *Kreiner* while paying its usual lip service to stare decisis.[fn] ...

The new majority assumed power in January 2009, and wasted little time in beginning its efforts to "undo" decisions of the previous majority.[fn] ...

It is quickly becoming a new favored practice of the majority to flag decisions of the past decade and invite challenges to those decisions. It is difficult to reconcile this practice with the majority's previous claims of fidelity to stare decisis. ...

In 2010, the majority has accelerated efforts to "undo" numerous cases decided by the former majority through express overrulings and additional orders asking parties to brief whether a case should be overruled. ...

The majority's work, however, has apparently only just begun. It has already teed up six more cases in its grant orders for possible overruling. ...

The new majority once purported to be concerned about the stability of the law,[fn] but that concern appears to have passed with the passing of the former majority. Indeed, it is difficult to consider anything more destabilizing to the law than to have the majority issue multiple orders continually requesting that the parties brief whether recently decided cases have been properly decided. Justices who once postured as champions of stare decisis now cannot act quickly enough to reverse disfavored precedents. The majority's past claims of fealty to stare decisis were greatly exaggerated, and obviously nothing more than a function of their opposition to *particular* decisions being decided by the Court at the time. ...

As discussed earlier, although virtually all legislation involves some sort of compromise, the no-fault act, in particular, entailed a substantial and well-understood compromise. In exchange for the payment of economic loss benefits from one's own insurance company (first-party benefits), the Legislature limited an injured person's ability to sue a negligent operator or owner of a motor vehicle for noneconomic losses (third-party benefits). [C] ...

At least two reasons are evident concerning why the Legislature limited recovery for noneconomic loss, both of which relate to the economic viability of the system. First, there was the problem of the overcompensation of minor injuries. Second, there were the problems incident to the excessive litigation of motor vehicle accident cases. Regarding the second problem, if noneconomic losses were always to be a matter subject to adjudication under the act, the goal of reducing motor vehicle accident litigation would likely be illusory. The combination of the costs of continuing litigation and continuing overcompensation for minor injuries could easily threaten the economic viability, or at least desirability, of providing so many benefits without regard to fault. If every case is subject to the potential of litigation on the question of noneconomic loss, for which recovery is still predicated on negligence, perhaps little has been gained by granting benefits for economic loss without regard to fault. ...

In addition, it has been repeatedly recognized that, due to the mandatory nature of no-fault insurance, the Legislature intended that its cost be affordable. [C] ...

The majority's decision will not only result in increased automobile insurance premiums, and more uninsured vehicles on our roads and highways, but it will also mean that substantially more lawsuits will be filed, even though an express goal of the no-fault act was to reduce "excessive litigation of motor vehicle accident cases." [C] Yet, under the majority's opinion, more lawsuits will make their way to juries for the consideration of noneconomic loss benefits, straining our already overburdened courts.[fn] As it is, no-fault automobile negligence cases remain a dominant factor in Michigan civil filings every year. Indeed, of the 47,300 new civil case filings in Michigan circuit courts in 2009, 9,067—approximately 20 percent of all civil cases—were automobile related.[fn] Given that many no-fault claims are settled without the filing of a lawsuit, the number of claims potentially affected by the majority's ruling is even higher. ...

Finally, and as a consequence of all of the above, the majority's decision will almost certainly call into question the long-term economic integrity of the present no-fault system in Michigan. By nullifying the legislative compromise that was struck when the no-fault act was adopted—a compromise grounded in concerns over excessive litigation, the over-compensation of minor injuries, and the availability of affordable insurance—the Court's decision today will restore a legal environment in which each of these hazards reappear and threaten the continued fiscal soundness of our no-fault system.[fn] ...

Because I do not believe that the lower courts erred in concluding that plaintiff has not suffered a serious impairment of body function, I would affirm the judgment of the Court of Appeals.

CORRIGAN and YOUNG, JJ., concurred with MARKMAN, J.

INQUIRY

Alternative Thresholds. Compare Michigan's "serious impairment of body function" no-fault threshold discussed in the above case to New York's "serious injury" threshold in the statute that follows. Do you think that the New York statute defines the threshold any clearer than the Michigan statute? How would you advise a client whose injury approached the threshold?

> **NEW YORK INSURANCE CODE §5102. Definitions**
> In this chapter:
> (a) "Basic economic loss" means, up to fifty thousand dollars per person of the following combined items... :
> (1) All necessary expenses incurred for: (i) medical, hospital (including services rendered in compliance with article forty-one of the public health law, whether or not such services are rendered directly by a hospital), surgical, nursing, dental, ambulance, x-ray, prescription drug and prosthetic services; (ii) psychiatric, physical therapy (provided that treatment is rendered pursuant to a referral) and occupational therapy and rehabilitation; (iii) any non-medical remedial care and treatment rendered in accordance with a religious method of healing recognized by the laws of this state; and (iv) any other professional health services; all without limitation as to time, provided that within one year after the date of the accident causing the injury it is ascertainable that further expenses may be incurred as a result of the injury. ...

(2) Loss of earnings from work which the person would have performed had he not been injured, and reasonable and necessary expenses incurred by such person in obtaining services in lieu of those that he would have performed for income, up to two thousand dollars per month for not more than three years from the date of the accident causing the injury. ...

(3) All other reasonable and necessary expenses incurred, up to twenty-five dollars per day for not more than one year from the date of the accident causing the injury. ...

(4) "Basic economic loss" shall not include any loss incurred on account of death ... .

(5) "Basic economic loss" shall also include an additional option to purchase, for an additional premium, an additional twenty-five thousand dollars of coverage which the insured or his legal representative may specify will be applied to loss of earnings from work and/or psychiatric, physical or occupational therapy and rehabilitation after the initial fifty thousand dollars of basic economic loss has been exhausted. ...

(b) "First party benefits" means payments to reimburse a person for basic economic loss on account of personal injury arising out of the use or operation of a motor vehicle... .

(c) "Non-economic loss" means pain and suffering and similar non-monetary detriment.

(d) "Serious injury" means a personal injury which results in death; dismemberment; significant disfigurement; a fracture; loss of a fetus; permanent loss of use of a body organ, member, function or system; permanent consequential limitation of use of a body organ or member; significant limitation of use of a body function or system; or a medically determined injury or impairment of a non-permanent nature which prevents the injured person from performing substantially all of the material acts which constitute such person's usual and customary daily activities for not less than ninety days during the one hundred eighty days immediately following the occurrence of the injury or impairment. ...

NEW YORK INSURANCE CODE §5104. Causes of action for personal injury

(a) Notwithstanding any other law, in any action by or on behalf of a covered person against another covered person for personal injuries arising out of negligence in the use or operation of a motor vehicle in this state, there shall be no right of recovery for non-economic loss, except in the case of a serious injury, or for basic economic loss. ...

(b) In any action by or on behalf of a covered person, against a non-covered person, where damages for personal injuries arising out of the use or operation of a motor vehicle or a motorcycle may be recovered, an insurer which paid or is liable for first party benefits on account of such injuries has a lien against any recovery to the extent of benefits paid or payable by it to the covered person. ...

(c) Where there is no right of recovery for basic economic loss, such loss may nevertheless be pleaded and proved to the extent that it is relevant to the proof of non-economic loss.

INQUIRY

Coverage. No-fault practice can be surprisingly complex. Seven major issues can arise in evaluating no-fault rights and benefits: (1) coverage, (2) exclusions, (3) priority, (4) benefits, (5) setoffs, (6) property damage, and (7) the third-party claims discussed in the above *McCormick* case. The coverage issue is simply whether the injury that arose is one that falls within the legislative no-fault scheme, for injuries arising out of the ownership, operation, maintenance, or use of a motor vehicle as a motor vehicle. No-fault laws generally cover injuries to occupants of automobiles colliding on the highways. No-fault laws generally cover injuries to pedestrians and other non-occupants when the accident involves the use of a motor vehicle. They may also cover injuries while loading and unloading vehicles, entering and alighting from vehicles, and maintaining and repairing vehicles—but not (again to suggest the complexity and subtlety of the schemes) injuries from use of a motor vehicle as a scaffold or hunting stand. *See* Morosini v. Citizens Ins. Co., 602 N.W.2d 828 (Mich. 1999) (no first-party coverage for injuries from fight between two drivers involved in minor collision); McKenzie v. Auto Club Ins. Assn., 580 N.W.2d 424 (Mich. 1998) (no first-party coverage for asphyxiation injuries from sleeping in camper attached to insured pickup truck). Also implicated in the coverage issue is what constitutes a motor vehicle. A typical definition would be a more than two-wheeled vehicle designed for operation on public highways and powered by other than muscular power—not including motorcycles, tractors, and other farm and purely off-road vehicles. Consider one coverage case.

Matter of Manhattan & Bronx Surface Transit Oper. Auth.
New York Supreme Court, Appellate Division
71 A.D.2d 1004, 420 N.Y.S.2d 298 (1979)

MEMORANDUM BY THE COURT.

In a proceeding to stay arbitration of a no-fault insurance claim, the appeal is from a judgment of the Supreme Court, Kings County, dated March 13, 1979, which granted petitioner's application to permanently stay arbitration.

Judgment affirmed, with $50 costs and disbursements.

The appellant was injured when, in the course of his duties as a bus driver, he was stabbed by a passenger whom he refused to discharge from the bus at a location other than a designated bus stop. In an effort to collect first party no-fault insurance benefits, the appellant demanded arbitration. He appeals from a judgment which permanently stayed arbitration of his no-fault claim.

First party no-fault benefits are available to "reimburse a person for basic economic loss on account of personal injury arising out of the use or operation of a motor vehicle" (Insurance Law, §671, subd. 2). At issue is whether the appellant was injured as a result of the "use or operation" of a motor vehicle.

There is no question that the use of a bus entails the discharge of passengers at designated locations, and that the appellant was injured while he was operating a bus. However, these factors are insufficient to establish that the injury resulted from the use or operation of a motor vehicle as contemplated by the no-fault provisions of the Insurance Law.

Three rules have been formulated to determine an insurer's liability under standard automobile liability policies. These rules are that:

"'1. The accident must have arisen out of the inherent nature of the automobile, as such; 2. The accident must have arisen within the natural territorial limits of an automobile, and the accidental use, loading, or unloading must not have terminated; 3. The automobile must not merely contribute to cause the condition which produces the injury, but must, itself, produce the injury'" (Goetz v. General Acc. Fire & Life Assur. Corp., 47 Misc.2d 67, 69, 262 N.Y.S.2d 305, 307, citing 7 Appleman, Insurance Law and Practice, s 4317, affd. without opn. 26 A.D.2d 635, 272 N.Y.S.2d 979, affd. without opn. 19 N.Y.2d 762, 279 N.Y.S.2d 521, 226 N.E.2d 310).

These rules are equally applicable to the determination of no-fault insurance coverage (cf. Amins v. Government Employees Ins. Co., N.Y.L.J., June 8, 1976, p. 13, col. 1), and when so applied, it is plain that the appellant is not entitled to first party benefits.

The appellant was not injured by the bus or an appurtenance thereof. Although the refusal to use the bus in an unauthorized manner may have been a motivating factor in precipitating the assault, contrary to principles one and three above, the injury neither arose from the intrinsic nature of the bus, as such, nor did the bus, itself, produce the injury. Regardless of whether injuries arise out of the performance of one's duties as an operator of a motor vehicle, first party no-fault insurance benefits are available only when a motor vehicle, by its use or operation, is the actual instrumentality which produces the injuries.

This requirement, that the vehicle itself actually produces injury, reflects the limitation of no-fault insurance to automobile torts as distinguished from the other types of tort. Here the injury resulted from a knife-wielding passenger and the appellant's operation of the bus was largely incidental. The assault may not be characterized as a motor vehicle tort as contemplated by the no-fault insurance law. It was therefore proper to stay arbitration of appellant's no-fault claim.

INQUIRY

Exclusions. Simply because coverage exists does not necessarily mean that the insurer must pay. Statutory no-fault schemes authorize insurers to exclude coverage around certain acts and circumstances. Insurers may wish to exclude many different kinds of conduct or conditions that affect underwriting costs (costs of insuring). Yet because no-fault schemes are statutory creatures, the exclusions where a policy will not provide coverage depend on statutory categories. Those statutory exclusions typically include claims by an intentional tortfeasor and by one whom law requires to have no-fault insurance in place but fails to do so. Statutory exclusions may include other misconduct such as drunk driving. Consider the following case reflecting that exclusion, present in New York but not necessarily available elsewhere.

Fafinski v. Reliance Insurance Co.
New York Court of Appeals
484 N.E.2d 121 (1985)

MEMORANDUM.
The order of the Appellate Division, [c,] should be affirmed for the reasons stated in the opinion of Justice Stewart F. Hancock, Jr., and judgment absolute granted to defendant, without costs, in accordance with the stipulation of the parties. We add only that there is nothing in the language of the insurance policy to limit the exclusion of benefits to only those individuals actually convicted under Vehicle and Traffic Law §1192. The policy exclusion, which tracks the governing statutory provision (Insurance Law § 5103[b][2], formerly § 672[2][b]), provides that an insurer may exclude from coverage a person injured "as a result of operating a motor vehicle while in an intoxicated condition" within the meaning of section 1192 of the New York Vehicle and Traffic Law. Plaintiff, who had a blood alcohol content of .276% when tested shortly after the accident, asserts that a conviction under section 1192 is required

by the subject exclusionary clause. His position would render the exclusion of coverage for intoxicated drivers inapplicable for those drivers who, by virtue of having blood alcohol content in excess of .10%, have committed a per se violation of Vehicle and Traffic Law § 1192(2), but who, for one reason or another, have not been charged, prosecuted or convicted under section 1192. Such an anomalous result contravenes the legislative purposes of denying coverage for losses resulting from violations of the law (*see,* Insurance Law § 5103[b]) and of keeping premiums low (*see generally, Montgomery v. Daniels,* 38 N.Y.2d 41, 62, 378 N.Y.S.2d 1, 340 N.E.2d 444). ...

... [O]rder affirmed, without costs, and judgment absolute granted to defendant in a memorandum.

INQUIRY

Priority. Two or more insurers frequently provide potential no-fault coverage for a single accident. The drivers of each involved vehicle, the owners of each involved vehicle, passengers within the involved vehicles, and even pedestrians injured by motor vehicle may all own motor vehicles and thus have motor-vehicle no-fault coverage. For ease and efficiency of administration, statutory no-fault schemes state priorities so that only one insurer, or in rare cases two insurers of equal priority, will pay any one claim for no-fault benefits. The priority schemes necessarily tend toward complexity because of the complex relationships and interests. They also vary. They may begin with the injured claimant's own no-fault insurer and, if none exists, may then look to no-fault insurers of the injured person's spouse or resident relatives, then to the no-fault insurers of the owner and driver of the occupied and involved vehicles, and finally (if no insurer anywhere) to an assigned-claims facility. Priority schemes are claimant and practitioner hazards. Submitting claims to the wrong insurer may result in delay that bars the correct insurer's payment of claims.

Benefits and Setoffs. As indicated above, first-party benefits in a no-fault scheme typically include one-hundred percent of reasonably necessary medical expense for accident-related injuries. No-fault schemes may permit no-fault insurers to coordinate those benefits with health-insurance benefits so that, if the no-fault policy provides, the health insurer pays first and the no-fault insurer pays co-pays and deductibles. For Medicare- or Medicaid-eligible injured persons, and those insured through ERISA plans, the order of payment reverses (no-fault insurer first, then Medicare or Medicaid) because of the supremacy of federal over state law. Medical-expense benefits are typically lifetime but capped at a gross amount (for instance, $1 million). Work-loss benefits for work the injured person could not perform because of motor-vehicle accident-related injuries may exist at a reduced percentage (for instance, 85%), limited duration (for instance, three years), and capped monthly amounts. Social Security and other disability-plan benefits may also coordinate or setoff against first-party no-fault work loss benefits. Some schemes also offer replacement-service expense at capped amounts for limited duration (for instance, $20 per day for up to three years) for home services the injured person usually performed but could not because of accident-related injuries.

Property Damage. Motor-vehicle accidents can cause substantial property damage to buildings and other structures along highways. Most no-fault schemes do not cover property damage caused by the use of a motor vehicle. No-fault schemes that do extend first-party coverage and third-party immunity from negligence claims not only to personal injury but also to property damage, guarantee payment by the first-party no-fault insurer of real and personal property damaged in a motor-vehicle accident, excluding the vehicles and their contents. *See* Mich. Comp. L. §§500.3121-.3127. Policyholders would purchase optional coverage for damage to vehicles and their contents separately from the no-fault property-damage coverage law required.

Procedure. No-fault schemes may have shorter limitations periods for first-party-benefits claims than the state's general negligence limitations period, such as one year rather than three years. They may also permit insurers to require the injured person to notify the insurer within a defined period after the motor-vehicle accident, such as one year. As an incentive to the insurer to promptly pay valid claims, no-fault schemes may have penalty-interest, attorney's-fee, and cost provisions for unreasonable failures and refusals to pay, and delays in paying, valid claims.

Uninsured Drivers. Large numbers of vehicle owners required by law to maintain motor-vehicle insurance operate their vehicles or allow others to operate them illegally without the insurance in place. Making matters worse, uninsured drivers cause a disproportionate percentage of motor-vehicle accidents. The percentage of uninsured drivers varies substantially from state to state depending on the administration of the insurance laws (whether, for instance, one must show proof of insurance to obtain registration and plates), their enforcement regimes (from fees to fines, license suspension or revocation, incarceration, and vehicle impoundment), insurance availability and cost, and driver demographics. Utah, for instance, saw its uninsured motorist percentage fall from 23% to 9% after implementing a system under which the insurer notifies the state license bureau when a policyholder fails to pay a motor-vehicle insurance premium under certain conditions, and the bureau then revokes driver's license and vehicle registration under other conditions. New York has one of the lower uninsured-motorist percentages at 7% (half the national average of 14%), even though it has a large urban and immigrant population. California, by contrast, has one of the higher rates, although not quite as high as Mississippi, which leads the nation at 26%.

Uninsured-Motorist Coverage. Some states require vehicle registrants to purchase uninsured-motorist (UM) coverage. Persons protected by uninsured-motorist coverage receive up to the policy limit when able to prove an injury compensable by one who failed to maintain the required motor-vehicle insurance. Even where a state does not require uninsured-motorist coverage, insurers may offer it as an option. The practitioner representing a person negligently injured by an uninsured motorist should check for uninsured-motorist coverage. Some motor-vehicle-insurance policies also provide for underinsured-motorist coverage. As indicated above in the introduction to this section, motor-vehicle-insurance policies have coverage limits varying from state minimums as low as $7,500 per person up to whatever the insured chooses to purchase—occasionally $1 million but more commonly $50,000, $100,000, or possibly $300,000. If the plaintiff's recoverable liability claim exceeds the defendant's insurance policy limits, and the plaintiff has underinsured-motorist coverage, then that coverage may make up the difference between the defendant's limits and the value of the plaintiff's claim (within the underinsured-motorist-coverage limits).

B. Workers' Compensation

OBJECTIVE: **Given a workplace injury, determine whether worker's compensation covers the injury, identify and describe the likely benefits, and determine whether those benefits are the injured person's exclusive remedy, as stated in this section.**

Case Study: A worker was injured while cleaning a plastic-injection molding machine at her workplace. The electrical circuitry was exposed in an area where the worker reached to vacuum dust and debris, with the result that the worker received a severe high-voltage shock, burns to the hands, and nerve injuries. A distributing company installed the machine. The worker does not expect to return to work for at least several months. Reports by OSHA investigators indicate that the worker's injury was the result of a combination of her carelessness, training and guarding violations by the employer, and a machine defect. ***What are the worker's legal rights for recovery for her injury?***

The workers' compensation acts that states began adopting shortly after the turn of the last century (New York's 1910 act, the first, did not pass constitutional muster in that state, but Wisconsin's in 1911 did) survive today in all states. American workers' compensation acts were to some extent drawn from other worker's compensation systems already in place in Germany and Great Britain. The acts were necessary because of the insufficiency of the common-law negligence action, restricted by an "unholy trinity" of contributory-negligence, assumption-of-risk, and fellow-servant defenses, to overcome the carnage accompanying Industrial Revolution employment. *See* Guy v. Arthur H. Thomas Co., 55 Ohio St.2d 183, 378 N.E.2d 488 (Ohio 1978). The acts were also politically wise, particularly in Bismarck's Germany where they first appeared during a time of substantial labor and political unrest. As the prosperity and stability of industrial societies increased, the early sense that workers should be grateful for any industrial employment slowly gave way to a more-mature judgment that the industrial system should bear its own human costs—rather than shift those very large costs to the backs of individual injured workers and their families. State legislatures gradually expanded the acts to include not only workplace injury but also occupational disease. Today, workers' compensation insurance representatives, administrative-law judges and systems, and a workers' compensation bar comprised of lawyers who tend to specialize in that field because of its discrete and complex statutory schemes and administrative procedures, maintain the worker's compensation system.

Fundamentally, worker's compensation acts offer a trade-off of relatively rare but make-whole negligence remedies (including not only wage loss and medical expense but also pain, suffering, and other provable economic and non-economic loss) for uniform coverage of workplace injuries without considering fault but limited as to recovery—typically to medical expense and a portion of wage loss. Instead of a few (those who can prove negligence) receiving all loss, all (the thought is) should receive part of their loss. The acts grant employer immunity from negligence actions brought by employees, abolish the traditional defenses, and establish a form of strict liability for employers (or their insurers) to promptly pay benefits limited in type and amount but periodic and continuing in duration—nearly like a form of health and disability insurance. The economic rationale includes that the enterprises causing the injuries should better and more efficiently internalize their costs—that the "transaction costs" of litigating negligence claims for a few should give way to a more-efficient administrative system that forces the employing enterprise to bear a portion (not including pain and suffering) of injury costs. Insurers rate the employer's workers' compensation insurance premium by the employer's accident experience and the type of work the employer requires of its employees. These justifications are not solely for academic interest. Indeed, lawyers who practice in the worker's compensation field must grow accustomed to communicating to clients the limited nature of worker's compensation benefit and, accordingly, its rationale.

Coverage. The first practical task in worker's compensation claims is, as in other no-fault schemes, to establish whether coverage applies. "Coverage" does not mean whether insurance in place—not whether the terms of a certain insurance policy cover the workplace injury. Instead, coverage means whether the substantive terms of the state's workers' compensation act and any interpreting case law provide that the claim under consideration falls within the strictures and benefit scheme of the worker's compensation act. To determine coverage, one looks to the state act and law, not to an employer or insurance policy. Coverage begins with determining whether the injury involved an employer and employee. Workers' compensation schemes commonly exclude casual, domestic, and agricultural workers from the employee definition. A few schemes exclude from the employer definition companies having fewer than six (or some other small number of) employees.

Incident to Employment. Beyond the initial determination defining employers and employees, proving coverage requires a showing that the injury occurred within the course of employment and arose out of employment. A connection must exist between the injury and work—not generally based on foreseeability (a narrower standard) but based on whether the activity in which the employee engaged when injured was during employment and because of the work. *See* Kolson v. District of Columbia Dept. of Emp. Services, 699 A.2d 357 (D.C. App. 1997) (act covers injury from criminal attack on employee walking from job to hotel); In the Matter of the Compensation of Burke, 929 P.2d 1085 (Or. App. 1996) (employee injured during rescue of person employee believed to be employer's patron, entitled to worker's compensation benefits); Nemchick v. Thatcher Glass Mfg. Co., 203 N.J. Super. 137, 495 A.2d 1372 (App. Div. 1985) (course-of-employment includes driving home from off-site work); *but see* Ralphs Grocery Co. v. Workers' Comp. Appeals Bd., 58 Cal. App.4th 647, 68 Cal. Rptr.2d 161 (1997) (heart attack at home from being offered re-employment at less than expected hours and wage is not within the course of employment for purposes of workers' compensation benefits); Hall v. Mason Dixon Lines, Inc., 743 S.W.2d 148 (Tenn. 1987) (truck driver's injury during attempted rescue of another motorist is not in the course of employment). The course-of-employment standard within the workers' compensation laws may be subtly different from standards applied to the same question for vicarious-liability purposes. Consider the following illustrative case.

Jaeger Baking Co. v. Kretschmann
Wisconsin Supreme Court
96 Wis.2d 590, 292 N.W.2d 622 (1980)

HEFFERNAN, J. Action was brought by the Jaeger Baking Company ... to review the [award of] worker's compensation for medical expenses and temporary total disability to the claimant, Heinrich Kretschmann, for injuries he sustained while walking to work on January 27, 1974. ...

The circuit court ... reversed the department's order and dismissed the claimant's application for compensation. Kretschmann then appealed to the court of appeals, which ... reversed the circuit court and reinstated the department's order awarding compensation. ...

The sole issue on review is whether sec. 102.03(1)(c)1, Stats., as amended by ch. 148, sec. 1, Laws of 1971, which provides workers compensation coverage to "any employee (injured while) going between an employer's designated parking lot and the employer's work premises while on a direct route and in the ordinary and usual way," covers an employee who, although he has made no use of the employer's parking lot, is injured on his way to work at a point on the direct path between the employer's parking lot and work premises.[fn] Stated another way, does the amended statute cover only those employees who are injured while proceeding to or from the employer's parking lot, or does it create a zone of coverage between the two portions of the employer's work premises. On the facts of this case, we hold that the statute only affords coverage to workers who have left the parking lot and are travelling on a direct route to the work premises. We reverse the court of appeals' decision and reinstate the circuit court's judgment dismissing the compensation claim. ...

The facts are undisputed. Heinrich Kretschmann was injured while walking to work shortly before 2:00 a.m. the morning of January 27, 1974, when two unknown persons attacked him on a public sidewalk in the City of Milwaukee. Kretschmann was on his way to work the 2:00 a.m. shift at the Jaeger Baking Company. On the night of the injury, he took a city bus to work. Upon alighting at the bus stop, at a location undisclosed by the record, Kretschmann walked directly toward the bakery's employee entrance. Kretschmann was walking on the public sidewalk adjacent to the bakery building and was about 50 feet from the employee entrance when attacked.

The place where the attack occurred was on the direct route which an employee using the parking lot would have taken in travelling from the lot to the employee entrance. Had Kretschmann used the parking lot and then walked to the employee entrance, his route would have taken him to the point where he was attacked. ...

The general rule prior to the amendment was that employees going to or coming from work were ordinarily not performing services incidental to their employment and thus were not covered unless actually on the employer's premises when injured. [Cc] ...

The argument advanced by the department, and the one which forms the basis for the court of appeals' decision, is that the term, "going between," is ambiguous and could reasonably mean only that the employee must be "going" in the sense of physical movement or ambulation and be "between" in the sense of being located between the two portions of the employer's business premises when injured. We disagree both with the premise that the statutory language is ambiguous and with the conclusion that the only construction of the provision which avoids absurd results is one which creates an employment zone between the employer's parking lot and business premises. ...

It is strained to conclude as a matter of fact that a worker falls within the compensable category merely because his route to work intersected the route that would have been taken by an employee walking from the parking lot to the work premises. Protection is afforded by the statute for the journey undertaken by an employee when he is going between two portions of the employer's premises when one of such portions is the employee parking lot. ...

The court of appeals reasoned, and the department argues on appeal, that following the plain meaning of the statute will produce absurd results by distinguishing between employees injured in the same manner and place on the basis of how they got to work.[fn] Although the argument has superficial merit, the construction of the statute urged by the department would produce even more arbitrary results.

The department's construction would differentiate between two employees proceeding to work from the same bus stop if one happened to be injured at a location on the direct route between the employer's parking lot and work premises and the other, following the same route to work, was injured several inches, yards, or blocks off the "route between." It was fortuitous that Kretschmann was injured at a point on the direct route from the employee parking lot to the bakery. ...

We find Professor Larson's discussion of the problem presented by this case persuasive. Professor Larson is generally critical of judicial attempts to broaden the time tested premises rule. He notes that: "It is a familiar problem of law, when a sharp, objective, and perhaps somewhat arbitrary line has been drawn, producing the kind of distinctions just cited, to encounter demands that the line be blurred a little to take care of the closest cases. For example, one writer says that there is no reason in principle why states should not protect employees 'for a reasonable distance' before reaching or after leaving the employer's premises. This, however, only raises a new problem without solving the first. It raises a new problem because it provides no standard by which the reasonableness of the distance can be judged. It substitutes the widely-varying subjective interpretation of 'reasonable distance' by different administrators and judges for the physical fact of a boundary line. At the same time, it does not solve the original problem, because each time the premises are extended a 'reasonable distance,' there will inevitably arise new cases only slightly beyond that point and the cry of unfairness of drawing distinctions based on only a few feet of distance will once more be heard." 1 Larson, Worker's Compensation Law, sec. 15.12 at 4-6 (1978). ...

We agree with Professor Larson's analysis... .

Accordingly, we resolve the question of statutory interpretation against Kretschmann and against the unwarranted broadening of coverage. We conclude that the legislature has not made the injury here compensable. The decision of the court of appeals is reversed and the circuit court's judgment dismissing the claim for compensation is affirmed. ...

INQUIRY

Recreation. Although the statutory language is certainly the starting point, and courts do not afford coverage where the statutory language does not provide it, the courts broadly interpret coverage under the course of employment. Should coverage exist when an employee suffers injury while engaging in some pastime or recreation on company time? *See* McCann v. Hatchett, 19 S.W.3d 218 (Tenn. 2000) (act covers injury occurring during a traveling employee's recreation incident to employment). What about for injuries occurring during horseplay on the job? *See* Carvalho v. Decorative Fabrics Co., 117 R.I. 231, 366 A.2d 157 (1976) (coverage afforded for perforated-rectum injury from customary horseplay with air hose used to clean off work clothes); *see also* Prows v. Industrial Comn., 610 P.2d 1362 (Utah 1980) (instigator of customary horseplay also entitled to coverage). What if the horseplay is, instead, conflict involving employees that results in serious injury from an intentional battery? *See* Kerr-McGee Corp. v. Hutto, 401 So.2d 1277 (Miss. 1981) (coverage for death occurring when employer's husband shot employee); Ford Motor Co. v. Industrial Comn., 78 Ill.2d 260, 35 Ill. Dec. 752, 399 N.E.2d 1280 (1980) (coverage afforded for intentional injury from job-related conflict).

Accidental Injury. Workers' compensation schemes typically restrict recovery to "accidental injury," generally ruling out compensation for disability from degenerative conditions. To be compensable, the injury must be due to a specific occasion or event. The classic example of a non-covered condition may be degenerative back problems, even if due to repeated heavy lifting at work. Everyone, some physicians will tell you, has a degenerative back condition even if in most of us those conditions remain asymptomatic. Employers do not bear the cost of disability from gradually declining capacities. If, on the other hand, an employee suffers a sudden back injury from the same work conditions that caused only degenerative changes in another employee, then the employee suffering the sudden injury receives benefits. *See* Harris v. Board of Educ., 375 Md. 21, 825 A.2d 365 (2003) (rejecting the "unusual activity" test and affording coverage for a sudden back injury from regular work of lifting boxes). Legislatures and courts have wrestled with heart attacks at work, some of them adopting an "unusual exertion" test. *See* Kan. Stat. Ann. §44-501(e); *see also* Wyo. Stat. §27-14-603(b) (also requiring that attack occur within four hours after the exertion); Farrington v. Total Petroleum, Inc., 442 Mich. 201, 501 N.W.2d 76 (1993) (must be significantly caused or aggravated by work). In addition to requiring an injury occasion or event, "accidental" also implies that the employee must not have intended the injury.

Disease. Workers' compensation schemes typically provide coverage for occupational disease. *See* Union Carbide Corp. v Industrial Comn., 196 Colo. 56, 581 P.2d 734 (1978) (death from lung cancer due to miner's uranium exposure is covered by act). The coverage afforded for occupational disease may be less generous than the coverage afforded for accidental injury. Cumulative, repetitive-stress injury may fall between accidental injury and disease, and thus not receive coverage. *See* Stenrich Group v. Jemmott, 251 Va. 186, 467 S.E.2d 795 (1996). Disease from exposure to conditions, like second-hand cigarette smoke, that are usual to the workplace, may not be within the act. *See* Palmer v. Del Webb's High Sierra, 108 Nev. 673, 838 P.2d 435 (1992); *but see* Johannensen v. New York City Dept. of Housing, 84 N.Y.2d 129, 615 N.Y.S.2d 336, 638 N.E.2d 981 (1994). Consider the following illustrative case.

Millison v. E.I du Pont de Nemours & Co.
New Jersey Supreme Court
101 N.J. 161, 501 A.2d 505 (1985)

[The facts of this case and a discussion of the exclusive-remedy provision appear in the chapter on products-liability defenses.]

IV

In determining whether these plaintiffs have stated a cause of action under the "intentional wrong" exception to the exclusive-remedy provision of the Compensation Act we must be faithful to the legislative goals of the workers' compensation system. To the end that the system and those goals may be fully understood, we pause to focus on the development of the Compensation Act and the underlying premises that support it.

The stimulus for workers' compensation legislation arose out of an increasing number of industrial accidents and the inadequacies of the common-law tort remedies that were available to aid injured workers. [C] Injured employees seeking tort recovery were confronted with the difficult task of persuading nonunion coworker-witnesses to testify against the employer. Even if successful at gathering witnesses, plaintiffs-employees were inevitably confronted with the "unholy trinity" of employer defenses-contributory negligence, assumption of risk, and the fellow servant rule-which served to protect the employer from legal liability even though he had failed in his duty as master to protect his servants. [C] Thus, various authorities have estimated that at common law up to 94% of industrial accidents went uncompensated. [C]

In 1911, in response to these common-law inequities, the legislature passed our Workers' Compensation Act. L. 1911, c. 95. This legislation involved a historic trade-off whereby employees relinquished their right to pursue common-law remedies in exchange for automatic entitlement to certain, but reduced, benefits whenever they suffered injuries by accident arising out of and in the course of employment. Thus the quid pro quo anticipated by the Act was that employees would receive assurance of relatively swift and certain compensation payments, but would relinquish their rights to pursue a potentially larger recovery in a common-law action.

However, claimants suffering from work-related occupational diseases were initially unsuccessful in their efforts to recover compensation under the Act because it could not be proved that they had been injured by "accident"-the operative term permitting recovery under the statute. ... Thereafter, the legislature, apparently recognizing that workers who had contracted diseases due to gradual exposure to certain potentially-hazardous working conditions were no less in need of the Compensation Act's protection than were employees injured by "accident," amended the Act to include occupational diseases within its coverage. L. 1924, c. 124.

Initially, only nine named occupational diseases were compensable under the terms of the Act: anthrax, lead poisoning, mercury poisoning, arsenic poisoning, phosphorus poisoning, all homologues and derivatives of benzene, wood alcohol poisoning, poisoning from chrome, and caisson disease. The right to compensation was conditioned on the employee notifying the employer of his disability due to occupational disease within five months of his last exposure to the harmful substances. In order to make additional occupational diseases compensable, the legislature passed various amendments over the years: L. 1926, c. 31 (mesothorium or radium necrosis); L. 1931, c. 33 (radium poisoning); L. 1945, c. 53 (dermatitis venenata).

Moreover, a totally separate system of elective compensation was enacted for the diseases of asbestosis and silicosis. L. 1944, c. 88, codified at N.J.S.A. 34:15-35.1 to -35.9. Compensation was to be awarded for death or total disability resulting from silicosis or asbestosis when "the disease was due to the nature of" the employment, id. at § 3, 34:15-35.3, and the Act specifically indicated that there shall be no liability in tort for damages on account of death or total disability from silicosis or asbestosis. Id. at § 5, 34:15-35.5. This separate system of compensation was repealed at L. 1951, c. 59, and asbestosis and silicosis were implicitly returned to the general occupational-disease coverage, which had since replaced its limited list of specific-named occupational diseases with a definitional phrase, "compensable occupational disease."

L. 1949, c. 29. The current definition of "compensable occupational disease" is codified at N.J.S.A. 34:15-31.

The point to be emphasized is that the express inclusion of occupational diseases as part of the Compensation Act reflects a general awareness of potentially-hazardous conditions in the workplace that may result in debilitating diseases necessitating compensation. Early versions of the Compensation Act relating to occupational diseases indicate that certain defined workplace diseases, i.e., asbestosis, are known to be an enemy of the workman, and that relief is to be awarded under the Act to employees stricken with these illnesses. In addition, the current statutory approach of providing only a general compensable occupational-disease definition rather than listing the specific compensable illnesses suggests either that the occupational-disease risks of the workplace are too numerous to list separately or that in the future employees may contract occupational diseases, as yet unknown, that should nonetheless be compensated under the terms of the Act (if such illnesses can be proven and their causes can be traced to conditions of employment). Suffice it to say that in revamping the Compensation Act over the years, the legislature has not been blind to the fact that each year an unspecified number of workers will be disabled with diseases contracted as a result of the hazards of the workplace.

INQUIRY

Benefits. Worker's compensation benefits vary state to state but tend to be just enough to sustain the injured employee while still providing an incentive to return to work for full pay. The most generous of the benefits tends to be medical expense, typically unlimited in amount and duration if reasonable and customary charges for reasonably necessary treatment of the work-related accidental injury. Medical-expense benefits generally coordinate against health insurance but do not require any co-pay or deductible—indeed, will instead cover the co-pay and deductible of the health insurer. Wage loss benefits are less, representing only a percentage (60%, 80%, or whatever similar amount the state regime provides) of the employee's income earned before the injury, and in some states also capped as to maximum amount. These limits provide the employee with an incentive to return to work while also accounting for tax and other employee savings. Disability may be temporary or permanent in duration, and partial or total in degree. The law adjusts wage-loss benefits accordingly to cover only the duration and degree of disability. "Scheduled" benefits, meaning benefits established not by disability but by the statutory scheme itself, are also usually available, without respect to disability, for certain serious injuries like loss of sight in one eye, loss of a finger, or other disfigurement even when not work disabling. This scheduled-benefit or "specific-loss" aspect of the workers' compensation schemes is the feature most like the lump-sum recoveries available under negligence law. Death benefits are typically to certain dependents defined by statute—spouses and resident relatives who either presumptively or in fact depended on the decedent employee's financial support.

Exceptions. Although most workers' compensation schemes are compulsory, a few permit the employer or employee to elect out of the system in favor of common-law rights and remedies. Where they apply, workers' compensation schemes do provide that their benefits are employees' exclusive remedy for workplace injuries.

However, the exclusive-remedy provision does not bar an action against a third party who is not the injured employee's employer. Thus, the employee injured by a combination of the employer's negligence and a defect in a product manufactured by an entity other than the employer may sue that other entity in a products-liability action—even though law bars the employee's negligence action against the employer. Although workers' compensation immunity usually extends to protect co-workers from suit, if the co-worker commits an intentional tort furthering some personal (rather than work) agenda, then the injured co-worker may sue the co-worker. *See* West Bend Mut. Ins. Co. v. Berger, 192 Wis.2d 743, 531 N.W.2d 636 (1995) (co-worker liable for sexual harassment if intending to physically injure). Worker's compensation acts also commonly include an intentional-tort exception with respect to the employer, whether explicitly or by limiting the statutory immunity to acts of negligence. If the employer intends to injure an employee, then the employee may bring an intentional-tort action notwithstanding the workers' compensation act's exclusive-remedy provision. The statutes define and the courts interpret "intent" in different fashions, as the following case illustrates.

Woodson v. Rowland
North Carolina Supreme Court
329 N.C. 330, 407 S.E.2d 222 (1991)

EXUM, C.J. This is a wrongful death action arising from a work-related trench cave-in which killed Thomas Alfred Sprouse on Sunday, 4 August 1985. Plaintiff is the administrator of Sprouse's estate. The principal question is whether the exclusivity provisions of the Workers' Compensation Act limit plaintiff's remedies to those provided by the Act. The courts below concluded plaintiff was so limited in her choice of remedies. We disagree. ...

On Saturday, 3 August 1985, workers from both Rowland Utility and Davidson & Jones were digging trenches to lay sewer lines. ...

Because the trenches were not sloped, shored, or braced, and did not have a trench box, Lynn Craig, the Davidson & Jones foreman, refused to let his men work in them. ...

A backhoe worked in front of of decedent Sprouse and his coworkers, who were laying pipe inside the freshly dug trench. A piece of heavy machinery called a front-end loader drove along the edge of the ditch and followed their progress, dumping loads of gravel onto the newly laid pipe. Workers tamped the gravel using a device similar to a jackhammer. Sprouse was the closest person in the trench to the front-end loader.

At about 9:30 a.m. one side of the trench collapsed, completely burying Sprouse and burying the man closest to him up to his armpits. The partially buried man was Alan Fry, son of project supervisor Elmer Fry. The workers pulled Alan Fry out of the trench, and Morris Rowland took him to the hospital.

Morris Rowland did not return to the site for several hours after the cave-in. The remaining workers continued to dig Sprouse out. ... By the time the workers had finished digging Sprouse out, he was dead.

The trench was approximately fourteen feet deep and four feet wide with vertical sides at the point of the cave-in. Craig, who saw the site later and commented on a photograph of it at his deposition, stated that the trench was being sloped less than it had been at the end of the previous day's work. He characterized it as "unsafe" and stated that he "would never put a man in it." ...

We first decide whether the forecast of evidence is sufficient to survive Rowland Utility's and Morris Rowland's motions for summary judgment, which are based on the ground that Sprouse's death was caused only by "accident" under the Workers' Compensation Act ("the Act"). If the death can only be considered accidental, defendants' summary judgment motions were properly allowed because Sprouse's death would fall within the Act's exclusive coverage, and no other remedies than those provided in the Act are available to plaintiff either against his employer, [c], or a co-worker, [c]. On the other hand, if the forecast of evidence is sufficient to show that Sprouse's death was the result of an intentional tort committed by his employer, then summary judgment was improperly allowed on the ground stated, because the employer's intentional tort will support a civil action. [C]

We conclude, for reasons given below, that the forecast of evidence is sufficient for plaintiff to survive defendants' motions for summary judgment because: (1) it tends to show that Sprouse's death was the result of intentional conduct by his employer which the employer knew was substantially certain to cause serious injury or death; and (2) this conduct is tantamount to an intentional tort committed by the employer. ...

Section 97-9 of the Workers' Compensation Act provides: *"Every employer subject to the compensation provisions of this Article shall secure the payment of compensation to his employees in the manner hereinafter provided; and while such security remains in force, he or those conducting his business shall only be liable to any employee for personal injury or death by accident to the extent and manner herein specified."* N.C.G.S. § 97-9 (1985) (emphasis added). ...

The Act seeks to balance competing interests and implement trade-offs between the rights of employees and their employers. It provides for an injured employee's certain and sure recovery without having to prove employer negligence or face affirmative defenses such as contributory negligence and the fellow servant rule. [C] In return the Act limits the amount of recovery available for work-related injuries and removes the employee's right to pursue potentially larger damages awards in civil actions. [Cc] ... Notwithstanding these important trade-offs, the legislature did not intend to relieve employers of civil liability for intentional torts which result in injury or death to employees. In such cases the injury or death is considered to be both by accident, for which the employee or personal representative may pursue a compensation claim under the Act, and the result of an intentional tort, for which a civil action against the employer may be maintained. [C] ...

... We hold that when an employer intentionally engages in misconduct knowing it is substantially certain to cause serious injury or death to employees and an employee is injured or killed by that misconduct, that employee, or the personal representative of the estate in case of death, may pursue a civil action against the employer. Such misconduct is tantamount to an intentional tort, and civil actions based thereon are not barred by the exclusivity provisions of the Act. Because, as also discussed in a subsequent portion of this opinion, the injury or death caused by such misconduct is nonetheless the result of an accident under the Act, workers' compensation claims may also be pursued. There may, however, only be one recovery. We believe this holding conforms with general legal principles and is true to the legislative intent when considered in light of the Act's underlying purposes.

Our holding is consistent with general concepts of tort liability outside the workers' compensation context. The gradations of tortious conduct can best be understood as a continuum. The most aggravated conduct is where the actor actually intends the probable consequences of his conduct. One who intentionally engages in conduct knowing that particular results are substantially certain to follow also intends the results for purposes of tort liability. [Cc] ...

... We have recognized the doctrine of "constructive intent" and have generally applied it where willful and wanton conduct is present. ...

... The substantial certainty standard satisfies the Act's purposes of providing trade-offs to competing interests and balancing these interests, while serving as a deterrent to intentional wrongdoing and promoting safety in the workplace. [C]

Other jurisdictions which have considered how egregious employer misconduct must be in order to justify a worker's civil recovery against the employer extraneous to workers' compensation statutes have reached different results. Some require that the employer actually intend to harm the worker, as in a classic assault and battery suit. [Cc] Others require the employer's misconduct to be willful and wanton.[fn] [C] Still others require intentional conduct which the employer knows is "substantially certain" to cause injury or death. [Cc]

It is true that some of the cases adopting the willful and wanton misconduct or substantial certainty standard have been modified by statute. Legislation enacted in Michigan modified the decision in *Beauchamp v. Dow Chemical Co.*, 427 Mich. 1, 398 N.W.2d 882. The legislation provides: "The only exception [to the exclusivity of workers' compensation] is an intentional tort. An intentional tort shall exist only when an employee is injured as a result of a deliberate act of the employer and the employer specifically intended an injury. *An employer shall be deemed to have intended to injure if the employer has actual knowledge that an injury was certain to occur and willfully disregarded that knowledge.*" Mich.Comp.Laws § 418.131 (Supp.1990) (emphasis added). ...

On the basis of these kinds of statutory modifications, Rowland Utility urges us to conclude that the willful and wanton misconduct and substantial certainty standards should be rejected as inconsistent with the legislative purpose of North Carolina's Workers' Compensation Act. We do not read the statutory modifications of judicial decisions in other jurisdictions to repudiate the standards adopted in those decisions. The statutory modifications seem more to narrow the application of, rather than to abolish, these standards. ... These legislative modifications confirm, rather than reject, the proposition that, in those states, actual intent to injure is not required in order for an employer to be civilly liable outside workers' compensation statutes. ...

... [B]oth courts and legislatures in a fair number of other jurisdictions have rejected the proposition that actual intent to harm is required for an employer's conduct to be actionable in tort and not protected by the exclusivity provisions of workers' compensation. Our adoption of the substantial certainty standard does the same. ...

... We thus examine Morris Rowland's conduct and attribute it to his principal, Rowland Utility. If plaintiff's forecast of evidence is sufficient to show that there is a genuine issue of material fact as to whether Morris Rowland's conduct satisfies the substantial certainty standard, then plaintiff is entitled to take her case against Rowland Utility to trial.

We conclude that plaintiff's forecast of evidence is sufficient to raise such a material issue of fact against Rowland Utility. Agronomist James Rees, offered as an expert in soil and environmental analysis, submitted an affidavit on the status of the soil where the cave-in occurred. He stated: "Based on my review of the physical conditions existent at the time of the trench collapse, as nearly as they can be determined, and on the nature and physical conditions of the surface and subsurface materials, my conclusion is that the trench as constructed by Morris Rowland Utility, Inc. consisting of sheer, vertical walls approximately fourteen feet deep, had an exceedingly high probability of failure, and the trench was substantially certain to fail."

From this evidence, a reasonable juror could determine that upon placing a man in this trench serious injury or death as a result of a cave-in was a substantial certainty rather than an unforeseeable event, mere possibility, or even substantial probability.

There is also evidence to indicate that Morris Rowland knew of this substantial certainty. Neither we, nor later the jury, need accept his characterization of his state of mind at face value. Other evidence is available from which his state of mind can be inferred. [C] There is evidence that Morris Rowland was capable of discerning extremely hazardous ditches. His career had been excavating different kinds of soil. He knew the attendant risks. He had been cited at least four times in six and one-half years immediately preceding this incident for violating multiple safety regulations governing trenching procedures. He was aware of safety regulations designed to protect trench diggers from serious injury or death. He knew he was not following these regulations in digging the trench in question. ...

Davidson & Jones foreman Lynn Craig testified that the trench at point of collapse was "unsafe" and that he would "never put a man in it" without a trench box or other precautions. ... His emphatic indication that the trench was unsafe could lead reasonable jurors to conclude that Morris Rowland, who was also at the trench and equally capable of observing its dangerous tendencies, shared Craig's knowledge and disregarded the substantial certainty of a cave-in resulting in serious injury or death. Rowland's attempts to rush Greene the previous day and his commencement of hasty, unsafe procedures, including his failure to use the available trench box, would offer the jury a motive for his conduct—swift completion of the project, whatever the risk.

Morris Rowland's knowledge and prior disregard of dangers associated with trenching; his presence at the site and opportunity to observe the hazards; his direction to proceed without the required safety procedures; Craig's experienced opinion that the trench was unsafe; and Rees' scientific soil analysis converge to make plaintiff's evidentiary forecast sufficient to survive Rowland Utility's motion for summary judgment. ...

In conclusion, and for the reasons given, we reverse the Court of Appeals' decision insofar as it affirms summary judgments in favor of Rowland Utility and Morris Rowland.... .

INQUIRY

Intentional Torts. The above *Woodson* case illustrates the principal pattern in the intentional-tort cases—that of an employer proceeding with the work in the face of severe risks of injury to employees reaching the point of substantial certainty. *See* Laidlow v. Hariton Machinery Co., 790 A.2d 884 (N.J. 2002) (employer disables rolling-mill safety guard, resulting in employee's crushed hand); Holtz v. Schutt Pattern Works Co., 626 N.E.2d 1029 (Ohio Ct. App. 1993) (employer removes pattern-making machine's safety guards, resulting in two-finger amputation for employee). Another pattern involves exposure to materials and conditions that are substantially certain to produce occupational disease—or have already done so in a manner that the employer has intentionally concealed, leading to the certain workplace aggravation of the workplace injury. *See* Martin v. Lancaster Battery Co., 530 Pa. 11, 606 A.2d 444 (1992) (exposure to lead dust and fumes, combined with employer concealment and alteration of employee blood tests showing positive for poisoning, establish fraudulent-misrepresentation, intentional-tort exception). As the above *Woodson* case shows, legislatures and courts adopt different definitions for the intention necessary to avoid the employer-immunity bar of the workers' compensation acts. Why would an employee wish to avoid the immunity bar? Some intentional torts do not produce the kind of disability that is compensable under workers' compensation schemes. *See* Fermino v. Fedco, 7 Cal.4th 701, 30 Cal. Rptr.2d 18, 872 P.2d 559 (1994) (employee's false-imprisonment claim against employer for coerced interrogation is not barred by the exclusive-remedy provision). Would the act bar a claim against the employer for sexual harassment and assault by a co-worker, if the claim against the employer was one for negligent hiring, training, and supervision? *See* Kerans v. Porter Paint Co., 61 Ohio St.3d 486, 575 N.E.2d 428 (1991) (claims against employer not barred); *but see* Driscoll v. General Nutrition Corp., 252 Conn. 215, 752 A.2d 1069 (2000) (exclusive-remedy provision bars employee's tort claim against employer for emotional harm from co-worker's forced sexual assault—employee receives only workers' compensation remedies). When they conflict, federal civil-rights laws, such as Title VII barring certain forms of workplace discrimination, the Americans with Disabilities Act, and the Family and Medical Leave Act, are supreme over workers' compensation provisions.

Administration. The above cases should have made it clear that when disputes arise over benefits—a relatively common occurrence despite the administrative nature of the schemes—administrative-hearing officers decide the disputes within state administrative systems. Lawyers usually represent the employer and employee in those proceedings, even though the administrative rules relax the evidentiary rules and requirements. The hearing process typically begins with filing and service of a notice of dispute and concludes with a decision following the administrative hearing. Appeals from adverse administrative decisions are to the courts. The courts apply administrative-review standards that do not challenge factual determinations but instead ensure that administrative decisions conform to the law and have substantial evidence in support.

Career

Resources can make a difference in finding employment and succeeding in tort practice. Law schools maintain Career and Professional Development offices and employ trained staff for those functions. Staff can provide substantial valuable guidance and advice. They will have worked with other students having similar interests in tort law, and will know of lawyers and law firms with torts practices. They can also direct you to a wealth of career, placement, and professional-development resources including resources on tort law and practice. Even if you already have a job when you graduate, interacting with placement staff can help prepare you for that job, by helping you understand, appreciate, and equip yourself for what your future employer is likely to most value. Get an early start with your law school's career, placement, and professional-development staff. Get to know their services before you think you need them. Doing so can make a substantial difference in the quality of your legal education, its outcome, and your satisfaction with it.

Chapter XVIII

MISUSE OF LEGAL PROCEDURE

As the previous two chapters on defamation and invasion of privacy may already have suggested, another nefarious way in which a wrongdoer can affect a person's reputation and well being is by misuse of the legal process itself. Tort law protects persons against the misuse of legal procedure. To be sure, other means exist to hold responsible and punish one who misuses legal process, including court sanction in the abused proceeding, grievance proceedings against the involved attorneys' licenses, and even criminal charge for making a false police report. Yet the tort system provides a way of both deterring wrongdoers and compensating the wronged. Two traditional torts address the misuse of legal procedure—malicious prosecution and abuse of process. The two torts address somewhat different concerns. Malicious prosecution has to do with improper initiation of criminal charges. Abuse of process has to do with improper use of legal proceedings once they have begun. Consider each in turn.

A. Malicious Prosecution

OBJECTIVE: Given facts indicating the dismissal of criminal charges, recall and apply the elements of the malicious-prosecution tort in order to determine whether that claim exists.

Case Study: The law-enforcement officer who had signaled the motorist to pull over for a non-working taillight regretfully informed her that she was going to jail—as courteous as she had been and as small of an infraction as was the darkened taillight. Stunned, the motorist asked why. The officer replied that there was a bench warrant for her arrest for uttering and publishing. Later the next day—after the motorist spent the night in jail and missed work the next morning—the motorist learned that a rental-store owner had falsely complained to the police that she had written the store a bad check. At the preliminary hearing on the owner's false charges, the motorist established to the magistrate judge's satisfaction that she had properly stopped payment on her check the moment she found out that the owner had fraudulently double-billed her. The court dismissed the charge. *Identify, discuss, and evaluate the motorist's tort claim against the rental-store owner.*

The malicious-prosecution tort is just as it sounds. It requires a plaintiff to prove that (1) defendant caused criminal charges to issue against the plaintiff, (2) the charges resolved in the plaintiff's favor, (3) defendant had no probable cause for the charges, and (4) defendant acted with malice. *See* Restatement (Second) of Torts §653. The defendant in malicious-prosecution actions is not a public-official prosecutor but rather the complaining-witness accuser—a private person—who by false police report or other communication induces the prosecutor to bring charges. *See* Restatement (Second) of Torts §656 (prosecutor has privilege). As in the case of defamation, the malice element of the malicious-prosecution tort takes on a special meaning other than ordinary ill will. Restatement (Second) of Torts §668 defines the malice element of the malicious-prosecution tort as when the proceedings "have been initiated primarily for a purpose other than that of bringing an offender to justice." The law traditionally presumes damage to reputation, as one might reasonably expect from the filing of criminal charges. However, a plaintiff would benefit by showing the specific form and extent of damages, which may include the humiliation of arrest and incarceration, mental distress, attendant medical care, and the attorney's fees spent defending the criminal action. Consider the following representative cases.

Rose v. Whitbeck
Oregon Supreme Court
277 Or. 791, 562 P.2d 188 (1977)

BRYSON, J. Plaintiff, Betty Rose, brought this action for malicious prosecution against her brother-in-law, Ted Rose, and sister-in-law, Nettie Whitbeck. This action arises out of a family quarrel involving the probate and distribution of assets in the estate of LeRoy D. Rose.[fn omitted] Defendants appeal from a judgment entered on a jury verdict in favor of plaintiff.

Defendants contend that the plaintiff failed as a matter of law to prove that the criminal proceedings against plaintiff were instituted by defendants, that defendants lacked probable cause, or that the proceedings were terminated in plaintiff's favor. Defendants maintain that for these reasons the trial court erred in denying their motions for nonsuit and directed verdict. ...

The evidence when so reviewed reveals the following facts. Joe, Betty's husband, and Nettie were the co-executors of LeRoy's estate. As a result of incidents relating to the management of LeRoy's property prior to his death on March 17, 1973, and the marshalling of the assets of his estate thereafter, animosity arose between Joe and the defendants.

Prior to his death on March 17, 1973, LeRoy gave Betty his 1964 Buick. At the time of the gift, the Buick was registered in the name of Mildred Rose, LeRoy's deceased wife. At LeRoy's request, Betty signed Mildred's name to the title and had it placed in her own name. Testimony was presented from which the jury could reasonably conclude that the title was delivered into Betty's possession by defendant Nettie, and that both defendants were aware that the Buick was a gift prior to May 10, 1973, the date Ted first complained to the sheriff's department in regard to Betty's possession of the Buick.

At Ted's request, Deputy Sheriff Kenneth Engh undertook to investigate Betty's actions. Ted gave Deputy Engh a copy of the title to the Buick, which he had procured from the Department of Motor Vehicles. He also related to the deputy statements made by LeRoy's housekeeper that she had seen Joe removing papers from Mildred's and LeRoy's safe immediately after Mildred's death. Ted did not inform the deputy that the Buick had been a gift from LeRoy to Betty. Deputy Engh learned of the gift characterization of the transaction only when he interviewed Betty the following month.

The information obtained by Deputy Engh was forwarded to District Attorney Robinett. Robinett decided that the matter should be sent to the grand jury and called Ted and Ettie to testify. The district attorney could not remember whether he spoke to Ted and Nettie before or after his decision to present the matter to the grand jury. Both defendants testified that they did not visit the district attorney's office prior to their being called as witnesses before the grand jury. However, Ted did admit to contacting the office several times thereafter to check on the progress of the case.

The grand jury, after hearing the testimony of Ted, Nettie, and Deputy Engh, and after reading the report of Detective Robert C. Phillips, returned an indictment for forgery against plaintiff.

Betty was never brought to trial. After the indictment, the probate court, having jurisdiction over LeRoy's estate, determined the Buick to have been a gift. In view of this adverse determination of the issue critical to the state's case against Betty, the district attorney moved that the indictment against Betty be dismissed. The indictment was dismissed by the court on December 20, 1974.

Public policy requires that those who have good reason to believe the law has been violated should be encouraged to bring that information to the law enforcement authorities to the end that those guilty of crime may be brought to trial and punished.[fn omitted] In order to recover for this tort, the burden is upon the plaintiff to prove each of the following elements: (1) the institution or continuation of the original criminal proceedings; (2) by or at the insistence of the defendant; (3) termination of such proceedings in the plaintiff's favor; (4) malice in instituting the proceedings; (5) lack of probable cause for the proceeding; and (6) injury or damage because of the prosecution.[fn omitted] If any element is left unproven, plaintiff's case must fail.

We review first as to Nettie Whitbeck. ... In order to find that Nettie participated in instituting the indictment, plaintiff must prove that Nettie was "actively instrumental in putting the law in force."[fn omitted] It is not, however, required that a defendant personally or single-handedly institute the criminal proceeding. A defendant may be held to have satisfied this prerequisite where she has urged or insisted that another institute the criminal proceeding[fn omitted] or where due to proof of agency or conspiracy she is made responsible for the acts and conduct of others.

As to defendant Nettie, there is no evidence to prove that her brother Ted acted on her behalf or that Nettie conspired with Ted "in putting the law in force." Plaintiff has also failed to present any evidence that Nettie urged or otherwise insisted that Ted institute a police investigation regarding Betty's possession of the Buick.

The evidence does reveal Nettie and Ted to have been closely allied in the intra-family arguments concerning the estate and that Nettie agreed with her brother's assessment that Betty was guilty of forgery. However, this evidence falls short of showing that Nettie urged her brother to seek a police investigation, or even that she condoned his action in doing so. If Nettie is to be held liable, that liability must be judged solely upon her actions and not upon her brother Ted's actions on his own behalf.

The evidence shows Nettie's only role in Betty's indictment to have been that of a witness called by the grand jury to testify before it. This limited participation is as a matter of law insufficient to render Nettie liable for malicious prosecution. ...

In the instant case there is no evidence of perjury. It is argued that Nettie acted improperly in failing to inform the grand jury that the Buick was a gift. But, it should be noted that the role of a grand jury witness is essentially a passive one. Nettie only responded to the questions of the district attorney and the frand jurors. No evidence was presented that Nettie had any opportunity or duty to make unsolicited disclosure that the Buick was a gift. ...

It follows from what has been said that defendant Nettie's motion for nonsuit or a directed verdict should have been granted. We turn now to the contentions of defendant Ted.

Defendant Ted first contends that, as in the case of his sister Nettie, the trial court should have granted his motions for nonsuit and directed verdict as plaintiff failed to prove that the criminal proceedings were instituted by him. The rule ... is that where the prosecutor, after an independent investigation and in the exercise of his independent discretion, decides to bring criminal proceedings, the defendant will be insulated from liability. This rule contains the limitation that the defendant must have been truthful and did not withhold information in his presentation of the facts to the prosecutor. ...

Evidence was presented in the instant case from which a jury could reasonably conclude that Ted knew that the automobile had been a gift to Betty. Betty testified that the entire family knew the Buick had been a gift and that Nettie had specifically informed Ted of their father's decision to give Betty the automobile. Since the crime of forgery is in the instant case dependent upon the transfer of title having been fraudulent, there would have been no prosecution if Ted had revealed that he knew the Buick to have been a gift. A jury choosing to believe Betty and not Ted could reasonably conclude that Ted did not make full and truthful disclosure to Deputy Engh, and that this failure to disclose led to Betty's subsequent indictment.

Defendant Ted next contends that a directed verdict should have been granted due to the plaintiff's failure to prove that the criminal proceedings terminated in her favor. Defendant Ted maintains that the indictment was dismissed as a result of compromise by the plaintiff.

Dismissal of an indictment at the request of the district attorney is generally sufficient to satisfy the requirement that the criminal proceeding has terminated in the favor of the plaintiff. [Cc] An exception is made, however, where the dismissal was pursuant to an agreement of compromise by the plaintiff. [Cc] In such cases the dismissal is not indicative of innocence.

In the instant case there is no evidence that the accused entered into any compromise. Plaintiff asserted her position that the Buick was a gift throughout the criminal and probate proceedings, until this issue was finally resolved in her favor by the probate court. The evidence further shows the prosecution's decision to move for dismissal of the indictment was unilateral and not the product of any agreement between himself and Betty or between Ted and Betty. The trial court court did not err in refusing to grant a directed verdict on this issue.

Lastly, Ted argues that a nonsuit or directed verdict should have been granted due to the plaintiff's failure to prove that Ted lacked probable cause for his complaint, or, in the alternative, that his requested instruction on probable cause should have been given. ...

In Lampos v. Bazar, Inc., [270 Or. 256, 267, 527 P.2d 376, 381 (1974)], we stated:

"... (F)or one to have probable cause to initiate a criminal prosecution he must have both a reasonable belief and a subjective belief in the guilt of the accused; that suspicion alone is not enough to constitute probable cause, although certainty is not required and belief beyond a reasonable doubt is not necessary; that the question of probable cause is one to be decided by the court and not by the jury, but that if the facts or inferences are in dispute the court must instruct the jury what facts constitute probable cause and the jury must then decide the facts; and that the question of probable cause 'almost has to be decided on an ad hoc basis because of the tremendous number of fact combinations possible.'"

Mere proof of improper purpose or malice raises no inference that defendant lacked probable cause. ...

We have also adopted 3 Restatement of Torts §662, which provides, at pages 403-04, as follows:[fn omitted]

"One who initiates criminal proceedings against another has probable cause for so doing if he

"(a) reasonably believes that the person accused has acted or failed to act in a particular manner, and

"(b) (i) correctly believes that such acts or omissions constitute at common law or under an existing statute the offense charged against the accused, or

"(ii) mistakenly so believes in reliance on the advice of counsel under the conditions stated in §666."

In the instant case, the facts relevant to determining whether or not Ted had probable cause are disputed. As has already been discussed, evidence was presented from which the jury could reasonably conclude that Ted knew the Buick to have been a gift. If the jury so found, defendant would, as a matter of law, have lacked probable cause to take his complaint to Deputy Sheriff Engh unless his acts were based upon the advice of counsel. If the Buick were a gift, there could have been no fraudulent transfer and hence there could have been no crime.

Defendant Ted cannot rely upon the safe harbor provided by the Restatement of Torts in §662(b)(ii), supra, as the record presents no evidence that he relied upon the advice of counsel prior to taking his complaint to Deputy Sheriff Engh. Ted's later conversations with the district attorney are insufficient to insulate him from liability as they occurred only after criminal proceedings had been initiated. Furthermore, the record is absent of any evidence that Ted disclosed to the district attorney that he knew the Buick to have been a gift. Under these facts, the issue of probable cause was properly left to the jury.

Defendant Ted's contention that the grand jury indictment constituted prima facie evidence of probable cause has been considered before by this court and rejected. ...

Affirmed as to defendant Theodore Rose; reversed as to defendant Nettie C. Whitbeck.

Murray v. Wal-Mart, Inc.
United States Court of Appeals
874 F.2d 555 (8th Cir. 1989)

BEAM, J. Wal-Mart challenges the district court's[fn omitted] judgment for the plaintiff, Mary Murray. Murray sued Wal-Mart and the City of Blytheville for malicious prosection, intentional infliction of emotional distress, and violation of 42 U.S.C. § 1983 (1982), after she was detained and prosecuted for shoplifting in a Wal-Mart store. The City agreed to a settlement after completion of the plaintiff's case-in-chief. The suit against Wal-Mart was heard to a conclusion by the district court sitting without a jury. The court awarded Murray compensatory damages, punitive damages, and attorney fees. We affirm.

I. BACKGROUND

Murray, a black female, was shopping at Wal-Mart on June 14, 1986, with her daughter and grandchildren. During her visit to the store, she put one hundred dollars' worth of merchandise on layaway, purchased fifteen dollars' worth of other items, and left the store with $207 in her possession. While shopping, Murray had been observed by Dana Elliot, a Wal-Mart loss prevention employee. Elliot testified at trial that she had seen Murray take a bottle of cologne, valued at $5.87, out of its box and place the bottle inside her halter top.

As Murray was leaving the store, Elliot, store manager Earnest Harris, and an assistant store manager detained Murray and inquired about the cologne. Murray denied the accusation of shoplifting and pulled her halter top down to show that she was not concealing any merchandise. Harris directed Murray to accompany him back into the store. Profane and racially derogatory comments were made by Harris at this time.

Murray was escorted to the second floor of the store. Harris or Elliot emptied the contents of Murray's purse onto the floor. More derogatory statements were made to Murray while this episode unfolded. The Wal-Mart employees then telephoned the local police and, based upon the advice of a local prosecutor, requested prosecution of Murray for shoplifting. Murray was taken into custody and was searched by a female officer at the station. The search revealed no concealed items. Murray was denied access to her heart medication when she requested it for pain. Following her release, she sought medical attention because of her nervous condition.

Wal-Mart has an established shoplifting policy which provides that (1) Wal-Mart employees should treat a suspected shoplifter with courtesy, (2) employees should let suspected shoplifters go when in doubt or when unable to find items on the person, and (3) store managers should check with the regional supervisor before prosecuting doubtful cases.

Despite this established policy, and notwithstanding the fact that a thorough search of Murray revealed no concealed merchandise, Wal-Mart continued to pursue Murray's prosecution. Subsequently, Murray was charged with shoplifting but, after trial, was acquitted.

... Addressing the merits, the district court found that Wal-Mart had pursued prosecution without probable cause, that the intentional and outrageous conduct of the Wal-Mart employees caused Murray to suffer severe emotional distress, and that the conduct was willful, wanton, and malicious. Consequently, the court awarded Murray $15,000 in actual damages, $10,000 in punitive damages, and $7850 in attorney fees.

II. DISCUSSION

...

C. Malicious Prosecution

On the issue of probable cause, Wal-Mart contends that because probable cause existed for Murray's arrest and prosecution, Murray's claim for damages for malicious prosecution is barred. The Arkansas Code provides that concealment of unpurchased goods gives rise to a presumption that the actor took the goods with the intention of depriving the owner of them, and a person engaging in such conduct may be reasonably detained without creating civil liability for false arrest, false imprisonment, or unlawful detention. [C] Wal-Mart contends that these statutes operate as a defense to malicious prosecution as well as to the enumerated actions. Wal-Mart claims that the district court should have found that probable cause existed as a matter of law and dismissed the case.[Fn2]

[Fn2. Wal-Mart also contends that, under Arkansas case law, the advice of the prosecutor to institute a prosecution acts as conclusive evidence of the existence of probable cause and thus is a complete defense to an action for malicious prosecution. [C] If, however, the evidence tends to show that a defendant did not impartially state all the facts to legal counsel when seeking his advice, then the defendant has no complete defense to a malicious prosecution action by relying on that advice. [C] The district court held that Elliot did not disclose all of the material facts to the prosecuting attorney. Elliot's incomplete rendition of the facts negates prosecutorial advice as a defense to this action.]

Murray argues that Wal-Mart had no probable cause to detain, arrest, or prosecute Murray for shoplifting or theft. While there may have been probable cause for the Wal-Mart employees to initially detain and confront Murray, we agree that no probable cause existed for further detention, or for arrest or prosecution. Probable cause to stop a customer does not necessarily give the merchant probable cause to prosecute. [C]

Murray proved that there was no cologne in her halter top when she was initially confronted. At that point, the actions of the store employees were no longer "reasonable" so as to be afforded protection under the state statutes. In addition, the employees ignored Wal-Mart's own shoplifting policy. After the employees searched Murray's purse, probable cause became more elusive, and after she was thoroughly searched at the police station and no items were found on her person, Wal-Mart policy dictated that there should be no prosecution.

The district court found that Murray was searched without a warrant and without probable cause. The evidence is more than sufficient to support the court's finding of malicious prosecution. …

III. CONCLUSION

For the foregoing reason, we affirm the district court award of $15,000 in actual damages and $10,000 in punitive damages. Furthermore, because attorney fees are available as part of a successful section 1983 action, we affirm the award of attorney fees in the amount of $7850.

INQUIRY

Criminal Proceedings. What a "criminal proceeding" means is usually clear—an action in which the "government seeks to prosecute a person for an offense and to impose upon him a penalty of a criminal character." Restatement (Second) of Torts §654(1). Juvenile-delinquency proceedings may be within the malicious-prosecution tort's scope. Also, the criminal proceeding need not go beyond the initial stage of an indictment, warrant, arrest, or preliminary hearing. *See* Ballard v. Cash, 191 Ky. 312, 230 S.W. 48 (1921) (arrest not necessary to malicious-prosecution suit based on entering of charge and issuing of warrant). One can imagine why—that indictment or arrest alone may inflict harm and ruin reputation. If, on the other hand, the government does not seek to punish but to protect the plaintiff or public, such as in commitment or regulatory proceedings, then the law does not regard the underlying action as a criminal proceeding for purposes of the malicious-prosecution tort, and the plaintiff must pursue other remedies. *See* Moser v. Fulk, 237 N.C. 302, 74 S.E.2d 729 (1953) (temporary protective incarceration for public drunkenness not a criminal proceeding for malicious-prosecution purposes).

Malice. The element that the plaintiff must show that the defendant caused the criminal proceeding primarily for some purpose other than bringing the plaintiff to justice requires the plaintiff to articulate the defendant's primary purpose. Sometimes the defendant's primary illicit purpose lies in the defendant's hatred or ill will toward the plaintiff—the desire to see the plaintiff harmed. *See* Smith v. Kidd, 246 S.W.2d 155 (Ky. 1952). More commonly, the plaintiff proves malice by showing that the defendant did not believe in the plaintiff's guilt and instead had a private interest in the plaintiff's prosecution. To establish the malice element, the defendant's ulterior purpose need not be improper. For instance, the plaintiff may owe the defendant a just debt that the defendant could properly pursue in a private civil action. Yet if instead the defendant knowingly causes the prosecutor to bring a groundless criminal charge, with the purpose of inducing the plaintiff to pay the debt, the defendant will have acted with the malice required to satisfy this element of the malicious-prosecution tort. *See* Peters v. Hall, 263 Wis. 450, 57 N.W.2d 723 (1953); Curly v. Automobile Finance Co., 343 Pa. 280, 23 A.2d 48 (1941); *see* Patterson v. Bogan, 261 S.C. 87, 198 S.E.2d 586 (1973) (criminal action initiated to recover property); *also* Suchey v. Stiles, 155 Colo. 363, 394 P.2d 739 (1964). As the above *Murray* case suggests, advice of counsel insulates a malicious-prosecution defendant from liability only when the defendant seeks the advice in good faith after a full and fair disclosure. *See* Bain v. Phillips, 217 Va. 387, 228 S.E.2d 576 (1976).

Probable Cause. Dismissal of the charges on preliminary hearing is usually conclusive that no probable cause existed. *See* Hawkins v. Hawkins, 32 N.C. App. 158, 231 S.E.2d 174 (N.C. App. 1977). Accordingly, bindover after preliminary hearing is also usually conclusive as to probable cause. *See* Davis v. Quille, 248 Md. 631, 237 A.2d 745 (1968); *see generally* Restatement (Second) of Torts §659. The prosecutor's dismissal of charges for lack of evidence indicates the absence of probable cause. *See* Exxon Corp. v. Kelly, 281 Md. 689, 381 A.2d 1146 (1978). The prosecutor's abandonment of the criminal proceeding for other reasons, such as mercy toward the accused, compromise with the accused, or the instituting of other proceedings, is not (for purposes of the malicious-prosecution tort) a termination favorable to the plaintiff. Restatement (Second) of Torts §660. Conviction establishes probable cause. *See* Earley v. Harry's I.G.A., Inc., 223 Kan. 32, 573 P.2d 572 (1977); Restatement (Second) of Torts §657 (guilt is complete defense), §667 (conviction establishes probable cause). Why would the majority rule hold acquittal to have no effect? *See* Meyer v. Nedry, 159 Or. 62, 78 P.2d 339 (1938).

Belief in Probable Cause. Probable cause for the plaintiff's prosecution does not necessarily insulate the defendant from malicious-prosecution liability. The defendant must also have *believed* in probable cause. The question of the defendant's belief is initially subjective, not objective—did the defendant genuinely believe in the plaintiff's guilt? *See* Hanson v. Crouch, 360 So.2d 942 (Ala. 1978). In other words, if the defendant knew that the plaintiff was not guilty even though another person might have reasonably believed that the plaintiff was guilty, then the defendant will have acted with malice in pursuing a charge. But the question of malice then turns to an objective standard because the defendant's belief must be reasonable for probable cause to exist. *See* Turner v. Chicago, 91 Ill. App.3d 931, 47 Ill. Dec. 476, 415 N.E.2d 481 (1980). A malicious-prosecution defendant who honestly believed that the plaintiff was guilty of the charged crime but whose belief was unreasonable remains liable. *See* Lambert v. Sears, Roebuck & Co., 280 Or. 123, 570 P.2d 357 (1977).

Although reasonable mistakes of fact protect the malicious-prosecution defendant from liability, under the majority rule mistakes of law (even reasonable ones) do not. *See* Ruff v. Eckerds Drugs, Inc., 265 S.C. 563, 220 S.E.2d 649 (1975); Meadows v. Grant, 15 Ariz. App. 104, 486 P.2d 216 (1971).

Damages. Damages ordinarily include harm to reputation, Browning v. Ray, 440 P.2d 721 (Okla. 1968), and humiliation and mental distress, Ejteljorg v. Borner, 502 P.2d 970 (Colo. App. 1972). Although the common law would presume damages for malicious prosecution, that presumption may raise the same constitutional issues that presumed damages in defamation cases raise. After all, the accusation of a crime is a form of speech in which the speaker and the public both have significant interests. The Supreme Court has not resolved whether the protections of *New York Times v. Sullivan* and *Gertz v. Robert Welch Inc.* extend to malicious-prosecution cases. Note, however, that most malicious-prosecution cases include proof that the defendant did not believe the defendant's own accusations—that which would presumably qualify as actual malice under the constitutional tests for presumed and punitive damages. Punitive damages may be available when ill-will (not merely ulterior-purpose) malice is present. *See* Montgomery Ward v. Wilson, 339 Md. 701, 664 A.2d 916 (1995); Sanders v. Daniel Intern. Corp., 682 S.W.2d 803 (Mo. 1984).

Civil Proceedings. Some courts apply the malicious-prosecution tort to a defendant's initiation of groundless civil, not just criminal, proceedings. The malicious-civil-prosecution tort sometimes goes by the same name as its criminal-prosecution sibling ("malicious prosecution") or under similar names such as "malicious civil prosecution." *See* City of Long Beach v. Bozek, 31 Cal.3d 527, 183 Cal. Rptr. 86, 645 P.2d 137 (1982), *after remand*, 33 Cal.3d 727, 190 Cal. Rptr. 918, 661 P.2d 1072 (1983). The elements for the civil form of the tort are the same (no probable cause, an ulterior purpose, resolution in plaintiff's favor) except that the plaintiff must also overcome a strong, policy-based presumption that the defendant's underlying civil action was appropriate. Many jurisdictions satisfy that policy interest by adding an element of "special injury" to the civil form of the malicious-prosecution tort. Consider the following case discussing and illustrating the policy concerns justifying a special-injury requirement.

Friedman v. Dozorc
Michigan Supreme Court
412 Mich. 1, 312 N.W.2d 585 (1981)

LEVIN, J. The plaintiff is a physician who, after successfully defending in a medical malpractice action, brought this action against the attorneys who had represented the plaintiffs in the former action. Dr. Friedman sought under a number of theories to recover damages for being compelled to defend against an allegedly groundless medical malpractice action. The trial court granted the defendants' motions for summary and accelerated judgment.

The Court of Appeals affirmed in part and reversed in part. We granted leave to appeal to consider what remedies may be available to a physician who brings such a "countersuit."

We hold that: ... [that t]he plaintiff has failed to state an actionable claim on a theory of malicious prosecution because his complaint did not allege interference with his person or property sufficient to constitute special injury under Michigan law.

We affirm the decision of the Court of Appeals dismissing plaintiff's negligence and abuse of process claims, and reverse its decision to remand plaintiff's malicious prosecution claim to the trial court for further proceedings.

I

Leona Serafin entered Outer Drive Hospital in May, 1970, for treatment of gynecological problems. * * * While in the hospital, Mrs. Serafin was referred to the present plaintiff, Dr. Friedman, for urological consultation. Dr. Friedman recommended surgical removal of a kidney stone which was too large to pass, and the operation was performed on May 20, 1970. During the surgery, the patient began to ooze blood uncontrollably. Although other physicians were consulted, Mrs. Serafin's condition continued to worsen and she died five days after the surgery. An autopsy was performed the next day; the report identified the cause of death as thrombotic thrombocytopenic purpura, a rare and uniformly fatal blood disease, the cause and cure of which are unknown.

On January 11, 1972, attorneys Dozorc and Golden, the defendants in this action, filed a malpractice action on behalf of Anthony Serafin, Jr., for himself and as administrator of the estate of Leona Serafin… . In December, 1974, the case went to trial in Wayne Circuit Court. No expert testimony tending to show that any of the defendants had breached accepted professional standards in making the decision to perform the elective surgery or in the manner of its performance was presented as part of the plaintiff's case. The judge entered a directed verdict of no cause of action in favor of Dr. Friedman and the other defendants at the close of the plaintiff's proofs. …

Dr. Friedman commenced the present action on March 17, 1976 in Oakland Circuit Court. … [The trial judge dismissed the malicious-prosecution claim because] the prior action was brought with probable cause and therefore precluded a subsequent action for malicious prosecution or abuse of process.

The Court of Appeals … reversed the dismissal of the cause of action sounding in malicious prosecution and remanded this cause to the trial court, declaring that an adverse ruling on a defendant's motion [for costs] … did not bar a subsequent malicious prosecution action and that the facts surrounding the filing and continuation of the prior action were in dispute. …

[The supreme court ruled in Part II that an attorney owes no duty to an opposing party, the violation of which would create a cause of action for negligence. The supreme court ruled in Part III that the plaintiff had not shown an act in the use of process which would support a claim for abuse of process.]

IV

… We agree with defendants that under Michigan law special injury remains an essential element of the tort cause of action for malicious prosecution of civil proceedings. Although the circuit judge did not rest decision on the plaintiff's failure to plead special injury, summary judgment … for failure to state a claim could be appropriately entered on that basis; the factual disputes asserted by plaintiff are immaterial.[fn omitted] …

A substantial number of American jurisdictions today follow some form of "English rule" to the effect that "in the absence of an arrest, seizure, or special damage, the successful civil defendant has no remedy, despite the fact that his antagonist proceeded against him maliciously and without probable cause."[fn omitted] A larger number of jurisdictions, some say a majority, follow an "American rule" permitting actions for malicious prosecution of civil proceedings without requiring the plaintiff to show special injury.[fn omitted] …

Most commentators appear to favor abrogation of the special injury requirement to make the action more available and less difficult to maintain.[fn omitted] Their counsel should, however, be evaluated skeptically. The lawyer's remedy for a grievance is a lawsuit, and a law student or tort professor may be particularly predisposed by experience and training to see the preferred remedy for a wrongful tort action as another tort action. In seeking a remedy for the excessive litigiousness of our society, we would do well to cast off the limitations of a perspective which ascribes curative power only to lawsuits….

Although this case arises upon the plaintiff doctor's assertions that the defendant attorneys wrongfully prosecuted a medical malpractice action against him, if we were to eliminate the special injury requirement that expansion of the tort of malicious prosecution would not be limited to countersuits against attorneys by aggrieved physicians. An action for malicious prosecution of civil proceedings could be brought by any former defendant-person, firm or corporation, private or public-in whose favor a prior civil suit terminated, against the former plaintiff or the plaintiff's attorney or both. In expanding the availability of such an action the Court would not merely provide a remedy for those required to defend groundless medical malpractice actions, but would arm all prevailing defendants with an instrument of retaliation, whether the prior action sounded in tort, contract or an altogether different area of law.

This is strong medicine—too strong for the affliction it is intended to cure. To be sure, successful defense of the former action is no assurance of recovery in a subsequent tort action, but the unrestricted availability of such an action introduces a new strategic weapon into the arsenal of defense litigators, particularly those whose clients can afford to devote extensive resources to prophylactic intimidation.

At present, a plaintiff and his attorney who know that they have less than an airtight case must, in deciding whether to continue the case or in evaluating a settlement offer, consider whether if they proceed to trial they will invest more and recover less or nothing. If the instant plaintiff's approach is adopted, all plaintiffs and their attorneys henceforth must also weigh the likelihood that if they persevere in the action and receive an unfavorable decision, they will not only take nothing but also be forced to defend an action for malicious prosecution of civil proceedings. Even if the plaintiff and his attorney had abundant cause for bringing and continuing the action and acted without malice, the expense and annoyance foreseeably involved in even a successful defense of the countersuit may induce them to abandon a problematic claim or to settle the case for less than they would otherwise accept. Some will say amen, but this would push the pendulum too far in favor of the defense, more than is necessary to rectify the evil to which this effort is directed.

Because many actions for malicious prosecution of civil proceedings will present questions of fact concerning what measures the former plaintiff and his attorney took, and with what state of mind, the prospect of having the countersuit submitted to a jury capable of returning a large verdict including damages for business loss, injury to reputation and emotional distress will loom large indeed, especially since many parties or attorneys do not have or may be unable to obtain insurance against such liability.

The cost of legal malpractice insurance is bound to increase, assuming coverage against such liability is available. … Litigators may be excluded from group programs and find that they cannot obtain coverage at reasonable rates. A legal malpractice crisis may arise as serious as the medical malpractice crisis. ...

The cure for an excess of litigation is not more litigation. Meritorious as well as frivolous claims are likely to be deterred. There are sure to be those who would use the courts and such an expanded tort remedy as a retaliatory or punitive device without regard to the likelihood of recovery or who would seek a means of recovering the actual costs of defending the first action without regard to whether it was truly vexatious. ...

In medical malpractice actions the facts relevant to an informed assessment of the defendant's liability may not emerge until well into the discovery process. Sometimes the relevant facts are not readily ascertainable. In the instant case, for example, defendants maintain that their efforts to acquire Mrs. Serafin's medical records were rebuffed until they commenced suit and thereupon became able to invoke established discovery procedures and the implicit power of the court to compel disclosure; it may be the practice of some doctors or hospitals to refuse to release medical records until a lawsuit has been commenced.[fn omitted] ...

While a client's decision to proceed with litigation although he knows that the facts are not as alleged, or that a proper application to the facts of existing law (or any modification thereof which can be advanced in good faith) will not support the claim, is indicative of the client's ulterior, malicious motive, that inference cannot so easily be drawn from conduct of a lawyer who owes his client a duty of representation and is unaware of the client's improper purpose. The lawyer who "acts primarily for the purpose of aiding his client in obtaining a proper adjudication of his claim," albeit with knowledge that the claim is not tenable, should not be subject to liability on the thesis that an inference of an improper purpose may be drawn from the lawyer's continuing to advance a claim which he knew to be untenable. [fn omitted] ...

The Restatement defines the mental element of the tort of wrongful civil proceedings as "a purpose other than that of securing the proper adjudication of the claim in which the proceedings are based." A finding of an improper purpose on the part of the unsuccessful attorney must be supported by evidence independent of the evidence establishing that the action was brought without probable cause.[fn omitted]

We affirm that portion of the Court of Appeals decision which upheld summary judgment in favor of defendants on plaintiff's claims sounding in negligence and abuse of process. With respect to plaintiff's claim for malicious prosecution, we reverse the decision of the Court of Appeals and affirm the trial court's grant of summary judgment; we do so on the ground that an action for malicious prosecution of a civil action may not be brought absent special injury and the plaintiff failed to plead special injury.

KAVANAGH, WILLIAMS and RYAN, JJ., concur.

INQUIRY

Special Injury. Substantial authority continues to support the special-injury requirement for malicious-civil-prosecution claims. See O'Toole v. Franklin, 279 Or. 513, 569 P.2d 561 (1977) (questioning but declining to reject the special-injury requirement). What is special injury? As the above *Friedman* case makes clear, it is not mere harm to reputation. Instead, it usually involves the taking of some person or property through the initiation of the civil action. Even where courts have abandoned the special-injury requirement, courts remain reluctant to impose malicious-civil-prosecution liability. The few cases that do find liability possible absent special injury stress the defendant lawyer's right to maintain even a weak action "'for the purpose of aiding his client in obtaining a proper adjudication of his claim.'" Nelson v. Miller, 227 Kan. 271, 283, 607 P.2d 438 (1980), *quoting* Restatement (Second) of Torts §674, comment d.

Alternatives. In addition to their chilling effect, another part of the problem with malicious-civil-prosecution suits is that they may not be necessary. Court rules and statutes will often give the aggrieved litigant the right in the underlying action to obtain sanctions against the party who maintains a frivolous claim or defense. *See* Fed. R. Civ. P. 11. The federal and state provisions typically construe the plaintiff's or plaintiff's lawyer's signature on the complaint or other pleading to be a certification that the pleading represents the best of the signer's knowledge, information, and belief after reasonable inquiry. Rule 11 allows the plaintiff twenty-one days after the defendant's filing of a motion for summary judgment within which to withdraw a complaint—without fear of sanctions. Rule 11 thus permits the plaintiff to file an action and maintain it long enough to see how the defendant will respond. Sanctions are to deter rather than to compensate and so, in the typical case, provide only a limited opportunity for the aggrieved party to recover the attorney's fees and costs incurred in defense of the frivolous action.

B. Abuse of Process

OBJECTIVE: **Given facts indicating that a party has used legal proceedings to gain an interest or advantage not lawfully sought within the proceeding, recall and apply the elements of the abuse of process tort to determine whether that claim exists, as stated in this section.**

Case Study: A corporation filed suit against its competitor to resolve disputed rights to the use and maintenance of the border between their mining properties. During the course of the litigation, the competitor's engineers worked closely with retained counsel to draft discovery requests that would disclose to the competitor the design of proprietary equipment and nature of secret methods used by the corporation in its mining operations. The corporation complied with the discovery requests on counsel's assurance that the disclosures would be used solely in defense of the corporation's action. The corporation discovered after the settlement of the litigation, from the competitor's former employee whom the corporation hired, that the competitor was now using the corporation's proprietary designs and secret methods in the competitor's mining operations. *Discuss and evaluate whether the corporation has claims against the competitor or counsel for abuse of process.*

Because they address the *initiation* of legal proceedings, the malicious-prosecution and malicious-civil-prosecution torts do not provide a remedy for other potentially harmful misuses *during* legal proceedings. Tort claims for abuse of process address those latter misuses. A claim—civil or criminal—that a party justly initiated and therefore cannot give rise to a malicious-prosecution action can still involve some abuse for an ulterior purpose that the proceeding itself cannot lawfully achieve. The elements of an abuse of process claim are thus misuse of legal process for an ulterior or improper purpose. The law does not require that the underlying legal proceeding have terminated in the abuse-of-process plaintiff's favor. *See* Brownsell v. Klawitter, 102 Wis.2d 108, 306 N.W.2d 41 (1981); *see also* DeVaney v. Thriftway Mktg. Corp., 124 N.M. 512, 953 P.2d 277 (1997) (tortious litigation tort does not require favorable termination for plaintiff). The abuse-of-process defendant's cause itself may be just, but the abuse-of-process defendant nonetheless misused it. To establish abuse of process, courts may also require proof of special damages in the nature of pecuniary loss. Consider the following illustrative case.

Board of Educ. v. Farmingdale Classroom Teachers Assn., Inc.
New York Court of Appeals
38 N.Y.2d 397, 343 N.E.2d 278 (1975)

WACHTLER, J. This appeal, arising in the context of an apparently bitter dispute between a school district and a teachers' association, concerns the seldom considered tort of abuse of process. The school district contends that the association and its attorney are liable for abusing legal process by subpoenaing, with the intent to harass and to injure, 87 teachers and refusing to stagger their appearances. As a result the school district was compelled to hire substitutes in order to avert a total shutdown. The issue on appeal is whether the complaint states a cause of action.

The controversy began in March, 1972 when a number of teachers employed by the district were absent from their classes on two successive days. The school district considered this illegal and the teachers' association was charged with violating the so-called Taylor law ([c]) by the Public Employees Relations Board (PERB). The association vehemently denied having engaged in or condoned a strike and the matter was scheduled for a hearing to be held on October 5, 6, 10 and 11.

The complaint contains the following version of the ensuing events. Sometime between September 5, 1972 and October 5, 1972, the attorney for the association prepared and issued judicial subpoenas duces tecum to 87 teachers in order to compel their attendance as witnesses on October 5. The school district learned of these subpoenas on or about October 3, 1972 when the individual teachers requested approved absences from teaching duties in accordance with the collective bargaining agreement. The complaint further alleges that the district's prompt oral request that the majority of teachers be excused from attendance at the initial hearing date was refused by the defendant. Indeed, the defendant refused even to grant the request to stagger the appearances. Consequently all 87 teachers attended the hearing and 77 substitute teachers were hired to replace them. Based on these allegations, the school district asserts three causes of action.

The first alleges an abuse of process in that the defendants wrongfully and maliciously and with intent to injure and harass the plaintiff issued 87 subpoenas with knowledge that all the teachers could not have possibly testified on the initial hearing date. As damages for this cause of action plaintiff seeks the amount expended to engage substitute teachers and an amount representing the aggregate salary of the subpoenaed teachers. ...

In its broadest sense, abuse of process may be defined as the misuse or perversion of regularly issued legal process for a purpose not justified by the nature of the process. It has been observed that this tort is an obscure one ([c]) which is rarely brought to the attention of the courts ([c]) and the vital elements of which are not clearly defined ([cc]).

Abuse of process, i.e., causing process to issue lawfully but to accomplish some unjustified purpose, is frequently confused with malicious prosecution, i.e., maliciously causing process to issue without justification. Although much of the confusion is dispelled on careful analysis, it must be noted that both torts possess the common element of improper purpose in the use of legal process....

Despite the paucity of New York authority, three essential elements of the tort of abuse of process can be distilled from the preceding history and case law. First, there must be regularly issued process, civil or criminal, compelling the performance or forebearance of some prescribed act. Next, the person activating the process must be moved by a purpose to do harm without that which has been traditionally described as economic or social excuse or justification ([c]). Lastly, defendant must be seeking some collateral advantage or corresponding detriment to the plaintiff which is outside the legitimate ends of the process.

... [W]e find that the complaint before us is sufficient to state a cause of action for abuse of process. The subpoenas here were regularly issued process, defendants were motivated by an intent to harass and to injure, and the refusal to comply with a reasonable request to stagger the appearances was sufficient to support an inference that the process was being perverted to inflict economic harm on the school district.

While it is true that public policy mandates free access to the courts for redress of wrongs ([cc]) and our adversarial system cannot function without zealous advocacy, it is also true that legal procedure must be utilized in a manner consonant with the purpose for which that procedure was designed. Where process is manipulated to achieve some collateral advantage, whether it be denominated extortion, blackmail or retribution, the tort of abuse of process will be available to the injured party.

The appellants raise several arguments against the sufficiency of this complaint. The most troublesome contention raised is that it is standard, appropriate and proper practice to subpoena all witnesses for the first day of any judicial proceeding. While we acknowledge this as appropriate procedure and in no way intend this decision to proscribe it, we are obligated to determine appeals in the context in which they are presented. Here we consider solely whether the complaint states a valid cause of action. If the proof at trial establishes that defendants attempted to reach a reasonable accommodation at a time when the accommodation would have been effectual, the cause of action will be defeated. However, on its face an allegation that defendants subpoenaed 87 persons with full knowledge that they all could not and would not testify and that this was done maliciously with the intent to injure and to harass plaintiff spells out an abuse of process. Another factor to be weighed at trial is whether the testimony of so many witnesses was material and necessary. As this complaint is framed, it may be inferred that defendants were effecting a not too subtle threat which should be actionable. ...

Turning to the question of damages, we note that to sustain the first cause of action plaintiff must allege and prove actual or special damages in order to recover ([c]). Plaintiff has satisfied this requirement by asserting damages in the amount expended to hire substitutes. However, we reject the claim for damages representing the salaries paid to the subpoenaed teachers. There is no justification for that element of damages, particularly in view of the fact that these were approved absences within the meaning of the collective bargaining agreement. Accordingly, that element of damages should be stricken from the complaint. As to the second cause of action for punitive damages we see no obstacle to its maintenance, contingent on the establishment of malice. ...

Order modified, with costs, in accordance with the opinion herein and, as so modified, affirmed. Question certified answered in the negative.

INQUIRY

Ulterior Purpose. Unlike the malicious-prosecution tort where the defendants' ulterior purpose is often to recover property or a debt by leveraging the prosecution, the ulterior purposes associated with abuse of process vary more widely. *See, e.g.,* Ginsberg v. Ginsberg, 84 A.D.2d 573, 443 N.Y.S.2d 439 (2d Dept. 1981) (abuse of process to win custody of child). Sometimes, as alleged in the case above and in Bell v. Icard, 986 S.W.2d 550 (Tenn. 1999), the ulterior purpose is to frustrate and defeat other litigation. The so-called SLAPP suit (Strategic Lawsuit Against Public Participation) is an example, in which the plaintiff aggressively pursues an anticipatory lawsuit against a longtime adversary relating to a public, to dissuade the adversary from pursuing the cause, whether the cause is legal, social, political, or financial. *See* Jackson v. Mayweather, 217 Cal.Rptr.3d 234 (Cal.Ct.App. 2017) (dismissing most of fame-seeking ex-girlfriend's claims against famous boxing world champion who spoke publicly about ex-girlfriend's abortion and cosmetic surgery). Some states have adopted anti-SLAPP provisions requiring that the party suspected of filing a lawsuit to discourage free-speech rights prove a probability of success before proceeding with pretrial discovery. *See* Entravision Communs. Corp. v. Salinas, 487 S.W.3d 276 (Tex. Ct. App. 2016) (dismissing defamation action of mayor and father against media defendants reporting on social media suspected payoffs). SLAPP statutes create a constitutional tension in that they attempt to create a new balance between two sides' equal rights to petition the government. *See* Baker v. Parsons, 434 Mass. 543, 750 N.E.2d 953 (2001) (affirming dismissal of SLAPP suit). Consider one such statute and a case upholding it as constitutional.

> **CALIFORNIA CODE OF CIVIL PROCEDURE §425.16. Anti-SLAPP actions; motion to strike; discovery; remedies**
> (a) The Legislature finds and declares that there has been a disturbing increase in lawsuits brought primarily to chill the valid exercise of the constitutional rights of freedom of speech and petition for the redress of grievances. The Legislature finds and declares that it is in the public interest to encourage continued participation in matters of public significance, and that this participation should not be chilled through abuse of the judicial process. To this end, this section shall be construed broadly.
> (b)(1) A cause of action against a person arising from any act of that person in furtherance of the person's right of petition or free speech under the United States Constitution or the California Constitution in connection with a public issue shall be subject to a special motion to strike, unless the court determines that the plaintiff has established that there is a probability that the plaintiff will prevail on the claim. ...
> (c)(1) ... [A] prevailing defendant on a special motion to strike shall be entitled to recover his or her attorney's fees and costs. If the court finds that a special motion to strike is frivolous or is solely intended to cause unnecessary delay, the court shall award costs and reasonable attorney's fees to a plaintiff prevailing on the motion... .

(e) As used in this section, "act in furtherance of a person's right of petition or free speech under the United States or California Constitution in connection with a public issue" includes: (1) any written or oral statement or writing made before a legislative, executive, or judicial proceeding, or any other official proceeding authorized by law; (2) any written or oral statement or writing made in connection with an issue under consideration or review by a legislative, executive, or judicial body, or any other official proceeding authorized by law; (3) any written or oral statement or writing made in a place open to the public or a public forum in connection with an issue of public interest; (4) or any other conduct in furtherance of the exercise of the constitutional right of petition or the constitutional right of free speech in connection with a public issue or an issue of public interest. ...

(g) All discovery proceedings in the action shall be stayed upon the filing of a notice of motion made pursuant to this section. The stay of discovery shall remain in effect until notice of entry of the order ruling on the motion. The court, on noticed motion and for good cause shown, may order that specified discovery be conducted notwithstanding this subdivision. ...

Dixon v. Superior Court
California Court of Appeals
36 Cal. Rptr.2d 687 (1994)

WALLIN, J. In this petition for writ of mandate we are asked to interpret recently enacted legislation (Code Civ.Proc., §425.16) designed to curtail a growing number of SLAPP (Strategic Lawsuits Against Public Participation) suits.[fn]

Factual and Procedural Background

At the heart of this controversy is a 22-acre portion of the California State University at Long Beach (CSULB) campus long believed by many Native American Indians to be part of an ancient Indian village known as Puvunga. In 1974, following nomination by petitioner Keith Dixon, an archaeologist and Professor Emeritus of Anthropology at CSULB, the Puvunga site[fn] was accepted for inclusion on the National Register of Historic Places.

Sometime in late 1979 or early 1980, CSULB contracted with Scientific Resource Surveys, Inc. (SRS) to perform archaeological tests on a portion of the Puvunga site on which it wanted to build a Japanese garden and museum. The 1980 report prepared by SRS concluded the proposed project would cause no "adverse effects to archaeological and/or historic resources." In early 1981, the director of CSULB's Physical Planning and Development Department forwarded a copy of SRS's archaeological report to the anthropology department for review and comments. Dixon, along with another faculty member, responded with a critique of the report. Dixon's detailed letter concluded the report was "poorly done," biased and should be withdrawn and revised. ... Despite Dixon's objection, CSULB proceeded with its Japanese garden project and, apparently, continued to contract with SRS to perform a variety of archaeological work on campus.

In 1992, CSULB planned to construct a strip mall (apartment buildings and retail stores) and a parking lot on the Puvunga site. In compliance with the California Environmental Quality Act, Public Resources Code section 21050 et seq. (CEQA),[fn] CSULB commissioned Envicom Corporation to conduct a study on the environmental effects of the proposed development. In December 1992, Envicom issued a report which concluded the proposed project would not significantly impact the local environment, result in alteration or destruction of an archaeological site, or affect cultural values or sacred or religious uses in that area. Based on those findings, the report recommended CSULB adopt a negative declaration.

Dixon learned of the proposed negative declaration and began a letter writing campaign challenging its findings in January 1993. He first wrote to a CSULB official, claiming the determination in the negative declaration that the environment would not be adversely impacted by development was based on the report of an unnamed archaeological firm[fn] that was "error-filled" and did not meet professional standards. Dixon also accused the unnamed firm of unprofessional secrecy. Following the meeting, CSULB agreed that it would conduct a "cultural review" of the Puvunga site and that neither SRS nor its president, Nancy Whitney-Desautels, would be involved in any further archaeological work on campus.[fn]

In March 1993, Dixon wrote three letters to CSULB's vice president. The first letter complained of the lack of response by the administration to his commentary on the negative declaration. In discussing the possible reasons for what he deemed his "excommunication" by CSULB administrators, Dixon cited his critique of the 1980 archaeological report prepared by SRS, which he claimed angered the administration. He further stated "[SRS] never did face the professional issues we raised or correct their factual errors. ..."

After learning that CSULB had contracted with SRS to perform continued consulting work related to the Puvunga site despite its agreement not to, Dixon wrote to the administration and complained... .

In May 1993, Dixon wrote to CSULB requesting to review progress billing submitted by SRS. In that letter, he stated, "I should mention as a reminder that many of the campus' present problems with SRS stem from their earlier work, which was found by me ... to be highly flawed and biased. ..." At the time bids for the cultural review of the Puvunga site were solicited, CSULB asked SRS not to bid the contract because of Dixon's outspoken opposition.

SRS responded by filing the underlying lawsuit against Dixon. The complaint sought $570,000 in damages for intentional and negligent interference with contractual relations and prospective economic advantage, libel, slander and trade libel. SRS alleged its contractual relationship with CSULB had been destroyed by Dixon's oral and written statements to CSULB officials concerning the accuracy of previous SRS reports, the quality of services rendered by them, and accusations that SRS aligned itself with developers and tailored its reports to that end. Attached to the complaint were the five letters written by Dixon to CSULB officials between January and May 1993.

After filing his answer, Dixon moved to strike the complaint, which he characterized as a SLAPP suit, under Code of Civil Procedure section 425.16, subdivision (b). ... In support of the motion, Dixon attached his declaration in which he averred that the statements he made to CSULB officials were for the sole purpose of participating in the CEQA public comment and review process by informing them about the cultural, historical and archaeological significance of the Puvunga site and the potential environmental effects that further excavation and commercial development would cause. His statements regarding the quality of SRS's work and their competence as an archeological firm were not based on personal animosity; rather, they were based on a professional review of the documents SRS generated. He denied any participation in the NAHC proceedings regarding CSULB's proposed development or discussing his opinion of SRS's work with any member of the Native American community. ...

SRS opposed the motion on the grounds the statements made by Dixon were not part of the CEQA review process and were not made to an official body in connection with an issue under consideration, nor in a place open to the public in connection with an issue of public interest. Since the negative declaration prepared by Envicom (but not yet adopted by CSULB) contained no mention of SRS's 1980 archaeological report, SRS contended Dixon's attack on that report, and its author, were outside the scope of the CEQA review process. SRS also argued that Dixon's statements were malicious and therefore not entitled to immunity. In support of its motions, SRS attached the declarations of its president, Nancy Whitney-Desautels, and several Native Americans who averred, among other things, that SRS is competent and respected by the Native American community as a whole. The declaration of a CSULB official indicated Dixon had been a "thorn in the side of CSULB" for years and had gone to great lengths to quash the opinions of professionals with whom he does not agree. Also included was a declaration of a Native American who averred that in February 1993, CSULB called a meeting of Native Americans for the purpose of discussing the proposed development of the Puvunga site. At that meeting, Dixon was said to have declared that SRS had earlier performed archaeological services on an unrelated Native American site which resulted in its desecration and destruction. The trial court denied the motion to strike and this writ petition followed.

The Origin of SLAPP Suits and the Legislature's Response

The *typical*[fn] SLAPP suit involves citizens opposed to a particular real estate development. The group opposed to the project, usually a local neighborhood, protests by distributing flyers, writing letters to local newspapers, and speaking at planning commission or city council meetings. The developer responds by filing a SLAPP suit against the citizen group alleging defamation or various business torts. [C] SLAPP plaintiffs do not intend to win their suits; rather, they are filed solely for delay and distraction ([c]), and to punish activists by imposing litigation costs on them for exercising their constitutional right to speak and petition the government for redress of grievances. [C]

And "[w]hile SLAPP suits 'masquerade as ordinary lawsuits' the conceptual features which reveal them as SLAPP's are that they are generally meritless suits brought by large private interests to deter common citizens from exercising their political or legal rights or to punish them for doing so. [Citations.] Because winning is not a SLAPP plaintiff's primary motivation, defendants' traditional safeguards against meritless actions, (suits for malicious prosecution and abuse of process, requests for sanctions) are inadequate to counter SLAPP's. Instead, the SLAPPer considers any damage or sanction award which the SLAPPee might eventually recover as merely a cost of doing business. [Citations.] By the time a SLAPP victim can win a 'SLAPP-back' suit years later the SLAPP plaintiff will probably already have accomplished its underlying objective.... [Citations.]" (Wilcox v. Superior Court, [] 27 Cal.App.4th [809,] 816-817, 33 Cal.Rptr.2d 446[(1994)].)

In 1992, the Legislature responded to the problem of SLAPP suits by enacting Code of Civil Procedure section 425.16.... .

Does the Complaint Filed by SRS Constitute a SLAPP Suit?

The party moving to strike a complaint under Code of Civil Procedure section 425.16 has the burden of making a prima facie showing that the lawsuit arises "'from any act of [defendant] in furtherance of [defendant's] right of petition or free speech under the United States or California Constitution *in connection with a public issue.*' [Citation.]" (*Wilcox v. Superior Court, supra,* 27 Cal.App.4th at [] 820[], emphasis added.)

There is no dispute the proposed development of the Puvunga site and its related CEQA proceedings were matters of public concern. What is in dispute is whether Dixon's allegedly tortious statements were made in connection with those proceedings. SRS argues they were not because: (1) They were made after the CEQA proceedings had terminated with the issuance of the negative declaration; and (2) they were directed against SRS, which was not part of the CEQA proceedings.

There is no merit to SRS's first contention that the CEQA proceedings had terminated by the time Dixon began his letter writing campaign. When a proposed project may have a significant effect on the environment, CEQA requires the lead agency[fn] to undertake an initial threshold study. If that study results in a finding the project will not significantly affect the environment, the agency may so declare in a negative declaration. [C] However, *before* adopting a negative declaration, the agency is required to give notice to the public and allow time for comments. [C][fn] During that time, any interested person or group has a right to express its views. [C]

Envicom's issuance of the negative declaration and the recommendation that it be adopted did not *end* the public review period; on the contrary, it *initiated* it. At that point Dixon began the first of many communications to the CSULB administration arguing against the adoption of the negative declaration. That being so, each of Dixon's allegedly slanderous and libelous comments were made during the public review period contemplated by CEQA and were, therefore, "in connection" with those proceedings.[fn]

SRS's second contention, that its reports were not relied on by Envicom in reaching its finding, does not protect it from exposure to public scrutiny. SRS has been involved with the Puvunga site since 1980, when it performed archaeological tests on another portion of the site CSULB sought to develop. At that time, SRS concluded development of that area would cause no "adverse effects to archaeological and/or historic resources." During the current heated debate over development of the site and the proposed adoption of the negative declaration, SRS was asked to perform further testing, presumably to assist CSULB in reaching a decision as to whether to adopt the negative declaration. Given SRS's involvement with the Puvunga site and its position as to its archaeological significance (or lack thereof), it strains credulity for SRS to argue it was not involved in the CEQA proceedings.

… We conclude the comments made by Dixon were in connection with a public issue and fall within the statutory definition of Code of Civil Procedure section 425.16. That being so, the burden shifted to SRS to establish a probability of prevailing on its claim. [C]

Did SRS Make a Prima Facie Showing of Facts Which Would Support a Judgment in its Favor?

Given our determination that Dixon made a prima facie showing that he was exercising his First Amendment right to petition the government in connection with a public issue,[fn] he was entitled to have the complaint stricken unless SRS established a probability of prevailing at trial.

SRS argues it did so by offering evidence that the statements made by Dixon were made with "actual malice [and] with knowledge of their falsity or with reckless disregard for their truth." Citing McDonald v. Smith (1985) 472 U.S. 479[,] for the proposition that "[t]he right to petition is guaranteed; the right to commit libel with impunity is not" (*id.* at 485[]), SRS argues if it can show Dixon acted with malice, he was not entitled to First Amendment protection and SRS has, therefore, established a probability of prevailing at trial.

In *McDonald,* an unsuccessful candidate for appointment as United States Attorney sued an individual who had sent letters to the President of the United States and other members of the administration falsely accusing the candidate of violating the civil rights of various individuals, fraud, extortion and blackmail. The complaint alleged the defendant knew the statements were false and they were made with malice. [C] In rejecting the defendant's claim of absolute immunity, the Supreme Court held the right to petition is "cut from the same cloth" as other guarantees of the First Amendment. And to grant absolute immunity would improperly elevate the right to petition above other First Amendment guarantees. [C] Under the law of the state in which the complaint was brought, plaintiff was entitled to damages on a showing of malice. [C] Dixon contends, and we agree, that *McDonald* does not apply where, as here, a statute exists which expressly invites public comment. ...

In [Matossian v. Fahmie, 161 Cal.Rptr. 532 (1980), the court] held, "The very idea of a government ... implies a right on the part of its citizens ... to petition for a redress of grievances. [Cc] [A]ny attempt to restrict those liberties must be justified by clear public interest, threatened not doubtfully or remotely, but by clear and present danger." [C] The court explained that "[w]here administrative agencies such as the Department must make factual determinations 'the widest possible dissemination of information from *diverse and antagonistic sources* is essential to the welfare of the public[.]' [Cc]" [C] And motive is irrelevant: "We are persuaded by the foregoing authority and considerations that where, as here, a statute expressly invites or allows interested persons to protest, or give their views or opinions concerning, proposed or requested governmental administrative action, such persons singly or in combination have a lawful right to do so; in such a case the law will not permit judicial or other inquiry into the persons' purpose or motivation.... 'the motive, even if malicious, of defendants is unimportant if legal ground existed upon which to predicate' their protests. Such a right may not be defeated, or abridged, or 'chilled,' by threat or fear of civil action for exercising it." [C]

Here, as in *Matossian,* the statutory invitation for public participation bars any inquiry into the motives behind the statements or comments made. To bring himself within the protection of section 425.16, all Dixon had to do was show his statements were made in response to a matter of public concern. He did. Therefore, SRS could not, *as a matter of law,* have established a probability of prevailing at trial because even if it proved Dixon acted with malice, his statements are still entitled to absolute immunity. [C]

Constitutional Challenges to Section 425.16

Finally, SRS raises several constitutional challenges to Code of Civil Procedure section 425.16. It first contends the section violates its right to due process by requiring a plaintiff to establish probability of success without the opportunity to conduct discovery. Specifically, it argues if it were permitted to conduct discovery, it would be able to show a triable issue of fact as to malice. But, as we hold, Dixon's motivation in making the complained of statements is irrelevant; thus, proof of malice is not material in this case. ...

The alternative writ is dissolved. Let a peremptory writ of mandate issue directing the trial court to vacate its order denying petitioner's motion to strike the complaint and enter a new order granting the motion and dismissing the complaint.

SILLS, P.J., and SONENSHINE, J., concur.

> **Career**
> Sides can make a difference in finding employment and succeeding in tort practice. Tort lawyers and law firms having torts practice groups tend to practice either on the plaintiff's side or on defense. They tend not to practice on both sides. Exceptions exist where a lawyer or law firm can defend in one niche and take plaintiff's cases in another niche. Yet insurers tend not to appreciate when one of their insureds forwards to them a demand letter from one of their own assigned counsel. The problem is not just that the lawyer would have a conflict of interest in representing a claimant against an insurer with which the lawyer was then working on other cases. A lawyer's mistake of that kind can quickly end a valuable assigned-counsel relationship. Because firms tend to take sides, you may want to reflect on which side you prefer, plaintiff's representation or defense. The differences can be substantial, not only in the payment model (contingency fee versus hourly) but in the client relationships (personal or impersonal) and financial and time commitments the work requires. Discuss these considerations with lawyers and law professors. If torts practice after law school interests you, then try externing while in law school for one side or the other to be sure you choose the side best suited to your talents and nature after graduation.

Chapter XIX

Harm to Commercial Interests

Tort law does not limit itself to addressing purely personal, dignitary torts. It also addresses commercial disputes that have little or no personal or dignitary component. Tort law addresses certain forms of business misconduct resulting in commercial loss. The commercial torts work similarly to the personal torts in their elements and applications. Yet they also vary among the states more than their personal-tort counterparts can. The first form of commercial tort involves injurious falsehoods—not, as in the case of defamation, against the person but against some property or commercial interest belonging to the plaintiff. A plaintiff may plead injurious falsehood in that name or in names like *slander of title* or *disparagement of title* when involving false statements regarding title to property, *slander of goods* or *trade libel* when involving false statements regarding the sale of goods, and, most broadly, *commercial disparagement* when involving false statements about commercial reputation and interests. In each case, though, the essence of the injurious-falsehood tort is the same, that the defendant with certain purpose has communicated false information affecting the value of the plaintiff's property, trade, or commercial interest.

The second major form of commercial tort involves the defendant's interference with the plaintiff's existing or anticipated contract or other business relationship with a third party. Depending on the jurisdiction and circumstances, this second form of commercial tort goes by various names including *interference with contract*, *interference with business relations*, or *interference with prospective economic advantage*. This second form of commercial tort differs from the injurious-falsehood tort, in which the defendant's falsehoods reduce the value of the plaintiff's property or commercial interest. In the interference forms of the business torts, the defendant prevents the plaintiff from realizing the full value of an existing or anticipated business relationship. Strangers should not interfere by improper means with the economic productivity of others.

Some especially reprehensible cases may involve both injurious falsehoods about the plaintiff's property, goods, or business, and (at the same time) interference with business relations preventing the plaintiff from realizing full value of various relationships and interests. Some courts have allowed these cases of mixed wrongs to fall under a general rubric of *unfair competition*, where the defendant's overriding motive was to take the plaintiff's business whether lawfully or unlawfully. *See, e.g.,* McRoberts Protective Agency, Inc. v. Lansdell Protective Agency, Inc., 61 A.D.2d 652, 403 N.Y.S.2d 511 (N.Y. Supreme Court, App. Div. 1978) (statements that the plaintiff was going out of business). Yet *unfair competition* is a label more commonly given to traditional trademark-infringement claims such as passing off one's own product for another's. To learn these business torts, retain the traditional distinctions rather than referring to these commercial torts as unfair competition. Consider then each of the two major forms of commercial tort—injurious falsehood and interference with business relations.

A. Injurious Falsehood

OBJECTIVE: Given a commercial loss due to false statements by another, recall and apply the elements of the injurious-falsehood tort to determine whether that claim exists for the loss, consistent with this section.

Case Study: Two manufacturers sell dies to the same automotive-parts-supplier market. A die is a component of industrial machinery that the die-maker must finely tool to precise manufacturer specifications and deliver timely to meet production schedules. The market for dies has grown competitive. The first manufacturer made several die sales to customers who were simultaneously considering purchasing the second manufacturer's dies. Sales representatives from the second manufacturer heard from some of those customers that the first manufactuer's sales representative said that the second manufacturer was having tooling problems, had lost customers, and was on the verge of going out of business. *What information would you want to know from the second manufacturer in order to be able to evaluate its potential commercial-disparagement claim against the first manufacturer?*

1. Title

From a historical standpoint within the common law, the first form of injurious falsehood involved slander-of-title actions redressing false statements about property. Gerard v. Dickenson, Cro. Eliz. 196, 76 Eng. Rep. 903 (1590), is an early representative case in which the defendant knowingly made a false claim against the plaintiff's castle. *See also* Ratcliffe v. Evans, 2 Q.B. 524 (1892) (popularizing the phrases "injurious falsehood" and "slander of title"). As that early *Gerard* case aptly illustrates, the elements of this slander-of-title form of injurious falsehood are (1) a false statement (2) calculated to harm the plaintiff's pecuniary interest by (3) publication to a third person with (4) malice (commonly meaning knowledge or reckless disregard of falsity) causing (5) special (usually meaning pecuniary) damage. Recognize the similarities of the slander-of-title elements to those of a defamation claim. The slander-of-title elements—especially the definition of malice—produce similar conceptual difficulties and boundary issues.

Slander-of-title actions can involve any real or personal, tangible or intangible property interest that the property owner can sell. A common way in which slander-of-title actions arise is with the recording of an unwarranted lien against the plaintiff's property. *See, e.g.,* Timeline, LLC v. Williams Holdings No. 3, LLC, 698 N.W.2d 181 (Minn. App. 2005). Another common slander-of-title action arises with the filing of a lawsuit involving other matters followed by the recording of a notice of pending litigation ("lis pendens") against the property. *See, e.g.,* Gudger v. Maton, 21 Cal.2d 537, 134 P.2d 217 (1943). False lien filings and title recordings readily interfere with, indeed prohibit, sale, thus reducing the value of the property against which the claimant records the claim or lien. Those who assert liens and give notices of claims should be cautious to avoid slander of title and should scrupulously follow any applicable statutes. Consider the following case as an example.

Marking v. Surwillo
Wisconsin Court of Appeals
298 Wis.2d 550, 727 N.W.2d 375 (2006) (Table)

KESSLER, J. Plaintiff Robert Marking appeals from an order granting defendant Mildred Surwillo's motion for summary judgment and dismissing Marking's complaint in its entirety. Marking also appeals from an order granting Surwillo's counterclaim and a money judgment awarding Surwillo damages in the amount of $5,885.[fn omitted] Because we conclude that the trial court properly found that, under WIS. STAT. § 706.02 (2003-04),[fn omitted] there was no valid and enforceable contract between the parties entitling Marking to specific performance, and further conclude that the trial court did not erroneously exercise its discretion when it determined that Marking had acted in bad faith and slandered the title of the subject property, in violation of WIS. STAT. § 706.13 when he filed a *lis pendens* on the property, we affirm. ...

BACKGROUND

On December 13, 2004, Marking emailed or faxed an unsigned Offer to Purchase (Offer) to Attorney Kevin Demet, Surwillo's attorney. Surwillo signed the Offer and faxed it back to Marking on December 15, 2004. ...

Marking informed Demet that he would not be able to close on December 28, 2004[, as the offer required]. Marking rescheduled the closing for December 29, 2004, but did not do so in writing. On Tuesday, December 28, 2004, at 2:06 p.m., Marking left a voicemail for Demet indicating that he could not close on December 29, 2004. ...

In a subsequent telephone call between Demet and Marking on December 28, 2004, Marking confirmed that he was "unable to obtain financing in time to close." On December 30, 2004, Demet faxed a letter to Marking reiterating the above information and then cancelling the deal, noting: "Your rights under the contract expired on December 28th when you failed to perform." At no time between December 13, 2004 and December 30, 2004, did Marking sign the Offer or deliver a signed Offer to Surwillo.

Marking commenced this lawsuit on January 11, 2005. On January 12, 2005, Marking caused a *lis pendens* to be recorded with the Milwaukee County Register of Deeds on the property that was the subject of the Offer. To date [the opinion is dated December 27, 2006], the *lis pendens* has not been released. ... Surwillo filed an answer, affirmative defenses and counterclaim on February 9, 2005. On February 24, 2005, Surwillo filed a motion for summary judgment. On April 11 and 25, 2005, a hearing was held on Surwillo's motion. The trial court granted the motion, dismissing Marking's amended complaint in its entirety and ordering the release of the *lis pendens*. ...

After a bench trial on Surwillo's counterclaim, the trial court [found in Surwillo's favor on Surwillo's counterclaim against Marking.] ...

DISCUSSION ...

II. Counterclaim

Marking filed a *lis pendens* contemporaneously with his filing of this lawsuit. In response, Surwillo filed a counterclaim against Marking which included claims of: (1) slander of title; (2) abuse of process; and (3) violation of WIS. STAT. § 814.025. Marking never filed a response to the counterclaim. After trial, the trial court made the following additional findings of fact and conclusions of law:

- Marking had "slandered title to Mrs. Surwillo's property"
- Marking "continued this action in bad faith"
- Marking "should not have maintained the *lis pendens* on this property"
- Surwillo "has incurred damages to clear title ... in the amount of $4,880.00, and statutory damages in the amount of $1,000.00." ...

Under common law, to prove a slander of title claim:

[A]n individual must show a publication which: (1) results in an injurious falsehood or disparagement of property and includes matters derogatory to the plaintiff's title or business in general, calculated to prevent others from dealing with the plaintiff, or to interfere with his relations with others to his disadvantage; (2) has been communicated to a third person; (3) plays a material or substantial part in inducing others not to deal with the plaintiff; and (4) results in special damage. ...

It is undisputed that when Surwillo withdrew her acceptance of the Offer on December 30, 2004, Marking had not signed the Offer. Accordingly, under WIS. STAT. § 706.02, the Offer never ripened into an enforceable contract. Consequently, at the time Marking filed his lawsuit in January 2005, he did not "have a reasonable ground for believing the truth of the pleading" and knew or should have known that there was no enforceable contract to convey real estate, making his *lis pendens* false, a sham or a frivolous claim impairing title. [C] Accordingly, we affirm the trial court's judgment in favor of Surwillo on her counterclaim, because Marking slandered Surwillo's title to the subject property by filing the *lis pendens*. ...

Judgment and orders affirmed and cause remanded.

INQUIRY

Privilege. The plaintiff's right to prevent or receive compensation for the false disparagement of the plaintiff's title is in tension with the defendant's right to pursue reasonable claims and protect legitimate interests against the plaintiff over disputed property. Absolute and conditional privileges protect the defendant's right to pursue disputed claims against the plaintiff's property. The absolute privileges are like those in defamation cases, including the privilege attached to the filing of court pleadings and statements within judicial proceedings. *See* Stewart v. Fahey, 14 Ariz. App. 149, 481 P.2d 519 (1971); Davis v. Union State Bank, 137 Kan. 264, 20 P.2d 508 (1933). The conditional privilege protects the defendant who subjectively believes that the defendant has the claim—even if the defendant's belief is objectively unreasonable. The plaintiff must in such cases prove the defendant's malice, defined (as in the defamation cases) as knowledge of or reckless disregard with respect to the claim's falsity. *See* Horning v. Hardy, 36 Md. App. 419, 373 A.2d 1273 (1977). Modern privilege cases like *Horning v. Hardy* expressly incorporate the constitutional forms and language of *New York Times v. Sullivan* and *Gertz v. Robert Welch, Inc.* Thus, as in the defamation cases, the constitutional structure tends to subsume the privilege defense in injurious-falsehood and commercial-disparagement cases.

2. Trade

The plaintiff's property is not always the interest that the defendant will have disparaged. In some instances, the defendant may have published false statements to a third person regarding the plaintiff's goods or business—what the law labels *commercial disparagement, trade disparagement*, or *trade libel*, the other form of the injurious-falsehood tort after the disparagement-of-title form discussed above. *See, e.g.*, Testing Systems, Inc. v. Magnaflux Corp., 251 F. Supp. 286 (E.D. Pa. 1966) (alleging false statements that the federal government had found plaintiff's product to be only forty percent as effective as defendant's product). The elements of trade disparagement include (1) publication of a (2) false statement (3) intended to cause (4) pecuniary harm to another's trade or business with (5) knowledge or reckless disregard that the statement is false. *See* Restatement (Second) of Torts § 623(A) (1977). Although their elements are quite alike, the difference between commercial disparagement and defamation is that commercial disparagement involves false statements about the quality of the plaintiff's goods or business, whereas defamation involves false statements about the plaintiff's own character or conduct—perhaps a slim distinction in some cases but a difference nonetheless. *See* U.S. Healthcare, Inc. v. Blue Cross of Greater Philadelphia, 898 F.2d 914 (3d Cir. 1990). Although slander of title is the earlier form of injurious falsehood, early English common law also recognized the slander-of-trade form, in a case, Dickes v. Fenne March N.R. 59, 82 Eng. Rep. 411 (1639), involving false criticism of a brewer's beer. Despite its long history, the commercial-disparagement tort remains viable today as a means of addressing falsehoods calculated to cause commercial loss. Consider the following case illustrating the potential reach of the commercial-disparagement tort.

Brunson Communications, Inc. v. Arbitron, Inc.
United States District Court, Eastern District of Pennsylvania
266 F. Supp.2d 377 (2003)

BAYLSON, J. * * * [T]his Court must determine whether Plaintiff's latest amended pleading states sufficient facts to sustain either, or both, of the two causes of action remaining in this case.

I. *Relevant Procedural History* [fn omitted]

… Plaintiff filed its Second Amended Complaint ("Sec.Am.Comp.") on March 3, 2003, reasserting claims for disparagement of commercial products and negligence.[fn omitted] …

Plaintiff alleges the following facts, which, for the purpose of deciding the instant motion, will be viewed in the light most favorable to Plaintiff. Plaintiff is the owner of Channel 48, WGTW-TV, a small non-network television station serving the Philadelphia area. [C] Defendant Arbitron is in the business of developing and operating measurement systems to monitor radio listeners and television viewers, to serve various industries, including the advertising industry. [C] Defendant has developed a new technology for measuring television viewership, known as the personal people meter ("PPM"). …

In the fourth quarter of 2001, Defendant began a "test" survey program to introduce its PPM technology into the Philadelphia market. [C] Defendant announced, in conjunction with its launching of the PPM test, that the survey would "accurately and creditably measure the performance of the entire market."[fn omitted] [C] This statement, Plaintiff claims, was "false and malicious," in that Defendant did not intend to include WGTW in the test. [C]

In order to measure a particular station's viewership, Defendant would have to install certain equipment at that station. Plaintiff alleges Defendant did not possess enough equipment to measure all stations in the Philadelphia market. According to the Second Amended Complaint, Defendant chose to omit Plaintiff's station from the PPM survey, despite the fact that WGTW's actual viewership is significant. [C] Moreover, Plaintiff alleges, Defendant embedded its PPM signal only in the transmitters of Plaintiff's competitors—the larger networks and cable systems—omitting Plaintiff's station from the PPM survey data. [C] Plaintiff claims that Defendant's motive in omitting Plaintiff was to obtain the benefits of working with the larger networks, plaintiff's competitors, who have most of the outlets in the markets. Therefore its pursuit of profits caused it to knowingly give preferential treatment to plaintiff's competitors and knowingly and [sic] exclude and subject to disparagement an independent non-network station that did not have the market power of the competitors. [C]

According to Plaintiff, Defendant then began to release periodic PPM survey data to advertising agencies, advertisers, television stations and other media sources, representing that the data were complete and accurate. [C] By failing to include Plaintiff's station in the PPM test measurements, Plaintiff claims, Defendant impaired WGTW's ability to be competitive in the market for sales of advertising time, in that advertising agencies would be unable to confirm from the survey that WGTW had a measurable viewership. [C] Plaintiff further maintains that even if advertisers had recognized that WGTW was omitted from the PPM test data, such omission by Defendant "de-facto reduced WGTW's standing in the eyes of the persons and companies it must solicit to buy the station's product, i.e. viewership watching time." [C] ...

In its commercial disparagement count, Plaintiff asserts that Defendant's false statements as to the accuracy and completeness of its test surveys caused substantial pecuniary loss to Plaintiff, in that prospective advertisers would conclude from the data that WGTW's viewership was "so insignificant as not to warrant either inclusion in the survey or recognition of the exclusion, as was foreseen by the defendant." [C] ...

IV. *Sufficiency of the Second Amended Complaint*

Defendant moves for dismissal of both counts, for failure to state a claim upon which relief can be granted.

A. *Disparagement of Commercial Products*

The Court of Appeals for the Third Circuit has recently predicted that the Pennsylvania Supreme Court would adopt a Restatement of Torts section regarding commercial disparagement. [C] That Restatement section, § 623A, provides that:

> One who *publishes a false statement harmful to the interests of another* is subject to liability for *pecuniary loss* resulting to the other if
>
> (a) he *intends* for publication of the statement to result in harm to interests of the other having a pecuniary value, *or* either recognizes or should *recognize that it is likely* to do so, *and*
>
> (b) he *knows* that the statement is *false* or acts in *reckless disregard* of its truth or falsity.

Restatement (Second) of Torts § 623(A) (1977) (emphasis added).

... Thus, to sustain its cause of action for commercial disparagement, Plaintiff must allege, 1.) that Defendant made a false statement, which caused pecuniary loss to Plaintiff, 2.) that Defendant intended for publication of the statement to result in harm to Plaintiff's pecuniary interests, or either recognized or should have recognized that it was likely to do so, and 3.) that Defendant knew that the statement was false or acted in reckless disregard of its truth or falsity.

Plaintiff alleges that Defendant announced, in conjunction with its launching of the PPM test, that the survey would "accurately and creditably measure the performance of the entire market," when, in fact, the survey omitted WGTW entirely. [C] Further, according to Plaintiff, Kevin Smith, a Senior Vice President of Arbitron, speaking at an industry meeting, "knowingly and intentionally falsely represented that the survey was fair, accurate and complete." [C] Plaintiff's theory is that these statements were false, and damaging to Plaintiff, in that prospective advertisers would conclude from the data that WGTW's viewership was "so insignificant as not to warrant either inclusion in the survey or recognition of the exclusion, as was foreseen by the defendant." [C]

Under notice pleading, these allegations fulfill the requirement of a "false statement," the requirement that Defendant should have recognized the potential harm the statement could cause, and the requirement that Defendant knew the statement was false or acted in reckless disregard of its truth or falsity. Restatement (Second) of Torts § 623(A). Although Plaintiff does not allege that Defendant made any statements *directly referring to WGTW*, this Court concludes that Plaintiff has made out a disparagement case strong enough to withstand the present motion to dismiss. While Defendant may not have expressly mentioned WGTW in any of its statements, Plaintiff may, nevertheless, be able to prove that the total effect of Defendant's various statements and actions was to disparage Plaintiff's business and to reduce WGTW's standing in the eyes of the persons and companies it must solicit to buy the station's product. [C]

However, as noted above, Plaintiff has not specifically identified a pecuniary loss resulting from the allegedly false statements. Rule 9(g) provides that "[w]hen items of special damage are claimed, they shall be specifically stated." Fed.R.Civ.P. 9(g). This Court has previously held that, to successfully plead a cause of action for disparagement, a plaintiff must allege facts showing an established business, the amount of sales for a substantial period preceding publication, and amount of sales subsequent to the publication, facts showing that such loss in sale were the natural and probable result of such publication, and the facts showing the plaintiff could not allege the name of particular customers who withdrew or withheld their custom. [C]

... In the case at bar, Plaintiff does not allege a general decline in business, much less a specific type of pecuniary loss. However, because the allegedly disparaging statements were made approximately one year ago, Plaintiff should now be able to readily determine and specifically allege the type and extent of its economic damages.
... Therefore, this Court will dismiss Plaintiff's commercial disparagement claim without prejudice to Plaintiff's right to file a Third Amended Complaint within twenty days, alleging facts showing specific types and amounts of damages, such as alleging the amount of sales for a substantial period preceding Defendant's statements, and the amount of sales subsequent to Defendant's statements, and also alleging specific facts

showing that such losses in sales were the natural and probable result of Defendant's statements.

V. *Conclusion*

For the foregoing reasons, Defendant's Motion to Dismiss Plaintiff's Second Amended Complaint Pursuant to Federal Rule of Civil Procedure 12(b)(6) will be granted; ... Plaintiff's Disparagement of Commercial Products claim will be dismissed, without prejudice to Plaintiff's right to file a Third Amended Complaint within twenty days; and Plaintiff's Motion for Leave to Amend will be denied as moot. An appropriate Order follows.

INQUIRY

Scope. As the above *Brunson Communications* case suggests, the defendant's disparagement need not necessarily be direct to satisfy the harmful-false-statement element of the commercial-disparagement tort. False statements that the plaintiff is going out of business, *see* McRoberts Protective Agency, Inc. v. Lansdell Protective Agency, Inc., 61 A.D.2d 652, 403 N.Y.S.2d 511 (1978), or that the plaintiff proprietor has died, Davis v. New England Railway Pub. Co., 203 Mass. 470, 89 N.E. 565 (1909), can effectively disparage and be the basis for a tort action. So, too, can a false report to the IRS that results in tax-defense costs, *see* Penn-Ohio Steel Corp. v. Allis-Chalmers Mfg. Co., 7 A.D.2d 441, 184 N.Y.S.2d 58 (1959), a false statement as to non-citizenship that requires defense of deportation proceedings, *see* Al Raschid v. News Syndicate Co., 265 N.Y.1, 191 N.E. 713 (1934), or a false wage assignment communicated to an employer resulting in the plaintiff's firing, *see* Barlett v. Federal Outfitting Co., 133 Cal. App. 747, 24 P.2d 877 (1933). The relief in a commercial-disparagement action may also be broader to include an injunction—not typically available in other tort actions.

Special Damages. As the above *Brunson Communications* case also suggests, the trade-disparagement form requires proof of special damages. The courts tend not to permit the plaintiff to claim a general decline in business due to the defendant's disparagement. *See* Amerinet, Inc. v. Xerox Corp., 972 F.2d 1483 (8th Cir. 1992), cert. denied, 506 U.S. 1080 (1993); *but see* Imperial Developers, Inc., v. Seaboard Surety Co., 518 N.W.2d 623 (Minn. App. 1994) (allowing general-damages claim for business but not product disaparagement). If the plaintiff's alleged loss is of prospective rather than current customers, then the courts generally require that the plaintiff identify the particular lost customers. *See* Barquin v. Hall Oil Co., 28 Wyo. 164, 201 P. 352 (1921). Where particular proof of loss is not reasonably available, some courts allow the plaintiff to satisfy the special-damages requirement with expert statistical treatments that reasonably exclude other factors unrelated to the defendant's disparagement. *See* Teilhaber Mfg. Co. v. Unarco Materials Storage, 791 P.2d 1164 (Colo. App. 1989). The special-damages element ensures the reliability of the causation and damages proofs, given the large number of other factors (beyond disparagement) that might influence business income.

Constitutional Protection. The First Amendment protects those who publish statements about public figures (including for-profit corporations) that lead to commercial loss, unless the plaintiff can prove actual malice. The Supreme Court in Bose Corp. v. Consumers Union of United States, Inc., 466 U.S. 485 (1984), held that the plaintiff speaker manufacturer must prove the defendant publisher's actual malice by clear-and-convincing evidence, where the manufacturer (a public figure) maintained that the defendant's false statements had caused the plaintiff commercial loss. The First Amendment protects criticism of another's trade when the businessperson or commercial entity criticized is a public figure and the criticizer does not know of or act recklessly as to the statement's falsity. Constitutional protection reminds us of the value of free expression within the marketplace to determine truth. Producers should be relatively free to criticize competitors' products. *See* Nonpareil Cork Mfg. Co. v. Keasbey & Mattison Co., 108 Fed. 721 (E.D. Pa. 1901) (statement that insulation product was a "fraud" is nonactionable expression of opinion). Consider the following case articulating the protections.

Dairy Stores, Inc. v. Sentinel Pub. Co.
New Jersey Supreme Court
516 A.2d 220 (1986)

POLLOCK, J.

This appeal requires that we declare the standard of liability of a newspaper, its reporter, and an independent laboratory retained by them for statements that allegedly defamed the plaintiff corporation's reputation and disparaged its product. Relying on the first amendment to the United States Constitution, the Law Division granted summary judgment for the defendants, finding that they had not published the statements with reckless disregard for their truth. [C] The Appellate Division affirmed. [C] We granted certification, [c], and now affirm the judgment of the Appellate Division. In reaching that result, we look to federal law for guidance, but we base our decision on the common-law privilege of fair comment.

-I-

During a drought in 1981, two weekly newspapers, The Sentinel and The Suburban, both owned by defendant Sentinel Publishing Co., Inc. (Sentinel), published a series of articles on the increased sale of bottled water in Milltown. ... Shortly after a period of heavy rain, Milltown residents noticed that their tap water tasted odd and had a strong odor. As a result, sales of bottled water increased. Plaintiff, Dairy Stores, Inc., t/a Krauszer's Food Stores (Krauszer's), sold [bottled water]... . Between January and February 1981, sales at Krauszer's Milltown convenience store increased more than 50 percent, and in one week sales jumped from an average of 40 gallons to 700 gallons.

Defendant Kathleen Dzielak wrote three articles that were published in Sentinel newspapers about the water shortage, Milltown's water problem, and the bottled water industry. In pursuing her story, she tried to learn the source of Krauszer's bottled water, which was sold under the label "Covered Bridge Crystal Clear Spring Water" (Covered Bridge). Krauszer's declined to identify the source, and Dzielak took a bottle of Covered Bridge water to an independent state-certified testing laboratory, New Jersey Dairy Laboratories. When Dzielak asked whether testing could prove that the water was spring water, the laboratory supervisor told her that a positive chlorine test result would exclude the possibility that the water came from a spring. Upon recognizing the Covered Bridge label, the supervisor advised Dzielak that Krauszer's was a customer of the laboratory, and that the supervisor was so sure Covered Bridge water did not contain chlorine that a test was "unnecessary." Nonetheless, at Dzielak's request, the supervisor tested the water and reported that it did not contain chlorine. Skeptical of the results, Dzielak took the bottle to another independent laboratory, defendant Paterson Clinical Laboratory (Paterson), for similar tests, stating that she was compiling information for an article. Paterson's laboratory director told her that exposure of the water to air made more difficult an accurate analysis of the sample. Nonetheless, in repeated tests, Paterson found that chlorine was present in the water. Dzielak took a second sealed bottle of Covered Bridge water to a third laboratory, Princeton Aqua Science, which submitted a report to Dzielak, who did not understand the results because they were expressed in a manner different from those in the other reports.

Based on her investigation, Dzielak wrote her stories and submitted them for publication. On March 11, 1981, Sentinel published the stories, two of which ran without a by-line under the headlines, "Water sales booming" and "Firms protect sources." The latter story concluded that current law did not require disclosure of the source of the water but that proposed regulations would require such disclosure. The third story was published with Dzielak's by-line and ran under a banner headline, "Spring water/Independent lab analysis casts doubt on content." The article began:

> A sample bottle of "Covered Bridge Crystal Clear Spring Water," sold at Krauszer's convenient food stores, does not contain pure spring water, according to a laboratory analysis obtained by the Sentinel Newspapers.
>
> Tests conducted on the product, purchased at the Krauszer's store at 23 N. Main Street, Milltown, showed a chlorine content of .1 parts per million. Ralph Pugliese, director of the state-certified Paterson Clinic Lab, which conducted the tests, said pure spring water should not contain any chlorine.
>
> "I can't see how it could possibly be spring water unless the spring source was contaminated and chlorine was added at the source. Since we thought we were dealing with a spring water sampling, when we received a .1 reading we ran the test again four or five times and had two chemists look at it to make sure."
>
> Because of the high rate of chlorine's dissipation, either by contact with air or other substances, Pugliese conjectured that at one point the water had contained a higher concentration of chlorine.
>
> When Jerry McCloskey, national sales manager for Krauszer's, was informed of the lab results, he insisted that no chlorine is added to Covered Bridge water at any step of the operation and that the water does come from springs.

Sentinel rejected Krauszer's request for a retraction, whereupon Krauszer's instituted its complaint asserting a claim against Sentinel and Dzielak for defamation, which the Law Division viewed as including a claim for product disparagement. [C] As against Paterson, Krauszer's asserted a claim for negligence and for interference with prospective economic advantage, which the Law Division treated as a claim for defamation. [C]

Defendants moved for summary judgment, arguing that the relevant principle for determining their liability was whether they published the story with actual malice. ... [The trial] court granted summary judgment in favor of all defendants.

In affirming substantially for the reasons set forth in the trial court's opinion, the Appellate Division referred to Bose Corporation v. Consumers Union of United States, Inc., 466 U.S. 485[] (1984), which was decided by the United States Supreme Court after publication of the Law Division's opinion. The Appellate Division read *Bose* as extending the actual malice test to product disparagement. [C]

At the outset, we must consider the distinction between causes of action for defamation and for product disparagement. ...

-II-

Plaintiff has pursued the cause as one for defamation, but the cause could also be viewed as one for product disparagement. Indeed, the concurring opinion treats the case as if it were exclusively an action for product disparagement. We are sensitive, as was the Law Division, [c], to the potential implication of product disparagement principles, but we are constrained to decide the case as the parties and the lower courts have viewed it, as an action for defamation.

Although the two causes sometimes overlap, actions for defamation and product disparagement stem from different branches of tort law. A defamation action, which encompasses libel and slander, affords a remedy for damage to one's reputation. [Cc] By comparison, an action for product disparagement is an offshoot of the cause of action for interference with contractual relations, such as sales to a prospective buyer. [Cc] The two causes may merge when a disparaging statement about a product reflects on the reputation of the business that made, distributed, or sold it. If, for example, a statement about the poor quality of a product implies that the seller is fraudulent, then the statement may be actionable under both theories. [Cc] Courts generally are reluctant to impute a lack of integrity to a corporation merely from a criticism of its product. [Cc] On the premise that the reputation of a business is more valuable than any particular product it sells, courts have responded more readily to a claim of damage to one's reputation than to a claim for product disparagement. [C] Semantics contributes to the confusion of the two causes because terms used to describe a product disparagement action, such as "trade libel" and "slander of title," tend to blur the distinction between such an action and one for defamation.

Recent decisions of the United States Supreme Court have further blurred the dividing line between the two causes. Traditionally, a plaintiff in a product disparagement action has borne the burden of establishing that the disparaging statement was both false and injurious. By comparison, in a defamation action, the plaintiff was entitled to a presumption that the defamatory statement was both false and harmful. [Cc] Just this year, however, the United States Supreme Court held that when a statement treats a matter of public concern, the plaintiff in a defamation action has the burden of proving that the statement is false. Philadelphia Newspapers, Inc. v. Hepps, [475 U.S. 767] (1986). Earlier the Court had ruled that a plaintiff was not entitled to presume damages from the publication of a statement about a matter of public concern, unless the statement was published with actual malice. Gertz v. Robert Welch, Inc., 418 U.S. 323, 349-50[] (1974); *see also* Dun & Bradstreet, Inc. v. Greenmoss Builders, Inc., 472 U.S. 749, 761[] (1985). As a result, the difference between product disparagement and defamation has narrowed further when a statement treats a matter of public concern.

Here, Sentinel's article reported the presence of chlorine in Covered Bridge water and stated that Krauszer's kept the source of its bottled water a "well-guarded secret." Arguably, these statements not only disparaged Covered Bridge water by casting doubt on whether it was spring water, but also defamed Krauszer's corporate reputation by implying that it was trying to hide something through non-disclosure of the source of the water, *e.g.*, that the water did not come from a spring or that the spring was contaminated.

Because this matter was presented on review of an order granting defendants' motion for summary judgment, we view the facts in the light most favorable to the plaintiff, giving it the benefit of all favorable inferences that may legitimately be drawn from the record. [C] Thus, for the purposes of this appeal, we assume that the articles were not only disparaging, but also false and defamatory. As a result, the distinction between defamation and product disparagement disappears, and our attention shifts to whether the publications were privileged and whether the defendants abused any such privilege.

-III-

... Insofar as defenses to product disparagement are concerned, a qualified privilege should exist wherever it would exist in a defamation action. [C] Because the common law historically has held the interest in one's reputation as more worthy of protection than the interest of a business in the products that it makes, it follows that the right to make a statement about a product should exist whenever it is permissible to make such a statement about the reputation of another.

One illustration of a qualified privilege is fair comment, which is sometimes described as rendering a statement non-libelous. No matter how described, the defense is lost upon a showing that the statement was made with malice. [C] The roots of fair comment are imbedded in the common law, but in recent years, those roots have intertwined with others arising from constitutional law. ...

... Although constitutional considerations have dominated defamation law in recent years, the common law provides an alternative, and potentially more stable, framework for analyzing statements about matters of public interest.

Another reason for turning to the common law is that the constitutional concepts do not comfortably fit the activities or products of a corporation. As the Law Division noted, the term "public figure" does not readily apply to corporate enterprises, and "public controversy" is poorly suited to describe the commercial activities of such an enterprise. [C] The term "public figure" includes individuals who engage in a public controversy and ill fits a corporation, which ordinarily is interested not in thrusting itself into such a controversy, but in selling its products.

Lower federal courts, although differing on the nature and amount of activity needed to support the characterization of a corporation as a public figure, have concluded that corporations and their products can be viewed as public figures. ...

To summarize, the "public figure" device provides an awkward and uncertain method of determining whether statements about corporations or their products are actionable. Although the United States Supreme Court has withdrawn constitutional protection from statements on matters of public interest, the Court has left open to state courts the prospect of protecting such statements through common-law privileges, including fair comment. Providing such protection would be consistent with the enhanced protection we have provided to speech in other areas. [C] Thus, we turn to the analysis of the scope of the fair comment privilege.

A

Generally speaking, the doctrine of fair comment extends to virtually all matters of legitimate public interest. Through the principle of fair comment, New Jersey courts have long accorded protection to wide-ranging statements about public officials. [Cc] The courts have likewise applied the principle to controversial public issues, such as internal security during the McCarthy era, [c], and to criticism of a proposed trailer park that was perceived as posing a threat to drainage, property values, and taxes, [c].

Drinking water, the subject of the present litigation, has also been held to be a topic of vital public concern and subject to fair comment. [C] ...

In like fashion, federal and state courts proceeding on constitutional analysis have recognized that information concerning products intended for human consumption, such as drinking water, or other matters of public health, require the plaintiff to prove actual malice to sustain a claim for defamation. [Cc] ...

We recognize that not everything that is newsworthy is a matter of legitimate public concern, and that sorting such matters from those of a more private nature may be difficult. In this regard, the assessment of public interest includes a determination whether the person "voluntarily and knowingly engaged in conduct that one in his position should reasonably know would implicate a legitimate public interest, engendering the real possibility of public attention and scrutiny." Sisler v. Gannett Co., Inc., 104 N.J. 256, 274, 516 A.2d 1083, 1092 (1986).

Some courts have developed criteria for determining whether the activities and products of corporations constitute matters of public interest. As previously indicated, matters of public interest include such essentials of life as food and water. [Cc] Widespread effects of a product are yet another indicator that statements about the product are in the public interest. [Cc] Still another criterion is substantial government regulation of business activities and products. [Cc] Historically, restaurants also have been the subject of critical review. [Cc]

It would be anomalous to consider food and drink to be a subject of public interest when purchased in a restaurant, but not when purchased in a store. This conclusion applies with particular force to bottled drinking water, which is the subject of state regulation. Since 1924, New Jersey has regulated the sale of bottled drinking water, and anyone engaged in the business of bottling and selling drinking water must be licensed by and comply with regulations of the Department of Health. [C] As an essential of human life, drinking water is a paradigm of legitimate public concern. We leave to the future a more complete definition of matters of legitimate public concern. For this decision, it suffices to conclude that drinking water is such a subject.

Because the present case involves a product that is unquestionably a matter of legitimate public concern, we believe it is more prudent to extend that standard for the time being only to such products, leaving to another day the determination whether the standard should apply to statements about all products no matter how prosaic or innocuous. To this extent, we disagree with our concurring colleague, who would extend the actual malice standard to a disparaging statement about any product.

B

Throughout the country, courts have divided on the issue whether fair comment should be restricted to statements of opinion or should extend to factual statements. Underlying the distinction is the premise that the widest possible latitude should extend to expressions of opinion on matters of public concern, but that factual misstatements should be more narrowly confined.

The majority view is that fair comment extends to opinion only, [cc], but a respected minority view holds that statements of fact should also be protected. [Cc] Although both strands are evident in our common law, the more traditional view has been that the fair comment "privilege" does not extend to factual statements. [C] ...

The need for the free flow of information and commentary on matters of legitimate public concern leads us to conclude that fair comment should extend beyond opinion to statements of fact. When confronting such a matter, a publisher should not be unduly inhibited in analyzing whether a statement is an immune opinion or a potentially culpable statement of fact. [C] We believe we come close to fulfilling the policy considerations that underlie fair comment if we evaluate factual statements as the subject of a qualified privilege. This conclusion leads to further consideration of the facts that will constitute an abuse of the privilege.

C

In traditional defamation analysis, one difference between absolute and qualified privileges is that an absolute privilege grants complete immunity to the publisher, but a qualified privilege accords immunity only if the statement is made without malice. [C] The defense of fair comment, like other qualified privileges, may be overcome by showing that a statement was made with malice. [C] ...

As the actual malice standard has evolved, the relevant test is not "whether a reasonably prudent man would have published, or would have investigated before publishing," but "whether the defendant in fact entertained serious doubts as to the truth of his publication." St. Amant v. Thompson, 390 U.S. 727, 731[] (1968). That test, which is substantially subjective, is akin to the common-law requirement that to qualify as fair comment, a statement must honestly express the writer's true opinion. [Cc]

The bald assertion by the publisher that he believes in the truth of the statement may not be sufficient. [C] Notwithstanding a publisher's denial that it had serious doubts about the truthfulness of the statement, other facts might support an inference that the publisher harbored such doubts. ...

"Malice" adds nothing to the legal analysis of an allegedly defamatory statement, and it can become a pitfall in the underbrush of the common law. Consequently, we lose nothing by striking "malice" from the vocabulary of the common law of defamation. [C] Indeed, the *Restatement* eschews the term altogether, speaking instead of the "abuse of privilege." *Restatement (Second), supra,* § 599. It is more direct to recognize the legal consequences of the publication of certain statements without recourse to so ambiguous a word with such a checkered past. ... With or without the term, the critical determination is whether, on balance, the public interest in obtaining information outweighs the individual's right to protect his or her reputation. [C]

As society in general, and the sale of goods in particular, becomes more complex, the general welfare requires the dissemination of more and more information to the consuming public. Consumers, who are often separated from those in the early stages of a chain of distribution, have a legitimate need to learn about the reputation of the business entities in that chain and of the goods that are being distributed. From that need emanates the right to publish information concerning the nature and quality of goods intended for human consumption, and the reputations of those who make, distribute, and sell those goods. ...

-IV-

Turning to Sentinel's articles, three statements are critical. The lead sentence in the article published under Dzielak's by-line states: "A sample bottle of 'Covered Bridge Crystal Clear Spring Water,' sold at Krauszer's convenient food stores, does not contain pure spring water, according to a laboratory analysis obtained by the Sentinel Newspapers." The next sentence states that the director of Paterson's laboratory said that "pure spring water should not contain any chlorine." The director continued by stating: "'I can't see how it could possibly be spring water unless the spring source was contaminated and chlorine was added at the source.'"

We conclude that the statement that the Covered Bridge bottle "does not contain spring water" and that "pure spring water should not contain any chlorine" may fairly be viewed as statements of fact. Although testing for the presence of chlorine is a scientific procedure that results in the formulation of an opinion, the statement is more a factual assertion than an expression of an opinion.

We find, however, that the statement of the director that he "can't see how it could possibly be spring water unless the spring source was contaminated and chlorine was added at the source" is an expression of pure opinion. It states the director's opinion, and the factual basis for it. For instance, the article recites that chlorine dissipates at a "high rate" on exposure to "air or other substances," and that tests were repeated several times to rule out testing error. It also states countervailing facts, such as that the seal had already been broken on the bottle containing the tested water. We conclude that the director's opinion was made on the basis of stated facts, and is a statement of "pure opinion," entitled to absolute immunity. [Cc] ...

... [P]laintiff has not raised a genuine issue of material fact that entitles it to a trial on the merits. [C] Implicit in that determination is our belief that the appropriate standard to resolve a motion for summary judgment is not whether a rational finder of fact could find actual malice as a matter of clear and convincing evidence, but whether the opposing affidavits have created a genuine issue of material fact that defendants published with actual malice. ...

The dispositive question, then, is whether there is a genuine issue that any of the defendants displayed reckless disregard in publishing the two factual statements. Because this issue implicates the defendants' state of mind, we approach it with due respect for the difficulty of granting summary judgment dismissing the complaint. [C] Nonetheless, we recognize also that summary judgment practice is particularly well-suited for the determination of libel actions, the fear of which can inhibit comment on matters of public concern. By discouraging frivolous defamation actions, motions for summary judgment keep open lines of communication to the public on such issues. [Cc]

As to the two defamatory statements, nothing in the record before us creates a genuine issue of material fact that any defendant knew the statements to be false or entertained serious doubts about their truth. Paterson, knowing that the water was supposed to be spring water, confirmed the positive test results through subsequent tests, all of which were reviewed by two other chemists. This procedure does not bespeak a reckless disregard for the truth.

Insofar as Sentinel and its reporter are concerned, Dzielak started out carefully enough by seeking the services of an independent testing laboratory. The first laboratory found that the water did not contain chlorine, but upon learning that Krauszer's was a customer of that laboratory, Dzielak understandably sought confirmation elsewhere. Upon obtaining Paterson's positive test results for chlorine, she consulted still another laboratory, but she did not understand its report. A more careful reporter might have deferred publication until all doubts were finally resolved, but we cannot conclude that Dzielak entertained serious doubts about the truth of her stories.

The judgment of the Appellate Division is affirmed.

INQUIRY

Statutory actions. State unfair-competition and deceptive-practices acts may provide alternative liability theories to the common-law commercial-disparagement tort, for instance under versions of the Uniform Trade Secrets Act or state antitrust laws. So, too, may the Federal Trade Commission Act, 15 U.S.C.§§41-58 (regarding price discrimination), Lanham Act, 15 U.S.C. §1125(a) (regarding trade marks and names), Sherman Antitrust Act, 15 U.S.C. §§1-7, and Clayton Antitrust Act, 15 U.S.C. §§12-27 (regarding restraints of trade), Robinson-Patman Act, 15 U.S.C. §§12 et seq. (regarding price discrimination), and federal copyright and patent infringement laws, 17 U.S.C. §§101 et seq. (copyright); 35 U.S.C. §§1 et seq. (patents). *See* Qualitex Co. v. Jacobson Prods. Co., 514 U.S. 159 (1995) (recognizing party's right to a trademark-infringement claim over competitor's use of a similarly colored product). The Supreme Court in Sedima, S.P.R.L. v. Imrex Co., 473 U.S. 479 (1985), also granted relatively broad application to the civil-remedy provisions of the Racketeer Influenced and Corrupt Organizations Act, 18 U.S.C. §§1961-1968—better known as RICO and for its criminal penalties. Statutory actions may grant broader remedies including injunctions and attorney's fees but may also impose procedural requirements (jurisdiction, venue, and notice requirements, and different limitations periods) different from the common-law action. Should the federal statutory actions preempt state business-tort laws? *See* Bonito Boats, Inc. v. Thunder Craft Boats, Inc., 489 U.S. 141 (1989); Rodime PLC v. Seagate Technology, Inc., 174 F.3d 1294, 1306 (Fed. Cir. 1999) (no preemption of state-law tortious-interference torts offering different protections from patents and other federal statutory rights).

B. Tortious Interference

OBJECTIVE: Given the loss of a commercial opportunity due to actions by another who was not an anticipated party to the commercial transaction, recall and apply the elements of the interference-with-economic-advantage tort to determine whether a claim exists for the loss, consistent with this section.

Case Study: A supplier supplies insulation material to a manufacturer for use in modular-housing products. The supplier supplies the material on an open-purchase-order basis in which the supplier ships the material at the last negotiated price, as soon as the manufacturer's purchasing manager emails the request for product. A second supplier offered an alternative insulation material to the manufacturer, offering to undercut the first supplier's price by three percent for a minimum of one year from the date of the manufacturer's first order. The second supplier's sales agent at the same time warned the manufacturer's purchasing manager that the first supplier was having supply-line difficulties—a statement for which the agent had no basis other than an unarticulated suspicion expressed by another customer of the first supplier. ***Evaluate the first supplier's tortious-interference claim against the second supplier.***

As the introduction to this chapter indicates, the second major form of commercial tort (after injurious falsehood) involves the defendant's interference with the plaintiff's existing or anticipated contract or other business relationship with a third party—

known variously as *interference with contract, interference with business relations,* and *interference with prospective economic advantage.* The interference tort has a colorful English common-law history beginning with Lumley v. Gye, 2 El. & Bl. 216, 118 Eng. Rep. 749 (Queen's Bench 1853). The defendant impresario Gye induced the famous singer Johanna Wagner (the niece of Richard Wagner) to break her contract to sing in London's Queens Theatre for competitor Lumley. The court granted judgment for Lumley and in a companion case Lumley v. Wagner, 1 De G.M. & G. 604, 42 Eng. Rep. 687 (1852), enjoined Wagner from singing for Gye—for five years depriving London of her fabulous voice. The English courts then gradually extended the interference tort to cover any wrongful interference with any contract causing its breach or preventing its performance. American courts continue to trace the interference tort's history to the *Lumley* affair. *See* Della Penna v. Toyota Motors Sales, U.S.A., Inc., 11 Cal. 4th 376, 902 P.2d 740 (1995).

The interference tort has as its elements the (1) intentional (2) harmful (3) interference with a (4) contract or business expectancy by (5) improper or wrongful means. *See* Restatement (Second) of Torts §766B. Perhaps too obviously, to be liable, the defendant must know of the contract or expectancy. *See* Continental Research, Inc. v. Cruttenden, Podesta & Miller, 222 F. Supp. 190 (D.C. Minn. 1963); *cf.* Mid-Continent Tel. Corp. v. Home Tel. Co., 319 F. Supp. 1176 (D.C. Miss. 1970) (willful ignorance not a defense). The tortious-interference tort also requires that the interference be with a contract or expectancy between other parties. The law will not hold a party liable in tort for interfering with the party's own contract. Breach of contract is the proper form of action in such cases. *See* Applied Equip. Corp. v. Litton Saudi Arabia Ltd., 7 Cal.4th 503, 2 Cal. Rptr.2d 475, 869 P.2d 454 (1994). The following early American case illustrates the interference tort including the fine point on which its central improper-or-wrongful-conduct standard may turn.

Tuttle v. Buck
Minnesota Supreme Court
107 Minn. 145, 119 N.W. 946 (1909)

This appeal was from an order overruling a general demurrer to a complaint in which the plaintiff alleged: That for more than 10 years last past he has been and still is a barber by trade, and engaged in business as such in the village of Howard Lake, Minn., in said county, where he resides, owning and operating a shop for the purpose of his said trade. That until the injury hereinafter complained of his said business was prosperous, and plaintiff was enabled thereby to comfortably maintain himself and family out of the income and profits thereof, and also to save a considerable sum per annum, to wit, about $800. That the defendant, during the period of about 12 months last past, has wrongfully, unlawfully, and maliciously endeavored to destroy plaintiff's said business and compel plaintiff to abandon the same. That to that end he has persistently and systematically sought, by false and malicious reports and accusations of and concerning the plaintiff, by personally soliciting and urging plaintiff's patrons no longer to employ plaintiff, by threats of his personal displeasure, and by various other unlawful means and devices, to induce, and has thereby induced, many of said patrons to withhold from plaintiff the employment by them formerly given. That defendant is possessed of large means, and is engaged in the business of a banker in said village of Howard Lake, at Dassel, Minn., and at divers other places, and is nowise interested in the occupation of a barber; yet in the pursuance of the wicked, malicious, and unlawful purpose aforesaid, and for the sole and only purpose of injuring the trade of the plaintiff, and of accomplishing his purpose and threats of ruining the plaintiff's said business and driving him out of said village, the defendant fitted up and furnished a barber shop in said village for conducting the trade of barbering. That failing to induce any barber to occupy said shop on his own account, though offered at nominal rental, said defendant, with the wrongful and malicious purpose aforesaid, and not otherwise, has during the time herein stated hired two barbers in succession for a stated salary, paid by him, to occupy said shop, and to serve so many of plaintiff's patrons as said defendant has been or may be able by the means aforesaid to direct from plaintiff's shop. That at the present time a barber so employed and paid by the defendant is occupying and nominally conducting the shop thus fitted and furnished by the defendant, without paying any rent therefor, and under an agreement with defendant whereby the income of said shop is required to be paid to defendant, and is so paid in partial return for his wages. That all of said things were and are done by defendant with the sole design of injuring the plaintiff, and of destroying his said business, and not for the purpose of serving any legitimate interest of his own. That by reason of the great wealth and prominence of the defendant, and the personal and financial influence consequent thereon, he has by the means aforesaid, and through other unlawful means and devices by him employed, materially injured the business of the plaintiff, has largely reduced the income and profits thereof, and intends and threatens to destroy the same altogether, to plaintiff's damage in the sum of $10,000.

ELLIOTT, J. (after stating the facts as above). ...

... It must be remembered that the common law is the result of growth, and that its development has been determined by the social needs of the community which it governs. It is the resultant of conflicting social forces, and those forces which are for the time dominant leave their impress upon the law. It is of judicial origin, and seeks to establish doctrines and rules for the determination, protection, and enforcement of legal rights. Manifestly it must change as society changes and new rights are recognized. To be an efficient instrument, and not a mere abstraction, it must gradually adapt itself to changed conditions. Necessarily its form and substance has been greatly affected by prevalent economic theories. For generations there has been a practical agreement upon the proposition that competition in trade and business is desirable, and this idea has found expression in the decisions of the courts as well as in statutes. But it has led to grievous and manifold wrongs to individuals, and many courts have manifested an earnest desire to protect the individuals from the evils which result from unrestrained business competition. The problem has been to so adjust matters as to preserve the principle of competition and yet guard against its abuse to the unnecessary injury to the individual. So the principle that a man may use his own property according to his own needs and desires, while true in the abstract, is subject to many limitations in the concrete. Men cannot always, in civilized society, be allowed to use their own property as their interests or desires may dictate without reference to the fact that they have neighbors whose rights are as sacred as their own. The existence and well-being of society requires that each and every person shall conduct himself consistently with the fact that he is a social and reasonable person. The purpose for which a man is using his own property may thus sometimes determine his rights... .

It is freely conceded that there are many decisions contrary to this view; but, when carried to the extent contended for by the appellant, we think they are unsafe, unsound, and illy adapted to modern conditions. To divert to one's self the customers of a business rival by the offer of goods at lower prices is in general a legitimate mode of serving one's own interest, and justifiable as fair competition. But when a man starts an opposition place of business, not for the sake of profit to himself, but regardless of loss to himself, and for the sole purpose of driving his competitor out of business, and with the intention of himself retiring upon the accomplishment of his malevolent purpose, he is guilty of a wanton wrong and an actionable tort. In such a case he would not be exercising his legal right, or doing an act which can be judged separately from the motive which actuated him. To call such conduct competition is a perversion of terms. It is simply the application of force without legal justification, which in its moral quality may be no better than highway robbery. ...

A majority of the Justices ... are of the opinion that, on the principle declared in the foregoing opinion, the complaint states a cause of action, and the order is therefore affirmed.

Affirmed.

INQUIRY

Scope. Tort practitioners recognize the varying situations in which the interference tort applies—in either its contract-relations or prospective-economic-advantage forms. Practitioners have pled the interference tort in cases where the defendant allegedly wrongfully excluded the plaintiff from a place of performance. *See* Bacon v. St. Paul Union Stockyards Co., 161 Minn. 522, 201 N.W. 326 (1924) (stockyard wrongfully excluding dealer from making transactions with other dealers). They have pled it when the defendant wrongfully prevented the plaintiff from making sales of a product, *see* Harber v. Ohio Natl. Life Ins. Co., 512 F.2d 170 (8th Cir. 1975), or from having access to a labor market, Lichter v. Fuller, 22 Tenn. App. 670, 125 S.W.2d 501 (1938). They have also pled it in cases where the defendant made the plaintiff's performance of a contract more difficult or expensive. *See* Piedmont Cotton Mills v. H.W. Ivey Constr. Co., 109 Ga. App. 876, 137 S.E.2d 528 (1964). Should the interference tort be available to prevent a lawyer who leaves a law firm from using the lawyer's knowledge of the clients' confidential matters to solicit the clients to follow the lawyer to a new law firm? *See* Adler, Barish, Daniels, Levin and Creskoff v. Epstein, 482 Pa. 416, 393 A.2d 1175 (1978) (yes), *cert. denied*, 442 U.S. 907. Should the interference tort be available when one wrongfully induces another to terminate a terminable-at-will contract? Is the plaintiff's prospective economic advantage of having a terminable-at-will contract enough to warrant the tort's recognition? Restatement (Second) of Torts §768 (yes); *see* Roy v. Woonsocket Instit. for Saving, 525 A.2d 915 (R.I. 1987) (no interference-with-contract claim but possible claim for loss of prospective economic advantage).

Improper Conduct. The key to the interference tort is determining what constitutes "improper" or "wrongful" means. To be improper, the defendant's conduct need not be illegal. That the conduct violates generally accepted moral standards, Sustick v. Slatina, 48 N.J. Super. 134, 137 A.2d 54 (1957), professional ethics, Herron v. State Farm Mut. Ins. Co., 56 Cal.2d 202, 363 P.2d 310, 14 Cal. Rptr. 294 (1961), or standards of fairness, Leonard Duckworth, Inc. v. Michael L. Field & Co., 516 F.2d 952 (5th Cir. 1975), may be enough. Fraud, defamation, and threats of violence or frivolous litigation may also be sufficient. *See, e.g.,* South Central Livestock Dealers, Inc. v. Security State Bank, 551 F.2d 1346 (5th Cir. 1977). Extortionate or manipulative acts—interference to obtain some unrelated but possibly lawful end—may also be sufficient. *See* Hill Grocery Co. v. Carroll, 223 Ala. 376, 136 So. 789 (1931) (interference with employment contract to obtain payment of debt). On the other hand, some cases abandon the *improper* element altogether, requiring the defendant to prove justification for the interference. *See* Alyeska Pipeline Serv. Co. v. Aurora Air Serv., 604 P.2d 1090 (Alaska 1979). Other cases strengthen the *improper* element to mean conduct that is in itself tortious (for example, fraudulent or defamatory) independent of the interference claim—especially if the interference claim involves prospective advantage rather than an existing contract. *See* Wal-Mart Stores, Inc. v. Sturges, 52 S.W.2d 3d 711 (Tex. 2001); Speakers of Sport, Inc. v. ProServ, Inc., 178 F.3d 862 (7th Cir. 1999). The Restatement (Second) of Torts §766B follows a multi-factor balancing approach to define improper conduct. *See also* Restatement (Second) of Torts §870 (new causes of action should be recognized where injury is caused by conduct that is "generally culpable and not justifiable under the circumstances").

Justification. Traditionally, the plaintiff has the burden of proving each element of a tort claim—including the interference-tort claim. *See* M & M Rental Tools, Inc. v. Milchem, Inc., 94 N.M. 449, 612 P.2d 241 (1980). Some cases employ shifting proof burdens to ease the challenge of determining whether the interference was improper. In those cases, once the plaintiff proves the defendant knowingly interfered with an existing contract, the burden of proof shifts to the defendant to justify the interference. *See* Duggin v. Adams, 234 Va. 221, 360 S.E.2d 832 (1987); Lowell v. Mother's Cake & Cookie Co., 79 Cal. App.3d 13, 144 Cal. Rptr. 664 (1978); Margolin v. Morton F. Plant Hosp. Assn., 342 So.2d 1090 (Fla. App. 1977) (anethesiologists required to prove justification for refusing to serve surgeon's patients). Justifications may include price boycotts, Julie Baking Co. v. Graymond, 152 Misc. 846, 274 N.Y.S. 250 (1934), protecting ethical standards, Harris v. Thomas, 217 S.W. 1068 (Tex. Civ. App. 1920), legal advice, Richardson v. La Rancherita La Jolla, Inc., 98 Cal. App.3d 73, 159 Cal. Rptr. 285 (1979), political action to end discrimination, NAACP v. Claiborne Hardware Co., 458 U.S. 886 (1982), and asserting genuine claims, Restatement (Second) of Torts §773. In the face of conflicting case law and no clear majority rule, the Restatement (Second) of Torts §767 declines to state whether the proof burden should shift.

Limits. As the above opinion suggests, not every effort to undermine a contract between other parties is necessarily actionable as tortious interference. The law will generally not hold a defendant to have interfered with a contract that terminates of its own terms—even if the defendant's conduct discouraged its renewal. *See* Sampson Investments v. Jondex Corp., 176 Wis.2d 55, 499 N.W.2d 177 (1993). Nor will interfering with an illegal contract, such as one to restrain trade, be actionable. *See* Fairbanks, Morse & Co. v. Texas Elec. Serv. Co., 63 F.2d 702 (5th Cir. 1933), *cert. denied*, 290 U.S. 655. Nor will interfering with an agreement to marry be actionable. Brown v. Glickstein, 347 Ill. App. 486, 107 N.E.2d 267 (1952). The expectancy must also be reasonably certain, meaning that the law will deny tortious-interference recovery when all that was lost was a gambler's chance. *See* Youst v. Longo, 43

Cal.3d 64, 233 Cal. Rptr. 294, 729 P.2d 728 (1987). Some courts have been reluctant to recognize tortious-interference claims when the defendant has frustrated a gift or bequest—especially when probate law would provide other equitable remedies for undue influence. *See* Labonte v. Giordano, 426 Mass. 319, 687 N.E.2d 1253 (1997); *but see* Harmon v. Harmon, 404 A.2d 1020 (Me. 1979) (recognizing tortious-interference claim in will contest). Of course, the usual challenge exists that the plaintiff must prove that the interference was improper or wrongful. *See* Windsor Secs., Inc. v. Hartford Life Ins. Co., 986 F.2d 655 (3d Cir. 1993) (no actionable wrong in fund's restriction prohibiting investor from transferring investments between accounts). When the motive is political or competitive, as in a boycott supporting union interests, law is unlikely to find a claim. *See* Caruso v. Local Union No. 690, 100 Wash.2d 343, 670 P.2d 240 (1983). Consider the following case illustrating the limits of the tortious-interference action.

Mason v. Wal-Mart Stores, Inc.
Supreme Court of Arkansas
333 Ark. 3, 969 S.W.2d 160 (1998)

NEWBERN, J. John M. Mason appeals from a summary judgment awarded to Wal-Mart Stores, Inc. ("Wal-Mart"), on Mr. Mason's claim for tortious interference with a contractual relationship and business expectancy. We affirm the judgment because the evidence presented by Mr. Mason did not demonstrate that Wal-Mart's conduct was improper.

Mr. Mason worked as an independent sales representative for three vendors who sold products to Wal-Mart for resale. Century Products Company ("Century"), Okla Homer Smith Furniture Manufacturing Company ("Okla Homer"), and Pentech International, Inc. ("Pentech"), each had an account with Wal-Mart, and Mr. Mason, on a purely at-will basis, served as their sales representative to Wal-Mart.

For more than a decade, Wal-Mart exhibited discontent with dealing with independent manufacturers' representatives like Mr. Mason. On November 6, 1991, David Glass, Wal-Mart president and CEO, issued a letter to some, if not all, of its vendors expressing Wal-Mart's preference for dealing directly with "principals" of the vendors.

The letter, which was reported in a major article in *The Wall Street Journal*, mentioned the rapid growth of Wal-Mart and the desirability on the part of Wal-Mart and its suppliers to be able to forecast each other's needs and to react quickly. It mentioned new computer systems by which Wal-Mart shared information with its vendors, and it referred to the extra reaction time created by dealing through a third party in addition to the "high risk of misunderstandings" inherent in the system using independent representatives. ...

Shortly after Wal-Mart issued that letter, Century, Okla Homer Smith, and Pentech removed Mr. Mason from their Wal-Mart accounts.... .

Mr. Mason sued Wal-Mart.... .

The interference with his contractual relationships and business expectancies was described as Wal-Mart's use of its economic power to coerce Mr. Mason's employers to terminate his contracts with them. The complaint referred to Mr. Glass's letter and mentioned an incident that allegedly occurred in 1982 when a Wal-Mart employee asked Century to terminate its relationship with Mr. Mason and pass on to Wal-Mart any savings thus achieved.

Mr. Mason argues first that the Trial Court "improperly imposed an element of proof on Mason which the law does not require"—namely, the requirement to prove that the alleged interference by the defendant was "improper" or "wrongful." Secondly, he contends that, even if impropriety or wrongfulness *is* an element of his claim, summary judgment was inappropriate because he adduced sufficient evidence of improper or wrongful conduct on Wal-Mart's part to create a genuine issue of material fact.

For an interference to be actionable, it must be improper. [C] The *Restatement (Second) of Torts* sets out the factors in determining when interference is improper as follows: ... "In determining whether an actor's conduct in intentionally interfering with a contract or a prospective contractual relation of another is improper or not, consideration is given to the following factors: (a) the nature of the actor's conduct; (b) the actor's motive; (c) the interests of the other with which the actor's conduct interferes; (d) the interests sought to be advanced by the actor; (e) the social interests in protecting the freedom of action of the actor and the contractual interests of the other; (f) the proximity or remoteness of the actor's conduct to the interference; and (g) the relations between the parties. [C] ...

Just as our cases seem to have reverted to requiring an allegation, or, at the summary-judgment stage, a showing of "improper" conduct on the part of the defendant, the RESTATEMENT (SECOND) OF TORTS, §766, now provides: "One who intentionally *and improperly* interferes with the performance of a contract (except a contract to marry) between another and a third person by inducing or otherwise causing the third person not to perform the contract, is subject to liability to the other for the pecuniary loss resulting to the other from the failure of the third person to perform the contract."

2. *Wal-Mart's conduct*

Mr. Mason's argument does not end with the suggestion that the Trial Court erred in including the requirement that Wal-Mart be shown to have interfered improperly in his contracts or business expectancies. He argues that, even if that is a requirement, the evidence he presented shows that Wal-Mart's conduct was indeed improper. The only suggestion of impropriety, however, is that Wal-Mart's intention was to increase its profits by eliminating manufacturer's representatives from its purchasing process. When questioned about whether the economic ends sought to be furthered by Wal-Mart were improper, Mr. Mason's counsel referred to Comment c of the Restatement (Second) of Torts following § 767. It reads as follows:

Economic pressure. Economic pressure of various types is a common means of inducing persons not to deal with another, as when A refuses to deal with B if B enters into or continues a relation with C, or when A increases his prices to B or induces D not to deal with B on the same condition. Or the pressure may consist of the refusal to admit B to membership into a trade association or a professional organization, as a medical or legal association. The question whether this pressure is proper is answered in the light of the circumstances in which it is exerted, the object sought to be accomplished by the actor, the degree of coercion involved, the extent of the harm that it threatens, the effect upon the neutral parties drawn into the situation, the effects upon competition, and the general reasonableness and appropriateness of this pressure as a means of accomplishing the actor's objective.

Although Mr. Mason uses the term "greed" to describe Wal-Mart's objective, the term "profit motive" could have been substituted. To hold that the evidence presented in this case requires that a jury evaluate Wal-Mart's conduct in accordance with the explanation contained in comment c to §767 would require it in any instance when a business threatens not to buy in order to get a better price. In short, we see nothing in the evidence presented by Mr. Mason that we could consider to be indicative of improper conduct on the part of Wal-Mart.

Affirmed.

INQUIRY

Relief. By stating above that the interference must be harmful, the court means that damage is an element of the interference tort. If the interference causes no loss, no tort action exists. *See* In re Alert Holdings, Inc., 148 B.R. 194 (Bnkr. N.Y. 1992). On the other hand, where compensable commercial loss exists, mental-distress damages and punitive damages may be available. *See* Duff v. Engelberg, 237 Cal. App.2d 505, 47 Cal. Rptr. 114 (1965); *see also* Texaco, Inc. v. Pennzoil, Co., 729 S.W.2d 768-866 (Tex. App. 1987) (interference-with-takeover-contract verdict in excess of $10 billion). In that respect, a tortious-interference claim may add a significant new arrow to the plaintiff's breach-of-contract quiver. As also indicated above, injunction may be available to prohibit the interference. *Cf.* Beverly Glen Music, Inc. v. Warner Communs., 178 Cal. App.3d 1142, 224 Cal. Rptr. 260 (1986) (no injunction if it would amount to specific performance of personal-services agreement).

Bad Faith. Although tortious interference involves the defendant's interference with a contract or expectancy between other parties (not with the defendant's own contract), tort law has one narrow area where it may provide a remedy for a party's misconduct in the performance of the party's own contract. A majority of states recognize an insured's cause of action in tort against an insurer for a breach of an implied covenant of good faith. *See* Careau & Co. v. Security Pacific Business Credit, Inc., 222 Cal. App.3d 1371, 272 Cal. Rptr. 387 (1990). Bad-faith issues arise when an insurer unreasonably refuses to settle a claim against its insured when the claimant's settlement demand is within the policy limits, and the insured subsequently suffers a judgment in excess of the insurance-policy limits within which the insurer could previously have settled the case. In such cases, some courts have recognized the tort claim for bad faith breach of the implied covenant. *See* Zoppo v. Homestead Ins., 71 Ohio St.3d 552, 644 N.E.2d 397 (1995). Other courts have held that the aggrieved insured must plead the claim instead as one for breach of contract. *See* Beck v. Farmers Ins. Exchange, 701 P.2d 795 (Utah 1985).

CONCLUSION

Law schools typically teach torts in the first year. Tort law is an appropriate subject for the first year because it, like much of law, combines a highly analytic framework with a highly practical application—but does so, unlike much of other law, in settings with which the law student is already familiar. The greatest challenge of learning tort law is not so much in acquiring the knowledge base—although surely plenty of challenge exists as to that. Nor is the greatest challenge (moving up through

Bloom's Taxonomy of Learning) to acquire the knowledge base, apply it, and synthesize it around its broad organizing principles of caring for one another to preserve human dignity and integrity, and improve the human condition. Tort law's great hidden challenge lies at the top of Bloom's Taxonomy in its evaluation—in connecting tort law to the cultures, worldviews, perspectives, truths, faiths, beliefs, and reference systems of those whom it so imperceptibly governs, until an incident happens, when tort law rears its powerful head. What the successful student of tort law acquires is a peculiar sagacity or wisdom—a familiarity with the workings of the world and, more importantly, a saving way of approaching the world's greatest failings. Tort-law wisdom is not a product of rigorous analysis or philosophical musing, although both can help. It involves not only possessing and applying knowledge to human experience but connecting its forms to underlying meanings and truths of the human condition—things that we can sometimes learn in books and professional schools but that we more often learn with the experience of life. Tort law is ultimately a healthy way of looking at the world, not through rose-colored glasses but instead confronting the worst of human conduct with the best of human compassion and redemption. Tort law holds us individually accountable to one another, yet at the same time, satisfies judgment and forgives—a story that will always need retelling and, within the course of human history, never be complete.

> **Career**
> References can make a difference in finding employment and succeeding in tort practice. Law firms hiring a new tort litigator make a substantial investment in that choice. A new tort lawyer may require months or years to develop to the point of contributing substantially to the economic welfare and reputation of the firm. Lawyers hiring other lawyers will request and investigate references to ensure that they make the right choice. Value your law-school relationships with professors, staff, and administrators, from your first day on campus. Get to know professors and deans outside of class, in circumstances where they can provide you with a strong positive recommendation. Volunteer and do other legal-service or law-related work with lawyers and other professionals who can provide you with a good reference. Think intentionally about developing relationships on which you can draw for this kind of placement and career-development support. Tort practice excites and rewards. Give yourself the best opportunity to participate in it.

APPENDIX

TORT-PRACTICE PROCESS MODELS

Project-Management Plan															
Matter Personal-Injury Litigation			Doe v ABC Corp.										Role Plaintiff's Counsel		
Stage	Time (Months)														
	1	2	3	4	5	6	7	8	9	10	11	12	13	14	
Intake	.2	*Minimal risk of conflicts arising.*												
Consult	1	1.6	*Minimal risk of termination of representation.*											
Investigate		7.2	*Some risk of discovering substantial defense.*											
Pleading		2.3	*No risk of counterclaim.*											
Discovery			13	*Some risk of discovering substantial defense.*										
Documents						*Small risk of private disclosures.*								
Interrogatories							*Small risk of private disclosures.*							
Depositions								*Small risk of private disclosures.*						
Experts								*Fair risk of additional experts.*						
Mediation			*Some risk of unwarranted disclosures.*						9						
Motions			*Some risk of summary judgment.*							12				
Case evaluation			*Some risk of sanctions.*							10				
Pretrial			*Some risk of adverse rulings.*								21			
Trial					*Fair risk of adverse verdict.*							21		
Judgment						*Low risk of relief from judgment.*							2	
Post-judgment							*Very low risk of non-collection.*					2	1
Closing														.5
Totals	1.2	11.1	13	2	3.5	2.5	4	4	9	22	21	23	2	1.5
														103.8

Matter General Practice	Client Intake			Role Plaintiff's Counsel
Task	Resource	Analysis	Improve	Control
1 Record contact.	Paralegal .1	Ensure ability to contact.	Build market database.	
2 Obtain conflict information.	Paralegal .1	Record all interested parties.	Automate into electronic conflict-check.	
3 Perform conflict check.	Lawyer .1	Compare to client list.	Automate into electronic conflict-check.	Managing partner review.
4 Complete intake information.	Intake form Paralegal .5	Record detailed information.	Ensure complete intake form. Develop client questionnaire.	Lawyer review to ensure complete.
5 Decide whether to consult.	Lawyer .1	Make preliminary decision.	Check against market study.	
6 Communicate consultation decision.	Firm brochure Paralegal .1	Contact client.	Confirm in writing to client. Provide firm brochure.	Lawyer review.
Total:	Lawyer .2 Paralegal .8		Reduce paralegal time.	

Matter General	Initial Consultation			Role Counsel
Task	Resource	Analysis	Improve	Control
1 Obtain completed client questionnaire.	Questionnaire Paralegal .1 Lawyer .1	Supplies preliminary information.	Convey and receive as electronic file.	Lawyer review completed questionnaire.
2 Calculate and calendar limitations periods.	Paralegal .1 Lawyer .1	Ensure timely handling of all matters.	Calendar with both lawyer and paralegal.	Lawyer review.
3 Schedule appointment.	Paralegal .1	Confirm time and place of meeting lawyer.	Confirm in writing. Limit to 30 minutes?	Lawyer approve appointment after questionnaire review.
4 Conduct initial consultation.	Lawyer 1.0	Determine achievable objectives.	Confirm consultation results in writing with client present.	Partner review.
5 Execute fee agreement.	Fee agreement template Lawyer .2	Confirm terms in writing using template.	Generate in client's presence.	Partner review
6 Assign follow-up tasks.	Lawyer .2	Initiate tasks promptly.	Use process models.	Partner review.
Total:	Lawyer 1.6 Paralegal .3			

Matter: Personal Injury	**Claim Investigation**			Role: Plaintiff's Counsel
Task	**Resource**	**Analysis**	**Improve**	**Control**
1. Preserve physical evidence.	Instruction and notice templates Lawyer .3 Paralegal .5	Ensure availability of evidence. Prevent spoliation.	Instruct client and notify others in writing. Develop instruction and notice templates.	Documentation of instructions and notices are in file.
2. Preserve electronically stored information	Instruction and notice templates Lawyer .5 Paralegal .5	Ensure availability of ESI. Prevent spoliation.	Instruct client and notify others in writing. Develop instruction and notice templates.	Documentation of instructions and notices are in file.
3. Obtain police and incident reports.	Request template Lawyer .1 Paralegal 3.0	Ensure review of incident reports before filing.	Include video, audio, and electronic-records request.	Lawyer review and approve before routing.
4. Obtain medical and employment records.	Request template Lawyer .1 Paralegal 3.0	Ensure comprehensive review of records before filing.	Ensure reasonable cost. Request notice if cost exceeds cap.	Lawyer review and approve before routing.
5. Consider order of weather, insurance, academic, and other records.	Lawyer .1	Determine whether other records are necessary.	Develop other-records list and criteria for ordering other records.	
6. Confirm corporate and assumed names.	Lawyer .1 Paralegal .8	Conduct corporate name search.	Document results of search.	Documentation of results are in file.
7. Perform internet and social-media searches.	Paralegal 1.0	Ensure no surprises over internet and social-media sources.	Develop standard search protocols.	Document completion of search protocol in file.
8. Determine necessity of experts.	Analysis template Lawyer 2.0	Evaluate necessity and cost of experts.	Develop template and make written analysis using template.	Managing-partner review. Documentation of analysis and approval in file.
9. Locate and interview experts.	Lawyer 2.0 Paralegal 1.5	Determine availability of supporting expert testimony.	Develop retention-letter template confirming all terms.	Retention letters are in file.
10. Confirm expert opinions after expert record review.	Lawyer 1.0 Paralegal 2.0	Document supporting expert opinions.	Ensure written opinions from retained experts.	Written confirmation is in file.
Total:	Lawyer 7.2 Paralegal 12.3			

		Matter Insurance Defense	**Receipt of Assignment**		**Role** Defense Counsel
	Task	**Resource**	**Analysis**	**Improve**	**Control**
1	Acknowledge assignment.	Correspondence template Lawyer .2	Confirm receipt and for whom to appear. Calendar answer due date.	Ensure immediate confirmation. Double-calendar due date.	Managing partner review.
2	Check conflicts.	Lawyer .1	Ensure no conflicts.	Adopt electronic conflict-check system?	Conflict-check documented in file.
3	Review file.	Lawyer .2	Evaluate file contents.	Develop file checklist.	Completed checklist in file.
4	Develop budget.	Budget form Lawyer .5	Communicate cost estimate to insurer.	Assess budget projections against actual.	Managing partner review.
5	Request extension.	Lawyer .1	Request in all cases for time to investigate and evaluate.	Calendar response to ensure timely follow-up and answer.	Copy in file.
6	Notify insured.	Lawyer .1	Instruct insured regarding conduct. Confirm party appearance.	Develop standard instructions. Provide firm brochure.	Copy in file.
7	Investigate.	Lawyer .5 Paralegal 2.0	Interview insured and witnesses. Obtain accident report and other public records.	Develop investigation checklist. Paralegal do witness interviews.	Completed checklist in file.
8	Decide on counterclaim.	Lawyer .1	Ensure insured understands and approves decision.	Develop counterclaim checklist.	Completed checklist in file.
9	Decide on third parties.	Lawyer .2	Evaluate and obtain approval for third-party claims.	Consider notice of non-party fault.	Documentation in file.
10	Answer complaint.	Answer template Lawyer 1 hour	Include all affirmative defenses.	Paralegal format answer. Use defenses checklist. Obtain file-stamped court copy.	Lawyer confirms filing on calendared due date.
	Total:	Lawyer 3.0 Paralegal 2.0			

Matter: Tort Litigation		**Pleading—Complaint**			Role: Plaintiff's Counsel
	Task	**Resource**	**Analysis**	**Improve**	**Control**
1	Re-confirm limitations period.	Lawyer .2	Ensure timely filing.		
2	Review file.	Lawyer .3	Identify relevant facts.	Confirm facts are complete.	
3	Choose court.	Pleading template Lawyer .1	Consider jurisdiction and venue.	Ensure client approves.	Confirm with client in writing.
4	Identify parties.	Lawyer .2	Join all parties.	Ensure client approves.	Confirm with client in writing.
5	Confirm counsel.	Lawyer .1	Identify all appearances.	Query co-counsel.	Managing partner review.
6	Confirm residence and incorporation.	Lawyer .2	Ensure correct corporate name.	Copy and file bureau name search.	Document in file.
7	Allege facts.	Lawyer .5	Draft from file documents.	Ensure accuracy—client review.	Confirm with client in writing.
8	Determine counts.	Lawyer .2	Ensure comprehensive pleading.	Develop counts checklist.	Document checklist in file.
9	Plead counts.	Lawyer .3	Ensure elements pled.		
10	Develop prayer for relief.	Lawyer .2	Ensure comprehensive request.	Develop prayer checklist.	Document checklist in file.
11	Prepare summons.	Paralegal .5			Lawyer review.
12	File pleading.	Cover letter template Paralegal .5	Obtain issued summonses.	Obtain file-stamped copy.	Lawyer review.
	Total:	Lawyer 2.3 Paralegal 1.0			

Pleading—Answer

Matter: Tort Litigation				Role: Defense Counsel
Task	**Resource**	**Analysis**	**Improve**	**Control**
1. Calculate and calendar due date.	Lawyer .1	Ensure timely filing.		
2. Obtain and review file.	Lawyer .3	Identify relevant facts.	List remaining questions.	
3. Confirm appearances.	Lawyer .2	Ensure defense of all assigned parties.	Confirm with insurer and insured.	Document confirmation in file.
4. Interview insured.	Lawyer 1.0	Address allegations of complaint.	Provide copy of complaint in advance.	Document copy in file.
5. Confirm court.	Lawyer .1	Consider both jurisdiction and venue.	Query federal-court jurisdiction.	Confirm options to client in writing.
6. Confirm residence and incorporation.	Lawyer .2	Ensure correct corporate name.	Search corporations bureau and confirm with client.	Document in file.
7. Deny false fact allegations.	Answer template Lawyer .5	Draft answer to fact allegations.	Client reviews and approves draft answer.	Document client review in file.
8. Deny disputed counts.	Lawyer .3	Preserve all reasonable fact disputes.	Client reviews and approves admissions.	Document client review in file.
9. Plead affirmative defenses.	Defenses template Lawyer .4	Preserve all arguable defenses.	Develop and use defenses checklist.	Document checklist use in file.
10. Develop prayer for relief.	Lawyer .2	Request all appropriate relief.	Ensure costs request.	Lawyer review.
11. File pleading.	Cover letter template Paralegal .5	Ensure timely filing.	Obtain file-stamped copy.	Lawyer review.
Total:	Lawyer 3.3 Paralegal .5			

Matter: Personal Injury Litigation		Discovery — Plaintiff's		Role: Plaintiff's Counsel
	Task	**Resource**	**Analysis**	**Improve**	**Control**
1	Plan discovery.	Lawyer 1.0	Articulate goals and methods of discovery.	Develop model discovery plan and checklist.	Document written plan in file.
2	Make & review mandatory disclosures.	Disclosure template Lawyer 2.5 Paralegal 1.0	Ensure timely disclosure of required information.	Calendar disclosures. Develop protocol.	Disclosures documented in file.
3	Conduct scheduling conference.	Lawyer 1.5	Negotiate reasonable pretrial schedule.	Prepare written case synopsis. Ensure settlement authority.	File reflects written synopsis.
4	Calendar scheduling order.	Lawyer .3 Paralegal .3	Ensure notice of timing for pretrial tasks.	Double-calendar with paralegal.	Two calendars reflect control dates.
5	Draft production requests.	Requests template Lawyer .5	Obtain documents, ESI, and tangible items.	Re-develop requests template to include ESI.	Copy of production requests in file.
6	Draft interrogatories.	Interrogs. template Lawyer 1.0	Investigate incident detail, location of records, witnesses, and theories.	Analyze past responses to improve template.	Copy of interrogatories in file.
7	Induce timely responses.	Lawyer .2 Paralegal .3	Calendar and remind on due dates.	Paralegal initiate reminders.	Document reminders in file.
8	Compel complete responses.	Lawyer 1.0 Paralegal 1.0	Ensure complete and timely responses.	Send draft motion requesting to consent order.	Document request in file.
9	Evaluate responses.	Lawyer 1.0	Determine case impact and need for additional discovery.	Develop proofs schema to chart evidentiary support.	Document schema in file.
10	Notice depositions.	Dep. notice template Lawyer .5 Paralegal 1.0	Schedule depositions.	Request convenient date before sending notice.	Document request in file.
11	Prepare for depositions.	Lawyer 1.5	Ensure comprehensive discovery.	Develop deposition checklist.	Document deposition checklist in file.
12	Conduct depositions.	Lawyer 4.0	Confirm admissions and test disputed issues.	Employ proofs schema to ensure comprehensive examination.	Document proofs schema in file.
13	Review discovery for completion.	Lawyer 1.0	Ensure discovery is complete.		
14	Analyze and communicate discovery results.	Lawyer 2.0 Paralegal 3.0	Evaluate effect of discovery on case and inform client.	Paralegal summarize depositions.	Document analysis and client communication in file.
	Total:	Lawyer 13.7 Paralegal 5.3			

Matter Personal-Injury Litigation		Discovery — Defendant's		Role Defense Counsel
	Task	**Resource**	**Analysis**	**Improve**	**Control**

	Task	Resource	Analysis	Improve	Control
1	Determine discovery plan.	Lawyer 1.0	Articulate goals and methods of discovery.	Choose elements from process model.	Document plan in file.
2	Obtain client approval of plan.	Lawyer .5	Communicate plan to client for review and approval.	Develop explanatory guide to discovery.	Document client review and approval in file.
3	Make & review mandatory disclosures.	Disclosure template Lawyer 2.5 Paralegal 1.0	Ensure timely disclosure of required information.	Calendar disclosures. Develop protocol.	Disclosures documented in file.
4	Conduct scheduling conference.	Lawyer 1.5	Negotiate reasonable pretrial schedule.	Prepare written case synopsis. Ensure settlement authority.	File reflects written synopsis.
5	Calendar scheduling order.	Lawyer .3 Paralegal .3	Ensure notice of timing for pretrial tasks.	Double-calendar with paralegal.	Two calendars reflect control dates.
6	Draft production requests.	Requests template Lawyer .5	Obtain medical, employment, insurance, academic, and other records.	Supply authorizations for release of information with answer, requesting record-keeper lists.	
7	Draft interrogatories.	Interrogs. template Lawyer 1.0	Confirm incident detail, medical & employment history, and theories.	Analyze past responses to improve template.	
8	Induce timely responses.	Lawyer .2 Paralegal .3	Calendar and remind on due dates.	Paralegal initiate reminders.	Document reminders in file.
9	Compel complete responses.	Lawyer 1.0 Paralegal 1.0	Ensure complete and timely responses.	Send draft motion requesting to consent order.	Document request in file.
10	Evaluate responses.	Lawyer 1.0	Determine case impact and need for additional discovery.	Develop proofs schema to chart evidentiary support.	Document schema in file.
11	Notice depositions.	Dep. notice template Lawyer .5 Paralegal 1.0	Schedule depositions.	Request convenient date before sending notice.	Document request in file.
12	Prepare for depositions.	Lawyer 1.5	Ensure comprehensive discovery.	Develop deposition checklist.	Document checklist in file.
13	Conduct depositions.	Lawyer 4.0	Confirm admissions and test disputed issues.	Employ proofs schema to ensure comprehensive examination.	
14	Review discovery for completion.	Lawyer 1.0	Ensure discovery is complete.		
15	Analyze and report discovery results.	Lawyer 2.0 Paralegal 3.0	Evaluate effect of discovery on case and report to client.	Paralegal summarize depositions for client.	Document analysis and report in file.
	Total:	Lawyer 18.5 Paralegal 6.6			

Matter: Civil Litigation		Mediation		Role: Plaintiff's Counsel
Task	**Resource**	**Analysis**	**Improve**	**Control**
1. Confirm fact of mediation.	Lawyer .5	Ensure agreement or order to mediate.	Confirm agreement or order in writing.	Document agreement or order in file.
2. Select mediator.	Lawyer .5	Choose qualified mediator.	Develop mediator catalog and criteria.	Associate review.
3. Confirm mediation place and date.	Lawyer .5 Paralegal .2	Ensure neutral site on convenient date confirmed in writing.	Develop mediation handbook for client.	
4. Draft and submit mediation brief.	Lawyer 2.5	Provide mediator case background.	Determine objectives and strategies.	Associate review. Objectives recorded in file.
5. Prepare client for mediation.	Lawyer .5	Ensure client understands process and outcomes.	Prepare draft settlement statements.	Draft settlement statements are in file.
6. Conduct mediation.	Lawyer 4.0	Facilitate settlement discussions.	Complete mediation training.	
7. Document mediation results.	Lawyer .5	Confirm outcome in writing.	Document before adjournment.	Results documented in file.
8. Notify tribunal of outcome.	Lawyer .2	Ensure tribunal receives prompt notice of outcome.		Notice to tribunal is in file.
Total:	Lawyer 9.2 Paralegal .2			

Matter: Civil Litigation		Case Evaluation		Role: Counsel
Task	Resource	Analysis	Improve	Control
1. Confirm time, place, and evaluators.	Lawyer .2	Review case-evaluation notice. Calendar.	Consider consent or order to limit scope. Check evaluator conflicts.	Obtain order or confirm consent in writing.
2. Notify client, confirming disclosures and objectives.	Lawyer .5	Confirm case-evaluation process, strategies, and disclosure of settlement figure.	Develop and provide case-evaluation client-information sheet.	Document information-sheet distribution in file.
3. Draft case-evaluation brief.	Lawyer 5.0	Present and analyze case facts, and supply key exhibits.	Determine objectives and strategies.	Associate review. Objectives recorded in file.
4. Serve case-evaluation brief.	Paralegal .5	Serve case-evaluation briefs on evaluators and counsel.	Convey evaluator checks with briefs.	Cover letter in file documents payment of fees.
5. Review opposing briefs.	Lawyer 1.0	Analyze opposing briefs preparing for evaluation hearing.	Draft hearing remarks responding to opposing briefs.	Associate review before hearing.
6. Conduct case evaluation.	Lawyer 2.0	Present argument justifying an award that client will accept.	Join evaluation panel for other cases.	File confirms that presenter is evaluator in that county.
7. Calendar response due date.	Lawyer .1 Paralegal .1	Ensure timely response.		
8. Communicate results to client.	Lawyer .4	Advise client regarding consequences.	Develop and use standard explanation enclosing rule.	File documents standard explanation enclosing rule.
9. Make timely response.	Lawyer .2	Ensure administrator receives timely response.	Paralegal confirm receipt of response.	Document paralegal confirmation in file.
10. Evaluate and communicate to client case-evaluation results.	Lawyer .4	Advise client of results of case evaluation and strategic responses.	Ensure prompt action if claims settle.	Associate review of results documented in file.
Total:	Lawyer 10.3 Paralegal .6			

Matter: Civil Litigation		Summary Disposition		Role: Defense Counsel
	Task	**Resource**	**Analysis**	**Improve**	**Control**
1	Evaluate case for summary disposition.	Lawyer .5	Determine basis and scope (all or fewer-than-all claims).	Partner consult. Also, ensure timely hearing.	Document evaluation in file.
2	Obtain client approval for motion.	Lawyer .5	Communicate recommendation.	Confirm approval in writing.	Confirmation documented in file.
3	Request opposing-party consent to relief.	Lawyer .2	Ensure that opposing party intends to dispute.	Send draft motion requesting consent?	Document date, time, and form of request in file.
4	Draft facts for brief.	Template brief Lawyer 2.5 Paralegal .2	Summarize evidentiary materials from file review.	Paralegal fit template to case.	
5	Research and draft argument and relief.	Template brief Lawyer 2.5 Clerk 3.0	State law supporting summary disposition.	Clerk perform preliminary research.	Clerk's research memorandum in file.
6	Assemble exhibits.	Lawyer .3 Paralegal .5	Ensure adequate evidentiary support.	Consider affidavit. Partner consult.	Document consult in file.
7	Notice for hearing.	Paralegal .3	Ensure timely hearing.	Contact opposing counsel for date.	
8	File motion.	Paralegal .5	Ensure appropriate filing, service, and distribution.	Back-copy client.	Document back-copy in file.
9	Review response for reply brief.	Lawyer 1.5 Clerk 2.0	Evaluate response and determine benefit of reply.	Partner consult. Clerk review and research.	Document clerk research in file.
10	Prepare for hearing.	Lawyer 1.0	Outline hearing points and rebuttal.		
11	Argue hearing.	Lawyer 2.0	Appear in court to argue granting of motion.	Confirm with clerk and opposing counsel.	Document confirmation in file.
12	Prepare and submit order.	Lawyer .5	Ensure order reflecting ruling.	Seek stipulation as to form.	
13	Report results.	Lawyer .5	Communicate outcome to client.	Confirm outcome in writing.	Confirmation in file.
	Total:	Lawyer 12.0 Paralegal 1.5 Clerk 5.0			

Matter: Personal-Injury Litigation		Pretrial		Role: Counsel
	Task	**Resource**	**Analysis**	**Improve**	**Control**
1	Prepare and file lay and expert witness lists.	List template Lawyer 2.0 Paralegal .5	Ensure timely disclosure of lay and expert witnesses.	Associate develop, partner review.	File reflects partner review.
2	File exhibit lists.	List template Lawyer 1.0 Paralegal .8	Ensure timely disclosure of evidentiary materials.	Associate develop, partner review.	File reflects partner review.
3	Develop demonstrative exhibits.	Lawyer 2.0	Ensure accessible presentation of evidence.	Include damages computations.	File documents demonstrative exhibit review.
4	Draft joint pretrial order.	Order template Lawyer 2.0 Paralegal .5	Ensure compliance with judge's form.	Partner consult on applicable theories.	File reflects partner consult.
5	Conduct final pretrial conference.	Lawyer 2.0	Negotiate reasonable trial conditions.	Prepare written trial synopsis and conference objectives.	File reflects written synopsis and objectives.
6	Prepare client witnesses.	Instructions Lawyer 4.0	Ensure informed testimony.	Develop brochure or video for client witnesses.	File documents client supplied instructions.
7	Prepare examination outlines.	Exam template Lawyer 6.0	Draft direct and cross examinations.	Use proofs points or chart.	File documents exam outlines.
8	Subpoena witnesses.	Subpoena template Letter template Lawyer .5 Paralegal 2.0	Ensure witness availability.	Paralegal telephone as courtesy.	File documents communication.
9	Complete trial notebook.	Notebook form Lawyer 3.0 Paralegal 3.0	Ensure organization of trial materials.	Associate review.	File includes trial notebook.
	Total:	Lawyer 21.0 Paralegal 6.8			

Matter: Personal-Injury Litigation		Trial		Role: Plaintiff's Counsel
Task	**Resource**	**Analysis**	**Improve**	**Control**
1. Conduct jury voir dire.	Lawyer 1.5	Ensure non-biased jurors. Foreshadow theme.	Consider jury consultant.	File reflects client consult on jury.
2. Make opening statement.	Opening template Lawyer 1.5	State framework & develop story.	Develop opening-statement template.	Partner review.
3. Present case in chief.	Lawyer 8.0	Make prima facie case.	Ensure all exhibit admission.	Exhibit checklist reflects admission.
4. Contest opposing party's case.	Lawyer 4.0	Challenge opposing proofs.	Develop story and theme.	Partner review.
5. Research and draft special instructions.	Lawyer 1.0 Law clerk 2.5	Ensure instruction on special issues.	Research special-instruction criteria.	Partner review.
6. Object to jury instructions.	Lawyer 1.0	Preserve law issues for appeal.	Associate review of law issues.	Trial record reflects objections.
7. Make closing argument.	Closing template Lawyer 2.0	State compelling story and theme.	Develop closing-argument template.	Partner review.
8. Receive verdict.	Lawyer 1.0	Ensure jury poll.		
9. Prepare and submit judgment.	Judgment template Lawyer 1.0 Paralegal .5	Ensure judgment reflects verdict.	Partner review.	File reflects review.
Total:	Lawyer 21.0 Paralegal 6.8			

Matter: Personal Injury		**Settlement—Plaintiff**		Role: Plaintiff's Counsel
Task	**Resource**	**Analysis**	**Improvement**	**Control**
1. Secure preliminary confirmation.	Lawyer .5	Memorialize basic terms to secure time for drafting detailed agreement.	Query disputable terms including confidentiality and its enforcement, and indemnity.	Review every material term with client, confirming those terms in writing.
2. Give preliminary notice.	Paralegal .5	Notify court or other tribunal, witnesses, and others to ensure no further costs.	Coordinate notice to tribunal with defense counsel. Defense counsel notifies tribunal.	Prompt notice is critical to cost control. Lawyer review paralegal actions to ensure all notice.
3. Prepare settlement statement.	Statement template Bookkeeper .5 Lawyer .1	Comply with conduct rule requiring disclosure of fee calculation.	Prepare settlement statement sooner, before settlement so client approves net then. Include all costs; bookkeeper confirm with suppliers.	Managing partner reviews all settlement statements for reasonableness of fees and expenses.
4. Review and approve proposed settlement agreement.	Lawyer .5	Determine which disputable terms to challenge.	Discuss with defense counsel when negotiating settlement. Do not assume standard settlement terms.	Managing partner review?
5. Obtain client approval of settlement agreement.	Correspondence template Lawyer .5	Fully inform client regarding meaning and consequences of signing, and as to disputable terms.	Cover letter should explain key features and offer meeting.	Lawyer confirms indemnity and confidentiality explained in writing.
6. Review and approve proposed dismissal order.	Lawyer .5	Confirm with-prejudice dismissal terms and identity of dismissed parties.	Discuss with defense counsel when negotiating settlement. Do not assume standard dismissal terms.	
7. Obtain client approval and signatures on settlement agreement and statement.	Correspondence template Lawyer .5	Alert in cover letter to key terms and disputable provisions.	Send settlement statement sooner, right after client approves settlement. Explain.	Calendar client response. Contact within one week of tender to ensure client response and satisfaction.
8. Convey signed settlement agreement and dismissal order to defense counsel.	Correspondence template Lawyer .2	Tender approved agreement and dismissal order under cover letter requiring escrow of signed documents until counsel conveys funds.	Calendar defense counsel response. Contact within two weeks of tender to ensure reasonably prompt response.	
9. Deposit funds in trust account.	Lawyer .1	Convey to bookkeeper with written instructions that funds are for trust account only.	Ensure funds clear before issuing client check. Notify client about clearance delay.	Managing partner review of deposit account.
10. Convey net funds to client.	Correspondence template Lawyer .2	Include copy of signed settlement statement.	Ensure prompt transmittal of funds. Have paralegal perform?	
11. Close file.	Lawyer .2	Correspondence to client should indicate file closing.	Include client-satisfaction survey.	
TOTALS:	Lawyer 4.8 Paralegal .5 Bookkeeper .5			

Matter: Civil Litigation	**Settlement—Defense**			Role: Defense Counsel
Task	**Resource**	**Analysis**	**Improve**	**Control**
1. Secure preliminary confirmation.	Lawyer .5	Memorialize terms for time to draft detailed agreement.	Query confidentiality and its enforcement, and indemnity.	Review every material term with client, confirming those terms in writing.
2. Give preliminary notice.	Paralegal .5	Notify tribunal and witnesses, to ensure no further costs.	Prompt notice is critical to cost control.	Lawyer review paralegal actions to ensure all notice.
3. Order funds.	Correspondence template Lawyer .5	Notify insurer of amount and payees to initiate funds processing.	Confirm that all plaintiffs and plaintiff's counsel will be on check.	Compare amount to settlement agreement and payees to claimants.
4. Draft settlement agreement.	Agreement template Lawyer .5	Use template. Determine terms to include. Convey to counsel.	Should the cover letter explain the choice of disputable terms?	Work from a template that includes all possible clauses.
5. Draft dismissal order.	Order template Lawyer .5	Confirm with-prejudice dismissal and identity of dismissed parties.	Have paralegal assemble?	Every dismissal should be with prejudice unless otherwise approved.
6. Obtain client approval and signatures on settlement agreement.	Correspondence template Lawyer .5	Alert in cover letter to key terms and disputable provisions.	Justify debatable choices. Anticipate client issues and concerns.	Calendar client response. Contact within one week to ensure client satisfaction.
7. Obtain counsel's approval and plaintiffs' signatures.	Correspondence template Lawyer .5	Tender agreement and dismissal order under cover letter. Escrow signed agreement to convey funds.	Call plaintiff's counsel in advance to discuss disputable terms.	Confer with managing partner over disputable terms.
8. Convey funds on receipt of signed agreement and order.	Correspondence template Lawyer .1	Standard cover letter conveying funds and confirming release of escrow.	Have paralegal assemble?	No staff conveys any funds. Lawyer must convey.
9. Submit and obtain dismissal order.	Correspondence template Lawyer .2	Include extra copies to conform and return.	Have paralegal perform?	Lawyer must review and approve any paralegal action.
10. Convey signed agreement and dismissal order to client and counsel.	Lawyer .2	Cover letter to client should indicate closing file.	Include client-satisfaction survey?	Review with managing partner to ensure appropriate closure.
TOTALS:	Lawyer 4.0 Paralegal .5			